Planning Policy and Politics

Smart Growth and the States

Planning Policy and Politics

Smart Growth and the States

John M. DeGrove

LINCOLN INSTITUTE
OF LAND POLICY
CAMBRIDGE, MASSACHUSETTS

Library of Congress Cataloging-in-Publication Data

DeGrove, John Melvin, 1924–
  Planning policy and politics : smart growth and the states / John M. DeGrove ; foreword by Armando Carbonell.
      p. cm.
  Includes bibliographical references and index.
  ISBN-13: 978-1-55844-142-2 (alk. paper)
  ISBN-10: 1-55844-142-5 (alk. paper)
      1. Regional planning—United States—States. 2. Land use—United States—States. 3. Sustainable development—United States—States. I. Lincoln Institute of Land Policy. II. Title.
  HT392.D443 2005
  307.1'2—dc22   2005030397

Designed and produced by Snow Creative Services

Composed in Granjon and Optima. Printed and bound by Webcom Limited in Toronto, Ontario, Canada. The paper is Legacy Offset, a recycled, acid-free sheet.

MANUFACTURED IN CANADA

Contents

Foreword

The "DeGrove interview," a highly interactive data-gathering method, was an essential source of the information in this volume, as it was in the two previous DeGrove books on planning and growth management. My first exposure to John DeGrove and his method came in the 1980s, when I was working on the development of the Cape Cod Commission. John came up to Barnstable, Massachusetts, from Florida—parachuted in is the image I have in mind—with an attaché case full of yellow legal pads, a load of questions, and much advice about the workings of our legislation, and about politics, strategy and tactics in general. Not merely an interview, it was an intervention. I felt like I was being inducted into an elite corps of planning commandos by a battle-hardened veteran.

Through John, I was introduced to the intrepid scouts who had penetrated the triple-canopy rain forest that was land use in America in the early days of the "quiet revolution." These were the roots from which sprang the growth management—later smart growth—insurgency. From that initial meeting onward, I had no doubt (nor did he, nor will you) about where John DeGrove stood on the issue of land use planning and control, and whom he considered to be the heroes and the villains of the story. When I later chaired 1000 Friends of Massachusetts, a call or visit from John was always either an occasion to celebrate a victory on the path to planning reform, or as often, to commiserate over a lost battle. He held, and holds, a simple conviction: if the forces of good prevail, the world will be a better place, through planning. I know of no one in the planning world more qualified to hold the title, "passionate observer of the smart growth insurgency."

As the reader of this volume will soon discover, the years have not diluted John's passion, nor has he abandoned a strong point of view in bringing us up to date on the policy and political happenings that have taken place since the publication of his second book, *The New Frontier for Land Policy: Planning and Growth Management in the States*. This new book is the story of nine key states that continue to play out a great American land planning experiment that by law and tradition has been the exclusive purview of the states. We learn of "positive developments and new assaults." But it is not a dry chronology of laws passed (or repealed) and smart growth programs implemented (or stymied). Rather, John has limned a drama animated by the exploits of flesh-and-blood politicians, bureaucrats and advocates: governors (especially governors!), chairs of legislative committees, state agency heads, home builders, farmers and environmentalists. At times, it is a nuanced story of amazing intricacy: where else will you see parsed the distinct positions on land use control held by the Oregon Farm Bureau, the Grange and the Wheat League? (And who else would have provided such a useful glossary, decoding the alphabet soup of state smart growth speak?) But there are also epic tales of pitched battles, unexpected coalitions, victories snatched from the jaws of defeat, and vice versa.

Not content to confine himself to the academy (where he ultimately had the unusual distinction of holding for a time an eponymous endowed Chair), John himself served on the front lines in the smart growth forces as secretary of the Florida Department of Community Affairs (DCA) and president of the powerful state smart growth advocacy group, 1000 Friends of Florida. He helped to draft and pushed for passage of the landmark Florida legislation described in this and earlier volumes, and he continues to be its staunch defender. With this personal background, and through his continued interaction with key players across the country, DeGrove is able to provide us with the perspective of not just a passionate, but a *participant* observer of the smart growth movement.

In an earlier Lincoln Institute volume, *Smart Growth: Form and Consequences*, I observed that the term *smart growth* means different things to different interests (Szold and Carbonell 2002). Much of its cleverness—and strength—as a policy term derives from this very ambiguity and its ability to provide an umbrella big enough to shelter stereotypically opposed groups—e.g., home builders and environmentalists—who, arguably, lacking only a unifying metaphor, could have been standing shoulder-to-shoulder all along.

During a recent Institute-sponsored meeting of state planning directors from the Northeast, all present reported that their states were pursuing what are, in terms of policy content, smart growth programs, although some have chosen to march under different banners. It might be tempting to conclude that the war is won, as what was once revolutionary has become the established, conventional wisdom. But all of these programs in the Northeast are incentive-based, and it remains to be seen whether, over time, they will be potent enough to have the dramatic effect on the ground of the muscular Oregon-style regulatory approach.

The big umbrella is beginning to show its years as well, with a few rips and leaks, and some stakeholders are still not comfortable standing under it. Mostly they are at the extremes—those fearing all development and those fearing all regulation. Moreover, increasing strength can be seen in a private property rights movement that seeks to impose restrictions beyond those required by the U.S. Supreme Court on government action in the land use sphere, including requiring compensation for *any* diminution in property value caused by regulation (see Jacobs 2004). This new strength was particularly manifest in the 60–40 percent approval of Measure 37 in Oregon, an event that took place toward the end of the research for this volume (November 2004). This is a significant development, since smart growth is all about the balancing of public and private interests. It relies on the promise of a bigger pie (better quality of life, greater prosperity), equitably distributed.

In this long-awaited volume, John DeGrove has brought his chronicle of the smart growth movement into the twenty-first century, providing us with a vantage point from which to glimpse an uncertain future.

Armando Carbonell
Cochairman
Department of Planning and Development
Lincoln Institute of Land Policy

References

DeGrove, John M. 1992. *The New Frontier for Land Policy: Planning and Growth Management in the States*. Cambridge, MA: Lincoln Institute of Land Policy.

Jacobs, Harvey M., ed. 2004. *Private Property in the 21st Century: The Future of an American Ideal*. Cheltenham, UK, and Northampton, MA: Edward Elgar (in association with the Lincoln Institute of Land Policy).

Szold, Terry and Armando Carbonell, eds. 2002. *Smart Growth: Form and Consequences*. Cambridge, MA: Lincoln Institute of Land Policy.

1

Introduction

Managing Growth in a Changing Environment

In two earlier books, I described and assessed the development and implementation of comprehensive planning and growth management systems in selected states and regions. *Land, Growth and Politics* (1984) examined the political climate and policy concerns that caused seven states to adopt comprehensive planning legislation with substantial emphasis on implementation. That focus, in turn, elevated the issue of funding the new systems to a higher place on the public policy agenda. In *The New Frontier for Land Policy: Planning and Growth Management in the States* (1992), the experiences of those state systems were updated to evaluate their sustainability over time and how they compared with several other state systems that evolved in the 1980s and early 1990s.

Now, in the early twenty-first century, important new questions must be examined in light of a shifting and volatile political and public policy environment that is challenging long-standing assumptions about public responsibilities in growth management. Are comprehensive efforts to plan for and manage growth an expression of governmental and private sector partnerships that no longer apply and are destined to fade away or be replaced by something else? How do the concepts of ecosystem management and sustainability—both very much alive—relate to comprehensive planning and growth management systems?

A related concern is how federal legislation such as the Clean Air Act, ISTEA (Intermodal Surface Transportation Efficiency Act) and its successor, TEA-21 (Transportation Equity Act of the 21st Century), influenced comprehensive growth management systems by requiring a stronger relationship between land use and transportation systems. In the same vein, what about the ability of the Clean Water and Endangered Species acts to reflect an ecosystem/habitat conservation planning approach and their relationship to state and regional planning and growth management?

Most important, is this nation in the midst of a political revolution that will turn back the clock to an earlier era? Will environmental and comprehensive land use systems designed with an important role for states and regions be terminated through repeal or drastic weakening of existing federal and state legislation? Will we return to a nonplanning or planning-in-isolation pattern for local governments, with little or no coordination between and among federal, state and local governments, or with the private sector? Or will we work toward a bipartisan commitment to smart growth—a proactive effort to limit sprawl patterns of development and build sustainable urban communities—to ensure the protection of natural systems, including important farm and forest lands?

Final answers to many of these questions are beyond the reach of this book, but important light can be shed on them by examining the following questions.

- How and why did certain states and regions get into the comprehensive planning and growth management business in the first place?

- How did the forces that supported such actions change over time?

- Why and how were the comprehensive systems adopted in the 1970s, 1980s and 1990s sustained over time, if in fact they did survive?

- Have those systems been joined by new state and regional efforts?

- How can we track the "new politics" that grew out of the 1990s in order to understand the prospects for growth management systems in the twenty-first century?

Smart Growth Principles

Looking more closely at the core of development patterns now being called smart growth, one significant development is the emergence of 10 to 12 frequently used principles. They all grow out of the rising concern about the negative impacts of sprawl and prescribe very similar sets of remedies aimed at renewing our cities and protecting natural systems, all in an integrated fashion. The smart growth principles endorsed by Minnesota's Smart Growth Network (1000 Friends of Minnesota) are representative.

1. Make efficient and effective use of land resources and existing infrastructure by encouraging development to areas with existing infrastructure or capacity to avoid costly duplication of services and costly use of land.

2. Provide a mix of land uses to create a variety of housing choices and opportunities.

3. Make development decisions predictable, fair and cost-effective.

4. Provide a variety of transportation choices, including pedestrian friendly neighborhoods.

5. Maintain a unique sense of place by respecting local culture and natural environmental features.

6. Conserve open space and farmland, and preserve critical environmental areas.

7. Encourage stakeholder collaboration and community participation rather than conflict.

8. Provide staged and managed growth in urban transition areas with compact development patterns.

9. Enhance access to equitable public and private resources for everyone.

10. Promote the safety, livability and revitalization of existing urban and rural communities.

The smart growth principles in other states and organizations are remarkable for their similarity to those crafted in Minnesota. Those not specific to a state or region include the 10 principles of the Smart Growth Network. The National Governor's Association adopted a similar list of Principles for Better Land Use at its annual meeting in 1999. Statements in support of smart growth strategies also have been adopted by the National Association of Home Builders (NAHB), the National Association of Counties (NACO) and other groups.

Building on this momentum and years of research on state growth management systems, this book documents developments that strengthen integrated growth management and smart growth systems in nine states: Oregon, Florida, New Jersey, Maine, Rhode Island, Vermont, Georgia, Maryland and Washington. A comparative assessment of the struggle to implement such systems (some for decades, some for a few years) seems especially timely in light of new forces—some positive, some negative—that are impacting existing efforts to manage growth and change in a way that will contain sprawl, renew our cities and protect our natural systems. But, first, a brief review of earlier studies of state-based growth management systems may help put current policy and implementation issues into perspective.

Concern for the Environment: The First-Wave States of the 1970s

Land, Growth and Politics examined the first wave of growth management states within a conceptual framework that included

- the issue context: the emergence of problems and issues that demanded action;

- the politics of adoption: the forces, both public and private, that were involved in opposing or supporting a strong state initiative to improve land and growth management;

- the politics of implementation: the major political and policy developments during the period in which the new legislation was put into practice, including the continuing roles of governors, legislators, and all key stakeholders, with a focus on efforts to weaken or strengthen the original legislation; and

■ the politics of the future: focusing on prospects for strengthening or weakening the systems that had been put into place. (DeGrove 1984, 1–2)

State governments were seen as occupying key leverage points in the federal system, having the ultimate authority (with minor exceptions) in the public policy arena of land and growth management if they chose to exercise it. Those that did were (and still are) ripe for examination as case studies in a comparative analysis framework that can yield rich results in the public policy subfield of growth management.

The seven states analyzed in *Land, Growth and Politics* fell into three categories, from weak to strong.

1. Comprehensive, but limited to coastal areas (California and North Carolina)

2. Statewide but limited to certain types of projects or geographical areas (Vermont, Florida and Colorado)

3. Comprehensive (Oregon and Hawaii)

Concern for the environment was the key factor in mobilizing stakeholders and in passing early growth management legislation in all seven states. Adoption efforts were not a partisan political issue in any state except Colorado, and the virtual demise of that program was directly linked to its political roots. The apparent rise of partisan politics, beginning in the late 1980s and continuing through the 1990s, is critical to ongoing efforts to weaken or even destroy long-standing state systems. In the case of Oregon, the passage of Measure 37 in November 2004 presents a real threat to that system, which is widely recognized as one of the oldest and strongest systems for managing growth and change.

Stakeholder opposition in the first-wave states came from home builders, developers, local governments and other private-sector groups, while support came from environmental and civic groups. Support by the governor and key legislators was critical in almost every successful adoption effort, and that

pattern continued for the most part into the second wave of growth management systems in the 1980s and early 1990s.

The process has become increasingly complex as many components of the private sector have come to recognize the economic downside of sprawl development patterns and have begun to support new initiatives to reverse sprawl. Funding was a significant issue in the implementation stage of the original state systems and remains a tough problem today. In light of the growing antiregulation environment of the early 2000s, it is important to ask whether some key stakeholders who opposed comprehensive growth management systems in the 1970s have shifted their positions and under what circumstances.

Results of the analysis of the first-wave states bear on the adoption and implementation of new efforts from the 1980s through 2004. First, both state and local governments gained authority from the comprehensive systems of the 1970s (although some regional and local governments were occasionally reluctant to fully exercise their new roles). Nevertheless, the first-wave states assumed new and important roles in planning and land use, and that trend has been sustained in the systems adopted in other states. Assuming that these new state roles continue, are they significant enough to represent a shift of major importance in federal/state/local relations and thus have a critical impact on the nature of the federal system in the area of intergovernmental relations?

The relationship between planning and regulation showed great promise in the 1970s and early 1980s, but failed to fulfill this promise into the new century. We are still struggling to make permitting the servant of the goals and policies of a comprehensive planning system. The expression of that effort is illustrated by attempts to move to an ecosystem approach in managing wetlands and related uplands, and to substitute broad-based habitat conservation planning for individual endangered species protection, thus attempting to move from reactive to proactive approaches.

The concept of sustainability, albeit subject to a wide array of definitions, always has at its core the demand for placing individual local and regional planning, and the resulting permit decisions, in a comprehensive planning and management framework to ensure the sustainability of the resource or community in question. State agencies generally have been reluctant latecomers to a comprehensive approach for planning and growth management. While there has been much stronger emphasis from the 1980s to the present on bringing state agencies into such systems, the success record is mixed. Typically, monitoring and enforcement were weak links in the implementation record of systems adopted in the 1970s. Whether this element has improved in the new or remodeled systems is a key question in assessing the effectiveness of those systems.

The concluding analysis of state and regional systems in *Land, Growth and Politics* questioned whether the comprehensive planning and growth management movement is a passing fad or one that will continue to evolve and expand. The answer was that state systems are here to stay, but will evolve with time and with the new demands placed on them.

Redefining Growth Management: The Second-Wave States of the 1980s and Early 1990s

Growth management was a powerful concept that produced at least three important outcomes during this period:

1. Redefining the practice of planning;

2. Redefining state/regional/local relations in important ways, including a reallocation of authority and responsibility for important public policy issues; and

3. Causing funding issues associated with growth management to be moved up on the public policy agenda (i.e., concurrency, or the costs of developing plans to meet new planning mandates and the funds needed for infrastructure to meet the impacts of growth).

In assessing the second wave of states that adopted comprehensive growth management systems in the 1980s and early 1990s, *The New Frontier for Land Policy* highlighted the evolving definition of growth management, which had shed its original, narrow label of "growth control/no growth/slow growth" associated with local government efforts and had come to mean

> a commitment to plan carefully for the growth that comes to an area so as to achieve a responsible balance between the protection of natural systems—land, air, and water—and the development required to support growth in the residential, commercial, and retail areas. Growth management...is deeply committed to a responsible "fit" between development and the infrastructure needed to support the impacts of development, including such things as roads, schools, water, sewer, drainage, solid waste, and parks and recreation. Thus growth management is closely linked to, and necessary for, the achievement of "quality of life," a concept that has emerged as a powerful if somewhat elusive framework for the planning and growth management systems described here. (DeGrove 1992, 1)

The New Frontier demonstrated this broadened definition in new state and regional initiatives ranging from Florida in 1985 to Washington State in 1990–1991 and Maryland in 1992. The book identified consistency, concurrency, compact urban form, natural systems, housing and economic development as the defining components of these evolving systems. The concluding chapter examined the future of growth management systems and noted that "the best guess now [spring 1992] seems to be that state growth management systems are of major importance, that they are here to stay, and that new systems will continue to emerge" (DeGrove 1992, 170).

In 2005, that prediction is holding, even in the face of threatening forces that could destroy or severely undermine the systems. Predicting the future is a risky business, so our focus in this volume is on (1) understanding what has happened in our case states, what is happening now, and why; (2) what difference the systems are making; and (3) how they seem destined to evolve. Beyond that, and most important of all, is the question of whether the move to a smart growth approach is here to stay, and whether it is powerful enough to lead to fundamental and lasting changes in managing growth and change.

The Shift to Smart Growth: The Third-Wave States of the Late 1990s and Early 2000s

This book expands and updates the earlier reviews of state systems and presents a comparative assessment of the key concepts that have emerged as common characteristics in nine important states. The chapters describe, compare and contrast those comprehensive state and regional systems by

- identifying the major problems and issues that caused the political system to adopt new or revise old systems;

- pinpointing the key stakeholders, both public and private, who supported and opposed the drafting and adoption of the new legislation, including governors and key legislators;

- describing the key features of the new (or amended old) systems, drawing from the legislation both process (governance) and substantive components;

- outlining the implementation record, including the major weaknesses and strengths that emerged as the systems were put in place; and

- examining the political prospects of existing new and potential future systems, especially in light of the highly charged political environment of the mid- to late-1990s, made even more uncertain by the declining economy from 2001 to 2003, the events of September 11, 2001, the war in Iraq and the political movements currently taking shape.

The "new politics" of the late 1990s and early 2000s have brought additional challenges to growth management systems that generally assume government has an important role to play in maintaining a sense of community and quality of life in our society. These systems involve creative and sometimes delicate partnerships between and among state, regional and local governments and the private sector, with support from the national level, making confident predictions about the future difficult. Some of the strongest systems have come under attack as never before; at the same time, significant attempts to adopt new systems and strengthen existing ones are also under way. The

analysis and conclusions in this volume attempt to pinpoint the forces at play and assess the prospects for sustaining and/or expanding existing systems. Front and center is the need to reconcile apparent conflicts between a strong economy and a healthy environment through consensus-building techniques that can result in win-win solutions.

Special treatment is given to issues that extend our understanding of the nature, significance and sustainability of growth management systems. In the area of implementation, Oregon's system was adopted in 1973 and Florida's in 1985. Both are comprehensive in scope, have significant mandatory elements, and enjoyed strong political support until the early 1990s. But in 2005 both systems are under attack from antigovernment, antiregulation and antiplanning forces. A related threat is the impact of the private property rights movement that gained strength in the 1990s.

On a more positive note, how does the greenways movement link to growth management systems, and does it lend support to more compact urban development patterns? Other positive efforts have emerged in Florida, Maryland and Oregon to develop affordable housing within the context of growth management systems. Are those successes exportable to other states?

Matters of process, substance and politics common to all state systems are examined and compared. For example, is consistency—"the tie that binds"— necessary for an effective growth management system, and, if so, are there bottom-up as well as top-down ways to achieve it? Is concurrency the "truth in planning" core of any responsible growth management system, and, if so, are there new, creative ways to fund its implementation? Is responsible management of growth possible without containing urban sprawl through compact urban form, and what are the incentives and disincentives that can do the job? Further, is it possible to strengthen the movement by documenting its fiscal as well as its environmental and social costs? Has affordable housing benefited from growth management systems, and can lessons be learned for other states?

In examining how the protection of natural systems fits into comprehensive growth management programs, do the concepts of sustainability and ecosystem management mean that compact urban form (containing sprawl) and protecting natural systems are inextricably entwined, and neither can be achieved in isolation from the other? Does economic development as a key component of growth management systems lead anywhere beyond a statement of goals, and, if there are successes to report, how did they come about and can they be shared successfully with other systems?

Economic development emerged as a key element for most states adopting growth management systems in the 1980s. This component was a strong part of the New Jersey and Georgia systems, as well as Maine and Vermont. Washington and Maryland, the two states that adopted growth management legislation in the midst of the national recession in the early 1990s, also focused on economic development. How have they fared as the economy recovered, given the growing negative political environment for almost all government programs, including growth management systems?

Organization of the Book

This book begins with an analysis of Oregon's comprehensive system, in place since 1973, which is far longer than that of any other state. It has more concrete results to show than any other system, and, in spite of severe political backlash in the Oregon legislature and ill-advised initiatives that aim to destroy the whole system, continues to move forward with innovative developments. Oregon allows us to set the benchmark for comparison with other states in such areas as containing sprawl, protecting important farmland, and promoting innovative links between land use, transportation and air quality, especially in the Portland metropolitan region. Further, Oregon is a logical starting point because it has had the greatest influence on other state systems.

An analysis of Florida's experience, with its comprehensive system in place since 1985, highlights its strengths and weaknesses, with a special focus on concurrency, the attempts to contain sprawl, and the bright spots of protecting natural systems and making affordable housing an important part of the growth

management system. The experiences of Oregon and Florida demonstrate that even the most highly regarded growth systems never settle into a stable implementation cycle free from crisis and challenge. Both states have come under heavy assault as the political environment shifted toward an antigovernment and antiplanning mode. These chapters examine the shifts in legislative support, assess the role of governors in sustaining or further undermining the programs, and give special attention to the contributions of broad-based support groups, such as 1000 Friends organizations, in sustaining the programs in the face of private and/or public sector attack.

New Jersey has attempted to craft a comprehensive system by integrating a state development and redevelopment plan with county, municipal and regional plans, through a complex negotiation process called cross-acceptance. Are there enough incentives (that is, targeted state agency investments) to hold the system together? If not, what are the prospects for strengthening the comprehensive planning mandate in order to ensure compact urban development patterns and resource protection on the ground? This chapter outlines recent developments and describes the Pinelands Commission, one of the most effective regional governance systems in the nation. Finally, it assesses the impact of Governor James McGreevey's resignation in 2004 and developments that followed, to determine the chances of sustaining New Jersey's system for managing growth and change.

The New England states of Maine, Rhode Island and Vermont adopted their growth management systems in 1988, and they are analyzed together for important lessons about political support, funding and implementation. Two of the programs have come under severe attack from hostile elements in the private sector and the legislature, and all three have had difficulty implementing the laws adopted in 1988 and later amended. As these states emerged from the recession of the early 1990s, there were positive signs that their systems were growing stronger, but the events of the past few years have presented new challenges, as well as hopeful responses from grassroots coalitions.

Georgia spotlights a nationally significant effort to achieve a comprehensive, coordinated growth management system in a state with some 700 local governments and wide differences among regions. This chapter examines the exportability of the unique consensus-building techniques that resulted in the most broad-based range of private and public sector support ever assembled for the original adoption of growth management legislation. The Georgia system is particularly important because of its bold effort to achieve comprehensive planning and land development regulations in all local governments, consistent with each other and with regional and state laws, without directly mandating those systems through a top-down or command-and-control approach.

The Georgia experiment is the most significant test of the ability of an incentive-based approach in achieving an integrated, comprehensive system. Negative factors stalled the full implementation of the system in the mid- to late 1990s, but the leadership of Governor Roy Barnes (1998–2002) and the increasing support of the private sector for antisprawl measures weighed in on the positive side. More recent developments, including the surprising defeat of Governor Barnes in November 2002, have put the future of the Georgia system in question.

In 1997 Maryland passed a major amendment to its Economic Growth, Resource Protection and Planning Act of 1992. Spearheaded by then-Governor Parris Glendening, this amendment aimed to contain sprawl through incentives, disincentives and strong efforts to encourage development and redevelopment in existing urban areas. The long-term success of this initiative will depend on the ability of his successors to bring all the relevant state agencies fully into the picture in order to channel education, transportation, housing, economic development and other infrastructure investments into areas earmarked for development and away from rural and environmentally sensitive areas.

The 2002 election of Republican Robert L. Ehrlich Jr., as governor has raised major questions about whether the smart growth strategies put in place in the Glendening administration would be continued, lost or greatly weakened. The result is mixed, with positive and negative actions still in play. Assessing Maryland also gives us an opportunity to address questions of whether smart growth is simply a more palatable term for comprehensive planning and growth management systems, or something markedly different.

In the state of Washington, one focus is on whether key stakeholder-based support groups such as 1000 Friends of Washington (renamed Futurewise in 2005) are making a difference, as that state struggles to sustain its system. The results of the November 1998 elections, featuring strong gains by Democrats, and the reorganization of the key state agency responsible for implementing Washington's growth management in 1998 and again in 1999–2000 seemed sure to strengthen the program. Negative factors also are at play, including the continued failure to enact a reliable and major funding source for public transportation initiatives, a challenge shared by the neighboring state of Oregon.

Several regional agencies are singled out for special treatment within the state chapters, because they highlight contrasting approaches and degrees of success in dealing with regional problems, largely within the framework of their state comprehensive systems. Two of the regions operate within strong statewide growth management systems: Metro in Portland, Oregon, and the Puget Sound Regional Council in Washington. Each is a dominant region in its state, from an economic and population perspective, and each has a special assigned role in the implementation of their state growth management systems. Both are applying innovative land use, transportation and air quality programs that involve light rail and other public transportation linked to mixed use, traditional neighborhood development patterns, and other techniques to contain population growth within defined urban growth boundaries. The strengths and weaknesses of those efforts are examined in some detail. As noted, the passage of Measure 37 in November 2004 in Oregon threatens the very future of that system. The political environment in Washington is more positive, but inadequate funding remains an unresolved problem.

The Atlanta Regional Commission has long done excellent planning, including an ambitious Vision 2020 strategy, funded liberally by the private sector, but it continues to have great difficulty implementing the essence of the vision. This region is examined within the framework of the Georgia Planning Act.

Many view the Atlanta region as out of control, with sprawl reaching out in all directions and insufficient emphasis on public transportation and the sustainability of natural and urban systems. However, Governor Roy Barnes in 1999 moved swiftly to establish the Georgia Regional Transportation Authority, which committed both resources and power to deal with land use, transportation and air quality issues in the Atlanta region and other parts of Georgia. Barnes's surprising defeat by Republican Sonny Perdue is analyzed, as well as how, after an uninspiring start, Perdue, in his second year as governor, took a number of actions that were clearly smart growth driven.

What can be said with certainty at the beginning of the twenty-first century is that support for containing sprawl by moving to smart growth approaches remains strong in many quarters. These approaches are moving from "talking the talk" to "walking the walk," with input from every stakeholder group—public, private, nonprofit, and even some real estate and homeowner organizations. At the same time, however, global political and economic developments in the first years of this century have produced new and significant uncertainty as to the prospects for smart growth strategies across the country.

A number of issues at the national, state and local levels have combined to call into question the George W. Bush administration's support for smart growth initiatives at any level, if indeed that support was there in the first place. It seems highly unlikely that his administration will somehow see the light and recognize that smart growth strategies, carefully conceived and wisely implemented, are not only good for natural systems, but also point the way to a strong economy, a high quality of life for all citizens, and a sustainable future for the nation as a whole.

References

1000 Friends of Minnesota. Principles for smart growth: Smart growth principles for Minnesota. http://www.1000fom.org/Smart_Growth/SG_Principles/sg_principles.htm.

DeGrove, John M. 1984. *Land, growth and politics*. Washington, DC: Planners Press.

———. 1992. *The new frontier for land policy: Planning and growth management in the states*. Cambridge, MA: Lincoln Institute of Land Policy.

National Governors Association. Principles for better land use. http://www.nga.org/pubs/policies/nr/nr13.asp.

Smart Growth Network. Smart growth principles. http//www.smartgrowth.org/about/default.asp.

2

Oregon

Contents

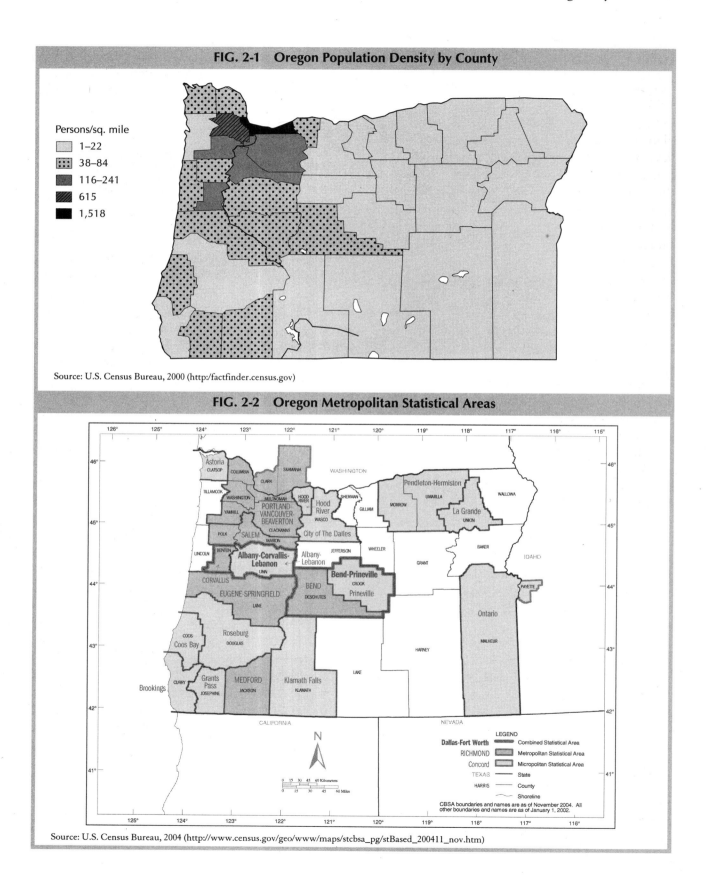

FIG. 2-1 Oregon Population Density by County

Persons/sq. mile
- 1–22
- 38–84
- 116–241
- 615
- 1,518

Source: U.S. Census Bureau, 2000 (http:/factfinder.census.gov)

FIG. 2-2 Oregon Metropolitan Statistical Areas

Source: U.S. Census Bureau, 2004 (http://www.census.gov/geo/www/maps/stcbsa_pg/stBased_200411_nov.htm)

Introduction

Oregon's Land Use Planning Act (SB 100) dates to 1973, and it is traditionally held up as the premier example of a comprehensive growth management plan to protect natural systems and confine urban development. However, the adoption of the law was a struggle, and it has required extensive changes over the past 32 years. The implementation process has been interrupted by several major initiatives to repeal or drastically weaken the legislation, which remains under attack by a hostile legislature and interests long dedicated to destroying it. At the same time, a renewed surge of growth in many parts of the state, primarily in the Portland metropolitan region, has brought growth management concerns to the top of the agenda in the minds of citizens across the state.

The old adage, "it's not over until it's over, and it's never over," certainly applies to the effectiveness and even the survival of the Oregon land use system. From the mid-1980s and into 2005 there has never been a time when opponents of the system were not busy trying to weaken or destroy it. These assaults have focused on the rural lands issue (how to protect the best agricultural and forest lands from rural sprawl), and on how to accommodate strong population growth inside urban growth boundaries (UGBs), thus diminishing the pressure on rural areas. How these challenges have played out tells us much about the key components of a smart growth system, and the challenges that must be overcome to assure long-term success.

This chapter examines the above complexities, including the ambivalence or steadfastness of groups that historically have supported the land use program. We are especially interested in Oregon's leading defender of the land use law, 1000 Friends of Oregon (formed in 1975), and its expanded scope from an almost exclusive focus on rural farm and forest lands to on e that extends to issues of urban form inside UGBs. We assess the impacts of Measure 7 (passed in November 2000, but later ruled unconstitutional by the state Supreme Court) and look at the potential for an improved political climate for full implementation of the system. Finally, we look at the latest efforts to greatly weaken or dismantle Oregon's land use system in the form of Measure 37, the "Son of Measure 7," and the efforts to defeat it led by 1000 Friends of Oregon and its allies, which reached its climax in the November 2004 balloting.

The Oregon Land Use Planning Program: Its Beginnings and Early Implementation

The Issue Context

Most residents of Oregon, native and newcomer alike, seem to have a special feeling for the unique features of the three major regions of the state: the rugged and beautiful coastal region; the expansive Willamette Valley, stretching from Portland in the north to southern Oregon; and the sparsely populated, relatively dry eastern part of the state. The Willamette Valley, some 100 miles long and 30–40 miles wide, features a central core of about two million acres of flat, extremely fertile land, ideally suited for both agriculture and urban development. The valley contains more than 80 percent of all the state's prime farmland, and produces about half of its agricultural goods. On either side of this finite valley, foothills rise to the Coast Range on the west and the Cascade Range on the east. The broad-based concern for the protection of the Willamette Valley drove the fight to adopt the nation's first comprehensive state land use law in 1973, which featured a unique partnership between state, regional (in the Portland area) and local governments.

A surge in population in the 1960s and into the 1970s fueled the forces that allowed the adoption of SB 100 by the 1973 legislature. The 1960 population of 1.8 million increased to almost 2.1 million by 1970, and two-thirds of that growth took place in the Willamette Valley's nine core counties. The same trend of concentrated growth in the valley continued in the 1970s, 1980s and 1990s. Between 1990 and 2000, the state's population rose by 579,062, an increase of 20 percent, to 3,421,399. According to the 2000 Census, 70 percent of state residents lived in Willamette Valley counties. The state's population for the year 2015 is projected to be 3,992,000 and for 2025, 4,349,000 (U.S. Census Bureau).

Perhaps as much as anything else that generated support for a broad-based land use law was the determination of Oregonians (including those who had recently moved to Oregon from California) to avoid being "Californiarized." In its natural features, the Willamette Valley was much like the Santa Clara and San Fernando valleys in California, where "uncontrolled development had turned a natural paradise into a polluted nightmare" (DeGrove 1984, 235). There was a widespread fear in Oregon that such development would spread to the valley if the state did not take care of its growth future. Concern for Oregon's quality of life was not confined to the valley. Increasing development along the state's rugged 400-mile coastline was sufficient to signal a coastal disaster for the future if not checked, particularly in Lincoln County in the north.

While the scattered coastal development and the "sagebrush subdivisions" of eastern Oregon were a concern, the heart of the matter was in Oregon's great central valley, where the visible urban encroachment on farmland was a key motivation for adopting a comprehensive land and growth management law. Farmland in the valley declined by some 36 percent in the 1960s. Charles E. Little's assessment of the growth pressures noted that, of the seven million acres in the entire valley, only two million acres of flatland were ideal for both agriculture and urban development. As Little put it, "Oregonians have reason to fear that Portland will ultimately merge with Salem, and Salem with Eugene to make one continuous conurbation...tract houses, clogged highways, factories, and commercial strips" (DeGrove 1984, 237).

Eastern Oregon had its own potential disaster, with a 1972 study showing 160,000 acres of dry rangeland, deserts and plains east of the Cascade Range subdivided into 43,000 lots. Land sales schemes, some legal, some not, threatened to damage a fragile landscape and defraud purchasers who believed the representations in the colorful brochures. Governor Tom McCall, surely one of the most creative phrase-makers ever to occupy a governor's chair, summed it up in his opening address to the 1973 Oregon legislature:

> There is a shameless threat to our environment... and to the whole quality of life...[that] is the unfettered despoiling of the land.... We are in dire

need of a state land use policy, new subdivision laws, and new standards for planning and zoning by cities and counties. The interest of Oregon for today and in the future must be protected from the grasping wastrels of the land. (DeGrove 1984, 237)

During the 1960s and early 1970s, Oregon enacted a series of laws that illustrated the state's environmental commitment. These included statutes mandating returnable bottles, earmarking funds for bicycle paths, issuing bonds for pollution abatement, reaffirming the public's right of access to beaches and enacting a billboard removal law. In addition, the successful drive during 1971–1973 to pass an historic comprehensive land use law was part of a growing nationwide movement during the 1960s and early 1970s, with the passage of major federal and state environmental legislation.

Yet, the Oregon law was not crafted and passed by well-organized environmental groups. A newly elected Republican senator from the Willamette Valley, dairy farmer Hector Macpherson, and the Republican Governor Thomas McCall, who was strongly committed to protecting Oregon's quality of life, led the charge. Their alliance illustrated the key importance of gubernatorial and legislative leadership in overcoming the natural resistance of private and public key stakeholders to any far-reaching changes in land use planning and implementation.

As in other states, the movement in Oregon was based on a profound citizen mistrust of the willingness or ability of local governments to protect the environment, including management of urban development patterns. The experience with SB 10 (Chapter 234), passed in 1969 by the Oregon legislature, reinforced that skepticism. The bill was the result of concern over the loss of agricultural land, and mandated that all counties and cities develop land use controls; if they failed to do so, the governor was empowered to develop such controls on their behalf. The law, however, had no funding and only very limited impact on land use planning and regulation (DeGrove 1984, 239).

From the time of his election in 1971, Macpherson was determined to work on legislation to protect Oregon's agricultural lands and, more generally, to ensure the wise management of all the state's land resources. In the 1971 session, he pushed for authorization of an interim study group to bring state land use legislation to the next session of the Oregon legislature in 1973. Failing to get that authorization, Macpherson assembled an ad hoc committee to draft proposed legislation. Cities and counties came to the bargaining table, but many key industry groups did not. The legislation, drafted with the help of the governor's office and legislative counsel, was an extensive change from the status quo, and featured a major role for the state. It mandated the development of comprehensive land use plans by cities and counties within the framework of and consistent with a set of state goals and policies. Local government efforts would be integrated by newly empowered regional agencies; a state agency would be authorized to designate and permit areas of critical state concern and activities of statewide interest.

This proved too much for the Oregon legislature to swallow. Though the legislation had the support of the Senate Environment and Land Use Committee chairman, it did not have a majority, and efforts to compromise several key parts of the bill seemed headed for failure. Macpherson next named another committee to redraft the proposed bill, headed by L. B. Day, former head of the state's Department of Environmental Quality and head of the Teamsters Union in Oregon. Day made his strategy clear from the beginning, "If we can get the right people on the ad hoc committee...the Home Builders Association...the governor's staff...the Association of Oregon Industries...the forest products industry, I think we can hammer out a bill that will do it" (DeGrove 1984, 242).

Day was right. In 10 days the bill was redrafted with three key features: a continued meaningful state oversight role; the removal of the mandated regional council authority; and the removal of state agency authority to establish and issue permits for areas of critical state concern. When Macpherson and his committee produced the first drafts of the proposed land use law, the emphasis was on state/regional responsibilities. But, "In the end...Oregon's new land use initiative represented more a state-local partnership than a state-dominated system" (DeGrove 1984, 244–245). This shift was typical of the state planning–land use–growth management efforts of the 1970s.

The success of Day's committee illustrates the value of a strong governor in full support of proposed legislation. With a generally supportive legislature, the odds were high that some legislation would pass, and staying on the sidelines seemed a higher risk than engaging in the process. Not all stakeholders came to the table, with the cities conspicuously absent after counties replaced regions as the center of the implementation effort at the local level. The Oregon Home Builders Association's support was given in part to try to use the legislation to ward off "no-growth" advocates in the Willamette Valley. The resulting legislation and its implementation, since 1973, have never been a no-growth system, despite widespread belief outside Oregon that stopping growth was the purpose of the legislation. The final votes were cast along geographical rather than political party lines. Willamette Valley legislators voted 5–1 in favor, while the 30 legislators from eastern, southern and coastal Oregon voted 2–1 against the bill (Abbott, Howe and Adler 1994, 4–6).

Key Provisions of the 1973 Land Use Planning Act (SB 100)

The Oregon Land Use Planning Act (SB 100) became effective in October 1973.[1] The law created the Land Conservation and Development Commission (LCDC) to oversee implementation of the law's requirements. The commission is composed of seven members appointed by the governor and approved by the Senate for four-year terms, with one member from each of the five state congressional districts and two from the state at large. At least one but no more than two must be from Multnomah County, the state's most urbanized county; one must be an elected city or county official when appointed; and one current or former elected city official must be included. Administration of the commission and the planning program was provided by establishing the Department of Land Conservation and Development (DLCD).

LCDC was charged with developing the goals and supporting policies by January 1975 for the commis-

---

1. The key requirements of Senate Bill 100, and the long and often painful efforts to implement those requirements, are detailed in DeGrove (1984); Knaap and Nelson (1992); Abbott, Howe and Adler (1994).

sion to adopt. After an aggressive effort to seek public input—10,000 people in workshops, hearings and other meetings, and 17 advisory committees of technical specialists—about what should be included, the commission adopted the first 14 goals and guidelines in late December 1974. The remaining five goals were adopted by LCDC in December 1976.

Of the 19 goals, five combine to form an impressive focus on urban policy: land use planning, agriculture land, economy of the state, housing, public facilities and services, and urbanization. The urbanization goal requires the establishment of a UGB by all Oregon cities that includes sufficient land outside the city limits to accommodate a 20-year population projection. The relevant county has the coordinating role of establishing and maintaining the boundary, except in the Portland Metro region. The economy, housing, public facilities and services, and transportation goals have a direct bearing on how urban development occurs within the UGB, but with the exception of housing their application has been uneven and sporadic.

Only in recent years have urban development patterns inside UGBs become a major issue. The focus of the program until the late 1980s was primarily on housing inside UGBs and farm and forest land outside UGBs. There was a continuing struggle to sustain the integrity of exclusive farm use (EFU) zones in the face of constant pressure to exempt or otherwise water down rules, so that large rural acreages could be converted to nonagricultural or nonforestry uses. Counties found it increasingly difficult to enforce their own rules in this regard, and, in a series of assessments, 1000 Friends of Oregon found widespread violations of local plans and land use regulations in allowing nonfarm dwellings in these zones.

Under SB 100, a local government must submit its comprehensive plan and implementing regulations to DLCD for review and recommendation to LCDC. The commission may deny, continue or approve the community's request for "acknowledgment," which is the Oregon version of consistency. Major updates (periodic reviews) were originally scheduled every five years, but the law now requires such review in four- to ten-year cycles. Once a local plan has been acknowledged, the local government carries out its

Goals of the Land Use Planning Act (SB 100)

1. Citizen involvement
2. Land use planning
3. Agricultural land
4. Forest lands
5. Open spaces and scenic, historic and natural areas
6. Air, water and land resources quality
7. Areas subject to natural disaster and hazards
8. Recreational needs
9. Economy of the state
10. Housing
11. Public facilities and services
12. Transportation
13. Energy conservation
14. Urbanization
15. Willamette River Greenway
16. Estuarine resources
17. Coastal shorelands
18. Beaches and dunes
19. Ocean resources

provisions, and the goals no longer apply directly. A variety of sanctions are available to help ensure plans are carried out.

Deadlines and Repeal Efforts, 1976–1986

Adoption of the planning goals and guidelines by LCDC under Day's leadership was the first and last time a deadline set by the law was met. The plans of Oregon's 230 cities and 36 counties were due in the commission's office by January 1, 1976. Never realistic, the deadline was made less likely by limited funding to DLCD to interact with local governments and review plans promptly. While appropriations to implement the law were substantial, by legislative direction most dollars were passed through to local governments to assist them in plan preparation. Some critics felt that LCDC, through its staff agency, DLCD, did not use its full authority by attaching more specific conditions to the pass-through dollars to local governments. By 1980 some $18 million in state funds had gone to local governments, and one estimate had local governments spending an additional $75 million. Yet only 94 city and county plans, out of a total of 266, had been fully acknowledged.

The process proved far more difficult than antici-pated. DLCD's limited staff tended to be reactive rather than proactive in working with local gov-ernments. Policies developed to flesh out the goals and guidelines continued evolving, giving local gov-ernments a moving target to meet. Perhaps most important, a succession of ballot initiatives in 1976, 1978, 1982 and 1984 focused on repealing or drasti-cally weakening Oregon's land use law. Although these ballot initiatives were unsuccessful, they slowed the implementation process, as local governments opposed to SB 100's requirements delayed action in the hope the bill would be repealed. Strong support from several governors, other key stakeholders and 1000 Friends of Oregon managed to turn what looked like certain defeat, especially in 1982, into impressive wins for SB 100. In each case, the repeal efforts were soundly defeated. Oregon, along with every other state examined in this book, is proof that no system for managing growth and change to establish and sustain a smart growth system ever reaches a point where success is easy and automatic.[2]

In spite of the stress and strain, all plans and regu-lations were approved by 1986, with enforcement actions by LCDC and appeals by 1000 Friends of Oregon playing an important role in bringing the final holdouts, mainly counties, into the system. The difficulty in bringing the acknowledgment process to closure should not obscure the fact that major accomplishments were reached in developing local plans that conformed with the state goals framework. The interface between the agriculture and urbaniza-tion goals resulted in the designation of more than 16 million acres of EFU zones and more than 8 mil-lion acres of exclusive forest zones. In turn, all urban development was scheduled to take place within des-ignated UGBs. While each component has major weaknesses, Oregon still maintains an impressive record unmatched anywhere in the nation.[3]

2. For additional information, see Abbott, Howe and Adler (1984, 10, 291); Oregon Business Council (1993); DeGrove (1984, 276–290); Knaap and Nelson (1992, 190–193, 204–205).

3. For more background and history on this process, see DeGrove (1984, 235; 1992, 170); Abbott, Howe and Adler (1994, 212); Knaap and Nelson (1992, 1–3).

Protecting Farm and Forest Lands

Key Issues and Evolving Policies

Much was at stake in the effort to protect the best agri-cultural and forest lands from being eaten up by rural sprawl. Of the 62 million acres of land in Oregon, the federal government owned about half, mostly forest and range lands. Of the remaining 30 million acres, about 17 million were used as some type of farmland. Diversity is a major factor in Oregon agriculture, and the state is a national leader in such crops as grass seed, filberts, nursery crops, snap beans, peppermint oil and Christmas trees.

Counties initially supported SB 100, while cities were more negative. However, the stresses of the acknowledgment process, which dragged on for more than a decade beyond the original deadline, caused both cities and counties to become more negative about the implementation process. Understaffed for proactive coordination with local governments, LCDC waited for the plans and regulations, then reviewed them for conformance with the goals. During this process, the guidelines and policies clari-fying the requirements of the often vague goals were still evolving. Few plans were acknowledged on first submittal—typically several rounds were required to reach closure. In the meantime, new guidelines and policies often appeared, attempting to streamline the rules of the game. When LCDC seemed to weaken in its firm application of the goals, 1000 Friends and others challenged approvals in administrative hear-ings or in the courts. A key issue concerned how tightly UGBs should be drawn and proper densities assigned outside those boundaries.

All plans were acknowledged by August 1986, and counties were charged with the task of denying constituents' requests to partition land or build non-farm dwellings in EFU zones. However, this task often was not carried out, and supporters of the law became convinced that the commercial agriculture and forestry protection backbone of the law was being eroded. Goal 3 of SB 100 (Agriculture) defines the best farmland in terms of the U.S. Soil Conservation Service classification system, including soil classes I–IV in western Oregon and I–VI in eastern Oregon.

Counties are mandated, not just enabled, to place such land in EFU zones.

Exception lands—those outside UGBs unsuitable for agriculture because of prior subdivision and development or for other reasons—were recognized from the beginning. Local governments (primarily counties) were required to identify such lands and justify their exclusion from EFU zones. The criteria were specific and difficult to meet, with the burden on the county to justify a parcel as an exception area. Goal 3 required all farmland outside UGBs and not approved as an exception by LCDC to be placed in an EFU zone. The restrictions on uses in those lands were defined in the 1973 Farm Land Tax Assessment Act (SB 101), which contained the public policy goals of maintaining farmland for agricultural production, and spelled out other profarming policies, including requiring county governments to review all land partitions in EFU zones that create one or more parcels less than 10 acres in size. It also made all farmland in EFU zones eligible for tax deferral, and exempted such lands from sewer and water district charges.

In spite of the burden of justifying exception lands with "compelling reasons and facts," some 750,000 acres of such lands were approved by LCDC, including about 300,000 acres in the Willamette Valley. Still, many local plans were rejected by LCDC, in part because of a failure to justify exception lands. As the acknowledgment process dragged on, the governor and the legislature pressured LCDC to be more flexible in applying exception land criteria.

Subsequent legislation in 1983 authorized LCDC to allow local governments to identify marginal lands of lesser agricultural productivity, and to relax the land use standards on such lands. LCDC amended Goal 3 to allow such marginal land identification, but only if the county doing so applied more stringent restrictions to prime farmlands. Most counties did not take advantage of this opportunity, and the struggle to find a solution to the exception areas and secondary lands debate wore on. Under pressure from the legislature to resolve the issue, LCDC launched a number of pilot studies in counties, to find appropriate criteria for identifying secondary lands and the land uses that should be allowed on them.

By 1985 the rural lands issue was far from settled,

with opponents of any strict application of the policies and standards fighting to free large acreages of rural lands from the limitations of EFU zoning. At the same time, 1000 Friends and its allies, including the Oregon Farm Bureau, pressed for stricter enforcement of EFU controls and resisted efforts to release additional rural lands from those controls.

In 1985 Robert E. Stacey Jr., 1000 Friends staff attorney, charged that while the 16 million acres in EFU zones looked good, their significance was being eroded by county governments' failure to enforce their own rules, as well as by LCDC approval of vague and contradictory standards that invited abuse. Stacey concluded that "the result of this pernicious combination...has been the continuation of the very thing SB 100 was supposed to stop: the alarming erosion of the state's rural areas by unnecessary and harmful development" (1000 Friends 1985, 9).

Richard P. Benner of 1000 Friends also expressed concern over the 1985 legislative action directing LCDC to identify secondary resource lands and define uses allowed on them. According to Benner, the legislative directive was "a compromise between the counties on the one hand and the Farm Bureau, Agriculture for Oregon and 1000 Friends of Oregon on the other" (1000 Friends 1986, 3). Benner argued that several safety valves allowed some noncommercial farm and forestry uses in rural areas, including the exception land process and the nonfarm or forest dwelling process, resulting in hundreds of homes each year on marginal lands.

A major handicap in addressing the rural lands problem in an informed, rather than an emotional, way was the failure to collect, analyze and compose data, including maps showing exactly where the nonfarm dwellings and parcelizations had occurred. The legislature recognized the problem, and in 1986 required that DLCD be notified of all land divisions and nonfarm dwellings in EFU zones, and in 1989 added the same reporting actions for exclusive forest zones. However, DLCD never had the resources to analyze these data, or at least never made it a high enough priority. The best map of land divisions under the exception lands provision was prepared by Robert Liberty of 1000 Friends and presented to LCDC on April 1, 1986. A year in preparation, the so-called map of shame showed all exception land approvals throughout the Willamette Valley, and identified the amount of nonfarm development being allowed in rural areas.

Efforts to "solve" the rural lands problem ran into a political deadlock in the 1991 legislative session. A Republican-controlled House blocked consideration of a bill that key supporters of the land use law could reluctantly support. In March 1991 LCDC, acting on its legislative mandate to produce new rules based on a 1990 pilot project with regard to rural lands, recommended a secondary lands program. This proposal was rejected by the House because it was too tough and by the Democratic-controlled Senate because it exposed too much land to rural sprawl.

The House and Senate then developed their own secondary land bills, HB 3570 and SB 91. HB 3570 "repealed existing farm and forest land protections, and gave counties broad discretion to designate new secondary lands" (1000 Friends 1991, 3). SB 91 outlined specific criteria to determine what land should fall into the secondary category. While it maintained the essence of the farmland protection program, by some estimates it would have resulted in the designation of four million acres as secondary lands. Introduced by Senator John Kitzhaber, the bill was supported by the Oregon Farm Bureau, the Oregon Forest Industries Council, the League of Oregon Cities, most home builders and developers, the League of Women Voters and 1000 Friends. Governor Barbara Roberts also supported SB 91 as the appropriate starting point for LCDC to try again to craft a new secondary lands rule.

1992 Secondary Land Rules

In December 1992 LCDC adopted a set of administrative rules on secondary rural lands in an attempt to put the issue to rest, so it could concentrate instead on problems of transportation, land use and air quality in Oregon's urban areas. The new rules followed the specific criteria approach of SB 91, rather than the "turn it all over to the counties" approach of HB 3570. Even though the December rules lasted only long enough for the 1993 legislature to reject them, they deserve close analysis because the follow-up bill, HB 3661, reflected significant parts of LCDC's rules.

The new rules specified designation criteria, land uses and minimum parcel sizes for six new zones: high-value farmlands, important farmlands, small-scale farmlands, high-value forest lands, small-scale forest lands, and mixed farm and forest lands (Pease 1994, 172–173). The high-value farm and forest lands criteria offered the most protection for commercial farm and forest production. High-value farmlands included lands with soils classified as prime, unique, Class I or II soils, and certain other lands suitable for intensive farming. High-value forest lands were "defined in terms of a tract's capacity to produce 5,000 cubic feet of commercial wood fiber in western Oregon and 4,000 cubic feet per year in eastern Oregon" (Pease 1994, 173). The new Goal 3 (Agriculture) and Goal 4 (Forest) rules were mandatory for eleven counties: nine in the Willamette Valley, plus Jackson and Hood River counties, which were required to be in compliance with the new rules by 1996. Banning such developments as golf courses and destination resorts as uses in the high-value farm and forest lands was a definite plus (Pease 1994, 173).

While the 1992 rules contained many of the specific criteria favored by 1000 Friends and its allies, they did not win that group's support in the 1993 legislative session, and were far too restrictive to win the support of the realtors, counties and their Republican allies in the legislature. Governor Roberts and a majority of the Senate, led by Kitzhaber, favored strong controls on rural land use, while the Republican majority in the House and their allies in the Senate wanted something much weaker. A bitter, session-long battle saw LCDC rules first rejected wholesale in the early versions of HB 3661 (dubbed the Big Land Use Bill, or BLUB), and a far more "liberal" (much less protection for rural land) approach in a wide-ranging new Omnibus Rule. Strong objection by the governor and 1000 Friends to this approach finally resulted in a compromise that revised HB 3661 to make adjustments in LCDC rules (DLCD 1993a; 1993b; 1993c; 1994).

The 1993 Legislative Fight over HB 3661

Republicans maintained their control of the House for the 1993 session, while Democrats narrowly maintained control of the Senate. The new House leadership moved early in the 1993 session to draft HB 3661. The bill in its original form ordered the repeal of LCDC's 1992 Secondary Land Rules and substituted provisions that conformed essentially to the procounty approach (HB 3570) supported by House Speaker Larry Campbell and others who advanced strong private property rights agendas. House Republican leaders and some Senate Republicans made it clear to LCDC that a bill acceptable to them was the tradeoff for LCDC's budget.

The House crafted a bill that, in the eyes of long-time supporters of SB 100, would totally destroy the program for which they had worked so hard. In the intense negotiations between the House and Senate to decide on a final form of the bill, the fight came down to the last days of an unusually long session. Although the House Republicans apparently had a majority to gut the land use program, they also understood that this would be opposed by both the Senate and the governor.

The debate within the Republican caucus dragged on, and when HB 3661 was finally introduced in May it was quickly blasted as too extreme. *The Oregonian* and other Willamette Valley press criticized it, and the Republicans found themselves near the end of a session without a viable bill. Finally, all sides agreed on a version that was not fundamentally destructive of Oregon's effort to protect important farm and forest land. They struck a reasonable compromise between stronger protection of agriculture lands in the Willamette Valley, where they were under greatest pressure from nonfarm dwellings and farmland parcelization, and weaker protection for such land in eastern and southern Oregon.

The new DLCD rules were approved by LCDC on March 1, 1994, incorporating the specific criteria and standards in HB 3661. That bill directed LCDC to repeal all the rules it had adopted in December 1992 and develop new rules based on "small-scale" farm and forest land, and to substitute a "lot of record" approach to solve the equity issue. Equity, in this case, meant giving relief to persons who had owned land for a certain time. Under HB 3661, if a person or his or her heirs had owned the property since 1985, in a farm or forest zone where under the old rules a dwelling was not allowed, a dwelling now could exist as a

matter of right, depending on the productivity of the land for farm or forest use.

A second major change designed to strengthen and simplify the protection of farm and forest land was the abandonment of performance standards in favor of a minimum lot size of 80 acres in all farm and forest zones, a standard more stringent than LCDC had been applying previously. If counties proposed any minimum lot size below 80 acres, they were required to justify it to LCDC. A 160-acre minimum lot size on rangeland, mainly in eastern Oregon, was also included in the bill. The impact of the minimum lot size provisions was seen as creating more dwellings in the short run but fewer in the long run.

A third major policy change had to do with the standard for farm dwellings on high-value land. HB 3661 left it to LCDC to solve the issue by rule, and it adopted a standard in high-value farmland of an $80,000 gross income in two of the last three years. This was a substantially higher standard than previously applied and helped assure that "farm dwellings" were really for farmers. The case-by-case parceling used previously resulted in small parcels that were not truly farm units. Together, the 80-acre minimum lot size and the new gross income standard were seen as a great improvement. Some 1000 Friends studies had shown that more than 75 percent of the farm dwellings being approved statewide were going to people who made no money on farming, and the new rules were expected to eliminate almost all of that abuse (1000 Friends 1991, 5–6).

Contrary to the experience in any other state, one of the most interesting sources of support for HB 3661's provision to tighten protection on the best agricultural lands was the Oregon Farm Bureau, and that support has continued over many years. Several county farm bureaus also evolved into outspoken supporters of land use planning, although internal conflicts linger, and the annual Oregon Farm Bureau policy statement has strong support for the land use law and EFU zoning right along side a strong private property rights plank.

Among other agricultural groups, the Grange was not seen as active in land use politics, though they were "quietly opposed" to land use controls. The Oregon Wheat League's involvement was seen as supporting the HB 3661 approach of being tough in the Willamette Valley but more hands-off in eastern Oregon. Because the eastern lands are generally not irrigated, and thus growth pressures are not as prevalent, supporters of strong land use planning such as 1000 Friends felt they could accept that tradeoff.

Urban Growth Management

While protection of rural lands was a primary stimulus for Oregon's land use planning legislation, five of the policy goals outlined in SB 100 addressed urban issues: Goal 14 (Urbanization); Goal 10 (Housing); Goal 11 (Public facilities and services); Goal 9 (Economy); and Goal 12 (Transportation).

Goal 14 and the Establishment of Urban Growth Boundaries

Goal 14 (Urbanization) aimed at providing an orderly, efficient transition from rural to urban land use by establishing UGBs, not to limit growth but to manage its location. LCDC based this UGB requirement on that adopted for the city of Salem and for Marion and Polk counties in 1974. As Oregon's first "development stop line," the UGB was an attempt to manage the area's growth better, in response to reports by the Mid-Willamette Valley Council of Governments that demonstrated the efficiencies of urban containment over urban sprawl. The action was a remarkable example of voluntary intergovernmental coordination, in which the city, counties and a number of water and sanitary sewerage districts agreed to establish

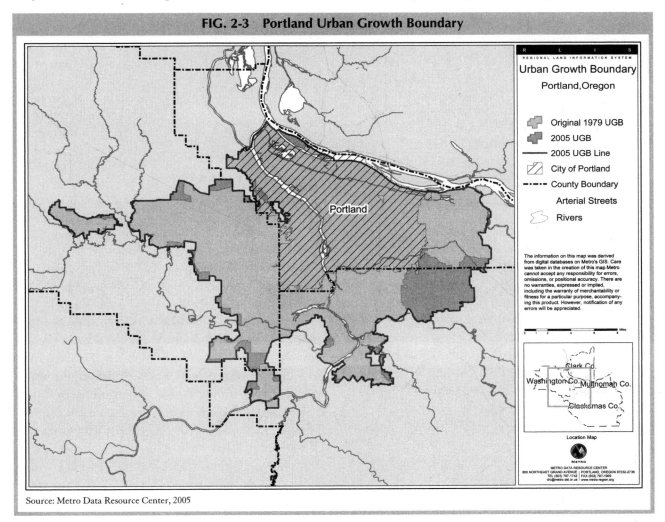

FIG. 2-3   Portland Urban Growth Boundary

Source: Metro Data Resource Center, 2005

the boundary. Other important elements in Goal 14 included the extensive downzoning of farmland outside the UGB to eliminate any urban development opportunities at even the lower densities. Another provision anticipated the exception lands category of SB 100 by zoning land not suitable for farming down to five- to twenty-acre tracts, but restricted their use to assure compatibility with nearby farm operations.

The effort to establish boundaries was a tough struggle in almost every case. Cities and counties typically proposed boundaries far too large to justify in light of the required 20-year population projections. The other urban growth management goals associated with Goal 14 could have resulted in the compact urban form crucial to successful sprawl containment. But there was the combined lack of a clear, compelling concurrency requirement, Oregon's very difficult annexation laws, and the assumption that once the boundary was established the urban form challenge would take care of itself. This led to two problems that continue to threaten the effectiveness of the law: urban sprawl inside the UGB and the high number of nonfarm dwellings and inappropriate land divisions outside UGBs.

The Portland metropolitan region is a special case because it has a unique regional governance system, known as Metro, and contains almost half the population of the state. According to the 2000 census, the population inside the UGB is approximately 1.3 million; the projection for 2020 is 1,730,000 (Metro 2002, 1; Metro Data Resource Center 1999). Metro's struggle is similar to that in Oregon's other urban areas, both in establishing the boundary initially and in establishing high enough densities to prevent the expansion of the UGB because of low-density development inside the boundary.

The market factor approach to drawing UGBs involved placing "25 percent more land than necessary to achieve 100 percent buildout in the year 2000, based on urban growth projections" (Knaap and Nelson 1992, 48–49). Salem used this approach in drawing its UGB in 1974, to ease charges that a growth boundary would drive up the cost of land. A 1976 study found little or no impact on land costs that could be attributed to the Salem UGB, and a 1977

study found the UGB impact on land and housing costs to be minor (DeGrove 1984, 275; Knaap and Nelson 1992, 48–51).

The recession that began in the late 1970s and continued into the mid-1980s caused most urban growth management concerns to slide off the public policy agenda (except housing policy, which was already being addressed). However, as the state began to feel strong growth pressures again during the late 1980s and early 1990s, the issue of urban growth management moved up on that agenda.

Implementation of Goal 10 (Housing)

Enforcement of LCDC's Goal 10 (Housing), "to provide for the housing needs of citizens of the state," was the product of a unique partnership between 1000 Friends, the Home Builders Association of Metropolitan Portland (HBAMP) and the state Association of Home Builders. This coalition brought key housing-related appeals to LCDC and persuaded the commission to adopt its rigorous interpretations of the goal as administrative rules. The coalition also lobbied successfully for adoption of the goal's requirements into the Oregon Statutes by the 1981 legislative session, increasing the certainty that the goal would be fully implemented by LCDC. Goal 10 stated in part:

> Buildable lands for residential use shall be inventoried and plans shall encourage the availability of adequate numbers of housing units at price ranges and rent levels which are commensurate with the financial capabilities of Oregon households and allow for flexibility of housing location, type, and density. (LCDC 1985, 11)

Beginning in 1977 LCDC interpreted the language of the goal to include the legal principles of "fair share" and "least cost" housing. This required each local government to reach its fair allocation of housing types (single-family versus multifamily) by examining the broader housing needs of the region, including manufactured housing. Furthermore, LCDC ruled that "local standards and procedures for reviewing applications to build 'needed housing types'...must be 'clear and objective'" (Ketcham and Siegel 1991, 2–3).

The coalition of 1000 Friends and the Home Builders was a matter of self-interest in each case: 1000 Friends needed support for the land use law, and its executive director, Henry Richmond, supported a meaningful affordable housing component. The Home Builders, unsuccessful in getting the law repealed in 1976, accepted a tradeoff between staying out of rural lands and having clear standards and a mix of densities to keep them busy inside UGBs. They got what home builders desire: more certainty and timeliness in getting permits than anywhere else in the nation. This partnership has endured since its inception, with equally long-lasting strains.

LCDC proceeded to implement Goal 10 aggressively in several early reviews of local plans. In two key decisions, it upheld the goal's policies by rejecting local government reductions in density that effectively excluded low-income residents (*Seaman v City of Durham*). LCDC also rejected a City of St. Helens plan that placed high-density development in a "conditional use" category that gave the city the ability to reject the applications on vague and uncertain grounds. This practice was common in many other local governments, and the St. Helens decision closed the loophole. LCDC stated that the housing goal

> clearly says that municipalities... are not going to be able to pass the buck to their neighbors on the assumption that some other community will open wide its doors and take in the teachers, police, firemen, clerks, secretaries and other ordinary folks who can't afford homes in the towns where they work. (DeGrove 1984, 272–273)

The Metropolitan Housing Rule (MHR) adopted by LCDC in 1981 (amended in 1987 and 1990) applied to the part of the Portland region within the UGB; parts of Clackamas, Multnomah and Washington counties; and 24 cities, including Portland (LCDC 1998). The rule is remarkable for the specificity of its policy requirements, and, together with Goal 10, made the housing component of Oregon's land use planning law stronger than that of any other state (with the possible exception of Florida). The basic goals of the MHR are to (1) provide adequate land for needed housing types; (2) ensure that land within the metropolitan Portland UGB accommodates the region's projected population growth; (3) provide greater certainty to the development process; and (4) reduce housing costs.

These cities and counties must prepare comprehensive plans allowing at least 50 percent multifamily or attached single-family units, and they must allow development at certain minimum densities, ranging from ten units per buildable acre to six or eight units per buildable acre in most suburban areas. The assumption was that higher densities would equal more affordable housing (Ketcham and Siegel 1991, 3).

In a study that examined vacant land only, 1000 Friends (1982) concluded that housing opportunities had been increased substantially by the MHR (a 400 percent increase in land zoned for multifamily units and a decline in average lot size from 13,000 to 8,000 square feet). A 1991 study by the Home Builders Association and 1000 Friends examined actual development patterns (Ketcham and Siegel 1991). The study was conducted during 1985–1989, when the state was recovering from the recession of the early 1980s and the Portland area, especially, was beginning to grow again.

The findings of the 1991 study yielded five conclusions.

1. The proportion of multifamily and attached single-family housing increased dramatically. Of all such units built, 74 percent were in projects of moderate- to low-density (less than 25 units per net buildable acre), while only 5 percent were higher than 60 units per net acre. Furthermore, 77 percent of households could afford to rent the region's median-priced apartments; 67 percent could afford the median-priced two-bedroom home; and 43 percent could afford the three-bedroom home. Even so, housing affordability for the Portland area was seen as two to three times greater than comparable West Coast areas.

2. The proportion of smaller and more affordable developed single-family lots increased. Multifamily and attached single-family housing accounted for 50 percent of all residential develop-

ment, compared to 30 percent before the MHR took effect, demonstrating that mandating higher densities had a substantial effect. In the post-MHR timeframe, density of new development increased from 13 to 32 percent, depending on its subregional location.

3. Jurisdictions where building activity was greatest came closest to achieving development mix and density targets. Rapid development of a finite amount of buildable land favored smaller lots and more multifamily housing, an important finding to policy makers deciding whether to expand the UGB.

4. Research into the causes of reduced project densities showed very little citizen opposition to development at higher densities. Of five density-limiting factors analyzed, citizen opposition was one of the least important. The top three were development economics, size constraints and regulatory constraints.

5. Land developed during the 1985–1989 study period was underutilized to the extent that remaining lands cannot absorb the region's projected housing needs under current zoning. This had great significance for the emerging debate over whether to expand the UGB. While residential development in this period exceeded density targets for the 20-year planning period for the UGB, single-family development occurred at substantially lower densities than those allowed. Multifamily development came in at about 90 percent of planned density, while single-family development achieved only 66 percent of potential or allowed densities. Most jurisdictions projected containing their population growth on the assumption of development at 100 percent of allowable densities. In a telling number, 12 percent of all single-family subdivisions developed were on lands zoned for multifamily. Because of shortfalls, the study concluded that "insufficient residentially zoned land remains to meet the region's projected housing needs over the remainder of the [20-year] planning period." (Ketcham and Siegel 1991, 9)

The study contained eight recommendations, a few of which are noted here. The first addressed man-

datory minimum density requirements: single-family development would not be allowed on land zoned for multifamily, and all development would have to reach a figure near the maximum allowed density, absent compelling reasons for not doing so (the city of Portland adopted a minimum density requirement in 1990). Another recommendation called for mandating a statewide Urban Housing Rule similar to the MHR, on the premise that the challenge facing the Metro region was emerging as a major problem in other urban areas as well. Other recommendations addressed monitoring and evaluating regional growth patterns, and stronger rules for local governments demonstrating compliance with regional housing objectives.[4]

LCDC Self-Assessment, 1989–1992

Spurred on by the approaching review of UGBs at the 20-year mark in 1993, and assisted by a 1989 legislative appropriation to support a comprehensive Urban Growth Management Study, DLCD, as the administrative arm of LCDC, examined what was happening inside UGBs and why. The purpose of the study was to evaluate the effectiveness of the growth management policies of the statewide planning program in confining growth within UGBs, and sharply limiting any nonfarm dwellings or land divisions outside those boundaries. DLCD hired ECONorthwest, a land use planning and economics consulting firm, to analyze urban growth issues in four urban areas, ranging from a small coastal community to the Portland metropolitan region.[5] The evaluation focused on two central issues: "(1) the amount of post-acknowledgment residential and nonresidential development outside UGBs; and (2) the density and configuration of development immediately outside and adjacent to UGBs as constraints on future development of urban lands" (Knaap and Nelson 1992, 58–59).

---

4. See Ketcham and Siegel (1991, 11–13); Abbott, Howe and Adler (1994, 105–116). See also Knaap and Nelson (1992, 77–96) for a description of the MHR, including a report on several evaluations of the impact of the MHR.

5. This information is taken largely from DeGrove (1992, 148–155), with additions and updating as required. It also draws on Knaap and Nelson (1992, 39–67), Abbott, Howe and Adler (1984, 25–45); ECONorthwest (1990).

The ECONorthwest study (1990) concluded that urban growth could be contained within the UGB, but that inappropriate development, inside and outside UGBs in the case study areas, called for significant policy changes to accommodate the great bulk of the state's population growth in compact urban areas. Actual densities within the Portland UGB were not so low as to demand immediate expansion of the UGB, but they were far enough below the densities permitted by zoning to be a major cause for concern: 34 percent underbuilt for single-family homes and 23 percent for multifamily residences.

Metro: Portland's Regional Government

The Portland metropolitan region and its elected government, know as Metro, are a major part of Oregon's growth management system. Much of the activity in the region is interwoven with state trends and legislation, but significant efforts are unique to the region. Growth in and around Portland is expected to continue to outpace that of the state as a whole, but the region's comprehensive urban growth strategy features a revamped, reempowered Metro and a new level of coordination by state agencies— especially the Oregon Department of Transportation (ODOT)—joining with LCDC and Metro to link land use and transportation for a more compact urban development pattern within the UGB.

The Origins of Metro

Portland's Metropolitan Service District (Metro) began operation in 1979 following a long evolution of regional planning efforts. In 1977 the Oregon legislature had put before the region's voters a plan to combine the Metropolitan Service District and the Columbia River Association of Governments (CRAG). The new entity was to be headed by the Metro Council composed of 12 council members, each elected from a single district within the region, and an executive director elected at-large. Voters approved the plan in May 1978 by a margin of 55–45 percent,

thus establishing the only elected regional government in the nation (Abbott and Abbott 2001).

Metro took over operation of the Washington Park Zoo and other regionwide services, including solid waste disposal facilities and the UGB established by CRAG in 1977. In its first decade, Metro limited its involvement in land use planning to reviewing applications for UGB amendments and local plans for the 24 cities and the unincorporated areas of the three counties lying within the UGB, for consistency with LCDC goals and policies (Metro 1989).

It was not until the late 1980s that Metro began the process of developing its own set of regional growth strategies. Part of the problem was money. Beyond an excise tax on fees for its operation of the zoo, the solid waste facility and later the Oregon Convention Center, Metro's funding sources were limited. Any additional revenues, including an ad valorem tax, were subject to a referendum, and the political climate in the early 1980s never seemed ripe for such an effort. Thus, local government dues were virtually the only flexible funding source for Metro, putting it in a poor position to assert its authority over local plan review.

Taking on Urban Growth Management Issues

In 1989 Metro became increasingly involved in urban growth management issues and formed a strong partnership with LCDC and other relevant state agencies. Led by Rena Cusma, Metro's second elected executive, Metro's Regional Urban Growth Goals and Objectives (RUGGOs) were developed through a two-year planning process initiated in early 1989. A series of workshops was held for public input and subsequent revision of the issues framework, concluding with a regional growth conference in January 1990. Key issues identified were traffic congestion, rising housing costs, loss of open space and declining environmental quality, all seen as demanding regional growth management solutions. Infrastructure funding shortfalls were also identified, with only about half of the needed funding available. As Cusma put it, speaking in early 1990:

> In the coming decade, Metro's effectiveness will be measured by the ability to plan for the future and manage our urban environment.... [P]ublic

policy decisions and infrastructure investments have to be made now in order to manage growth so we can also maintain our livability. In addition to managing the UGB, I believe Metro's planning role will be expanded in the following areas: parks, natural areas and recreational facilities; affordable housing; water quality; and transportation. By working together, regional government, local government, and the private sector—we create a partnership that will lead us into a more livable future. (Metro 1990)

In September 1991 the Metro Council adopted the final version of the RUGGOs to replace those originally adopted by CRAG in 1976. Given the home rule sensitivity of local governments and the realities of Metro funding, RUGGOs were used initially to guide the preparation of Metro's functional plans, including air and water quality, transportation and any other matters deemed regionally significant, and for setting the standards and procedures for managing the UGB. City and county comprehensive plans would then be reviewed for consistency with those Metro plans and standards.

A goal of urban form provided the substantive framework for growth management in the region, and had three subgoals: the natural environment, the built environment and growth management, each with a series of objectives for implementation of the goals. For example, the objectives for growth management called for a compact urban form with a clear demarcation between rural and urban land; mixed-use urban centers throughout the region, at densities sufficient to support an efficient public transportation system; and neighborhood-oriented, pedestrian-friendly communities.

In the midst of these planning efforts, a separate but closely related movement was undertaken by a group of citizens and regional leaders to substantially change Metro by giving it a home rule charter. In 1990 a constitutional amendment passed in a statewide vote granting home rule authority to the voters of the district. The ballot measure provided for the legislature to appoint a commission to draft a proposed home rule charter to be placed on the ballot in November 1992. In the final version endorsed by the commission and approved by the voters, Metro's ability to adopt and implement a regional plan was substantially strengthened.

The new Metro charter mandated the development of a long-range vision of the future and a regional framework plan to address transportation, the UGB, urban design, housing density, water supply, open space and other topics of regional significance. Having been authorized but not mandated to do almost all such regional growth management activities before the charter adoption, Metro now had to change its primary focus from the operation of regional facilities to regional urban planning and growth management.

The charter specifically required Metro to adopt a Future Vision by 1995 and a Regional Framework Plan to implement the vision by 1997, and to review all local plans for consistency with the framework plan by December 1999. A mandated Metropolitan Policy Advisory Committee (MPAC), consisting of city, county and special district representatives, could give input to any Metro action that would assume a service delivery function or amend the plan.

On the matter of funding for Metro, the picture remained difficult and uncertain. The charter gave Metro a broad range of possible fiscal sources, but Metro must refer significant ones to the voters for approval (e.g., a regional sales, income or property tax). A Tax Study Commission, whose membership was specified in the charter, also must give its opinion of a proposed tax increase before it can be submitted to a referendum. This requirement left Metro with only its so-called niche taxes—an excise tax on its enterprise funds, of which solid waste tipping fees comprised 80 percent. Yet, the charter also mandated that the Metro Council had to fund its planning responsibilities at an "adequate" level.

In the area of governance, the charter provisions reduced the number of council districts from twelve to seven, all single-member districts as before. They also kept the at-large elected executive officer, Mike Burton, who had won the post in the fall 1994 elections and was committed to implementing a strong vision for Metro. Most observers felt that the new seven-member council would be more visible on regional planning and urban growth management issues than had the previous larger council, and that has proven to be the case. Amendments to the charter in 2000 consolidated the executive and council offices further and created a new elected leadership position of council president.

The Region 2040 Planning Process

Out of the development and adoption of RUGGOs came the Region 2040 growth management planning process, a cooperative effort among Metro, TriMet (the regional public transportation agency), ODOT, LCDC and the cities and counties in the region (DeGrove 1992, 151–155).

Given the political upheaval in drafting and adopting the home rule charter and changes in Metro Council membership, the major planning and implementation programs moved along remarkably well. Several key elements of a new 2040 strategy were being put in place to move Metro into an even stronger position.

As mandated by the 1992 Metro charter, the 18-member Future Vision Commission worked for 18 months to develop the regional vision. Adopted by the Metro Council in July 1995, it concluded with a statement about future growth management:

> In 2045 growth in the region has been managed. Our objective has been, and still is, to live in great cities, not merely big ones. Performance indicators and standards have been established for our vision and all other growth management efforts, and citizens of the bi-state region annually have an opportunity to review and comment on our progress. The results of that review are used to frame appropriate actions needed to maintain and enhance our regional quality of life. (Metro 1995, 10)

The Region 2040 Growth Concept "is a long-range outline of what the region will look like from now until the year 2040," focusing on urban as well as rural–open space issues (Metro 1995, 4). Using a 50-year timeframe starting from 1990, it outlines the policies needed to establish a new urban form inside the UGB, aimed at moderate, carefully planned increases in density inside the UGB, so as to require only a small increase in the size of the UGB; fight traffic congestion; and improve air quality. Another element in the 2040 process was the Urban Growth Management Functional Plan, approved in 1996 to provide tools to meet the Growth Concept goals.

The entire development and redevelopment strategy is aimed at inner and outer neighborhoods, and centers and corridors. Residential and nonresidential density targets are set for each area (e.g., inner-city neighborhood lots averaging 5,000–6,000 square feet; larger outer area lots, but small enough to reduce the average lot size in the region from 7,200 to 6,600 square feet). The Metro Council formally adopted the Growth Concept by ordinance in December 1995. Burton summed up the concept, saying, "We chose to grow 'up' rather than 'out'; preserve open space and natural areas; redevelop urban areas when and wherever possible; create new development that is less auto-dependent and is oriented along transit corridors; and plan for affordable housing" (Metro 1995, 1).

The 2040 Framework, sometimes called the Regional Framework Plan (RFP), was designed "to develop strategies for implementing the growth concept. The plan will develop performance standards and model ordinances for local governments to meet" (Metro 1995, 4). The Metro charter required the plan's adoption by December 31, 1997, in effect mandating local governments' full participation as partners in planning for the region. The following are the basic elements of the 2040 Framework:

- *Use of land*, including "the urban growth boundary, housing densities, and affordability; urban design, urban reserves, rural reserves, and economic development."

- *Transportation*, including an update of the RTP, focusing on how best to move people and goods, "including strategies for cars, transit, freight, bikes, and pedestrians."

- *Natural areas*, starting with Metro's Greenspaces Master Plan and local plans, to establish "an interconnected system of parks, natural areas, greenways, and trails."

- *Water*, focusing on developing a Regional Water Supply Plan for watershed management and water quality and supply issues. (Metro 1995, 5)

Local comprehensive plans are where the Future Vision, the Growth Concept and the Framework Plan are implemented, to shape the future of the region for better or worse. These plans must address how local jurisdictions will meet the regional standards contained in the 2040 Framework (Metro 1993; 1994). The city and county elected officials on MPAC had a major role in the development of the 2040 strategy, and many of them had a stake in its success. Full implementation also depends on sustaining and strengthening Metro's partnership with the state, especially LCDC and ODOT, as well as the implementation of a new transportation planning rule (TPR). Metro's strategy could be greatly diluted or lost altogether if a hostile state legislature is able to weaken the state land use planning program and its emerging link with transportation planning.

The RFP is the final step in managing the very substantial growth taking place and projected to continue within the UGB. It integrated previous regional policies to produce a land use, transportation, and parks and open spaces planning framework. It was then passed to local governments and citizens of the region for input, especially on new mandates for the areas within the UGB. Citizens showed very strong support for all the key actions needed to limit the expansion of the UGB; this support included protecting natural areas within the UGB and a strong preference for transportation dollars to be spent on public transportation rather than roads (Metro 1996–1997; 1997a).

During a 1996–1997 review of Metro's UGB, the issue of urban form in general and density inside the UGB in particular was central to whether the boundary needed to be expanded to accommodate future population growth. It was hoped that the success or failure of Metro to design and implement policies to increase densities inside the UGB—thus limiting the need to extend the growth boundary into the rural countryside—would influence other urban areas in Oregon (e.g., Salem, Eugene and Medford). Furthermore, the effort to blend land use and public transportation systems has significance for other areas of the nation attempting to cope with sprawl patterns of development.

Metro used extensive (and expensive) databases to decide how much added land would be needed to meet the 20-year housing need projection, comparing the dwelling unit capacity with and without the full implementation of the Region 2040 Growth Concept. The analysis showed that the capacity to absorb growth within the existing UGB was much greater under the Region 2040 growth scenario, thus requiring a much smaller expansion of the UGB to meet projected population increases. These data determined the need to expand the UGB by only 4,000–4,800 gross acres to meet the year 2017 demand, when calls for expansion had ranged from none to at least 50,000 acres (Metro 1997a; 1997b). No other region currently planning its growth into the future has committed the resources to assure such a comprehensive database from which key decisions can be made, except possibly in the Puget Sound region of Washington state.

The decision by the Metro Council to add just 3,500 acres to the Metro UGB in December 1998 was far less than some development interests wanted, but was strongly encouraged by land use advocates supporting the full implementation of the RFP. It set the stage for a spirited debate as to whether the boundary needed further expansion. A decision had to be made by October 2000 on whether there was enough land inside the boundary to satisfy the state's 20-year supply requirement. The Home Builders Association of Metropolitan Portland—with other development interests, organized as the Partnership for Sensible Growth—failed in court action "to force Metro to 'immediately' expand the boundary" (1000 Friends 2000c, 24). On October 26, 2000, the Metro Council voted not to expand the UGB on the grounds that Metro's 2017 Land Need Report showed "there is enough land inside the boundary to satisfy the state's 20-year supply requirement" (Metro 2000a, 1).

Clearly, the decision not to expand the UGB was based on the assumption that the RFP would be fully implemented and not sabotaged by a hostile legislature or an initiative, such as one proposed for the 2000 ballot by Oregonians in Action (OIA), an antiplanning organization. The initiative, the Neighborhood Preservation Act, would have repealed "any existing Metro ordinances establishing density requirements on residential land," and the UGB would have been unnecessarily expanded onto farmland outside the boundary (1000 Friends 2000c, 24). The proposed initiative did not qualify for the May 2000 ballot, but it did qualify in May 2002, illustrating the significance of continuing efforts to weaken or destroy the Oregon land use system, particularly with regard to Metro's move toward smart growth (1000 Friends 2001b, 9).

The Green Infrastructure Component

One of the key factors in maintaining livable communities in Portland involved planning for and implementing a green infrastructure throughout the region. The goal of a regional network of parks, natural areas, trails and greenways to support, among other things, fish and wildlife populations goes back to the adoption of RUGGOs, the predecessor to Region 2040. A comprehensive effort led to the adoption of the Metropolitan Greenspaces Master Plan in 1992, which identified "57 regionally significant natural areas and 34 trail and greenway corridors for protection," including "forests, meadows, wetlands, lakes, and streams interconnected by more than 350 miles of trail and greenway corridors" (Metro 1996–1997, 4).

Funding to support green infrastructure was and continues to be a challenge. In May 1995 voters approved a $135.6 million bond issue to begin acquisition of the open spaces identified in the Greenspaces Master Plan. Six thousand acres were targeted, including 40 miles of trail and greenway corridors, and by fall 1996, 1,158 acres had been acquired. As of August 15, 2001, Metro had acquired more than 7,121 acres of land in 216 separate transactions. The acquisitions included 14 regional natural areas from 43 acres to more than 1,000 acres, for a total of 6,835 acres. In the regional trails and greenways category, six acquisitions were reported, ranging from one to 608 acres (Metro 2001b). A July 2001 report by Metro noted the "willing seller" status of all the transactions, including "more than 50 miles of stream and river frontage, and thousands of acres of natural area properties including wetlands, riparian areas, meadows and forests" (Metro 2001e). Of the original $135.6 million bond issue, a total of $98.2 million had been spent by May 31, 2001.

The local share portion of the measure contributed $25 million to 26 local parks providers. As of May 31, 2001, almost $21 million of those funds had been spent for 76 separate projects. Metro's Regional Parks and Greenspaces Department had also managed to secure more than $5 million from state and local sources for the purchase of "regionally significant" open space. While the acquisition phase of the 1995 bond issue moved along very well, Metro's Mike Burton noted, "significant financial challenges regarding the future management of these new open spaces" remain (Metro 2001e, 14–16).

Affordable Housing

Affordable housing received a substantial amount of attention in the countdown to final adoption of the 2040 Regional Framework Plan. In fall 1997 a three-part series of discussion sessions entitled "Housing Choices for Our Region" involved Metro, MPAC, the Home Builders Association of Metropolitan Portland, and the Coalition for a Livable Future. Additional sponsors were Fannie Mae, Washington Mutual and 1000 Friends. The series brought into focus the need to put affordable housing high on the list of policy challenges in adopting and implementing the RFP (Metro 1997a). Clearly, the push to increase densities inside the UGB offered additional opportunities for increasing the supply of affordable housing and assuring the best location regarding jobs or other needs.

The allocation of jobs and housing units to all of the 24 cities and parts of the three counties within the UGB (with the support of almost all of the local government units) was a long step toward keeping the expansion of the UGB below 5,000 acres. Ridership on the Westside light rail line was well ahead of projections; public transportation was being heavily used everywhere in the Portland region where it was easily available. There is and will continue to be a market for housing at a density that will keep the expansion of the UGB to a minimum.

The Metro Council adopted the RFP on December 18, 1997, and "all of Metro's efforts in developing regional housing policies came into play" (Metro 2000b, 5). The original policy included an inclusionary zoning provision strongly objected to by some local governments and home builders, which led to amending the policies in September 1998 (Metro Ordinance no. 98-769). The amended policy was the result of mediation between local governments, Metro and providers of affordable housing. John Fregonese of Metro noted later that he did not feel the mediated changes had kept Metro and local governments from making significant progress in the provision of housing, including affordable housing.

The Regional Affordable Housing Strategy (RAHS), adopted by the Metro Council on June 22, 2000, was the product of the Metro-appointed Affordable Housing Technical Advisory Committee, a broad-based group of 25 voting members from both the public and private sectors. In response to its charge to review and advise Metro on policies and strategies related to affordable housing, the committee recommended RAHS, which included "affordable housing goals and objectives, implementation strategies, and an assessment process" (Metro 2001d, 1).

Metro Ordinance 00-882C amended the RFP and Urban Growth Management Functional Plan to be consistent with RAHS. The new broad policy directions in the Framework Plan are not directly binding on local government, but they are significant because they set the framework for Functional Plan changes that are directly binding on local governments. New policy directions in the Framework Plan add sections on affordable housing production goals; changes in the Functional Plan that apply to local governments; and regionwide efforts to provide funding for affordable housing (Metro 2001d, 2–3).

Changes to the Functional Plan that are directly binding on local governments include requirements that

■ cities and counties adopt voluntary affordable housing production goals;

■ cities and counties shall ensure their comprehensive plans and implementing ordinances include strategies that ensure a diverse range of housing types, including action plans and implementation measures to maintain the existing supply of affordable housing and increase new affordable housing in dispersed locations and methods of increasing opportunities for households of all income levels to live in housing affordable to them; and

■ each jurisdiction completes progress reports 12, 24 and 36 months after adoption of Metro's ordinance. (Metro 2001d, 3)

Local governments were also given a list of seven land use tools that they must use in implementing the RAHS, including but not limited to

■ allowing for density bonuses;

■ providing for replacement housing;

■ encouraging voluntary inclusionary zoning;

■ allowing for TDRs;

■ addressing elderly and disabled housing needs;

■ correcting existing regulatory constraints;

■ reviewing surface parking requirements; and

■ reporting on tools considered but not adopted and why they were not adopted. (Metro 2001d, 3)

The amended RFP and the Functional Plan contain an impressive list of policies and recommended or required actions to implement them in the housing and especially affordable housing area. As always, implementation is the key, and as Metro put it: "While the tools and strategies identified in the RAHS will help to address the problem, we need more money to make a large dent in the need" (Metro 2001d, 2). However, many observers agree that the Metro region has done very well in producing affordable housing even without the inclusionary zoning mandate.[6]

Developments in the Transportation–Land Use Area

The evolution of a much closer land use–transportation connection started in 1984, when Metro and Washington County, supported by LCDC, agreed to consider a Westside Bypass Expressway that originated inside the Metro UGB, passed outside the boundary through valuable farmland west of the city, and then reentered the boundary. First introduced in 1968, the expressway was pushed aside in 1977 due to a conflict over a proposed Mount Hood freeway in

---

6. Changes to the Functional Plan directly binding on local governments, and the tools local governments use in implementing RAHS, are listed at www.metro-region.org/article.cfm?ArticleID=269.

southwestern Portland (Oliver and Hamilton 1999). When Metro returned to a study of Westside transportation needs in 1984, the bypass was again put on the agenda and was close to approval in 1988, when Sensible Transportation Options for People (STOP), led by 1000 Friends, took an appeal to the state Land Use Board of Appeals (LUBA). They argued that an evaluation should be done prior to the project analysis stage, since they feared that some alternatives that could make the bypass unnecessary would go unexplored. LUBA agreed with STOP, and the issue was appealed to the Oregon Court of Appeals, which overturned LUBA (1000 Friends 1995, 27).

In the meantime, in 1989 the Oregon legislature authorized the Urban Growth Management Study, which confirmed the fears of LCDC and others: densities were too low inside UGBs, and transportation and infrastructure needs were not keeping up with LCDC rules. In 1991 LCDC authorized an Urban Growth Management Task Group of local officials and interested groups to study the issue further and make detailed recommendations (DLCD 1992). In April 1992 DLCD adopted a new rule allowing all Oregon cities and Metro to adopt an urban reserve area to protect land just outside the UGB from inappropriate land division (e.g., one- to five-acre "martini farms") to keep it available for expanding the UGB if needed (DLCD 1993d, 5–7).

The early Westside Bypass–inspired discussions between LCDC and ODOT on the development of a new Transportation Planning Rule (TPR) were concurrent with LCDC's Urban Growth Management Study, Metro's RUGGO and its subsequent Region 2040 process. All of these efforts were focused on the same set of issues: reducing sprawl, both inside and outside UGBs, and lessening the reliance on the automobile. Modestly increased housing densities were seen as improving the affordable housing picture and as the key to avoiding large extensions of the UGB. Inside the boundary, more compact urban developments would encourage increased reliance on public transportation, thereby reducing trips and improving air quality.

By 1991 Metro, LCDC and ODOT all opposed the Westside Bypass, in favor of the land use, trans-portation and air quality (LUTRAQ) approach, applying smart growth principles to the traffic and other problems the bypass was supposed to address. As these efforts moved forward and LCDC's TPR was adopted in April 1991, Metro's position supported a mandatory TPR for the Portland region, where the rule set a goal of a 20 percent reduction in vehicle miles traveled (VMT) over the next 30 years (Brody 1991). A 1993 ODOT study estimated savings in excess of $11.5 billion over the 20-year period in avoided road construction costs, just by the VMT reductions necessary to meet the TPR in Oregon's four largest metropolitan areas (DLCD 1993d, 7; ODOT et al., 1993).

The Transportation and Growth Management (TGM) program of LCDC and ODOT was the most powerful expression of the integration of land use and transportation planning in Oregon and the nation at the time (early 1990s). The Urban Growth Management Study task group convinced LCDC that local government plans, developed in the 1970s and early 1980s, were not working to contain sprawl and accommodate growth without unbearable infrastructure costs and substantial loss of rural lands. Beyond personnel, funding for the joint program came almost exclusively from ODOT via the flexibility given for transportation programs by the federal government through ISTEA (Intermodal Surface Transportation Efficiency Act). Support by Governor Roberts and her appointments to the Oregon Transportation Commission (OTC) were key to the program's success.

The 10-point growth management tool kit required by TPR, and the TGM program itself, was scheduled to start using $6.5 million in ODOT–ISTEA dollars for grants to local governments, but two items needed approval from the hostile 1993 legislature. First was the revision of Oregon's virtually impossible annexation laws to allow cities to move logically in stages out to their UGB; second was a requirement that special districts coordinate their activities with local plans. To the surprise of many, both LCDC proposals were approved by the legislature.

Of the $6.5 million in ISTEA funds, $4.8 million went for grants to local governments to revise their transportation system plans for consistency with the

TPR; rethink land use patterns to be supportive of public transportation; and try out the growth management tool ideas generated by DLCD's Urban Growth Management Study. Grants were generally up to $440,000 per project and $80,000 for focused investment plans (ODOT/DLCD 1994). The hope was that good results would cause the 1995 legislature to authorize a second phase of the effort with similar funding. Instead, legislation that would have gutted the TPR passed the 1995 legislature, but Governor Kitzhaber vetoed it, leaving the TPR and TGM programs intact.

Despite an unsupportive legislature and other challenges, Metro's 2040 Framework Plan began to be implemented across the region by local governments, state agencies and Metro, backed by 1000 Friends, other organized groups and citizens. The Metro Council adopted the Regional Transportation Plan Update in July 1996. The guiding principles made it clear that the revised RTP would focus on supporting the Region 2040 Growth Concept, including making the transportation–land use connection the heart of the update.

Another RTP was adopted by ordinance by the Metro Council on August 10, 2000, as a blueprint for directing new transportation investments in the Metro region over the next 20 years. The goal was to provide additional travel options in the Portland region, which was expected to see a 50 percent increase in population and a 70 percent increase in jobs by 2020 (Metro 2001c, 1), thereby ensuring an enhanced quality of life for the Metro region. The plan, to be updated every three years, set out targets and guidelines for pedestrian access, bicycles, transit, light rail, freight and railways. The Metropolitan Transportation Improvement Program (MTIP) was used by Metro and the ODOT to allocate federal and state transportation funds for a broad array of multimodal projects (Metro 2001f, 2).

In a related development, Portland was one of nine cities chosen in 1996 by the Federal Highway Administration to examine the potential of peak-period pricing to reduce traffic congestion. The Traffic Relief Option Study was a three-year effort (1996–1999) jointly sponsored by Metro and ODOT (Metro 2000c). Peak-period pricing involves charging drivers variable fees for the use of roads (higher during congestion periods) and includes incentives to use noncongested routes or public transportation. The study's initial results showed substantial support for peak-period pricing, especially if the money generated would be used for improving public transportation. The study showed that peak pricing could be beneficial, but that building public support would be required before a demonstration project was proposed (Metro 2000c). While peak pricing has become part of the RTP, its implementation remains a hot potato. Land use management supporters favor the system, seeing it as a way to raise additional revenue to strengthen public transit systems and benefit especially low- and moderate-income groups. Others view it as a barrier to maximum flexibility in development and use of the land in general.

On the plus side, results in transit ridership have been very positive. The popularity of public transit that is safe and dependable is made clear by the fact that transit ridership from 1990 to 2000 grew faster than the average daily vehicle miles traveled or the population increase. During the 1990–1996 period, transit ridership in the region increased 24 percent to some 50 million rides per year, and it increased to over 80 million by 2000. Some tangible results of the focus on public transit over the past several years included an 18-mile light rail extension to the western suburbs in 1997; a 5.5-mile light rail connection to the airport in fall 2001; and a 2.5-mile downtown Portland streetcar in summer 2001. A six-mile north light rail extension from downtown Portland through the inner city to the Expo Center at the Columbia River is scheduled to open in 2004. Known as the Interstate MAX, this is the first leg of a long-discussed plan to connect Portland to the Clark County (Washington) suburbs across the Columbia River.

Unlike many transit systems developed around the country, Portland Metro's transit routes have typically exceeded ridership projections. Tri-Met, which is the main provider of public transportation in the region, is committed to providing sufficient levels of transit service to meet the objectives of the 2040 Growth Concept. For example, in 1999, 193,000 riders used the region's bus and rail systems on an average weekday (Metro 2001c, 1). Given the population and job increases by 2020, that could grow to 450,000 riders "if expected funds are available for transit improvements...[and] could increase to as many as 590,000 per weekday by 2020 if additional funds are found for transit improvements identified" in the 2020 RTP (Metro 2001c, 1). By 2002 the 2.5-mile downtown streetcar had ridership well ahead of schedule with 4,000 passengers on weekdays, 4,600 on Saturdays and 3,300 on Sundays.

Metro's stronger role in implementing transportation and land use planning means that Tri-Met and any other provider of public transportation projects can only apply for federal funds for projects included in the RTP (Metro 2001c, 2). Cities and counties likewise are required to adopt a transit system map that conforms to the RTP and adheres to a sizable list of other smart growth land use–transportation requirements, such as amending development regulations to require that commercial development be located near major transit stops and designating pedestrian districts that are consistent with the plan. In short, there are now enough new "teeth" in the land use–transportation system to make the implementation of smart growth strategies far more likely than in pre-Metro charter and 2040 planning process days.

However positive Metro's experience with public transit has been, and it has been remarkable, there remains the challenge of finding the funds to expand the system as proposed in the 2000 RTP over the next 20 years. The plan calls for more than 650 transportation projects at an estimated cost of $7.6 billion, including

- $3.14 billion to double existing transit service to meet an expected 89 percent increase in bus and light rail riders by 2020; $2.1 billion for expanding and building new freeways and highways;

- $1.5 billion for arterial street expansions and new connections;

- $252 million for bridge maintenance and preservation;

- nearly $406 million for bicycle lanes, sidewalks, multiuse paths, trails, safer street crossings and improved bus stops and shelters;

- nearly $84 million for programs to ensure the system works efficiently, such as ramp metering and signal timing; and

- $7.1 million to promote transit ridership, walking, biking and telecommuting in the region. (Metro 2001a)

Of the money required to fund all the projects by 2020, about $3.16 billion is expected to come from state, local and federal sources. The challenge will be to expand those sources, since the primary goal of Metro's 2000 RTP is to link transportation investments to land use. In short, "collectively, these strategies can help the region maintain clean air, conserve energy, and reduce pressure to expand the urban growth boundary" (Metro 2001a, 2). Metro and ODOT are working together to ensure that monies are expended appropriately according to that plan.

Challenges to Oregon's Land Use Planning Program, 1995–2002

The balancing of Oregon's land use planning program between rural lands issues and urban growth management was just gaining momentum in the early 1990s when the program came under serious attack in the Oregon legislature. In spite of earlier challenges to SB 100 in 1991 and 1993, the result was surprisingly moderate: some weakening of land use controls in southern and eastern Oregon seemed to be balanced by stronger criteria to protect the best farmlands in the Willamette Valley.

Legislative Sessions and Elections, 1995–1998

Supporters anticipated a renewed assault on the smart growth program in the 1995 legislative session. The political action committees of the realtors, construction industry and OIA had raised $500,000 to support candidates opposed to the program, and both the House and Senate were taken over by the Republican party, whose legislative leadership was almost without exception opposed to the program. The chairs of the Senate Water and Land Use Committee and the House Natural Resource Committee had two of the worst scores of the Oregon Growth Management Policy Advisory Committee (PAC) for anti–land use bills in the 1993 legislature (Liberty 1995a). However, land use planning supporters were encouraged by the 1994 election of Democrat John Kitzhaber as governor, because he had strongly supported the program while serving in the state Senate.

As of mid-March 1995, 85 land use bills had been introduced, 41 of which, if passed and signed into law, would have weakened the land use program to greater or lesser degrees. Three bills were considered especially damaging to the program, and would have resulted in a very substantial expansion of UGBs into rural areas. HB 2114 would have ended LCDC's authority to protect farm and forest lands and require affordable housing and major transportation improvements that did not cross UGBs. HB 2117 would have allowed counties to rezone as secondary lands at least 85 percent of lands then in EFU zones, and 50 percent of lands in exclusive forest zones. HB 2709 would have required every city to expand its UGB to maintain a 20-year supply of land, based on the last 10-year rate of land consumption. This bill would have left no room to combat urban sprawl inside UGBs by requiring higher densities, thus reducing the need to expand the boundary.

The good news was that 1000 Friends and its allies immediately mounted a broad-based campaign to mobilize support for the program and to oppose crippling bills, which helped keep the worst of them from advancing. The Oregon Farm Bureau Federation and some county farm bureaus also supported efforts to block the worst assaults on the program, as did some timber interests.

1000 Friends opposed 63 bills in the 1995 session that would have weakened the land use law in various ways, including HB 2117 and HB 2114. Two Senate bills also seemed especially subversive. SB 600, the Ecotake Landowner Compensation Bill, would have required compensation for those affected by new state and local regulations aimed at protecting wildlife habitat, wetlands, open space and scenic resources, if the

regulations reduced the value of the land by $10,000 or 10 percent. This pernicious cousin of similar bills introduced in other states would have called a halt to much of the present system for managing growth and change in Oregon. SB 1114 addressed the secondary lands issue and would have taken 10 million acres of EFU land (about 60 percent) and made them available for very low-density development. Robert Liberty, executive director of 1000 Friends, signaled the critical factor for the survival of the Oregon program (1995b, 4).

> A lot is going to depend on the governor's willingness to veto bad bills. Right now we think we have the votes to sustain those vetoes (in some cases, in only one house), but the other side is discussing organizing a special session to override the vetoes (and effectively cripple the governor).

The last days of the regular 1995 legislative session saw renewed efforts by opponents of the land use law to revive the bills that would weaken the system the most. The strategy involved a "stuff and gut" procedure, by which previously defeated bills were added to other bills, including HB 2114 and SB 1114. Defenders of the law devised a counter-strategy, and so the 1995 regular session adjourned on June 10 without reviving the "bad" bills. By adjourning at that point, however, the legislature failed to approve the state's $375 million contribution to the proposed South/North Light Rail Line in the Portland metropolitan area, requiring a special session later that opened up the land use law to a renewed assault.

While many of the worst bills did not clear the legislature, a large number did pass. The critical question then became whether Governor Kitzhaber would veto them. The first and perhaps worst bill passed, then vetoed, was SB 600, the Oregon version of extreme property rights laws. The governor cited the protection of Oregon's land use planning program as the main reason for his veto. While Kitzhaber did not veto every bill that 1000 Friends and other supporters of the land use planning program opposed, he sustained the hopes of those who saw him as the last bastion of support among a misguided legislative majority. Had Kitzhaber not been elected governor, even worse bills would very likely have passed in the first place, and they almost certainly would not have been vetoed.

At the special session on July 28, the governor's vetoes of these bills were upheld in each case. The funding for Metro's light rail project also was approved, but without concessions to the Republican majority. Probably the most "iffy" of the special session bills, from the perspective of maintaining the principles of the land use system, was a variant of a regular session bill (HB 3458) on "regional problem solving," including provisions that would have allowed substantial rezoning of farm and forest land in two, and perhaps other, Oregon counties. The governor assured 1000 Friends that the special session version of the bill would not be used to weaken the land use program. Technical problems with the light rail funding necessitated another special session, which convened on February 1, 1996, and confirmed that funding without further damage to the land use law. Once again, Oregon's land use planning program had avoided eradication (Liberty 1996).

It did not take long for defenders of the system to begin planning to ward off disaster in the 1997 session of the legislature. The state Senate lineup for this session was seen as even more anti-planning than in 1995. However, the November 1996 elections had produced a closely divided House (31 Republicans and 29 Democrats), deemed more sympathetic to the land use system. Again, on the plus side for defenders of the land use law, the Oregon Farm Bureau maintained its support for most parts of the program. In a strategic decision, 1000 Friends crafted a long list of proposed changes to strengthen the system under the heading, "Agenda for Livability" (1000 Friends 1997, 9).

The legislative proposals attempted to give Oregon and its local governments revenue sources that are used in a number of other states, (i.e., impact fees on new development for schools and funding for mass transit), but they did not pass. Other 1000 Friends agenda items also failed, but raised key issues for the future, including requiring taxpayer impact statements for UGB expansions; conflict of interest standards for land use decision makers; and expansion of state parks—linked to a Kitzhaber administration initiative calling for a new bottle tax to pay for state park expansions (1000 Friends 1998, 6–7).

The April–May 1997 timeframe in the legislature saw the introduction of some 70 bills that (1) would undermine the land use system through weakening laws protecting farm and forest lands from sprawling development; (2) would attempt to weaken the authority of the LCDC; and (3) would have made it harder for citizens to challenge decisions they believed to be inconsistent with the land use system. The first test of the 1997 legislature's stance on these issues came in a vote on HB 2643, which would have gutted LCDC's authority to enforce its own land use laws. The bill was defeated 34–26, an embarrassing defeat for the Republican leadership. When the legislature adjourned, only SB 379, a truly "bad" bill from the perspective of land use supporters, had passed the legislature. This bill would have increased residential development in forest zones and was vetoed by the governor. Thus, the legislature was even more successful in 1997 than in 1995 in defeating legislation that would have gutted the land use planning system.

With no legislative session in 1998, the important developments centered on the elections for governor and the legislature, and on several ballot measures, all with the potential for major impacts on the 1999 legislative session and beyond. As the fall elections approached, Oregon Taxpayers United, headed by Bill Sizemore, was promoting an initiative to eliminate all regional governance systems in Oregon. Sizemore later withdrew it and announced his intention to run for governor as a Republican against incumbent Kitzhaber, who later won by a margin of 65 percent to Sizemore's 30 percent. No single development in the political arena was more significant to the ability of Oregon's land use planning program to survive and move forward in a smart growth direction (Thompson 1998).

On the legislative side, the results were mixed. While Republicans maintained their majority in the House and Senate, their 20 to 10 majority in the Senate was reduced to 17 to 12 to 1, with one former Democrat becoming an Independent. In the House, Republicans gained three seats, increasing their majority from a narrow 31 to 29, to 34 to 25 to 1, with one Democrat switching to Independent. The Republicans selected Lynn Snodgrass as speaker, an outspoken critic of the planning program who had tried to weaken protection of productive farm and forest land. Most if not all key committee posts in the House seemed certain to be held by strong opponents of the program (Tucker 1998). Thus, supporters of the land use planning program saw the Senate as a better place to fight bad bills than the House since Senate Republicans had lost their "veto-proof" majority.

Several initiatives on the fall 1998 ballot were promoted by OIA. The most hotly contested was Measure 65, which would have established an initiative process allowing citizens to require their elected representatives to review state agency administrative rules. The measure lost by a narrow margin, but land use program supporters expected to see it revived.

Legislation and Ballot Measures, 1999–2002

From the perspective of the growth management coalition led by 1000 Friends, the 1999 legislative session was a qualified success. Governor Kitzhaber vetoed eight bills that these supporters opposed, most of which would have weakened the system's capacity to protect rural lands (1000 Friends 2000a). The coalition and its allies claimed credit for defeating a long list of "bad" bills either in the House, the Senate or in conference committees, although three of these bills were signed into law. Perhaps the biggest disappointment was Kitzhaber's signing of HB 2658, which prohibited local governments from adopting inclusionary housing policies. "By signing this bill, the Governor has pre-empted local governments by taking a very effective tool out of their tool box" (1000 Friends 1999b, 2). A long list of affordable housing advocates decried the governor's action, and he later pledged that after the session he would work to provide more incentive-based efforts for affordable housing (1000 Friends 1999a).

The Westside Bypass Expressway idea was revived again in 1999 as a legislative mandate due to very heavy growth in that part of Washington County. A Senate Transportation Committee agreed, on April 28, 1999, to have a statewide vote in May 2000 on whether to build the long-debated expressway. Not surprisingly, 1000 Friends opposed the idea. The surprise was that the Washington County Commission and Beaverton's mayor also expressed doubt that the bypass would be good for the county, given a long

list of other needs, including roads, that were more pressing. The bill, however, died when it reached the Ways and Means Committee, so no statewide vote took place.

While it can be argued that the gains by the Democrats in the 1998 election kept extreme anti–SB 100 bills from clearing the Senate, those committed to weakening or destroying the system were as determined as ever. Indeed, the 1999 legislative session could be seen as the lull before the storm.

Measures 2 and 7 qualified for the November 2000 ballot in July, and set the stage for an all-out war between supporters and opponents of Oregon's land use system. The essence of Measure 2 was the same as Measure 65, which Oregon voters rejected in 1998: it would establish a process for requiring legislative review of administrative rules, some of which made up the core of Oregon's land use planning system, as well as EFU and exclusive forest zoning and UGBs. Other rules at risk included those that set standards for clean air and drinking water and the cleanup of toxic pollution (1000 Friends 2000d, 2).

Measure 7 had the full support of OIA and other groups dedicated to undoing Oregon's land planning and management system. It would amend the state's constitution to require that landowners be paid for any reduction in value caused by government enforcement of laws and regulations. Measure 7 amounted to one of the most extreme "takings" measures that have surfaced over the years. As the Oregon chapter of the American Planning Association put it: "Passage of Sizemore's 'takings' constitutional amendment would force Oregon into an impossible choice: either pay out millions or billions of dollars in 'compensation' to special interests—or simply stop enforcing the basic safeguards that protect our quality of life" (APA 2000). An initial polling by Measure 7's key sponsor showed some 70 percent of respondents favoring the measure.

For 1000 Friends and the 80-member Oregon Community Protection PAC, the challenge was to raise enough funds to make clear to the citizens what the true impacts of the measures would be (1000 Friends 2000b, 1–3). In late August 2000 the name of the "anticampaign" by the Oregon Community Protection PAC was changed to "No on 2 and 7."

Substantial contributions had allowed the campaign to hire a strong management team, move into a working office and expand their endorsement list. The campaign against Measure 7 included the active support of Audrey McCall, widow of the former governor Tom McCall, who had led the fight to pass SB 100, the 1973 landmark land use planning legislation. A strong show of opposition also came from farmers throughout the Willamette Valley, some leading developers and U.S. Senator Ron Wyden. Opponents of Measures 2 and 7 also included the League of Oregon Cities, Association of Oregon Counties, mayors, sheriffs and many others.

Editorials in a substantial number of Oregon newspapers focused on opposition to Measure 2, and it was rejected by a 56–44 percent margin, including support from rural counties that often opposed SB 100 and related statutes and regulations. Measure 7 passed, however, with 53 percent voting *yes* and 47 percent *no*. Given the certainty that Measure 7 would undermine implementation of the core values of Oregon's land use planning and management system, efforts to mount a constitutional challenge began immediately. Tom Christ, a Portland lawyer, volunteered his services to 1000 Friends to head the legal challenge, and the League of Oregon Cities filed a separate challenge. Christ argued that Measure 7 amended more than one part of the constitution, which, under Oregon law, requires a separate vote. OIA was confident that the suit had no chance of success, but on December 6, 2000, circuit court Judge Paul Lipscomb issued an injunction that blocked implementation of Measure 7, and on February 6, 2001, he ruled Measure 7 unconstitutional and made the injunction permanent (1000 Friends 2001c, 8). The measure was appealed to the Supreme Court, which agreed with Lipscomb on October 4, 2002.

The 2001 legislative session was seen as making a modest but potentially helpful gain, because bills to weaken Oregon's planning program were defeated. In the Senate, Democrats gained a seat, making it 16 Republicans and 14 Democrats. In the House, the result was 32 Republicans, 27 Democrats, and one Independent; when the Independent switched over to the Democrats, the margin became 32–28. 1000 Friends saw these shifts as making it harder for prosprawl forces to pass laws weakening the land use system (1000 Friends 2001c).

Legislative priorities in the 2001 session for 1000 Friends, other than defeating bad bills still sure to be introduced in the Republican-controlled legislature, focused on an eight-point Agenda for a Livable Millennium (1000 Friends 2001a, 17). It offered a familiar list of actions to

- defend citizen participation and promote ethical decision making;

- protect taxpayers' interests in growth issues;

- save special places (i.e., Columbia River Gorge, the Oregon coast) from intrusive development;

- protect farm, forest and range lands;

- use urban land wisely;

- increase transportation choices;

- respond to Measure 7; and

- encourage better development.

To counter Measure 7–type assaults on the system, most supporters agreed that a compromise was needed to offer limited compensation under narrowly drawn rules. However, actions by OIA during the 2001 legislative session had killed legislation that promised to find a compromise to Measure 7 (1000 Friends 2001b, 1), and the group later put forward four initiatives aimed at reinstating Measure 7 itself, regardless of the Supreme Court decision. Two of them would require any initiative overturned by the courts, including Measure 7, to be "corrected" and automatically re-sent to the ballot. The other two would strip the courts of powers retroactively, thereby declaring Measure 7 constitutional (1000 Friends 2001d, 8–9).

In anticipation of the November 2002 election, supporters of Oregon's land use system saw their hope for a smart growth future hinging on the election of a governor strongly supportive of the land management system, a legislature at least modestly supportive, and success in mobilizing citizens to vote against initiatives that undermine the system and for those that strengthen it. Prospects for a Democratic takeover of the legislature in 2002 looked promising before September 11, 2001, and the downturn in the Oregon economy also played a role in the campaign.

In the end, Democrat Ted Kulongoski was elected governor, and the 72nd Legislative Assembly, which convened in January 2003, included 15 Republicans and 15 Democrats in the Senate and 35 Republicans and 25 Democrats in the House.

Positive Developments and New Assaults in 2003–2004

The 2003 Legislative Session

The 2003 legislative session, lasting from January to August 27, was the longest in the state's history. The House, controlled by Republicans eager to dismantle Oregon's growth management system, launched its attack early in the session. In the Senate, evenly divided between Democrats and Republicans, "efforts to work toward consensus rather than conflict, caused most of the worst bills to become mired in committee and die... with the session finally behind us, Oregon's land use program emerged relatively unscathed." 1000 Friends concluded that after 227 days of trying, "the legislators and interest groups who worked overtime to roll back the laws that protect Oregon's communities, countryside, and quality of life have little to show for their efforts" (1000 Friends 2003a, 1).

As supporters of Oregon's system saw it, bad bills that did not pass or were vetoed by Governor Kulongoski included:

■ HB 3013, which "would have allowed almost limitless aggregate mining on farmland, regardless of the quality of the farmland or gravel involved";

■ HB 2617, which "would have allowed cities in central and eastern Oregon (mainly Bend) to expand their UGBs without demonstrating any need for such expansion"; and

■ HB 3631, which continued OIA's assault on land use laws by allowing individuals (e.g., long-time owners) to "further subdivide and develop their forest properties." (1000 Friends 2003a, 2)

1000 Friends and the Oregon Association of Realtors worked together on SB 515, which did pass the 2003 session. The intent was to simplify the process of notifying landowners about zoning changes. Another

success was the passage of a "bipartisan bill to help rural economies by allowing old mill sites to be redeveloped for industrial development" (1000 Friends 2003a, 3).

Metro Activities, 2000–2003

A major change in Metro's governance arrangement took place as a result of a charter amendment approved by the voters in the fall 2000 election. The action, effective at the end of 2002, eliminated the elected executive position, held by Mike Burton, and replaced it with a president who is elected at-large and presides over the council, which was reduced to six districts. The council president appoints a chief operating officer who in turn appoints Metro's department heads. Burton initiated and supported the governance change, which was widely backed by supporters of Metro and Oregon's land use planning system. Burton noted that during his eight years as elected executive, tension was constant between him and the Metro Council as to what role each should play.

David Bragdon was elected president in the May 2002 nonpartisan primary, on a platform of promoting economic opportunity, improving the coexistence of nature with a dynamic urban area, and transforming Metro into a more accountable and efficient organization (Metro 2003c).

Bragdon's goals for 2003 included increased efficiency and cost savings in Metro operations; development of a second open space acquisition measure for voter consideration; work on development of a regional economic strategy; and identification of the land necessary for development of new jobs in the region. Metro remains the only directly elected regional agency in the nation, and if a significant number of supporters of Metro and Oregon's land use planning system are correct, it may become even more effective with the governance changes described above.

In other actions, the May 2002 ballot in the Metro region included a measure put forward by the Neighborhood Preservation Committee, an arm of OIA, that would prohibit Metro from making local governments meet minimum housing density requirements. In the view of supporters of the land use system, the result would be "mandatory sprawl: immediate, unnecessary, and massive expansions of the urban growth boundary, increased traffic and pollution, and the loss of thousands of acres of farmland" (1000 Friends 2001d, 9).

After extensive studies, the Metro Council approved an expansion of the UGB on December 12, 2002, primarily to ensure sufficient available land to meet employment and housing needs. As required by state law, LCDC reviewed the recommended expansion, and on July 7, 2003, issued its approval of the bulk of Metro's recommendations. Citizens involved in the process then had 60 days to file an appeal to the decision. The expansion added 18,638 acres to the UGB, including 2,851 acres dedicated to employment purposes (Metro 2003c).

In March 2003 Metro published an assessment of its progress since the 1995 adoption of the 2040 Growth Concept (Metro 2003c). It stated that density in existing single-family neighborhoods has remained stable, and new residential development has become more compact, with the result that "the region is consuming fewer acres per residential development while accommodating more population inside the UBG" (Metro 2003c, 4). Metro has acquired 7,877 acres of natural area, exceeding the goal of 6,000 acres set in 1995. Transit ridership has increased, and residents are driving shorter distances on a regular basis. Since 1997 Metro's air quality has remained stable and in compliance with the Federal Clean Air Act of 1990.

However, despite efforts to encourage a wider variety of housing options in the area, permits for single-family homes continued to outnumber those for multifamily dwellings. Affordability of homes in the region is shrinking, with the median selling price of a home in Portland increasing from $79,700 in 1990 to $166,000 in 2000, while median family income increased from $37,100 to $55,900. And although nearly 28,555 acres of parks and greenspaces and 107 miles of regional trails within the Metro region are accessible, another 22,000 publicly owned acres are yet to be improved and opened to the public (Metro 2003c, 4–17).

New Actions by 1000 Friends of Oregon

An important example of creating a smart growth community occurred in the Bethany area of Washington County. In a negotiation, 1000 Friends agreed not to appeal a UGB expansion in Bethany, "while city and regional governments agreed to create a strong land use plan for the area." As a result, "the Beaverton City Council adopted, and Metro Council endorsed, a set of conditions to be integrated into the Bethany area concept plan—conditions that developers must follow." The list of conditions had a smart growth focus, and included

- a mix of commercial and civic uses, allowing residents to meet most of their daily needs in their neighborhood;

- a system of streets, sidewalks and bicycle paths that connect the neighborhood and provide strong connections beyond the neighborhood;

- "green" street designs where practicable, protecting the watershed;

- using development densities and design that support frequent transit service; and

- building a variety of housing, including affordable housing. (1000 Friends 2003a, 7)

1000 Friends director Bob Stacey saw the remarkably strong affordable housing conditions as a possible model for other developments around the state.

> At least 20 percent of the housing developed for ownership will be available at prices affordable to households at or below 80 percent of median income, and at least 20 percent of rental housing will be available at rents affordable to households at or below 60 percent of median income. (1000 Friends 2003a, 7)

1000 Friends also formed a Smart Development Advisory Committee, which held its first meeting in June 2003. The committee advises 1000 Friends' board and staff on how to promote more compact livable cities, and its members include a cross-section of key players in that area. The formation of this committee, and another group, the Farmers' Advisory Committee, illustrates 1000 Friends' active efforts to assure a smart growth future for Oregon (1000 Friends 2003a, 11–12).

Another significant effort is the group's Coastal Futures Project, made possible by a three-year,

$150,000 challenge grant from the Meyer Memorial Trust, and an additional $58,000 from 153 contributors to match the first-year challenge. Noting that the Oregon coast "is in danger of being loved to death," the project will be a key to establishing a permanent coastal office of 1000 Friends. Among the goals are to

■ bring public and private stakeholders together to identify, design and implement alternatives that curb sprawl and promote vibrant, livable communities;

■ conduct a three-year outreach campaign to increase understanding of coastal development pressures, Oregon's planning program and smart growth alternatives; and

■ help coastal communities envision, design and work toward a better future. (1000 Friends 2003b, 13)

Measure 37 and Actions to Defeat It

Having lost in their effort to dismantle the Oregon growth management system via Measure 7, OIA began circulating proposed language for two initiatives for the 2004 ballot: Initiative 36 (later renamed Measure 37), the so-called Son of Measure 7; and a second initiative that would "prohibit local governments and state agencies from adopting new land use or forestry laws, unless they first get written approval from a majority of landowners whose property values would potentially be decreased by more than 10 percent" (1000 Friends 2003a, 3).

The Oregon Community Protection Coalition (OCPC) had a steering committee of 1000 Friends, Audubon Society of Portland, Oregon Chapter of the American Planning Association, Oregon League of Conservation Voters, and the Sierra Club's Oregon Chapter. The organization saw its "ability to keep Oregon a great place to live" as being at risk and formed a PAC to fight Measure 37, a ballot measure "that directly assaults our 30-year legacy of using land use planning to protect our farmland, forestland, and neighborhoods." As the coalition saw it, OIA hoped "that voters caught up in national politics and the looming battle over taxes won't notice their Son of 7 until it's too late" (Oregon Community Protection PAC 2003, 1).

Measure 37 would rip the heart out of Oregon's land use planning system, while drastically curtailing regulations limiting clearcut logging in sensitive areas. How? By stating that any regulation of "land use," including "forest practices," cannot be enforced if it lowers the value of property, unless taxpayers pay for the reduced value. In an era of budget shortfalls, backers know full well that the answer will be to stop enforcing regulations. If it only applied to new regulations, Measure 37 would be bad enough, freezing all zoning and regulations in place, regardless of need. But its "pay or waive" scheme is far worse—it applies retroactively to the enforcement of any existing regulation if the property owner or a family member owned the property prior to the regulation's adoption (Oregon Community Protection PAC 2003, 1–2).

The coalition saw the consequences of adopting and enforcing Measure 37 as disastrous for Oregon, because (1) a large proportion of Willamette Valley farms could suddenly be converted into subdivisions and congested strip development—creating an explosion of rural sprawl; (2) many timber companies—whose ownership of forests far pre-dates Oregon's forest practices regulations—would be free to engage in virtually unlimited clearcutting; and (3) dozens of other city, county, regional and state safeguards would be waived, including UGBs, limits on highrises or industrial uses in residential neighborhoods, requirements that developers provide open space or coastal access and many more (Oregon Community Protection PAC 2003, 2).

To defeat Measure 37, OCPC launched a major public education effort, including making 90 presentations to a variety of key interest groups. It "built an arsenal of stories and spokespeople. We know that sound land use planning *protects property values and helps the economy*. We need to provide it in a way that Oregonians can relate to—through the stories of individual landowners" (Oregon Community Protection PAC 2003, 2). The coalition stressed that Measure 37 was a statutory measure that avoids the legal flaw that led the courts to throw out Measure 7, and must be defeated at the polls.

By December 2003, 1000 Friends and other players in the campaign to defeat Measure 37 had become convinced that a broader-based campaign would be needed to defeat that measure. Just before Christmas, OCPC was disbanded and the Take a Closer Look Committee was established, its key goal being to broaden the stakeholder base of the campaign.

In spite of the vigorous effort throughout 2004 to defeat Measure 37, it carried with a winning margin of 60 to 40 percent, and a majority in 35 of Oregon's 36 counties. 1000 Friends director Stacey (2004) wrote after the November results were announced, "Election day brought bad news for Oregonians who care about smart land use planning...we could not overcome the misleading ballot title and deceptive rhetoric pushed by the backers of Measure 37. But we're not giving up." He suggested that the next steps would include assessing legal theories for challenging the measure, tracking claims for compensation that are filed following passage, and continuing to educate citizens about the tangible benefits of smart planning, as opposed to the destruction that can be caused by unmanaged development.

Bob Clay, president of the Oregon chapter of APA, noted, "Our most immediate task is to help find ways of administering the law—a law rife with loopholes and ambiguities that seem to create boundless confusion" (APA 2004). He outlined several actions that OAPA would take, including calling on Governor Kulongoski to name a commission or task force to advise legislators on how to deal with claims and mobilizing chapter members to help local governments develop operating procedures to address the complex implications of the measure. Another challenge is to "find an acceptable balance between land use planning and individual property rights," which clearly is at the crux of the entire issue (APA 2004).

A comment on the city of Eugene and Mayor Jim Torrey illustrates how contentious the stuggle over Measure 37 will be for localities that have been strongly committed to traditional planning principles. He stated, "The city of Eugene will not automatically waive anything" (Oppenheimer 2004). The governor also asked cities and counties to minimize waivers from landowners while the state worked on a compensation plan. Nevertheless, while waiting for the governor and legislature to come up with a strategy to protect the state's land use planning system from the most destructive impacts of Measure 37, local governments still face the threat of lawsuits and other actions that will impact budgets that are already strained to the breaking point.

Conclusion

The passage of Measure 37 clearly calls into question the future of the nation's leading system to manage its growth and change. A positive factor is Governor Kulongoski, a moderate Democrat who strongly supports Oregon's land use system and has moved aggressively to find ways to challenge Measure 37 in the courts, by legislative action or any other means necessary so it does not destroy that system. Predicting the outcome of that struggle with any degree of certainty is not possible at this time.

Certainly 1000 Friends and its allies in the public, nonprofit and corporate sectors are mobilizing their forces to save Oregon's system from total destruction or at least drastic weakening. On the other side are the powerful forces of those building on their success to dismantle the system, including Oregon Taxpayers United and Oregonians in Action, which spearheaded support for the property rights measure. The fiscal crisis in the state makes the task even harder, as the state and local governments struggle with budget shortfalls at the same time as added resources are needed to minimize the negative impacts of Measure 37.

Despite the strong opposition to Oregon's land use planning and growth management system, there have been some successes in protecting rural lands and in shaping sustainable urban systems. Portland's Metro, still the only elected regional governance system in the nation, is well on its way to the full implementation of the Region 2040 process mandated by the home rule charter adopted in 1992. A unique blend of citizen input, staff and political leadership has led to a regional coordination effort involving Metro, state agencies and local governments, taking the region strongly in a smart growth direction. Challenges remain, including better funding in a time when the state has been in a recession, which tends to push growth management concerns off the agenda.

Portland and indeed Oregon as a whole remain a great success story for the nation, although one that is once again in a fight for its life.

References

1000 Friends of Oregon. 1982. The impact of Oregon's land use planning program on housing opportunities in the Portland metropolitan region. Portland, OR.

———. 1985. Anniversary issue. *Landmark*. Portland, OR.

———. 1986. *Landmark*. Summer.

———. 1991. *Landmark*. September.

———. 1995. *Landmark*. January.

———. 1997. *Landmark*. May.

———. 1998. *The story of land use in the 1997 Oregon legislature*. Portland, OR.

———. 1999a. Governor signs bill banning affordable housing strategy. Press release. July 23.

———. 1999b. *Landmark*. Winter.

———. 2000a. A brief overview of land use and the 1999 Oregon Legislature.

———. 2000b. Anti-planning forces declare WAR on Oregon's land use laws. *Landmark*. September.

———. 2000c. *Landmark*. Spring.

———. 2000d. Measure 2: Undemocratic, unaccountable process to repeal Oregon's statewide planning goals. *Landmark*. September.

———. 2001a. Agenda for a livable millennium. *Landmark*. Winter.

———. 2001b. *Landmark*. December.

———. 2001c. Life after Measure 7. *Landmark*. Winter.

———. 2001d. Oregon's land use system: Hanging by a chad? *Landmark*. December.

———. 2003a. *Landmark*. Fall.

———. 2003b. *Landmark*. Winter.

Abbott, Carl and Margery Post Abbott. 2001. *Historical development of the Metropolitan Service District*. Portland: Metro. May.

Abbott, Carl, Deborah Howe and Sy Adler. 1994. *Planning the Oregon way: A twenty-year evaluation*. Corvallis: Oregon State University Press.

American Planning Association (APA), Oregon Chapter. 2000. Oregon ballot measures. Electronic message sent to APA network. August 10.

———. 2004. Message from the President: Measure 37. Electronic message sent to APA network. November 9.

Brody, Susan. 1991. Transportation planning rule. Memorandum. Salem: Oregon Department of Land Conservation and Development. May 9.

DeGrove, John M. 1984. *Land, growth and politics*. Washington, DC: American Planning Association/Planners Press.

———. 1992. *The new frontier for land policy: Planning and growth management in the states*. Cambridge, MA: Lincoln Institute of Land Policy.

ECONorthwest with David J. Newton & Associates and MLP Associates. 1990. *Portland case study: Urban growth management study*. Salem, OR: Department of Land Conservation and Development. November.

Ketcham, Paul and Scot Siegel. 1991. Managing growth to promote affordable housing: Revisiting Oregon's Goal 10, executive summary. Portland: 1000 Friends of Oregon and the Home Builders Association of Metropolitan Portland.

Knaap, Gerrit and Arthur C. Nelson. 1992. *The regulated landscape: Lessons on state land use planning from Oregon*. Cambridge, MA: Lincoln Institute of Land Policy.

Liberty, Robert. 1995a. Memorandum to NGMLP colleagues, re update on legislative attacks on Oregon's growth management laws and other odds and ends. Portland, OR: 1000 Friends of Oregon. March 16.

———. 1995b. Memorandum to 1000 Friends and Oregon's land use planning program, re update on the assault on Oregon's land use planning laws in the 1995 legislature. Portland, OR: 1000 Friends of Oregon. May 22.

———. 1996. The battle over Tom McCall's legacy: The story of land use in the 1995 Oregon legislature. *Environmental and Urban Issues* 23:(3) Spring. Ft. Lauderdale, FL: FAU/FIU Joint Center for Environmental and Urban Problems.

Metro (Portland Metropolitan Service District). 1989. *Facts about Metro*. January.

———. 1990. Metro planning news. March.

———. 1993. Metro 2040 framework update. Fall/Winter.

———. 1994. Metro 2040 framework update. Fall.

———. 1995. Metro 2040 framework update. Spring/Summer.

———. 1996–1997. Metro 2040 framework update. Fall/Winter.

———. 1997a. Metro's regional framework plan update. Fall.

———. 1997b. Urban growth report. Final draft. Portland, OR: Portland Metro Growth Management Services Department. December 18.

———. 2000a. It's official—No expansion of UGB, neighborhood-level success stories add up to regionwide win. Press release. October 26.

———. 2000b. Regional affordable housing strategy. June.

———. 2000c. Traffic relief options study: Peak period pricing incentives to relieve congestion. November.

———. 2001a. A summary of the 2000 RTP.

———. 2001b. Open spaces: Acquiring land for parks and natural areas. http://www.metro-region.org/metro/parks/openspaces/opensp.html.

———. 2001c. Planning for transit.

———. 2001d. Regional affordable housing. http://www.metro-region.org/growth/tfplan/affordable.html.

———. 2001e. Six years and 6,920 acres: Metro's open spaces land acquisition report to citizens. July.

———. 2001f. Transportation planning.

———. 2002. Metro facts: 2002 urban growth boundary. September.

———. 2003a. Metro President David Bragdon. Inaugural address. January 6.

———. 2003b. The Portland region: How are we doing? March. http://www.metro-region.org/library_docs/land_use/2040_report.pdf.

———. 2003c. Urban growth boundary. http://www.metro-region.org/article.cfm?articleid=266.

Metro Data Resource Center. 1999. *Metro regional data book.* November.

Oliver, Gordon and Don Hamilton. 1999. Westside bypass idea faces a rough road. *Oregonian.* April 30.

Oppenheimer, Laura. Defenses aimed at Measure 37. *Oregonian.* November 28.

Oregon Business Council. 1993. Oregon values and beliefs, summary. Results of study conducted during July and August 1992. May.

Oregon Community Protection PAC. 2003. Letter. December 17.

Oregon Department of Land Conservation and Development (DLCD). 1992. *Recommendations.* Urban growth management task group on development inside urban growth boundaries. Salem, OR. October 29.

———. 1993a. An outline of House Bill 3661's criteria for new farm dwellings in exclusive farm use (EFU) zones. Salem, OR. September.

———. 1993b. *HB3661: New law on land use planning in Oregon.* Salem, OR. September.

———. 1993c. New laws about new dwellings in farm zones: A summary of key provisions from 1993's House Bill 3661. Salem, OR. September.

———. 1993d. *Shaping Oregon's future: The biennial report for 1991–1993 to the sixty-seventh legislative assembly.* Salem, OR. March.

———. 1994. *Rules for new farm dwellings.* Salem, OR. March.

Oregon Department of Transportation (ODOT), Association of Oregon Counties and League of Oregon Cities. 1993. Forward Oregon: Roads in a new context, 1993 Oregon road finance study. Salem, OR.

Oregon Department of Transportation (ODOT) and Department of Land Conservation and Development (DLCD). 1994. Transportation and growth management program, request for applications. January. Salem, OR.

Oregon Land Conservation and Development Commission (LCDC). 1985. Oregon's statewide planning goals. Salem, OR.

———. 1998. Division 7: Metropolitan housing.

Pease, James R. 1994. Oregon rural land use: Policy and practices. In *Planning the Oregon way: A twenty-year evaluation,* Abbott, Howe and Adler, eds., 163–188. Corvallis, OR: Oregon State University Press.

Stacey, Robert. 2004. Memo to 1000 Friends supporters. November.

Thompson, Courtenay. 1998. GOP gains, loses in the legislature. *Oregonian.* November.

Tucker, Randy. 1998. Summary and analysis of election results. Memorandum to 1000 Friends of Oregon Legislative Committee and Board of Directors. November.

U.S. Census Bureau. Projections of the total population of states: 1995 to 2025. http://www.census.gov/population/projections/state/stpjpop.txt.

Appendix

Governors

Thomas L. McCall (Republican)	1967–1975
Robert William Straub (Democrat)	1975–1979
Victor G. Atiyeh (Republican)	1979–1987
Neil E. Goldschmidt (Democrat)	1987–1991
Barbara K. Roberts (Democrat)	1991–1995
John A. Kitzhaber (Democrat)	1995–2002
Ted Kulongoski (Democrat)	2003–present

Acronyms

BLUB	Big Land Use Bill (HB 3661)
DLCD	Department of Land Conservation and Development
EFU	exclusive farm use
LCDC	Land Conservation and Development Commission
LUBA	Land Use Board of Appeals
MHR	Metropolitan Housing Rule
MPAC	Metro Policy Advisory Committee
OCPC	Oregon Community Protection Coalition
ODOT	Oregon Department of Transportation
OIA	Oregonians in Action
OTC	Oregon Transportation Commission
RFP	Regional Framework Plan
RTP	Regional Transportation Plan
RUGGOs	Regional Urban Growth Goals and Objectives
TGM	Transportation/Growth Management Program
TPR	Transportation Planning Rule
UGB	urban growth boundary

Contacts

1000 Friends of Oregon
534 S.W. Third Avenue, Suite 300
Portland, OR 97204
503-497-1000
http://www.friends.org

Home Builders Association of Metropolitan Portland
15555 S.W. Bangy Road, #301
Lake Oswego, OR 97035
503-684-1880
http://www.homebuildersportland.com

Metro
600 N.E. Grand Avenue
Portland, OR 97232-2736
503-797-1700
http://www.metro-region.org

Oregon Building Industry Association
375 Taylor Street, N.E.
Salem, OR 97303
503-378-9066
http://www.obia.net

Oregon Department of Land Conservation and Development
635 Capitol Street, N.E., Suite 150
Salem, OR 97301-2540
503-373-0050
http://www.lcd.state.or.us

Oregon Farm Bureau
3415 Commercial Street, S.E.
Salem, OR 97302
503-399-1701
http://www.oregonfb.org

State of Oregon
http://www.oregon.gov/

3

Florida

Contents

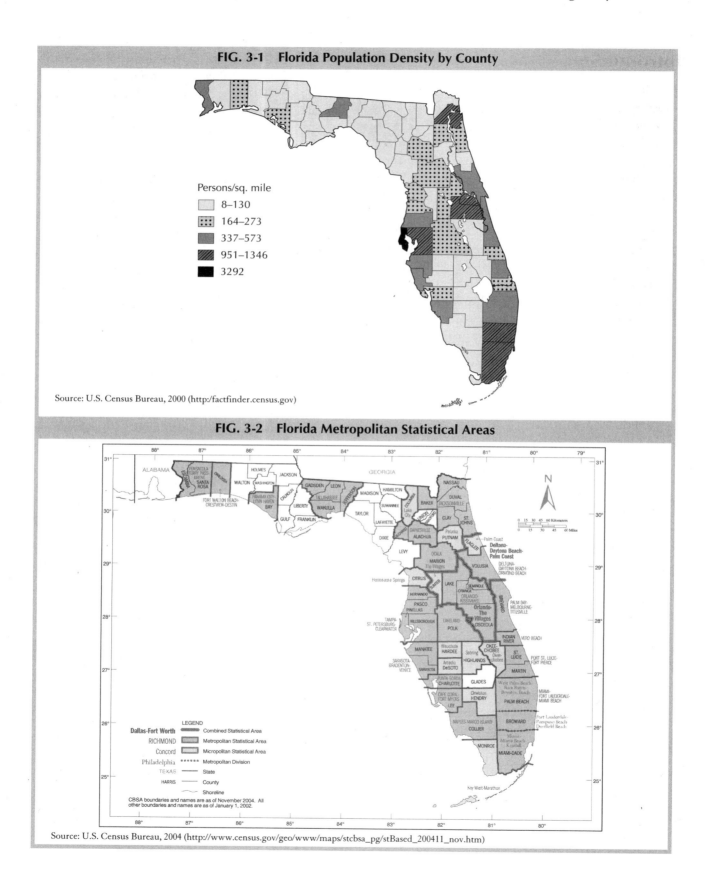

FIG. 3-1   Florida Population Density by County

Persons/sq. mile

- 8–130
- 164–273
- 337–573
- 951–1346
- 3292

Source: U.S. Census Bureau, 2000 (http:/factfinder.census.gov)

FIG. 3-2   Florida Metropolitan Statistical Areas

Source: U.S. Census Bureau, 2004 (http://www.census.gov/geo/www/maps/stcbsa_pg/stBased_200411_nov.htm)

Introduction

The title of the Florida chapter in the book *The New Frontier for Land Policy: Planning and Growth Management in the States* (DeGrove 1992) was "Florida: A Second Try at Managing Massive Growth Pressures." During the past decade and more, that "second try" system has been tested and, in some important dimensions, found wanting as never before. The framing concepts of the system, especially consistency and concurrency, seem as sound as ever. However, implementing those and related concepts so that growth is managed in a way that will produce sustainable urban and natural systems has produced planning, regulatory and funding challenges that have yet to be resolved.

Florida ranks fourth among all states in population, behind California, Texas and New York, and is the only one of those states to have launched a comprehensive effort to manage its growth, although California has elements of such a system in place.

The state's growth management system has evolved through three phases over the past 34 years. Phase One (1970–1982) was necessitated by massive, unmanaged population growth that brought with it the threat of major negative impacts on the state's environment, especially its sensitive water systems. Governor Reubin Askew's strong commitment to pass legislation to address these problems was a model for the nation in terms of public land acquisition and water resource protection. The first Environmental Land Management Study Committee (ELMS I) was established in 1972. Legislation adopted in 1972 and 1975 moved Florida to a leading position in efforts to manage its growth. However, the system as a whole suffered from loopholes and experienced implementation and funding problems.

During Phase Two (1982–1996), two important sets of legislation were introduced by successive Environmental Land Management Study Committees (ELMS II in 1982–1986 and ELMS III in 1991–1992). A thorough examination of ELMS II and III and their implementation successes and failures depicts the complicated journey of achieving successful plan development and review, consistency, intergovernmental coordination and concurrency. This period also highlights challenges for such key growth management goals as containing sprawl, protecting natural resources, promoting economic development and providing affordable housing.

Phase Three (1996–2003) is characterized by early efforts at a "sustainable communities" approach, which aimed to shift the emphasis from command-and-control to incentives and disincentives for achieving the goal of sustainable urban and natural systems. However, negative factors still threaten the success of the Florida system, including the continuing failure to fund the system adequately and the challenge of sharply reducing sprawl development in favor of more compact urban communities. Florida also faces a dilemma in introducing creative new planning and regulatory systems in view of widespread negative attitudes toward government, the private property rights movement and the emergence of a legislature and governor much less supportive of growth management than in the past several decades.

We look at the recommendations of Governor Chiles's Commission for a Sustainable South Florida and the efforts to implement those recommendations, including sustainable communities legislation passed in 1996. We also have a special interest in the Eastward Ho! Initiative to apply sustainability concepts to a development/redevelopment/infill corridor in southeast Florida. We also assess the impacts of the 1998 and 2002 elections on Florida's continuing struggle to craft and implement a smart growth system for the state, and examine both positive and negative developments under Governor Jeb Bush's administration.

As in other chapters in this book, the existence (or nonexistence) of the linchpins of growth management—leadership by the governor, legislative and popular support, and adequate funding—are woven throughout our discussion. In analyzing the prospects for Florida's future, the optimist's view is that a clear majority of the state's citizens still support managing growth to assure livable urban and healthy natural systems, and public opinion surveys continue to show that to be the case. Florida's experience demonstrates, however, that significant challenges remain to prevent the system from being weakened drastically or even destroyed by political action. Better ways of mobilizing citizen-based support through organizations like

1000 Friends of Florida must be found if the state is to achieve the goals of the smart growth movement.

Phase One, 1970–1982: Responding to Concerns about Rapid Growth and the Environment

The Issue Context

Like other states that took action in the 1970s, Florida's first efforts to better manage its growth were centered on environmental concerns, but the challenge was especially difficult because of significant population increases. From a relatively modest population of 2.7 million in 1950, the state grew to 4.9 million by 1960, 6.8 million in 1970. By 2000 the population had soared to 15.9 million, with a projected increase to 16.3 million in 2005 (U.S. Census Bureau).

The large number of new citizens moving to the state was seen at first as a boon to the economy, with little concern for any potential negative impacts associated with unmanaged growth. By the mid-1960s, however, problems began to emerge. The extensive destruction of wetlands, beaches and dune systems, and the continued threat of saltwater intrusion into drinking water aquifers (particularly in southeast Florida and the Tampa Bay area) began to sour Florida's love affair with growth.

Florida was not alone in its concerns. The national environmental movement had emerged during the 1960s and early 1970s, and protecting the environment from the negative effects of unmanaged growth became part of the national political discourse. However, it was not long before discourse turned to discord. A severe drought, unparalleled in Florida's history, hit the southeastern and Tampa Bay areas in 1970 and 1971, and many long-time residents saw unchecked growth as an important contributing factor.

Early Legislation and Implementation, 1971–1978

The 1970–1971 drought coincided with the election of Reubin Askew as governor. After taking office in

January 1971, as the water level of Lake Okeechobee dropped to an all-time low, Governor Askew took action that became a major step forward in efforts to manage the state's growth more wisely. He established the Governor's Conference on Water Management in South Florida. Addressing the conference in August 1971, Askew became the first statewide elected official to challenge the necessary goodness of growth, especially unplanned growth, for Florida. The conference, encouraged to take bold action by the governor, produced a short but hard-hitting report that called for a comprehensive approach to managing growth.[1]

Following up on the conference report, Askew convened a task force on land use in fall 1971, to craft the legislation necessary to implement its findings and recommendations. In a remarkably short period of time, the task force drafted four major pieces of legislation to present to the 1972 legislature, each of which was passed:

- Environmental Land and Water Management Act (Chapter 380, *Florida Statutes*, 1972)

- Water Resources Act (Chapter 373, *Florida Statutes*, 1972)

- State Comprehensive Planning Act (Chapter 23, *Florida Statutes*, 1972)

- Land Conservation Act (Chapter 259, *Florida Statutes*, 1972)

These laws comprised Florida's first major effort to address the issue of balancing the needs of the environment with the need to accommodate growth

---

1. Governor Askew's charge to the conference and the policy statement the conference submitted to the governor can be found in Central and Southern Florida Flood Control District (December 1971–January 1972, 4). For a more detailed description of the conference and the water crisis and other issues that led up to it, see DeGrove (1984, 106–109).

in a responsible way. Along with a subsequent companion law—the Local Government Comprehensive Planning Act (Chapter 163, *Florida Statutes*, 1975) mandating that local governments adopt growth management plans—these laws were viewed as far-reaching, progressive and even radical in what they proposed.[2]

The first Environmental Land Management Study Committee (ELMS I) was established as part of the adoption of Chapter 380 in 1972. Over the two years of its existence, ELMS I played a key role in getting Florida's initial effort at managing its growth off to a good start. It was charged, among other things, with making recommendations for threshold criteria that would cause a development to be a development of regional impact (DRI) when it had an impact on the citizens of more than one county. ELMS I also crafted the recommendations for what became the Local Government Comprehensive Planning Act (Chapter 163).

The membership of ELMS I was set by the statute at 15 members and was mandated to include representation of the key stakeholders, including "environmental interests, organized labor, business interests, the home construction industry, the academic community, the land sales industry, the real estate profession, agricultural interests, and other professions and occupations affected by the provisions of Chapter 380, *Florida Statutes*" (ELMS I 1973). The governor appointed nine members, and the Senate president and Speaker of the House each appointed three. ELMS I issued a series of reports in late 1972 and 1973, with its final report produced in December 1973.

Getting legislative approval of the four land use laws in 1972 and the Local Government Comprehensive Planning Act in 1975 was far from easy. Support by Askew and the House of Representatives did not negate problems in the more conservative Senate. There, the fight for the legislation, especially the Environmental Land and Water Management Act (Chapter 380), was led by then State Senator Bob Graham, a

member of the Task Force on Land Use that drafted the legislation. A series of compromises were worked out, and a number of hostile amendments were narrowly defeated (DeGrove 1984, 111–116).

Early efforts to manage growth in order to cope with the population boom enjoyed some important successes, but on balance the system could not cope with the infrastructure and environmental impacts of new growth. It was a case of "too little, too late," and of a failure to appreciate some central realities of the growth management process. First and foremost was the failure to recognize, or the inability to act on the recognition, that substantial funding would be needed to make the system work. During much of the 1970s, Florida still moved in a kind of fool's paradise, believing that growth paid for itself and that sooner or later the new growth would cause the needed infrastructure to be put in place to support the impacts of that growth. It was not until that notion was recognized as fundamentally false that Florida began, in the late 1970s and 1980s, to fully face its growth management problems.

The weaknesses of Florida's first set of growth management laws should not obscure the fact that some good things were accomplished. The Water Resources Act was a progressive law that put Florida in the forefront nationally in managing its water resources, including subsequent efforts to restore and sustain the Everglades ecosystem. With an initial $200 million from a bond issue approved in a statewide vote, the Land Conservation Act set the stage for the development of the nation's most extensive public land acquisition program. The Environmental Land and Water Management Act introduced a special state and/or regional review of DRIs and Areas of Critical State Concern (ACSC). Urban development projects that took shape under the DRI process came closer to the concept of good design and adequate infrastructure than other projects.

By the late 1970s, a particular weakness became apparent: the loopholes and incompleteness of the 1975 Local Government Comprehensive Planning Act (Chapter 163). This law certainly did facilitate (in some cases, force) local governments into the planning process, although many had done little or no planning in the past. Chapter 163 required each city and county

---

2. See DeGrove (1984, 109–116) for further details on these laws and the negative impacts of unplanned growth that led to the work of the Task Force on Land Use and the details of the fight to get the legislation passed in the 1972 session.

to put a plan in place, and that was accomplished by the late 1970s. However, the requirements of the law were merely oriented toward process, not substance, and the implementation requirements were weak. The state undermined its credibility in mandating local planning when it failed to carry out a commitment to share plan preparation costs with local governments. Furthermore, local plans were subject to review and comment—not review and approval—at the state and regional levels.

Implementation difficulties were not limited to local planning. At the state level, Governor Askew encountered political and legal resistance to the Environmental Land and Water Management Act, particularly as it pertained to the section on ACSC. Acting as the state's Administration Commission, the governor and his cabinet designated these critical areas by rule. The first two designations were the largely undeveloped but important water resource areas of the Big Cypress Swamp in southwest Florida (1973) and the Green Swamp in central Florida (1974). The third designation covered all of the Florida Keys (1975) and was the first to combine rural and urban areas. Because these areas could be subject to strict growth and development controls, the City of Key West legally challenged the state's designation.

In 1978 the Florida Supreme Court declared that ACSC was unconstitutional as an improper delegation of legislative authority to the executive branch. Immediately after the court's ruling, Askew called a special session of the legislature, which redesignated the Florida Keys and Green Swamp as critical areas. Surprisingly, the new language for reestablishing the critical area designation had little trouble winning approval by the 1979 legislature. The Administration Commission retained the power to designate critical areas, but a designated area would not go into effect until after the next legislative session, giving the legislature the opportunity to negate it. In addition, before a new area could be designated, a Resource Planning and Management Committee, named by the governor, would prepare a resource management plan addressing the area's problems. If this "voluntary" approach, led by the state's Department of Community Affairs (DCA), did not solve the problems, then DCA was empowered to recommend a formal critical

area designation to the Administration Commission (DeGrove 1984, 126–128; Stroud 1979, 4–8).

Reassessing the Growth Management System, 1978–1982

During the 1970s, Askew had shown unprecedented commitment to managing growth while protecting the environment, and he expanded the focus of the system beyond water management to land use issues. Bob Graham, elected governor in 1978, showed equal determination, but the time was ripe for a thorough reappraisal of the system.[3]

In early 1979 Governor Graham undertook a comprehensive reassessment of the state's capacity to manage growth by naming a Resource Management Task Force. Its most immediate charge was to study the feasibility of reenacting the ACSC section of the Environmental Land and Water Management Act (Chapter 380) and to make recommendations as to how that should occur. The task force wisely chose a well-respected chair, James H. Shimberg, head of the Florida Home Builders Association (HBA) and a member of the ELMS I committee.

The final report of the Florida Resource Management Task Force (1980) was key to the major revisions of the growth management system in the mid-1980s. It called for, and the 1980 legislature accepted, a more proactive planning approach for DRIs, by authorizing the designation of an entire downtown area as a DRI, to expedite the development and redevelopment of such areas. The City of Tampa had pushed for this change to avoid extended delays caused by a building-by-building DRI approval process, or the construction of inappropriately sized office buildings in order to fall below the threshold that would trigger the DRI process. In a later change, the concept was extended to locations outside of downtown in the form of an areawide DRI process, also intended to promote proactive planning.

The most significant part of the final report, however, clarified and restated the need for an integrated

---

3. See DeGrove (1984, 99–121) for a full assessment of Phase One of Florida's growth management efforts in the 1970s.

policy framework to reshape the fundamentals of Florida's growth management system. A set of legislatively approved goals and policies was called for at the state level, as well as strong comprehensive regional policy plans. In addition, a much stronger local government comprehensive planning system was recommended, along with state and regional review and approval, not just review and comment.[4]

Phase Two, 1982–1996: Crafting and Implementing Growth Management Legislation

Continued growth pressures during the 1970s and 1980s shifted and broadened the issue context that led to changes in the growth management system during the 1984–1986 legislative sessions, and again in the 1991–1993 period. The environment continued to be important, but other issues were pushed toward the top of the policy agenda. The long-held assumption that growth would pay for itself was abandoned in the face of massive infrastructure backlogs. The citizens of Florida, natives and newcomers alike, began to feel the effects of the negative impacts of unmanaged growth. Congested traffic, crowded schools and polluted water bodies were clear examples of the deterioration of their quality of life.

ELMS II Recommendations and Legislative Action, 1982–1986

Despite making headway in the legislation adopted in 1972 and 1975, Florida failed to craft a growth managment system that could cope with the continued influx of large numbers of people. In 1982 Governor Graham established a second Environmental Land Management Study Committee (ELMS II) and directed it to "review all Florida resource and growth management programs governed by and related to Chapter 380 and ... recommend improvements to these programs" (ELMS II 1984). An interim report was required by February 15, 1983, on matters calling for "immediate improvements to existing programs." A final report to the governor was called for a year later, "for specific legislation to improve land and water management programs." DCA employed the executive director and other staff with funding under the Federal Coastal Zone Management Act of 1972, via the State Depart-

ment of Environmental Regulation. The 20-member ELMS II committee heard testimony from the public, private and nonprofit sectors in meetings held around the state. The report's conclusion stressed the heart of the committee's work:

> To meet the challenge of growth management for Florida's future, the ELMS committee has designed, and set out in this report, a statewide framework for planning, coordinated plan implementation, and greater citizen participation in state, regional, and local planning processes. This framework should serve as a guide for planning and growth management at all levels of Florida's government. (ELMS II 1984, 105)

The committee debated over what to do with the DRI process, with views ranging from abolishing it to strengthening it, and ended up with the following:

> The Committee's recommendations are designed to overcome the shortcomings of the DRI program; to provide greater incentives, and remove disincentives, for developers, local governments, and the public to enter into the process; and to relieve the DRI program from the burden of having to address a large portion of Florida's growth problems. (ELMS II 1984, 105)

Finally, the committee made "recommendations for maintaining and strengthening the Florida Coastal Management Program and the ACSC program to make each an integral part of a coordinated growth management system" (ELMS II 1984, 106).

Like the earlier Resource Management Task Force, ELMS II included a cross-section of stakeholders, including all the principal adversaries. When it was clear that the governor and legislature were

---

4. See Florida Resource Management Task Force (1980, III: 1–19); DeGrove (1984, 128); Stroud (1980, 2, 3, 19).

prepared to pass new legislation, even the reluctant players came to the bargaining table. Developer and home builder groups joined the League of Cities, environmental and civic groups, and others in supporting the legislation. The state Association of Counties sat on the sidelines, although there was substantial support for the proposed new system at the county level.[5]

ELMS II reached a consensus on recommending both new laws and changes to existing laws, including the importance of funding the state's fair share of any new mandates. That concern was clearly expressed in the final report in the proposal to establish a Growth Management Trust Fund with a continuing earmarked funding source. The message was clear: if you can't or won't fund it, don't enact it.

Remarkably, legislative action over the 1984–1986 period placed into law virtually every recommendation made by ELMS II. The Florida State and Regional Planning Act (Chapter 186), passed by the 1984 legislature, required that the Office of the Governor prepare a state plan and present it to the 1985 legislature. It also reasserted the mandate for regional planning councils (RPCs) to prepare comprehensive regional policy plans, with the crucial difference that this time the legislature appropriated funds (initially $500,000, and later, more) to support the preparation of the plans.

Responding to ELMS II's call for either funding or abandoning the effort, the 1984 legislative session also appropriated substantial additional funds to strengthen the state land planning agency component of DCA, to increase its staff and other fiscal capacities. Between 1984 and 1985, the Governor's Office of Planning and Budgeting drafted the proposed State Comprehensive Plan and held hearings across the state to garner support for the document (DeGrove 1992, 11–12).

The 1985 session passed two key pieces of legislation. First, the legislature held extensive hearings on the proposed State Comprehensive Plan and adopted it into law as Chapter 187. It was more like a strategic plan in emphasizing outcomes and ways of reaching goals than a traditional comprehensive plan that

tried to cover everything. Critics of the plan's 26 goals and policies claimed there were too many goals and that they were either too specific or too general. The goals ranged from healthcare for children and families to protection of water resources, property rights, downtown revitalization and agriculture. However, the comprehensive plan constituted a clear and meaningful framework for regional and local plans and provided a foundation for a workable growth management system (DeGrove 1989, 35; 1992, 12).

The second piece of legislation, the Omnibus Growth Management Act of 1985, encompassed changes to three existing statutes: the Local Government Comprehensive Planning Act (Chapter 163), later renamed the Local Government Comprehensive Planning and Land Development Regulations Act; the coastal setback line regulations (Chapter 161); and the Environmental Land and Water Management Act (Chapter 380).

The Omnibus Act established an integrated policy framework involving vertical implementation of goals, policies and implementation strategies, as well as a provision for horizontal compatibility within and among plans at the state, regional and local levels. With the state plan in place, state agencies had to prepare functional plans by July 1986 in the form of strategic documents consistent with the state plan, to become the source of state agency budget submissions. At the regional level, comprehensive regional policy plans had to be prepared and adopted by July 1987 and be consistent with the goals and policies of the state plan.

Finally, local governments were to prepare and submit plans to DCA, to bring coastal cities and counties into the process first, and remaining local governments in over a period of several years. The Omnibus Act also provided new opportunities for citizen participation in the preparation, adoption and implementation of local plans and regulations, including challenging (under certain circumstances) a consistency finding by DCA. At long last, a policy framework would now drive the budget process instead of the other way around.

The 1986 Glitch Bill (SB 978, Chapter 86-191) completed the substantive framework for the growth management system. The bill

---

5. For a more extended discussion of the issue and political context, see DeGrove (1984, 169–176; 1989, 35–36).

- attempted to clarify responsibility for setting concurrency levels;

- altered windload requirements for the coastal zone, thereby weakening the more stringent 1985 requirements; and

- included a clarification of the consistency requirement for local government plans that opponents hoped would weaken it but, in fact, served to strengthen it.

This bill reconfirmed the requirement that local plans be consistent with the relevant provisions of the Local Government Comprehensive Planning and Land Development Regulations Act; the state comprehensive and regional plans; and other relevant statutes and rules. Most important, local plans had to be consistent with the DCA minimum criteria rule (Rule 9-J-5, Florida Administrative Code) mandated by the 1985 legislation and prepared by DCA with input from local planners and others. Rule 9-J-5 required "approval" by the 1986 legislature and was accepted essentially as submitted, including a directive to "discourage urban sprawl" (DeGrove 1989, 35–36; 1992, 12–15).

Implementation Challenges and Mixed Results

Phase Two of growth management occurred under a variety of circumstances, several different governors and legislatures, and difficult economic conditions. What remained constant was a significant number of constituents—builders, developers, business interests and even local governments—opposed to growth management, at least in part. Not surprisingly, the 1986–1996 decade was characterized by many challenges and problems in achieving consistency, integration and cooperation between state and local agencies, and successful plan development and review—the cornerstones of growth management. Moreover, these challenges had a cumulative effect on the related substantive concepts of concurrency as a means of containing sprawl, protecting natural resources, providing affordable housing and supporting economic development.

Consistency

The consistency requirement is the central concept for effective growth management systems, because without a meaningful consistency requirement, the "natural" tendencies of local governments and state and regional agencies to plan and act unilaterally cannot be overcome. Inconsistency, in turn, leads to what has been the major development pattern in this nation for more than four decades: sprawl.

It is fair to say that the consistency requirement of the Florida system set the framework for implementing the substantive requirements. It significantly affected the way local governments paid attention to the internal consistency of the various elements of their plans and, to a lesser degree, to the impacts of their plans on neighboring governments. On the downside, the intergovernmental coordination element of the mandated local plans was widely viewed as a weak link in the system, and later efforts to strengthen that key element through the recommendations of ELMS III did not bear out.

DCA was responsible for ensuring that local land uses identified on its Future Land Use Map (FLUM) fit the projected population of a local government through its long-range planning period. Both Rule 9-J-5 and Chapter 163, Part II, require that the FLUM "be based upon the amount of land needed to accommodate anticipated growth" (Florida DCA 1995b). Any significant surplus produces sprawl. However, analyses have shown that, in spite of a brave beginning by DCA Secretary Tom Pelham, local governments consistently failed to balance their FLUM with their population projections—typically by having densities too high in rural areas—thereby encouraging sprawl development patterns.

Integration and Cooperation Between State and Local Agencies

A common characteristic of all comprehensive growth management systems across the U.S. has been the difficulty of drawing local governments and state agencies into the integrated policy framework, and Florida has been no exception. Creating plans, implementing the review process and maintaining internal consistency were not limited to struggles between the state and its cities and counties. State agencies met the technical requirements of the State Comprehensive Plan (Chapter 187) by preparing and updating functional plans to meet statutory deadlines. However, those same plans did not serve as the framework for the agencies' own programs and budgets. For the most part they were unused, and there was no clear requirement in the law that state agency actions had to be consistent with approved local plans.

Efforts to integrate state agencies more fully into growth management occurred after the election of Lawton Chiles as governor and Buddy MacKay as lieutenant governor, in November 1990. They led an aggressive effort to create a common growth management strategy among seven state agencies: Community Affairs; Transportation; Environmental Regulation; Natural Resources; Labor and Employment Security; Commerce; and the Game and Freshwater Fish Commission. The DCA secretary or the lieutenant governor chaired the meetings, and the governor or his chief of staff almost always attended, which meant that agency heads, not their subordinates, were also present.

An agreement, signed in early 1991, committed the agencies to an ongoing collaborative effort to bring their actions into focus with the state plan and with each other. Unfortunately, the significance of the agreement was diluted by an increasingly hostile legislature, even though the agreement remained in place. These efforts to make state agency actions a supportive part of the integrated policy framework illustrate two points: the basic difficulty of integrating state agencies, each with its own mission and constituents; and the importance of sustained support from both the governor's office and the legislature. Furthermore, the implementation of the state agency effort was undermined because a weak Office of Management and Budget was unable to reinforce statewide efforts.

Plan Development and Review

The process of plan development at the local level, plan review at the regional and local levels, and certification of local plans as being in or out of compliance with the requirements of the system went forward, aided by the state's commitment of substantial funding to support local governments' efforts. Oregon and California had set very short deadlines for local governments to prepare plans and have them certified as consistent, and Florida did not repeat that error. A specific date was set for every one of the state's 457 cities and counties, requiring that plans be submitted for consistency review over the 1988–1992 period. Land development regulations consistent with the local plans were required to be in place one year after submission of a plan to the state planning agency (DCA).

A balanced assessment of this phase of the implementation process yields the conclusion that the character and quality of plan making and at least the potential for plan implementation were drastically improved. State reviews, especially under the aggressive leadership of DCA Secretary Tom Pelham, were much more than process-oriented checklists. In addition to an insistence that consistency with state and regional goals, policies and rules be taken seriously, DCA worked hard to achieve key substantive growth management concepts. The problems in implementation become evident when one considers that about half of all local plans initially submitted were found to be "not in compliance" by DCA (Florida DCA 1990a, 5). The emergence of the compliance agreement as a key in negotiating differences between DCA and local governments to bring local plans into compliance was important in moving the process along (Florida DCA 1992, 2).

Concurrency

No element of Florida's growth management system has attracted as much attention around the nation as the concurrency requirement. Concurrency was Florida's attempt to introduce accountability into growth and change in the state. It was the most powerful requirement of the growth management system put in place over the 1984–1986 period, and its charge was clear. "It is the intent of the legislature that public facilities and services needed to support development shall be available concurrent with the impacts of development" (Chapter 163.3177[10] [h], *Florida Statutes* 1985). Rule 9-J-5 provided, among other things, the specifics for implementing concurrency by setting levels of service for six kinds of public services: transportation, water, sewer, solid waste, parks and recreation, and stormwater management.

State agency responsibility for some of these services shaped local governments' options. This was especially true for transportation. The Florida Department of Transportation (DOT) set levels of service on a network of 11,000 miles of state roads ranging from rural routes to the major highways through cities. For the most part, DOT had originally ignored location and set the same level of service everywhere. That problem led to the first modifications to the transportation concurrency requirement.

As the date for enforcing the concurrency requirement approached, in 1987–1988, one year after local governments submitted their plans to DCA, Pelham calmed fears that rigid enforcement would shut down all development in the state. The concept of a "fair and flexible" concurrency management system would clarify the treatment of infrastructure—strict adherence for new development and more flexibility for backlogs (Florida DCA, 1989b, 1). The struggle to find the "right" balance in this area has continued throughout the implementation process. Ironically, some relaxing of the concurrency system has come from an increased sensitivity to another central concept of the system: the need to limit sprawl by promoting more compact urban growth patterns.

With population and economic expansion at high levels in the late 1980s, there were concerns that setting the same levels of service on all state roads, many of them in urban areas, would exacerbate sprawl, as developers fled to the edge where roads still had available capacity. Without firm urban growth boundaries in place, the problem was real, as illustrated by the first county plan (Broward County) found in compliance by DCA. Broward set the same level of service on all state roads in the county. Since most major roads in the county's urban areas were included, development was in effect shut down in the very areas where compact urban development patterns were called for. The exception was for vested development not subject to concurrency (admittedly substantial). The approval of the counterproductive Broward plan was a wake-up call for DCA, which began to work on the problem in the late 1980s. The "solution" was to include in plan reviews a compact development policy drawn from language in the state plan, such as "encourage the use of existing infrastructure," "promote infill and

redevelopment" or "separate urban and rural uses." The effort to set meaningful urban service boundaries called for a close examination of the concurrency requirement, especially in transportation.

Governor Bob Martinez (1986–1990) appointed a Governor's Task Force on Urban Growth Patterns that called for amendments to the growth management laws to include much stronger policies to contain urban sprawl, but the amendments failed to pass in the 1989 legislature. DCA also undertook creative efforts to define urban sprawl clearly as leapfrog development, ribbon or strip development, and large expanses of low-density, single-dimensional development. These definitions were expanded and incorporated into DCA's urban sprawl rule in 1996 as an amendment to Rule 9-J-5. Nevertheless, these multiple efforts to contain sprawl and move in a smart growth direction were not successful.

This was not for lack of trying. Flexibility was introduced into the transportation concurrency requirement to allow development in downtowns and other urban areas in exchange for public transportation improvements. For example, Dade County set a series of transportation levels of service: most lenient (congested) in urban infill areas; modestly strict outside that area but within Dade's urban development boundary; and most strict outside the boundary. This case prompted DCA to work with DOT in allowing local governments to establish Transportation Concurrency Management Areas (TCMAs) in the early 1990s. The TCMAs gave local governments greater flexibility in the transportation concurrency area to encourage infill or redevelopment in existing urban areas, to contain sprawl at the edge. The greatest negative aspect to all these efforts was the failure to fund the system adequately, especially the costs of implementing the concurrency requirement.

Natural Resources

Concern for Florida's natural systems has been a high priority for the state's citizens since the 1960s, and that concern has not been weakened by the broadening of the growth management agenda in recent decades. To a considerable extent, protection of natural systems is the flip side of the anti-urban sprawl policy. Success in combating sprawl means less pressure on rural lands, including wetlands, water recharge areas, critical habitats, and farm and forest lands. Sprawl threatens all of these resources, in addition to having negative social and fiscal impacts.

In the plan review process, DCA pushed hard, both to achieve local plans that would limit densities and intensities of land uses in rural areas, and to require the investment of public infrastructure funds in areas designated for urban growth. For example, DCA found the plan submitted by Hillsborough County to be internally inconsistent, since it documented a $400 million annual agricultural industry and then designated a density of one dwelling unit per acre for all agricultural lands. In the ensuing negotiations, the county lowered rural densities to a range of 1-in-5 to 1-in-20 dwelling units per acre, but even these densities were considerably higher than DCA had advocated. The state was also diligent to limit development on barrier islands and coastal high-hazard areas. DCA rejected one southwest county's plan because it projected a transportation level of "F" (virtual gridlock) on roads leading to the only surface evacuation route.

In the implementation phase of the growth management system, efforts to contain sprawl by limiting rural densities were not always successful, so the burden for protecting natural systems fell on programs to raise large sums of money (Florida DCA 1989c, 1; 1989d, 5–6). While there was never an expectation that this could be achieved solely through the local plan review and implementation process, the state has been fortunate to have the best funded program for protecting environmentally sensitive lands in the nation, arguably including that of the federal government.

The present program has deep roots. In 1972, as part of Phase One of the state's growth management system, voters overwhelmingly approved a constitutional amendment authorizing a $200 million bond issue to acquire environmentally sensitive lands. This measure, the Environmentally Endangered Lands (EEL) program, was supplemented by $40 million for outdoor recreation land purchases. The land acquisition effort has grown steadily, sometimes in spectacular fashion, since then. In 1979 the Conservation and Recreational Lands (CARL) program succeeded the

EEL program, with earmarked funding initially from severance taxes and later from documentary stamp taxes. The Save Our Rivers program was established in 1982 and administered through the state's five water management districts, and the Preservation 2000 program was approved in 1990. Together, those programs comprised the largest conservation lands acquisition program in the nation, with some $4 billion committed over the 1990s.

Before leaving office in 1990, Martinez named a blue ribbon panel to evaluate Florida's environment. This Commission on the Future of Florida's Environment was chaired by Nathaniel Reed, a prominent environmentalist and leading Republican dedicated to environmental values. The commission's view of the "state" of Florida's environment was not a happy one; it documented 56 percent of the state's historic wetlands lost to dredging and filling, and 32 percent of upland forests converted to agricultural or urban use. "At the 1990 rate of development," the commission warned, "about three million acres of wetlands and forest lands would be converted to other uses by the year 2020, dooming unique plant and animal species and threatening the state's drinking water supplies" (The Nature Conservancy 1996; Commission on the Future 1990).

Poll results cited by the commission in 1990 showed "that 88 percent of Floridians believed state government should give more attention to the environment, and 63 percent favored spending more money in environmental protection." This information was taken to heart by the state's political leaders—Democrat and Republican, liberal and conservative (The Nature Conservancy 1996). It was clear by the late 1990s that the full commitment of $3 billion over 10 years would be met, and the coalition of environmental and other groups, led by the Nature Conservancy, was exploring ways to continue a similar level of funding into the new century.

The legislature has had to review its commitment of funds for the Preservation 2000 program each year since 1991. In spite of a severe recession and a legislature increasingly hostile to government programs, every legislature has provided the funds necessary to support the annual issuance of $300 million in bonds, due to strong voter support for the program (Drake and Sullivan 1997). The Preservation 2000 funds were channeled to existing land acquisition programs: 50 percent to the Conservation and Recreational Lands program; 30 percent to the Save Our Rivers program; and 10 percent to the Florida Communities Trust. The remaining 10 percent went to such programs as Rails to Trails, and agencies such as the Division of Forestry and Recreation and Parks in the Department of Environmental Protection and the Florida Game and Fresh Water Fish Commission.

A report by the Nature Conservancy (1997) showed that more than 820,000 acres of important environmental lands had been preserved by funds from the program. Achievements ranged from protecting "48,000 acres of rare Florida prairie in Okeechobee and Osceola counties (lower central Florida)...to a landmark purchase preserving 98 miles of river frontage near Florida's 'Big Bend' (upper west coast)."

The Florida Communities Trust (FCT) component of the Preservation 2000 funding was $30 million, or 10 percent of each bond issue. This amount was directly aimed at supporting the implementation of Florida's growth management system by making competitive grants to local governments to assist them in implementing the conservation elements of their comprehensive plans. The 1997 round of awards amounted to "over $44.3 million in project grants to 36 local governments for acquisition of urban natural areas and open space. The local governments committed to match the FCT funds with nearly $30 million in local funds." The program, administered by the DCA, was slow to get under way, but "since 1990, FCT has awarded grants to 188 different local governments, funded 193 local projects, and protected over 40,000 acres of urban parks, greenways, and open space" (The Nature Conservancy 1997, 5).

Another important by-product of Preservation 2000 funding and the state's land acquisition agenda has been the encouragement of local governments to initiate their own bond issues to provide a match for state or regional funds to acquire environmentally important lands in their communities. In the process, citizens have demonstrated support for bond issues while they reject bonds or other funding efforts for schools and infrastructure. The Nature Conservancy (1996) listed 19 counties and one city that had issued voter-approved bonds. These typically were backed by an increase in ad valorem taxes or by other means that amounted to $696 million, at a time when citizens were reluctant to approve revenue increases at any level, for any other purpose.

All of this adds up to at least one bright spot in the future for funding critical public needs. By 1998 some 900,000 acres of "natural Florida" had been protected through the use of about $1 billion in new land conservation funding (The Nature Conservancy 1998). Environmental groups led by the Nature Conservancy and many other organizations were determined to find a way to extend the Preservation 2000 funding levels into the next decade.

Affordable Housing

DCA Secretary Pelham and his successor, Bill Sadowski, pushed hard to make meaningful the affordable housing component of the growth management system. However, with virtually no funding available to back up the State Comprehensive Plan (Chapter 187), the Local Government Planning and Land Development Regulations Act (Chapter 163, part II), and other statutory and rules language, their task was a difficult one. Using language in the state plan and the requirements of the housing element of local plans, Pelham stressed that inadequate attention to the affordable housing issue was grounds for denial of consistency.

A Governor's Task Force on Affordable Housing, named in 1986, made a number of recommendations to strengthen Florida's affordable housing programs, and Governor Martinez supported those recommendations in legislation presented to the 1988 legislature. The legislation that passed included funding for several new programs, one of which was the State Apartment Incentive Loan (SAIL) program to stimulate the production of rental housing affordable to people with very low incomes. SAIL received $30 million dollars from the legislature in 1988, and that funding has continued.[6]

The dramatic breakthrough in the affordable housing arena came in the form of the adoption of the William E. Sadowski Affordable Housing Act,

---

6. See Affordable Housing Study Commission (1987); Elder (1988, 3–4); and FAPA (1988, 4).

signed into law on July 7, 1992. Named in honor of DCA Secretary Sadowski, who was killed in a plane crash in 1991, the law had emerged from the recommendations of Governor Chiles's Ad Hoc Working Group on Affordable Housing and skilled coalition building by Jaimie Ross, affordable housing director for 1000 Friends of Florida. The legislation provided for a dedicated revenue source for affordable housing by increasing the documentary (doc) stamp tax on deeds from 60 cents per $100 to 70 cents per $100 beginning August 1, 1992. The act also transferred another 10 cents per $100 of existing doc stamp revenues from general revenues to housing as of July 1, 1995. With the additional 10-cent equivalent transfer from general revenue, annual dollars to housing were estimated to reach over $114 million. The dollars from the first dime were divided equally between state and local governments. Those from the second dime would go 12.5 percent to the state and 87.5 percent to local governments, yielding a distribution from both dimes of 31 percent to the state and 69 percent to local governments (Ross 1992, 13).

To overcome differences between the House and Senate versions of what became the Sadowski Affordable Housing Act of 1992, Ross worked out a compromise supported by all key actors: county and city organizations; the Florida Home Builders Association; the Florida Association of Realtors; Florida Legal Services; Florida Catholic Conference; DCA; the State Housing Finance Agency; and 1000 Friends.

The heart of the new law was the State Housing Initiative Partnership (SHIP), the vehicle by which money was passed to eligible local governments—any county or eligible municipality (an entitlement city for Community Development Block Grant purposes). Local governments had to meet a number of criteria to receive the SHIP funds from DCA and the Housing Finance Agency. The SHIP program was complemented by the funds for existing housing programs at the state level, primarily SAIL and the Homeowners Assistance Program (HAP).

The critical test of the Sadowski Act coalition came during the 1995 legislative session, in an attempt to win approval of the 10-cent equivalent from general revenue. Ross and 1000 Friends again took the lead in reactivating 1992's successful coalition. The budget environment could hardly have been worse for shifting millions of dollars from general revenue to earmarked funding for affordable housing, yet the coalition held firm. The transfer of funds increased Sadowski Act funding by 120 percent, from $53 million to $116.8 million. The appropriation for fiscal 1996–1997 totaled $130 million, with $86 million going directly to local governments for implementing SHIP programs and the rest for state programs. By far the largest commitment of the state program's $44 million share was to SAIL, with $31.6 million.[7]

Economic Development

Along with consistent funding to meet the concurrency requirement, economic development was a weak link in Florida's system. The problem was not the barriers to economic development, but rather the lack of a positive, well-funded economic policy. Such a policy must have appropriate incentives and disincentives to assure the creation of jobs and housing throughout the state, especially in rural areas of northwest Florida, where economic development is the number one priority. By early 1990 DCA was beginning to address the problem, and widespread support continues for a more proactive state program to support economic development in rural areas. What these actors and groups do not support is the solution sought by some who see the growth management system as the cause of all the state's economic ills, especially the recession of the early 1990s. Their solution was to repeal the laws establishing the system, or to at least gut them by removing the requirements for consistency and concurrency.

Ongoing Funding Struggles

Florida's failure to provide its promised $50 million share of funds to prepare the plans required by the 1975 Local Government Comprehensive Planning Act undermined the state's moral authority to mandate key elements of a comprehensive growth management system. Only a small fraction of the funding proposed in the 1970s was ever delivered, but the state

---

7. See Gluckman et al. (1996, 25); Florida DCA (1995c, 3, 7); (1994b, 1, 5); and 1000 Friends of Florida (1997, 5).

did not repeat that mistake after renewing its mandate for local planning in 1985. From 1985 through the 1991 legislative session, about $44 million in planning support was distributed to cities and counties, according to a formula developed by DCA and based on a set amount for each local government, with added funds based on population and coastal status. All local governments that were required to prepare a coastal element in their plans were given a double allocation. As local governments moved into the land development regulation and plan amendment stages, the state continued to provide planning funds (Florida DCA 1989a, 12; 1990a, 6; 1991, 8).

The state was reasonably generous in providing planning funds to local governments (and, to a lesser degree, to regional governments), but the same cannot be said of the infrastructure costs associated with the concurrency requirement. The story here centers around the work of the State Comprehensive Plan Committee (SCPC or the Zwick Committee), chaired by Charles J. Zwick, then-chairman of Southeast Banking Corporation based in Miami (1985–1987). The 20-member committee was mandated by the State Comprehensive Plan (Chapter 187) and was charged "with calculating the costs of implementing the state comprehensive plan and with recommending specific ways of paying for those costs."

The committee's members represented the development and financial community, as well as state and local governments. Implementation of the committee's key funding recommendations stand out as the high-water mark in the state's effort to behave responsibly and predictably in funding the growth management system. The opening pages of the committee's report (Florida SCPC 1987) made the fundamental point that Florida lacked a tax structure that would allow it to reach the goals of the state comprehensive plan, including a healthy economy. To achieve this, the report stated, Florida would have to become nationally and internationally competitive, with the following "keys to competition" in place.

- A sound physical infrastructure

- Well-managed natural resources

- An educated and motivated workforce supported by adequate human services

- Quality universities and research and development institutes

- An attractive quality of life

- A regulatory atmosphere that encourages enterprise

- Fiscal stability characterized by reasonable tax rates and prudent spending policies

The committee next analyzed the state "as it is" and found it lacking in the ability to achieve these keys to success without making major changes to the state's tax policies. Florida's shortcomings included the failure to provide needed infrastructure, such as roads, solid waste and schools (concurrency); the failure to balance growth to protect natural systems; an education system not up to the standard needed to compete successfully; and rankings of last among the 50 states in per capita spending for basic human services, and 47th "in state and local taxes as a percentage of state personal income." The Zwick Committee report (Florida SCPC 1987, 3) concluded:

> Florida is a state with boundless economic potential—a state we can keep on the competing edge. Florida is also a state with jammed highways, polluted natural resources, struggling schools, poorly paid teachers, teeming jails, neglected children, needy senior citizens, inadequate health care, a shortage of affordable housing, and a declining quality of life. Florida is a state on a collision course with painful realities that must be faced—now.

To achieve the goals of the state plan and overcome a negative future, the committee estimated that the total costs to state and local governments of implementing the state comprehensive plan would be $52.9 billion ($35 billion at the state level and $17.9 billion at the local level) over the next 10 years, not including making up backlogs.

The committee's main recommendation called for "fundamental tax reform that will give a stable source of revenue for state government in Florida that will keep pace with the demands of our growing state." The committee found just three possibilities for such a revenue source: the extension of the sales tax to services, a business receipts tax and a personal income tax. Noting that the 1986 legislature had decided to "sunset" all sales tax exemptions except for "food, medicine, feed, seed, fertilizer, and some minor and miscellaneous exemptions for business and not-for-profit organizations," the Zwick Committee made its fundamental tax reform proposal. "Our committee's strong belief is that the state should tax sales of services for which exemptions from the sales tax are scheduled to 'sunset' on July 1, 1987." The report noted that such a broadened sales tax would initially yield some $1.36 billion annually and would grow over time, and later estimates indicated that the amount might be substantially higher (Florida SCPC 1987, 41).

The 1987 legislature, with the full support of recently elected Governor Bob Martinez, allowed the sales tax exemptions on services to sunset, and the state began the collection of the new revenues. The additional funds from the initial six months of collection were earmarked for an Infrastructure Trust Fund, which in turn would be the state's source of revenue to keep its commitment to paying its share of the concurrency requirement imposed on local government by the system.

Following this brave and bold effort to reform the state revenue system, revenue collection over the first six months quickly built up $500 million in the fund. However, Martinez suddenly reversed himself on the issue, calling for the repeal of the sales tax on services and the substitution of a one-cent increase in the historic, narrowly based sales tax on commodities. Martinez thus turned against the fiscal solution needed to implement the state plan fully and fairly. After a series of extraordinarily bitter special sessions of the 1988 legislature, the sales tax on services was repealed and replaced by a one-cent increase in the sales tax on commodities, a tax with much less revenue potential, especially during an economic downturn (Colburn and deHaven-Smith 1999, 73; deHaven-Smith 1998, 251–260).

Reasons for Martinez's reversal have never been fully explained, but they clearly involved his role as national finance cochair of George H. W. Bush's 1988 presidential campaign. Many observers, including this author, hold that Martinez's action led directly to his defeat in his bid for reelection in 1990, and set off a struggle to find the revenues necessary for the implementation of the growth management system. Most important, the repeal of the sales tax on services

deprived the state of the ability to offer incentives to local governments from the Infrastructure Trust Fund, which, by the end of 2000, would have produced more than $25 billion for that purpose. That outcome could have led to greater trust and cohesion in the whole system, as well as better quality plans at the local level that fully reflected the goals of the system.

In 1992 Governor Chiles's attempt to return to the sales tax on services as part of a $1.4 billion revenue enhancement initiative encountered a hostile legislature. As a result, state and local governments and the private sector have tried to patch together an assortment of revenues and fees to fund the system's implementation (DeGrove and Stroud 1987; 1988). Many believe that repeal of the sales tax on services was the biggest public policy setback in the history of the state.

The burden of the concurrency requirement falls squarely and finally on local governments—not on developers, regional or state agencies, or any other actor in the system. Faced with the state's failure to sustain its commitment to fund its fair share of the costs of concurrency, local governments, supported from time to time by home builders and developers, have pushed hard for more revenues from a variety of sources. Their main thrust has been to persuade the state to approve often promised but reluctantly delivered fiscal home rule. While these efforts have been somewhat successful, they have failed to provide the funds needed to pay for the costs of growth.

By the late 1990s the local option gas tax (now called the fuel tax) amounted to 12 cents per gallon; six cents had been authorized in 1983; a "ninth" cent tax was adopted earlier; and an additional five cents per gallon was approved by the 1993 legislature upon the recommendation of ELMS III. However, these sources fell short of true fiscal home rule for local governments because they called for either a referendum or a large majority for adoption.

In a modest transportation-related breakthrough, the 1990 legislature had approved and Governor Martinez did not veto a funding package that increased transportation funding from $1.6 billion to $3.6 billion over the 1990–1998 period. Nevertheless, this amount was inadequate to meet transportation infrastructure needs according to Donald R. Crane, head of Floridians for Better Transportation. This group had put together the public-private coalition that won approval of the 1990 legislation, and also had persuaded Governor Martinez not to veto it.[8]

Another local option tax, the Local Government Infrastructure Surtax, was directly aimed at providing local governments with revenues needed to help meet the demands of the concurrency requirement. Both houses of the legislature strongly supported the ability of local governments to levy the tax without a referendum, but Martinez insisted that the referendum requirement be added. The tax could be levied at either one-half cent or one cent, pursuant to an ordinance adopted by the county governing body *and* approved by voters in a countywide referendum. While there were some exceptions, especially for small counties, the proceeds had to be used to "finance, plan, and construct infrastructure; to acquire land for public recreation or conservation or protection of natural resources," and to finance the closure of certain solid waste landfills required by the state.

Most counties (29 of 67) imposing this levy at a one-half or one-cent rate have been small, except for a cluster of counties on the west coast such as Hillsborough (half-cent levy) and Pinellas, Sarasota, Charlotte and Manatee (full-cent levy). Efforts by other larger counties to levy the tax have failed at the ballot box (Broward) or have not been put to a vote (Palm Beach). The tax, where imposed, produces substantial revenues to help meet the concurrency demands of the growth management system. Had it been available without a referendum as the legislature proposed, the concurrency funding picture might have been much stronger for local governments.[9]

---

8. The gas (fuel) tax data are taken from *The Local Government Finance Information Handbook*, Florida Legislative Committee on Intergovernmental Relations and Florida Department of Revenue (1998, 331–337), and the cumulative dollar numbers are found in Table 1 (337). See in the same handbook "1 to 6 Cents Local Option Fuel Tax" (369–375) and "1 to 5 Cents Local Option Fuel Tax" (377–380). See also Crane (1998) and Floridians for Better Transportation (Undated).

9. For more information, see Florida Legislative Committee on Intergovernmental Relations and Florida Department of Revenue (1998, 309–326); and DeGrove and Turner (1998, 187–188).

Two of the state's leading participant-observers of the system made the same point as the Zwick Committee. Professor Susan MacManus (1998), of the University of South Florida, an expert in state and local finances, stated that the challenge is "how to meet the rising expenditure demands associated with rapid population growth in a fiscally conservative political environment." Lance deHaven-Smith (1998), head of Florida State University's public administration program, concluded that "the most serious problem caused by growth is an endemic fiscal crisis" and the demise of the sales tax on services removed the "final component needed to manage Florida's growth."

ELMS III Recommendations and Implementation, 1991–1996

The election of Lawton Chiles as governor in 1990 coincided with a severe recession in Florida, which was in part responsible for the legislature becoming increasingly hostile to the growth management system. For those favoring the system, Chiles's strong support was the difference between disaster for the program and fighting more or less successful rearguard actions aimed at defeating the worst bills springing up in the legislature. His strategy to ward off these assaults on the program in the 1992 legislative session (January 14–July 1, including special sessions) was to establish the third Environmental Land Management Study Committee (ELMS III) on November 19, 1991. Chiles made it clear that he would not support major changes in the system until ELMS III had done its work and reported to him and the legislature in December 1992 (FAPA 1992a; 1992b).

Nevertheless, a "fine-tuning" bill for the growth management system did pass in 1992 (Murley, Draper and Durrence 1992). SB 1882 was the first growth management legislation passed since 1986, and it contained useful though not major items that encouraged innovative urban and rural planning policies aimed in part at curbing sprawl. The bill also required DCA to review the DRI process and recommend whether it should be "replaced, repealed, or incorporated in whole or part into the comprehensive planning process," a task undertaken by ELMS III. On another positive note, the first 1992 special session included legislation to transfer the Coastal Zone Management program from the Department of Environmental Regulation, where it had been given a very narrow regulatory focus, to DCA, in order to strengthen its planning framework, among other things.

However, a bill did pass that would sunset regional planning councils in 1993 unless their enabling legislation was specifically reenacted by both houses, and a number of other bills that would have drastically weakened the system cleared House or Senate committees. Although these latter bills did not pass in the full legislature in 1992, their considerable support in both houses was a danger signal for the future (Murley, Draper and Durrence 1992). When legislative elections in late 1992 saw those hostile to the growth management system gain strength in both houses, even though the Democrats retained majorities, the prospects for positive growth management action in the 1993 session became even more uncertain.

Early Consensus on an Action Agenda

ELMS III was the latest in a long line of committees trying to move the process forward, but probably none had been convened in an environment so hostile to the growth management system. Governor Chiles's charge to the committee was very broad but was worded in such a way that the members had considerable flexibility in setting its agenda. James Harold Thompson, the chair, was a former Speaker of the House who supported the adoption of the growth management system in 1985, but was also seen as a conservative on many issues and sensitive to concerns about the system in north Florida's cities and counties. Vice chair Linda Loomis Shelley had been general counsel for both DCA and the governor during the Graham administration and was highly respected by local government, environmental groups and others.

The 51-member ELMS III committee first met on December 19, 1991, in Tallahassee, amid skepticism as to whether the group would be able to reach a consensus on anything of any importance. Fourteen meetings were held within the year, and to the surprise of many, including most of its members, the committee did reach a consensus on a wide range of

issues, helped greatly by the facilitation services of the Florida Growth Management Conflict Resolution Consortium led by Robert M. Jones.

ELMS III Recommendations

Several controversial issues faced the ELMS III committee: whether to maintain the integrated policy framework bound together by the consistency concept that was the bedrock of the existing system; what to do with DRIs and the related issue of a stronger Intergovernmental Coordination Element (often referred to as "ICE with teeth"); what to do for or with regional planning councils; and whether to modify and how to fund concurrency. As to solutions, views among the 51 members ranged across the spectrum, but they reached agreement on the most fundamental issue.

On March 19, 1992, the group met in plenary session and issued a statement in favor of planning and the growth management system that led directly to Recommendation 1 of the ELMS III final report (1992, 13 and 112):

> Florida should retain and improve its integrated comprehensive planning and growth management system. The State should perform the leadership role while preserving for local governments reasonable flexibility to carry out their responsibilities and enhancing their ability to meet State goals, objectives, and policies.

That dramatic endorsement of the system's primary concept was followed by 173 additional recommendations organized around eight key topics that formed the contents of the final report.

1. The State Role in Planning and Growth Management (Recommendations 1–17)

Major recommendations included the provision of "adequate financing for these programs [as] the most important task now confronting the legislature in implementing the state leadership role in growth management" (Rec. 2). This was another remarkable recommendation considering that many members of the group were determined to eliminate the system in whole or in part. Recommendation 5 called for "the use of incentives and rewards where possible as the means for executing the state leadership role in planning and growth management programs." It has become a central concept of the sustainable communities focus of Florida's growth management system.

Recommendations 7, 8 and 9 focused on a visioning process, including legislative enactment of a state vision as a preamble to the State Comprehensive Plan. Recommendation 13 called on the legislature to amend the Florida State and Regional Planning Act of 1984 (Chapter 186) "to authorize the preparation of functional plans to address goals, objectives, and policies in the state comprehensive plan that are logically related to each other. Functional plans should integrate related matters from the state comprehensive plan in order to provide detailed guidance to all levels of government." The full implementation of this recommendation alone has yet to be achieved, but it would go far toward integrating state agency functional plans into the growth management system.

Recommendation 14 called for amending Chapter 186 "to direct preparation of a Strategic Growth and Development Plan, a functional plan that would... integrate land use, water resources, transportation... and identify state resources, facilities." Such a plan, when developed and approved by the legislature, would be the direct link between the state comprehensive plan and local, regional and state agency plans, and such plans would have to be consistent with it.

ELMS III Action Agenda

The Governor's Office (in Executive Order 91-291, dated November 19, 1991) requested the ELMS III committee to specifically address and, if appropriate, make recommendations for improving the growth management system with respect to the following issues.

1. The roles and adequacy of the State Comprehensive Plan, the State Land Development Plan, the Florida Transportation Plan, the State Water Use Plan, the State Water Policy, the Surface Water Improvement Plans for Water Management Districts and long term objectives for the coastal program in the State's system for managing growth.

2. Methods to enhance and strengthen intergovernmental coordination in the planning process, including recommendations regarding annexation.

3. Improvements in coastal zone management including potential roles for the Interagency Management Committee, the role of the coastal management program, the potential to have a State consistency process to supplement the existing Federal consistency process and for additional funding for the coastal management program.

4. Whether additional elements should be included in local government comprehensive planning. Such elements could include education, public safety, health care, air quality, corrections, economic development, energy conservation, and such others as the committee may choose to consider.

5. Identification of what, if any, adverse effects the growth management system has created in respect to the ability of citizens to obtain credit. Recommend steps to mitigate any such adverse effects consistent with the goals and purposes of growth management.

6. Adequacy of provisions related to enforcement of local plans.

7. Funding public infrastructure.

8. The appropriate role of the development of regional impact process in the context of implementation of local comprehensive planning.

9. The role and character of regional units of government, metropolitan planning organizations and their relationships to state and local governments.

10. The implementation of state policies such as post-disaster planning, interbasin transfers of water, wellfield protection, pricing of water and near-shore water quality through local plans.

11. Standardizing and computerizing data from local plans, especially future land use maps.

12. Assuring concurrency in an efficient, predictable, and reasonable manner.

13. The content requirements for Evaluation and Appraisal Reports and recommended procedures for their review by the department.

14. The establishment of a statewide system for transferring or purchasing development and water rights.

15. Establishing a "quality communities" program that provides incentives to local governments that are willing to implement comprehensive plans that exceed minimum requirements.

16. Methods for dealing with platted subdivisions.

17. The relationship between state agencies and local comprehensive plans.

18. Appropriate integration of rural planning areas into the growth management system.

Source: ELMS III, 1992, 125–127

2. The Regional Role in Planning and Growth Management (Recommendations 18–35)

The fate of regional planning councils (RPCs) was clearly shaky. To some, RPCs were the critical middle level in the growth management system, but were to others a useless added layer of government. The enabling statute had been sunsetted by the 1992 legislature, and all sides agreed that reenactment by the 1993 legislature would be difficult. The legislature had sought ELMS III's recommendations on both the regional councils and DRIs. In the end, ELMS III recommended that RPCs be retained, but with a substantial refocusing of their mission from "regulatory" actions built largely around the DRI process back to planning. The ELMS III final report stated that RPCs should be reauthorized prior to the sunset of the Florida State and Regional Planning Act in 1993. Recommended changes involved new, more focused regional plans with only five goals mandated, instead of trying to relate to all 26 of the goals of the State Comprehensive Plan.

While Recommendation 18 called for reenactment of RPCs, Recommendations 20–31 addressed ELMS III's views on how the regional level should be changed to serve more effectively as the middle level in the system. Highlights included a new coordinating role for RPCs involving all other relevant regional agencies such as water management districts and MPOs in developing the new Strategic Regional Policy Plans (Rec. 19). In addition, ELMS III proposed amending the Local Government Comprehensive Planning Act so that RPCs focused on "regional resources and facilities as identified in the regional policy plans, and extrajurisdictional impacts inconsistent with the comprehensive plan of the affected local government" (Rec. 21). The aim here was to get RPCs out of matters that were local rather than regional, with regard to the review of local plans. Recommendation 23 called for RPCs to focus on their new roles in coordinating and facilitating conflicts between local governments regarding the impacts of "greater than local" issues, including establishing a dispute resolution and mediation process (Rec. 24). This related to recommendations for the elimination of the DRI process for most jurisdictions and the implementation

of a much tougher intergovernmental coordination element for local plans.

Recommendation 25 called for more state dollars to fund RPC activities, noting the reduction for state-mandated activities from $2.2 million in fiscal 1992 to $1.4 million for fiscal 1993. Recommendation 27 called on RPCs to move more aggressively in the critical areas of regional transportation and land use in order to coordinate such policies more efficiently.

Recommendations 28–31 related to the Strategic Regional Policy Plans, which were mandated to address just five areas: affordable housing, economic development, emergency preparedness, natural resources of regional significance and regional transportation (although an RPC could address other areas if it wished). The recommendations with regard to RPCs came after much debate among ELMS III members. Most supporters of RPCs viewed the recommendations as enhancing their chances of survival at the next legislative session and strengthening their ability to address critical regional issues through strategic planning.

The committee also made a number of recommendations regarding the relationship between two federal laws (ISTEA and the Clean Air Act) and transportation at the regional level.[10] The result was a strong recommendation to overcome the downside of single county MPOs that did not cover the "real" transportation region by combining them or at least requiring that they develop joint transportation plans (Rec. 33). The committee next called for appointment by the governor of a study group "to make recommendations on the legal relationship that should be established between the water management district plans and strategic regional policy plans and local comprehensive plans," a recommendation that would (and did) force a head-on attack on the "proper" relationship between land planning and water use issues.

3. Local Planning and Intergovernmental Coordination (Recommendations 36–68)

The committee's recommendations in the area of local comprehensive planning and intergovernmental

---

10. U.S. Public Law 95-95, *Clean Air Act Amendments of 1977*; U.S. Public Law 102-240, *Intermodal Surface Transportation Efficiency Act of 1991*.

coordination carried forward the visioning recommendation made for the state and regional levels (Recs. 36–39). After spirited debate on whether additional mandatory elements (in particular, an economic element) should be added, the prevailing view was that since the whole process was underfunded, no further mandatory elements were justified. However, optional elements should be included, especially an economic element that would allow governments to levy an additional local occupational license tax (Rec. 42).

The Intergovernmental Coordination Element (ICE) was billed for substantial strengthening "to address the extrajurisdictional impacts of development projects and other greater-than-local planning issues" (Rec. 44). This was to be the tradeoff for phasing out the DRI process for most local governments. A number of recommendations were aimed at simplifying the local plan amendment process, with DCA plan amendment review not required in many cases, but preserving the right to call up an amendment for review if DCA deemed it necessary. The Growth Management Trust Fund, recommended by ELMS II to help local governments develop mandated plans, had never received the suggested $20 million per year from a specified source of funding. Recommendation 56 called for an earmarked funding source for the trust fund, linked to development and reserved for local governments whose plans were in compliance with state law. Several affordable housing recommendations called for stronger local actions to increase the efficiency of the use of Sadowski Act funds at the local level. A series of recommendations pushed for closer coordination between cities, counties, school boards and higher education facilities, and for expediting the annexation of enclaves within incorporated areas (Recs. 62–68).

4. Evaluation and Appraisal Reports (Recommendations 69–87)

Continuing to address local plans, the report included a number of recommendations concerning Evaluation and Appraisal Reports (EARs), the process by which local governments review their plans and implementing regulations at designated intervals. ELMS III's concern was to provide direction for what the EARs should contain, and at the same time simplify the process, especially for smaller units of local government. The full requirement would be maintained for updating the key local plan elements (future land use, intergovernmental coordination, conservation and capital improvements).

5. Concurrency and Public Facilities (Recommendations 88–116)

This section of the report recommended substantial changes in concurrency but did not recommend major abandonment of this key concept of Florida's growth management system. The committee stressed that additional revenue sources were critical to the success of growth management. Recommendations 88, 90 and 91 called for the state to provide additional funding itself, and to give local governments more fiscal home rule. A key recommendation was for the legislature to repeal the referendum requirements for the Local Government Infrastructure Surtax, allowing counties to adopt it by a strong majority vote of their commissions.

ELMS III said no to expanding the concurrency requirement to schools, but maintained that education should be the first area considered for future expansion of concurrency. Other recommendations included making it clear by statute that "roads, sanitary sewer, solid waste, stormwater management, potable water, parks and recreation, and mass transit (where required) were the only facilities subject to concurrency by the state, previously spelled out only by Rule 9-J-5." Other suggestions involved adding flexibility in timing for transportation and parks and recreation to promote downtown development, urban infill and public transportation. However, there would be no relaxation of timing for potable water, sanitary sewer, solid waste, or stormwater management "because these public facilities and services are essential to public health and safety" (Rec. 101). Other concurrency recommendations were included in Recommendations 94–105.

A special series of recommendations (106–116) was aimed at greatly increasing the timeframes and introducing flexibility into mandates for local governments to meet the transportation concurrency requirements. Most were adopted by the 1993 legislature, including a transportation exemption provision to promote various forms of urban development. In sum, ELMS III's recommendations were significant in calling for more flexibility for some concurrency requirements, and for more state action to provide funds needed to make concurrency work. Of equal significance was the fact that ELMS III made a strong case for maintaining the concurrency requirement as one of the key concepts of Florida's system.

6. Programs Pre-Dating the 1985 Growth Management Act (Recommendations 117–134)

The development community and some local interests were determined to eliminate the DRI process, while others were just as determined to maintain the state's ability to account for the "greater than local" impacts of local government decisions. Finding common ground was difficult, and while consensus was reached, it is fair to say that no one was very happy with it. In essence, the DRI process would be phased out in most local jurisdictions, coincident with the substantial strengthening of ICE for local plans to ensure regional impacts of local development would be accounted for. Recommendations 117–128 set forth the details of that strategy at some length.

The ACSC process was given attention in an interesting way. In addition to calling for the use of the critical area approach in smaller areas to protect important state interests, ELMS III recommended that the legislature amend the provision, "so that the critical area program can be utilized as a means for assuring compliance in the local comprehensive planning program." When all efforts to reach compliance for a local program had failed, the State Administration Commission would designate the local government as an ACSC, in lieu of applying fiscal sanctions (Rec. 132).

7. Coastal Management (Recommendations 135–156)

Recommendations addressing coastal management aimed at clarity in defining the coastal zone (designated as the 35 coastal counties) and a uniform definition of coastal high hazard areas. ELMS III called for strengthening the Coastal Resources Interagency Management Committee as the principal body responsible for coordinating policy for multijurisdictional coastal issues (Rec. 137). Other recommendations involved coastal water quality problems, especially nonpoint sources; issues of water dependent land uses (protecting ports and other areas for such uses); and postdisaster redevelopment plans (strengthening local and regional action in this area).

ELMS III also called for a targeted effort to link coastal policies and land acquisition, utilizing the 10 percent of Preservation 2000 set aside to acquire locally identified properties that serve to implement a wide range of coastal policies (Rec. 153). Determined to follow its predecessor ELMS II's focus on funding what was requested, ELMS III called on the legislature to identify special funding mechanisms, including coastal management improvement districts as a possible funding source (Rec. 155).

8. Land Preservation (Recommendations 157–174)

The last set of recommendations in the ELMS III final report included a review of Florida's efforts to acquire important resource lands, beginning with the 1972 Environmentally Endangered Lands (EEL) program and continuing through Preservation 2000. The recommendations addressed a wide range of issues.

- Better intergovernmental coordination in deciding what lands to buy

- The importance of using an ecosystem approach in land preservation

- The use of mitigation techniques to support ecosystem goals

- Full funding for Preservation 2000

- Streamlining the Florida Communities Trust land acquisition efforts

- A series of recommendations on the importance of and the need for flexible techniques to keep agricultural lands in production

- Less than fee, transferable development rights, and other techniques to protect important resource lands

In summary, ELMS III's year of intensive effort produced 174 wide-ranging recommendations that were significant for their breadth and depth, and the remarkable consensus to sustain the basic foundations of the growth management system and strengthen it through better coordination and funding. Major changes were agreed on that impacted regional planning councils, the DRI process and concurrency, among others.

The Political Environment

We turn now to an assessment of the 1993 legislature's actions on ELMS III's recommendations and how those actions set the stage for state efforts to move to the sustainable communities phase of the late 1990s. The fragile consensus reached by ELMS III in its unanimous adoption of the final report was expected by some to hold up through the legislature's consideration of the committee's recommendations. However, as former ELMS III vice chair Linda Loomis Shelley put it after assuming the post of DCA secretary, "There may be pushing and shoving by some special interests in an attempt to use the legislative process to gain an advantage which they did not achieve in the ELMS process" (Florida DCA 1993). Nevertheless, the consensus achieved by the 51 members of ELMS III held, and the legislature adopted, without significant changes, all the major and many minor recommendations, representing 75 percent of the 174 items (Murley, Powell and Draper 1993, 10). Agreement on legislative action was possible in part because, as former DCA Secretary Pelham put it, "Both the Final Report...and the ELMS III legislation are primarily process oriented; neither confronts and deals with substantive growth management issues. However, the new legislation set the stage for some major debates over substantive growth management policy" (Pelham 1993, 1, 4). His assessment turned out to be right on target.

The major and tough-to-implement items that did pass included a new state planning mandate to carry out a biennial review of the state plan by the governor, with recommended changes considered by the Administration Commission, and given to the legislature with proposed revisions, including measurable objectives. The ELMS III legislation also required the preparation of a Growth Management Portion (GMP) of the state plan (arguably required but never implemented by the 1984 act) to generate "a more focused and strategic plan component address-

ing land, water, transportation and other issues closely related to physical growth and development." The legislation called for the GMP to be proposed by the governor in October 1993, given to the legislature by December 1993 and taken up by the legislature in 1994. Presumably, this document would address the complaints of some local governments and others that the requirements of the state plan were vague, general and uncertain. In one view, "If the legislature adopts such a measure and so provides, it will become a new cornerstone for planning and growth management in Florida" (Murley, Powell and Draper 1993, 10).

For RPCs, the ELMS III legislation was a good news/bad news package. RPCs were not sunseted, their statute was reenacted, and in some areas their responsibilities were broadened. But to those RPCs whose energies had been largely focused on DRI reviews, it doubtless seemed a big loss. An RPC boundary review by the governor's office was required by January 1, 1994; RPCs were required to establish a dispute resolution process to resolve inconsistencies between regional and local plans; and each council had to adopt, by a two-thirds vote of the governing board, a new strategic regional policy plan, including the five required areas recommended by ELMS III. The plans had to focus on regional rather than local resources and facilities, "to be used for planning, not regulatory or permitting purposes." The governor's office was directed to adopt a rule to "coordinate preparation and review of strategic policy plans with the new EARs review process" (Pelham 1993, 4).

The ELMS III legislation made changes to three mandatory local plan elements: housing, transportation and the Intergovernmental Coordination Element. Of the three, the new ICE was by far the most important, since it had to be implemented in order for the DRI process to be largely phased out. If implemented, the new ICE requirement would be much stronger than the existing ICE. To get the process moving, DCA was directed to (1) prepare and get to local governments a model element; (2) adopt a rule setting up minimum criteria that local governments would have to meet to comply with the new "ICE with teeth" rule; and (3) adopt a rule with a schedule for local governments to follow in transmitting to DCA the proposed amendments to their ICE.

For local governments where the DRI process was to be terminated (counties with 100,000 or more people, all cities in those counties with 2,500 or more residents, and others electing not to be covered by the process), the new ICE had to be developed, adopted and submitted to DCA for approval by December 31, 1997. Where the DRI process remained, changes were made to thresholds for certain land uses in downtowns and regional activity centers to make DRI-scale development easier in such areas. DCA was directed to adopt uniform statewide standards for reviews, and these changes were aimed at making the process easier to work with (Murley, Powell, and Draper 1993, 10; Pelham 1993, 4).

The concurrency recommendations of ELMS III were adopted by the legislature essentially as recommended. They gave the requirement a clear statutory base for the first time and greater flexibility for transportation concurrency, including exemption from the transportation concurrency requirement in certain cases. The legislation also required revision of existing Transportation Concurrency Management Areas (TCMAs) to make them easier to use by local governments, and authorized 10- or even 15-year backlog reduction plans for roads (Murley, Powell and Draper 1993, 11–12).

The 1993 ELMS law was a bold statute in many of its dimensions, and it gave local governments an additional five cents optional gas tax without a local referendum, to be added to the five-cent option local governments already had. Tom Pelham's point, that when process moved to substance the going would get tough, has proven to be all too accurate. Not one of the major requirements of the ELMS III legislation has been fully implemented, and some very important requirements are dead in the water.

More Failures than Successes

The capstone of the effort to make the integrated policy framework more meaningful was put on a fast track by the 1993 legislature. At first, the implementation effort moved more or less on schedule, with the Executive Office of the Governor appointing a technical advisory committee and a series of subcommittees to draft the GMP of the state plan. The game plan was

for the governor to appoint a growth management policy advisory committee to review the GMP before it was transmitted to the governor and cabinet, on the road to the 1994 legislature. The policy advisory committee held its first meeting in August 1993 to look at input from the technical advisory committee and its subcommittees. This 12-member policy committee included a good cross-section of public- and private-sector actors, including DCA Secretary Shelley and 1000 Friends' Jim Murley, both ELMS III veterans.

Soon sentiment began to surface that the timetable was too short to develop a "quality" GMP in time for the 1994 legislature. How the GMP should relate to the mandated review of the whole state comprehensive plan, the lack of adequate data with which to make decisions, the need to further educate the public—all these issues and more led the advisory committee to recommend not developing a GMP of the state plan until the whole plan was updated. It was downhill for the GMP after that. Many observers, including this author, felt that a GMP of the state comprehensive plan was badly needed and had been part of the original state comprehensive plan enabling legislation in 1984. The real reason it was "deep-sixed" goes to Tom Pelham's point about substance. Questions of exactly what would be in the GMP, who would have to be consistent with it, and how it would be implemented proved to be too hot to handle (Elder 1993a; 1993b; FAPA 1993).

The review of the state comprehensive plan mandated by ELMS III has not fared any better than the GMP. The fall 1994 issue of DCA's newsletter, *Community Planning*, reported that the governor's office was leading a thorough review of the state comprehensive plan, presumably to set the stage for its recommended revisions (Florida DCA 1994a, 5). In fact, no such review resulted in recommendations for action from the governor through the Administration Commission to the legislature. The fundamental reason seemed to be that the governor's office viewed opening up the plan to legislative review as being too risky in light of an increasingly hostile Republican-controlled legislature after the November 1996 elections.

The ELMS III "deal" that no one loved but that was ultimately embraced by ELMS III and the 1993 legislature (involving the tradeoff between phasing out most of the DRI process in exchange for a much stronger intergovernmental coordination element) had no more success than changes to the state comprehensive plan. By 1996 both changes were essentially dead, with a return to a pre-ELMS III weak ICE and a somewhat more flexible DRI process that seemed destined to be around for the indefinite future.

The crux of the implementation problem was that when local governments and many developers got a good look at the requirements of ICE with teeth, the old processes began to look better and better. DCA's February 1995 *Community Planning* set out, in great detail, what local governments would have to do to meet the new ICE rule adopted by the 1994 legislature (Florida DCA 1995a, 1, 4–6). To shed the DRI process, local governments would have to

■ develop an ICE element for the local plans that included a process clearly identifying development that would impact state and regional resources and facilities;

■ define significant impacts;

■ describe mitigation criteria;

■ demonstrate intergovernmental compatibility;

■ install a development review process to replace the DRI review;

■ incorporate a dispute resolution process into their plan; and

■ agree to submit DRI-size development orders to DCA (not to RPCs) for review and possible appeal.

After struggling with the new ICE for a year, the 1995 legislature directed Secretary Shelley to establish a 15-member ICE Technical Committee to consider changes to the department's 1994 ICE rule. The upshot of the review was a recommendation that the legislature authorize a return of ICE to its pre-1993 status and eliminate provisions for the termination of the DRI process (Florida DCA 1996, 3). The 1996 legislature responded to the Technical Committee's recommendations by deleting the ELMS III language adopted in 1994 and returning to the pre-1994 status

for both ICE and DRIs. In the process, the threshold for DRI review of marina projects was changed from 400 to 200 boat slips (Gluckman et al. 1996, 22).

Not all ELMS III recommendations fell by the wayside. The changes in the roles of regional planning councils have, for the most part, been implemented. With the reenactment of the DRI process, RPCs no longer have a right of administrative appeal of the final DRI development order, but they continue to be the sole agency that issues the assessment of the regional impacts of the proposed DRI: the ADA-Application for Development Approval Assessment. Involvement in the DRI process was viewed by friend and foe of the RPCs as a distraction from their planning role. This was especially true after the passage of the growth management legislation of the mid-1980s, when RPCs had a major role to play in the review (and even preparation in many regions) of local plans. In their post-ELMS III roles, RPCs will be focusing much more on planning in the preparation of the Strategic Regional Policy Plans and through their newly acquired roles of coordinator and mediator.

The concurrency changes recommended by ELMS III and accepted by the legislature are of special significance, providing much-needed flexibility in the area of transportation concurrency and, to a lesser degree, for the parks and recreation concurrency requirement. Yet, they kept intact the basic concept of providing the facilities needed to take care of the impacts of new development as they occur, and making up backlogs over time. Those changes have provided valuable options in meeting the concurrency requirement as the sustainable communities modification of the system moved forward in the last part of the 1990s. The transportation exemption provision approved by the legislature for areas designated in amended local comprehensive plans was aimed at promoting infill development and redevelopment where most growth would occur. That, in turn, would facilitate the effort to contain sprawl and promote sustainable communities by establishing effective urban limit lines.[11]

---

11. For further details on the ELMS III changes, see DeGrove and Gale (1994) and FAU/FIU (1993, 12–13).

The Property Rights Issue

In the midst of the state's worst recession in recent memory and a period of growing antigovernment attitude, the timing was clearly bad for any proposal that would raise new revenue or reform the system to provide for new revenue in the future. Nor was the legislature particularly pleased with the implications of the ELMS III recommendations for property owners. The issue of what is and is not appropriate regarding the issue of property rights is complex. Supporters of an effective growth management system argue that protecting private property rights is important but must be balanced against the public's interest in managing growth and change. Opponents of having such a system argue that any plan and implementing regulations that reduce the value of property, however small the reduction and whatever the public purpose, must be compensated. The "you can't tell people what they can do with their property" theme is supported by some developers, realtors and individuals, and is an ongoing issue in every state or region that attempts any kind of growth management system.

The 1993 legislature developed the first in a string of "takings" bills aimed at giving private property owners much more compensation for *any* regulatory action that decreased property values by more than 40 percent (FAU/FIU 1993, 9). The 1994 session saw a flurry of private property rights (some would say wrongs) bills, with the 40 percent reduction in value bill resurfacing. A new set of tax cap amendments to the Florida Constitution was proposed, but three of the four were removed from the ballot by the State Supreme Court as violating the single subject rule for amending the constitution. In 1995 the legislature finally passed and the governor signed a private property rights act, the Bert J. Harris Jr., Private Property Rights Protection Act. It was seen by some as necessary to avoid a much more extreme "private property wrongs" constitutional amendment, and viewed by others as an unwise giving in to forces bent on undermining all land use planning and regulation efforts. The results of the law and its implications are still being debated, but it certainly had a chilling effect, at least temporarily, on the readiness of many local governments to amend their plans and develop new implementing regulations (Henderson, Drake and Ross 1995, 2–3; Pelham 1995; DeGrove and Turner 1998, 169–192).

Accomplishments and Disappointments, 1986–1996

Efforts to implement Florida's growth management system, based on the recommendations of ELMS II and ELMS III over the 1986–1996 decade, present a mixed picture of accomplishments and disappointments, with the political environment growing less favorable over the last half of that period. Local government plans and land development regulations were created, reviewed by the state land planning agency (DCA) and, to greater or lesser degrees, implemented. The failure of the state to provide its fair share of the cost greatly limited the capacity to implement the system, especially in areas such as consistency and concurrency. The recommendation of the Zwick Committee to pass a sales tax on services was briefly adopted and then repealed, leaving a multibillion dollar shortfall that has never been corrected, in spite of efforts by the Tax Reform Commission and Governor Chiles's administration in the early 1990s. Bright spots in the funding area were in natural resources, with the adoption of Preservation 2000 in 1990, and in affordable housing, with the adoption of the Sadowski Housing Act in 1992.

Regional planning councils survived an effort to eliminate them, but they present a mixed picture: some are more effective than others, but all lack the tools needed to implement their comprehensive regional policy plans and other goals and objectives. The importance and effectiveness of water management districts increased with the move toward ecosystem approaches to restoring and sustaining natural resources.

The challenge of integrating state agencies fully and effectively into the system remained, with only limited success, in spite of special efforts by the Chiles-MacKay administration. Finally, the failure to implement key recommendations of ELMS III to strengthen the system by updating the State Comprehensive Plan and developing a growth management component as a more directive framework for the system left those issues on the unfinished agenda.

Phase Three, 1996–2003:
A Strategy for a Sustainable Florida

By 1996 it had become clear that a new approach would have to be found if Florida, still faced with substantial growth pressures, would find a way to implement the integrated policy framework as recommended by ELMS II and III. The Chiles-MacKay administration's efforts to strengthen the system by substantially increasing state-level funding and greater fiscal home rule for local government had, with limited exceptions, been rebuffed by an increasingly hostile legislature, where both houses were controlled by the Republican party after the 1996 elections. In the House especially, with a very conservative Republican speaker, prospects for any movement without a new approach seemed virtually nil.

Because Phase Three of growth management centers on the concept of sustainability, a brief discussion of its origin and meaning is warranted. The idea of sustainable development first gained international attention in a 1987 World Commission on Environment and Development report, where it was defined as "development which meets the needs of the present without endangering the ability of future generations to meet their own needs" (World Commission 1987). Sustainability gained momentum in June 1992 during the United Nations Conference on Environment and Development Earth Summit, when a document was adopted to promote the integration of environmental, economic and social planning (Brown 1994–1995, 31; United Nations 1992). In the case of Florida, with its decades-long struggle to integrate land use, transportation, water, air quality and other factors, the essence of sustainability was clear: everything is related to everything else.

Restoring the Everglades

The sustainability concept in Florida can be traced as far back as the mid-1980s, with the efforts to protect and restore the greater Everglades (Florida Office of the Governor 1997). The Everglades ecosystem is home to a large number of threatened and endangered wildlife species, including the only living coral reef in the continental U.S. The Everglades also provides the major source of fresh water for almost five million people. This figure was projected to increase to more than eight million by the year 2020 in the 16 counties that constitute the Everglades ecosystem. In short, the Everglades was seen as essential to the sustained health of South Florida in all its dimensions: environmental, social and economic.

By 1994 a series of state and federal actions had led to a major effort to "retrofit" the Central and Southern Florida Flood Control Project, to undo the massive environmental damage done to the Everglades by past drainage and reclamation efforts.[12] The 1994 Florida legislature, responding to strong support by Governor Chiles, passed the Everglades Restoration Act. The act charged all the key actors to "pursue restoring and sustaining the ecosystem that begins at the headwaters of the Kissimmee River (Reedy Creek and Disney World), continues along the Kissimmee to Lake Okeechobee, and fans out to encompass the entire watershed." The watershed also is the boundary of the South Florida Water Management District (DeGrove 1995, 1, 15). On March 31, 1994, Chiles appointed the Governor's Commission for a Sustainable South Florida (Governor's Commission 1995).

The original commission consisted of 37 voting members and five nonvoting members (representing federal agencies), with several other members added over time. The voting members included representatives from the business and economic community, public interest and environmental organizations, county and city officials, relevant state and regional agencies, the Seminole and Miccosukee Indian tribes, and one member each from the Florida House and Senate. When the Governor's Commission convened its first meeting on April 27, 1994, there was widespread distrust and skepticism that such a group could reach a consensus on anything, as occurred

---

12. For a historical perspective on efforts to drain and reclaim the Everglades for useful purposes, see DeGrove (1958, 13–53).

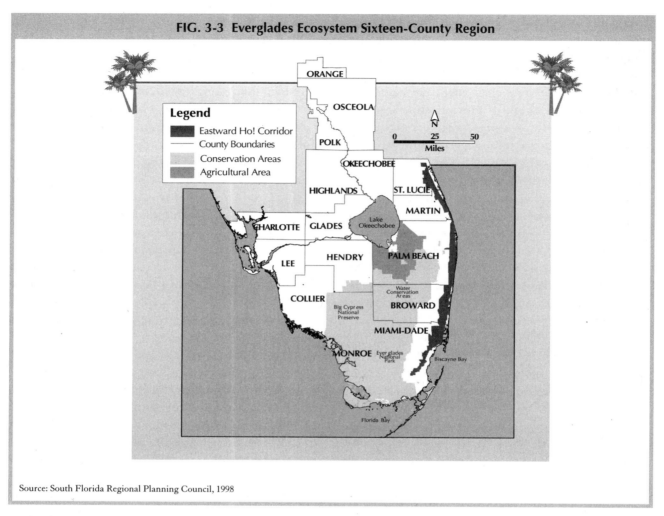

FIG. 3-3 Everglades Ecosystem Sixteen-County Region

Source: South Florida Regional Planning Council, 1998

at the first meeting of ELMS III. Yet, a unanimous consensus was reached in September 1995, on two major recommendations that set the stage for the development of Phase Three of Florida's growth management system.

First, the commission came down firmly on the side of restoring all of the available natural Everglades (two million of the original four million acres) that had not been taken up by urban development or other irreversible uses. Next, it accepted the recommendation of its Urban Form, Intergovernmental Relations, and Governance Committee that the natural and urban systems in South Florida were not and could not become sustainable unless the population growth in the region, especially in Palm Beach, Broward and Dade counties, was absorbed in communities of moderate densities that encouraged the use of

public transit and discouraged the predominance of the single occupancy vehicle. The commission went further by recommending a development and redevelopment corridor utilizing a wide range of incentives to encourage much of the population growth to locate there. It called for a pilot project to demonstrate the feasibility of radically shifting future population growth to a corridor stretching generally from Palm Beach (with a later expansion to Martin and St. Lucie counties to its north) south, through Broward and into Dade County.

The Eastward Ho! Initiative

This strategy for luring population growth back to urban centers on the east coast and away from the

Everglades came to be called the Eastward Ho! Initiative, and soon became the catalyst for an added sustainable communities component to Florida's growth management system. The Governor's Commission's initial report (1995) defined several barriers to implementing Eastward Ho!, including crime and inadequate schools. The report also cited the reluctance of banks and other financial institutions to fund infill development projects. It concluded by challenging all relevant actors to work together to overcome the barriers and move Eastward Ho! from vision to reality. A description of the effort noted the Governor's Commission's twin recommendations to protect and restore the Everglades ecosystem and to slow the suburban sprawl and urban decay that were displacing the urban environment and degrading the quality of life (Florida DCA 1997b, 1).

The challenges of Eastward Ho! were and remain awesome. The whole effort might have foundered in its infancy if DCA had not stepped forward and taken the lead in coordinating the effort. Jim Murley, former director of 1000 Friends of Florida (1987–1995), succeeded Linda Loomis Shelley as DCA secretary in August 1995, when Shelley became Governor Chiles's chief of staff. Murley had played a major role as division director of Resource Planning and Management for DCA in the mid-1980s, when he helped craft the growth management system and pushed hard at 1000 Friends to implement the system. He was in a unique position to recognize the need to provide an added component to the system if it were to thrive or even survive, and he seized on the sustainable communities concept as that component. During the 1996–1999 period, DCA invested $3,530,000 in the effort (primarily from the Petroleum Violation Escrow Fund).

Working closely with the South Florida and Treasure Coast RPCs, South Florida's local governments, and the business community, DCA moved rapidly to keep the Eastward Ho! momentum going. The redevelopment framework envisioned a corridor through an economically depressed area in the tricounty region. The boundaries of the corridor, while not fixed, generally parallel Interstate 95 and the CSX railroad tracks on the west and the Florida East Coast (FEC) tracks on the east, including the area between these tracks, with fluctuations to incorporate the region's major seaports, airports and downtown centers. DCA expressed an ambitious vision for the redevelopment corridor (Florida DCA 1997b).

It is easy to see why this vision was so potentially powerful as a major model for sustainable communities anywhere in the state, and so difficult to implement. To build support for the effort, DCA undertook a vigorous outreach and policy development effort. It included strengthening the ability to assemble land in the corridor, hiring an infill development and redevelopment ombudsman, and assessing financial impediments to development in the corridor and strategies to overcome them. It also included a mixed-use plan book for use by local governments and the development and financial communities, to guide development in the corridor, as well as demonstration projects "to provide positive examples of sustainable urban design" (Florida DCA 1997b, 3; FAU/FIU 1998).

During the 1996 legislative session, DCA succeeded in gaining approval for legislation for an initial demonstration project (Sustainable Communities Demonstration Project, HB 2705). The aim of the project was to demonstrate the feasibility of achieving the fundamental goals of the growth management system by a more incentive-based sustainable communities approach and, assuming success in the pilot program, to expand the concept statewide. The sustainable principles outlined in Section 15 of the 1996 legislation were to

- restore key ecosystems;
- achieve a cleaner, more healthful environment;
- limit urban sprawl;
- protect wildlife and natural areas; and
- create quality communities and jobs.

Given the negative attitudes of many key legislators (including most of the leadership in both houses), it is remarkable that the legislative language on sustainability was as strong as it was. The law set out important criteria for DCA to use in deciding whether a local government (all or part of its territory) should be designated a sustainable community. A key criterion was that DCA "assure that the local government has set an urban development boundary or functionally equivalent mechanisms, based on projected needs and adequate data and analysis." Three key objectives were included in the legislation:

> Encourage urban infill at appropriate densities and intensities, separate urban and rural uses, and discourage urban sprawl development patterns while preserving public open spaces and planning for buffer-type land uses and rural development consistent with respective character along and outside the urban boundary. (HB 2705 Section 15 (3)(a) 1)

In a June 1996 letter to local officials regarding the sustainable communities legislation, DCA Secretary Murley stressed the benefits for local governments:

> The Department will substantially reduce its oversight of local comprehensive plan amendments and developments of regional impact within the local government's jurisdiction. In addition, state agencies will give priority to programs and projects that assist designated local governments to create and maintain self-sustaining communities.

Twenty-eight cities and/or counties responded to DCA's call for proposals, and by January 1997 five sites had been chosen, including the City of Boca Raton and Martin County in the Eastward Ho! corridor; the cities of Ocala and Orlando in central and north central Florida; and the City of Tampa and surrounding Hillsborough County. While negotiating detailed contracts with the five "winners" to meet the criteria in the 1996 law, Murley made it clear that DCA would work with the "losers" to develop, to the extent possible, the same kind of agreements. Beyond that, DCA organized a Florida Sustainable Communities Network (composed of 30 cities and counties and still growing) that stretched from Fort Walton Beach in the Florida panhandle to Dade County. This organization was an important potential source of support in any effort to broaden the sustainable communities legislation in later legislative sessions (Sherrod 1997, 28–36).

DCA kicked off the first phase of moving Eastward Ho! from vision to reality by funding an issues and options report for the corridor, prepared by the South Florida Regional Planning Council (SFRPC) in conjunction with the Treasure Coast Regional Planning Council (TCRPC) and in partnership with local governments and interested citizens (SFRPC

1996). This report included a geographic, economic and demographic assessment of the corridor, and identified options for implementing Eastward Ho! The implementation phase developed during 1997 and 1998 with contracts executed with the South Florida and Treasure Coast RPCs, the State University System, the FAU/FIU Joint Center for Environmental and Urban Problems (an applied research center) and 1000 Friends. The activities and programs that emerged from these contracts included

- community outreach involving forums and workshops to broaden understanding and build support for the Eastward Ho! concept;

- development of recommendations and proposed legislation regarding the fragmentation of land ownership in the corridor;

- a land assembly component;

- establishment of ombudsman positions at the SFRPC to assist developers through the regulatory process and serve a "matchmaker" role regarding potential sites and projects;

- an assessment of financial impediments to find solutions to financial roadblocks, including extensive outreach to financial institutions and developers;

- creation of the mixed-use plan book discussed earlier;

- promotion of demonstration projects to show examples of sustainable urban design; and

- development of a wide range of incentives, including funds for retrofitting infrastructure in the corridor, the cleanup of brownfield sites, streamlining permitting processes, and revising land development regulations to make them supportive of Eastward Ho! goals.

As the Eastward Ho! Initiative attracted more interest, new partners appeared, ranging from neighborhood organizations to the National Audubon Society's Everglades Restoration program to the MacArthur and Ford Foundations (Florida DCA 1997b).

A significant example of the expanding interest in and support for Eastward Ho! was its Brownfields Partnership, which developed as part of the National

Brownfields Partnership, led by the Environmental Protection Agency and involving numerous other federal agencies. The National Partnership pledged support to 16 Brownfields Showcase Communities that could show collaborative action on brownfields cleanup and reuse, and a group of Floridians took the challenge. The first meeting of the Eastward Ho! Brownfields Partnership in February 1997 included more than 70 people from environmental, urban planning, housing, economic development and other community activist groups. The two-day meeting included reports on brownfield cleanup efforts in the corridor and across the nation, and concluded with a commitment to pursue aggressively the further development of the partnership (SFRPC 1997, 1).

After an unsuccessful effort by Dade and Palm Beach to be designated as individual counties, the three core counties in the corridor (including Broward) managed to present one application in March 1998—remarkable evidence of the ability of the Eastward Ho! Initiative to promote *regional* cooperation. The three counties also became one of the National Brownfields Showcase communities. The designation holds the potential for greater financial and other assistance from the 15 federal agencies that are part of the program. In turn, the three-county partnership committed to a series of actions in the next several years to further Eastward Ho! implementation, including undertaking at least four demonstration projects with federal agencies to show how the partnership can be used.

A December 1998 publication, prepared by the SFRPC and TCRPC, contained an update on progress in implementing the Eastward Ho! Initiative (SFRPC 1998, 1–9). The report projected a population for the now five-county southeast Florida region (adding St. Lucie and Martin counties) of 6.8 million in 2025, with a statewide projection at that time of 21 million. The report also described the status of implementation efforts as of 1998 and discussed the challenge of water management and overcoming barriers to redevelopment. The report underscored the concept of sustainability, using the definition drawn from the 1987 report of the UN Commission on Environment and Development, as well as the principles of sustainability in the 1996 legislature's

action, previously discussed. The report also included highlights from a study prepared for the five-county Eastward Ho! corridor, which showed potential savings of $6.1 billion in infrastructure costs, and other major benefits of implementing the Eastward Ho! concept versus the "trend" plan: continued sprawl (SFRPC 1998, 32).

Strengthening Economic Development and Job Opportunities

DCA Secretary Murley saw the sustainable communities addition to the integrated policy framework developed in the mid-1980s as the most important legacy he could leave for the state and his department. Working with leaders of the Florida chapter of the American Planning Association (APA) and 1000 Friends, city and county officials, and other stakeholders, Murley reached out to the economic community by stressing the department's Memorandum of Agreement (MOA) with Enterprise Florida, a quasigovernmental group charged with finding better ways to attract quality economic growth to the state. DCA invested $5 million in Energy Office funds in 1996 and recommended another $6 million in 1997, to further support Enterprise Florida's loan pools and other economic development programs.

Under Murley's leadership, DCA also worked with Enterprise Florida on the state's Work and Gain Economic Self-Sufficiency (WAGES) program, Florida's version of a welfare-to-work initiative, by making job creation for former welfare recipients one of DCA's top priorities for 1997 and 1998. Finally, the department executed an MOA with the Governor's Office of Trade, Tourism, and Economic Development (OTTED), agreeing, along with other state and regional agencies, "to streamline development approval processes for projects meeting the job creation targets established by the 1996 legislature." Under a 1997 legislative action, local governments had the option of joining this streamlining effort, potentially stimulating positive economic development actions in the Eastward Ho! corridor and in Florida in general (Florida DCA 1997a).

Florida's Sustainable Communities Demonstration Project received widespread and valuable coverage, setting the stage for a strong coalition from the public and private sectors to support the governor's and DCA's possible recommendation to the 1998 legislative session to make the sustainable communities approach available to all local governments. It was meant to become the critical vehicle for the full and fair implementation of the state's growth management system.

However, a generally hostile legislature needed to be persuaded that urban sprawl is a fiscal loser of major proportions, and that well-designed, more compact urban communities were the smart way to go. Despite elements of uncertainty, a sustainable communities blueprint for Florida's future that emphasized environmental protection *and* economic development was seen by supporters of a smart growth system as the approach that could succeed into the next century. The degree to which the Governor's Commission's vision for Eastward Ho! could be made a reality would have a major impact on whether the sustainable communities approach could overcome the resistance to government programs in general and adequate funding for them in particular (Mullins 1997, 5, 11; Murley 1997, 6, 7, 41).

As the campaign for governor approached, the politics of the 1998 legislative session prevented the hoped-for expansion legislation from going forward. However, the concept remained at the core of Secretary Murley's vision for Florida's future and was outlined in the final assessment of priorities issued by DCA just before Murley left office in early January 1999. DCA's 1998 report on accomplishments focused on creating a sustainable Florida by promoting sustainable communities in all the complex dimensions of that concept.

The 1998 Election: Changes in Florida Politics and Policies

The 1998 gubernatorial campaign pitted Republican Jeb Bush against Democratic Lieutenant Governor Buddy MacKay. This was Bush's second run, having narrowly lost to Lawton Chiles in 1994. During the campaign, Bush indicated some support for protecting the state's environment and adopting strong policies to breathe new life into urban areas undermined by sprawl. He made clear his support for a new version of Preservation 2000, the restoration of the Everglades and Eastward Ho!

Nearly two-thirds of registered voters went to the polls, which was the key to Bush's 55 to 45 percent victory. Observers agreed that Bush ran a stronger campaign than he had in 1994 by focusing on the environment, growth management and education. As veteran editorial writer Tom Blackburn (1998) put it, "The '98 model Bush ran differently than the 1994 model. Four years ago he had answers to all problems. The answers had the inky smell of conservative think tanks." Blackburn's main point was that many of Bush's fellow Republicans were still firmly committed to the ultraconservative line that Bush took in 1994. This was especially true in the House, so the apparently moderate candidate would have to confront an extreme legislature.

The MacKay campaign never really got organized to tap the traditional sources of Democratic support and was unsuccessful in mobilizing a strong turnout of Democratic voters. Tom Fiedler, *Miami Herald* political editor and a highly regarded observer of Florida politics over the past several decades, concluded that the only reason Bush was able to prevail in 1998 was that he "cloaked himself in Democratic clothes"; the voters favored Bush personally while preferring Democratic issues (Fiedler 1998).

Constitutional Amendments: Strong Support for Smart Growth

The Florida Constitution mandates a major new look at that document every 20 years by a Constitution Revision Commission, with members named by the governor, the Speaker of the House, the president of the Senate and ex officio members from the judicial branch. The previous commission's recommendations were on the November 1978 ballot, and all went down to defeat. In 1998 there were 13 amendments on the ballot covering a wide range of subjects, and 12 were winners.

The biggest surprise, and the one with the potential to produce major changes in Florida's governance system, especially its unique plural executive—the so-called cabinet system—was the passage of Amendment 8. The change took effect in 2002 and left only three elected cabinet officers: the attorney general, a chief financial officer taking over the jobs of treasurer and comptroller, and the commissioner of agriculture. The offices of secretary of state and education were eliminated. Instead, the governor would appoint a board of education, which would appoint an education commissioner. Opponents of the elected cabinet, some of whom had struggled for decades to reduce or eliminate what they considered a dysfunctional relic of post–Civil War politics, were very surprised and pleased to see its size cut in half and the office of governor significantly strengthened (Robles 1998; Elmore 1998).

Amendment 5, which had several components, was the one most strongly supported by environmental protection and growth management (smart growth) proponents. It created a Fish and Wildlife Commission as an independent agency composed of seven members appointed by the governor, thus replacing the existing Game and Fresh Water Fish Commission and the Marine Fisheries Commission and combining responsibility for fresh and saltwater resources in one agency. In a move important to the continuation of Preservation 2000 for another 10 years, Amendment 5 also continued indefinitely the constitutional authority to sell bonds to purchase lands for whatever version of Preservation 2000 might be adopted by the legislature. The amendment also contained language expanding protection of natural resources. It passed with a commanding 72 percent of the vote.

Taken together, the constitutional amendments undermined any notion that the 1998 elections in Florida were a victory for right-wing extremists. Doubtless, some were elected, but, on balance, the results support the assessment of Tom Fiedler and others that the voters were not interested in approving radical right-wing measures and, indeed, strongly supported actions opposed by such groups (Robles 1998; Elmore 1998).

The Bush Administration

During his campaign, Jeb Bush seemed clear in his support of growth management in Florida. In the early days of his administration, however, he asserted that it was not working as intended and that emphasis should be placed on correcting the system's failures rather than dismantling it altogether. To supporters of the system, his positions seemed to be a mixed message: stop the sprawl patterns, but at the same time weaken the ability of the state, regional agencies and local governments to plan and act in harmony with, not in isolation from, one another. With so much at stake, the new governor's appointments to critical positions were seen by many as important signals of how he intended to proceed in his first term.

Supporters of environmental protection and growth management were surprised and generally pleased by Governor Bush's key appointments. For secretary of DCA, Bush named Steve Seibert, a Republican member of the county commission in Pinellas County (the Tampa Bay area). They also welcomed the naming of David Struhs as secretary of the Department of Environmental Protection (DEP). Struhs, who left a similar position in Massachusetts to come to Florida, had been chief of staff for the Council on Environmental Quality under President George H. W. Bush, and served as an executive assistant at the U.S. Environmental Protection Agency. A final key appointment, as Everglades Policy Coordinator, was J. Allison DeFoor II, a seventh-generation Floridian, former sheriff of Monroe County and a member of Florida Audubon's board of directors. In announcing DeFoor's appointment, Bush noted that "the Everglades will become one of the most dominant issues over the next five years, and, if done right, will be a legacy for all of us" (Kleindienst 1999). How these appointees would interact with some of Bush's ultraconservative colleagues in the legislature and that component of his constituency in the state remained to be seen. Certainly, they gave hope to supporters of the effort to restore and sustain the Everglades ecosystem in particular, and to environmental and smart growth advocates in general.

The 1999 Legislative Session

The new version of Preservation 2000 was one of several major pieces of legislation passed by the 1999 legislature. Entitled Florida Forever, the act was made possible in 1998 by Amendment 5, which continued indefinitely the constitutional authority to sell bonds to purchase lands for any version of Preservation 2000 approved by the legislature. Florida Forever was introduced in the Senate by Jack Latvala as SB 908 and in the House as HB 641 and HB 653. Given that both houses of the legislature were controlled by Republicans, many of whom (especially in the House) were hostile to environmental and growth management issues of any kind, passage of Florida Forever was seen by many as a major victory.

As finally passed, Florida Forever provided, among other key provisions, a major increase in funds for the Florida Communities Trust (FCT). It provided $300 million a year for the first decade (2000–2010), and the allocation of dollars for the FCT was to be increased from 10 to 24 percent annually to provide grants to local governments for acquisition of community-based greenspace.

A Florida Forever Coalition included 14 environmental and growth management groups, including 1000 Friends, the Florida Audubon Society, Sierra Club, the Nature Conservancy, the Trust for Public Land, the Florida Rails-to-Trails Conservancy and the Florida APA chapter. The allocation of some $72 million per year (24 percent of $300 million) to the FCT to acquire significant natural areas in an urban setting will generate greater than $720 million over the decade, given the matching fund requirements of the program. When considering Florida Forever along with the continuation of the Conservation and Recreational Lands (CARL) program and Save Our Rivers, which will generate about another billion dollars over the decade, Florida continues to have the most liberally funded program to protect environmentally important lands in both rural and urban settings in the nation, including the federal level.[13]

The 1999 legislative session produced other legislation to move Florida in a smart growth direction. The Growth Policy Act was intended to "promote fiscally strong urban centers as a benefit to regional

and state economies and as a method to reduce future urban sprawl" (Florida DCA 1999, 4). This lengthy act was introduced in the 1998 legislative session as the Urban Infill and Redevelopment Act, but it failed to pass. The 1999 act addressed four major topics:

1. Creation of infill and redevelopment areas and plans

2. Improved transportation and land use coordination

3. School siting and concurrency

4. Municipal incorporation and annexation

1000 Friends (1999b) summarized this potentially significant legislation as follows:

> This [Growth Policy] Act promotes the vitality of downtowns as a means of curbing sprawl, benefiting the environment, and enhancing regional and state economies.
>
> Proposed changes to Chapter 163 provide for the adoption of urban infill and redevelopment areas into local comprehensive plans. These plans will address affordable housing, school coordination, transportation alternatives, job creation, crime reduction, neighborhood revitalization, and financial and regulatory incentives. After their adoption, additional financing options become available, including bonding, tax increment financing, and special assessments. Additionally, all state agencies providing infrastructure funding are required to give such areas priority in their programs. As a planning incentive, designated areas will receive special consideration for concurrency and plan amendments. Substantial deviation standards for developments of regional impact under Chapter 380.06 are increased by 50 percent.
>
> Changes are also proposed for Chapter 187 (State Comprehensive Plan) to strengthen urban redevelopment goals and policies. Other statutory changes include modifications for eminent domain, annexations, efficiency in government services, brownfield designations, and incorporation of municipalities.

Another bill focused on creating stronger incentives for economic development, especially in rural areas and certain urban areas. It added to the duties of OTTED by creating an Office of Urban Opportunity to promote Governor Bush's Front Porch Initiative (designed to promote planning and to implement certain urban development and redevelopment projects) and creating a task force to recruit the digital industry to Florida (Florida DCA 1999, 8).

---

13. Remarks prepared by John M. DeGrove for the conference "Smart Growth: From Rhetoric to Reality," held July 23–24, 1999, in Portland, Oregon, sponsored by 1000 Friends of Oregon. See also 1000 Friends of Florida (1999a, 4–5; 1999b, 2–5).

HB 107, an Administrative Procedures Act, introduced by Representative Ken Pruitt, aimed to reverse a case before the first district court of appeals, which ruled that the St. Johns River Water Management District "had the authority under Chapter 373 to establish reasonable regulations to protect the Tomoka River and its floodplains" (1000 Friends 1999a, 4). 1000 Friends was a party to the case and joined with the Florida Wildlife Federation and Florida Audubon to oppose the bill. Although Pruitt agreed to two amendments that lessened the bill's negative impacts, opponents maintained that the bill would jeopardize "400 state environmental rules and 1,000 other administrative rules" by requiring that agency rule-making under Chapter 120 (Administrative Procedures Act) require "specific" authorization to adopt rules and "require all administrative agencies to re-review the authority to adopt rules under this new standard" (1000 Friends 1999a, 5). The amendments passed, and the state agencies admitted they no longer had authority to enforce certain rules and policies. The bill will continue to pose a chilling effect on the adoption of new environmental rules, and over time existing rules will be subject to challenge under these amendments.

The 2000 Legislative Session

The 2000 session provided a sharp contrast to 1999 because a group of term-limited legislators concentrated in the Florida House of Representatives launched an all-out attack to dismantle or drastically weaken the growth management system. At the same time, 1000 Friends, the state APA chapter and other organizations were promoting a smart growth agenda to address the weaknesses of the growth management system. In a January 11, 2000, letter to DCA Secretary Steve Seibert, Charles Pattison, executive director of 1000 F , laid out the goals and objectives of a coalition of growth management and environmental organizations for the 2000 legislative session and beyond.

The coalition members stressed a smart growth agenda, illustrated by 10 principles for smarter growth in Florida adopted by 1000 Friends' Board of Directors on December 8, 1999, and six principles of unity

for smarter growth in Florida (1000 Friends 2000e, 4–7). For implementation, this agenda depended on the ability of a broad-based coalition to enlist the support of the governor and the legislature, who in turn needed evidence that key groups and the citizens around the state supported the agenda. Two surveys provided that evidence.

First, DCA mailed 10,000 copies of its growth management survey to a nonscientific sample of individuals whom the department considered to be actively involved in growth management. DCA received 3,671 responses, of which 70 percent were submitted on the Internet and the rest were mailed.

Smart Growth Agenda

1000 Friends of Florida's Ten Principles for Smarter Growth in Florida[a]

1. Better implement the laws that are already on the books.
2. Maintain reasonable state oversight of local planning.
3. Thoughtfully evaluate Florida's Growth Management Act to refine and improve it.
4. Improve the ability of citizens to help enforce their local comprehensive plans.
5. Think regionally.
6. Take a hard line on sprawl.
7. Encourage better movement of people and goods, not just cars.
8. Establish a statewide rural policy to better help rural communities protect their distinctive lifestyle.
9. Establish green connectors.
10. Improve the process to evaluate local comprehensive plans.

Six Principles of Unity for Smarter Growth in Florida[b]

1. Increase the ability of citizens to help shape the future of their communities.
2. Create stronger, healthier communities.
3. Reduce the amount of sprawl.
4. Protect rural areas, greenspaces and natural resources.
5. Recognize that transportation, land use and water management decisions are interrelated and regional in nature.
6. Maintain a state presence in managing growth in Florida.

a. As adopted by the board of directors, December 8, 1999
b. As adopted by concerned Florida organizations, January 11, 2000

Some 60 percent of the 3,671 respondents "believed that the general quality of life in Florida had changed for the worse," with the most serious growth management problems being traffic congestion (72 percent), urban sprawl (70 percent), loss of wildlife and habitat (66 percent) and limited water supplies (60 percent).

There was remarkably broad support for a wide range of changes that would move Florida in a smart growth direction if implemented. These changes would

- provide incentives for urban redevelopment (83 percent);

- place limits on urban sprawl (79 percent);

- provide incentives for community visioning and design (74 percent);

- develop requirements for intergovernmental coordination (72 percent);

- provide incentives to keep land in agricultural uses (69 percent), including financial;

- provide incentives to discourage conversion of such land (78 percent);

- strengthen links between transportation and land use (86 percent);

- establish urban growth boundaries (76 percent);

- develop a state comprehensive plan with clear priorities for growth (75 percent); and

- support the DRI process (53 percent).

The survey also showed "wide support for the continued roles of state, regional, and local governments in growth management" (Florida DCA 2000b, 7). Residents considered it very important for DCA to protect identified state interests (60 percent), develop a state vision (57 percent), and develop a state plan that guides growth (55 percent). On the subject of concurrency, there was strong support for continuing and expanding the requirement to schools, other modes of transportation and emergency management facilities (over 90 percent). Finally, more than 75 percent of survey respondents favored strengthening citizen participation, including more public involvement in local plan and land development regulations, and in the ability of citizens to petition state agencies to investigate local actions (Florida DCA 2000b, 1, 2, 7).

The second survey, conducted on April 21–25, 2000, by Cherry Communications Company in Tallahassee, randomly surveyed 439 adult Floridians who were year-round residents (the margin of error was 5 percent). This scientific survey, conducted for 1000 Friends (2000c), produced results similar to DCA's nonscientific survey. Participants were strongly or somewhat opposed to: (1) making it easier for developers to build new projects in Florida (65 percent); (2) making it harder for citizens to challenge new development (80 percent); and (3) weakening local government's authority to pass laws to protect the public from agricultural and timber operations already in operation (60 percent). They strongly or somewhat supported establishing a study commission to evaluate growth management and bring back changes next year, rather than making quick changes this year (76 percent).

This second survey also showed that most Floridians were not aware that the legislature was considering changes that would substantially weaken the growth management laws. "More than 70 percent of respondents indicated that they would be inclined to vote against legislators who played a role in relaxing growth management and environmental laws in Florida. Republicans, Democrats, and Independents were almost equal in their opposition to weakening growth management," according to a press release from 1000 Friends (2000c). As Pattison stated, "It is clear that the residents of Florida favor effective growth management in this state. Many legislators do not seem to be getting this message and are bent on rushing dramatic and damaging changes through this session" (1000 Friends 2000b).

Nevertheless, a significant number of bills designed to weaken the system were introduced in the legislature, and at one time seemed likely to pass. While there is no single explanation for this change, one important factor was that some 63 legislators in the House and Senate were term-limited, and many wanted to weaken or even repeal key parts of the growth management system. Ocala Representative George Albright led the fight for the single worst bill aimed at accomplishing this goal, introducing a "shell" bill with no details, early in the session. By mid-March Albright filled in the gaps on his proposal to dismantle the system.

Representative Bill Sublette and others came up with a "strike everything" amendment for Albright's bill. Albright then filed an amendment to that bill that included his proposal to turn growth management controls back to the local level, and another to repeal the entire growth management act. In an effort to make the bill look balanced, Albright then withdrew his amendments. However, as APA's Florida chapter saw it, "The bottom line on the bill is that it doesn't improve growth management (and represents a significant setback in many respects), it has been hurriedly drafted and, in large measure, it second guesses the proposed growth management study commission" (Elder 2000a, 1–5). 1000 Friends' "take" on the bill was much the same: while better than Albright's original proposals, the amended bill still would weaken the system in important ways. For example, 1000 Friends (2000a, 3) noted the bill

- opens the door for increased development and sprawl by relaxing requirements on small-scale amendments;

- significantly weakens the DRI process;

- gives DCA the ability to relax growth management compliance requirements;

- exempts electric utilities from local planning and land use requirements;

- authorizes public schools on agricultural lands;

- allows certain inappropriate developments on rural and agricultural lands; and

- calls for a study commission to make further changes in 2001 dominated by business/development/agricultural interests.

The politics of the House legislators were revealing. As Wade Hopping, a long-time prominent development lobbyist, told the *St. Petersburg Times,* "I think the legislators, as a group, suddenly see their ability to do things in areas that were once considered sacred cows" (Hauserman 2000). The same article noted that Senate leaders "have vowed to kill any attempt to revamp growth management this year." That prediction turned out to be prophetic, even though the article was written several weeks before the legislature adjourned on May 5, 2000.

Albright's growth management "overhaul" bill (HB 2335) was scheduled for a final vote in the House on May 1, 2000. When it became clear that the Senate would not accept this bill, but would support its "good" version proposed by Senator Tom Lee as SB 758, the House refused to act, and in the end no growth management bill passed. The Senate bill was acceptable to supporters of growth management, but most were happy with the no-bill option.

The key role of the Senate leadership in supporting a deliberate approach to any changes to the growth management system is illustrated by the fact that the Senate Comprehensive Planning Chair, Senator Lisa Carlton, supported the Lee bill, as did Senate Majority Leader Jack Latvala who cosponsored the legislation. Lee was elected to the Senate in 1996 from the Tampa Bay area and served on Carlton's Comprehensive Planning and Military Affairs Committee, which had lead responsibility in addressing growth management issues. In an article written for the Florida APA newsletter, Lee stated his and his Senate colleague's goal of "producing a framework for change that is sensible, fair, deliberate, and inclusive" (Lee 2000).

Continuing the litany of "bad" bills, HB 659 sought to amend the Bert J. Harris Jr., Private Property Rights Act, by defining "inordinate burden" so as to make it virtually impossible to regulate land uses, however justified. Inordinate burden was defined by the bill to include "action by a governmental entity that changes the density, intensity, or use of areas of development below the equivalent of one residence per five acres." The bill had some 22 cosponsors in the House, but died when it was not even considered there, in view of the virtual certainty that it could not pass the Senate.

HB 1807, the Submerged Sovereign Lands Bill, sponsored by Republican Senator Paula Dockery and others, was seen by many as a land-grab giveaway of state submerged sovereign lands. It passed in the House, 70–45, but died on the last day of the session when the Senate refused to consider either that bill or the Senate version, SB 1824. State Attorney General Bob Butterworth and others strongly opposed HB 1807, and it was puzzling that it was filed at all, given that the issue had been litigated almost 100 years earlier and again in 1986, presumably confirming that navigable lakes and rivers were held in trust for public use (Elder 2000b).

SB 2556, relating to administrative procedures, as proposed by DCA and the Bush administration, would have restricted citizen standing in environmental permit appeals. It died in the Senate, although the House companion bill, HB 2023, passed 106–11. The original language in the bill was narrowed when growth management and environmental groups entered strong objections and Governor Bush called on the House to change its language (Elder 2000b).

HB 1599/SB 1976, the Rodman Dam bill, also passed the House but failed in the Senate. This was an attempt to prevent the dam from being removed by declaring it a state recreational area. Governor Bush has since stated his support for removing the dam.

Some "good" bills were supported by growth management and environmental advocates and did pass. They included HB 221, the Everglades Funding Bill, which ensured that Florida would pay its half of the $7.8 billion restoration costs; HB 941/SB 2310, the Lake Okeechobee restoration bill; and the Neighborhood Revitalization Bill, CS/SB 2578, which included improvements to allow more flexibility in administering State Housing Initiatives Partnership (SHIP) and the Predevelopment Loan Program. Funding for the Sadowski Affordable Housing Act continued to be one of Florida's few funding success stories, with the legislature appropriating $176 million in 2000 (Ross and Hendrickson 2000).

The Governor's Growth Management Study Commission and the 2001 Legislative Session

When it became clear that a legislative commission to examine Florida's growth management system and recommend changes for the 2001 session would not come to pass, Governor Bush established his own Growth Management Study Commission on July 3, 2000. An intense schedule ensued to meet the commission's broadly defined mission and the February

15, 2001, deadline for submitting its findings to the governor and the legislature. The first meeting was held on August 9, 2000, and meetings were scheduled every three weeks. Among the commission's 23 members, only one, a board member of 1000 Friends, was drawn from the coalition formed in 1999 to advocate for "reasonable" growth management reform. Most commission members either had no record of involvement with the issue or were known to be hostile to the existing growth management system.

The chair was Mel Martinez, chair of the Orange County Commission. Four members were drawn from the legislature with the advice (not the consent) of the president of the Senate and the Speaker of the House. DCA Secretary Steve Seibert and Commissioner of Agriculture Bob Crawford were voting members, and the heads of DOT, DEP and the Fish and Wildlife Conservation Commission served as nonvoting members. In a press release issued along with the signing of his Executive Order, Bush stated that "Floridians deserve to be part of a growth management system that not only preserves their quality of life but is less complex, less regulatory, and more community based." His double message stated the need for a system to better manage continued population growth and its significant impacts to the state's natural resources and public infrastructure, but that it should be less regulatory and more decentralized (1000 Friends 2000d, 5, 13; Florida DCA 2000a).

After considering the establishment of seven Technical Advisory Committees that would include both commission members and "volunteers" from interested community groups, the commission decided not to have these advisory committees at all, and instead set up five committees composed *only* of members of the commission: Urban Revitalization; Rural Policy; Citizen Involvement; Infrastructure; and State, Regional, and Local Roles.

The December 14, 2000, meeting of the Study Commission received reports from the five subcommittees, with the commission acting on a stepped-up schedule when Martinez was appointed U.S. Secretary of Housing and Urban Development by President George W. Bush. The commission issued its *Draft Report and Recommendations* on January 4, 2001, with a "final" draft version to be voted on at the January 31–February 1 meeting in Orlando. The commission's third *Draft Report and Recommendations*, dated January 25, 2001, included a signal that more changes would be made before the "final" report to the governor and legislature. By mid-January, groups opposed to hasty change by the 2001 legislature (e.g., 1000 Friends, the Florida APA chapter) summarized their views.

Bush Narrows the Agenda

Just before the 2001 legislative session got under way on March 6, Governor Bush seemed intent to act on most, if not all, of his commission's recommendations, but that expectation was dashed. Either directly or through DCA Secretary Seibert, Bush made it clear that he would not propose highly controversial changes such as repealing the state plan, ending the DRI process and limiting DCA's capacity to review local plans. The "politics of passage" in the 2001 session obviously got the governor's attention. In a press release dated March 9, 2001, Bush outlined his three major growth management priorities, as prepared by Seibert in a draft bill for the 2001 session.

1. Schools

- Develop better joint planning between school boards and local governments

- "Prohibit approval of increased residential densities where there is inadequate school capacity"

- "Provide greater flexibility for school construction and school siting"

2. True (Full) Cost Accounting

- Develop a model for uniform fiscal impact analysis to provide better information and more accountability for the true costs of new development

- Create a nine-member commission to ensure the model developed is practical and useful

- Test the model in six areas

3. State's Role

- Define issues of compelling state interest

- Refocus the state's oversight role to a limited number of compelling state interests

- Expand the technical assistance provided by the DCA

- Leave control of local issues at the local level

In his speech to the legislature on opening day of the session, Bush noted Florida's strong economic growth and seemed to call for strong moves in a smart growth direction. Even with his sharply scaled-back agenda, however, the Bush proposals did not have smooth sailing. In hearings before the Senate Comprehensive Planning, Local and Military Affairs Committee, one senator warned that special interests

---

Views on 2001 Legislation by Smart Growth Advocates

What We Like

1. Citizen participation is somewhat better, with more opportunities for access and challenges, but we don't have all the details.

2. We like most the urban infill ideas for revitalizing and redeveloping already settled areas.

3. We like the linkage between additional natural resource protection, heightened development scrutiny, and optional density credits, if it remains linked.

4. We applaud the concept of full cost or true cost accounting.

5. We like the idea of a compelling state interest focus when and if they are sufficiently defined.

What We Have Concerns About

1. The commitment to the package as a whole, especially incentives for better growth and more natural resource protection.

2. Eliminating the state comprehensive plan in favor of a single vision sentence.

3. Not committing to mapping natural resource areas.

4. Explaining in adequate detail how many ideas will work; is full cost accounting really adequate to replace concurrency, including the school overcrowding issue?

5. Limited time to complete the work.

6. Adequacy of funding issues, including RPC's ability to accept new duties and tasks.

7. Clear and definitive recommendations on citizen ability to challenge development orders.

8. Compelling state issues should expand at a minimum to include affordable housing, education and citizen participation.

Source: Pattison, 2001

would try to tag their pet projects onto whatever smart growth legislation was proposed. Senator Tom Lee stated flatly, "If you don't provide funding options, it sets up false expectations.... It really all does come down to money, ultimately." Lee noted further that "every special interest advocating some position will endeavor to find a sponsor" (Hull 2001).

The whole issue of funding was seen by almost every stakeholder as a key matter for the 2001 session. The challenge was illustrated by the Florida Home Builders Association's (HBA) effort to persuade 1000 Friends and other growth management supporters to join the 14,000 member HBA in its initiative, *Fund Florida's Future: Schools for Our Children.* The HBA saw an increase in the documentary stamp (real estate transfer) tax as a likely source of new funds, to be bonded to produce $200–$300 million per year to be collected by the state and returned to the area generating the funds, with a minimum for rural counties with little real estate activity. 1000 Friends worked with the HBA to hammer out details it could support, on the grounds that no new initiative to strengthen the growth management system would succeed without new funding sources (Gentry and Buck, Undated). The Florida School Boards Association estimated the cost of needed school facilities at $13 billion, and worked with the HBA to push for more education facility funds. Further, a broad-based group of organizations, including the Florida League of Cities, the HBA, the SBA, the state APA chapter and 1000 Friends, met regularly, although DCA no longer coordinated the group meetings as it did previously (FAPA 2001, 2–3).

The outlook was not bright for finding new funding to implement the core concepts of Florida's growth management system. However, an important positive factor emerged during the third week of the 60-day session in the form of Senate President John McKay's announcement that, given budget realities, he could not justify any tax cuts for the fiscal year ahead. Beyond that, in what was called "intense media questioning," McKay made it clear that even without tax cuts, it would be very hard to meet critical budget demands for human services and education. Such a stand, which was apparently supported by many of McKay's colleagues, put the Senate in a diametrically opposite position from the House of Representatives and Governor Bush's proposed tax cut package. The House had already passed a $222 million cut in the intangibles tax and was moving to approve a "sales tax holiday" that would mean some $42 million in lost revenues. To add to the budget bad news, the Revenue Estimating Conference announced that some $228 million in tax receipts for the fiscal year starting July 2001 would not be realized (Center for Florida's Children 2001).

Results of the 2001 Legislative Session

When the final bell sounded just before midnight on May 4, most advocates of an effective smart growth system could agree with the summary of 1000 Friends (2001): "The 2001 legislative session is over, and growth management as we know it remains basically the same. Considering the changes that could have been made, this outcome is not so bad." This conclusion was in sharp contrast to what might have been expected early in the session, when Bush narrowed his growth management agenda to feature a full cost accounting proposal and to link planning for schools with local comprehensive plans.

These proposals were included in the Senate's growth management bill (SB 310); however, the House companion bill (HB 1617) was loaded down with numerous bad amendments that would have seriously undermined the growth management system (very similar to what happened in the 2000 session). SB 310 passed the Senate, but the House never took it up, objecting to the inclusion of a modest amount of fiscal home rule that would have allowed school boards to adopt a half-penny sales tax by a super-majority vote with no public referendum attached. The Senate was not willing to pass a bill without some form of funding for the schools proposal, and the House was adamant in its opposition. Negotiations between the governor, House and Senate were not successful (Elder 2001, 3–4).

While the growth management bill itself never gained approval, a number of other legislative actions were approved, some negative and some positive in their impacts on the system. On the negative side, the DRI component of Chapter 380 was weakened by attaching DRI provisions to other bills. SB 460/HB

1225, an economic development bill, increased by 150 percent the threshold for DRI review in all counties designated as rural areas of critical economic concern. In 1999 Bush had designated eight Panhandle counties in this category, and in January 2001 he added six southwest counties.

The big push for the threshold change in the 2001 session came from the St. Joe Corporation, which owns about one million acres of land in the Panhandle area. In a designated rural county, the DRI threshold would go from 250 houses to 750 houses with no DRI review. Supporters of growth management viewed this action with dismay, and many state newspapers called it a "special interest giveaway." One assessment stated, "The loophole will allow St. Joe and other developers to save millions when they develop parts of the Florida Panhandle, including some valuable stretches of coast" (Hauserman 2001). The DRI process was further weakened with the passage of the Senate Transportation bill (SB 2056), which exempts airports and petroleum storage facilities from such review. An attempt to include marinas in the exemption was not successful.

A Livable Communities Certification Program (SB 432) would have expanded the sustainable communities demonstration project to any qualifying local government. Growth management advocates could support that concept, but not without measurable standards regarding exactly what local governments would have to do with regard to putting sustainable planning principles, including an urban growth boundary, in place. The bill did not pass but will no doubt be back with, one would hope, clear standards that justify removing oversight of local plan amendment and DRI review. Another bill with negative impacts was SB 910, which would have limited the ability of citizens to challenge state agency decisions on the environment and imposed new threats of sizeable attorney's fees.

To many supporters of sustaining a close link between smart growth and environmental protection, the raid on Preservation 2000 and its successor Florida Forever funds (in the amount of $75 million due to the Senate's efforts to limit tax cuts) led the list of bad outcomes for 2001. Because about $100 million in Preservation 2000 funds were still in the process of being committed to specific projects, they were seen as "surplus." The danger for Florida Forever is that such raids could well continue in the future and in the process would drastically weaken the nation's best-funded environmentally important land acquisition program.

However, the 2001 legislative session was not a total loss for smart growth. 1000 Friends played a key role in two pieces of legislation favorable to affordable housing. SB 1132 made clear "local government's ability to adopt inclusionary housing ordinances, a land use tool that can require new development to include a set percent of affordable housing." SB 446 strengthened the state's ability to provide housing for the homeless. 1000 Friends also sustained its support for the Sadowski Act's annual funding for affordable housing, with dedicated revenue for the next fiscal year totaling more than $185 million.

The Rural and Family Lands Protection Act, part of SB 1922, the main agricultural bill, received little notice compared to the attention given to other major battles during the session. Noting that each year 130,000 acres of farmland in Florida are converted to other uses, 1000 Friends (2001) explained that "this act enables the state to purchase conservation easements in perpetuity and enter into 30-year agreements with farmers to ensure that land remains in agricultural use." The easements would stay in place if the land were sold. Supporters, including an unusual joining of agriculturalists and environmentalists, sought $100 million in new tax dollars each year for 10 years to implement the program, but those dollars were not appropriated. Included in the bill was a Rural Land Stewardship Area pilot program in which up to five rural communities could "designate large rural areas by plan amendment for future community development." Through transfer of density credits conditioned on "specified sustainable development practices," it also provided for "agricultural and conservation easements to permanently protect open space" (Hauserman 2001).

Finally, the 2001 legislature approved significant funds for agencies critical to the growth management program. RPCs received $2,236,250, of which $250,000 was for the Northeast RPC to develop an Internet-based data center. An additional $400,000 was established as a new general budget line for RPCs. Further, the community planning budget at DCA received $525,000 for technical and planning assistance to local communities (Elder 2001). While Bush did not get his top priorities approved by the legislature, he directed DCA to expand its rules to allow the state to deny local comprehensive plan amendments that would contribute to school overcrowding. This action confirmed the belief that much of what Bush wanted to do could be accomplished without new legislation.

The basic framework of the growth management system remained in place in the 2001 legislature, although it was somewhat weakened by changes in the DRI area. Above all, it was not possible to put forward and pass a positive agenda to correct weaknesses in the system that even its strongest supporters agreed were there. After the session ended, McKay announced his intention to push for a major reform of Florida's tax structure as the only way to cope with continuing growth. The basic change he proposed was another extension of the sales tax to cover services. Over the 17-year history of the comprehensive growth management system, his was far from the first to attempt to establish an adequate source of funding for its implementation. However, it remains clear that a sustainable future for the state depends on such funding.

To make matters worse, the slowing of the economy that began in early 2001 saw tax collections fall short of projections, and after the September 11th attacks, which hit Florida's tourist industry very hard, state economists projected a $1.3 billion shortfall. Democrats and Republicans were sharply divided as to how to make up the deficit, and Republicans disagreed among themselves on how and what to cut. Democrats favored postponing or deleting tax cuts, a move that the Republican-controlled House strongly opposed. Senate Republican leaders supported at least the postponement of a scheduled reduction in the intangible tax.

Governor Bush called a special session of the legislature on October 22 to make the necessary cuts. In the end, however, Senate President John McKay and House Speaker Tom Feeney were not able to agree on how to cut $800 million, and the session ended on a bitter note. Bush then called a second special session

on November 27. When that session adjourned on December 6, Senate and House leaders agreed on nearly $1 billion in cuts (primarily in the areas of education and social services) plus postponement of the intangibles tax cut (Fineout 2001, B1 and 10; Date, Ash and Klas 2001, 1-A, 18-A).

Over three years, Republicans had cut taxes by some $1.6 billion, with Senate Democratic leader Tom Rossin calling for rolling back many of those tax cuts rather than making deep cuts in programs such as education, healthcare and other areas critical to Florida's quality of life. A central lesson to be taken from this dismal fiscal picture takes us back to the Zwick Committee's assessment of Florida's tax structure as being inadequate to support the demands of a rapidly growing state. It was inadequate before the economic decline of 2001 and was aggravated further following the events of September 11.

The 2002 Legislative Session and Election Results

The 2002 legislative session ended in a mix of legislative and budget actions that had both positive and negative impacts on the state's growth management system. SB 1906 "streamlines development orders and provides for an optional special master process to resolve disputes; waives certain concurrency requirements for urban infill and redevelopment areas; and creates a Local Government Planning Certification Program to succeed the Sustainable Communications Demonstration Program." The bill was created and supported by a coalition of the state's HBA, League of Cities, Association of Counties, APA chapter and 1000 Friends (1000 Friends 2002, 10).

HB 813 provided for issuing bonds at the rate of $100 million a year for eight years to pay the costs of Everglades restoration. While smart growth supporters led by the Growth Management Coalition supported the use of bonds to pay the state's share of restoration costs, they objected strongly to a Governor's Office proposal early in the session to take State Housing Trust Fund dollars to pay part of the cost of retiring the bonds. The Sadowski Act Coalition succeeded in blocking that proposal, but that success was tainted by an amendment added to HB 813 providing that only "affected citizens" as well as "environmental groups registered in Florida with more than 25 members in the county in question may challenge proposed developments under the act." Some environmental groups opposed HB 813, but 1000 Friends believed that funding for Everglades restoration was absolutely essential and continued to support the bill, pledging to find a way to neutralize the negative impacts of the citizen standing provision. HB 257 and SB 280, "which would have overly complicated litigation and imposed attorneys' fees on citizens engaged in administrative proceedings" with regard to citizen standing, were eventually withdrawn late in the session (1000 Friends 2002, 1, 9).

In the area of transportation, HB 261 had a number of negative impacts, both immediate and potential. It stated that the financial feasibility of turnpike projects does not have to be taken into consideration, and funds can be taken from other toll roads that are profitable to pay for new projects. Moreover, turnpike projects can be advertised before environmental permits are issued, and the Turnpike Authority is authorized to build such things as hotels and meeting facilities. The bill also exempted all airports from the state's DRI process. Supporters of smart growth saw this provision as having the potential to promote sprawl in rural parts of the state. The bill also authorized the Orlando-Orange County Expressway Authority to build roads without oversight from the Division of Bond Finance. Such projects no longer have to pass through the city and/or county approval process, thereby creating the potential for jeopardizing environmentally important areas such as the Wekiva River and parts of the Green Swamp (1000 Friends 2002, 9–10).

HB 715 allowed the DOT to delegate permit authority, authorized local governments to increase the height limits for signs, and called for owners required to take down billboards to be reimbursed by local governments. The bill also allowed improvements to the Florida interstate highway system to be counted for concurrency purposes if placed within the five-year work plan (1000 Friends 2002, 10). As HB 715 is implemented, the potential for undermining the state's quality of life is clear.

In other areas, efforts to raid the Sadowski Housing

Act Trust Fund to help pay for Everglades restoration were defeated, and the House and Senate ultimately funded full implementation of the Sadowski Housing Act by providing almost $250 million to continue funding the nation's leading affordable housing program. A timely veto by Governor Bush blocked the $100 million proposed to be taken from the Florida Forever debt reserve, but supporters of smart growth feared that such raids would continue in future legislatures unless the state's tax structure were subjected to a fundamental reform (1000 Friends 2002, 3, 10).

Democrat Bill McBride ran a surprisingly strong campaign for governor, but Bush won by a wide margin, as did the Republican candidates for attorney general and agricultural commissioner. Republicans also scored significant gains in the Florida House (81 Republicans and 39 Democrats) and Senate (26 Republicans and 14 Democrats), and in the state's congressional delegation (18 Republicans and 7 Democrats). Ironically, all but one of the constitutional amendments on the ballot, most of which were strongly opposed by Bush and his Republican colleagues, were approved by voters (Bridges 2002).

The 2003 Legislative Session

House Speaker Johnnie Byrd led a hardcore majority absolutely opposed to any new taxes and seemed ready to further dismantle efforts to manage Florida's growth. Senate President Jim King and other key leaders in the Senate pushed hard to reach some kind of compromise with the House and the governor to find new dollars to meet a substantial budget shortfall. Nevertheless, the regular 60-day session ended without action on any of the key bills before it, including the budget.

Governor Bush immediately called a 16-day special legislative session beginning May 12, and the budget deadlock was finally resolved with the passage of a $53.5 billion budget. Some $225,668,171 was swept from DEP trust funds, and another $200 million from transportation trust funds. Thanks largely to strong support in the Senate, these actions did not reduce Florida Forever appropriations (Killinger 2003, 2–3). One thing can be said with certainty about the budget adopted in 2003: by using nonrecurring funds and reserves of all sorts to make up the budget deficit without addressing the shortfalls produced by the state's inadequate tax structure, the budget shortfalls can hardly do anything but get worse.

Three bills passed by the legislature and signed by Governor Bush in 2003 have the potential to seriously undermine local controls over actions in the area of growth management.

■ SB 1660, ostensibly intended to loosen local government restrictions on farmers, was seen by opponents as decreasing protections for water bodies and other natural areas and enhancing the potential for the siting of intensive agricultural activities adjacent to urbanized areas.

■ SB 676 exempts state transportation projects from local regulations and, according to public officials, will have an adverse effect on restrictions relating to such things as wetland mitigation, billboards and beautification.

■ HB 601 allows the Cape Canaveral Hospital Authority to supersede the local government comprehensive plan and land development regulations of the City of Cocoa Beach relating to height, density and the filling of submerged lands. The bill creates a dangerous precedent of allowing an independent special district to exempt itself from specific provisions of a local plan and regulations. In the case of height restrictions, the City of Cocoa Beach charter was amended by a referendum of the voters to establish maximum height limitations. Hence this bill also undermines the will of the voters in Cocoa Beach by superseding a charter provision that came directly from the electorate. (1000 Friends 2003)

In another example of continuing struggles over state versus local control in these matters, DOT is involved in a battle with Jacksonville's metro government over Jacksonville's right to enforce its tree law on state road projects (Salinero 2003).

Conclusion

Florida's effort to manage growth and change in a comprehensive, effective and equitable fashion developed because of pressures that began in the 1950s and have continued into the twenty-first century. The growth pressures of the 1950s and 1960s, together with the rising strength of the environmental movement nationally and in Florida, led to actions over the 1970–1975 period that were truly amazing. The destruction of wetlands, damage to beach and dune systems, saltwater intrusion into critical freshwater aquifers and other concerns led to the legislative components of Phase One of Florida's growth management system. The adoption of five major laws in 1972 and 1975 and related actions represented a giant leap forward for Florida. The state moved from being a laggard to a leader nationally in growth management.

As the 1970s drew to a close, the shortcomings of the system, led by the state's failure to fund its fair share of mandates, especially on local governments, brought about a reassessment that led to Phase Two

(1982–1996). By the mid-1980s it was possible to see at least two common threads critical to a comprehensive growth management system: a governor strongly supportive of such action and a legislature willing to follow the lead of the governor. A third emerging thread was the importance of bringing together broad-based coalitions including the public, private and nonprofit sectors, to support the adoption and implementation of such systems. A mixed picture of accomplishments and disappointments in implementing Florida's growth management system summarizes the 1986 to 1996 decade, with the political environment growing less favorable over the last half of the period.

The early years of Phase Three (1996–2003) focused largely on restoring and protecting the greater Everglades ecosystem and on implementing the sustainable communities legislation passed by the 1996 legislature, which seemed capable of moving the whole state in a smart growth direction. The good news was that the Everglades program had strong statewide support, and its $7.8 billion funding was approved by the U.S. Congress. The bad news was that the planned expansion of the sustainable communities legislation to the rest of the state stalled and looked unlikely in the near future.

The election of Governor Jeb Bush in November 1998 started what has been considered by some the demise of Florida's move to a smart growth system. While at times Governor Bush seemed to support a more deliberate effort to simplify the system, and thus make it more effective, at other times he and his administration have seemed ready to turn almost all decisions on growth back to local governments, with no state or regional oversight and coordination. The governor's Growth Management Study Commission seemed promising, but both friend and foe agreed that there was not enough substance to predict the results of implementing its recommendations.

So, where does Florida stand in late 2004, in the decades-long effort to manage land and water resources in ways that will assure a sustainable future for the state? To move smart growth initiatives from concept to reality almost always calls for significant executive policy decisions and legislative changes, and always calls for substantial funding to underwrite their implementation. Given the current political environment in Florida, it would be easy to conclude that there is no chance we can strengthen our system for managing growth and change in the foreseeable future. Some would even conclude, either in despair or with joy, that the threat of raids on such landmark programs as Florida Forever and the Affordable Housing Trust Fund for implementing the Sadowski Housing Act will become a reality.

With the growth management system in danger of being drastically weakened or dismantled, there is clear evidence that a substantial majority of Florida's citizens instead favor strengthening it. However, even the boldest prophet would hesitate to predict the future. It seems clear that Florida's system, which in the past was held in high regard by supporters of smart growth around the nation, is at the very best destined to tread water until a new governor and legislature more supportive of the system are in place.

Indeed, only one solution that will produce the substantial funds required to salvage the system has any chance of success in our present political environment: the reextension of the sales tax to services—the Zwick Committee's solution. Is there hope that this can happen? The state is fortunate to have some Republican leaders in the Senate who seem determined to do something about it, including former Senate President John McKay. In addition, Bush has recently named as lieutenant governor former Senate President Toni Jennings, who helped block some of the worst efforts to totally dismantle Florida's growth management system. She recognized the need to face up to the inadequacy of the tax system and find ways to correct it.

1000 Friends, in an open letter to DCA Secretary Thaddeus Cohen in June 2004, stated that "growth management in Florida is at a crossroad" and set forth an ambitious agenda for strengthening Florida's smart growth system by advocating these actions:

- Provide adequate state funding and resources for growth management, and directing their investment to limit sprawl and promote better communities

- Encourage vision-based planning, starting at the neighborhood level

- Empower citizens to participate more meaningfully in community planning

- Upgrade local comprehensive plans to exceed minimum state standards

The organization also confirmed its opposition to the Hometown Democracy Amendment, a constitutional ballot initiative that sought to amend the Florida Constitution so that every future land use amendment to a local government comprehensive plan would require a plebiscite vote of the community's residents (1000 Friends 2004a). The initiative later failed to get enough signatures to go on the ballot in November 2004.

At the same time, 1000 Friends released a position paper outlining its agenda for proposing and implementing far-reaching changes to Florida's growth management system.

- Encourage communities to address the physical design of development and redevelopment with attention to its impact on lifestyle, health and livability

- Identify sensitive natural lands that must be acquired or otherwise protected, and identify funding

- Create regional plans that, among other things, define the ultimate geographic limits of urban development

- Develop a meaningful state plan (1000 Friends 2004c, 5)

One section of the position paper is devoted to revenue and investment policies of the state. While all six recommendations put forward by 1000 Friends in this section are critical to a smart growth future for Florida, two go to the heart of what must be done: (1) provide a sustainable state tax system with an expanded tax base to continue to meet growing infrastructure funding needs over time, and (2) provide local government with tools to raise additional funds locally in order to implement their comprehensive plans (1000 Friends 2004c).

A smart growth future for the state can not and will not come about unless a way is found to mobilize broad-based support to move such actions from vision to reality. 1000 Friends' strategy in this regard, states that

> 1000 Friends intends to partner with other players in the growth management process (citizens, developers, environmentalists, business leaders, affordable housing advocates, and others) to refine these recommendations into a workable program of reform. Initial legislation will be introduced in the 2005 session, with additional legislation to be introduced in 2006 and beyond. (1000 Friends 2004c, 5)

Certainly, there seems to be little hope of implementing the smart growth agenda discussed above unless a strong coalition is pulled together that can move the governor and legislature (both houses) to support such actions.

One positive action in the 2004 legislative session was the passage of the Wekiva Parkway and Protection Act that implemented the recommendations of the final report of the Governor's Wekiva Basin Coordinating Committee. The act provides for building the Wekiva Parkway, allowing for the completion of a beltway around Orlando and the construction of a related connector road. Four buffer areas are to be publicly acquired, and local governments must update their comprehensive plans so that they address the road's impacts. DCA and the St. Johns River Water Management District will work in coordination to assure a balance in the revised plans between increased growth and availability of water. 1000 Friends believes the act "can serve as a model process for resolving tough growth issues in other areas of Florida" (1000 Friends 2004b).

In times of crisis, remarkable things can and do happen. If Florida continues on its current path, the state is surely headed for a crisis unmatched in the state's history. That in itself could produce the actions needed to resolve the state's funding shortfall and allow the implementation of smart growth strategies for Florida.

References

1000 Friends of Florida. 1997. *Foresight* 10: 5.

———. 1999a. Legislative update: 1000 Friends prepares for the 1999 session and Florida Forever Coalition. *Foresight* 12.1. Spring.

———. 1999b. Legislative update: 1999 legislative wrap-up. *Foresight* 12.2. Summer.

———. 2000a. Attack on growth management in Florida continues! April 7.

———. 2000b. Floridians' attitudes toward proposed changes to Florida's growth management laws. April 26.

———. 2000c. Floridians oppose weakening growth management. Press release. April 26.

———. 2000d. Governor Bush appoints study commission. *Foresight* 13.3. Fall.

———. 2000e. Six principles of unity for smarter growth in Florida and 10 principles for smarter growth in Florida. *Foresight* 13.1. Spring.

———. 2001. Summary of the 2001 legislative session. Updated May 21.

———. 2002. *Foresight*. 15.1. Spring.

———. 2003. *2003 Legislative Session*. July 16.

———. 2004a. An open letter to DCA Secretary Thaddeus Cohen. June 10.

———. 2004b. *Foresight* 17.1. Spring/Summer:1, 7.

———. 2004c. Growth management for Florida's future: 1000 Friends of Florida position paper. June.

Affordable Housing Study Commission. 1987. Final report of the affordable housing study commission: An agenda for Florida housing policy. Tallahassee, FL. December.

Blackburn, Tom. 1998. Bush and GOP: Same party but not yet on same page. *Palm Beach Post.* November 8:1E, 5E.

Bridges, Tyler. 2002. GOP's strategy flips Florida politics. *Miami Herald.* December 1.

Brown, Donald A. 1994–1995. The relevance of "Agenda 21" to the states. *Environmental Law, Newsletter of the Standing Committee on Environmental Law* 14.1. Fall/Winter.

Center for Florida's Children. 2001. 2001 Legislative update #2. March 16.

Central and Southern Florida Flood Control District. 1971. Statement to Governor Reubin O'D. Askew from the Governor's Conference on Water Management in South Florida. *Water Management Bulletin* 5.3. December–January.

Colburn, David R. and Lance deHaven-Smith. 1999. *Government in the Sunshine State.* Gainesville, FL: University Press of Florida.

Commission on the Future of Florida's Environment. 1990. *Facing Florida's environmental future.* Tallahassee, FL.

Crane, Donald R. Jr. 1998. When is the right time to address a $5.21 issue? *FBT Focus.* Floridians for Better Transportation. Year end report.

Date, S. V., Jim Ash and Mary Ellen Klas. 2001. Legislators approve $1 billion in cuts, prepare for tax fight. *Palm Beach Post.* December 7:1A, 18A.

DeGrove, John M. 1958. *Approaches to resource development in Central and Southern Florida, 1845–1947.* Gainesville, FL: University of Florida, Public Administration Clearing Services, Studies in Public Administration, no. 17.

———. 1984. *Land, growth and politics.* Washington, DC: APA/ Planners Press.

———. 1989. Consistent, concurrent, compact: Florida's search for a rational growth management system. *Political Chronicle* 1:(2):35–36.

———. 1992. *The new frontier for land policy: Planning and growth management in the states.* Cambridge, MA: Lincoln Institute of Land Policy.

———. 1995. Sustaining South Florida. *National Wetlands Newsletter* 17.5(September/October):1, 15. Washington, DC: Environmental Law Institute.

DeGrove, John M. and Nancy E. Stroud. 1987. State land planning and regulation: Innovative roles in the 1980s and beyond. *Land Use Law and Zoning Digest* 39.3(March):3–8.

———. 1988. New development and future trends in local government comprehensive planning. *Stetson Law Review* 17(3):573–605.

DeGrove, John M. and Dennis E. Gale. 1994. Linking infrastructure to development project approvals: Florida's concurrency policy under statewide growth management. Paper presented at the 36th Annual Conference of the Association of Collegiate Schools of Planning, Phoenix, AZ. November 3–6.

DeGrove, John M. and Robyne Turner. 1998. Local government: Coping with massive and sustained growth. In *Government and politics in Florida, second edition*, Robert J. Huckshorn, ed. Gainesville, FL: University Press of Florida.

deHaven-Smith, Lance. 1998. Unfinished agenda in growth management and environmental protection. In *Government and politics in Florida, second edition*, Robert J. Huckshorn, ed. Gainesville, FL: University Press of Florida.

Drake, Debbie and Terry Sullivan. 1997. *Preservation 2000: Memo to Preservation 2000 allies.* Tallahassee, FL: The Nature Conservancy. May 20.

Elder, Marcia. 1988. Capitol update. *Florida Planning.* 8.8(April):3–4. Florida Chapter, American Planning Association (FAPA).

———. 1993a. Capital update: The state plan. *Florida Planning* V.7. September. FAPA.

———. 1993b. The challenge continues as ELMS implementation gets under way. *Florida Planning* V.6, (July/August):1, 8. FAPA.

———. 2000a. Action alert/growth management legislation. Memorandum to FAPA members. April 28.

———. 2000b. Legislative update. Memorandum to FAPA members. May 9.

———. 2000c. Technical advisory committees. Memorandum to FAPA members. August 2.

———. 2001. Legislative session results. Memorandum to FAPA members. May 8.

Elmore, Charles. 1998. Revision vote trims Cabinet by 3 seats. *Palm Beach Post.* November 4:1, 8.

ELMS I. 1973. Environmental land management: Final report to the governor and legislature. December. Tallahassee, FL: ELMS I Committee.

ELMS II. 1984. Final report of the Environmental Land Management Study Committee. February. Tallahassee, FL: ELMS II Committee.

ELMS III. 1992. Final report: Building successful communities. December. Tallahassee, FL: ELMS III Committee.

Fiedler, Tom. 1998. For Florida democrats, it's rebuilding time. *Miami Herald.* December 6:6L.

Fineout, Gary. 2001. Session to target education funding. *Gainesville Sun.* November 25:B1, 10.

Florida Atlantic University/Florida International University (FAU/FIU). Joint Center for Environmental and Urban Problems. 1993. Staff analysis of 1993 Planning and Growth Management Act, 1993 Florida Environmental Reorganization Act, and 1993 Jobs Siting Act. Fort Lauderdale, FL.

———. 1998. Eastward Ho! Financial impediments and solutions to redevelopment. Fort Lauderdale, FL. January 15.

Florida Chapter, American Planning Association (FAPA). 1988. Housing tops DCA's legislative program. *Florida Planning* 8.7. March.

———. 1992a. 1992 Legislative session: Growth management policies under attack. *Florida Planning* 3.6, March.

———. 1992b. Legislative session concludes…special session gets underway. *Florida Planning* 3.7, April.

———. 1993. Growth Management Committee reports to the Governor. *Florida Planning* 5.9, November.

———. 2001. *Capital Highlights* 4, March 9.

Florida Department of Community Affairs (DCA). 1989a. $7.6 million in grants to locals approved; No amendments to Chapter 163, F.S. enacted. *Technical Memo* 4.3. Summer.

———. 1989b. Reflections on 1988: An interview with Paul Bradshaw. *Technical Memo* 4.1. Winter.

———. 1989c. Responding to ORC reports. *Technical Memo* 4.3. Summer.

———. 1989d. *Technical Memo* 4.4. Special issue.

———. 1990a. Comprehensive planning back in Florida: Past, present, and future. *Technical Memo* 5.8. September.

———. 1990b. *Technical Memo* 5.8. September.

———. 1991. Planning notes. *Technical Memo* 6.4. September.

———. 1992. 163 Amendments now in effect. *Technical Memo* 7.3. August.

———. 1993. *Community Planning* 2.1. February.

———. 1994a. *Community Planning* 3.3. Fall.

———. 1994b. Regulatory reform: Three solutions for affordable housing. *Community Planning* 3.3. Fall.

———. 1995a. *Community Planning* 4.1. February.

———. 1995b. *Community Planning* 4.2. June.

———. 1995c. SHIP program helps Floridians achieve the affordable dream. *Community Planning* 4.1. February.

———. 1996. *Community Planning* 5.1. March.

———. 1997a. *Community Planning* 6.1. Spring.

———. 1997b. The Eastward Ho! Initiative. January.

———. 1998. Making a difference in Florida's communities, a portfolio of accomplishments for the Florida Department of Community Affairs. December.

———. 1999. Florida growth management legislation 1999, summary. Division of Community Planning.

———. 2000a. Governor Bush creates Growth Management Study Commission. News release. July.

———. 2000b. Growth management survey. *Community Planning* 9.1. Winter.

———. 2000c. Growth management survey report. February.

Florida Legislative Committee on Intergovernmental Relations and Florida Department of Revenue. 1998. Local government financial information handbook. September.

Florida Office of the Governor. 1997. Governor's Save Our Everglades update. June.

Florida Resource Management Task Force. 1980. Final report to Governor Bob Graham, volumes 1 and 2. Tallahassee, FL.

Florida State Comprehensive Plan Committee (SCPC). 1987. Keys to Florida's future: Winning in a competitive world. Tallahassee, FL. February.

Floridians for Better Transportation. Undated. Florida's transportation system: Leading us into the next century—A blueprint for building Florida's competitiveness in the world market. St. Petersburg, FL: Floridians for Better Transportation.

Gentry, Richard and Douglas P. Buck. Undated. Florida Home Builders Association letter to Charles G. Pattison, executive director, 1000 Friends of Florida.

Gluckman, Casey, Vivian Young, Debbie Drake and Jaimie Ross. 1996. 1996 Legislative session update. *Environmental and Urban Issues* 24.1. Fort Lauderdale, FL. FAU/FIU Joint Center for Environmental and Urban Problems. Fall: 25.

Governor's Commission for a Sustainable South Florida. 1995. Initial report. Coral Gables. October 1.

Hauserman, Julie. 2000. GOP targets land use limits. *St. Petersburg Times*. April 10.

———. 2001. Year's push to curb growth falls short. *St. Petersburg Times*. May 6.

Henderson, Clay, Debbie Drake and Jaimie Ross. 1995. 1995 legislative session update. *Environmental and Urban Issues* 25.1. Fort Lauderdale, FL: FAU/FIU Joint Center for Environmental and Urban Problems. Fall.

Hull, Victor. 2001. Governor narrows focus of growth-management agenda. *Sarasota Herald Tribune*. March 7.

Killinger, Lee. 2003. Memorandum re: 2003 regular legislative session and 2003 special session A. The Nature Conservancy. June 9.

Kleindienst, Linda. 1999. Bush taps coordinator for Everglades policy. *Sun-Sentinel*. January 9:16B.

Lee, Thomas. 2000. Managing growth: The process of change. *Florida Planning* 12.1. January.

MacManus, Susan A. 1998. Financing government. In *Government and Politics in Florida, second edition,* Robert J. Huckshorn, ed. Gainesville, FL: University Press of Florida.

Mullins, Sue. 1997. Sustainability already declared a winner. *Florida Planning* 9.1. January.

Murley, James F. 1997. Sustainable Communities Demonstration Project. *Quality Cities* 70.9. March.

Murley, James F., Eric Draper and J. Larry Durrence. 1992. 1992 legislative session update. *Environmental and Urban Issues* 20.1. Fall: 5. Fort Lauderdale, FL: FAU/FIU Joint Center for Environmental and Urban Problems.

Murley, James F., David L. Powell and Eric Draper. 1993. 1993 Legislative session update. *Environmental and Urban Issues* 21.1. Fall: 10. Fort Lauderdale, FL: FAU/FIU Joint Center for Environmental and Urban Problems.

Newman, Joe and Julie Hauserman. 1998. Commissioner in Pinellas takes job with Bush. *St. Petersburg Times*. December 23.

Pattison, Charles. 2001. Memo to John DeGrove concerning the growth management commission's draft recommendations.

Pelham, Thomas. 1988. Letter to Senator Gwen Margolis. March 7. Tallahassee, FL: Florida DCA.

———. 1993. Implementing the ELMS III legislation: New challenges for Florida's planners. *Florida Planning*. May/June.

———. 1995. Florida legislature enacts Private Property Rights Protection Act. *Capital Highlights* 95.9. May 8.

Robles, Frances. 1998. Sweeping changes lie ahead for Constitution: 12 of 13 amendments pass. *Miami Herald*. November 5, 5B.

Ross, Jaimie. 1992. The William E. Sadowski Affordable Housing Act. *Environmental and Urban Issues* 20.1. Fort Lauderdale, FL: FAU/FIU Joint Center for Environmental and Urban Problems. Fall: 13.

Ross, Jaimie and Mark Hendrickson. 2000. Affordable housing in the 2000 Florida legislative session. *Housing News Network* 15.3. Summer.

Salinero, Mike. 2003. About-face: GOP lawmakers OK bills curbing local power. *Tampa Bay Online*. May 26.

Sherrod, Alice. 1997. Sustainable Communities Demonstration Project. *Journal of the Public Interest Environmental Conference* 1.1. Spring. Florida 2020: Visions of Our Future, The Third Annual Public Interest Environmental Conference.

South Florida Regional Planning Council (SFRPC) with Treasure Coast Regional Planning Council (TCRPC). 1996. *Eastward Ho! Revitalizing South Florida's urban core*. Hollywood, FL. July.

———. 1997. *Eastward Ho! Brownfields partnership: A collaborative approach to action*. Hollywood, FL. February.

———. 1998. Building on success: A report from Eastward Ho! Hollywood, FL. December.

Stroud, Nancy E. 1979. Areas of Critical State Concern: Legislative actions following the Cross Keys Decision. *Florida Environmen-tal and Urban Issues* 6.4. Fort Lauderdale, FL: FAU/FIU Joint Center for Environmental and Urban Problems. April.

———. 1980. Regionalism reaffirmed. *Florida Environmental and Urban Issues* 8.1. October. Fort Lauderdale, FL: FAU/FIU Joint Center for Environmental and Urban Problems.

The Nature Conservancy. 1996. Preservation 2000: 1996 annual report. Tallahassee, FL.

———. 1997. Keeping the promise. Preservation 2000. Tallahassee, FL. Winter.

———. 1998. Letter from Lawton Chiles. Preservation 2000: 1998 annual report. Tallahassee, FL: The Nature Conservancy.

United Nations. 1992. Earth Summit Agenda 21: The United Nations Programme of Action from Rio. New York, NY: United Nations.

U.S. Census Bureau. State and country Quickfacts, Florida. http://quickfacts.census.gov/qfd/states/12000.html.

World Commission on Environment and Development. 1987. *Our Common Future*. Oxford, UK: Oxford University Press.

Appendix

Governors

Reubin Askew (Democrat)	1971–1979
Daniel Robert (Bob) Graham (Democrat)	1979–1987
Robert Martinez (Republican)	1987–1991
Lawton Chiles (died in office) (Democrat)	1991–1998
Kenneth (Buddy) MacKay (Democrat)	1998–1999
John Ellis (Jeb) Bush (Republican)	1999–present

Acronyms

ACSC	Area of Critical State Concern
APA	American Planning Association
CARL	Conservation and Recreational Lands Program
DCA	Department of Community Affairs
DEP	Department of Environmental Protection
DOT	Department of Transportation
DRI	development of regional impact
EAR	Evaluation and Appraisal Report
EEL	Environmentally Endangered Lands Program
ELMS	Environmental Land Management Study Committees
FCT	Florida Communities Trust
FLUM	Future Land Use Map
GMP	Growth Management Portion
HAP	Homeowners Assistance Program
HBA	Home Builders Association
ICE	Intergovernmental Coordination Element
ISTEA	Intermodal Surface Transportation Efficiency Act of 1991 (federal legislation)
OTTED	Office of Trade, Tourism and Economic Development
RPC	Regional Planning Council
SAIL	State Apartment Incentive Loan Program
SCPC	State Comprehensive Plan Committee (Zwick Committee)
SFRPC	South Florida Regional Planning Council
SHIP	State Housing Initiative Partnership
TCMA	Transportation Concurrency Management Areas
TCRPC	Treasure Coast Regional Planning Council

Contacts

1000 Friends of Florida
926 East Park Avenue
P.O. Box 5948
Tallahassee, FL 32314-5948
850-222-6277
http://www.1000fof.org

The Catanese Center for Urban and Environmental Solutions at Florida Atlantic University
formerly the Joint Center for Environmental and Urban Problems at Florida Atlantic University/Florida International University (FAU/FIU)
111 East Las Olas Blvd., Suite 709
Fort Lauderdale, FL 33301
954-762-5255
http://www.catanese.org

Eastward Ho!
South Florida Regional Planning Council
954-985-4416
http://www.sfrpc.com/eho.htm

Enterprise Florida, Inc.
325 John Knox Road, Suite 201
Tallahassee, FL 32303
850-488-6300
http://www.eflorida.com

Growth Management Coalition
c/o Florida Chapter, American Planning Association
2040 Delta Way
Tallahassee, FL 32303
850-201-3272
http://www.floridaplanning.org

The Nature Conservancy
222 South Westmonte Drive, Suite 300
Altamonte Springs, FL 32714
407-682-3664
http://nature.org/wherewework/northamerica/states/florida/contact

South Florida Regional Planning Council
3440 Hollywood Boulevard, Suite 140
Hollywood, FL 33021
954-985-4416
http://www.sfrpc.com

State of Florida
http://www.myflorida.com

4

New Jersey

Contents

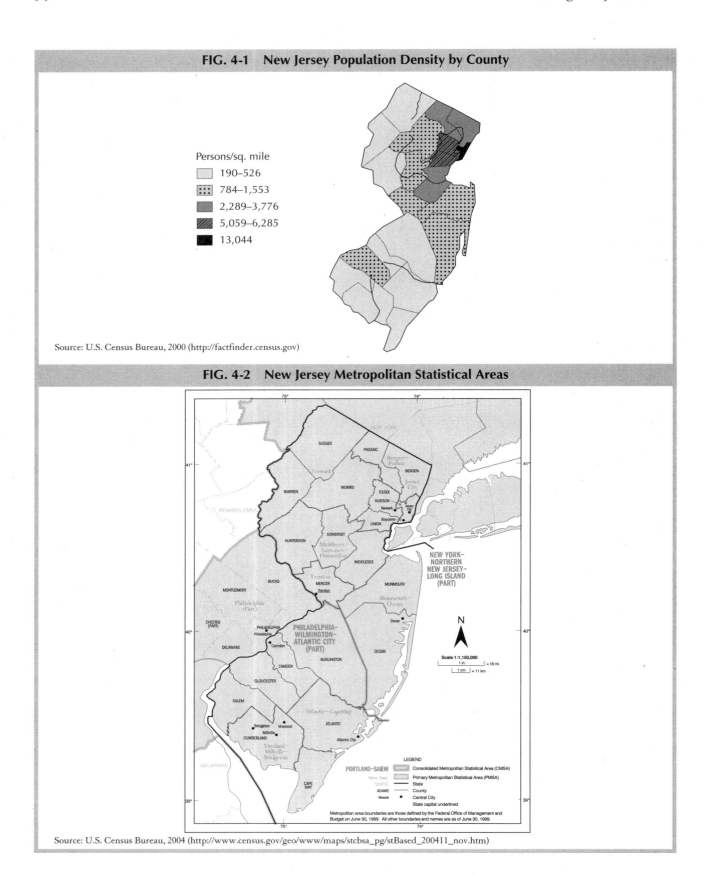

FIG. 4-1　New Jersey Population Density by County

Persons/sq. mile
190–526
784–1,553
2,289–3,776
5,059–6,285
13,044

Source: U.S. Census Bureau, 2000 (http://factfinder.census.gov)

FIG. 4-2　New Jersey Metropolitan Statistical Areas

Source: U.S. Census Bureau, 2004 (http://www.census.gov/geo/www/maps/stcbsa_pg/stBased_200411_nov.htm)

Introduction

New Jersey's attempt to implement a comprehensive strategy to contain the sprawling development that has dominated the state's growth since the early 1950s has been a mixture of successes and setbacks. Located between the large metropolitan regions of New York City and Philadelphia, New Jersey has been subjected to growth pressures from outside its boundaries for decades. Most of the substantial population growth in the 1950s and 1960s occurred in suburban development belts around those cities and along the Garden State Parkway. And, as in many other states, the postwar decline of urban manufacturing centers contributed to suburban expansion of both commercial and residential development and the concomitant decay of older cities.

By the early 1980s New Jersey was among a limited number of states taking up the challenge of better managing its suburban growth to mitigate the negative impacts. A rising conviction that the state's existing planning system was broken fueled demands that motivated the state's political system to act. However, it is debatable whether increasing awareness of such impacts alone would have caused the legislature to adopt and the governor to sign New Jersey's State Planning Act in January 1986 without the added factor of the state Supreme Court's Mt. Laurel decisions on affordable housing (discussed below). Those two forces interacted to help produce the initial state planning and affordable housing laws.[1]

Implementation of the State Planning Act of 1985 and the subsequent State Development and Redevelopment Plan in June 1992 moved slowly, however, as new governors in alternating political parties produced delays that at times threatened the very survival of the state planning system. Legislative support eroded further after the Republicans took control of the legislature in 1992, when Democratic Governor James Florio was thwarted in his effort to increase state revenues by substantially increasing the state income tax. The state plan moved to the bottom of his agenda, but he never wavered in his public support of the effort.

Only in mid-1996, during Governor Christine Todd Whitman's tenure, did it become clear that the planning effort would survive a series of crises, and from then through 2001 the challenge of implementing the plan continued with mixed outcomes. By late 2000 the prospects for full implementation of the plan's goals appeared better than at any time since its initial adoption as law in 1986. Voters had approved a statewide ballot question proposed by Whitman in 1998, aimed at providing $1 billion over the next 10 years to preserve half of the state's remaining farmland, woodlands and other open spaces. In addition, that year some 50 towns and seven of New Jersey's 21 counties voted *yes* to referenda proposing property tax increases to buy open space outright or purchase development rights. With new resources in hand to stop paving over New Jersey's open spaces, the challenge for the next decade would be choosing which areas to protect.

On March 1, 2001, the State Planning Commission adopted the most recent version of the State Development and Redevelopment Plan with a number of provisions emerging from the cross-acceptance negotiation process. Nevertheless, concerns remained whether the goals, policies and other requirements could be implemented in a timely way to bring smart growth to New Jersey through a sustainable development strategy. If the effort succeeds, New Jersey residents should enjoy a quality of life far superior to what they would experience if it fails. As the state moved into 2003 under Governor James McGreevey, a mix of positive and negative forces were at work, with McGreevey's determination to support a smart growth agenda being a major positive factor. Other developments through 2004 are covered below, with the same mix of forces still at work.

The Land Use Planning Context

A complex set of judicial, governance and planning policies dating back to the mid-1930s shape the components of New Jersey's state planning law. The governance system consists of an institutionally strong

---

1. For an assessment of Mt. Laurel decisions, see MSM Regional Council (1990). See also *Southern Burlington County NAACP v Mount Laurel* 336 A.2d 713,728 (1975) and *Southern Burlington County NAACP v Mount Laurel* 456 A.2d 390,410 (1983).

governor who appoints virtually all statewide officials, and 566 municipalities incorporating all the lands of the state. The Municipal Land Use Law empowered each municipality to develop a master land use plan focusing primarily on zoning ordinances (New Jersey P.L. 1975, revised 1977).

Public regional agencies generally have a low profile in New Jersey, although counties and municipalities may form such agencies and delegate planning to them. In spite of the 1935 County and Regional Planning Enabling Act (amended 1981), prior to 1986, New Jersey's 21 counties had limited authority to review municipal master plans for consistency. In certain narrowly drawn areas, however, counties had some influence over municipal zoning.

There are several notable exceptions to this weak regional picture. The Pinelands Regional Commission, formed in 1979 in partnership with the state and federal governments, has jurisdiction over a million acres of land in southern New Jersey and is considered one of the most successful regional growth management systems in the nation (New Jersey P.L. 1979; Association of NJ Environmental Commissions 1987). In the northeastern part of the state, the Hackensack Meadowlands Development Commission (now renamed the New Jersey Meadowlands Commission) was created by the state legislature in 1969 to balance strong urban development with wetlands protection, though with more modest success (New Jersey P.L. 1968).

One of several nonprofit agencies that promote regional cooperation is the Regional Planning Partnership (RPP), formerly named the Middlesex-Somerset-Mercer (MSM) Regional Council, a civic planning and research organization for central New Jersey. Another nonprofit, Morris 2000, was formed in 1984 as a "citizens' education and research organization that advocates balanced growth and regional planning" for Morris County and its 39 municipalities (DeGrove 1992, 35). The Highlands Coalition was established in 1988 as a grassroots association representing more than 90 local, state, regional and national citizens' organizations to protect the environmentally sensitive highlands area covering parts of New Jersey, New York and Connecticut.

State planning efforts in New Jersey date back to the passage of the State Planning Act of 1934.

During the mid-1970s, under the administration of Governor Brendan Byrne, the Department of Community Affairs' (DCA) Division of State and Regional Planning prepared a State Development Guide Plan. This plan first used the term *cross-acceptance,* which was to become the heart of the New Jersey growth strategy in the 1980s and beyond. Cross-acceptance, in the context of DCA's plan, meant an informal process of negotiation among county planners, the Tri-State Regional Planning Commission (in northeast New Jersey) and DCA's Division of State and Regional Planning.

At about the same time, DCA's plan was developed, the New Jersey Supreme Court in 1975 entered the land use scene with the first of the Mt. Laurel cases, a series of class action suits that challenged the zoning ordinances of Mt. Laurel, a small community near Philadelphia. The court asserted that suburban communities such as Mt. Laurel had to accept their fair share of regional housing needs and to zone land use accordingly. In response Byrne issued Executive Order 35, directing the development of a statewide housing allocation plan to help determine a given municipality's fair share. When a lower court required a municipality to accept a certain number of affordable units, and when a builder pursued the so-called "builders' remedy" and demanded permission to construct such units, DCA's plan would be used to determine a community's fair share. The builders' remedy, established in an early Mt. Laurel case, was a reward system allowing developers to build four market-price units for every low- or mid-priced unit built, thus contributing to sprawl development.

Even as the court expressed preference for a new state plan to guide the Mt. Laurel process, Governor Thomas Kean's administration abolished the Division of State and Regional Planning after taking office in 1982. When legal challenges to the builders' remedy using the State Development Guide Plan were unsuccessful, the stage was set for new legislation that could mandate state planning and replace court decisions with legislative and administrative procedures in the housing area.[2]

---

2. See Epling (1989, 7–8, 10); Hoskins (Undated, 1–3); Woodrow Wilson School (Undated).

Crafting and Passing the State Planning Act of 1985

The abolition of the Division of State and Regional Planning appeared to bode ill for the drafting of a state plan. Yet the twin forces of the Mt. Laurel decisions and a persistent group who believed that the state needed a system to manage the explosive growth of the 1980s led to the establishment of an ad hoc committee to present a new state planning law to the governor. Key members of the committee were Jack Trafford, executive director of the New Jersey League of Municipalities, and James G. Gilbert, president of the New Jersey Federation of Planning Officials.

W. Cary Edwards, Governor Kean's special counsel and later attorney general, indicated that the governor would support a state planning bill if it were relatively noncontroversial (Gottlieb 1988, 1, 20–23). The committee began meeting in summer 1983 to start building broad-based support for the bill's recommendations. In debating how to give a state plan some teeth without losing the support of Trafford and the municipalities, the group used cross-acceptance, which was sufficiently vague to satisfy local governments, but had the potential to bring state and local plans into conformance. Edwards played a major role in the effort to get a bill drafted and passed. At the same time, he was working with a Mt. Laurel housing group, so the two efforts were closely linked. Edwards noted that although the law as passed had no direct teeth, it tied the state capital budget process to the planning process, thus putting state agencies in a key position to implement the state plan.

In the legislature, Senator Gerald R. Stockman, a Democrat from Mercer County, sponsored the ad hoc team's draft planning law and enlisted the help of several leading New Jersey "thinkers and actors" on effective state planning and fair housing. They included Samuel Hamill, executive director of the MSM Regional Council; Peter Buchsbaum, an advocate of the link between the fair housing and state planning laws; and Thomas O'Neill of the Partnership for New Jersey Board. After considerable debate, the State Planning Act of 1985 passed easily: 62–9 in the Assembly and 33–4 in the Senate (DeGrove 1992, 37).

Goals and Provisions of the Act

Governor Kean signed the act into law in January 1986, stating that, "When we attract new jobs and industry we must think of the impact that development is going to have on local roads, on the quantity of open land…and examine those questions before development occurs—not after, when it is too late to do something about it" (DeGrove 1992, 37–39; NJF 1986a). Anticipating and planning for the effects of development are key to any sound system for managing growth, and the act set forth a policy framework that clearly expressed its major objectives:

> New Jersey, the nation's most densely populated state, requires sound and integrated statewide planning and the coordination of statewide planning with local and regional planning to conserve its natural resources, revitalize its urban centers, protect the quality of its environment, and provide needed housing and adequate public services at a reasonable cost while promoting beneficial economic growth, development, and renewal. (New Jersey P.L. 1985b)

To achieve those goals, the act established a 17-member, governor-appointed, Senate-confirmed State Planning Commission in the Treasury Department. Drawn from urban and rural areas and both political parties, the commission's membership represented a cross-section of state, county and municipal officials, as well as the public. The law also created an Office of State Planning within the Treasury Department to monitor and report on progress toward the plan's goals.

Superseding the old DCA State Development Guide Plan, the new State Development and Redevelopment Plan would "provide a coordinated, integrated and comprehensive plan for the growth, development, and renewal and conservation of the state and its regions" and *identify areas for growth, agriculture, open space conservation and other appropriate designations*" (emphasis added; New Jersey P.L. 1985b, section 4). This language formed the basis for the geographic "tiers" or "policy areas" to be mapped in successive drafts of the state plan. In addition to establishing the cross-acceptance process, the plan would also address infrastructure and capital improvements, both for economic growth and for a balance of development and conservation objectives. In keeping with the mandates of the Mt. Laurel cases, the new state plan would add affordable housing to its list of concerns.

Many believe that cross-acceptance is central to New Jersey's planning process, but there was no ultimate "hammer" in the law to enforce consistency among plans. The law assigns a key role to counties, traditionally weak partners in planning and land use in the state.

> [T]he term cross-acceptance means a process of comparison of planning policies among governmental levels with the purpose of attaining compatibility between local, county, and state plans. The process is designed to result in a written statement specifying areas of agreement or disagreement and areas requiring modification by parties to the cross-acceptance. (New Jersey P.L. 1985b, section 7b)

Success of the state's growth management system largely depended on how well the commission, the Office of State Planning and other state agencies could fulfill the requirements of the law; their effectiveness depended heavily on adequate funding and on the governor's active and sustained support. The act appropriated an initial $750,000 toward implementation of the plan.

Another significant feature of the law was the requirement that state agencies' capital projects be consistent with the state plan. Each year, agencies were required to submit a report to the State Planning Commission detailing proposed projects for the next three years, and the commission would in turn develop a Capital Facilities Improvement Plan consistent with the state plan. Assuming that most county and municipal plans achieved consistency with the state plan, allocating all state agency capital expenditures to projects consistent with the plan would be a powerful implementation tool for the act. Section 15 of the act provided thresholds for a regional impact review process by requiring the commission or its designee, such as a county, to review large-scale developments involving more than 150 acres or 500 housing units. Finally, the act called for the adoption of the new state plan within 18 months of the bill's enactment and for revision of the plan every three years.

Links to the Fair Housing Act

Language in the 1985 State Planning Act linked it to the passage of a fair housing bill, guaranteeing that growth management and housing policy would proceed in tandem. The New Jersey Fair Housing Act also cleared the legislature in 1985. The law established a nine-member Council on Affordable Housing, "in but not of the Department of Community Affairs" (New Jersey P.L. 1985a). Membership included municipal representatives, some from cities of a certain population density, people representing households in need of low- and moderately priced housing, a representative of builders of such housing, and people representing the public interest.

The purpose of the Fair Housing Act was to substitute legislative and administrative remedies for judicial ones, thus assuring that a municipality met its constitutional obligation for affordable housing. Under the act, the Council on Affordable Housing was to delineate the housing regions of the state, estimate (with the assistance of the State Planning Commission) the needs for low- and moderate-income housing at the regional and state levels, and adopt guidelines for determining regional and municipal fair share in numbers of housing units. With the council's approval, a municipality could transfer up to 50 percent of its fair share of units to another municipality within its housing region.

The fair housing law provided substantial funding to achieve its goals: a neighborhood preservation, nonlapsing trust fund with a $2 million appropriation, augmented by an anticipated $8 million annually from an increase in the real estate transfer tax. The act also appropriated $15 million to the New Jersey Mortgage and Finance Agency and directed that agency to appropriate 25 percent of its revenue-bond authority for the program, with $20 million to be made available for below market rate mortgages.

The Planning Commission Begins Its Work

The State Planning Act was broad enough and its impact on key stakeholders uncertain enough to bring about broad support and easy passage by the legislature. There was something in the law for a wide range of interests:

- Home builders, who hoped for more timeliness and for development approvals

- Municipalities, who saw little threat to their treasured home rule powers but hoped for more state dollars for their planning and zoning efforts

- Environmentalists, who considered the separation of rural and urban land uses and protecting natural resources as major pluses

- State professional planners, who viewed the law as a major expansion of planning in the state

- Key elements in the corporate community, who saw the act as a way to sustain New Jersey's quality of life (DeGrove 1992, 39)

Even so, implementation of the act got off to a slow start. Governor Kean signed the bill into law in January 1986, but the first commission meeting was delayed until September. The commission was made up of strong individuals, who, for the most part, were committed to making the system work. Several members had been active in pushing for the law, including Jim Gilbert, the commission's first chairman, and Candace Ashman, a New Jersey environmental leader. A representative of the home builders was conspicuously absent but was added later; top corporate talent was well represented, and two members were affordable housing advocates (DeGrove 1992, 40–41).

The governor's state agency appointments included the commissioner of transportation, who supported a strong growth management system. The strongest state agency in New Jersey was the Treasury Department, which included both the State Planning Commission and the Office of State Planning. The state treasurer, Feather O'Conner, had experience in land use and housing, having served as Kean's executive director of the New Jersey Housing and Mortgage Finance Agency and as director of the Division of Policy Development in the U.S. Department of Housing and Urban Development.

If the commission was late in getting organized, it moved with dispatch to meet the 18-month deadline for producing the new State Development and Redevelopment Plan. Newly appointed executive director John W. Epling brought extensive experience

in planning and growth management, having served for 14 years on the Northern Virginia District Planning Commission.

A variety of actors exhorted the commission to craft a balanced growth management system that promoted growth where needed, and also protected and restored the state's natural systems. In addressing the issue of enforcing compliance, Gilbert noted that "it will be difficult for any level of government in the state to ignore the results of our efforts without serious consequence." Fears of too much state direction were expressed by the deputy mayor of rapidly growing West Windsor township (one of the controversial sites of the Mt. Laurel cases), who said that the proper attitude of the state toward municipalities "should be one of cooperation, not coercion; of conciliation, not confrontation" (NJF 1986b, 2).

At its second meeting on October 31, 1986, the commission approved a statewide poll to explore citizen attitudes about land use and planning issues. The poll produced encouraging findings. Concern for the environment ranked high, as did the view that development threatened natural resources. Somewhat surprising was the finding that citizens were not as devoted to home rule as expected. When asked which level of government could best manage growth, 35 percent answered local towns; 23 percent named counties and 30 percent named the state. Most held that existing government control of development was "not very strict" and felt that it should be "very strict" (MSM 1987). Other early business of the commission established a schedule for a preliminary state plan by June 1987, with a draft plan to be in place by April 30, 1987. The commission made the decision, later the subject of great controversy, to undertake preliminary computer mapping of the state showing growth, limited growth and protection areas.

Significant to the success of the state growth strategy was the founding of New Jersey Future (NJF), a nonprofit organization dedicated to supporting implementation of the State Planning Act. Representing an impressive cross-section of corporate, development and environmental groups, the organization kept citizens informed of the work of the State Planning Commission. Concurrently, the New Jersey Business and Industry Association announced its intention to join other groups in helping the commission achieve its goals.

In February 1987 the commission published a report, *Trends and Hard Choices*, which summarized the group's activities and listed the new planning goals for the state (NJSPC 1987b, 29–30). It offered a hard-hitting account of the negative consequences of unmanaged growth, especially on agriculture and open space, water resources, air quality, roadways, housing and the state's declining cities. The commission's had eight goals.

1. Conserve natural resources
2. Revitalize urban centers
3. Protect the quality of the environment
4. Provide housing at a reasonable cost
5. Provide adequate public services at a reasonable cost
6. Accomplish these goals while protecting beneficial economic growth, development and renewal
7. Preserve and enhance the historical, cultural and recreational lands and structures in the state
8. Ensure sound and integrated statewide planning coordinated with local and regional planning

The remainder of the report outlined policies for achieving these goals. The document set the framework for the first draft state plan (made public in April 1987), which remained essentially unchanged in succeeding drafts and the final State Development and Redevelopment Plan adopted in June 1992.

The Senate considered several bills in December 1986, aimed at strengthening the state's ability to achieve the goals of the State Planning Act. The most significant was a Municipal-County Planning Partnership, mandating county planning and county master plans and an amendment to the Municipal Land Use Law requiring consistency between municipal and county master plans, with expanded county review of developments of regional impact. This was strong medicine for a state whose municipalities treasured their home rule powers—as was an effort to pass clear transfer of development rights (TDR) legislation and two very pro-growth management laws proposed by the New Jersey Department of

Transportation (DOT). Had those laws cleared the legislature, the prospects for implementation of the goals and policies of the State Planning Act would have been greatly enhanced. That they failed to do so, and most remained on the unfinished agenda into 2002, says much about the rocky road to smart growth in New Jersey over the past 17 years.

The State Development and Redevelopment Plan

The plan development process in New Jersey has been convoluted, but it has also produced creative and innovative ideas that survived in draft after draft. The process has been attacked, especially by home builders and agricultural interests, yet it has received sustained support from political leaders, public interest groups, and local government and planning organizations. The State Planning Commission kept Jim Gilbert as chair and John Epling as executive director throughout the process and, in the case of the chair, well into the postplan adoption period. A relatively small staff in the Office of State Planning (OSP) was stretched to accomplish a multitude of complex tasks, but performed well under pressure. Urged on by NJF and other groups, the staff improved its outreach to stakeholders over time, although some believed that not enough was done.

The First Draft Plan, April 1987

The first draft plan (NJSPC 1987a) was a hardhitting document that built on the commission's 1987 report (NJSPC 1987b) as did subsequent drafts. It drew largely from the State Planning Act for its goals and objectives, although professional consultants and staff produced the strategy to realize those goals. Policies and standards were proposed at the state, county and local levels to assure that growth went where it was designated. The key element was an eight-tier system to designate geographic areas appropriate for development, and other areas that should have limited or no development (DeGrove 1992, 42).

1. Urban centers
2. Older suburbs

3. Growing suburbs

4. Freestanding towns

5. Planned urbanized areas

6. Future urbanized areas

7. Agricultural areas

8. Conservation areas

Within each tier, different growth management policies would be applied, resulting in a pattern of corridors and nodes with growth channeled into existing urban centers and primarily at nodes along major highways and transit corridors (Lawrence 1988, 20).

The plan's mandate was clear: focus state infrastructure spending for transportation, water, sewer and parks in designated urban areas and growth corridors, while providing no such assistance in limited growth areas. Recognizing that achieving these goals depended mostly on cities and counties, the draft plan set out policies on the location, intensity and character of development to be negotiated through the cross-acceptance process, such as one dwelling unit per 20 acres in the conservation areas.

The April 1987 draft was a shock to many, including Jack Trafford of the League of Municipalities, because it specified what municipalities could and could not do to be consistent with the plan's goals and policies. While OSP staff wanted a strong draft plan to clarify the challenges of full implementation, the plan's "premature" release through a newspaper article meant that the State Planning Commission had neither reviewed nor approved it in advance. OSP's John Epling and SPC Chair Jim Gilbert subsequently worked hard to modify some of the toughest parts of the draft, to bring stakeholders like Trafford back on board, while retaining requirements critical to implementation. The mapped tiers in the 1987 draft were of concern to many municipalities, which saw them as zoning maps. Trafford also objected to "unnecessary" demands on small municipalities that lacked professional staff.

The Second Draft Plan, January 1988

The second draft of the plan also closely tracked the goals and policies in the NJSPC (1987b) report, but condensed the number of goals to seven (NJSPC 1988b, 20–56).

1. Promote beneficial economic growth, development and renewal

2. Provide adequate public services at a reasonable cost

3. Protect natural resources

4. Revitalize urban areas

5. Provide housing at a reasonable cost

6. Preserve and enhance historic, cultural, open space, and recreational lands and structures

7. Ensure sound and integrated planning statewide

This draft proposed seven instead of eight tiers, showing where public interest would be best served (NJSPC 1988b, 77–78). The growth areas were in the first four tiers and the limited growth areas in the last three tiers.

1. Redeveloping cities and suburbs (merging tiers 1 and 2 from the 1987 draft)

2. Stable cities and suburbs

3. Suburban and rural towns

4. Suburbanizing areas

5. Future suburbanizing areas

6. Agricultural areas

7. Environmentally sensitive areas

Critiques of the second draft plan, both positive and negative, came from a number of stakeholders. A Peer Review Technical Advisory Committee, chaired by this author, included leading experts on such systems as well as a number of state participants. The committee found the draft plan a good start toward planning and growth management in New Jersey, but identified significant gaps and weaknesses in implementation, infrastructure and funding. It recommended that new legislation and funding initiatives be part of the plan, including substantial state funds for municipalities and counties to increase local government capacity to implement the planning system (Peer Review Committee 1988).

The committee also noted that the new agricultural policy, a retreat from stronger language in the April 1987 draft, was "too weak," and expressed concern over areas left out of the plan, including some 46 percent of the state, such as the Hackensack Meadowlands, coastal areas under the Coastal Area Facility Review Act (CAFRA) and the Pinelands. The committee recommended that the legislature authorize a TDR system and identify a more aggressive strategy for both infrastructure and affordable housing needs, along with funding sources to meet those needs (Peer Review Committee 1988, 6–9).

New Jersey Future's critique of the January draft called for attention to four areas: a "clarification of the visions for the future of the state"; better defined measures "to bring state and local plans into alignment," thus improving the cross-acceptance process; "refinement of key planning and management concepts" aimed at more effective implementation; and an effort to shorten and simplify the draft to ensure better public participation and understanding. Key policy issues raised by the report were much the same as those of the Peer Review Committee (NJF 1988b, 2–4).

The NJF report called for measurable goals in two areas: "An urban growth boundary—the line between tiers 4 and 5—to be agreed to by all levels of government and adopted as a state policy"; and state agency support and enforcement of the state plan as it is ultimately adopted (NJF 1988, 2). Other groups weighing in on the draft plan included the New Jersey chapter of the American Planning Association, which pledged its support to implement the plan, and the MSM Regional Council, which saw the plan as the only way to reverse the sprawl pattern of development destroying New Jersey's quality of life (NJAPA 1988; MSM 1988).

On the negative side, a response prepared for the New Jersey Builders Association found nothing good about the plan, reflecting the association's deep hostility toward the State Planning Act and its own $1 million-funded Foundation for the Preservation of the American Dream dedicated to doing away with the draft plan (Foundation 1988, 43).

Preliminary Plan, November 1988

The State Planning Commission released the Preliminary State Development and Redevelopment Plan (Preliminary Plan) on November 14, 1988, in two volumes (NJSPC 1988). On January 27, 1989, the commission voted to release the third volume, containing the standards and guidelines necessary to allow the cross-acceptance process to begin (NJSPC 1989). Volumes one and two were "user friendly," including charts, maps and large print, with the goals of the planning act remaining the same. The vision section of the first volume was strengthened; statewide objectives clarified; and projected levels of population and employment growth made for each county and region, for use as initial targets in cross-acceptance negotiations. Focusing on an unfinished agenda for the planning act, the first volume addressed implementation capacity, in particular strengthening the capacity of state and local governments to meet the costs of growth.

■ Establish a statewide Infrastructure and Affordable Housing Trust Fund, with a statewide tax on new developments varying from tier to tier, presumably least in tier 1 and greatest in tier 7.

■ Give local governments the power to assess impact and linkage fees, as an alternative.

■ Provide more state dollars for all planning done in response to the plan.

■ Strengthen county planning as called for in the Municipal–County Planning Partnership amendments.

■ Establish a stable funding source to allow more dollars for open space and agricultural easements, including use of the state's bonding capacity. (NJSPC 1988a, 31)

The second volume stressed the need for greater coordination between the preliminary plan and the previously neglected New Jersey Pinelands, Hackensack Meadowlands and the coastal zone; and the third volume provided the details to make the cross-acceptance process meaningful.

Cross-Acceptance: The Heart of Plan Making

Cross-acceptance is defined as

a process of comparison of planning policies among governmental levels with the purpose of attaining compatibility among local, county and state plans. The process is designed to result in a written statement specifying areas of agreement or disagreement and areas requiring modification by parties to the cross-acceptance. (New Jersey P.L. 1985b, 8)

The cross-acceptance process has three phases—comparison, negotiation and issue resolution—each originally estimated to require six months. Comparison begins when the county, as the local "negotiating entity," receives the preliminary plan from the State Planning Commission. This phase called for 21 public informational meetings (one for each county) and additional public hearings as required by the act or the state planning rules.

Each county, its municipalities and the public took the following steps to carry out the first phase.

- Compare the county and municipality plans with the preliminary plan, and report "findings, recommendations, and objections to the preliminary plan. Any municipality disagreeing with the county's report may file its own report with the commission."

- Recommend ways to resolve "inconsistencies and incompatibilities" between local and state plans.

- Identify errors in mapping of tier boundaries.

- Recommend revisions in tier boundaries or criteria for their establishment.

- Indicate whether the projected level of growth for the county is reasonable or not, and why.

- Estimate the cost of additional infrastructure needed to support the level of growth anticipated. (NJSPC 1988a, 26–27)

The negotiation phase takes place after counties have submitted written reports, including municipal dissents, to SPC, which then negotiates with the county or municipality to reconcile issues by changes in the state, county or municipal plans. The final phase, issue resolution, follows after "the maximum possible consistency and compatibility among plans is agreed upon, and an interim plan, which will be aired before the state legislature and at a minimum of six hearings held across the state," is adopted in draft form (NJSPC 1988a, 27). Based on comments received, SPC reviews the interim plan to make changes. Thirty days after the last public hearing, the issue resolution phase

of cross-acceptance ends, and SPC adopts the final State Development and Redevelopment Plan. If any county or municipal plan still is not in harmony with the state plan, they "should make any appropriate changes to local and county plans and regulations to achieve compatibility." This whole process is repeated every three years (NJSPC 1988a, 27).

No "hammer" existed to compel compliance by a county or municipality, but the process depended on the ability of the key actors to resolve most differences in the cross-acceptance process. The effectiveness in implementing the state plan, even if no issues remained, hinged on subsequent events including full state agency participation, sustained support from the governor, adequate funding for the system (for both planning and infrastructure costs) and the strengthening of the county's capacity to play the regional role in the system. Whether counties would assume the key integrating role in the process was unclear. New Jersey's counties had long been viewed as weak on planning and land use controls, but they quickly assumed the cross-acceptance role, a step that required a positive vote of the county freeholders (commissioners).

By March 1989 13 counties had held meetings and agreed to play the lead role in cross-acceptance, perhaps due to the presence in each county of professional planners able to articulate cross-acceptance to the county government. By September, well past the six-month period allocated to the comparison phase, all 21 counties had filed work programs and undertaken the time-consuming cross-acceptance process, but only Mercer and Bergen counties submitted comparison reports. All other counties asked for extensions ranging from six months to a full year after the comparison phase of the cross-acceptance process began; SPC granted these requests. By mid-1990 the commission had received all county cross-acceptance comparison phase reports, and preparations for the negotiation phase were underway. Clearly, the process had invigorated the counties as key actors in planning and facilitated communication among counties and their municipalities that had never occurred before (NJF 1990).

In 1989 the Corporate Alliance for Intelligent Growth (CAIG) published a report that analyzed the comparison phase of the process in some detail.

Overall, it praised the process, noting that "in virtually every case the reports demonstrate a highly professional approach and considerable knowledge of the complex concepts and specific prescriptions contained in the state plan." The report identified six key issues from a review of the county cross-acceptance reports: fiscal and economic impacts; state regulatory and judicial mandates and their impact on home rule; infrastructure needs and costs; land equity; the tier system; and public participation (CAIG 1989, 1–2).

One of the more interesting developments in the comparison phase of cross-acceptance was the degree to which municipalities were willing to have counties handle the process, and the relatively few municipalities that filed separate reports, as the law allowed. On balance, the number of issues that were not resolved in the comparison stage was relatively small, leading to a potentially manageable situation for the negotiation stage.

On May 25, 1990, SPC moved to the negotiation phase of cross-acceptance, six months behind schedule, but with considerable optimism for a successful conclusion with the final state plan. The commission amended the State Planning Rule to

- eliminate specific dates for the cross-acceptance and planning process, leaving the commission to set dates as appropriate;

- authorize "counties, municipalities, and the commission as a whole to act on issues discussed during negotiations";

- provide the authority to "make the negotiating sessions open to the public and make periodic reports available"; and

- clarify the commission's authority to guide the negotiations. (NJF 1990, 2)

After meetings of SPC's Plan Development and Intergovernmental Relations committees in May 1990 to review issues, the full commission authorized the Plan Development Committee to consider the following points:

- Eliminate municipal distress as a criterion for designation as a tier 1 area; determining centers as the focus for growth within newly constituted tier 1 areas; and addressing urban revitalization through a statewide set of policies.

- Change the tier system so that tiers 5 and 6 include exurban policy areas where appropriate low-density development (hamlets, villages) could occur without threatening long-term agricultural use.

- Develop strategies and policies for agricultural development.

- Change "tiers" to "policy areas" in the interim plan, to clarify the difference between tiers and zoning.

- Identify appropriate elements of the interim plan's third volume that may be moved to the second volume so the remaining parts of the third volume can become a technical guide or manual. (NJF 1990, 2)

Supported by these guidelines, the negotiation process began in fall 1990 with each county planning board naming a negotiating team of at least two members from its planning board and staff. Municipalities that had filed a dissenting report (a total of 44 out of the state's 566 municipalities) also named a team. The local teams met with the Plan Development Committee, which presented negotiating results as recommendations to the full SPC. Periodic reports on negotiating sessions were published by the commission, with action on such agreements required by counties and municipalities within 45 days. The Plan Development Committee, once it had reached the highest agreement possible, submitted its findings, "including a list of agreements and disagreements resulting from each negotiation session, to SPC, each county and each municipality" (NJF 1990, 5).

The negotiation phase of cross-acceptance ended in early 1991, with the following major issues remaining (DeGrove 1992, 47):

- Funding for implementation

- Implementation of the final plan, especially the role of state agencies

- Municipal distress index, especially whether its removal as a criterion would weaken the commitment to redevelopment in tier 1 municipalities

- Tier criteria too narrowly drawn on existing or planned sewer service areas

- Loss of equity in the process of maintaining land in agriculture

- Home rule, expressed by almost every county on behalf of its municipalities

- Impact of new development on existing communities and their quality of life

- The need to better coordinate coastal planning

- The need to make the third volume of the preliminary plan a technical manual

The Interim Plan, July 1991

The Office of State Planning next prepared the Interim State Development and Redevelopment Plan, based on the first two stages of cross-acceptance (comparison and negotiation), for adoption by SPC, which released the plan on July 12, 1991, setting the stage for the issue resolution phase and the preparation of the final plan. The interim plan stressed that "the State Plan is not a regulation but a policy guide for state, regional, and local governments to use when they exercise their delegated authority" (NJSPC 1991, 7).

The interim plan was the fourth attempt in state plan adoption, and it provided a contrast to the previous preliminary plan that had described a five-part growth management system: tier, regional design, statewide strategies and policies, monitoring and evaluation, and the cross-acceptance process. The interim plan retained these five components in different formats. The term *tier* was replaced with *planning areas,* but the five new planning areas (reduced from seven tiers) still had a specific geographic identity and a unique set of policy objectives. The five areas were (1) metropolitan planning; (2) suburban planning; (3) fringe planning; (4) rural planning; and (5) environmentally sensitive planning (NJSPC 1991, 100–114).

The schedule for the adoption of the final plan started with the release of the interim plan. Before its adoption by SPC, counties and municipalities had 150 days to work with the commission on any deferred issues from previous cross-acceptance negotiations. The issue resolution phase of cross-acceptance would begin after SPC approval of any interim plan amendments reflecting negotiated issues.

In fall 1989, just as SPC and OSP were pushing to get the interim plan finalized and adopted, New Jersey elected a new governor, Democrat James Florio, whose term began in January 1990. He suc-

ceeded two-term Republican Thomas Kean, who could not run for reelection. Speculation about the new governor's attitude toward the state plan was widespread, since New Jersey's strong state executive system gives the governor direct control over almost all state agencies. Many planning advocates hoped to see a strong and early push by Florio to bring about the adoption of the state plan and the full engagement of state agencies in the subsequent implementation process.

In fact, the new governor did support the effort to complete the interim plan so the process could continue. The state treasurer appointed by Florio, however, did not rank the state plan adoption as high on his priority list as had the Kean administration's treasurer. More significant, Florio was totally engaged during his first year in winning support for a massive tax increase to cover a deficit inherited from the previous administration and provide for a more equitable distribution of state support for New Jersey's public schools as required by the court. In what many observers considered a rare display of political courage, the governor pushed a massive tax increase through the 1990 legislature (controlled by the Democrats). A subsequent Republican-led backlash further engaged the governor's time and energy, and later the Republicans, many of whom opposed the state plan, gained control of both houses of the legislature in the 1992 elections. In a mid-1991 speech to the New Jersey Association of Planning Officials, Florio expressed his support for the state plan by directing state agencies to do everything possible to bring about its full implementation.

Impact Assessment

An impact assessment study, mandated by the legislature, called for "an evaluation of the economic, environmental, infrastructure, community life, and intergovernmental coordination implications of the plan." The study was conducted by the Rutgers Center for Urban Policy Research (CUPR), headed by Professor Robert W. Burchell (Rutgers University 1992, 3). The year-long research effort was the most comprehensive assessment of the costs of sprawl development patterns ever made. The results gave the plan's supporters a boost, but were a bitter disappointment to the Republican legislative opponents who had pushed for this study, hoping it would show that the costs of implementation would far outweigh any cost savings resulting from plan implementation.

The massive, three-volume report was delivered to OSP in March 1992. The entire analysis was designed to contrast the impacts of growth under the current "trend" plan (continuing past development patterns) with what would happen if the proposed State Development and Redevelopment Plan were adopted and implemented. The comparisons focused on (1) the economy; (2) the environment, including subcategories of land capacity, environmentally sensitive and agricultural lands, and air and water pollution; (3) the infrastructure (local and state roads, transit, water and sewer and school capital facilities); (4) quality of community life, i.e., housing supply, demand and costs; and (5) intergovernmental coordination (NJF 1992, 3–4).

The most dramatic advantage of the state plan over the trend plan was a saving of almost $1.4 billion over the 20-year period (1990–2010) in roads, water, sewer and school costs. Moreover, the state plan was either equally "good" or substantially better in every category, including less land consumed in meeting development needs, more agricultural land saved, substantially greater protection of environmentally sensitive lands and less water pollution. Air pollution was the same in either plan, reduced because of stricter emissions controls (Rutgers University 1992, 3).

Adoption and Implementation of the Final Plan, 1992–1996

The 1985 State Planning Act had scheduled adoption of the final state plan in 18 months, but final adoption by the 17-member State Planning Commission did not take place until June 12, 1992, some 60 months overdue. The political backlash associated with the early work of the Office of State Planning, especially in the first (1987) draft, plunged the plan development process into major political conflicts, with powerful legislative forces dedicated to ending the whole process. Efforts to establish legislative oversight of the plan's adoption were either vetoed by Governor Kean as an unconstitutional intrusion by the legislature into

executive authority, or they failed to clear the 1992 legislative session; in any event, they faced an almost certain veto by Governor Florio.

After the plan was adopted, SPC and OSP had hoped to turn their attention to full-scale support of the implementation process, but those plans were abruptly put on hold by a budget crisis. The FY 1993 budget of the 1992 legislature, with a newly elected Republican majority hostile to the State Planning Act and its implementation, imposed a 45 percent budget cut for OSP, which was forced to shift focus from implementation to fiscal survival, as one crisis followed another. Director John Epling left OSP in mid-1992, and bad news continued in efforts to reconstitute SPC, restore funding and eventually reverse the dismissal of virtually the entire OSP staff. Herbert Simmens, a planner who had been administrator of several local governments and served two years as a member of the State Planning Commission, was appointed OSP director in December 1992.

Lame duck Governor Florio, defeated for reelection by Christine Todd Whitman in November 1993, issued a dramatic executive order just before leaving office, directing all state agencies to conduct their plans and programs to be consistent with the state plan—a belated expression of support that was needed much earlier in the process. Florio also called on the legislature to restore the drastic cuts in OSP funding, and challenged SPC and OSP to finish the urban center designation process in two years. This process permitted a municipality or group of municipalities to bring a request for designation before the Plan Implementation Committee, a subcommittee of SPC. The designation of centers, the drawing of meaningful development boundaries around them and the protection of the environs around the centers as low-density rural areas were essential to the success of the whole system.

Simmens found a number of vacancies in his commission, although several members, including the Chair James Gilbert, were continuing to serve until Whitman made her own appointments. In the uncertain environment of late 1993 into early 1994, Simmens, Gilbert and other veteran SPC members attempted to implement the center designation process and patch together enough resources to maintain a skeleton staff. When Whitman reinstated Simmens and his OSP staff after they had been fired by her own treasury head, she indicated that she was not ready to abandon the state planning effort entirely, even though the Republican-controlled legislature strongly supported its abandonment.

In his effort to sustain his small staff, Simmens got support from the Department of Transportation (DOT) by contracting to prepare a Scenic Byways Program, marginal to OSP's work plan but providing $50,000 toward a survival budget. Another DOT-supported project, developing population and demographic projections for potential use by all state agencies, was more central to OSP's program. Both contracts were key elements in fiscal survival, while the fight moved to restore OSP's budget in the legislature.

In March 1994 Whitman actually proposed doubling OSP's funding from $700,000 to $1.4 million. The recommendation went to a still-hostile legislature, especially the chair of the Appropriations Committee, who attached a pair of potentially devastating riders to the budget increase (NJF 1994, 1). The riders would have prevented the state plan from being implemented by state agencies and included a proviso that any funds received by OSP from other sources would reduce the OSP budget dollar for dollar. As she had done before when actions by her own administration or the legislature threatened to weaken or destroy New Jersey's planning program, Whitman used her line item veto to eliminate these riders. The budget increase allowed Simmens to stabilize the office, but still fell far short of resources needed for a proactive effort to attain OSP's major goals.

OSP's attempt to bring state agencies into the implementation process was made more difficult by the agencies' reluctance to reshape their plans and program components for consistency with the state plan. For New Jersey, where agency heads are appointed by the governor, the key to bringing agencies into line was the willingness of the governor to direct and monitor them for compliance. The State Development and Redevelopment Plan's goals and policies particularly required a process of state agency support for plan implementation, but until late 1995 and 1996 the governor did not take much initiative on the state plan.

The potential for moving the state planning process through state agency collaboration was significant but difficult. State agency plans (e.g., the Department of Environmental Protection's Watershed and Open Space Plans, DOT's multimodal grants and DCA's block grants) had to be consistent with each other by incorporating state plan policies. Such consistency would result in substantial funds flowing into growth centers designated through the planning process.

There were 20 staff members at OSP in March 1994. The cost of supporting the staff was about $1.1 million, leaving little room for expansion out of the $1.4 million 1994–1995 appropriations. With this staff and any expansion made possible with augmented funding, Simmens had three major tasks to accomplish to advance the implementation process: state agency coordination efforts; hastening the center designation process; and creation of a high-caliber research unit to scan population and economic data being collected, for use as a basis for issue papers, conferences and workshops, to inform and facilitate implementation.

Getting the center designation process off the ground was a key factor needed to convince skeptics that the state plan was going to have real meaning. In the first year after plan adoption (June 1992–June 1993), Simmens and SPC members attempted to convince state agencies and towns that the process was moving forward and that each of them was needed to make it a success. Out of this effort, a number of memoranda of understanding (MOU) were negotiated with state agencies, and in June 1993 OSP started to receive applications from municipalities. By fall 1993 three centers had been designated, representing variety in both geography (north, central, south) and size (village, town, regional). By March 1994 SPC had designated eight urban centers: Atlantic City, Camden, Elizabeth, Jersey City, Newark, New Brunswick, Paterson and Trenton. Seven other urban centers had completed applications, and 10 to 25 others had expressed varying degrees of interest.

Whitman's statements and actions in late 1995 and early 1996 supported state agency participation and strengthened the state planning process. She filled all SPC vacancies in October 1995, including Michele E. Byers as the only environmentalist among the appointments, and named Jay Crammer, a real estate developer, as the commission's chair. However, most of these new members had little previous involvement in the evolution of the state planning system and needed time to get up to speed on the issues.

In a letter dated November 17, 1995, Whitman directed all state agency heads to bring their plans and programs in line with the state plan, and to submit a progress report. Noting that some agencies had made progress, the governor went on to say that, "to ensure that state plan implementation is coordinated among all departments, please prepare a report describing your department's initiatives in incorporating state plan polices into your planning, decision making, and resource allocation." Reports were to be submitted to the governor's new Office for Policy and Planning and to Herbert Simmens as director of OSP (NJ Planning Officials 1995, 5; NJF 1995, 4).

In her State of the State address in January 1996, and in remarks to the reconstituted SPC in February 1996, the governor reinforced her support for the state plan. On the downside, the legislature was still hostile to the planning effort, and the attention the governor and her staff could give to the plan appeared problematic, since many other priorities took precedence.

All stakeholders appeared to agree that the state's system of land use governance needed reform. NJF noted that, "Land use governance in New Jersey comprises a vast and complex system of often uncoordinated interactions among all branches and all levels of government, a system that is widely perceived as hindering development and conservation alike" (NJF 1996a, 1). In arguing for appropriate reform legislation, the organization listed a set of outcomes that included something positive for all stakeholders: lower government costs, greater certainty for the private sector, lower development costs, more transportation options, and lessened environmental impacts (NJF 1996a, 1).

By early July 1996 no legislation had been introduced into the session, but the "builders' bill" draft, promoted by the New Jersey Builders Association, became controversial, with strong objections to its central concepts by the New Jersey State League of Municipalities, New Jersey Planning Officials and NJF (NJ State League 1995, 22; NJ Planning Officials

1995; NJF 1996a). In the eyes of a number of critics, the proposal would constitute the ultimate balkanization of land use decisions in a state where the pressures for planning in isolation by 566 municipalities were already great.

NJF led a consortium of public interest groups that advanced a set of principles for land use reform that became the basis of legislation in 1996. With the goal of a sustainable state as the framework for the principles, the objectives were to

■ advance the statewide planning process through implementing the State Development and Redevelopment Plan;

■ speed up and simplify the approval of projects where growth is called for in the state plan;

■ increase consistency among municipal, county, state and regional plans;

■ encourage faster regional decision making;

■ promote meaningful public engagement in the planning process; and

■ provide for tradeoffs between competing goals through comprehensive decision making. (NJF 1996a, 4)

The difficulty of bringing state agencies to support state plan implementation is seen in a 1996 study on how departments were incorporating the tenets and policies of the state plan into their own planning, decision making and resource allocation (NJF 1996b, 1). While all agencies reported that they were doing something to support the state plan, NJF viewed many of these efforts as being "at the margins" (NJF 1996b, 1–3). More important was the fact that many key state agencies had not used their most powerful tools to further implement the state plan: their infrastructure and development investments (millions and in some cases billions of dollars). The following are some examples of state agency action (or inaction):

■ In 1995 DOT established a Local Aid for Centers program that earmarked $1 million for "nontraditional transportation improvements in communities participating in the state plan centers program." DOT planners enthusiastically supported this and other initiatives, such as a traditional neighborhood development and livable communities program. However, NJF's analysis found that the multibillion dollar investments were not impacted by the state plan, nor was there evidence that metropolitan planning organizations (MPOs) paid much attention to the state plan in drawing up capital project lists (NJF 1996b, 3).

■ At the Department of Environmental Protection (DEP), efforts were made to bring Watershed Management Planning and CAFRA into consistency with the state plan. Other DEP rules, however, including those under revision, were viewed as undercutting the state plan, including a stipulation about wastewater management guidelines. NJF thought that DEP should "adopt rules that mandated conformance of wastewater management plans with the state plan" (NJF 1996b, 4). In the case of DEP—whose plans, programs and resource allocation could have the greatest potential for encouraging compact development patterns—the prospects of further changes to support the state plan were strengthened by the appointment of Robert Shinn as head of DEP. A longtime supporter of the state plan both in and out of the legislature, Shinn's experience with the Pinelands program made him supportive of the concept of consistency.

■ DCA was another key agency in the effort to implement the state plan, given its emphasis on investments in urban areas. DCA's commissioner reported to the governor that DCA's adopted goals were entirely consistent with the state plan. As of spring 1996, however, NJF noted that if the DCA goals were consistent, then its recent actions were not (NJF 1996b, 4). Such actions included its involvement with the New Jersey Builders Association on the "builders' bill," which completely ignored the state plan.

■ NJF also cited actions of the Council on Affordable Housing (COAH) in approving development in rural planning areas where agricultural lands, wetlands and other open space would be replaced by large-scale development (NJF 1996b, 4).

Given the experience in other states where agencies have been reluctant to integrate their plans, programs and resource allocations with state goals and policies, even in the face of clear mandates, it was clear that Governor Whitman would need to monitor her agencies, perhaps by strengthening the capacity of the governor's Office of Planning and Policy to be her eyes and ears in this matter.

State Planning and the Cross-Acceptance Process, 1996–1999

As of mid-1996, efforts to bring state agencies fully into the planning process in the implementation of the state plan remained difficult, but DEP and DOT were still considered the two key agencies critical to success. DEP's participation could affect whether the last million acres of land developed in New Jersey would maintain some rural areas intact (open space, farmland, environmentally sensitive areas). The main transportation network was already in place, but the water and sewer network was not. DEP had to redraft its programs and budgets to meet the state plan, with future development to be concentrated in centers and corridors. Key supporters of implementation wanted new state agency rules to block the extension of water and sewer infrastructure into the rural countryside, thus keeping growth inside designated centers.

DOT was viewed as a mixed bag by most advocates of strong linkage between the state plan and programs and budgets of state agencies. As of 1996 the planning staff at DOT was seen as "missionaries in their own department," because the department had not embraced linking its plans closely to the state plan with much enthusiasm. On a positive note, DOT did earmark $1 million for designated centers identified in the state plan and had an MOU with the State Planning Commission.

The bottom line in bringing state agencies into line came back to the governor. However, in mid-1996 Governor Whitman did not request DEP head Shinn to issue new CAFRA rules by a certain date, and she did not request that they integrate coastal policies and programs closely with those of the state plan. In hindsight, the governor's request, prepared with input from OSP, should have been more specific. It should have asked for a report on specific actions that had been taken to support the implementation of the state plan, not just a general statement of support.

As in all efforts to establish and maintain sustainable communities, the attraction of the center designation process to the municipalities in New Jersey depended heavily on state agencies "rewarding" those centers with "privileged" treatment on broadly defined infrastructure funds, including housing. But the process moved slowly, as OSP tried to focus on existing regional centers, such as the county seat towns that were more responsive than rural-suburban areas. By mid-1996, 19 centers had been designated, but as the process accelerated OSP saw itself quickly running out of resources to work with the centers. With little prospect of a substantial (or even modest) increase in OSP staff, the strategy was to delegate the hands-on work with centers to counties that had the capacity and willingness to undertake the task.

Updating the Plan, 1996–1997

The State Planning Act requires SPC to reexamine the state plan every three years, and 1996–1997 was such a time. As the deadline approached, supporters believed it was too risky—with a still-hostile state legislature—to try to amend the law to postpone this process, so their strategy was to reformulate and simplify the structure without compromising key concepts such as centers and policy areas. They would focus on ways to strengthen the vision of what the state would be like if the plan were implemented by adding indicators and targets that would also be integrated into the state plan. OSP's goal was to reduce by one-third to one-half the number of policies through consolidation, while also clarifying the policies. Since the SPC chair and most members were new and were still exploring what their roles would be, the governor and her staff were seen as crucial to how much and in what direction the cross-acceptance process would result in changes to the state's planning process.

During 1997 SPC and OSP moved forward, agreeing early on that the 1997 preliminary plan, which would serve as the basis for the second round of cross-acceptance, could not offer additional teeth for implementation, and that pressure for implementation should come out of the cross-acceptance process

itself. The preliminary plan was adopted and released by the commission in June 1997, along with a reexamination report not subject to the cross-acceptance process, which included changes in the economy, demographics, location of population and employment growth, housing needs and infrastructure needs. The report showed how and where land had been used by the state since the adoption of the state plan in 1992. It also outlined the preliminary plan's proposed responses to deal with those changes, and government and private sector actions taken to implement the 1992 plan (Lawrence 1998, 14).

A number of significant changes were included in the preliminary plan for discussion in the cross-acceptance process, including the concept of sustainable development, 17 indicators of the achievement of plan goals, and new statewide policies for design considerations and for coastal areas. Other changes involved the center designation process, which was intended to strengthen the requirement for drawing firm community development boundaries, and the inclusion of land uses in the environs of centers when drawing their master plans (Lawrence 1998, 15).

The cross-acceptance process remained similar, with comparison, negotiation, impact assessment and final review stages. The process got under way in October and November 1997, and as of mid-1998 NJF saw it as much less adversarial than the first round. Local governments and citizens were willing to focus on substantive issues, including state agency plans and programs as they affected the local level. Plan advocates did stress two changes in the cross-acceptance process. The first involved an effort to encourage urban centers to participate in the process, and included a grant of $15,000 to each of the eight urban centers designated in the 1992 Development and Redevelopment Plan. The second change required state agencies to explain to SPC how their various programs supported (or failed to support) the goals of the plan. Supporters of the plan hoped this process would pressure state agencies to take seriously the governor's mandate to bring them fully into the process (Lawrence 1998, 15).

Among the many challenges in keeping the improvements and the original implementation processes going was that they both had to go forward simultaneously. The center designation process was moving under the 1992 plan, despite weaknesses that would presumably be corrected in the new state plan. By November 1997 the planning commission had approved the designation of 21 centers, in addition to the eight urban centers designated by the 1992 plan. Since not all actors were participating fully in the system, especially state agencies, the incentives for municipalities to seek center designation were not as strong as they could have been. Effective implementation depended on the changes growing out of Whitman's increased involvement in the process.

Slow Progress Through the Late 1990s

As of late 1998, the question of whether the goals of the 1985 State Planning Act could be achieved remained uncertain. Barbara Lawrence, executive director of NJF, said the challenge was to assure that "each municipal, county, regional, and state agency's land use regulations, master plans, functional plans, and capital spending are consistent with the policies and strategies of the state plan" (Lawrence 1998, 7).

The bad news was that efforts between late 1998 and mid-2001 to craft and implement the state's version of a smart growth system fell far short of the goals set some 15 years after the passage of the act. Sprawl development patterns continued to consume natural systems and farmland at an alarming rate; local government implementation of the plan's goals was minimal; and state agency use of the plan was the exception rather than the rule. The good news was that after a slow start in her first term, Whitman began her second term with a strong commitment to reenergize the implementation of the state plan. In her second inaugural address on January 20, 1998, and earlier in her State of the State speech, she spelled out a vision for making New Jersey "truly the best place to live in America."

Whitman called on the legislature to give municipalities the power to control their pace of development and asked her Property Tax Commission to recommend ways to help local governments avoid destructive property tax competition. She had already directed her cabinet "to use the state plan as a funda-

mental guide in making permit and funding decisions," and "to give priority to applications that meet the plan's goals of developing where infrastructure is already in place." She went on to promise "one of the greatest incentives that state government can offer a town: a pledge to get out of your way." In return for a true commitment to build in concert with the state plan, she offered towns "up-front approval on all your development projects," with the approval time reduced to weeks instead of years (Lawrence 1998, 8). Those who track efforts to manage growth will recognize the kinds of promises the governor made as the key to effective smart growth strategies, and they will also recognize that all too often promises made are not implemented.

Whitman also pledged a strong push for something dear to the hearts of all New Jerseyans: protection of open space and farmland. Noting that the state had accomplished much in recent decades, including preserving 115,000 acres in the past four years, she called for a major new initiative to "preserve another 300,000 acres in the next four years," and "a million acres in the coming decade" (Lawrence 1998, 8).

If all the governor's efforts to implement the state plan goals were as successful as her open space initiative, the prospects for success would have been much brighter than they seemed to most plan advocates (and opponents) in her first term. The source for the funds needed to issue a billion dollars in bonds over the next decade was changed by the legislature from an increase in the gasoline tax to setting aside two cents of the sales tax. While environmental groups applauded the passage of the ballot initiative authorizing the bonds, many regretted that the governor had to compromise with the legislature over her original proposal to raise New Jersey's gasoline tax (one of the lowest in the country) by seven cents per gallon to help underwrite an annual fund of $170 million for 10 years to protect open space and farmland. In addition, the gas tax increase would have raised $210 million per year to repair bridges and highways and buy new buses and trains (*New York Times* 1998).

Two key components needed to achieve the goals of the planning act involved (1) spending the bond issue dollars to preserve the million acres of farmland

and open space, and (2) maximizing efforts to encourage state agencies to strengthen implementation of the state's planning and regulatory systems. The MSM Regional Council, celebrating three decades of promoting land use planning, advocated spending the money "in the context of sound comprehensive planning that is consistent with the state plan." It supported using the effective New Jersey DEP's Greenacres Program prioritization system as a foundation for the new $1 billion initiative, which would allocate the funds so as not to undermine other important planning goals such as encouraging growth in the right location and following the recommendations of the Governor's Council on New Jersey Outdoors. Furthermore, the challenge included integrating state spending with the funds that could flow from the 50 towns and seven counties that approved raising their property tax rates to buy open space outright or buy development rights (MSM 1998b, 1).

New Jersey's governance structure supports a strong governor, with department heads appointed by and serving at the pleasure of the governor. Through Whitman's second term she was determined to use that power aggressively to make state agency plans and budgets fully consistent with the goals of the state plan. Supporters of the plan hailed her appointment of Joseph T. Maraziti as chair of SPC, in early 1998. Maraziti is an environmental lawyer with a long record of support for good planning and urban revitalization and opposition to sprawl, who, until his appointment, served as chair of NJF. "By naming a leading plan advocate, the governor has—one month after her second inaugural address—signaled her commitment to a new day for state planning" (Lawrence 1998, 17).

Whitman's determination to bring state agencies into line was clearly good news, although more funding was also essential for OSP to proceed with the center designation process and other key components of the plan. That, plus more support for planning in key state agencies such as DEP, DOT and DCA, was not forthcoming from a still-reluctant legislature. With strong evidence that the citizens of New Jersey were behind Whitman, however, it was a fight many believed she could win (MSM 1998a, 1; Lawrence 1998, 17).

Moving to Smart Growth, 1999–2001

In early 1999 Governor Whitman initiated the transfer of OSP from the Treasury Department to the Department of Community Affairs (DCA). Viewed with some skepticism at the time by plan supporters, the transfer was actually a major plus for the implementation of the 1992 plan and preparations for the new plan to be adopted in March 2001. DCA head Jane M. Kenny, OSP Director Herbert Simmens, and SPC Chair Joseph Maraziti worked together with Whitman's full support to move smart growth initiatives forward. Kenny established a new unit, headed by Martin Bierbaum, "devoted on a full-time basis to increasing awareness and compliance by state agencies with State Plan principles," and added to the staff capacity of OSP (NJOSP 2000a, 2).

Released in March 1997, the preliminary plan aimed to strengthen the basic concepts of the 1992 plan by adding several new features: a vision statement for 2020; indicators to measure progress in meeting state plan goals; new design policies; and more specific strategies on plan implementation. In the comparison phase, the 21 counties reviewed their own plans and those of their municipalities for conformance with the preliminary plan, leading to the negotiation phase, highlighting areas of agreement and disagreement in 40 public negotiation meetings. The State Planning Commission accepted most of the suggested changes, leading to its adoption of the interim plan on March 6, 1999 (NJSPC 1999). Next steps included the impact assessment by Robert Burchell of Rutgers University and the adoption of the final plan in March 2001 (NJOSP 2000b, 12).

Strengthening the Implementation of the 1992 Plan

The 1992 plan remained in effect until the adoption of the new Development and Redevelopment Plan in 2001. Through Whitman's leadership, the new team at DCA, the staff of NJF and increasing support for smart growth initiatives by citizens, counties, municipalities and others, substantial plan implementation took place during 1999–2001.

Whitman's state budget for FY 2000 included $3 million, approved by the legislature, for smart growth planning grants. She later included another $3 million in the FY 2001 budget, and $3 million for FY 2002. In announcing the first round of awards under this program, involving 92 municipalities and seven counties, Whitman noted that the grants were aimed at developing plans that will lead to more livable and sustainable communities. She also stressed that "smart growth doesn't mean no growth. It means building where it makes sense and preserving land as much as we can. It means seeking a balance." Whitman added, "I'm proud of the level of commitment for smart growth we are seeing around the state. Communities are serious about fighting sprawl, and I'm pleased to say that they are crossing municipal boundaries to work together on regional solutions" (NJOSP 2000d, 6).

DCA and OSP administered the previously unavailable smart growth planning grants to encourage counties and cities to implement smart growth approaches. The largest awards were announced by the governor in March 2000 (NJOSP 2000d; NJSPC 2000).

- $300,000 to Sussex County for a countywide strategic plan

- $250,000 to Atlantic County for a growth management plan

- $250,000 to Monmouth County for its Route 9 corridor project

- $250,000 to the City of Trenton for its Canal Banks/West End community schools planning

- $200,000 to Hudson County Riverfront Walkway

The state's Brownfields Redevelopment Task Force was another example of putting dollars on the table to further smart growth initiatives. Chaired by DCA Commissioner Kenny and staffed by OSP, the task force involved a wide range of agencies aimed at promoting better utilization of brownfield sites in redevelopment efforts. In the FY 2001 budget, the legislature appropriated $15 million for brownfields redevelopment as part of an Urban Site Acquisition Program to "be used for acquisition and/or cleanup of certain sites when there is a gap in financing." The task force was busy in a number of other activities "to encourage more and better utilization of brownfield sites as part of smart growth initiatives" (NJOSP 2000c, 18–19).

Another aspect of the smart growth movement was New Jersey DEP's Watershed Management Planning Initiative. DEP divided the state into 20 watershed management areas as part of the long-awaited move toward a watershed-based approach to water quality and supply issues. The boundaries were drawn along natural, not political, lines, with smaller watersheds grouped together, much like Florida's widely praised regional water management districts. DEP contracted with the Regional Planning Partnership (RPP, formerly MSM Regional Council) to lead the development of watershed plans over the next four years. RPP's reputation in land use planning and research and computer modeling capacity should allow the Public Advisory Committee overseeing the development of comprehensive plans for each watershed to achieve its goal of "developing policies to reduce impervious cover, preserve important natural resources, and direct growth to areas where infrastructure already exists" (RPP 2000, 1–2).

New Jersey Future and Governor Whitman: A Unique Partnership

On May 20, 1999, NJF convened a Sustainable State Leadership Conference at which the organization unveiled an agenda featuring the following 11 goals (NJF 1999c):

1. Economic vitality

2. Equity

3. Strong community, culture and recreation

4. Quality education

5. Good government

6. Decent housing

7. Healthy people

8. Efficient transportation and land use

9. Natural and ecological integrity

10. Protected natural resources

11. Minimal pollution and waste

Whitman gave the keynote address at the conference, noting that in her second inaugural address she had set a goal for New Jersey "to become a fully sustainable state." She went on to endorse NJF's sustainability goals and announced an executive order that directed all state departments and agencies to: (1) pursue, as appropriate, policies that comport with the sustainability goals outlined in NJF's agenda; (2) collaborate in the exchange of information among departments and agencies, and establish institutional mechanisms to encourage and facilitate achievement of these goals; and (3) report to the governor on June 1, 2000, and every year thereafter, on their progress toward goal attainment (NJF 1999a; 1999b).

Without question, NJF and Whitman were united in their smart growth goal, but New Jersey also foresaw major roadblocks to achieving that goal: the uncertain political future marked by Whitman's impending departure to join the Bush administration, and what NJF (2000a, 1) called the state's "dirty secret"—lack of affordable housing for New Jersey's workers. A Rutgers University projection of 908,000 new residents and 802,000 new jobs in the next 20 years showed that workers would most likely have to live in Pennsylvania because they could not afford New Jersey's housing prices. New Jersey's Council on Affordable Housing estimated that since 1985 it had provided 24,000 houses against a need for 86,000; independent sources put the need much higher. Clearly, the affordable housing component of the state's smart growth effort fell far short of providing appropriately located affordable housing.

At a conference held on September 15, 2000, sponsored by NJF, Executive Director Barbara Lawrence stressed another unfinished agenda item: New Jersey's counterproductive tax system. She pointed out that New Jersey relied more on property taxes than any other state, in effect pushing local governments to a "race for development" to increase revenues. Lawrence saw significant failures in three interrelated systems: taxes; affordable housing; and the failure of the planning system to overcome local governments planning and acting in isolation from each other. In particular she noted that local zoning is largely untouched by regional needs (NJF 2000b, 5).

Smart Growth and the Legislature

New Jersey's legislature is in session all year, with only occasional breaks. The 1999, 2000 and 2001 legislative sessions had 25 Republicans and 15 Democrats in the Senate and 45 Republicans and 35 Democrats in the Assembly. Republican majorities generally have not been supportive of the smart growth initiatives (i.e., the State Planning Act of 1985 or the first [1992] or second [2001] State Development and Redevelopment Plans). With rising support for such actions by citizens and organized groups, and Governor Whitman's support of budgets with funding incentives (such as the smart growth grants), however, the legislative leadership was pressured to approve some bills, especially budget items, favorable to smart growth.

The general rule was that "bad" bills that would weaken the planning and growth management system either did not clear the legislature because they faced a sure veto by the governor or, if they did get through, were vetoed. Conversely, bills supportive of moves to strengthen the system typically did not clear the legislature at all. For example, Democratic Senator John Adler introduced bills to the 2000 legislature that would, had they passed,

- encourage municipal plan consistency with the state plan (SB 1499);

- appropriate $150 million for a Brownfields Redevelopment Grant Program (SB 1498);

- strengthen provisions of the Coastal Area Facility Review Act (CAFRA) of certain coastal developments (SB 298); and

- authorize bonds to create a $250 million fund for the upgrading or replacement of infrastructure and production of affordable housing in designated urban and rural centers (SB 1500).

Senator Adler and moderate Republican Senator William Schluter also introduced a bill calling for a constitutional convention on property tax reform.

An example of legislative action with negative impacts for smart growth involved the Transportation Trust Fund, itself a positive move to provide funds for rebuilding roads and bridges and for mass transit. The initial draft of the legislation "cited the state plan for guidance on where new construction should occur. State officials and legislators, nervous about offending builders, removed this language from the final bill, greatly weakening it as a guide for smarter growth" (NJF 2001, 1 and 4).

Adoption of the Second State Plan, March 2001

The adoption on March 1, 2001, of the new State Development and Redevelopment Plan took longer than smart growth supporters in New Jersey had hoped. They viewed the final result as potentially

moving toward a sustainable future by improving coordination among state, regional and local plans, assuming its implementation would be more effective than the 1992 plan. The new plan "presents new concepts such as sustainable development, new urbanism, strong connections between transportation and land use, and capacity-based planning" (NJSPC 2001, 2). The plan included the following components:

- Vision statement: Describes New Jersey in 2020 when the goals of the state plan are to be achieved.

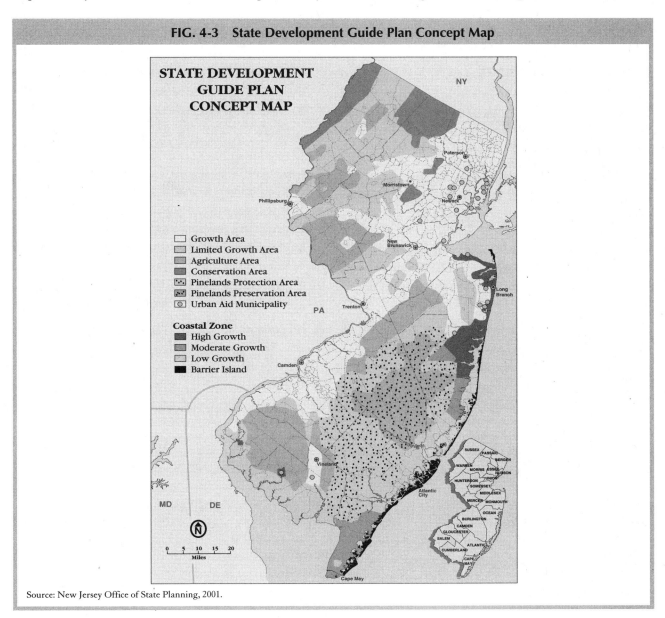

FIG. 4-3 State Development Guide Plan Concept Map

Source: New Jersey Office of State Planning, 2001.

■ Goals and strategies: Describes the eight goals that came from the State Planning Act and strategies for achieving each goal.

■ Statewide policies: Provides specific guidance to state and local officials on a broad range of issues in 19 different categories.

■ State plan policy map: Identifies areas for growth, limited growth, agriculture, open space, conservation and other appropriate designations required by the State Planning Act. (NJSPC 2001, 2, 8)

The plan aimed at achieving eight state planning goals by coordinating public and private actions to guide future growth into compact, ecologically designed forms of development and redevelopment. It also listed 19 statewide policies meant to guide municipal, county, regional and state planning initiatives.

The plan defined five planning areas (metropolitan, suburban, fringe, rural and environmentally sensitive) and outlined their importance in guiding the application of the plan's statewide policies. The "centers and environs" section defines *centers* as "compact forms of development that, compared to sprawl development, consume less land, deplete fewer natural resources, and are more efficient in the delivery of public services," and *environs* as "the land outside centers, including farmland, greenbelts, open spaces, and large forest tracts, that are protected from inappropriate development" (NJSPC 2001, 21–25, 27–31).

The impact assessment of the second state plan was carried out under the direction of Robert Burchell of Rutgers University, who had also directed the impact assessment of the first plan, and the results were much the same. The basic methodology used in the first analysis was used again, showing estimates of costs and other savings when comparing the trend plan (continuing to sprawl) with outcomes that assumed the full implementation of the state plan to 2020. The savings in the various categories assessed were summarized as follows (NJSPC 2001, 32):

■ Savings of $160 million annually to towns, counties, school districts

■ 870 fewer centerline miles of roads; savings of $870 million in local road costs

■ Savings of $1.45 billion in water and sewer costs

■ A 27,000 increase in work trips by transit users

■ 122,000 fewer acres of land (one-third less than current trends) would be converted to development, including 68,000 acres of farmland and 45,000 areas of environmentally fragile land

■ Reversal of a projected $340 million loss in household income in urban communities, to a gain of $3 billion

■ Improvements in the quantity and quality of intergovernmental contacts and relationships

Goals and Policies of the Second State Plan, 2001

State Planning Goals	State Planning Policies	
1. Revitalize the state's cities and towns	1. Equity	11. Water resources
2. Conserve the state's natural resources and systems	2. Comprehensive planning	12. Open lands and natural systems
3. Promote beneficial economic growth, development and renewal for all state residents	3. Public investment priorities	13. Energy resources
4. Protect the environment, prevent and clean up pollution	4. Infrastructure investments	14. Waste management, recycling and brownfields
5. Provide adequate public facilities and services at a reasonable cost	5. Economic development	15. Agriculture
6. Provide adequate housing at a reasonable cost	6. Urban revitalization	16. Coastal resources
7. Preserve and enhance areas with historic, cultural, scenic, open space and recreational value	7. Housing	17. Planning regions established by statute (i.e., the Pinelands and Hackensack Meadowlands)
8. Ensure sound and integrated planning and implementation statewide	8. Transportation	18. Special resource areas
	9. Historic, cultural and scenic resources	19. Design
	10. Air resources	

Source: NJSPC, 2001, 9, 13–19

The second Development and Redevelopment Plan was thus finally in place as the implementation arm of the State Planning Act adopted more than 16 years earlier in 1985. The failure of the system to achieve its goals during that time can be attributed to the failure to implement the first Development and Redevelopment Plan of 1992 in all its dimensions.

Post-Whitman Politics and the 2001 Election

One of the few early appointments by President George W. Bush favored by smart growth advocates was his nomination of Governor Whitman as administrator of the U.S. Environmental Protection Agency. However, features of the New Jersey governance system affected the implementation of smart growth actions in the state after Whitman left office.

New Jersey has no lieutenant governor, so the president of the Senate keeps that position and becomes acting governor until an election can be held. Accordingly, Republican Senate leader Donald DiFrancesco was sworn in as acting governor on January 31, 2001. Primaries were scheduled for June 5, and the general election in November 2001. Until May, when he was persuaded to drop his candidacy, DiFrancesco's term as acting governor was largely taken up with his run for governor, although he tried to position himself as supportive of funding some smart growth initiatives. His opponent in the Republican primary was Bret Schundler, mayor of Jersey City, who is very conservative and against anything involving smart growth. The unopposed Democratic candidate for governor, James McGreevey, mayor of Woodbridge, had run a strong race against Whitman in the November 1997 governor's election and expressed strong support for smart growth in his campaign.

In a move supported strongly by Republicans and opposed just as strongly by Democrats, the primaries were moved to June 26, 2001 (Halbfinger 2001a). In addition, a new legislative map for the Assembly and Senate, drawn up under a procedure set by the New Jersey Constitution, involved a Legislative Apportionment Commission and resulted in a political free-for-all. Furthermore, the Republican party leadership became convinced that Schundler had little or no chance of defeating McGreevey, who enjoyed a well-established record as a moderate. After DiFrancesco dropped out of the race, in part because of questionable financial practices brought up by Schundler, the leadership persuaded the Republican legislature to delay the election by three weeks to give Robert Franks time to organize his campaign. Franks was a moderate former New Jersey congressman who ran a strong race for the U.S. Senate in 2000 but lost against Democrat Jon S. Corzine. A survey by Fairleigh Dickinson University showed Franks and McGreevey in a "dead heat" in a face-to-face match-up, but McGreevey as a strong winner if Schundler were his opponent in the November election. It was not clear at the time whether Franks would support smart growth strategies for New Jersey, while McGreevey certainly would (Halbfinger 2001b).

The primary election results went against the tradition in New Jersey of moderates in either party winning over extremists of the right or left, when rightwinger Schundler won over middle-of-the-roader Franks by a margin of 193,342 to 143,606. Schundler's victory set the stage for the November 2001 general election in which McGreevey reinforced his standing as a moderate and Schundler tried to assure everyone that he believed in "everything in moderation" (Purdy 2001b, 22; Purdy 2001a, 20). McGreevey defeated Schundler by 1,256,853 votes to 928,174. In the legislature, the Democrats came close to realizing their goal of gaining control of both the General Assembly and the Senate for the first time since 1991, partly as the result of the reapportionment battle. The election resulted in 42 Democrats, 37 Republicans, and one Green party member in the General Assembly, and a 20–20 tie in the Senate.

The Early Years of the McGreevey Administration, 2002–2003

Just after he took office in January 2002, Governor McGreevey signed Executive Order No 4., which put in place two actions proposed by NJF: creating a cabinet-level Smart Growth Policy Council and a "smart growth shield." The executive order "promise[d] to change the way [the] state makes the thousands of decisions annually that help shape where and how development takes place in New Jersey"—certainly an aggressive, comprehensive call for specific actions in the direction of smart growth (New Jersey Office of the Governor 2002; NJF 2002a, 1). The key components of the order

- authorized the state attorney general to defend or intervene on behalf of towns, when their smart growth planning or zoning is challenged in cases of statewide significance;

- ordered that school construction abide by smart growth principles, helping to revitalize existing communities and preserve open space;

- required streamlined initiatives and points of contact for redeveloping communities;

- ordered transportation and infrastructure rules and spending to be consistent with the principles of smart growth and the state plan; and

- created a Smart Growth [Policy] Council made up of cabinet officers and other leaders from the executive branch of government, to coordinate their planning, spending and regulations with each other, and with New Jersey's State Plan. (NJF 2002a, 1)

The council's duties were awesome to say the least, but this good news came only a week after very bad news for New Jersey's smart growth advocates. In the face of probably the largest budget deficit of any state in the nation, the entire OSP staff was cut, possibly incorrectly in the midst of political chaos, but creating a "firestorm" of opposition led by NJF. OSP was later renamed the Office of Smart Growth, and funding was returned to rehire about 70 percent of the former OSP staff.

Addressing the Budget Shortfall: A Mix of Pain and Gain

Every state faced a budget shortfall in 2002, but according to McGreevey, if his budget proposals were not enacted, New Jersey's shortfall would be "more than 20 percent of the total budget.... No state has ever had a deficit as high on a percentage basis." Various estimates placed the gap from $5.3 to $6 billion of a total of $23.6 billion. Efforts to raise taxes

as part of the solution were haunted by the "Florio factor," referring to the backlash against a much-needed tax increase by Governor Florio in 1990 that led to Democrats losing both the governorship and the legislature for the next decade. Clearly, a tax increase was needed, but the new governor had pledged not to raise taxes if elected. McGreevey—justifiably blaming the preceding Republican legislature and governors for the budget shortfall—was forced to find some new sources of revenue.

In his budget proposal for fiscal 2003 (put forward March 26, 2002), McGreevey proposed both budget cuts and tax increases to deal with the crisis. Spending cuts included parks ($10 million in maintenance funds) and universities (state aid reduced by $64.3 million), a 5 percent cut for all state departments, and a $133 million reduction in funds for capital projects such as roads, buildings and dams. On the tax front, McGreevey proposed an increase in cigarette taxes and the sale of $1.1 billion in bonds against the state's tobacco settlement claim. He also ordered a revision of the state's corporate tax code that would cause major companies to pay $500 million a year more to the state. A number of other funds were tapped or shifted in an effort to make up the shortfall. While some Republicans admitted that McGreevey had little choice in the cuts and tax increases he proposed, many others felt the increase in corporate taxes would do more harm than good. In any event, some of the governor's proposals would require legislative action (Kocieniewski 2002).

On the plus side, in 2002, voters in New Jersey, as many in other states across the nation, approved funds to buy and preserve open space. As noted previously, New Jersey voters had supported Governor Whitman's 10-year plan to protect some one million acres of land from development, and 185 towns in 19 of New Jersey's 21 counties had already taken some actions related to open space preservation. The issue is especially critical in New Jersey, the state with the highest percentage of developed land in the nation—some 41 percent. However, while saving a "patchwork" of open spaces can be an important victory, "it is never going to take the place of real land use planning that directs development toward areas that can sustain it and preserves open space in the places that need it most" (*New York Times* 2002, A-26).

In early winter 2002, NJF reiterated its belief that full implementation of the state plan could save $2.3 billion over 20 years, stressed the need for "bold leadership at the state level," and listed five key priorities drawn from its policy guide (NJF 2002b, 2–3).

1. Create a Cabinet-level post for smart growth

2. Adopt new watershed protection rules to protect water quality and preserve vital open land

3. Defend all municipalities that adopt master plans and zoning ordinances consistent with the state plan

4. Revitalize communities and reduce traffic through new priorities for transportation spending

5. Give municipalities new tools for redevelopment and conserving open space

Support from Smart Growth Advocates

With a new governor promising greater attention to planning and growth management, NJF saw the 17-member State Planning Commission as ideally suited to lead the way to smarter growth. One key positive was SPC's ability to focus on the implementation of the state plan adopted in March 2001, having put to rest the debate over updating and revising it. On the negative side, NJF noted that urban viewpoints were "sorely underrepresented" as were local governments (NJF 2002b, 1, 5).

McGreevey made his first six appointments to SPC in early 2002, and all were confirmed before the end of the year. Timothy J. Touhey, named chair on July 22, 2002, had a strong record of affordable housing initiatives in New Jersey, and his appointment was seen by smart growth advocates, including NJF, as a positive step (NJF 2003a, 2–3). Touhey remarked that the governor's charge to move the state plan forward was greatly strengthened by naming smart growth as his first priority. By making it clear that the state would not subsidize sprawl, the governor had given "a focus to our priorities and a challenge to put action with his words." Like Maraziti and others before him, Touhey stressed the importance of all key actors, confirming that their priorities would be on

> **Governor McGreevey's
> Ten Smart Growth Principles**
>
> 1. Mix land uses
> 2. Take advantage of compact building design
> 3. Create a range of housing opportunities and choices
> 4. Create walkable neighborhoods
> 5. Foster distinctive, attractive communities with a strong sense of place
> 6. Preserve open space, farmland, natural beauty and critical environmental areas
> 7. Strengthen and direct development towards existing communities
> 8. Provide a variety of transportation choices
> 9. Make development decisions predictable, fair and cost effective
> 10. Encourage community and stakeholder collaboration in development decisions
>
> Source: NJMC, 2003b

implementing the state plan, as well as bringing state agencies, especially their funding decisions, fully into support of smart growth (NJF 2003a, 2).

RPP continued to advocate sound planning practices and promote regional cooperation in the three central state counties: Middlesex, Somerset and Mercer. Its aims were to prevent the corridor from being overrun by inappropriate growth and to ensure the availability of affordable housing and viable transportation options. Vision 2050, RPP's new concept plan, was aimed at demonstrating how smart growth measures can be implemented. The emphasis was on access and density, since density "helps us to reduce land consumption and mitigate the impact of development on the environment." Planning for both was seen as providing the key elements of smart growth: "A pedestrian-friendly environment [that] provides opportunities for social interaction, commerce, affordable housing and public amenities." RPP was pushing the adoption of this smart growth strategy statewide, but was also realistic about how far New Jersey had to go to get there. In a blunt assessment of just where New Jersey stood on smart growth in early 2003, RPP held

> While smart growth shows us the way forward, it is completely opposite to the current system of planning practices, state and local regulations, and infrastructure decision-making. Turning this

system around is not just about turning around an ocean liner; it means turning around a fleet of ocean liners. It is an enormous challenge. It is, however, the only way out of our lose/lose debate over congestion. (RPP 2003a, 2)

In his speech to a joint session of the New Jersey legislature on January 14, 2003, McGreevey issued a fervent call to legislators to curb the development and sprawl that was devouring 50 acres a day: "Let me say to those who profit from strip malls and McMansions, if you reap the benefits you must now take responsibility for the costs." The speech stressed overdevelopment as the root cause of rising property taxes. The governor also proposed legislation to let towns enact year-long moratoria on development, counteract the costs of new building by imposing fees, and discourage or halt development in environmentally sensitive locations through adoption of new rules and regulations. Smart growth advocates praised the speech, but were concerned about the demonization of builders; the New Jersey Builders Association condemned it as an effort to stop all construction of new housing in the state. Many of McGreevey's smart growth strategies would require incentives and disincentives requiring new dollars as part of the equation, and while the governor's budget proposals did call for a variety of new revenues, the "ghost of Governor Florio" still blocked something like an increase in the income tax (Mansnerus 2003, C-12).

RPP's response to this State of the State address was strongly favorable, noting that the governor had cited sprawl as the biggest threat to the state's quality of life and pointed to regional planning as the way to halt that sprawl. Once again, however, RPP sounded a note of realism about some key difficulties in implementing the governor's vision for a smart growth future:

> Although New Jersey residents recognize the need for regional planning and, when polled, say they would accept a shift away from local controls, most stakeholder groups are opposed: builders don't want another regulatory layer, environmentalists fear weaker protections, counties fear the lack of resources and Home Rulers don't want to lose control. (RPP 2003b, 1)

RPP has proposed a smart growth "to do" list for the governor covering most of the smart growth landscape, stressed the importance of water conservation measures, called property tax reform the key to smart growth, and laid out seven recommendations for tax reform in a November 2003 Symposium on Property Tax Reform, stressing such things as regional tax sharing.

The Pinelands, Meadowlands and Highlands Cases

One of the goals of the State Planning Act was to assure the integration of special regional efforts with the full implementation of the state plan. A brief analysis of the origins and developments of the Pinelands, Hackensack Meadowlands and Highlands initiatives is included here to illustrate how planning has moved forward and the degree to which there is consistency between regional and state goals.

The Pinelands

The New Jersey Pinelands effort is widely viewed as a significant success of national and even international significance in balancing growth and natural systems to preserve the best of both. The Pinelands is surrounded by one of the nation's most densely populated regions and constitutes over one million acres of unique forests of pygmy pines and oaks, the ruins of long-deserted towns and factories, barely passable sand roads, cedar swamps, and inland marshes and bogs (see NJ Pinelands Commission Web site). The Pinelands covers 22 percent of the total land area of the state and includes 56 municipalities and seven of New Jersey's 21 counties.

Threatened with being overrun by tides of urban development from metropolitan Philadelphia, northern New Jersey and New York, plus Atlantic City's casino boom, something approaching a miracle has occurred in the last 25 years. A unique partnership between the federal government and the state has led to one of the most successful efforts in the nation to manage growth and change in a complex and vulnerable region. The Pinelands experience is a model of where the state plan needs to lead the rest of New Jersey.

In 1978 the U.S. Congress designated the Pinelands National Reserve, the first in the nation, where governments at every level—from Washington, DC, down to local planning boards—could help shape the Pinelands' future in keeping with some basic guidelines. By executive order in early 1979, Governor Brendan Byrne established the Pinelands Commission, through which the state was to take the lead in evaluating the Pinelands' resources and how best to balance their protection with new development. Of the 15 members of the commission, seven were appointed by the governor, one by each of the seven counties in the region, and one by the U.S. Secretary of the Interior.

The state legislature passed the Pinelands Protection Act in June 1979, confirming the temporary limits on development that Byrne had established. County and municipal master plans and land use ordinances were required to conform with the comprehensive management plan the Pinelands Commission would develop. The act also set the key parameters of the plan: highly regulated development in the nearly 300,000-acre preservation area (large tracts of unbroken forest and most of the blueberry and cranberry area), and a larger protection area that contained a mix of valuable environmental features, farmland, hamlets, subdivisions and towns.

Much was at stake in the effort to devise and implement a plan to protect natural areas and channel development into areas suitable for growth. A shallow aquifer was estimated to hold over 17 trillion gallons; native plants, birds, reptiles and mammals (many threatened or endangered) had been identified. The comprehensive plan's land classification scheme was broken down into several subareas: agricultural production areas, forest areas, and rural development areas. These areas involved limiting development, yet with a commitment to accommodating projected growth in the region. Incentives and disincentives were designed to make increased densities acceptable, even welcome, in the designated growth areas. The comprehensive plan estimated that 175,000 new housing units could be built in urban growth areas.

Pinelands development credits were allocated to landowners in areas where development would be prohibited or limited; the credits could be purchased by developers who would, through the credit system, be allowed increased densities in the growth areas. While efforts in other areas to use such credits have faltered or failed without political support, the Pinelands development rights system has steadily grown in scope and been a key to directing growth away from preserve ("sending") areas and into growth ("receiving") areas.

Success in the early years was assisted by the Pinelands Development Credit Bank, which was established to acquire development credits from landowners who had their right to develop restricted. The bank held the credits until there were developers ready to purchase them in order to receive higher densities in the growth areas. Other incentives included state and federal dollars, allocated to the receiving areas that local governments earmarked as growth areas under the plan, to help in providing the infrastructure needed to accommodate the added development (a way to fund a concurrency requirement). A 1986 bond issue provided much of the infrastructure funding.

The Pinelands transfer of development rights (TDR) system is regarded by many as the most successful use of such a credit concept in the nation. Unlike other efforts in New Jersey and around the country to implement smart growth systems, the Pinelands Protection Act gives the Pinelands Commission the power to reject projects that fail to meet the standards of the Pinelands Comprehensive Management Plan. The Pinelands also offers a regional governance system that enjoys sustained political support. Both sending and receiving areas are clearly defined, and the regulatory system requires that local government actions be consistent with the regional comprehensive plan. At the same time, local government participation is made much more palatable by the funding of infrastructure by state and federal sources needed to support the density allocations to the growth centers. It is ironic that New Jersey, which has struggled to devise an effective regional component for its state plan, has at hand an example of one of the most effective systems in the nation to manage growth and change in a complex region subject to heavy growth pressures.

The Hackensack Meadowlands

The effort to devise an effective regional system in the Hackensack Meadowlands region of northeastern New Jersey also has some important accomplishments to its credit, but has not been nearly as successful as the Pinelands experience. The Hackensack Meadowlands District is a 30-square mile area, including all or part of 14 municipalities and two counties. The area once contained 17,000 acres of wetlands, about half of which were lost to filling and draining for development; the remaining acres have suffered from widespread damage due to landfills and unregulated dumping.

The Hackensack Meadowlands Development Commission (HMDC) was created by the New Jersey legislature in 1969 to regulate economic development, protect the environment and provide for the solid waste needs of the region. It was renamed the New Jersey Meadowlands Commission (NJMC) in August 2001. During its first 20 years, the commission managed to protect some wetland areas and eliminate almost all garbage dumping, ending an era during which 40 percent of the state's garbage was heaped into some 27 sites located throughout the wetlands area. All but one of the dumps were closed, although the leaking of toxic materials was halted in only five of the 26 closed dumps.

The master plan of NJMC, which amends the original 1970 plan, focuses additionally on curbing urban sprawl; cultivating desirable housing, community facilities and mass transit; and strengthening coordination between public and private stakeholders shaping land use. While balancing environmental and economic needs, the vision of the master plan includes thoughtful development on upland sites, creating an integrated multimodal transportation network, and securing better commercial enterprises on brownfield sites (NJMC 2003b). All of these initiatives fall under the general goal of smart growth.

NJMC uses Governor McGreevey's principles for smart growth for decisions about how and where to develop the meadowlands district. NJMC's master plan also includes the Sustainable Meadowlands initiative, which tracks sustainability of the district. It reinforces NJMC's dual commitment to preserving the area's natural resources and fostering a sustainable regional economy.

Another effort to deal with land use issues in the Meadowlands has involved the development of a Special Area Management Plan (SAMP) to address long-term environmental protection and cleanup, as well as balance additional development against these goals. SAMP is a collective effort of NJMC, the U.S. EPA, the U.S. Army Corps of Engineers, and the New Jersey DEP. SAMP goals are to "(1) provide for natural resource protection and reasonable economic growth and (2) to provide a program of environmental benefits for the district" (U.S. EPA 1999).

The 1995 environmental impact statement for the project describes its major features: 840 acres of wetlands designated for development; some 3,400 acres of wetlands designated for enhancement and restoration; and 7,600 acres of wetlands slated for permanent protection through deed restrictions, TDRs and outright purchase. A billion-dollar program for environmental cleanup, enhancement and management is included in the SAMP proposal, involving a comprehensive and cumulative impact analysis to address the problems of a significant ecological resource. Carol Browner, director of the U.S. EPA under the Clinton administration, described it as "one of the first land use planning efforts in the country to fully integrate environmental needs and human uses" (U.S. Water News Online 1996). While most observers agree that SAMP would be an improvement over past efforts, for some it was too little in the way of environmental protection and restoration and too much in the way of development. Some development interests, however, thought the opposite.[3]

In June 1999 the U.S. EPA selected the Hackensack Meadowlands Development Commission to be part of a brownfields pilot program. Focusing on 210 acres in the Paterson Plank Road area, in Bergen

---

3. For a positive view, see U.S. EPA Director Carol Browner's comments in U.S. Water News Online (1996). For a negative view, see New Jersey Audubon Society (1994). For a general description of the Meadowlands and the development of SAMP, see U.S. Environmental Protection Agency, Hackensack Meadowlands District (http://www.epa.gov/ecoplaces/part2/region2/site9.html).

County, the pilot is a joint effort by EPA and HMDC (now NJMC) to promote environmental preservation; economic development for increased revenue for infrastructure improvements; and brownfield cleanup and redevelopment. To achieve these goals, NJMC has inventoried brownfields, prepared environmental assessments and cleanup strategies, created a comprehensive land use plan, identified funding sources, and educated the community about the pilot's activities and encouraged citizen participation (U.S. EPA 1999).

In September 2003 NJMC announced a redevelopment plan for Paterson Plank Road consisting of four pedestrian-friendly zones of development. Two zones will include banks, galleries, restaurants, shops and theaters; one will offer offices and research centers; and one will focus on parks, trails and pedestrian water-crossings that take advantage of the surrounding scenic wetlands. "Working together with the state, the Meadowlands Commission has charted a course for development that is both wise and consistent with Governor James McGreevey's vision for balanced growth," said Susan Bass Levin of NJMC. "This redevelopment plan sets the stage for a new gateway into the Meadowlands...that will exhibit both the Meadowlands District's economic strength and ecological value" (NJMC 2003a).

The Highlands

The vast Highlands landscape—a region stretching from western Connecticut across New York's Lower Hudson Valley, northern New Jersey, and into east-central Pennsylvania—is rich in wilderness areas, natural resources and recreational opportunities, including some 200,000 acres of public open space. The area cuts across the heart of the most urbanized region in the U.S., yet provides clean drinking water for 12 million metropolitan residents and large patches of unfragmented forest critical to the survival of migratory songbirds. The Highlands still functions as an effective greenbelt, but its future ability to provide such shape and form to the region is in jeopardy. The towns that encompass the Highlands are likely to grow by more than 250,000 people in the next 20 years. Accommodating these new residents (and businesses, roads and public services) in typical

development patterns could result in the Highlands simply becoming a more mountainous part of the suburban sprawl north and west of New York City (Porter and Wallis 2002).

Significant public and private initiatives are now underway to answer this challenge, highlighted by the commitment of the state and other public and private institutions to spend hundreds of millions of dollars over the next 10 years to acquire valuable land. However, increasing land costs mean that funding may not be adequate to conserve more than a fraction of the most critical resources at risk. The Highlands Coalition, established in 1988, leads a grassroots movement comprised of more than 110 local, state, regional and national citizens' organizations that seek to influence government policy to protect the region.

In 2000 Congress directed the U.S. Forest Service to revise its 1992 *New York–New Jersey Highlands Regional Study*, and the update was completed in 2002 (Phelps and Hoppe 2002). It reassessed the region's natural resources, analyzed land cover and potential land use change, identified significant areas to be conserved and protected, and developed eight conservation strategies to protect the long-term integrity of the Highlands. The strategies were to be accomplished through a broad public and private partnership, including information sharing on the region's resource values and management issues; improving state and local planning practices; coordinating regional, interstate and intrastate conservation and stewardship efforts; and measuring and monitoring changes in the area.

Advancing the implementation of these strategies, President George W. Bush signed legislation to protect the forested Highlands Region in Connecticut, New York, New Jersey, and Pennsylvania on November 30, 2004. The measure authorizes $10 million a year over the next 10 years to help protect the Highlands. All four states may apply for money the federal government sets aside to help them buy land. An additional $1 million a year is authorized over the next 10 years for Forest Service programs in the region.

On the state level, the New Jersey Highlands are recognized in the State Plan as a "special resource area," demonstrating the critical environmental importance of the area covering portions of seven counties and 88 municipalities in the northwestern corner of the state. On June 10, 2004, the legislature passed the Highlands Water Protection and Planning Act, and Governor McGreevey signed it on August 10. This historic law institutes protective environmental standards for some 1,250 square miles within the region and provides assistance for coordinated planning efforts through the Office of Smart Growth.

NJF praised the act as an important step in protecting lands that supply drinking water for more than half of all New Jersey residents, but only a first step. The organization detailed six recommendations that it encourages the Highlands Council and local and state officials to take to safeguard water and ensure a high quality of life for the region. The recommendations include a detailed land use plan based on a regional land-and-water capacity analysis, permanent preservation of designated lands, use of land acquisition and transfer mechanisms, monitoring to ensure achievement of master plan goals, and consistency between the Highlands plan and the statewide development plan (NJF 2005b). Taken together the recommendations are far-reaching and will require substantial additional funds for implementation over a considerable timeframe.

Recent Progress Toward a Sustainable Future

Over the 1998–2003 period New Jersey led the nation in the approval of county and municipal conservation-related ballot measures with a total of 250 such measures approved, far ahead of the second highest state, Massachusetts, with 83. New Jersey's local governments were spurred on by former governor Whitman's successful push for a $1 billion bond issue that provided matching funds for local governments (Conservation Fund 2004, 7). New Jersey in 2003 led the nation in passing 32 of its 40 conservation ballot measures. Statewide, 65 percent of voters approved spending $150 million to continue its open space, farmland and historic preservation activities. Voters in Bergen County approved the dedication of one cent per $100 of property taxes to preserve open space,

farmland and historic properties and to improve recreation. This $214 million measure was the largest local measure in the nation in 2003 (Conservation Fund 2004, 1, 3). Much of this success can be linked to the efforts of two key and long-established nonprofit organizations: New Jersey Future and the Regional Planning Partnership.

NJF has continued its vigorous advocacy for a smart growth future for New Jersey. With regard to the 2003 legislative session, NJF called for far-reaching action with an emphasis on implementation:

> While New Jersey's leaders have yet to tackle the fundamental changes necessary for smarter growth, we talked about the issues more and better than ever before. For a long time, people thought smart growth was simply buying open space. Today, there's an increased awareness that smart growth doesn't mean no growth. Instead, it means using government's regulatory and spending powers to shape how and where development occurs, using growth to enhance our communities in ways that save taxpayers the cost of new and redundant infrastructure and protect the best remaining open lands and natural resources, without the need to buy it all. (NJF 2003b, 6)

A major package of bills to address sprawl, promised by McGreevey in January 2003, went largely undelivered that year, including two different bills to expand the use of TDRs statewide and action on impact fees to expand the fees assessed on new development to help cover the cost of new school facilities (NFJ 2003b, 6). "One of the nation's best TDR bills" did pass in 2004, however; it will be particularly useful because there is nowhere near enough money from government or private sources to simply buy all the land that needs protection. With the new law, towns all over New Jersey can now use this important smart growth tool (NJF 2004b, 1, 5).

In another action with a positive potential for smart growth, in November 2003 voters approved a statewide ballot dedicating one-third of new preservation funds for the Highlands region and additional funds for the purchase of open space. McGreevey also set up a Highlands Task Force of state and local officials to make recommendations for managing development and protecting the region's critical resources. The group's report was released on March 13, 2004, with six key recommendations for enactment of more stringent protections through a regionwide, coordinated program of land acquisition, regulation and comprehensive planning (Highlands Task Force 2004).

With passage of the Highlands Water Protection and Planning Act (Senate Bill 1) on June 10, 2004, those goals are being addressed. The state of New Jersey has a critical interest in conserving its water supply, and in order to assure that happens, the governor and legislature proposed "strict protections for some 370,000 acres of core watershed lands through land purchases, new environmental regulations, and a regional plan that dictates strict limits on development. These measures represent a bold step by state leaders rightfully concerned about development pressures in the region with a history of five droughts in the past 13 years" (NJF 2004b, 5).

The governor left no doubt about his pleasure at the legislature's passage of the bill. "New Jersey has been waiting for decades for this day," he stated. "Local and state officials along with members of the public have sought protection for the Highlands for years, and today, this administration and this Legislature got it done" (McGreevey 2004, 1). Given the fact that there is still strong opposition in New Jersey to almost any move toward smart growth, much less one as sweeping as this one, the strong support of the governor will be critical to its full and timely implementation.

Another critical issue in 2004 is public review of cross-acceptance, as required every three years. The special challenges of this process include the anticipated heavy amount of public comment and the State Planning Commission's plan to "accept public comments and begin refining a new process for endorsing county and municipal plans as consistent with the State Plan simultaneous with the collection of cross-acceptance feedback on the state plan itself" (NJF 2003b, 1). NJF and its smart growth allies do not believe the state is prepared for either of those challenges.

The schedules for the cross-acceptance and plan endorsement processes are very demanding, stretching from November 2003 to May 2005, with the adoption of the new state plan. To meet such a schedule and be assured of quality projects at the various stages, NJF has called for four specific actions, noting

that "the upcoming 18-months of update and cross-acceptance [will be] the most critical the state has ever undertaken."

- The Office of Smart Growth needs reallocation of resources and additional professional expertise.

- The State Planning Commission must engage municipalities on their plans for growth, not merely preservation, by providing growth projections and requiring growth plans to be a part of the municipal response.

- A more detailed proposal for Plan Endorsement is needed for public hearings to be meaningful.... Key questions: What are the final criteria for endorsement? What incentives will be used to encourage compliance? What happens to communities ready to enter into Plan Endorsement now? Is the process simple and quick enough to be attractive?

- The state must require its other departments to follow the lead of the DEP in drafting regulations and especially spending plans, that support the State Plan, even as the update is underway. (NJF 2003b, 5)

New Jersey Future also supported four important bills in the 2004 session:

- S 441, to amend the state's Municipal Land Use Law to require that municipal master plans be consistent with the State Development and Redevelopment Plan.

- A 1099, to establish a process to encourage inter-municipal cooperation in planning for developments that have impacts beyond municipal borders and would establish a procedure for the review of such development applications.

- S 274/A 1356, the "Smart Growth Tax Credit Act," to provide a corporate business tax credit and a gross income tax credit for certain smart growth developments.

- S 198, to require State Development and Redevelopment Plan consistency review upon introduction of each legislative bill. (NJF 2004b, 2)

While their fate is still being debated by the 2004 legislative session, the fact that they have been introduced by key legislators and have strong support from the smart growth coalition suggests a successful outcome. That, of course, is no easy task given the state's budget shortfalls.

Another development of importance to smart growth strategies in the state was the departure of Barbara Lawrence of NJF in October 2004, after 12 years of effective advocacy and leadership. Her successor, George S. Hawkins, assumed his duties in December 2004, after seven years as executive director of the Stony Brook Millstone Watershed Association, where he built the central New Jersey nonprofit into one of the country's largest watershed organizations. Among the challenges he sees for the state and for NJF are sprawl, income disparities and urban decay. While admitting that seeking to preserve the environment and strengthen the economy at the same time is difficult, he stated that is "what makes our approach unique" (NJF 2005a, 2).

RPP, established in 1968 as MSM, is another key nonprofit dedicated to furthering smart growth in New Jersey. While it focuses on regional cooperation and sound land use planning for smart growth in central New Jersey, its key goals are significant anywhere in the state. According to RPP, "Regional planning is needed to determine where to locate growth and conservation areas to balance jobs and housing and protect the environment." RPP has six components of a smart suburb.

1. Protect natural resources and agriculture

2. Develop an urban center containing mixed uses, and be pedestrian oriented

3. Encourage new development or redevelopment in already built areas

4. Provide a full range of housing choices

5. Provide good access to transit

6. Reflect an equitable distribution of the costs and benefits of growth (RPP 2003c, 1)

Citing the major challenges still facing proponents of a smart growth future for New Jersey, RPP noted that, "Smart growth is defined as achieving sustainable development by promoting a prosperous economy, a healthy environment and social equity....

RPP believes that there is no sector more important to achieving smart growth in New Jersey than transportation" (RPP 2003d, 1). The crisis in the state's Transportation Trust Fund could mean a loss of federal money requiring a state match for transportation projects. The result: a major blow to New Jersey's economy, which is dependent on an efficient transportation system. Failure to improve the state's capacity to move goods by rail and truck could be devastating if distributors seek "other ports to forge new sources to the NAFTA markets, bypassing the northeast" (RPP 2003c, 1).

Regarding the environment, New Jersey's air is the second most polluted in the country. Shifting from cars and trucks to other modes such as transit and rail is essential, but will require significant increases in funding. As for equity, "New Jersey is one of the most economically segregated states in the nation. Poverty is concentrated in cities (and spreading to inner ring communities) while the jobs have moved to the suburbs. Public transportation is critical for connecting the labor force to the jobs" (RPP 2003c, 1).

So, if a stable funding source for the fund is a key component to a smart growth future for New Jersey, how to do it? The Governor's Blue Ribbon Commission has recommended a 12.5 cent gas tax increase to be dedicated to the fund. While admitting that increasing taxes is difficult, RPP argues that it is the duty of the governor and the legislature to solve problems facing the economy, environment and society, and RPP holds that a well-presented case would win the support of the public (RPP 2003c, 2).

From January to May 2004, RPP issued a series of reports outlining significant smart growth strategies being pushed by RPP and its allies. Major points from these reports are as follows:

- "Advocate a regional approach to land use planning, with growth targets set for appropriate locations informed by: the needs of the economy, the constraints of the environment, and the opportunities for public transportation." (RPP 2004a, 1)

- With a grant from the Geraldine R. Dodge Foundation, "define hot spots of growth pressure and opportunities for conservation in South Jersey's five Delaware Estuary counties...called variously the 'next big growth area in New Jersey' and a hidden treasure of natural resources." (RPP 2004b, 1)

■ Change the Meadowlands Master Plan to correct the lack of housing and especially affordable housing. (RPP 2004c, 1)

■ Strengthen key elements of smart growth for central New Jersey, where "over half the population lives in communities that are categorized as fiscally distressed or at risk." (RPP 2004d, 1)

■ Relocate its headquarters from Princeton to Trenton to place RPP in a better position to interact with the legislature and state agencies, the press and other nonprofits in promoting its smart growth agenda. (RPP 2004e, 1)

Conclusion

As we look at the prospects for a smart growth future for New Jersey, there are positives and negatives that constitute a significant unfinished agenda. A key plus has been the strong support for many of the principles of smart growth by governors Whitman and McGreevey, and by Acting Governor Richard J. Codey, who took office after McGreevey resigned in November 2004. The General Assembly is firmly controlled by Democrats, who generally support smart growth legislation, but the Senate is evenly split between Democrats and Republicans. However, powerful interest groups remain that do not support critical smart growth actions, including the League of Municipalities, Home Builders Association, and even some environmental groups that have resisted efforts to shape how and where development occurs.

A major positive has been the strong advocacy by New Jersey Future, the Regional Planning Partnership and their allies to strengthen and ensure the full implementation of a comprehensive smart growth system, including funding. New Jersey has in place the kind of network called for in any smart growth strategy to ensure the implementation of its key ingredients, including the full and fair implementation of state, regional and local mandates.

Perhaps most important of all will be the ability of the governor and legislature to mobilize support for significant funding sources that will ensure a strong system of incentives and disincentives, and can bring reluctant local governments, regional systems and state agencies into the process. Major changes in the tax structure are needed to achieve this goal, and in this New Jersey shares the challenge with most other states examined in this book.

References

Association of New Jersey Environmental Commissions. 1987. *The land market in New Jersey's Pinelands: Past and present trends in land use and transfer.* Mendham, NJ. September.

Conservation Fund. 2004. *Common Ground* 15.1 (January/March).

Corporate Alliance for Intelligent Growth (CAIG). 1989. The state plan for development and redevelopment: A report on cross-acceptance.

DeGrove, John M. 1992. *The new frontier for land policy: Planning and growth management in the states.* Cambridge, MA: Lincoln Institute of Land Policy.

Epling, John W. 1989. State growth management: The New Jersey experience. Proceedings of the Institute on Planning, Zoning and Eminent Domain. Dallas, TX: Southwestern Legal Foundation.

Foundation for the Preservation of the American Dream. 1988. Summary and Discussion Paper of Draft Preliminary State Development and Redevelopment Plan. Prepared by John Rahen Kamp Consultants, Inc. February 26, March 8.

Gottlieb, Harry. 1988. For statewide planners, it's policy (and politics). *New Jersey Lawyer* 122(10): September 8.

Halbfinger, David M. 2001a. New Jersey Legislature votes to delay primaries three weeks. *New York Times.* April 24.

———. 2001b. Two Republican candidates and swinging (and stinging). *New York Times.* May 4.

Highlands Task Force. 2004. Action plan: Recommendations to preserve New Jersey's highlands. March. http://www.state.nj.us/highlands/highlands_report.pdf.

Hoskins, Anne E. The structure of land use planning in New Jersey. Undated, unpublished paper. Princeton, NJ: Woodrow Wilson School of International and Public Affairs.

Kocieniewski, David. 2002. In Trenton, plan to avert worst deficit in the nation. *New York Times.* March 27.

Lawrence, Barbara. 1988. New Jersey's controversial growth plan. *Urban Land* 47.1(January):20.

———. 1998. Implementing a statewide plan with (small) carrots and (few) sticks: The New Jersey state development and redevelopment plan. *Environmental and Urban Issues* XXV.2

Fort Lauderdale, FL: FAU/FIU Joint Center for Environmental and Urban Problems.

———. 2004 *Smart growth in New Jersey*. Trenton: NJ: New Jersey Future. June 10.

Mansnerus, Laura. 2003. New Jersey governor speaks fervently on sprawl, but is silent on taxes. *New York Times*. January 15.

McGreevey, James E. 2004. Statement on passage of historic Highlands act. New Jersey Governor's Office. June 10.

Middlesex-Somerset-Mercer (MSM) Regional Council. 1987. Shaping our future: A report on the New Jersey growth management conference. Held at Woodrow Wilson School, Princeton University on February 28, 1986. Princeton, NJ.

———. 1988. Review of the draft preliminary state development and redevelopment plan.

———. 1990. Providing affordable housing in Central New Jersey, 1990: Consequences of the Mount Laurel II Decision and the Fair Housing Act.

———. 1996. *MSM Reports*. March.

———. 1998a. *MSM Reports*. April.

———. 1998b. *MSM Reports*. December.

New Jersey American Planning Association. 1988. NJAPA comments on draft preliminary state development and redevelopment plan. May.

New Jersey Audubon Society. 1994. Hackensack Meadowlands Special Area Management Plan (SAMP), NJAS opinion. Fall. http://njaudubon.org/conservation/opinions/94aut.html.

New Jersey Future (NJF). 1986a. *Newsletter*. September 10.

———. 1986b. *Newsletter*. October 16.

———. 1988. Analysis of the draft preliminary state development and redevelopment plan. May 16.

———. 1990. *The New Jersey Future State Plan Monitor*. June/July.

———. 1992. *The New Jersey Future State Plan Monitor*. March/April.

———. 1994. Up to date. February.

———. 1995. *Newsletter*. November/December.

———. 1996a. *Newsletter*. January/February.

———. 1996b. *Newsletter*. March/April.

———. 1999a. Excerpts from Governor Christine Todd Whitman's keynote address: Let's take sustainability to heart. *Newsletter*. Special edition. Summer.

———. 1999b. Executive order. *Newsletter*. Special edition. Summer.

———. 1999c. Goals and indicators for New Jersey's quality of life. *Newsletter*. Special edition. Summer.

———. 2000a. Current issue: NJ's dirty secret—not enough housing affordable to NJ's workers. *Facts and Current Issues*. December 8.

———. 2000b. Sober realities, solutions with promise. *Newsletter*. Fall.

———. 2001. 2001 smart growth report card. *Newsletter*. February.

———. 2002a. Letter to "Dear Friend of New Jersey." February 4.

———. 2002b. *Newsletter*. Early winter.

———. 2003a. *Newsletter*. First quarter.

———. 2003b. *Newsletter*. Third and fourth quarters.

———. 2003c. Property tax reform: Smart growth recommendations from New Jersey Future. Issue 2, September.

———. 2003d. Smart growth: The basics—smart growth recommendations from New Jersey Future. Issue 3, October.

———. 2004a. Impact fees: Smart growth recommendations from New Jersey Future. Issue 4, January.

———. 2004b. *Newsletter*. Issue 1.

———. 2004c. Transfer of development rights. Smart growth recommendations from New Jersey Future. Issue 1, revised January 2004.

———. 2005a. *Newsletter*. Issue 1.

———. 2005b. Success in the Highlands: Smart Growth Recommendations from New Jersey Future. May.

New Jersey Meadowlands Commission (NJMC). 2003a. New Jersey Meadowlands Commission adopts redevelopment plan for Paterson Plank Road. http://www.hmdc.state.nj.us/news/2003/092903ppr.html.

———. 2003b. NJMC draft master plan. http://www. hmdc.state.nj.us/masterplan/summary/index.html.

New Jersey Office of the Governor. 2002. Executive Order No. 4. January 31.

New Jersey Office of State Planning (NJOSP). 2000a. Message from the director and chairman. State Planning Year in Review: Fiscal Years 1999 and 2000 Annual Report. August.

———. 2000b. Plan adoption. State Planning Year in Review: Fiscal Years 1999 and 2000 Annual Report. August.

———. 2000c. Redeveloping cities, towns and brownfields sites is getting more emphasis. State Planning Year in Review: Fiscal Years 1999 and 2000 Annual Report. August.

———. 2000d. Smart growth grants help 92 municipalities. State Planning Year in Review: Fiscal Years 1999 and 2000 Annual Report. August.

———. 2001. State development guide plan concept map. http://www.nj.gov/dca/osg/docs/stateplanconcept1980map.pdf.

New Jersey P.L. 1968. Hackensack Meadowlands Reclamation and Development Act. Chapter 404 (C13:17-1 et seq.).

———. 1975. Municipal Land Use Law. Chapter 291 (C40:55D-1 et seq.).

———. 1979. Pinelands Protection Act. Chapter 111 (C13:18A-1 et seq.).

———. 1985a. Fair Housing Act. Chapter 222A (C52:27D-301 et seq.).

———. 1985b. State Planning Act of 1985. Chapter 398 as amended, New Jersey Statutes Annotated (C52:18A-196 et seq.).

New Jersey Pinelands Commission. Undated. A summary of the New Jersey Pinelands Comprehensive Management Plan. http://www.state.nj.us/pinelands/cmp.htm.

New Jersey Planning Officials. 1995. *The New Jersey Planner* 55.6.

New Jersey State League of Municipalities. *New Jersey Municipalities*. December 1995.

New Jersey State Planning Commission (NJSPC). 1987a. First Draft Preliminary State Development and Redevelopment Plan. April.

———. 1987b. Trends and hard choices: Setting objectives for New Jersey's future. February.

———. 1988a. Preliminary State Development and Redevelopment Plan, Communities of Place: Volume I: Building a Legacy and Volume II: Strategies, Policies and Standards. November 14.

———. 1988b. Second Draft Preliminary State Development and Redevelopment Plan. January.

———. 1989. Preliminary State Development and Redevelopment Plan, Communities of Place: Volume III: Planning Standards and Guidelines. January 27.

———. 1991. The Interim State Development and Redevelopment Plan for the State of New Jersey. July 12.

———. 1992a. The Amended Interim State Development and Redevelopment Plan for the State of New Jersey. April.

———. 1992b. The Development and Redevelopment Plan for the State of New Jersey. June.

———. 1999. Commission approves smart growth vision. *State Planning Notes* 6.1. Summer.

———. 2000. $2.4 million in smart growth grants to help 92 communities and 7 counties. *State Planning Notes* 7.2. Spring.

———. 2001. The New Jersey State Development and Redevelopment Plan, Executive Summary. March.

New York Times. 1998. Bold decisions in New Jersey. Editorial. May 23.

———. 2001. The 2001 campaign: New Jersey governor. May 7.

———. 2002. Greening the Garden State. November 16.

Peer Review Technical Advisory Committee. 1988. Report on the Draft Preliminary State Development and Redevelopment Plan. June.

Phelps, Marcus G. and Martina C. Hoppe. 2002. New York–New Jersey Highlands regional study: 2002 update. Newtown Square, PA: U.S. Department of Agriculture, Forest Service, Northeastern Area. December.

Porter, Douglas R. and Allan D. Wallis. 2002. *Exploring ad hoc regionalism*. Cambridge, MA: Lincoln Institute of Land Policy.

Purdy, Matthew. 2001b. In the middle of the road, a politician can be run over, twice. *New York Times*. June 26.

———. 2001a. Without a little dirt, it wouldn't be the Garden State. *New York Times*. June 17.

Regional Planning Partnership (RPP). 2000. RPP's leadership role in watershed management. *Reports*. October.

———. 2003a. *Reports*. February.

———. 2003b. *Reports*. March.

———. 2003c. *Reports*. October.

———. 2003d. *Reports*. December.

———. 2004a. *Reports*. January.

———. 2004b. *Reports*. February.

———. 2004c. *Reports*. March.

———. 2004d. *Reports*. April.

———. 2004e. *Reports*. May.

Rutgers University Center for Urban Policy Research. 1992. *CUPR Reports* 3.2. Spring.

U.S. Environmental Protection Agency. Meadowlands District. http://www.epa.gov/ecoplaces/part2/region2/site9.html.

———. Region 2 Superfund: About brownfields. http://www.epa.gov/region02/superfund/brownfields/.

U.S. Environmental Protection Agency. 1999. Brownfields assessment pilot fact sheet: Hackensack Meadowlands District, NJ. www.epa.gov/swerosps/bf/html-doc/hcknsck.htm.

U.S. Water News Online. 1996. N.J. management plan takes regional approach. March. http://www.uswaternews.com/archive/96/policy/region.html.

Woodrow Wilson School of International and Public Affairs. Undated. Chronology of State Planning in New Jersey, 1934–1986. Princeton, NJ.

Appendix

Governors

Brendan Byrne (Democrat)	1974–1982
Thomas Kean (Republican)	1982–1990
James Florio (Democrat)	1990–1994
Christine Todd Whitman (Republican)	1994–2001
Donald T. DiFrancesco, acting (Republican)	2001–2002
James McGreevey (Democrat, resigned)	2002–2004
Richard J. Codey (Democrat)	2004–present

Acronyms

CAFRA	Coastal Area Facility Review Act
CAIG	Corporate Alliance for Intelligent Growth
COAH	Council on Affordable Housing
CUPR	Center for Urban Policy Research, Rutgers University
DCA	Department of Community Affairs
DEP	Department of Environmental Protection
DOC	Department of Commerce
MOUs	memos of understanding
MSM	Middlesex-Somerset-Mercer Regional Council
NJAPA	New Jersey Chapter, American Planning Association
NJF	New Jersey Future
NJMC	New Jersey Meadowlands Commission
NJSPC	New Jersey State Planning Commission
OSP	Office of State Planning
RPP	Regional Planning Partnership
SAMP	Special Area Management Plan
SPC	State Planning Commission
TDR	transferable development rights

Contacts

Highlands Coalition
PO Box 126
Titusville, NJ 08560
609-737-7263
www.highlandscoalition.org

New Jersey Audubon Society
9 Hardscrabble Road
PO Box 126
Bernardsville, NJ 07924
908-204-8998
www.njaudubon.org

New Jersey Chapter, American Planning Association
www.njapa.org

New Jersey Council on Affordable Housing (COAH)
101 South Broad Street
Trenton, NJ 08625
609-292-3000
www.state.nj.us/dca/coah

New Jersey Future
114 West State Street
Trenton, NJ 08608
609-393-0008
www.njfuture.org

New Jersey Meadowlands Commission
1 DeKorte Park Plaza
Lyndhurst, NJ 07071
201-460-1700
www.njmeadowlands.gov

New Jersey Pinelands Commission
15 Springfield Road
New Lisbon, NJ 08064
609-894-7300
www.state.nj.us/pinelands

Pinelands Preservation Alliance
17 Pemberton Road
Southampton, NJ 08088
609-859-8860
www.pinelandsalliance.org

The Regional Planning Partnership
(formerly The Middlesex-Somerset-Mercer Regional Council [MSM])
870 Mapleton Road
Princeton, NJ 08540-9538
609-393-9434
www.planningpartners.org

State of New Jersey
www.state.nj.us

State of New Jersey Office of Smart Growth
(formerly Office of State Planning)
Department of Community Affairs
101 South Broad Street
PO Box 204
Trenton, NJ 08625-0204
609-292-7156
www.nj.gov/dca/osg/

U.S. Environmental Protection Agency
Brownfields Cleanup and Redevelopment, Hackensack Pilot
www.epa.gov/brownfields/cities/hackensack.htm

5

New England

Introduction

In 1970 Vermont adopted Act 250, a regulatory system for managing its growth, in what was a remarkable step in a conservative New England state. However, it never evolved into the comprehensive planning and regulatory system it was originally designed to be. No other New England state managed to adopt any comprehensive public sector growth strategy until 1988. While the region's population growth numbers have not been as large as in Florida or Oregon, the negative impacts of unmanaged growth are very real, especially in particular parts of each state, such as southern Maine.

Maine, Rhode Island and Vermont have had similar experiences in adopting and implementing their growth management systems. Extensive outreach efforts were mounted in each state; there was strong leadership from the legislature or the governor's office, or both; and the print media were strongly supportive of efforts to adopt the legislation. The early optimism generated by the adoption of these growth management systems continued through 1990 and into 1991, but soon gave way in each state to a struggle to keep the systems from being repealed or severely weakened. The national recession of the early 1990s turned out to be especially severe in all three states, with Maine being the hardest hit, and that affected implementation efforts.

As we sketch the details of the fights to save these growth management systems in the early to mid-1990s, and efforts to reinvigorate them into 2005, we look for common themes among the states, particularly the shifting sources of support and opposition. We also examine the increasing determination to find new ways to overcome the reluctance of local governments to plan and act in concert with each other to address urban sprawl, promote the development of sustainable urban communities, and protect and sustain natural systems, including forest and farming areas.

Each of these New England states has had to face unique problems, but each has managed to move beyond the stage of simply avoiding further weakening or destruction of growth management goals to take proactive efforts to implement the original objectives of those systems. While none has provided the funding sufficient to put their systems fully back on track, there have been important moves in that direction, supported by broad-based public and private coalitions calling for smart growth and sustainable development.

Contents

Contents

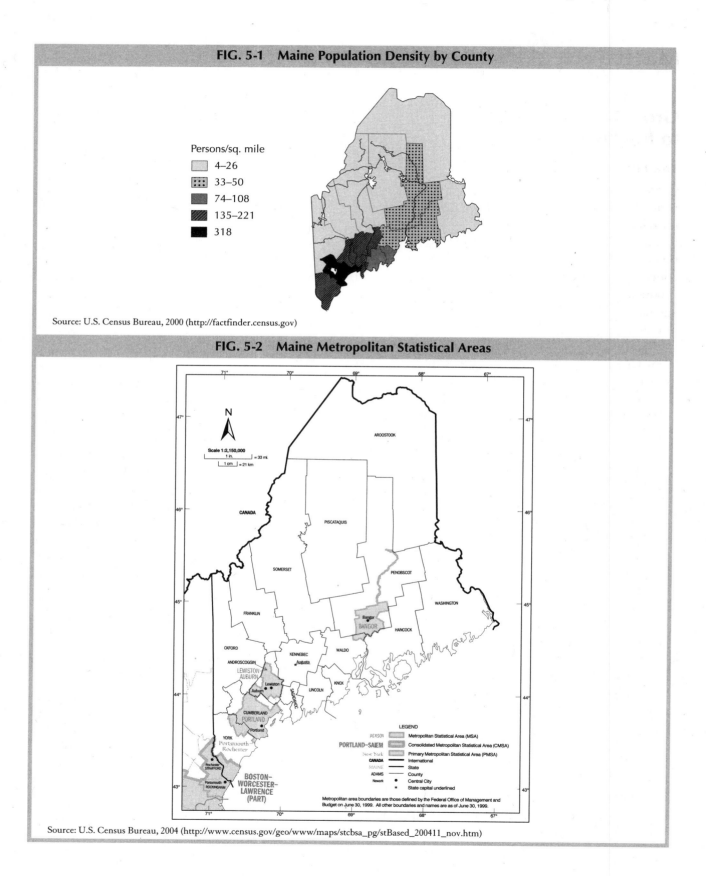

FIG. 5-1   Maine Population Density by County

Persons/sq. mile
- 4–26
- 33–50
- 74–108
- 135–221
- 318

Source: U.S. Census Bureau, 2000 (http://factfinder.census.gov)

FIG. 5-2   Maine Metropolitan Statistical Areas

Source: U.S. Census Bureau, 2004 (http://www.census.gov/geo/www/maps/stcbsa_pg/stBased_200411_nov.htm)

Maine

Growth Pressures Come to the Pine Tree State

The Issue Context

Benjamin Chinitz, former research director of the Lincoln Institute of Land Policy, noted that it is a mistake to confine the assessment of forces that lead to a need for growth management to either population or economic growth alone. In his view, the twin concepts of growth and change come into play in producing an issue context favorable to growth management (Chinitz 1990). Maine is a prime illustration of that point.

Between 1980 and 1997 Maine's population grew from 1,125,000 to 1,242,000, an increase of just over 10 percent. The 2000 population was 1,274,923, up 3.8 percent from 1990, and it is projected to grow to 1,285,000 by 2005; 1,362,000 by 2015; and 1,423,000 by 2025 (U.S. Census Bureau). Until the mid-1980s the perception of two distinct Maines was evident: the faster growing, prosperous south and the struggling north, eager for economic development with no questions asked. By 1986 the distinction was beginning to blur, and concern was spreading from south to north about the rising costs of growth and degradation of the environment. There was a general unease at losing the qualities that made Maine unique: easy access to the shore, uninterrupted open spaces, clean rivers and unspoiled lakes.

From 1986 to 1988, in a powerful illustration of the influence of the print media, the state's major newspapers bombarded the citizens of Maine with a steady barrage of editorials and articles documenting exploding growth pressures in a variety of ways:

"Building boom overwhelms controls on development"

"The land rush is on: Fever pushes prices to unprecedented level"

"Traffic headache for Maine"

"Fighting to save coastal jewels: Growth jolts Camden-Rockport"

"Developers pricing Mainers out of the state's market"

"Taking aim at the land speculators"[1]

Interviews with key participants in the evolution of growth management legislation in Maine yielded a consensus on the issue context that led to broad-based support for a legislative initiative aimed at better management of the emerging growth pressures. Kay Rand, the key lobbyist for the Maine Municipal Association (MMA) from 1986 to 1988, noted that much of the impetus came from the unprecedented growth in York and Cumberland counties in southern Maine and along the entire coast. Representatives of Maine's strongest environmental advocacy group, the Natural Resources Council of Maine (NRCM), also pointed to strong growth pressures in southern and coastal Maine, as well as rampant land speculation in rural areas, including central and northern Maine.

The cumulative impacts of the failure to keep up with a variety of infrastructure needs (not just roads) were also important. From 1985 to 1987 more than 60 towns faced serious growth pressures but had no plans or land development regulations. They turned to moratoriums to avoid being overwhelmed. The first moratoriums were environmentally driven but soon expanded to issues of infrastructure and related problems. Finally, the "quality of life" concept in Maine—translated into a fear of losing Maine's special sense of place, the rural character that had made Maine unique in the eyes of its citizens—was very important.

Michael Michaud, the state legislator from Penobscot County from 1981 to 1995, took the lead in crafting a growth management proposal and nursing it through the legislature. He pointed out that municipal officials then struggling to make difficult land use decisions, such as siting landfills, were operating without plans or regulations. The time had come for the state to help the towns help themselves.

---

1. These headlines appeared in issues of the *Maine Sunday Telegram* and the *Maine State Times* (Portland), the *Kennebec Journal* (Augusta) and the *Times Record* (Brunswick).

Drafting and Adopting Growth Management Legislation

The widespread belief that Maine was not planning properly to manage its growth had created a political environment friendly toward legislative action. This section describes the key interests and actors, and the approach used to bring the issue before the 1988 legislature through a process that would build the consensus necessary to assure passage of the proposed legislation. Governor John McKernan, Representative Michael Michaud and three major interest groups—MMA, NRCM and the Maine Real Estate Development Association (MEREDA)—were active in the compromises that led to agreement on a new growth management statute.

The burst of growth that occurred in Maine in the mid-1980s created a wave of anxiety and fear among citizens that quickly communicated itself to the state's political leaders. It is important to note that the issue was never framed as a "no-growth versus growth" issue. Even towns that adopted moratoriums in response to growth pressures did so to get plans and regulations in place to accommodate growth, not to stop it. Maine did not shed its long-standing desire for economic development, especially in the central and northern parts of the state.

The first official document on the negative impacts of unplanned growth was based on a 1986 study by the Maine State Planning Office (SPO) under Governor Joseph Brennan (Maine SPO 1987b). The executive summary included the following comment: "The major conclusion of this report is that negative cumulative effects are caused by haphazard growth. These can be minimized by planning, which anticipates and appropriately sites land uses to avoid harmful impacts." The report led to the formation of a working group in late 1986 that included most of the key organizations, including MMA, NRCM and MEREDA. The group at first explored the option of simply strengthening environmental and subdivision review laws to solve the problem. But they concluded that merely strengthening a permitting process could not incorporate consideration of cumulative impacts; nothing short of a comprehensive planning approach would do. The SPO then crafted a proposal out of the working group's efforts and called for legislation to mandate local planning, strengthen the role of the regional planning councils, and expand state involvement to include formulation of state goals and review of local plans in the light of those goals.

This SPO proposal came in late 1986, during the last days of Brennan's Democratic administration. The subsequent shift to Republican Governor McKernan strained the bipartisan coalition that had supported the effort to address growth issues. The incoming governor was clear in his support for the issue, but he wanted time to craft his own plan. His rejection of the SPO recommendations caused the growth proposal effort to take two tracks: one led by Governor McKernan and one led by a special Commission on Land Conservation and Economic Development, formed by the 1987 legislature.

The nine-member commission tapped three joint legislative committees for three members each: Energy and Natural Resources, State Government, and Taxation. The result was a bipartisan group led by Michaud, the Democratic House cochair of the Joint Committee on Energy and Natural Resources. In fall 1987 the commission held a number of public hearings attended by environmental representatives, municipal officials (including planning board members), land developers, home builders and realtors.

Although there were important differences about how to solve the problem of unplanned growth, there was little dispute about the nature and importance of the problem and the need to act. In the meantime, the state's press continued to hammer away at the need to manage Maine's growth better, emphasizing that growth management was compatible with economic development. The commission heard proposals from the governor, MMA, NRCM and MEREDA in the fall and winter of 1987. The key issues were whether to mandate local plans; the nature of the state's role, especially whether the state would review and approve local plans; and the amount of funding required to put the system on line and assure its implementation.

The biggest surprise was in the proposal submitted by MEREDA, which called for a stronger state role in growth management: a state comprehensive plan with mandatory local comprehensive plans consistent with the state plan and approved by the state. The proposal also called for mandatory zoning ordinances consistent with state and local comprehensive plans. The explanation for this emphasis on the state role lay in MEREDA's reaction to the wave of moratoriums that had swept across Maine, especially in the southern counties, in the previous three years. A firm state role, along with a strong limitation on the imposition of local development moratoriums, would offer some defense against what MEREDA saw as a budding no-growth movement in many of Maine's towns.

The NRCM proposal (1987b) built on an earlier document titled *An Analysis of Maine's Land Use Management System and Goals for Proposed Changes* (1987a), and called for the establishment of state goals that included

- combating urban sprawl;

- protecting environmental resources;

- providing affordable housing;

- establishing a new state agency to coordinate the state's role;

- developing mandatory town plans and implementing regulations;

- implementing state review and approval of local plans for their consistency with state and regional goals;

- assuring that state agency actions would be compatible with local plans;

- requiring strong public participation; and

- developing a financing mechanism involving a statewide land speculation tax and a local option real estate transfer tax to help fund the system.

The MMA proposal was more cautious, focusing on the need to provide more state resources and technical assistance, both directly and through strengthened regional planning councils. The proposal did not support mandated local comprehensive plans or state review and approval of such plans (MMA 1987).

Governor McKernan's proposal was closer to MMA's in defining the state role. While supporting the principle that all local governments should develop local plans consistent with state goals and policies, this proposal depended on incentives rather than any state mandate to bring about the desired result. The state would develop broad policy objec-tives that balanced economic growth and environmental protection as the basis for locally developed comprehensive land use plans. Local governments would be offered financial and technical assistance and other incentives to encourage the consistency of their plans with state goals. The governor's proposal called for an accelerated process that would require much less planning support to local governments than the other proposals (Maine SPO 1987a).

In late January 1988 the commission adopted for recommendation to the legislature a proposal that included some of the essential ingredients of the NRCM proposal and some elements drawn from the other three. The commission's proposal included MEREDA's recommendation for mandatory planning for all towns, but it did not pick up fully on MEREDA's call for uniform state standards through the adoption of a state land use plan. The key differences with the governor's proposal were in the commission's recommendations for mandatory planning, state review and approval of local plans for consistency with state goals, a longer time period for local governments to prepare plans, and substantially more dollars for implementing the new system.

In pushing hard for a strong state role, Michaud as commission chair went against not only the governor's preferences, but also those of MMA. However, funding was a central concern of MMA and was an important basis for its ultimate support of the new law. The commission's proposal included an NRCM recommendation for a land speculation tax, general fund revenues, and a local option real estate transfer tax to support the cost of planning, as well as the acquisition of open space and the provision of affordable housing.

The legislature referred the commission report to the Joint Committee on Energy and Natural Resources. Michaud's role as chair of the commission had given him an opportunity to send to the legislature, through his own committee, a stronger bill than even he would have thought could clear the legislature and gain the approval of the governor, and put him in a position to assert strong leadership in shaping a compromise bill with bipartisan support. In a key commission vote on the final report to the legislature, all nine members favored comprehensive planning by towns, but split five–four on whether the plans should be mandated.

During the first four months of the 1988 legislative session, the Energy and Natural Resources Committee held numerous hearings and workshops that sharpened and clarified the commission's earlier proposal. Michaud's aim was to "veto-proof" the bill by bringing the committee's 13 Democratic and Republican members to unanimous agreement (Turkel 1988b). At one standing-room-only hearing in March, more than 200 "Mainers" heard and participated in a spirited debate on the key issues: mandated planning and plan approval. Citing the home rule issue, some town officials opposed mandated planning, but (significantly) others supported it (*Kennebec Journal* 1988a).

By early April the battle lines were clearly drawn, but intense negotiations were continuing between Michaud and his committee, MMA, NRCM and the governor's office. The press also maintained its persistent, unanimous support for a strong law that mandated local planning, required state review and approval (and a state planning agency to insure effective implementation), and provided significant state funding to local government.

The governor maintained his strong opposition to any form of mandates and was far apart from the committee on the funding issue. His position was both philosophical and fiscal, leading to widespread concern that "his opposition may cause the hard fought growth management compromise to unravel" (Turkel 1988c). However, Michaud guided a series of compromises to prevent a partisan split from threatening the legislation. The key elements were mandatory town planning, a "voluntary" certification system and a generous funding package. The mandated planning and certification were critical to NRCM and MEREDA, while funding was the crucial element for MMA, which had agreed to mandated planning, but only if tied to an offer of state funding of 75 percent of the costs of planning before the mandate would trigger.

In another compromise, McKernan agreed to support voluntary certification. After further negotiations with Michaud, "Brownie" Carson (executive director of NRCM) and others, the governor also agreed to the significantly higher level of funding proposed by the

committee ($3.2 million). Michaud was further aided in his efforts by the strong feeling of several committee members that the compromise was already too weak and could not be diluted any more. However, when the committee met on the evening of April 13, with the legislative session coming to a close, the agreement began to fall apart in the face of lobbyists' efforts to amend the proposal.

The very open and informal process of the committee's work resulted in a number of changes that by 10 p.m. had seriously eroded the agreements reached earlier in the day. The next day, only Michaud's vigorous "shuttle diplomacy" among small subgroups of the committee, lobbyists and the governor's representatives patched the consensus back together. By day's end, he had salvaged the compromise. Michaud called the committee into formal session, "slammed down the gavel, and with no public discussion the measure was approved within seconds" (Turkel 1988c; *Kennebec Journal* 1988b, 1988c; NRCM 1988).

All sides expressed support for the final product. Developers could hope for a greater degree of consistency in planning across the state, as well as clear rules of the game on impact fees and moratoriums. MMA's desire to avoid state review of all land development regulations was realized when review was confined to zoning ordinances. NRCM and other environmentalists got much, if not all, of what they wanted in the provisions for mandatory planning and state review and better protection of natural resources. The governor avoided full state review and approval by means of the voluntary certification system. The amount of state funding for the process was still to be negotiated, with the committee supporting more than $3 million, and the governor wanting less. In spite of all the agreements and compromises, Michaud had achieved his goal: a meaningful growth management bill unanimously approved by the bipartisan Energy and Natural Resources Committee.

Knowing that any substantial debate or amendments in the legislature would shatter the compromise, Michaud hoped the bill would move quickly through the House and Senate, and that is exactly what happened. The appropriations committees and the governor settled on funding at a much higher level than the governor had originally supported. In a last-minute cliffhanger, Maine put in place a major growth management system with substantial funding to back it up.

Growth Management Act of 1988

Maine's Comprehensive Planning and Land Use Regulation Act was comprehensive with regard to both governance and substance. Also referred to as the Growth Management Act of 1988 (Title 30-A), it took a broad approach to growth management that embraced goals for economic development, housing and protection of natural resources, as did other states during that time.

The 10 statutory state goals that framed the entire growth management system were relatively brief and straightforward statements about a desired future for Maine. Like all such statements, the key to their importance is whether or not they are reflected in a meaningful way in plans and implementation strategies.

The Governance Structure

The governance system established by the act defined important new growth management roles at the state, regional and local levels. The law charged a new state Office of Comprehensive Planning (OCP) with providing technical and financial assistance programs to aid local governments in meeting the requirements of the act and with establishing a process for local program review by OCP and the regional councils to ensure consistency with state goals. Before adopting their growth management programs, the towns were required to submit them to OCP for comment. During its review, OCP sought comments on the program from the appropriate regional council, state agencies, and adjacent towns regarding the program's consistency with state goals. The towns were to submit the zoning ordinance of the growth management program to the state agency for consistency review one year after the plan's submission. The act authorized OCP to issue findings on local program deficiencies and to make recommendations to remedy them.

This OCP review was a "review and comment," not a "review and approval" procedure. Local governments, though required to develop a local growth management program, were not required to seek certification of consistency with state goals. However, there were substantial incentives for them to do so, including eligibility for state assistance for a variety of programs such as technical and financial aid in administering and enforcing local land use ordinances; "Maine's Future" funds for acquiring land for conservation, natural resource protection, and open space or recreational facilities; multipurpose community development block grants; and a new "municipal legal defense fund," a unique provision among state growth management systems designed to calm local government fears of lawsuits based on private property rights questions. Furthermore, local governments could impose impact fees for offsite improvements in such areas as transportation, parks and recreation, and water management only if they

---

Ten State Goals, 1988

1. Encourage orderly growth and development in appropriate areas of each community, while protecting the state's rural character, making efficient use of public services and preventing development sprawl.

2. Plan for, finance and develop an efficient system of public facilities and services to accommodate anticipated growth and economic development.

3. Promote an economic climate which increases job opportunities and overall economic well-being.

4. Encourage and promote affordable, decent housing opportunities for all Maine citizens.

5. Protect the quality and manage the quantity of the state's water resources, including lakes, aquifers, great ponds, estuaries, rivers and coastal areas.

6. Protect the state's other critical natural resources, including without limitation, wetlands, wildlife and fisheries habitat, sand dunes, shorelands, scenic vistas and unique natural areas.

7. Protect the state's marine resources industry, ports and harbors from incompatible development and to promote access to the shore for commercial fishermen and the public.

8. Protect the state's agricultural and forest resources from development which threatens those resources.

9. Preserve the state's historic and archaeological resources.

10. Promote and protect the availability of outdoor recreation opportunities for all Maine citizens including access to surface waters.

Source: Maine Legislature, 1989

had their growth management system certified for consistency.

The act required each of the nine listed state agencies, and any others with "regulatory or other authority" affecting the state goals, to submit to OCP by January 1, 1990, a written report addressing how the state goals had been incorporated into their plans. After that date, those agencies were to conduct their activities in a manner consistent with the state goals. This provision illustrates the broader effort to bring state agencies into state growth management systems during the 1980s, a task that experience indicates is very difficult, given the predilection of state agencies for independent action.

At the regional level, the new system gave Maine's traditionally weak regional councils major new responsibilities: to review and comment on local plans as to how they addressed regional needs, consistency with state goals, and compatibility with adjacent municipalities; and to offer technical assistance to local governments. The regional needs identification process was part of the councils' local plan review responsibility and did not constitute a regional plan. However, it did involve important components of such a plan, such as inventories of public infrastructure and agricultural and commercial forest lands; analyses of housing, recreation and open space needs; and projections of regional growth and economic development.

The high level of technical assistance necessary to meet the needs of many Maine towns, most of which had no professional staff, made it imperative for regional councils to assume a major role in the growth management process. These provisions, with the additional funding to be discussed later, constituted a substantial broadening of the responsibilities of Maine's regional agencies, which became a critical link in the success of the implementation phase.

The local level in every statewide growth management system is the heart of the planning and implementation process, and MMA was the primary actor for Maine's local governments during the adoption process. Its twin goals were to minimize the state role and to maximize state funding. MMA support of the new law was based on the provision for voluntary plan certification; the limitation of implementation

strategy review to zoning ordinances; and approval of the high-end funding proposals. Another of MMA's concerns was satisfied by the law's provisions that the mandatory planning schedule be based on "the availability of state assistance" and that towns could come in before the deadlines if they wished.

The act called for Maine's towns to submit their plans and zoning ordinances to OCP for review according to a schedule that gave priority to larger communities with higher growth rates (as determined by state growth and population data). The act divided the state's 496 towns into three "tiers" that were to submit their plans by 1991, 1993 and 1996, respectively. The local growth management program was to be prepared with the assistance of a local planning committee required to conduct its deliberation in "open, public session with adequate notice of public hearings," and citizen participation was strongly encouraged.

Funding

Funding, or the lack thereof, was the rock on which many state growth strategies in the 1970s foundered, and adequate funding for Maine's new law was a prime concern of all the key interest groups. MMA was concerned that even the higher level of funding approved by the governor was not sufficient to fully support a state grant to each municipality of 75 percent of its planning costs. The total appropriation to fund the first year of the program was $3.5 million, with $1 million earmarked for tier-one towns, $0.6 million for regional planning councils, and $1.8 million for the creation of the new OCP and strengthening the field enforcement capacity of the Department of Environmental Protection (DEP).

The legislature also recognized the importance of adequate data to support the new growth management system. About $750,000 was appropriated to several state agencies to expand existing or build new databases, including funds for the Maine Geological Survey for aquifer and freshwater wetland mapping, the Department of Conservation for a geographic information system (GIS) for natural resource identification, and the Department of Inland Fisheries and Wildlife for critical habitat identification. These funds were especially important to NRCM and constituted

---

Three Basic Components of the Local Growth Management Program

1. The inventory and analysis section was to include a 10-year projection of local and regional growth, the need for public facilities, and potential impacts on natural resources. It could also contain data relating to each of the goals (e.g., water resources, critical areas, forestry and agricultural lands, transportation systems and housing stock including affordable housing). This section also linked land use and infrastructure planning through a description of current and projected land use patterns, capital facilities and public services necessary to support growth and development and the costs of these facilities and services.

2. The policy development section linked the inventory and analysis section to the state goals, and addressed conflicts between state goals or between regional and local issues. Policy requirements are notable because they illustrated the persistent effort to link the state goals with other requirements of the system, and they demonstrated how to integrate other laws, such as the Shoreland Zoning Law of the 1970s, into the new system.

3. The implementation strategy section was key to the entire system, consisted of a timetable for implementation, including a requirement that land use ordinances and others

"significant ordinances" must be adopted within one year of the plan. At least two types of geographic areas had to be identified: growth areas and rural areas. Growth areas are suitable for orderly residential, commercial and industrial development over the next 10 years. Rural areas are areas where protection should be provided for agricultural, forest, open space and scenic lands within the municipality. The fact that no unincorporated areas exist in Maine, except in the northern unorganized territory, enhances the importance of this requirement. Most Maine towns contain extensive rural areas.

Other guidelines relate to implementation goals in areas of water quality, critical natural resource protection, access to coastal waters and protection of agricultural and forest resources. Guidelines for housing set a goal for affordable housing at a level of 10 percent of new residential development, and encouraged towns to use cluster zoning, reduced minimum lot and frontage sizes, and increased densities. To assure municipalities have the authority to carry out actions, the guidelines provided that policies and ordinances adopted as part of a town's implementation strategy may also include density limits, acquisition of land as development rights or performance standards.

Source: Maine DECD, 1989

---

a substantial legislative commitment to providing an adequate database underpinning for the system in the natural resources area (Turkel 1988a).

The Implementation Record, 1988–1992

Maine's 1988 law clearly refuted the notion that growth management is linked to no-growth or slow-growth programs. Rather, it was concerned with careful planning, including timing and location, and with promoting economic development in areas that need and want it. One of the first implementation tasks was to establish OCP, which was given the lead responsibility for administering the growth management program. Located within the Department of Economic and Community Development (DECD), OCP inherited several important programs from other parts of state government (e.g., the Flood Plain Management Program), but its primary task was to put the new growth management system in place. The $3.5 million appropriation in 1988 provided enough

funds to establish OCP with 16 staff positions, and Kay Rand was named director. As the chief lobbyist for MMA she had participated in the development of the legislation and was well regarded by Maine's town officials, legislators and state administrators.

Early Successes for the Growth Management System

Under Rand's direction, the organization of OCP quickly fell into place. Along with its first distribution of state funding to help towns prepare their plans, OCP published its first major product, *Guidelines for Maine's Growth Management Program* (Maine DECD/ OCP 1988). This practical document was written in nontechnical language that carefully distinguished between what was required as opposed to optional. It provided specific advice and instructions to municipalities on every stage of the process of developing a local growth management system. This impressive technical assistance effort is worthy of careful review by any state starting a similar program.

The first step in implementing the local growth management program requirements was OCP's offer of planning grants to 58 of the 145 tier-one municipalities. By January 1990, 54 of the 58 towns had completed the work program, received local approvals and executed the planning grant process. For the 1990 fiscal year, OCP requested and received $1.3 million to enable the remaining 87 tier-one towns to receive planning grant offers in July 1989. This schedule allowed all tier-one towns to have their plans in place by July 1, 1991. Total state funding of tier-one towns for the 1989 and 1990 fiscal years was $2.4 million, with the local 25 percent match bringing the total cost to $3.2 million.

Under the OCP funding formula, grants ranged from a minimum of $11,250 for towns of 500 or less in population to a maximum of $60,000 for towns of more than 25,000. Approval by both the governor and the legislature for the additional funding in 1990 was a clear signal of continued support for the program. That level of funding was meant to provide planning assistance to tier-two and tier-three towns on a schedule that would complete the towns' plan-making process by July 1, 1996, just six months short of the original target date. The total in state planning grants to local governments was almost $7.5 million (Maine DECD/OCP 1990a, 2–21).

The implementation grant program for towns is separate from the planning grant program, and funding for the implementation component was less clear. In the early stages, no funds were required, but the legislature did appropriate $100,000 for the 1991 fiscal year. Funding all tier-one towns under the implementation grant program amounted to an additional $70,000. The grants would average $7,500 per town and would fund the preparation of the required land use zoning ordinance portion of the implementation strategy (Maine DECD/OCP 1990a, 10–12).

At the regional level, OCP brought the state's regional councils fully into the growth management process. Those agencies had existed in Maine for 35 years but typically were underfunded, weak and often irrelevant in efforts to better manage the state's growth. To enhance their capacity to carry out their new responsibilities and duties, OCP was directed to work with the councils to develop regional education and training programs, policies for assessment of state goals and regional needs, and guidelines to ensure methodological consistency among the various regional councils (Maine DECD/OCP 1990a, 4–7).

State funding for regional councils included $600,000 per year of Growth Management Act appropriations, $194,000 in general fund dollars, and $230,000 under the Coastal Zone Management program. However, it remained to be seen if the regions would take an important role in the local plan and implementation review process. As elsewhere, the regional agencies remained somewhat schizophrenic in their efforts to serve two masters: state and local governments.

Maine had one of the strongest requirements for state agency involvement among the new, statewide growth management systems passed in the 1980s, and in the early stages OCP vigorously encouraged the full participation of state agencies. In addition to reviewing state agency reports on the consistency of their plans and activities with state goals, OCP asked state agencies to show how they had incorporated or planned to incorporate the consideration of local growth management programs in their own actions, "to ensure that actions taken by the agency are consistent, to the maximum extent feasible, with adopted local growth management programs" (Maine DECD/OCP 1990a, 11–12). A review of the first set of state agency reports (from 11 state agencies) to OCP in December 1989 suggested that those agencies were taking their role seriously for the most part. OCP's 1990 *Biennial Progress Report* and interviews with OCP's director and others also supported that view (Maine DECD/OCP 1990b).

Maine's growth management system also called on OCP to coordinate the collection of data necessary to meet the demands of the law. The first product of that effort was OCP's *Directory of State Data Resources* (DECD/OCP 1989). State agencies played a major role in the preparation of the directory for local governments. Agencies that administered grant or other financial assistance programs were working with OCP to ensure that they knew which municipalities were failing to put appropriate plans and ordinances in place (Maine DECD/OCP 1990a, 8–10). However, OCP's 1990 report (Maine DECD/OCP 1990b) addressed significant gaps in the data.

A Planning Advisory Committee of seven lay

members was appointed by the governor to advise OCP on all rules, guidelines and reports, and to report annually to the governor and the Joint Committee on Energy and Natural Resources Committee on funding or statutory changes needed to meet the purpose of the act. The committee pointed out major shortfalls in funding needed to complete the natural resources inventory (wildlife habitat, unique natural areas, endangered plants, and various critically significant water resources). The committee also noted that it would cost $4.5 million over five years to do the job well, a funding goal that even it knew was unlikely to be met.

Among its actions, the Planning Advisory Committee recommended that the governor appoint a GIS Steering Committee to advise the Department of Conservation on how to implement the newly funded GIS program. Furthermore, it supported the efforts of the Office of Informational Services to engage a consultant to devise a GIS strategy to meet local and regional agency needs and avoid duplicative and potentially wasteful efforts in developing separate and incompatible systems.

Although the state agencies supported the growth management system, two negative factors posed problems for the future. First, the responsibility for assuring the full participation of state agencies in the system was given to a sister agency, DECD. Only strong signals from the governor, along with an OCP director fully supported by the governor and legislature and possessing unusual diplomatic and persuasive skills, could succeed in that awkward situation. The second potential problem was the lack of funds to allow state agencies to discharge their responsibilities fully under the law. The recession of the early 1990s exacerbated this problem and called into question the very survival of the system.

Perhaps the most compelling testimony for the successful implementation of Maine's growth management system through 1991 came from the key actors who supported its adoption. Representative Michaud gave the implementation effort high marks and gave much of the credit to the governor's appointment of Kay Rand as OCP director. MMA leaders felt that, while local governments had been generally positive about it, the need for more funding, for both planning and infrastructure, posed a major problem for the future, especially if the economic downturn persisted. MEREDA, the real estate development group, and NRCM both rated implementation as *good*, with much credit going to Rand, who was pleased because both the governor and the legislature strongly supported the effort.

Economic Recession and Drastic Cutbacks

The conventional wisdom is that people support growth management efforts when the economy is booming, but quickly withdraw that support when the economy slows down. Maine was an important test of that point since its economy slowed in 1990, two years after the law was adopted. All of those interviewed at the time saw continued strong support for the law, but many felt that the focus would shift to the economic development component of the system. Kay Rand was optimistic, but felt that major challenges were ahead in maintaining town support as OCP began the consistency review process.

The growth management program continued to draw support through the 1991 legislative session, but in late 1991 the legislature went along with the governor's recommendation to discontinue the program, presumably on the assumption that planning was not needed when the economy was in a major downturn. The Office of Comprehensive Planning was eliminated.

When the legislative session resumed in January 1992, supporters, led by Michaud, reinstated the basic statute, put back limited funding for grants to local governments, and allocated three staff positions to DECD to administer grants and review plans and ordinances. However, OCP was not reinstated, and thus Rand's leadership was at least temporarily missing from the state scene. The system was modified to take a more permissive approach to what had been local government mandates. Review of plans and ordinances by the state was required only when an implementation grant was applied for and received; that in turn depended on the state having funds available for local governments to do the planning needed to fulfill the 10 goals of the law.

Overall funding for the planning program was cut by some 80 percent. By 1992, 222 of Maine's 494 towns had received planning grants, and 75 of them had plans that were found to be consistent with the planning law. Thirty other towns were in the process of drafting ordinances to carry out their plans. However, the process slowed, largely because state funds were not available to local governments standing in line for grant support.[2] Despite the subsequent partial reinstatement of the basic framework of the Growth Management Act, the 1992 legislative session was a major setback.

The Struggle to Strengthen the Growth Management System, 1993–1998

Even after the substantial weakening of Maine's system, Kay Rand and Michael Michaud provided much of the leadership for attempts to strengthen the system as the state emerged from the recession. Rand was hired by a real estate development group, the Maine Alliance, which had been formed by merging MEREDA with other real estate and development groups. They believed that only a strong state mandatory framework for an integrated system of planning and regulation could give the development community timeliness and certainty in the development process as well as protection from no-growth efforts at the local level.

Because of her experience at OCP, Rand was enthusiastic about working to develop proposals to reform and streamline the state agency regulatory process. She had dealt with state agencies, such as DEP, that saw no connection between their regulatory mandates and the need to keep their actions consistent with local plans. According to Rand, DEP's site plan review process in effect drove development to rural areas because undertaking a traffic and infrastructure analysis in developed areas, where the growth management act called for development to be concentrated, would have been much more costly and complex than moving out to the fringe. Since DEP did not link site plan review to consistency with an

2. See Natural Resources Council of Maine (1992, 1–2); Carson (1992, 3); National Growth Management Leadership Project (1992, 10). For more on the funding cuts, see Natural Resources Council of Maine (1993, 2).

approved local plan, developers got their "at the edge" site plans approved with much less difficulty.

Rand's key position in ongoing attempts to revive and strengthen the growth management legislation was enhanced significantly when she became the campaign manager for Angus King, the winning Independent Party candidate in the 1994 gubernatorial race. King shared many of Rand's frustrations with the existing political environment in Maine, and both were dedicated to a reform agenda.

The Land Use Regulatory Reform Committee

The first session of the 116th legislature in 1993 saw the introduction of an Act to Improve Environmental Protection and Support Economic Development under the State's Land Use Laws (LD 1487), a product of the Maine Alliance, with the assistance of Rand and others. Under the state's land use laws, this proposed act raised tough questions about Maine's land use and natural resource management system, the roles of state agencies and local governments in land use issues, and the need to coordinate better the various regulatory agencies.

Because LD 1487 raised such critical issues and tough remedies, the legislature's Joint Standing Committee on Energy and Natural Resources asked the legislative council to authorize a study committee to review the issues and report to the second session of the 116th legislature in 1994. The result was the naming of the Land Use Regulatory Reform Committee (LURRC) with eight members, six from the House and two from the Senate; Michaud was one of the House members.

The committee issued its final report in January 1994, after conducting hearings and receiving testimony from individuals representing numerous public and private interests. The report is a remarkable document, considering that Maine's growth management system had narrowly escaped total repeal as a reaction to the severe recession from which Maine still had not recovered in 1994. The committee concluded, "there is an inadequate framework and mechanism for state agencies and local governments to administratively coordinate their efforts and evolve new approaches to both land use and natural resource management" (Maine LURRC 1994, i).

The report stated that to achieve the required greater state and local cooperation there needed to be "a reaffirmation of the legislature's commitment to the growth management program." Throughout the report, the committee made clear its support for the practice and concepts of growth management to offer Maine communities a wide array of benefits they would otherwise forego. The report also made it clear that regional coordination would be needed to achieve such benefits. The committee gave special attention to what it saw as the most important goal of the growth management act: "to encourage orderly growth and development in appropriate areas of each municipality, while protecting the state's rural character, making efficient use of public services, and preventing development sprawl" (Maine LURRC 1994, 11).

Other sections of the LURRC report called for

■ integrating mandatory shoreland zoning and growth management, and restoring the wide range of technical and financial assistance and incentives to encourage and facilitate the adoption and implementation of local growth management programs;

■ establishing a Municipal Infrastructure Investment Trust Fund capitalized initially by a $10 million bond issue approved by Maine's voters. Eligibility for such funds would be restricted to towns that had adopted a certified local growth management program;

■ locating new school construction in growth areas designated by towns through the growth management program (taking up a theme that is being heard more and more around the nation); and

■ enacting new legislation to require water and sewer districts to cooperate in municipal plan development.

A Reinvigorated State Planning Office

There was little evidence that Governor McKernan would take action to support the recommendations of the committee, but with the election of Angus King in fall 1994, the prospects improved. In the same election, however, Republicans won control of the Senate, and the Democratic margin in the House was reduced to one. Michael Michaud won a Senate seat by defeating an incumbent Republican.

Shortly after his election, Governor King moved the functions of Maine's growth management system from the DECD to the State Planning Office (SPO), which had existed all along as the political arm of the governor's office but with no direct involvement in the growth management program. Evan Richert was named SPO director. He had long been involved in growth management issues in Maine as a planner for the city of South Portland and as head of his own consulting firm, Market Decisions, Inc., where he worked with towns in preparing their comprehensive plans.

The status of Maine's growth management system was the subject of a three-month study by the *Portland Press Herald* and *Maine Sunday Telegram,* in July 1997. While the series, titled "Spoiled by Sprawl," focused on southern Maine (York and Cumberland counties), it raised some of the key issues Maine faced in strengthening its growth management system. Furthermore, the series included discussions with Richert that made clear his determination to follow the recommendations of the LURRC report. The opening article cited the predominant sprawl pattern of suburban growth in southern Maine over the previous three years (1995–1997), and how efforts to contain it were hampered by the failure of Maine's citizens to understand the high costs of sprawl (Pochna and Canfield 1997a). A second article focused on efforts by SPO to document the costs of sprawl and begin to build support for changes needed to reverse those relentless development patterns (Pochna and Canfield 1997b).

A year-long "costs of sprawl" study for SPO (O'Hara 1997) concluded, among other things, that sprawl costs Maine about $450 million per year, in the process "damaging wildlife habitat, swallowing up farms and rural lifestyles, and increasing property taxes" (Pochna and Canfield 1997b). Richert toured the state to present the findings to town officials and community groups. Perhaps the toughest and most important new challenge was to strengthen Maine's ability to act regionally, rather than each town (and each state agency) planning and acting in isolation from one another.

Continuing Challenges and Opportunities, 1999–2000

An SPO report offered both good news and bad news (Maine SPO 1999). The bad news was that most of LURRC's recommendations in 1994 had not been fully implemented. The good news was that with the reelection of Angus King as governor in November 1998, support for significantly strengthening Maine's growth management system seemed likely to continue. With Richert's leadership at SPO, Rand as the governor's chief policy person dealing with the legislature, and Michaud in the Senate, a strong team was in place to lead support for the growth management program. The key question was how much support could be assembled to strengthen it along the lines of the 1994 LURRC recommendations, which in essence were reasserted in SPO's report five years later.

Challenges to Be Met

The 1999 SPO report made it clear that a fully effective growth management program had a long way to go.

> Local growth management has achieved some notable successes.... Nevertheless, local planning efforts alone are insufficient to protect natural resources and get the greatest return from public investment in infrastructure. In particular, by itself local growth management will not achieve the statutory objective of "orderly growth" as long as: state fiscal and investment policies work against it; state agencies fail to fully embrace the program; regional planning and cooperation are relegated to afterthoughts; and local governments discourage traditional, compact forms of development within their borders. (Maine SPO 1999, 1)

Two other key findings cited the need for more state support for local growth management efforts and the need to "devise and fund a cost-effective, coordinated development tracking system," so that the effectiveness of the investment in growth management could be measured. The report further cited the failure, as of early 1999, to return state funding for local planning to anything like the levels available before the cuts during the early 1990s recession. "The most significant barriers to compliance with the goals of the act" include "inadequate funding to meet the need for local planning and implementation" and "lack of staff to administer grants, provide technical assistance, and undertake necessary research and policy development" (Maine SPO 1999, 11).

A summary of the 1998 and 1999 grant budgets, compared to projected funding needs to complete the planning and implementation grant phases of the program, shows a major shortfall for towns and for SPO staff. One key example was the Municipal Infrastructure Bond Program, recommended by LURRC in 1994 and approved by the legislature but never actually funded. The aim was to help towns with low-cost loans and grants to provide the infrastructure (water, sewer, etc.) so communities with consistent growth management programs would have funds to concentrate development in designated centers and growth areas. The recommendation also called for state agencies to review and modify their programs supporting local infrastructure investments to give preference to communities whose projects were needed to implement consistent growth management programs.

Another important recommendation of the 1994 committee dealt with greater linkage between state programs and grants recognizing good local planning. It called for increasing "the number of state programs and policies that recognize and reward local planning efforts that are consistent with the act" and thus provide "meaningful incentives for communities to do good planning" (Maine SPO 1999, 21).

Given the increasing recognition in Maine and elsewhere that regions play a critical role in smart growth, Richert favored making legislative and administrative changes that increased substantially the state's ability to address regional issues on a regional basis. The Growth Management Act required a regional coordination program aimed at managing shared resources such as rivers, aquifers and transportation facilities, but it was not until 1999–2000 that significant progress was made in this area.

Meaningful regional cooperation among local governments and state agencies is difficult even in the best of circumstances. After the funding cuts in 1991–1992, most regional councils stopped commenting on local comprehensive plans and their treatment of regional issues and coordination. The report stated that, with some "notable exceptions, attention to regional planning and cooperation is oftentimes superficial and most plans focus more on local planning issues and local means to implement solutions than regional approaches" (Maine SPO 1999, 41). Some progress had been made to support the 10 regional councils more fully through a shared contract by several state agencies, including SPO and the departments of Transportation, Environmental Protection, and Economic and Community Development. Still, the failure to restore funding for the growth management program left regional councils with neither the funding nor the mandates to play the significant role required.

Areas of Progress

One area that showed important advances involved efforts to correct the spending of all school construction dollars on new schools in fast growing suburbs and almost none on new or rehabilitated schools in designated growth areas. As in many other states, the location of new schools had become a key instrument of sprawl development patterns. SPO's study of the cost of sprawl (O'Hara 1997) provided important documentation of the school location challenge. The 1998 legislature adopted LD 2252, which took significant steps to change the way school construction and renovation needs were identified, assessed and financed. The law established a new Revolving Renovation Fund capitalized at $20 million to improve the condition of *existing* school buildings. Other changes favored the location of new or renovation of old school buildings in designated growth centers (Maine SPO 1999, 10–11).

In the area of transportation, the SPO worked with the Maine Department of Transportation (DOT) on a number of initiatives to enhance public transportation and change the allocation of road dollars to encourage growth in designated centers and other urban areas rather than to support sprawl development at the edge (Maine SPO 1999, 44).

The Task Force on Regional Service Center Communities was established by the 118th legislature in 1998 "to recommend ways of reversing the decline of Maine's principal service center communities and strengthening them as centers of job creation and for the delivery of critical services to surrounding

regions." It offered a series of recommendations aimed at facilitating compact development in 69 designated service centers and urban areas including an expansion of SPO's regional infrastructure planning grants; expansion of special home ownership programs; expanding the redevelopment of brownfield sites; exploring ways to provide state matching funds for urban parks and trails in urban growth areas–regional service center communities; and other initiatives to discourage sprawl (Task Force 1998, 18–25).

Finally, the regional task force called for the implementation of the recommendations of the Task Force on Intergovernmental Structure, which had been created by an executive order of Governor King in 1996 to strengthen intergovernmental coordination. Not all its proposals were approved by the legislature, but LD 2244 (to encourage intergovernmental cooperation), which did pass, clarified the general authority of county government to provide a broad array of services to municipalities that were willing to contract for them on a voluntary basis. LD 2244 also created a permanent Task Force on Intergovernmental Coordination.

The Political Climate

With the economic recovery in the late 1990s, there were strong signals that Maine was ready to take legislative, administrative and fiscal steps to put teeth into the state's effort to substitute smart growth for growth dominated by sprawl, in spite of renewed growth pressures. The political framework at the executive level had improved dramatically under King's leadership, with SPO taking the lead in reshaping the growth management initiative. However, important actions remained on the unfinished agenda, and some clearly required legislative, not just executive, action. That raised questions about Maine's political climate and how much support could be mobilized in the Maine legislature to move the smart growth implementation process forward.

The King administration submitted a number of bills to the first session of the 119th legislature (the "long" session, January–June 1999), and some that addressed growth management and sprawl issues were carried over to the second session (January–June 2000). They addressed the following policies:

- State investment policy, involving the location of state office buildings vis à vis their contribution to making downtown centers viable and the effects of decisions by the state with regard to capital investment and siting. These proposals were reflected in LD 1080 and LD 1414.

- Fiscal policy, involving those that resulted in rural lands not being used for production, unduly burdened service center communities, and contributed to sprawl development.

- Transportation policy, with a focus on state and local transportation planning, streamlining of local and state land use rules and regulations, highway access management, and permitting and encouraging efficient neighborhood and economic development in growth areas. Obviously, land use was a key item under this heading, as reflected in LD 2550.

- Agricultural policy, aimed at ensuring optimum use of farms and woodlands and preserving open space adjacent to development. LD 449 "requires the seller of land abutting registered farmland to provide notice to prospective purchasers of the land that the State policy is to conserve, protect, and encourage the development and improvement of agricultural land and that farming activities on the land may cause noise, dust, and odors."

Sources of Input to Smart Growth Legislation in 2000

Numerous committees and reports had influenced the development of the smart growth legislative package for the 2000 session. First, SPO's cost of sprawl report noted four broad categories in defining the problems of sprawl.

1. Fiscal costs for taxpayers to essentially "re-create" a new infrastructure of roads, schools and public services in rural areas, while continuing to support the older set of public infrastructure in urban areas, even when the population base is declining.

2. Environmental costs of more air pollution from automobiles, more lake degradation from development runoff and more fragmentation of wildlife habitats.

3. Economic costs from the loss of rural and natural resource-based economies and enterprises when farms, forests and working waterfronts are converted to low-density residential or commercial development.

4. Social costs of the isolation of the poor and elderly in cities, the disruption of traditional farming and forestry activities in the countryside, and the loss of community connection and social character with the disappearance of traditional neighborhoods. (O'Hara 1997, 7–13)

Another key set of recommendations came from a report by the Task Force on Regional Service Center Communities. The highlights were intended to promote investment in service centers by

> capitalizing the Municipal Infrastructure Investment Trust Fund; expanding the State Planning Office's regional infrastructure planning grants; targeting Community Development Block Grants to support service centers; increasing home ownership through Maine State Housing Authority's "New Neighbors Program"; promoting revitalization of downtowns through an Executive Order for State office buildings to remain in service centers and downtowns; supporting redevelopment of brownfield sites in service center communities; and investing in urban green spaces and cultural arts grant programs. (Task Force 1998, 6–7)

A third source of input was SPO's 1999 report noting that while the voluntary local growth management approach to municipal participation had achieved positive results, that approach alone was not enough (Maine SPO 1999, 1–2). The state, the report held, would have to provide

- incentives and rewards for communities with consistent growth management programs;

- increased funding for local planning and implementation grants to meet new statutory deadlines;

- wider regional protection of wildlife and fisheries habitat; and

- strategies that go beyond regulatory approaches in addressing habitat fragmentation.

A key group contributing to the 2000 legislative package was the Smart Growth Task Force, consisting of five members from the Senate and eight members from the House, representing the key committees concerned with growth issues. Formally named the Task Force on State Office Building Location, Other State Growth-Related Capital Investments, and Patterns of Development, it was adopted by the legislature as Resolve 1999, Chapter 63, LD 304. An Emergency Preamble to allow it to go into effect immediately was signed by the governor on June 10, 1999. Normally, Resolves do not go into effect until 90 days after adjournment of the legislature. The justification for the Emergency Preamble cited the key elements needed to move Maine from sprawl to smart growth, well illustrated by the whereas clause that stated, "A long-standing goal of the state, as expressed in Maine Revised Statutes, Title 30-A, section 4312 (the 1988 Growth Management Act) is to encourage orderly growth and development in appropriate areas of each community while protecting the state's rural character, making efficient use of pubic services and preventing development sprawl." Time was of the essence because a report needed to be submitted to the next session of the legislature (January–June 2000).

The Smart Growth Task Force was convened on September 17, 1999, and held eight meetings through early January 2000. Its mission was to encourage orderly development and discourage sprawl in order to enhance the historic role of downtowns, strengthen the state's regional service center communities, promote rural enterprise and preserve the open lands on which rural enterprise depends. The task force was even bold enough to define sprawl:

> Low density development beyond the edge of service and employment, that results in escalated costs for schools, services and infrastructure, and that impacts the viability of a national resource-based economy and the vitality of Maine's traditional downtowns. (Maine Office of Policy and Legal Analysis 2000a, 1)

To achieve its mission, the task force committed itself to six objectives, all key elements of moving Maine to smart growth. Among these objectives were: to meet the demand of municipalities for establishing new or updating existing comprehensive plans and to assist in their implementation; and to provide ongoing and broad-based legislative involvement in the issues related to development and sprawl (Maine Office

of Policy and Legal Analysis 2000a, 1–2). Of special significance is that this assessment of the downsides of sprawl development in Maine is very similar to assessments made in other states and regions, as are the actions that must be taken to move in a new smart growth direction.

Another significant group was the Eco-Eco Civic Forum, based at the College of the Atlantic in Bar Harbor. Eco-Eco is described as "a statewide, nonpartisan group comprised of business, environmental, government and civic leaders pursuing common goals that enhance the economy and ecology of Maine." In its report *The Paradox of Sprawl* (Eco-Eco Civic Forum 1997), the group made it clear that new approaches would be needed to change long-established sprawl development patterns. Eco-Eco hosted eight statewide regional smart growth forums during 1998 that were well attended and well received. Eco-Eco continued its work in 1999 and into 2000 as the Maine Smart Growth Forum. The emergence of these broad-based coalitions is one of the key reasons why smart growth approaches in Maine and across the nation are more likely to be sustained and strengthened.

The last important source of input was the recommendations of Governor King's Smart Growth Sub-cabinet, chaired by Transportation Commissioner John Melrose. This working group consisted of 11 agencies represented by the commissioner or director and a designee, including Evan Richert and John DelVecchio for SPO. The committee stated as its goal: "To maintain Maine's competitive advantage as one of the most livable places in the United States—a place with growing, vital cities and towns, a productive countryside, and a revered natural environment" (Governor's Smart Growth Sub-cabinet 2000, 2). This report, *Smart Growth: The Competitive Advantage*, meshed closely with the findings of the Smart Growth Task Force and Eco-Eco.

The governor's subcabinet developed nine measurable objectives to be achieved by 2010, really a series of "visions" of what Maine would be like 10 years later (Governor's Smart Growth Sub-cabinet 2000, 1–2).

1. An increased population of Maine's job centers in urban and rural areas

2. Thirty years of stagnation and decline reversed

3. Reduced highway congestion and improving air quality

4. Increased use of both passenger mass transportation opportunities and air, rail and marine freight transportation over the use of traditional highway transportation

5. Assured that the number of new homes in designated growth areas will account for 65 percent of all new homes in the state

6. Increased protection of marine and coastal environments

7. Livelier downtowns developed

8. The amount of cropland harvested stabilized and possibly increased

9. Better managment of forests

The second part of the report outlined a three-year action plan built around four priorities, with specific actions needed to achieve them.

1. *State capital investments: enhancing public benefits.* Included an increase in state funding of local comprehensive plans and implementation programs from $250,000 to $500,000 per year to speed up the rate at which towns developed consistent comprehensive plans with designated growth areas. As of 1999 only 165, or about one-third of organized municipalities, had consistent plans.

2. *Keep rural lands ecologically and economically productive.* A Farm and Open Space Tax Act, proposed to be submitted to the 2000 legislature, included wildlife habitat and waterfront tax benefits; a Strategic Plan for Land for Maine's Future, targeting substantial portions of land acquisition funds for purchase of threatened rural lands around spreading urban areas; and a number of other fiscal measures.

3. *Resurgent service centers.* Included implementing the Main Street Maine Downtown initiative, including a multimodal transportation investments program and a joint investment program to improve infrastructure that served high-density mixed uses. Another item was to create and capitalize a Downtown Fund from the state surplus to support low-interest loans to municipalities with designated downtowns. Other items called for using a state income tax credit to cover brownfields redevelopment and giving priority to locating leased and owned state office space and civic buildings to downtowns and designated growth areas. Another goal was to review codes that could inhibit development of historic buildings and other downtown properties, with recommendations for needed changes. Also included were a home ownership program for service center downtown areas to encourage owner-occupied three- and four-unit buildings in high rental, low-income areas, and a proposal to support service centers losing population by making up for lost school funding and community revenue-sharing formulas.

4. *The Great American Neighborhoods.* Addressed traditional neighborhood development (TND) and healthy commercial centers. It included reforming local land use ordinances to allow the development of traditional neighborhoods (i.e., compact, walkable, mixed-use neighborhoods). A series of implementing actions called for preparing model ordinances for TNDs to be incorporated into local land use ordinances, and a design manual for towns and home builders, including case studies of Maine towns that "approach this concept." State funding of a "patient" sewer and water extension loan program was proposed, so that municipalities and sewer and water districts could finance extensions but delay repayment of loans until development takes place and charges are made to developers, provided the development takes place in designated growth areas that allow three or more units per acre in the service area of the extensions. Another item called for a governor's executive order "that requires state agencies to review their regulations for secondary impacts that may tend to discourage the development of traditional neighborhoods and commercial centers, or that tend to encourage development sprawl throughout the state." (Governor's Smart Growth Sub-cabinet 2000, 7)

The report's fiscal item charged "the Land and Water Resources Council with maintaining a biennial 'report card' on progress toward this initiative's measurable objectives within each of the state's 'extended communities'—that is, areas defined by the State Planning Office that consist of one or more service centers and surrounding suburbs and rural towns that are bound together economically" (Governor's Smart Growth Sub-cabinet 2000, 7).

Legislation Recommended by the Smart Growth Task Force

The legislature's Smart Growth Task Force heard presentations that reinforced the collaboration between and among the task force, the governor and his key agencies, Eco-Eco Civic Forum, the State Planning Office, and the Smart Growth Sub-cabinet. At its last meeting on January 7, 2000, the task force reached a consensus on its wide-ranging recommendations. Given the breadth and depth of those recommendations, the substantial funding called for, and the strong focus on the land use dimension of smart growth, that consensus was remarkable.

The Smart Growth Task Force eventually recommended three laws for consideration by the 2000 legislature as integral to its Smart Growth Initiative. The first and most extensive was LD 2600, relating to state office building location, capital investments and patterns of development. As proposed, LD 2600 set up the Maine Downtown Center to encourage downtown revitalization and a Downtown Leasehold Improvement Fund to encourage state agencies to secure space in downtowns. There was also a mandate that SPO and municipalities collaborate in selecting "priority locations" for new schools and state growth-related capital investments in locally designated growth areas designated in a comprehensive plan. In a move to implement the Municipal Investment Trust Fund, a Maine Municipal Bond Bank would be authorized to make loans to municipalities for downtown improvements, with an initial $5 million appropriation.

Other features of the bill included establishment of the 16-member Task Force to Study Growth Management; an evaluation of incentives to keep rural lands undeveloped and ways to expand the redevelopment of brownfields; and a directive to SPO regarding the development of model land use ordinances with smart growth design standards and flexibility in zoning regulations to allow traditional neighborhood development in designated growth areas. Finally, the proposed bill appropriated grants to municipalities and regional councils for planning, financial and technical assistance.

The second bill, LD 2550, focused on better highway access management and included a long list of other requirements to achieve smart growth by promoting land use–transportation linkages, including a special study of transit funding and ridership and innovative transit and transportation projects that address sprawl and air quality issues (Maine Office of Policy and Legal Analysis 2000b, 1). The third bill, LD 2510, aimed at implementing the task force's tax policy recommendations, included tax changes to strengthen service center communities and the protection of farmland for farming.

The Smart Growth Task Force's final report listed its objectives and recommendations and assigned a cost of $31.1 million for their full implementation. Of special significance for reviving and expanding the 1988 Growth Management Act were major funding increases for municipalities and regional planning councils for plan updates and implementation grants. The SPO was given a directive to give priority "to innovative projects that focus on smart growth around the state" and "make 'smart growth' a theme throughout the planning process" (Maine Office of Policy and Legal Analysis 2000a, 13).

Recognizing that its recommendations and the substantial dollars necessary to implement them might seem excessive to some, the task force defended its recommendations and accompanying costs by concluding, "Managing growth and development is an investment in Maine's future while ensuring we maintain the character of our state. These efforts are costly up front, but as noted in *The Cost of Sprawl* (O'Hara 1997) will help Maine avoid more expensive investments in the future and help maintain Maine's traditional rural character" (Maine Office of Policy and Legal Analysis 2000a, 21).

Given the broad-based support for the task force's recommendations, one would expect to see them easily adopted into law. To a considerable extent that happened, but not without resistance from some local governments, developers and others, and a substantial reduction in the amount of dollars appropriated to support reenergizing the goals of the 1988 Growth Management Act. Even so, the new dollars for planning for smart growth were significant and gave SPO important flexibility in how those dollars would be allocated. Of at least equal importance, actions by the governor, supported by the legislation, went far toward making state agency spending part of the solution instead of part of the problem.

Actions by the 2000 Legislature

The most extensive and remarkable single piece of legislation, LD 2600, aimed at implementing the land use recommendations of the Smart Growth Task Force. General fund appropriations to SPO, as originally presented in LD 2600, totaled more than $8.5 million, including some $3,835,000 in planning grants to municipalities, $4,000,000 in grants to regional councils for technical assistance to municipalities, and $700,000 for grants to municipalities for plan implementation and updates, including funding for pilot projects focusing on regional projects. This proposed funding was later reduced to $1.7 million and most of it was moved to LD 2510, the comprehensive state budget bill. The only SPO appropriation item that stayed in LD 2600 was a $100,000 appropriation to SPO to support the Downtown Center program.

Other Smart Growth Task Force recommendations adopted by the legislature in LD 2510 included establishment of the Task Force to Study Growth Management, charged with reviewing the growth management laws to make them more responsive to the issues of sprawl.

LD 2510 also reduced the withdrawal penalty under the Farmland Tax Law to the minimum required by the state constitution. However, the recommendation to reimburse municipalities for up to 90 percent of lost tax revenue resulting from valuing farmland at its current use did not succeed. In another significant funding action, the act allowed additional state-municipal revenue sharing for municipalities having property tax burdens that were above the average. One-time funds in the amount of $3.6 million were appropriated to be distributed in June 2002 (Maine Office of Policy and Legal Analysis 2000b, 1–2).

While not all of the Smart Growth Task Force recommendations were approved by the 2000 legisla-

ture, especially in the area of funding, there was at last a reversal of the drastic funding cuts of the early 1990s that had crippled the effective implementation of earlier legislation. The difference is significant for our purposes: a strong focus on promoting smart growth and reversing sprawl development patterns was at the core of many of the initiatives. The conclusion of the task force report noted the "growing tendency" of state public agencies to place their capital investments in the "wrong" places that encourage sprawl. This "shift of population outward into rural communities and the expense of services necessary to support that shift has created unintended consequences: fiscal, environmental, economic and social costs all related to a spread-out pattern of development often known as sprawl" (Maine Office of Policy and Legal Analysis 2000a, 21).

To a substantial degree, the recommendations of the Smart Growth Task Force had included the views of Eco-Eco Civic Forum, Governor King's Smart Growth Subcommittee, King himself, and other supporters of the better management of growth and change in Maine. There were dissenters to some of the legislative actions, including MMA, as well as some in the development and corporate communities. But Eco-Eco's leadership and membership included many of these interests, and the very name of the group—Eco (ecology) and Eco (economy)—was intended to make the point that not only are the two not in conflict, but "you just can't have the one without the other." However, MMA (2000) thought the marriage of antisprawl financial assistance with consistent comprehensive plans was unfair because it would limit state assistance to just the one-third of Maine's municipalities that qualified. MMA and the State Board of Education also objected to the original wording of the school siting recommendations.

What can be said with certainty is that the Smart Growth Initiative supported by stakeholders from all the key sectors—public, private, nonprofit and citizen groups—was ultimately put in place by the first and second sessions of the 119th Maine legislature in 1999–2000. Not only were new policies adopted to supplement and reinforce the goals and objectives of the 1988 Growth Management Act, but for the first time since the drastic cuts of the early 1990s, Maine's budget surplus was used to fund the system to draw the remaining municipalities into full compliance with the system.

Furthermore, the approval of state spending legislation directed a wide range of capital investment dollars into municipalities whose comprehensive plan included designated growth areas, or into identified surrogate areas for those municipalities whose plans were not yet completed under the 1988 legislation. The very substantial planning and plan implementation funds put in place for municipalities, while less than recommended by the Smart Growth Task Force and other supporters, seemed sure to speed up the process of developing certified plans and implementation regulations.

Smart Growth Actions, 2001–2004

The 2001 Legislature

After the November 2000 election, the 2001 Maine legislature was made up of 89 Democrats, 61 Republicans and 1 Independent in the House, but 17 Democrats, 17 Republicans and 1 Independent in the Senate. Despite the even party split in the Senate, the first session of the 120th legislature (January–June 2001) adopted additional laws moving Maine in a smart growth direction.

The actions of the second session of the 120th legislature (January–May 2002) grew out of *The Final Report of the Joint Study Committee to Study Growth Management* (2001). That committee was cochaired by Senator Lynn Bromley and newly elected Representative Ted Koffman, who had been an effective advocate for smart growth from his base at Eco-Eco Civic Forum.

According to the report, the committee's main concern "was the need to establish an entity that can, on a more consistent basis, confront issues dealing with planning for growth and preserving the character of Maine's communities" (Maine Joint Study Committee 2001, 5). To meet this need, the committee's first priority for the upcoming legislative session was the establishment of a long-term, continuing Community Preservation Advisory Committee (CPAC) that would "allow the Legislature to meet the challenges

Selected Legislative Actions in 2001

- LD 578 addressed the design of a statewide geographic information system local governments could use for planning. The study committee made recommendations that resulted in LD 2116, adopted in the second session of the 120th legislature.

- LD 669 established priorities for award of the Municipal Investment Trust Fund dollars (service centers, communities with certified growth management programs and consistent comprehensive plans, and projects involving one or more communities that benefit the region). The Task Force to Study Growth Management recommended that the fund be capitalized at $20 million, but that was rejected, with first-time funding approved in the amount of $300,000.

- LD 1278 amended the definition of subdivisions and prohibited municipalities from adopting ordinances that expanded that definition except as provided by law. It also required the SPO to report on local government subdivision ordinances before December 15, 2001.

- LD 1693 authorized the SPO to adopt rules to specify and clarify what local governments could and could not do in the requirement of consistency between local land use regulations and comprehensive plans. The law required that after January 1, 2003, the "rate of growth, zoning, and impact fee ordinances must be consistent with a comprehensive plan." The law also enhanced coordination efforts between state agencies in support of local planning.

- LD 1783 related to siting new school construction where state monies are involved. The State Board of Education, in considering a new school on a new site, must take into consideration those "preferred areas" identified in a local government's comprehensive plan as a locally designated growth area. If there is no plan, the board should consider a site that would not add to sprawl. The board must collaborate with appropriate federal, state and local entities when making such a decision (Maine Office of Policy and Legal Analysis and SPO 2002, 1, 3–4). Efforts to bring local governments on board in planning and acting in a coordinated fashion through a combination of mandates and incentives moved forward, but with strong resistance from the Maine Municipal Association.

of planning for the impacts of growth and development in Maine with more consistency, yet it would be structured to provide flexibility and promote new ideas" (Maine Joint Study Committee 2001, 5).

CPAC would review and make recommendations on all aspects of efforts to move toward smart growth: fiscal, transportation, education funding, school siting and land use policies. The name of the new committee was derived from the Joint Study Committee's belief that the term *growth management* did not adequately cover the issues to be addressed in the new century. The term *community preservation* focused on "preserving the character of communities in Maine, while planning for growth and development" (Maine Joint Study Committee 2001, 5–6).

Strongly supported by Ted Koffman and other smart growth advocates, CPAC began meeting in October 2002. All parties agreed on the need to correct "three structural barriers to addressing sprawl: Maine's taxation system; lack of effective regional mechanisms; and the need for an ongoing interdisciplinary advisory committee." The establishment of CPAC met this last need (SPO 2003, 12).

CPAC has introduced a new dimension in Maine's smart growth agenda. Unlike other smart growth task forces in the 1990s, CPAC was given five years to develop and pursue an agenda during several sessions of the legislature. The remarkable progress CPAC has made in furthering the smart growth cause in Maine comes in large part from its first pair of cochairs, Senator Peter Mills and Representative Koffman, as well as its broad membership representing state departments, nonprofit organizations and the private sector.

The Joint Study Committee outlined other priorities, including action to support regional planning by towns and adequate funding of the Municipal Investment Trust Fund. The committee noted that after several failed efforts to finance the fund since 1994, "In the First Regular Session of the 120th Legislature, a $300,000 bond issue for grants and loans to municipalities for public infrastructure was passed by the Legislature and approved by voters in the November 2001 election" (Maine Joint Study Committee 2001, 5).

The committee also called for amending Maine's Growth Management Act "to clarify that towns can work together to plan for growth...replacing the term 'municipality' with the terms 'multimunicipal region' and 'planning district.'" Finding that financial incentives were necessary to involve towns, the committee called upon the legislature to approve a general fund bond issue of $8 million in order for the trust fund to provide revolving low-interest loans (Maine Joint Study Committee 2001, 5–7).

Other findings and recommendations in the report addressed familiar issues of transportation, municipal growth ordinances, land and water resources and transfer of development rights. In the area of affordable housing, the committee outlined the following obstacles that often lead to failed policies (Maine Joint Study 2001, 6).

■ Restrictions on growth without careful planning can drive affordable housing out of a community and create additional housing development pressures in neighboring towns.

■ Overly restrictive and exclusionary zoning can create insurmountable financial obstacles for affordable housing development.

■ Unpredictable and inconsistent land use planning adds time and money to the development process and causes housing costs to escalate.

To say that the recommendations of the Joint Study Committee were far-reaching in strengthening Maine's growth management system would be an understatement. For every recommendation, the report included draft legislation for implementation. When and if implemented, the role of the state and region would be greatly strengthened, a fact bound to draw the fierce opposition of the MMA unless it could be persuaded that such a smart growth system would be an advantage, including an accurate understanding of the home rule rights of municipalities.

The 2002 Legislature and Election

The 2002 legislature moved Maine forward substantially in its smart growth agenda. A remarkably large number of the bills recommended by the Joint Study Committee were sponsored by Representative Koffman from his position as chair of the House Natural Resources Committee. One of the most significant bills, LD 2094, amended laws relating to land use regulations and comprehensive planning. With regard to growth management, the bill added and amended definitions, strengthened the roles of local governments, and specifically called for multimunicipal planning. It also increased "the flexibility in designating growth and rural areas by including a provision for critical rural areas, critical waterfront areas, and transitional areas, and by placing multimunicipal planning projects on an even footing with single town planning efforts" (Maine Office of Policy and Legal Analysis 2002, 1–3).

Angus King's term as governor was limited, and in the November election voters chose John E. Baldacci, a Democrat. He had served as a state senator for 12 years and served eight years as a Congressman from Maine, never losing an election in that timeframe. Ted Koffman and other smart growth supporters were positive about Baldacci's support for smart growth initiatives in Maine.

Public and Private Stakeholders

The far-reaching report, titled *We Have a Choice*, prepared by the Maine State Planning Office in February 2003, examines actions at all levels of government to achieve smart growth in Maine. It singles out Governor King's Smart Growth Sub-cabinet, made up of the SPO and 10 state agencies, for focusing on "a strong rate of return on public investment, a renewed commitment to environmental stewardship, and stepped up efforts to build and strengthen community" (SPO 2003, 4). This report offers a thorough evaluation of Maine's growth management program, outlines many aspects of the Smart Growth Initiative that had been established over the previous several years, and proposes nine priority areas for action over the next four years (to 2008).

1. *Support collaborative forums of smart growth interests.* Continue to work with public, private and nonprofit groups to bring and keep multiple interests involved in the pursuit of smart growth principles and to continually refine strategies to achieve the goals.

2. *Evaluate tax reform options.* Evaluate tax reform proposals to assess their impact on sprawl.

3. *Coordinate planning and investment.* Work with state, regional and local partners to make service centers attractive, affordable places to live in order to retain and attract residents.

4. *Plan for local street and infrastructure investment.* SPO will work with the Maine DOT and other agencies to establish a framework and technical assistance for local street network platting and capital investment for infrastructure that supports livable, compact development patterns.

Selected Legislative Actions in 2002

- LD 2049 involved TDRs and clarified that a municipality can implement a TDR program within its jurisdiction. Only when two or more municipalities have an interlocal agreement may they provide for TDRs.

- LD 2059 established that on-site parking was required only to assure reasonable public access and to accommodate staff and/or visitors with disabilities. Parking for employees could be located off-site as long as it was within reasonable walking distance.

- LD 2061 amended the priorities for Municipal Investment Trust Fund grants and loans, making the top priority funding for projects involving two or more local governments.

- LD 2062 mandated that municipalities having rate of growth ordinances review them at a minimum of every three years. However, the final version of the bill did not include the recommendations of the Joint Study Committee to Study Growth Management.

- LD 2070 established the Community Preservation Advisory Committee to study issues related to growth and report on them to the governor, legislature and State Planning Office.

- LD 2082 amended subdivision review requirements for traffic so that speeds of a mobility arterial would not be reduced by the proposed development.

- LD 2099 amended how affordable housing is defined in statutes relating to growth management but did not include the more substantive recommendations of the Joint Study Committee.

- LD 2116 created the Maine Library of Geographic Information and Maine Library of Geographic Information Board, to establish policies and standards on GIS data.

- LD 2119 amended the definition of *subdivision* and removed the 40-acre lot exemption from the definition, and prohibited local governments from expanding the definition in their ordinances, unless provided in state law.

- LD 2120 called for including $2.3 million in the November 2002 environmental bond issue.

- LD 2130 fell short of the Joint Study Committee's recommended $8 million, but called for including $4 million in the Economic Development bond issue approved by Maine voters in June 2002.

5. *Optimize school construction funds.* SPO will continue to work with the Board and Department of Education to invest state school construction funds in a way that...incentiv[izes] community preservation and smart growth.

6. *Focus environmental regulation.* Assure that environmental regulations do not have the unintended consequence of driving development outward. To this end, SPO will continue to work with the state's natural resource agencies to enhance the current policy framework, moving from piecemeal regulation to one that considers multiple resources simultaneously.

7. *Provide housing choices.* Market studies show that many people want to live in traditional, compact neighborhoods within walking distance of services and facilities. Many residents cannot afford suburban, large-lot subdivisions, which prevail in many towns today.

8. *Build capacity to measure outcomes of smart growth efforts.* There are some promising initiatives that should be considered, [which] require good data.... SPO will continue to design/build systems to measure the success of smart growth efforts so that the next evaluation can be more quantitative.

9. *Set priorities.* Progress has been made over the last four years, yet significant effort lies ahead. Given resource limitations, SPO must carefully select where to invest its limited resources over the next four years to assure continued progress. (SPO 2003, 7–9)

The formation of a number of smart growth policy advocacy groups also has spurred action throughout the state. Friends of Midcoast Maine, for example, began in 2000 "when 14 land trusts and advocacy groups met to discuss the increasing impacts of sprawl in the Midcoast Route 1 Corridor. Friends was launched as a grassroots initiative to reduce unplanned development in the Midcoast region through encouraging smart land use and transportation planning" (Friends of Midcoast Maine 2003a, 1). The group's Regional Smart Growth Principles are the key components of smart growth strategies to

- encourage development that maintains the New England tradition of compact towns separated by rural countryside;

- direct public funding to guarantee investment in existing schools, neighborhoods and infrastructure in compact mixed-use centers;

- protect and preserve the economic vitality and diversity of farmlands, forests and working waterfronts;

- protect the quality of our environment, open space, scenic landscapes and historic features;

- provide a range of housing alternatives, especially in fast-growing communities;

- promote transportation choices that reduce auto dependency;

- ensure stakeholder and regional collaboration in land use–transportation planning;

- save taxpayers money by balancing the location of growth with the availability of public utilities and services;

- support economic vitality by encouraging business enterprises in downtowns and villages, especially locally owned businesses; and

- promote smart growth goals and strategies through coalitions linking state planning with local planning. (Friends of Midcoast Maine 2003b, 1)

The organization is working with other groups on a Route 1 Corridor Planning Initiative, which seeks regional consensus on a long-term vision for the corridor and that will develop a strategy to implement the vision. The Maine DOT, SPO and other state transportation agencies are moving forward with just such a process. Entitled Gateway 1, MDOT has invested $300,000 to get it started, and federal funds of $1 million are being requested to move it along (Friends of Midcoast Maine 2003c, 5).

Another new group is GrowSmart Maine, the only statewide organization focused on stopping sprawl in the state. Since its first public meeting in December 2002, GrowSmart Maine has built a broad-based organization with a cadre of part-time professionals and volunteers providing expertise on growth-related public policy. They disseminate information through publications and presentations, community-based activities, and an extensive media communications program. One of the organization's early campaigns opposed a proposed casino referendum in 2003 because it had no regional planning mechanism to deal with the major infrastructure and housing impacts on the affected towns. In December 2004 more than 500 citizen planners, public officials, business interests, land trust advocates, farmers and others attended the organization's first summit, titled "Sprawl, Smart Growth and Maine's Future."

GrowSmart Maine's current initiatives are looking at proposed legislation and links between sprawling growth patterns, the growing cost of government, and the state's ability to compete for jobs and economic growth. This work complements Governor Baldacci's economic development strategy, announced in January 2004, which states that Maine must embrace four fundamental economic drivers: (1) the creation of a fair and stable business environment to attract investment; (2) investment in people; (3) a clear focus on key sectors of the state's economy; and (4) building infrastructure.

This emphasis on linking economic development with smart growth is also reflected in the work of the Maine Service Centers Coalition, which focuses on about 80 (out of 500) municipalities where most jobs and commerce occur and where most medical, educational and cultural institutions are located. The coalition was formed in 2001 under the auspices of the Maine Municipal Association "with the mission of providing a mechanism to articulate the needs of service centers to elected officials; to educate the citizenry as to the importance of healthy and thriving service centers; and to network and collaborate with all municipalities in the pursuit of promoting opportunities for all who visit, work or live in Maine" (MMA 2001).

Updating the 1998 report of SPO's Task Force on Regional Service Center Communities, the coalition developed a strategic plan in 2003 with contributions from GrowSmart Maine and CPAC, as well as MMA, SPO and other state agencies. The emphasis of the plan is on conserving Maine's economic, natural and human resources through revitalizing and reinvesting in the service centers. Matters of public expenditures, tax policy, government organization and service quality and regulatory issues are of primary concern as the group seeks to "level the financial playing field" among municipalities through property tax relief, greater private sector investment and other initiatives (Maine Service Centers Coalition 2003).

Urban revitalization was also the focus of a May 2004 executive order by Governor Baldacci "to strengthen and restore the vitality of Maine's downtowns." The Maine Downtown Center and SPO issued a follow-up report in October 2004 that addressed a number of barriers at the state and local levels that discourage downtown redevelopment efforts. Among its recommendations are integrating downtown revitalization as a key component of the state's economic development strategy, including funding and marketing; adopting a statewide model building rehabilitation code and state fire safety code for existing building renovations; and providing permanent capitalization of the Municipal Investment Trust Fund program. The center has already leveraged more than $11 million in total new downtown investment over the past four years since its establishment (Maine Downtown Center 2004).

The Community Preservation Advisory Committee (CPAC), established by the 2001 legislature and authorized through mid-2008, also meets regularly to review legislation and make recommendations on timely policy matters relating to growth management, economic development in rural and downtown centers, location of schools and other public buildings, and tax policy as it affects land use decisions. In 2003 CPAC's mandate expanded to address barriers to affordable housing and undertake reviews of municipal comprehensive plans by the SPO for consistency with the state's Comprehensive Planning and Land Use Regulation Act. Other priorities for the committee in 2004 included supporting better integration of transportation investments and land uses; a sustained campaign to increase public awareness of community preservation and smart growth; and support of SPO's Maine regional service center communities and its Great American Neighborhoods program (CPAC 2004).

Governor Baldacci has generally been supportive of Maine's recent moves toward smart growth, as has been the legislature. In addition, on November 4, 2003, voters approved a plan for statewide bonds raising some $63 million to improve transportation facilities (e.g., highways, bridges, rail corridors), making the state eligible for $17 million in federal funding. Tax reform was the most controversial issue for voters in 2004, when they soundly defeated a California-style tax cap referendum as being too extreme. Following that election, Governor Baldacci and the legislature moved quickly to make property tax relief a top priority of the 122nd First Regular Session, as a movement for a Taxpayer Bill of Rights initiative also was established.

Conclusion

After lying largely dormant following the severe funding cutbacks in the early 1990s, Maine's sound but never fully implemented growth management system has benefited from major moves during the early 2000s aimed at its revival and strengthening. Significant leadership came from former Governor Angus King and his planning director Evan Richert, and current Governor John Baldacci is continuing their efforts.

They all pinpointed the increasing downsides of small towns in Maine acting in isolation from each other, creating unplanned sprawl and rising costs due to duplicate services. Baldacci has stated that Maine is on a "full collision" course between competing values of home rule and a penchant for frugal government (Peirce 2004). But the state is beginning to address a regionalization program with cash incentives for localities that agree to curb local tax rates through sharing services among towns and school districts.

Other important recent developments have been the emergence of the Eco-Eco Civic Forum led by Ted Koffman and his leadership in the Maine House after his election in 2000; Kay Rand's strong advocacy from her base as the governor's chief of staff; the outstanding work of the Community Preservation Advisory Committee beginning in 2002; and the strong leadership of the Maine State Planning Office.

Maine, then, has a number of new laws, initiatives and funding programs that, through incentives (and disincentives), are helping to bring Maine's municipalities into the system to ensure a balanced local/regional/state partnership supportive of smart growth. What are the prospects that Maine's smart growth strategies can be fully implemented over the next decade and beyond? Emerging new leadership

Selected Legislative Actions in 2003–2004

- LD 1617 prohibits subdivisions that convert the primary use of the land from timberland to nontimberland use when the land being subdivided has changed ownership in the five years preceding a subdivision application and when a subdivision exceeds 100 acres.

- LD 1668 requires a state agency, when awarding grants or making discretionary investments, to give first preference to a municipality that has received a certificate of consistency for its growth management program and has adopted land use ordinances and a capital investment plan.

- LD 463 requires the Department of Transportation to adopt a major substantive rule that establishes linkage between the Sensible Transportation Policy Act and comprehensive planning and land use regulation laws.

- LD 1025 creates the Maine Model Building Code, composed of the International Residential Code and the International Building Code. Adoption of the Maine code is voluntary, but a town, city or municipality may not adopt a residential or nonresidential building code other than the Maine Model Building Code.

- LD1858 amends the point system for clearing vegetation adjacent to protected natural resources (Joint Order 2004, S.P. 684). It changes the definition of "well-distributed stand of trees" by increasing the area from a 25' × 25' square area to a 25' × 50' rectangular area and by changing the rating system. The bill also prohibits a landowner or lessee from aggressively eliminating all woody vegetation higher than three feet.

in the public, private and nonprofit sectors, along with a recent boost in the state's economy, make a smart growth future for Maine much more likely than in the recent past.

Maine References

Carson, Everett (Brownie). 1992. The next step. *Maine Growth Management News.* Augusta: Natural Resources Council of Maine. Summer.

Chinitz, Benjamin. 1990. Growth management: Good for the town, bad for the nation? *Journal of the American Planning Association* 56(1).

Community Preservation Advisory Committee (CPAC). 2003. First annual report of the Community Preservation Advisory Committee. February.

———. 2004. *Second annual report of the Community Preservation Advisory Committee.* January.

Eco-Eco Civic Forum. 1997. *The paradox of sprawl.* Bar Harbor, ME: College of the Atlantic. October 30.

Friends of Midcoast Maine. 2003a. Annual report 2002–2003. Camden, ME. November 6.

———. 2003c. *Newsletter* 2 (Fall).

———. 2003b. *Regional smart growth principles: What can be done?*

Governor's Smart Growth Sub-cabinet. 2000. *Smart growth: The competitive advantage.* Augusta, ME. January.

Kennebec Journal. 1988a. Land use bills win support, but state's role hits snag. March 17.

———. 1988b. Last lap toward managing growth. April 18.

———. 1988c. Panel gives unanimous O.K. to growth management bill. April 15.

Maine Department of Economic and Community Development (DECD). 1989. Highlights of the new growth management law. Augusta, ME. April.

Maine Department of Economic and Community Development, Office of Comprehensive Planning (DECD/OCP). 1988. *Guidelines for Maine's Growth Management Program.* Augusta, ME. December.

———. 1989. Directory of state data resources. Prepared by Market Decisions, Inc. (MDI) with Stevens Morton Rose and Thompson, Inc. Augusta, ME. April.

———. 1990a. Biennial progress report. Augusta, ME. January.

———. 1990b. Report of the Planning Advisory Committee. Augusta, ME. January.

Maine Downtown Center and Maine State Planning Office. 2004. Revitalizing Maine's downtowns: A report resulting from Executive Order 16 (FY04/05): An order to strengthen and restore Maine's Downtowns. October.

Maine Joint Study Committee to Study Growth Management. 2001. Final report of the Joint Study Committee to Study Growth Management. December.

Maine Land Use Regulatory Reform Committee (LURRC). 1994. *Integrating land use and natural resource management.* Augusta, ME. January.

Maine Legislature. 1989. Title 30-A, 4312. Statement of findings, purpose and goals. http://www.janus.state.me.us/legis/statutes/30-a/title30-asec4312.html.

Maine Municipal Association (MMA). 1987. *Growth management strategy.* Augusta, ME. November 18.

———. 2000. *Legislative Bulletin.* March 31.

———. 2001. Maine's service center communities to organize. Press release. September 4.

Maine Office of Policy and Legal Analysis, Maine Legislature. 2000a. Final report of the task force on state office building location, other state growth-related capital investments, and patterns of development (known as the Smart Growth Task Force report). Augusta, ME. January.

———. 2000b. Smart growth initiatives in the 119th Maine legislature. May 12.

———. 2002. Summary of growth management measures enacted by the 120th legislature.

Maine Office of Policy and Legal Analysis and State Planning Office (SPO). 2002. Growth management and sprawl legislation, 119th and 120th legislatures, summary of activity.

Maine Service Centers Coalition. 2003. A strategic plan for revitalizing Maine's service centers. Prepared by Maine Tomorrow. September 22. http://www.memun.org/public/MMA/Gov/Svc_Ctrs/MSCCStrategic_Plan9-22-03.htm.

Maine State Planning Office (SPO). 1987a. A legislative proposal for land use management in Maine. Augusta, ME. November.

———. 1987b. Land use and cumulative impacts of development: A study summary. Augusta, ME. December.

———. 1999. Continuing challenges and growing opportunities: Report to the Joint Standing Committee on Natural Resources on implementing Maine's growth management program. Augusta, ME. February 2.

———. 2003. We have a choice. Report to the Joint Standing Committee on Natural Resources to evaluate Maine's growth management program. Augusta, ME. February.

National Growth Management Leadership Project. 1992. Hard times in Maine: Growth management down—but not out. *Developments* 3(2).

Natural Resources Council of Maine (NRCM). 1987a. An analysis of Maine's land use management system and goals for proposed changes. Augusta, ME.

———. 1987b. A legislative strategy to manage growth in Maine. Augusta, ME. November 18.

———. 1988. *Maine growth management news.* Augusta, ME. Spring.

———. 1992. Comprehensive planning continues. *Maine Growth Management News.* Augusta, ME. Summer.

———. 1993. Growth management: Scant funding remains. *Maine Growth Management News.* Augusta, ME. Winter.

O'Hara, Frank. 1997. *The cost of sprawl.* Augusta: Maine SPO.

Peirce, Neal. 2004. Collaborate or collapse—tough New England message. http://www.postwritersgroup.com/archives/peir0417.htm.

Pochna, Peter and Clarke Canfield. 1997a. The pattern of growth in southern Maine has its costs. *Portland Press Herald* and *Maine Sunday Telegram.* July 6.

———. 1997b. State policies fostering suburban sprawl. *Portland Press Herald* and *Maine Sunday Telegram.* July 8.

Task Force on Regional Service Center Communities. 1998. *Reviving service centers.* Augusta, ME. September.

Turkel, Tux. 1988a. Growth: Maine enters a new era. *Maine Sunday Telegram.* April 24.

———. 1988b. Land use proposals set stage for debate. *Maine State Times.* January 29.

———. 1988c. Opponents hammer out accord on controlling growth in Maine. *Maine Sunday Telegram.* April 17.

U.S. Census Bureau. State and county QuickFacts: Maine. http://quickfacts.census.gov/qfd/states/23000.html.

———. Projections of the total population of states: 1995 to 2025. *http://www.census/gov/population/projections/state/stpjpop.txt.*

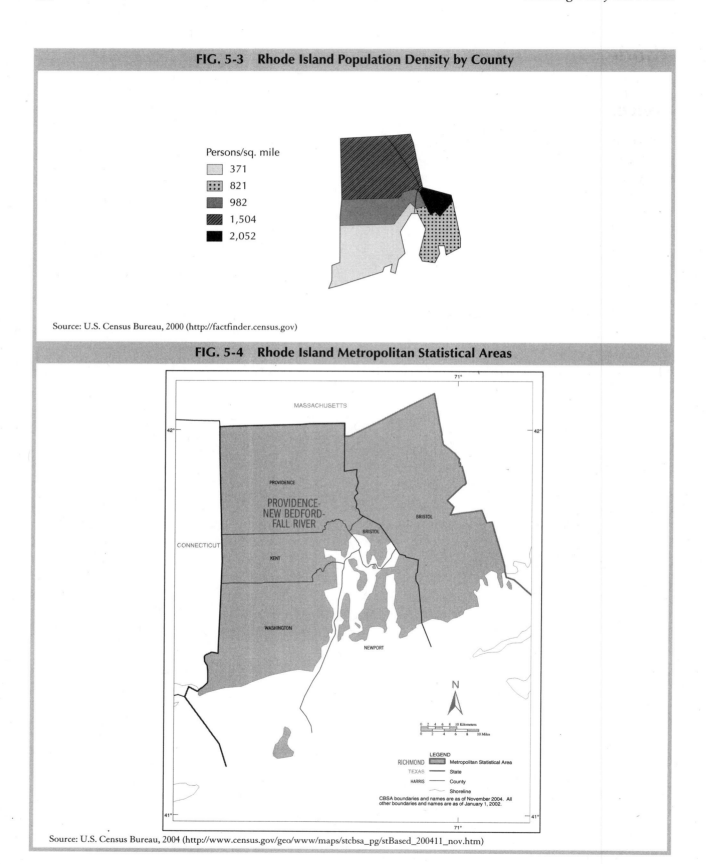

FIG. 5-3   Rhode Island Population Density by County

Persons/sq. mile

	371
	821
	982
	1,504
	2,052

Source: U.S. Census Bureau, 2000 (http://factfinder.census.gov)

FIG. 5-4   Rhode Island Metropolitan Statistical Areas

Source: U.S. Census Bureau, 2004 (http://www.census.gov/geo/www/maps/stcbsa_pg/stBased_200411_nov.htm)

Rhode Island

Concern for a Special Place

The Issue Context

Rhode Island is the nation's smallest state in land area, with just over 658,000 acres, yet it is the second most densely settled state, with a population of 1,048,319, according to the 2000 U.S. Census Bureau. Beginning with 400,000 persons in 1900, the state grew steadily until 1970, when it reached a population of 950,000. During the 1970s the closing or reduction of several U.S. Navy bases resulted in a loss of more than 25,000 military personnel and their families. Civilian population increases did not make up that deficit, and the state had a net loss for the decade of slightly more than 2,500. Growth resumed in the 1980s and 1990s, and the population is projected to reach 1,062,441 in 2005, and 1,128,260 in 2025 (RIDA/SPP Web site, see appendix).

Rhode Island is incorporated within 39 municipalities (8 cities and 31 towns). Although the state is subdivided into five counties, they act only as judicial districts and have no inherent governmental powers. Some cities and towns (primarily in suburban and exurban areas) saw substantial growth in the 1980s and 1990s, and that growth was projected to continue. The towns of Richmond and Charleston were expected to have the highest rates of growth (more than 50 percent) from 1990 to 2010. Thirteen towns were predicted to grow by more than 20 percent during that same period, with the statewide increase estimated at a modest 9.54 percent (RIDA/DP 1989c, 4.7–4.8).

Rhode Island had more than its share of economic problems, even in the context of the Northeast's recession. Heavy dependence on manufacturing has limited Rhode Island's ability to sustain economic growth on a level with the rest of the region. Land available for industry is limited. The departure of the navy in the 1970s vacated substantial industrial and commercial land, but a strategy for its effective reuse was slow to develop. Relatively low incomes in a high-income region have meant that the state's per capita income has been lower than the rest of its southern New England neighbors, although by the late 1990s the state had pulled even with the nation (RIDA/DP 1989c, 4.13).

Some of Rhode Island's leading products, including textiles, jewelry and shipbuilding, were susceptible to foreign competition and were on a level or downward growth curve. The state as a whole, and certain areas in particular, faced economic stagnation in the 1980s and into the 1990s, and there remained a need to pursue strong policies to assure a prosperous economic future. At the same time, the opening of key interstate highways in the 1980s brought an influx of people from the Boston and New York areas looking for more affordable housing and jobs requiring limited skills.

Given its demographic and economic profile, one might ask why Rhode Island, in 1988, put in place one of the nation's strongest growth management systems and why that system continued to enjoy substantial support in spite of the economic recession of the early 1990s. In fact, the notion of a statewide growth management system was not new to Rhode Island.

As early as the mid-1970s, Dan Varin, director of the Division of Planning in the state's Department of Administration, led a movement to create such a system. Varin was active in the Council of State Governments' National Land Use Project, and pushed to pass a land use law. The proposed law was a variation on the American Law Institute–American Bar Association Model State Land Development Code, with provisions for a strong state role in regulating developments of regional impact and areas of critical state concern. The proposed legislation could never muster enough support for passage due to opposition largely from the development community, smaller home builders and local zoning boards. As one developer who later supported the 1988 legislation put it, the 1976 bill "smacked of a Big Brother approach." A friendlier observer noted that the timing was bad, developers were "already hurting," and cities and towns still viewed growth and land use issues in a parochial manner.

A number of factors during the 1980s contributed to changing the attitudes of key stakeholders toward a state growth management system. The return of economic prosperity to New England in general brought strong growth pressures to Rhode Island for the first time in its recent history. With the completion of Routes 128 (I-95) and I-495, New York and Boston came within commuting distance. Many Bostonians looking for more affordable housing moved to northern Rhode Island. Second-home development along the coast also increased substantially.

The numbers tell the story. One source noted that the state's 1984–1988 building boom saw the issuance of 24,000 permits for residential development, valued at almost $6 billion (Holtzman 1988, 14–18). The costs and negative impacts of this unmanaged growth surge, real or perceived, included the loss of open space, higher taxes to pay for infrastructure and sharply rising housing costs. By the mid-1980s all relevant interests—developers, environmentalists, local governments and citizens—were finding the existing development process inadequate for managing the unprecedented growth pressures facing the state.

While Rhode Island's developers found strong markets for their residential and commercial products, they faced an unpopular regulatory environment. In spite of economic hard times during the 1970s, the environmental movement had gained strength in Rhode Island, and new regulations governing septic tanks, coastal areas, wetlands and other natural resources came on line. Some projects took 18 months or more to get through state and local regulatory processes. One state official noted that it could take three months to get any response at all from the system, much less approval. The development community wanted to ward off moratoriums, simplify an increasingly complex system of environmental permitting, and establish a development approval system that was more timely and predictable than that of the 1970s.

For some local governments, the initial response to strong development pressures was large-lot zoning; later they passed moratoriums to set rules and regulations to cope with the growth. Few towns had comprehensive plans and land development regulations in place, but their citizens were increasingly unhappy with what they saw as the negative impacts of growth. Like many citizens of New England, Rhode Islanders feel a special connectedness to the land, and they saw the boom of the 1980s breaking that connection. Save the Bay, Rhode Island's largest environmental organization, founded in 1970, was already moving from a concentration on restoring water quality in Narragansett Bay to a broader growth management agenda that included, but was not limited to, protecting the entire bay region.

An unwritten state tradition held that citizens would have access to the shore by traversing private but undeveloped land, which was often held in large tracts. The second-home boom along the coast ruptured that tradition as access was closed by developers or residents "from somewhere else." The custom of "private property functioning, very discreetly, as public open space" was sharply curtailed. This "loss of access made Rhode Islanders willing to throw their bodies in front of bulldozers, and helped persuade them to spend a great deal of money to do something about the situation" (Hiss 1989, 58).

Two actions that pre-dated the 1988 growth management legislation illustrate the concern of citizens and environmentalists alike. First, the need to protect rural open spaces and shoreline access led to an unusual bipartisan and apolitical coalition of environmental groups and government officials. They backed up their plan by launching the largest per capita open-space financing program in the country. State action was matched at the town level. The state responded to citizen concern first in 1985 with approval of a $9 million bond issue for open space protection. In 1986, a $16–18 million issue was approved. The same year, the town of Jamestown (population 4,500) spent $2.1 million to buy a large parcel scheduled for golf course development, and a year later voted to spend another $5 million to buy farms and ponds all over town. Then, in 1987, the General Assembly approved a $65 million bond issue, largely to buy land for open space, and passed a law to assist towns in adopting open space bond acts. Thirty-four of Rhode Island's 39 municipalities responded positively, including "both the poorest ones and the richest ones," adding $61 million to the effort (Hiss 1989, 57–58).

The second response to growth pressures was an attempt to address rising housing costs. A proposed law would have withheld all state aid from towns unless they zoned a certain percentage of their land in quarter-acre lots to encourage the construction of affordable housing. The towns never adopted the law, but Governor Edward DiPrete supported the approach and continued to call for mandated small-lot zoning. Later, during the development and adoption of the growth management system that passed in 1988, the governor again called for other quantitative affordable housing requirements (Holtzman 1988, 14–18).

Building a Consensus for Growth Management

One key legislator, House member Bob Weygand, emerged as the leader in the effort to fashion support for a new partnership for managing growth, with a major role for the state. Elected in 1985, Weygand was a landscape architect and professional planner who had also served as chair of the East Providence Planning Board. In the 1986 legislative session, he laid the groundwork for a consensus building effort to bring relevant interests together on a comprehensive approach to growth management in Rhode Island. By 1987, Weygand was ready to introduce a bill to create a Land Use Commission (LUC) with a broad-based membership representing all the relevant interests.

In 1987 a 23-member LUC was appointed by the governor, the lieutenant governor, the Senate majority leader and the House speaker. Appointees included members of the House and Senate; representatives from cities and towns, Save the Bay, and the League of Women Voters; four state agency heads (one voting, the others nonvoting); and representatives from the real estate development community. The executive director of Rhode Island's League of Cities and Towns was included, as was a representative of the Executive Office of the Governor. The law included a $50,000 appropriation, but the burden of staffing the commission fell on the Division of Planning. DiPrete was slow to make his appointments, perhaps because the commission approach was not on his agenda, but he completed the process, and in December 1987 LUC held its first meeting.

Given the failure to pass a state land use statute in the 1970s and early 1980s, there was considerable skepticism about whether the "warring factions" could be persuaded to agree on anything. As the work of the commission proceeded, however, the skeptics were proven wrong, due to the changed environment of the 1980s and the choice of Weygand as chair. His various experiences enabled him to gain the confidence of key interests on the commission. Weygand's first meeting was a workshop encouraging all the interests to air their frustrations with the existing system. LUC members were surprised to find that they shared with their traditional "opponents" many of the same dissatisfactions and concerns with the existing land development process.

The commission established three subcommittees to study identified problems more closely: the planning process, subdivision regulations and zoning regulations. From December 1987 to March 1988, the full commission and its subcommittees held 35 public hearings, during which the commission reached a consensus on a number of important issues, including the need for comprehensive local plans and for zoning consistent with those plans; for special attention to historical, cultural and, especially, environmental resources; and for documenting infrastructure needs and assuring that services such as transportation were provided as development occurred.

As chair of the Corporations Committee in the House, Weygand handled the proposed bill drafted by the commission. It passed easily, with the support of the Speaker of the House and the lieutenant governor in the Senate. The consensus building over the previous four months paid off as key interests from environmentalists to developers signed on to the bill. As in Maine, every group felt there was enough good in the bill to balance things they did not like. The strong state role offered developers more protection from moratoriums and no-growth efforts at the town level. Towns hoped the new system would be heavy on process and light on substance and would provide substantial dollars to participate in the process. Environmentalists saw important substantive requirements in the provisions for protection of natural areas, open spaces and agricultural lands. The state bureaucracy also strongly supported the effort.

Governor DiPrete alone was unhappy with the proposed legislation because it did not include a stronger affordable housing component. When both the Speaker of the House and the lieutenant governor in the Senate (both Democrats) made it clear that they had large enough majorities to make the bill veto-proof, the governor ultimately let the bill become law without his signature.

Key Features of the 1988 Growth Management Legislation

The Rhode Island Comprehensive Planning and Land Use Regulation Act and its companion statute, the State Comprehensive Plan Appeals Board Act, had the potential to be the most complete state growth management program of the 1980s.[1] The program provided a blueprint for the state's growth and development, with strong state and local roles. The comprehensive planning act stated that local governments were required to "plan for future land use which relates development to land capability, protects our natural resources, promotes a balance of housing choices, encourages economic development, preserves and protects our open space, recreational, historic and cultural resources, and provides for orderly provision of facilities and services" (R.I.G.L. 45-22.1-5[A]). To ensure this requirement was met, the state was given responsibility for review and approval of local plans.

State Goals

Rhode Island's two comprehensive planning laws set forth the state's goals relating to growth and development. They covered specific procedural and substantive requirements for development of local plans and implementing programs; a process for state review of local plans for consistency with state goals and guidelines; a process for recourse to an appeals board; the roles of state agencies in the system; and state technical and financial assistance for local planning. The substantive goals focused on

■ compatibility of growth with the natural characteristics of the land;

■ economic development to assure jobs and overall economic well being for Rhode Island;

■ affordable housing; and

■ protection of natural resources, open space and recreational resources, as well as cultural and historic resources.

The process-oriented goals focused on

■ use of innovative development regulations and techniques;

■ consistency of state actions and programs with municipal comprehensive plans;

■ review procedures to ensure that state goals and policies are reflected in municipal comprehensive plans and the State Guide Plan;

■ consistency of development regulations with plans;

■ the provision of adequate and uniform data to municipal and state government as the basis for comprehensive planning and land use regulation;

■ a call for consistency between mandated plans and the required implementing regulations at both local and state levels; and

■ involvement of citizens in the planning process. (R.I.G.L. 45-22.1-3[c])

The State Guide Plan is actually a collection of plans that have been adopted over many years, beginning in 1974, as a means for centralizing and integrating long-range goals. It contains 30 elements in the following functional areas: general goals and policies; economic development; energy; historical preservation and cultural heritage; housing; land use; natural resources; recreation and open space; solid waste management; state facilities; transportation; and water resources. The content of the State Guide Plan is prescribed only in general terms. Any matter of importance to the state's residents, government, cities or towns can be included. Local governments and the public participate in the planning process, which must be closely coordinated with the budgeting process.[2]

---

1. Rhode Island General Laws (R.I.G.L.), Chapter 45-22.2 and Chapter 45-22.3, respectively. The quotations and references in the following paragraphs are taken from various sections of these chapters. See http://www.rilin.state.ri.us/Statutes/title45/index.htm.

---

2. See the most recent overview of the elements of the State Guide Plan (R.I.G.L. 42-11-10) at http://www.planning.state.ri.us/sgp/sgp.htm.

Governance of Local Comprehensive Plans

The provisions of the comprehensive planning act required cities and towns to "adopt, update and amend comprehensive plans, including implementing programs consistent with the provisions of this chapter" (R.I.G.L. 45-22.6). Towns were to adopt a zoning ordinance and map consistent with the comprehensive plan within 18 months of plan adoption and approval. The state would review amendments to an approved plan in the same fashion as the original plan, with amendments limited to four times in any calendar year. Towns and cities were required to update plans at least once every five years.

The section in the act on regional elements contained both process and substantive requirements. The process requirements included internal plan consistency and a capital improvements program specifying costs of needed public facilities, the funding sources to pay for infrastructure costs, and the schedule for bringing the zoning ordinance and map into conformance with the comprehensive plan. Substantive elements dealt individually with land use, housing, economic development, natural and cultural resources, services and facilities, traffic circulation/transportation, and open space and recreation. The specific requirements were set forth in a concise and nontechnical paragraph emphasizing implementation of plan elements, including necessary coordination between elements.

Regional agencies are not part of the Rhode Island governance system, but the section on the "coordination of municipal planning activities" addressed problems that spilled across municipal boundaries and authorized joint planning and regulatory programs. Whether or not they entered into such joint efforts, all municipalities were expected to coordinate land uses with contiguous municipalities, with a special emphasis on rivers, aquifers and transportation facilities. The act outlined procedures for preparing and adopting comprehensive plans, including the roles of planning boards or commissions and the local legislative body. It also required citizen input.

The provisions for state review of local comprehensive plans placed that responsibility on the director of the Division of Planning. Local plans had to be consistent with the State Guide Plan, and with the goals and policies of the Comprehensive Planning and Land Use Regulation Act. The act spelled out timeframes for the plan review process; the review of an individual plan could not exceed 180 days.

The State Planning Council is authorized by statute to create committees to assist in carrying out its responsibilities. Standing committees conduct continuous operations, while special committees are appointed as needed to study a specific topic or to deal with an issue of current interest. The Technical Committee is comprised of public members from different geographic areas of the state who represent diverse interests and officials of all levels of government. It reviews major plans and advises the State Planning Council, ensuring representation of a range of interests and views in the state's planning activities. The committee holds regular monthly meetings and reviews staff reports throughout the year. State Guide Plan elements and documents are reviewed by the Technical Committee before being recommended to the State Planning Council.

Should a municipality fail to meet the consistency test applied by the division director, it can appeal the decision to the Comprehensive Plan Appeals Board, which can support, amend or overturn the director's decision. The appeals board is composed of 11 members appointed by the governor, the Senate and the House, and is carefully crafted to include members from large, medium and small municipalities. All members are either elected or appointed local officials, come from a different city or town, and have a "reasonable knowledge of land use, planning, zoning" and related matters (R.I.G.L., 45-22.2-1-8). The provision that the minority leader in the House and the Senate each have one appointment to the board ensures a bipartisan balance. If a city or town loses an appeal, it can then appeal directly to the state Supreme Court. The state planning director can also appeal a board reversal of a department decision to the Supreme Court.

Rhode Island is unique in its provision concerning the consequences for a local government's failure to develop a plan consistent with the requirements of the state's growth management system. In such a case, "the Director shall...prepare and the State Comprehensive Plan Appeals Board shall adopt...

a comprehensive plan which satisfies the requirements of this chapter" (R.I.G.L., 45-22.1-1-13). The provision itself is the best assurance that it will not be used; no city or town wants to place its fate wholly in the state's hands.

Rhode Island's provisions for bringing state agencies fully into the growth management system go further than most states. The heart of the link between state agency actions and state-approved local comprehensive plans is the requirement that "Once a municipality's comprehensive plan has been approved, plans and projects of state agencies shall conform to that plan. In the event that a state agency wishes to undertake a project or to develop a facility which is not in conformance with the comprehensive plan, the state planning council shall hold a public hearing on the proposal" (R.I.G.L., 45-22.1-IO[E]). At the hearing, the state agency is required to meet a four-part test: (1) conformance with the comprehensive planning act; (2) conformance with the State Guide Plan; (3) the need "to promote or protect the health, safety and welfare of the people of Rhode Island"; (4) a design that "varies as little as possible from the comprehensive plan of the municipality" (R.I.G.L., 45-22.1-1-13).

Rhode Island's program was comparatively generous in providing state technical and financial assistance to cities and towns for the preparation of their plans and implementing regulations. The planning division director administered the planning grants program that allocated up to $125,000 to each municipality according to a funding formula based in part on land area and population. The act also charged the division director with providing a statewide database for use by local governments, and with the duty of validating data from other sources used by the municipalities.

Implementing the Growth Management System, 1988–1992

As impressive as Rhode Island's Comprehensive Planning and Land Use Regulation Act was, its impact on growth management reflected the high level of implementation efforts that began in the summer of 1988. A clear indication of a state's commitment can be found in how much funding is allocated for implementation and how that funding is made available. In Rhode Island, as elsewhere, the softening of the economy in the late 1980s did not critically affect the implementation effort at first. However, as state revenue surpluses turned to deficits, all programs came under scrutiny in an effort to reduce spending. The key issue that emerged in the early 1990s was whether Rhode Island's system could survive the economic downturn.

Planning and Infrastructure Funding

The proposed $3 million appropriation to support local plan preparation in 1989–1990 was deemed too high by the governor. A compromise was to appropriate $900,000 in the 1989 fiscal year and fund the remaining $2.1 million in a $78 million bond issue originally intended to support land acquisition for open space and recreation, address water pollution problems and support an oil spill clean-up fund. Thus, in spite of an economic downturn and some initial uncertainty about support from the governor's office, "full" funding to assist local planning efforts was achieved in the early years of the implementation effort. The $3 million in planning funds were estimated to represent about 75 percent of the local costs of preparing plans. The first funds were granted to support local data collection for the plan. A town or city was required to pass a resolution indicating its intent to apply for state planning dollars, and to make a commitment to use the funds to carry out the mandates of the growth management law.

Infrastructure funding was another story, for both backlogs and keeping up with the impacts of new growth on water, sewer, transportation and open space needs. Sanitary sewer systems had been the subject of special attention for some time, so the "catch-up" requirements were minimal. An effort in the mid-1980s to quantify a substantial transportation backlog (roads and transit) failed due to incomplete or nonexistent data. The bond issues of the 1980s addressed the need for additional open space acquisition, but more funding would be necessary. Water supply and water quality issues, including better storm water management to control nonpoint source pollution, constituted a potentially large but not fully documented concern.

There was, then, a need for new infrastructure funding, but politics and finances made securing such funds difficult. It would seem that, at least until the economic downturn of the early 1990s, the people were ahead of the politicians in their willingness to support new revenues for infrastructure. The lack of gubernatorial leadership was the main deterrent to action.

Implementation Documents

The Division of Planning produced four major implementation documents from 1988 to 1990. The first, the *Grant Application and Management Handbook* (RIDA/DP 1988), explained the formula for determining the amount of each planning grant: 50 percent of the planning funds to be equally divided among the 39 municipalities (and one Narragansett Indian entity); 20 percent based on each municipality's total land area; and 30 percent based on population as recorded in the most recent Census data. The handbook listed the eligible amount for each city or town and made it clear that the grants program was not a competitive program. It also included advice about engaging consultants, outlined the plan review process, and set the tone for subsequent implementation documents issued by the Division of Planning: simple, straightforward and designed to draw cities and towns into the system as quickly as possible (RIDA/DP 1988, 71). Three additional documents were prepared and issued by the division over the following 10 months.

The *Handbook on the Local Comprehensive Plan* (RIDA/DP 1989b) addressed steps in plan preparation, adoption and implementation; the role of the State Guide Plan; the central purposes of the law; the process and content requirements of the nine local plan elements; the process for local government plan adoption; the process for local plan review by the state; the appeals process and the consequences of failure to develop an acceptable plan. On a more optimistic note, the handbook addressed the advantages of plan acceptance. Most notable were the parts that clarified the links between the State Guide Plan and the local plan elements.

The handbook described the land use plan portion as the principal element of any local government comprehensive plan, and considerable attention was given to what must go into it, including the required land use map. It highlighted the importance of the housing element with housing requirements, including implementation strategies that were relatively specific. The section on services and facilities strongly recommended but did not require a capital facilities program, and while the principle of concurrency was recommended it was not required. The section on transportation stressed close coordination with land use and other elements.

One of the key features of Rhode Island's growth management system was its emphasis on implementation. The handbook summed it up nicely: "The Implementation Program is significant because it is in this final element that a program of actions is devised and scheduled to lead to the attainment of local goals and the implementation of local policies emanating from all the plan elements" (RIDA/DP 1989b, IV-41). It has been the experience of every state adopting a comprehensive growth management system that goals stand little chance of attainment and even well-conceived and documented plans will be unrealized without a carefully formulated program of implementation. For Rhode Island, minimum requirements for implementation were specific, and planning dollars were available to ensure initial involvement by most if not all of the 39 local governments in the system. However, that was not enough to ensure achieving the goals of the system.

As in other states in New England, Rhode Island made a strong commitment to collect and make available to local governments data sources to assist them in preparing the mandated local plans. The *Data Catalog* provided agency names, contact persons and telephone numbers for the seven functional local plan elements (RIDA/DP 1989a). Special attention was given to how cities and towns might request data from the Rhode Island Geographic Information System (RIGIS) at the University of Rhode Island. A final implementation tool, the handbook titled *State Agency Goals and Policies*, provides municipalities with a brief synopsis of 17 state agencies, along with special commissions and other groups (RIDA/DP 1990).

Local Plan Review Criteria

The Division of Planning's development of substantive local plan review criteria gave important clues as to where it would put the emphasis in reviewing local plans. The three main concerns were housing, economic development sites and sensitive environmental areas. With regard to housing, the division developed a target number of low- and moderate-income units for each community based on the 1980 Census data, with some updates. Local communities could adopt a different number, but it had to be approved by the state. Setting numerical targets for affordable housing units provided a capacity for implementation and enforcement that could make affordable housing a reality.

Economic development emphasized sites because existing data indicated that few sites were available for industrial development. Of an estimated 35,000 acres zoned industrial, perhaps 15,000 acres remained vacant, in part because of proximity to an environmentally sensitive area or a lack of needed infrastructure. New industry was seen as a necessity in Rhode Island because of the mismatch between the labor force and available jobs.

Concern for sensitive environmental areas focused especially on developments in locales subject to flood hazards and on preserving wetlands and protecting water recharge areas, and ground and surface water. Protection of important agricultural land can be included in this category; there were about 31,000 acres of farmland and some 700 working farms at the time the program was adopted. Local plan land use elements were required to address the protection of those lands, and funds were provided for the purchase of development rights through the bond issues of the 1980s. TDR systems had not been authorized but were being considered.

The Division of Planning's technical assistance to cities and towns in preparing their plans was unusual, if not unique. Because Rhode Island lacks regional agencies to provide direct assistance to local governments, such assistance must come from the state. However, some felt that since the state was responsible for plan review, a conflict of interest might arise were the state to help municipalities with their plan preparation. Therefore, the division initially assigned technical assistance staff for towns' day-to-day planning and regulatory activities in order to free the towns' own staffs for long-range comprehensive planning.

Positive Legislative Actions

By 1990 the implementation of Rhode Island's new growth management system was well under way. However, it was clear to the creators of the system that local governments could not implement their mandates fully without a complete overhaul of both the zoning and subdivision regulation enabling acts. The growth management legislation of 1988 addressed primarily the issues studied by the planning subcommittee of LUC, while the recommendations of the rezoning and subdivision subcommittees had been postponed in order to put the growth management system in place.

Of major concern was the state's original Zoning Enabling Act, which allowed zoning boards of appeal to grant special exceptions to zoning ordinance land use provisions. The zoning boards in Rhode Island had long been viewed as out of control. Their discretionary powers can be (and have been) used to justify almost any exception to the regulations. Observers have noted that the boards did not keep good records and had a reputation for selling development approvals. The courts have frequently reversed and severely criticized the boards, and many citizens have concluded that their zoning boards were "giving away the town." A fierce battle to revise the law and clip the wings of these powerful boards was anticipated.

Things looked good for a revision of the Zoning Enabling Act early in 1990. Introduced by Weygand, there was strong support in the House for the subsequent amendment, and it passed without a dissenting vote. After much debate in the Senate, the bill eventually was passed successfully in the 1991 legislative session.

LUC and other supporters of the growth management system also gave a high priority to revising the Subdivision Regulations Enabling Act, which had some unusual provisions. For example, an "approval not required" provision allowed the subdivision of lots with 10 feet of frontage on a public road without review under subdivision regulations. The result has been the widespread creation of "spaghetti lots" that have substandard access to public rights-of-way. The rewrite of the Land Development and Subdivision Review Enabling Act, passed in 1992, was the second major challenge in ensuring implementation of Rhode Island's growth management system.

Another significant piece of proposed legislation was the Rhode Island Housing and Conservation Trust Fund Act, which sought to create and sustain low- and moderate-income housing while conserving and protecting Rhode Island's important natural areas, recreational lands and agricultural lands. The Coalition for Housing and Open Space, made up of more than 50 nonprofit affordable housing and conservation groups, together with Weygand and others in the General Assembly, drafted the proposed law. The trust fund would have been authorized to receive appropriated state funds or funds from any other private or public source approved by the board. Part of the funding was to come from a surcharge on property transfer fees over $100,000, which would have raised $3–$5 million annually. At least 25 percent of the trust's funds in a given year would have to be spent for housing, 25 percent for conservation, and the other 50 percent for either category where proposed projects met criteria.

The General Assembly passed the act in 1990, but did not provide funding. A 13-member study commission to determine appropriate sources and levels of permanent funding encountered difficulty gaining support from financial sources, so the act never went into effect. The governor proposed a $10 million bond issue to fund the trust, which was subject to both General Assembly and voter approval, but it failed. Subsequently, several attempts were made to establish funding for the trust, but only one passed. In June 1994 the Senate bill was put into law, which authorized the trust fund board to accept "any private grant, device, bequest, donation, gift, or assignment of money, bonds, or other valuable securities for deposit in and credit of the Rhode Island Housing and Conservation Trust Fund" (R.I.G.L. 42-113).

Prospects looked good in 1990 and 1991 for the full implementation of Rhode Island's growth management system. Governor Bruce Sundlun, a Democrat who defeated incumbent Republican Edward DiPrete in the November 1990 election, seemed supportive,

and he signed into law the Zoning Enabling Act following the 1991 legislative session. LUC, with Weygand at its head, continued to function. The plan review process was well under way, with 17 of 40 plans submitted as of spring 1992. One plan had been approved, 16 were still in the review process, and, at that time, no plans had been rejected.

However, the recession and funding cuts in 1991 left many agencies without sufficient staff to make a full review of the local plans submitted. Somewhat surprisingly, however, no one believed the downturn of the economy would actually jeopardize the system, partly because economic development was one of its major features.

Progress and Complications, 1993–1998

Winning legislative approval of three key growth management laws (1988 Comprehensive Planning Act, 1991 Zoning Enabling Act, and 1992 Subdivision Regulations Enabling Act) within four years was a major accomplishment, especially in view of the lukewarm support of governors DiPrete and Sundlun. In a Division of Planning report, staff member Derwent (Derry) Riding noted, "the end of 1995 will signal the effective date of the last of the three new planning acts, and with that Rhode Island will become one of [the] few states with fully effective, modern land use planning acts" (RIDA/DP 1994, 1–3). These laws certainly did provide a strong framework for a fully effective growth management system, but not until late 1999 to mid-2000 did the system evolve in such a way as to justify that claim.

Adoption of Local Plans

Town adoption of plans in accordance with the 1988 comprehensive planning act, the first step in the process, went forward much more slowly than originally intended. It was not until the end of 1995 that all 39 cities and towns had approved their plans and submitted them to the state Division of Planning to review consistency. The fact that all 39 cities and towns entered into the process and ultimately adopted a local plan that supposedly met the requirements of the law was due in considerable part to a relatively generous planning grant that was available from already approved bonding proceeds. The grants ranged from $125,000 for the three largest cities (Cranston, Providence and Warwick) to almost $44,000 for the smallest jurisdiction, New Shoreham. The Narragansett Indian Tribe lands, comprising the fortieth jurisdiction, participated in the process on a voluntary basis and received almost $40,000. By September 30, 1995, some $3 million had been provided to the 40 jurisdictions, with a commitment by those receiving the money to adopt a plan under the 1988 planning act (Rhode Island 1995).

The end of 1995 was long past the originally scheduled deadline for implementation of the local plans, but the delays were worse with regard to state review for compliance with the law. A key factor in the delays in certifying local plans was the drastic cuts in the Division of Planning's local assistance staff just as the first plans started coming in for review in 1992. Given their very small size, many Rhode Island towns had few, if any, professional planning staff, so the cuts in the Division of Planning were a major setback in getting the system in place.

Other factors contributed to delays in getting all local plans adopted and ultimately certified as consistent with the planning act, including the added requirements of the zoning and subdivision regulations statutes. LUC had insisted that the town's or city's governing body approve the plan, because otherwise there would be no local political "buy-in" and the chances of implementation would be reduced. However legitimate that premise, it complicated the process. Once adopted by the local government, the local plan went to the state for review (coordinated by the Division of Planning), and a number of state agencies suggested changes. The Division of Planning then gave its assessment of changes needed for the plan to be eligible for consistency certification. Those changes then had to go through the local governing body approval process again. Towns and cities were responsible for the costs of making these changes, and the recession of the early 1990s obviously made that part of the process more difficult.

Another complicating factor was that towns and cities were expected to change their plans to meet the zoning and subdivision requirements, even if they had not been certified as consistent. The Division of Planning's response was to insist that local governments press forward with changes to their existing plan, since it was their best effort at the moment. The consistency doctrine was not familiar to many Rhode Island cities and towns, and Varin, Weygand and others had successfully supported clear and compelling language in the state planning law and the zoning and land use regulation statutes.

However, the Rhode Island courts did not support a consistency concept, and case law pre-dating the 1988, 1991 and 1992 statutes did not recognize comprehensive plans as providing an essential basis or guide for zoning. A state Supreme Court ruling (*Town of East Greenwich v Narragansett Electric Company*) on December 19, 1994, recognized the primacy of the local comprehensive plans. In powerful language supporting the consistency doctrine, the Supreme Court stated:

> We believe a comprehensive plan is not simply the innocuous general policy statement the town contends it is . . . the comprehensive plan . . . establishes a binding framework or blueprint that dictates town and city promulgation of conforming zoning and planning ordinances. . . . The General Assembly has clearly instructed . . . *each city and town to conform its zoning ordinances and zoning map to be consistent with this comprehensive plan* [emphasis by the court].[3]

In rejecting decisions prior to the 1988 planning act and subsequent zoning and land use regulation laws, the court stated that those cases decided before the General Assembly enacted the Comprehensive Planning and Land Use Regulation Act were no longer sound authority (Varin 1995, 1–3). The court's ruling certainly strengthened the argument for an integrated growth management system for Rhode Island, but it was still unclear that cities and towns could actually be persuaded or forced to honor their own plans and regulations even after they had been certified as consistent by the state.

By the end of December 1998, in spite of the many delays in moving the process along, the state had

---

3. *Town of East Greenwich v Narragansett Electric Company*, no. 93-589-M.P., Supreme Court of Rhode Island, 651 A.2d 725; 1994 R.I. Lexis 298, December 19, 1994, decided, filed.

certified as consistent all 39 cities and towns, with the Narragansett Indian Tribe still participating on a voluntary basis. This certification was not synonymous with state approval of all municipal plans, however. The true test of the system was still to come—whether the cities and towns would actually implement their new plans and regulations in a manner that was consistent with and giving full meaning to Rhode Island's growth management system.

Organizational Changes

The Statewide Planning Program has survived a number of reorganizations over the years since it was created in 1964 by an interagency agreement between the Rhode Island Development Council and the state Department of Public Works. The program was designed to serve as a guide for future development policy by the state agencies and other entities involved with land use planning and transportation. State planning functions expanded significantly in the 1970s, when the program was placed within the Department of Administration. Following a major reorganization of that department in 1986, a Division of Planning was created legislatively to consolidate and reorganize planning functions. It included three major subdivisions: the Office of Strategic Planning, the Office of Systems Planning, and the Office of Municipal Affairs. However, in 1997 the division was dissolved and its component units were reassigned, which left the Statewide Planning Program far down in the organizational structure. The Office of Systems Planning was later renamed Statewide Planning and was assigned responsibility for maintaining and developing the State Guide Plan. The program's mission was "preparing and maintaining plans for the physical, economic, and social development of the state; encouraging their implementation; and coordinating the actions of state, local, and federal agencies and private individuals within the framework of the state's development goals and policies" (RIDA 1998a, 1).

Updating the State Guide Plan

Updates and new elements have been added to the State Guide Plan, with special importance for implementing the growth management system. These include establishing a course of action for the main-

tenance or the restoration of all of the state's fresh waters, as well as their immediate environment (Rhode Island Rivers Council 1998). Another key element, Transportation 2020: Ground Transportation Plan, was adopted by the State Planning Council in 1998 to set the direction for state transportation policy and action and complement elements dealing with land use, economic development, green space and greenways, and other related topics (RIDA 1998b). It provides a framework with which local comprehensive plans must be consistent. The secondary purpose of the plan is for federal transportation funding, which will support desired land use patterns; preserve assets and manage them well; add services to reflect new travel demands and shifts in usage; and have a financial base adequate for supporting needed services.

The changes to the State Guide Plan are significant for measuring the consistency of local comprehensive plans, programs and projects with state policies. However, the changes also make the full implementation of the growth management system more complicated because, as the elements are updated, they call for action by local governments to bring their plans into consistency. On the positive side, the common thrust of many updates is to strengthen the state growth management framework. The integration of state, local and federal actions, including stronger citizen participation, has the potential to bring Rhode Island closer to achieving the goals of its growth management system.

Developments in the Growth Management System, 1999–2000

Rhode Island governors traditionally have not provided strong leadership to either the original adoption of the growth management system or the subsequent steps needed to bring the system fully on line. Governor DiPrete objected to the 1988 comprehensive planning act because it did not include a stronger affordable housing component. Governor Sundlun also did not support the measures needed to ensure the full implementation of the system, including sustained funding for the state's technical assistance and oversight functions. Finally, Republican Governor Lincoln

Almond, elected as Rhode Island's first four-year-term governor in 1994 and reelected in 1998, only reluctantly began allocating any of the surplus produced by the state's strong economic recovery in the late 1990s for bolstering the Statewide Planning Program.

The growth management program was finally moving forward faster than in the past. However, one negative aspect was local governments' heavy reliance on the property tax, because this tax is not sensitive to regional and statewide interests. There was no system of tax base sharing in place to ease the negative impacts of tax-rich commercial or residential development, which may be lost to a neighboring local government in order to adhere to the requirements of a local plan, even one certified by the state.

In spite of this and other negative factors, all 39 local governments and the Narragansett Indian Tribe had prepared plans under the 1988 planning act, and by 1999, 21 of those local governments had met the requirements of the system for state certification. As noted above, that does not guarantee that the local governments will implement all the components of even the certified plans, but it does indicate that local governments are in the game.

One key goal of the Statewide Planning Program is to partner with other players in the system, including Grow Smart Rhode Island (see next section), key state agencies and federal programs to overcome the conviction firmly held by many Rhode Islanders that planning, and especially planning with a regional and state dimension, is in conflict with economic development. Far from being in conflict, however, careful planning by local governments within a clear state and regional framework can be a major plus in ensuring long-term economic prosperity for the state. Rhode Island's weak economy, relative to other New England states, makes economic development a central issue on every agenda.

A related Statewide Planning Program goal was to marshal available state, federal and other fiscal resources in such a way as to reward those local governments that have certified plans, especially those that implement them within a regional framework that is in close collaboration with their neighboring local governments. Among the positive developments was an evolving recognition that the cost of failing to implement a smart growth system for Rhode Islanders would have negative impacts not only on the quality of life for all residents, but also for the economic prosperity of the state.

The 1999 General Assembly passed An Act Relating to Valuation of Farm, Forest, and Open Space Land (Ch.252. 99-H 5452A) which was aimed at bringing some uniformity to how Rhode Island's 39 municipalities deal with key components of a smart growth system. The existing growth management act had not functioned well because of the discrepancy between assessment values and a true current use value. The new act called for establishing a process to determine current use rates and make them available to communities. It illustrated the increasing strength of Grow Smart Rhode Island in bringing about changes needed to move the state strongly in the direction of smart growth. In particular, it saw these assessment reforms as promoting open space conservation and the preservation of Rhode Island's rural character.

Grow Smart Rhode Island

Grow Smart Rhode Island, a nonprofit corporation founded in 1998, has emerged as a catalyst for bringing together key stakeholders in Rhode Island to push for public- and private-sector changes to move the state toward smart growth. At a spring 1997 conference some 600 citizens and representatives from organizations and agencies met to discuss the need for a new organization to educate citizens, business leaders and elected officials about the impacts of sprawl and about state and local policies and strategies to promote smart growth. Over the next year Grow Smart established itself with a "diverse, powerful 40-person board of directors representing business leaders, college and university presidents, heads of urban revitalization organizations, public transportation, the religious community, environmentalists, historic preservationists, realtors, and builders" (Grow Smart Undated a, 2). It also formed a technical committee (later renamed the Advisory Council) to establish public-private partnerships for specific smart growth efforts to bring together agencies that had not been communicating about the sprawl issue. A distinguished and broad-based board was successful in attracting significant funds to support the achievement of its adopted mission statement:

> To bring together diverse interests to protect and improve Rhode Island's quality of life, economic vitality, and environmental health and the unique physical character created by the state's historic cities, towns, and villages and by its farms, forests and open spaces. This will be achieved by promoting business and residential growth in urban and town centers and advancing open-land conservation and the preservation of rural character. (Grow Smart Undated a, 8)

Grow Smart's progress on funding has been impressive, although it still must expend a lot of energy to sustain itself. In 1998 the organization received a U.S. EPA Sustainable Development Challenge Grant to help pay for bringing focus groups together to discuss smart growth issues, fund a cost of sprawl study (noted below) and provide some operational support through 2000. The organization received other significant funding from the Rhode Island Foundation, the Prince Charitable Trusts, the Doris Duke Charitable Foundation and the Van Buren Foundation.

Armed with funding and strong leadership under Scott Wolf, its first executive director, Grow Smart established links with other smart growth efforts around the country, mainly through participation in the Growth Management Leadership Alliance. In the area of policy initiatives, Grow Smart made recommendations to the governor about strengthening the effectiveness of the Statewide Planning Program and the state's overall approach to planning major development projects. A 1999 report to the governor's chief of staff and his director of administration recommended further changes in the state's approach to planning. Out of this dialogue came a major governor's executive order in 2000 creating a Planning Council on Growth.

Grow Smart outlined a number of "bad news-good news" scenarios. On the bad news front, "Rhode Island's current inefficient use of land and infrastructure is having very negative social, economic, and environmental impacts on both our urban centers and on outlying areas. We are experiencing a steady drain of jobs, people and tax revenues from our urban centers while accelerated development in outlying areas is consuming open space rapidly" (Grow Smart

---

Other Key Issues and Measures Promoted by Grow Smart Rhode Island in Its Early Years

■ Creation of a user-friendly rehabilitation code

■ A state urban investment tax credit

■ An amendment to the farm, forest and open space act

■ An expansion of Rhode Island's historic preservation tax credit

■ Establishment of a state housing fund

■ An urban revitalization project for the south side of Providence

■ A proposed $50 million open space bond issue

Source: Grow Smart, Undated a and b

Undated a, 5). To illustrate this trend, Grow Smart cited *The Costs of Suburban Sprawl and Urban Decay in Rhode Island*, its landmark study published in 1999 and funded in part by U.S. EPA's Sustainable Development Challenge Grant (H.C. Planning Consultants 1999). Key points cited from that report included the following:

■ Between 1961 and 1995, residential, commercial and industrial land has been developed here at nine times the rate of our population growth;

■ The total value of property in our core cities between 1988 and 1998 declined by 24 percent, a drop of more than $31.3 billion. At the same time, effective tax rates in these communities rose by 44 percent, three times the rate of increase in rural areas;

■ Using conservative assumptions, our study demonstrates that continued sprawl, instead of switching to a more compact model of development, will cost Rhode Island more than $1.5 billion over the next 20 years. (Grow Smart Undated a, 5)

In spite of this gloomy picture, Grow Smart saw hope if Rhode Island could act quickly to "institute policies and practices that will enable Rhode Island to promote growth in areas where it can best benefit all our citizens. Changes in policies and practices are critical: if we do not alter our current pattern of development, then we will limit our ability to grow long term and undermine our high quality of life" (Grow Smart Undated a, 5). This is a strong statement from a group led by some of the state's leading corporate, business and development citizens, as well as almost every other relevant land use stakeholder group.

Grow Smart then went on to stress that, while it supports economic growth for Rhode Island, growth projects must be evaluated "not only for their local job creation, but also for their potential impacts on statewide industrial and commercial vitality, on the environment, and on the quality of life in the community" (Grow Smart Undated a, 6). To accomplish that, Grow Smart listed a number of actions aimed at strengthening cities and town centers; reforming the property tax system; promoting affordable housing; providing more transportation choices; and preserving farms, forests and other natural resources. To achieve these goals, the group recognized that state, local and private funds had to be committed to protect open space in perpetuity and to fund specific farmland efforts. It also had to ensure that Rhode Island towns have appropriate planning expertise and resources to conserve open spaces through creative development.

Growth Planning Council

In an unprecedented move toward smart growth in Rhode Island, Governor Almond issued the executive order "Creation of Growth Planning Council" on February 17, 2000. It established a 28-member council representing the private sector, environmental community, municipalities and the state. The 10-member steering committee included key state agency heads from the DEM, Department of Transportation and the Economic Development Corporation; the chief of the Statewide Planning Office; executive director of the Economic Policy Council; the Governor's policy director; and representatives of Grow Smart, the League of Cities and Towns, the Rhode Island Builders Association and the Nature Conservancy. Other council members represented several other municipal groups and nonprofit organizations. All were appointed by the governor except the legislative members (Rhode Island Office of the Governor 2000, 2–3).

Governor Almond directed the council to

- examine the economic, environmental and social impacts of Rhode Island's current development patterns;
- inventory all existing state programs, policies and expenditures to evaluate their effect on sustainable development and the preservation and enhancement of environmental quality and resources;

The "Whereas" Clauses of the Growth Planning Council

- The quality of life of the citizens of Rhode Island is inextricably linked to a balance of social, economic and environmental values; and
- Our economic development policy and ability to attract businesses and employees to our state is interdependent with our efforts to preserve our environmental, cultural and historic resources; and
- The state recognizes the responsibility of local communities in the development of balanced land use plans, taking into consideration the need for both an adequate tax base and the preservation of the environmental resources of each area; and
- The state understands the value of the resources that local communities, the business community, and nonprofit organizations can bring to the issue of the land use planning; and
- Direct public investments to reuse, revitalize or enhance existing infrastructure and resources can promote the preservation of natural resources as part of long-term economic strategy.

Source: Rhode Island Office of the Governor, 2000, 1

- recommend ways to encourage growth in economically and environmentally sound locations; and
- foster partnerships among state agencies, communities and the private sector to build local capacity to plan for and implement sustainable growth. (Rhode Island Office of the Governor 2000, 3)

The order went on to direct the council to advise local communities on the development of their land use plans; recommend to the governor and the General Assembly any changes in state and federal laws, regulations or procedures that would encourage sustainable growth; and prepare an annual report for the governor.

The governor had first announced his Growth Planning Council at his State of the State address in January 2000. Several reasons can be given for his shift toward smart growth, including his serving on a committee chaired by Maryland Governor Parris Glendening. Grow Smart's ability to persuade the governor to embrace what will amount to a revitalization of Rhode Island's growth management system was clearly another important factor. Friendly pressure coming from the private nonprofit sector with a strong corporate presence was more effective than from such sources as the Statewide Planning Program (*Providence Journal* 2000).

Other Positive Developments

In November 2000 voters approved a $34 million, five-year bond issue for open space, supported by the governor, Grow Smart and others. It allocated $23.5 million for open space and land acquisition and $10 million for a recreation development program. Earlier in the year the governor, Grow Smart and others had proposed a $50 million, 10-year bond, allocating $40 million for open space and land acquisition, $10 million for the recreation development program and $800,000 for local planning grants. While the amount of the bond was reduced, at least the spirit of the program and the allocation was maintained.

Another favorable action in 2000 was the passage of legislation mandating a single code for building rehabilitation projects, supported by Grow Smart, the governor, the state Senate's Democratic majority leader, Paul S. Kelly, and the Republican minority leader. Grow Smart pushed for the adoption of the Rhode Island State Building Rehabilitation Code by convening a meeting of 150 Rhode Islanders to hear about New Jersey's 1998 rewritten building code that helped spur urban redevelopment and contain sprawl (*Design/Build* 1999). New Jersey was the first state to adopt a separate construction code for existing buildings, and the results dramatically increased spending on old-building rehabilitation. Rhode Island also had many vacant structures, but the building codes were unnecessarily lengthy, costly and unpredictable. Old buildings had to be brought up to the most recent building and fire standards, which often were unnecessary and ended up driving developers to greenfields at the urban edge. Kelly met with the New Jersey visitors and later announced his intent to introduce a bill that would "make it easier for developers to invest in traditional downtown areas and bring new life to existing buildings and structures" (Sabar 2000a, B1).

The challenge became how to implement the codes as directed in the legislation, since 80 percent of the houses are at least 50 years old and many are in central cities. The new law provided for setting up a separate combined building and fire code for rehabilitation projects and holding such projects "to standards that vary according to the size and scope of the job" (Sabar 2000b). The new law assigned the task of drafting the code to a committee including building and fire officials, representatives of the Rhode Island Builders Association, Grow Smart and the State Historical Preservation Commission. The code would then have to be approved by the State Building Code Commission and Fire Safety Code Board of Review (see also Grow Smart Undated b; Rhode Island 2000).

The Rhode Island Statewide Planning Program has recently expanded its staff, in part to strengthen the Transportation Improvement Program (TIP). The state Department of Transportation has become much more supportive of increased spending for alternative modes of transit such as commuter rail and ferries, including funds for upgrading the existing highway system and for new initiatives focused on public transportation.

Another positive initiative is a state inventory to pinpoint spending by state agencies on transportation, housing and education, to refocus state spending on towns with good plans and implementing regulations as opposed to towns with weak systems. The goal, similar to initiatives in other states, is to use such funds to reward towns that are practicing smart growth and to withhold funds from those that are not.

Grow Smart is leading an effort to establish a training institute for town officials and boards, with strong support from the Statewide Planning Program and the Growth Planning Council. As Grow Smart sees the problem, "Some towns are offered multiple opportunities for training while others are offered none, there is a duplication of effort in the development of materials, and the information delivered is sometimes inconsistent. We decided that there could be a much better use of resources if we combined forces" (Grow Smart 2000, 1). The strategy is to establish a planning institute as a nonprofit corporation that will be self-supporting in the long run and will help to free up program staff to focus on its core duties.

Other legislation important to smart growth passed by the 2000 General Assembly was an Impact Fee Enabling Act placed in the statutes right behind the 1988 Planning Enabling Act. Some towns had enacted impact fees, but without any such enabling legislation.

Continuing Support for Smart Growth, 2001–2002

Grow Smart's executive director Scott Wolf noted in 2001 that "perpetuating our sprawling development pattern could cost Rhode Island taxpayers nearly one and a half billion dollars more over the next 20 years than a land use scenario that is modestly more compact and urban" (Grow Smart 2001a, 2) He added that saving that kind of money by growing smarter would allow the state to enhance its investment in areas such as education and public infrastructure. Indeed, a number of important new laws and other actions in late 2000, 2001 and 2002 (almost always led directly or indirectly by Grow Smart) favored smart growth.

Growth Planning Council Actions in 2001

The council, in keeping with the governor's original charge, focused in its first year on "those programs that are perceived to influence growth and for which there appears to be opportunity to readily refocus that influence" (RIDA/SPP 2001, 3–4). Its analysis was based on results of standardized questionnaires sent to each state agency, personal interviews and the agencies' commenting on SPO's draft program summaries and recommendations (RIDA/SPP 2001, 3–4). The results of the analysis pinpointed 21 programs located within eight departments: Administration (DOA); Economic Development Corporation (EDC); Elementary and Secondary Education (DOE); Environmental Management (DEM); Rhode Island Historical Preservation and Heritage Commission; Rhode Island Housing and Mortgage Finance Corporation (RIHMFC); Transportation (DOT with DOA); and the Water Resources Board. We limit our discussion here to key agency programs and how they support smart growth objectives of sustainable development and environmental protection (RIDA/SPP 2001, 3).

With regard to Rhode Island's Comprehensive Planning and Land Use Regulation Act, the council concluded that there were far too few incentives for local governments to get their plans approved by the state. In fact, the 24 communities with state-approved plans were, for the most part, treated the same as those communities that had not complied with the requirements for approval. The council's recommendation

was that grant and other financial programs administered by state agencies include incentives for local governments with comprehensive plans approved by the state (RIDA/SPP 2001, 6–7).

Rhode Island has significant untapped potential for using state agency dollars as incentives for communities to bring their plans and regulations into compliance with the state's growth management system and to implement those plans fully, to move Rhode Island toward smart growth. For example, the state's Transportation Improvement Program (TIP) allocated $558 million in federal and state matching funds to a number of projects, including the state highway, congestion mitigation–air quality, and transportation enhancement programs, all of which required separate evaluations.

The problem is that incentives were not strong enough to target such investments to designated growth areas. The council's recommendation was to adapt the criteria for TIP project scoring so that projects supporting development in designated growth areas would gain an advantage and "provide for higher cost caps and/or additional projects in enterprise zones or communities with State-approved comprehensive plans" (RIDA/SPP 2001, 7–8).

The Governor's Growth Planning Council's 2001 annual report stated that the first year was devoted to assessing growth patterns and evaluating the state's impact on those patterns (R.I. EDC, SPP and DEM 2001, 1). The verdict was that while state agencies had the potential to promote smart growth for Rhode Island, they actually often contributed to more sprawl development. Ways to decrease local government reliance on property taxes were examined, and the results confirmed the absolute need for change. In 2002 a special subcommittee considered means for providing infrastructure in rural areas to promote community development so that open space, community character and a healthy economy might be maintained.

The council focused on the *Inventory of State Programs* report by asking, "What can the state do better?"

- State investment: Increase the focus of government investment in urban communities.

- Targeted growth: Target growth toward areas that can accommodate sustainable development.

■ Support for local planning processes: Use state administered grants to provide incentives for proactive planning [and] support local transportation corridor preservation initiatives. (R.I. EDC, SPP and R.I. DEM 2001, 6)

In addition to adopting and monitoring the recommendations contained in its inventory report and 2001 annual report, the council stated its future commitment to the development of a Strategic Investment Policy that focuses public investments to areas that have been prioritized for growth; developing policy recommendations for supporting brownfields reuse in the state; and the examination of the affordable housing crisis facing all of Rhode Island's communities (R.I. EDC, SPP and R.I. DEM 2001, 10).

The council's plans for its second year included establishing a planning institute to increase local government capacity in growth management by enhancing training and programs.

Grow Smart Rhode Island Efforts

In 2001, Grow Smart added to its outreach efforts by posting a Web site and briefing gubernatorial candidates about the organization's research and policies. Grow Smart also pushed for coordination between Rhode Island's EDC and the DEM regarding brownfield regulations and policies, and played a key role in creating the Legislative Commission on Brownfields. Brownfields are defined as "vacant or underused industrial and commercial properties where the existence of contamination or even the perception that contamination may exist discourages reuse" (Grow Smart 2002a, 22). Grow Smart was a major player in the passage by the 2001 General Assembly of H 5547, characterized as "the most ambitious tax credit in the nation for rehabilitation of commercial historic properties" (Grow Smart 2001b, 1). Historic structures undergoing commercial rehabilitation can now qualify for a 20 percent federal credit and a 30 percent state credit (Rhode Island 2001; Grow Smart 2001a, 1).

Three major successes, backed by Grow Smart, included the adoption of the user-friendly Rhode Island Rehabilitation Building and Fire Code; the passage of a brownfields bill; and the creation of the Neighborhood Opportunities Program.

The Rhode Island Rehabilitation Building and Fire Code

In February 2002 Rhode Island adopted a new rehabilitation code that went into effect on May 1 of that year, drawing on rehab codes adopted in Maryland and New Jersey. The code removed many existing obstacles for those involved in redeveloping older commercial and industrial buildings who found their rehab projects financially impossible because they had to meet all the latest code requirements for new construction. While meeting health and safety standards, the Rhode Island rehab code sets out a more user-friendly process for those redeveloping older buildings. This has resulted in a significant reduction in the number of requests for variances for rehab projects; variances, when required, are heard by a single joint appeals board rather than two boards. "As is the case with rehab codes in Maryland and New Jersey, the Rhode Island Rehab Code emphasizes the notion of proportionality—the philosophy that code requirements...should generally be limited to the part of the building on which work is being done" (Grow Smart 2002a, 24–25). Grow Smart cautioned that a significant amount of training is required for those in the public and private sectors with regard to the new rehab code. Grow Smart urged the governor and General Assembly to support sufficient funding to ensure continued training in the new code (Grow Smart 2002a, 24–25).

The Brownfields Initiative

With a new rehab code and commercial historic tax credit in place, supporters of a sustainable, prosperous and equitable future for Rhode Island marshaled their forces to get a strong brownfields bill passed in 2002. In February 2001 Grow Smart organized the state's first conference on brownfields policy, which led to the formation of a Brownfield Task Force by the state's DEM. In addition, Groundworks Providence, a nonprofit organization, received a grant from the U.S. EPA to start a brownfields job training program. Other federal support came from legislation sponsored by Rhode Island Senator Lincoln Chafee and signed into law by President G. W. Bush in 2002. It authorized $350 million per year, from 2002 to 2006, for the assessment and clean-up of brownfield sites, and provided legal protection for innocent parties involved in redeveloping these sites. The Rhode Island House created the Legislative Commission on Brownfields to heighten awareness of and recommend legislation related to brownfields (Grow Smart 2002b, 1, 4).

The significance of Rhode Island's efforts to better utilize its numerous brownfield sites must be viewed in the context of that state's very limited land area for development, and the fact that there are an estimated several hundred brownfield sites in the state, primarily within urban areas and often on the waterfront. Since brownfields are essentially a "wasted resource," their cleanup and redevelopment "can provide new opportunities for revitalization of our urban centers, sites to house new jobs for Rhode Islanders, increased property tax revenues for municipalities and reduced pressure for development of greenfields" (Grow Smart 2002a, 22).

The Legislative Commission on Brownfields and the Governor's Office introduced two bills that passed in amended form in the 2002 General Assembly that strengthened the utilization of brownfields through (1) language changes to bring existing state law concerning brownfields into line with new federal brownfields legislation; and (2) mandates to Rhode Island Economic Development Corporation (RIEDC) and Rhode Island Department of Environmental Management (RIDEM) to research and make recommendations on environmental insurance, a Licensed Environmental Professional Program, and maintenance of a brownfields inventory (Grow Smart 2002a, 22).

Certainly the adoption of H 7489 Sub-A, an act relating to industrial property remediation and reuse, was a significant step toward full utilization of brownfield sites in Rhode Island, but some key actions were still needed (Rhode Island 2002a). Grow Smart called on the next governor to support the adoption of a state income tax credit of 30 percent of a brownfield's assessment and remediation costs, and encourage brownfield redevelopment (Grow Smart 2002a, 23).

The Neighborhood Opportunities Program

Rhode Island has a real crisis in providing housing for low- and moderate-income residents. The 2001 budget included $5 million for the Neighborhood Opportunities Program (NOP), described by Grow Smart as Rhode Island's "first significant financial commitment to affordable housing and neighborhood revitalization" (Grow Smart 2001a, 1). The goal was to develop approximately 1,000 new units of affordable housing for families whose annual income fell below $20,000. However, Governor Almond, facing a severe budget crunch, froze the $5 million, although, according to Grow Smart, the funds could leverage as much as "$32 million in additional neighborhood investment, while producing over 1,000 jobs and up to $30 million in wages" (Wolf 2001, 1). Eventually Almond and the 2002 General Assembly found an alternative method for funding NOP through a $10 million bond (Dodge 2001; Grow Smart 2002a, 27).

Because the availability of long-term funds for NOP was uncertain, Grow Smart addressed a number of strong recommendations to the state's next governor.

■ Make a commitment for future NOP funding in a predictable way

■ Provide a more permanent and reliable source of funding for affordable housing and land conservation through appropriations and/or a dedicated funding stream to the Rhode Island Housing and Open Space Trust Fund that had never been funded

■ Ensure that at least 10 percent of the housing in all municipalities is affordable, in accordance with the statutory definition (Grow Smart 2002a, 27)

Closely related to NOP, the Urban Revitalization Fund focused on revitalizing Rhode Island's urban centers in order to reduce development pressures and enhance economic opportunities for residents. The fund was established by the Southside Investment Partnership to focus initially on the South Providence urban core area, but with the flexibility to expand to all five of Rhode Island's urban core areas. The revitalization fund aimed at giving "community development corporations an equity financing vehicle to participate in the revitalization of nonresidential buildings in existing urban centers" (Grow Smart 2002a, 26). Grow Smart called on the next governor to include in his budget sufficient state monies to support an expansion of the fund (Grow Smart 2002a, 26).

A common thread running through all the promising smart growth initiatives described above is that even in the best case there was a significant shortage of dependable funds to fully achieve goals and objectives. Further, the heavy reliance on property taxes by municipalities was a significant deterrent to smart growth by making it difficult for Rhode Island's 39 municipalities to work with one another in dealing with growth management issues on a regional basis.

Other Grow Smart Recommendations

To further strengthen land conservation efforts, Grow Smart recommended funding the Housing and Open Space Trust Fund, in place since 1990 but never funded. While trying to establish dedicated funding streams, Grow Smart recommended that both the state and local governments be encouraged to support bond issues for the preservation of open space (Grow Smart 2002a, 32–33).

The 2002 General Assembly passed "an amendment to the state's current cluster development zoning regulations, [which] makes it easier for farmers and owners of forestland to participate in conservation-oriented cluster developments by allowing them to retain ownership of a portion of their property in an underdeveloped state, while the remainder of the property would be developed. A conservation easement, held either by the city/town or nonprofit organization, would be required to prevent the open space portion of the cluster development from being developed in the future" (Rhode Island 2002b; Grow Smart 2002a, 32–33). While far from a total solution to the threat that all of Rhode Island's rural communities might eventually turn into suburbs, the new legislation was at least a start in the right direction.

The state was not in a position to offer much-needed training for public officials and municipal staff, although the Office of Statewide Planning helped coordinate training by others. Grow Smart began offering its own nine-hour curriculum for municipal officials in late fall 2001, with funds to continue the courses until the end of 2003 (Grow Smart 2002a, 30).

Grow Smart urged the next governor to make long-term, broad training and technical assistance available to municipalities. Possibilities included implementing the Growth Planning Council's call for a Rhode Island Planning Institute, making it a "free-standing non-profit organization, funded by the state and private sources, that would coordinate, market, and deliver training and technical assistance" (Grow Smart 2002a, 30–31).

Grow Smart also recommended increasing the number of staff positions within the Office of Statewide Planning and charging the office with coordinating training and providing technical assistance to municipalities. Such strengthening of the office would then complement the Rhode Island Planning Institute.

Governor Carcieri and the Future of Smart Growth

According to a Grow Smart report (Grow Smart 2002a, 1), which was prepared for gubernatorial candidates in the 2002 primaries and general election, "staying on a sprawl course through 2020...will cost Rhode Island taxpayers almost $1.5 billion...[and the] 11,000 vacant lots in our five core cities [represent] an estimated $1.3 billion in lost property values for those cities." A modest shift to compact urban development patterns could have reduced the vacant lots to 3,000 by 2020, but continuing sprawl would raise the total to 20,000.

During his campaign Republican Donald Carcieri strongly supported targeting state public investments to growth centers, calling for a "coordinated development plan...[that would] lay out where and how we want development to grow in this state" (Arsenault 2002, A6). The governor-elect also called for concentrating growth centers through a statewide zoning effort and strengthening statewide planning by means of a "prioritized view of all development in the state" (Arsenault 2002, A6).

As Governor Carcieri took office, a constitutional amendment was implemented to downsize the General Assembly by 25 percent, with the total number of legislators reduced from 150 to 113 (75 in the House and 38 in the Senate); both houses remain heavily Democratic. In 2003 the Republicans had only 11 members in the House and 10 in the Senate (the

House has one Independent). That does not necessarily result in a partisan fight between the governor and the General Assembly, however, as they try to implement a smart growth agenda backed by Grow Smart's coalition and other smart growth advocates in Rhode Island. The agenda remains a struggle to bring the 39 municipalities fully into the game and to strengthen the support of the governor and General Assembly for bold smart growth initiatives.

Legislative Actions in 2003

The following is a brief review of successful and unsuccessful actions by the 2003 General Assembly related to smart growth.

In the area of brownfields redevelopment, House Resolution 270 (H 6564) renamed, amended and extended the existing Special House Commission with a charge to develop necessary legislative recommendations to be introduced in the January 2004 legislative session which would complement and strengthen the existing brownfields programs administered by the Rhode Island Economic Development Corporation and the Rhode Island Department of Environmental Management. The Commission would expire at the close of the 2004 legislative session. The resolution has good potential to strengthen Rhode Island's brownfield redevelopment initiative. A bill to create a tax credit for brownfield remediation (H 6333) failed to pass, a temporary setback for brownfields remediation.

In an earlier boost to Rhode Island's brownfields program (mid-2003), the U.S. EPA awarded a total of $3.45 million to the Rhode Island Economic Development Corporation and the Trust for Public Land in Providence, Warwick and Woonsocket, "to help assess, clean up and redevelop brownfields." Governor Carcieri supported this dimension of Rhode Island's smart growth strategy, saying, "This funding is of critical importance in helping to boost sound economic development opportunities in Rhode Island. The industrial history of this state has left a legacy of brownfields sites available for potential reuse, and seizing on that potential is an important and practical way to expand our economic base." Part of the grant will be used to clean up a former landfill in Providence, which, "once restored will become part

of the Woonasquatucket River Greenway Project" (*Providence Business News* 2003).

In response to the nightclub fire tragedy that resulted in 100 deaths in West Warwick in 2002, the General Assembly also passed fire safety reforms that went into effect February 20, 2004. A key action was the adoption of the National Fire Protection Association Standards (NFPA) 101, for existing buildings. Based on specific legislative language contained in the reforms, NFPA 101 would override the rehabilitation codes whenever the two codes came into conflict. The full ramifications of this development are still being assessed, but Grow Smart and several of its key allies are concerned that the viability of the rehabilitation codes could be in danger. However, a process has been established to resolve conflicts between the two sets of codes, and there is some hope that this process can be a vehicle for maintaining the viability of the rehabilitation codes.

The only action by the legislature in the area of urban infrastructure was the passage by the House (H 6067, Chapter 100) and Senate (S 0588, Chapter 236) to create an Urban Infrastructure Commission, presumably to make recommendations on how to promote various types of urban infrastructure to further the cause of smart growth in Rhode Island.

A key open space protection bill (S 0420) did pass the General Assembly and became law without the governor's signature on August 6, 2003. The act enables cities and towns to exempt farmland from taxation when the owner has conveyed the development rights of that land.

A very strong proposed bill to encourage low- and moderate-income housing (H 6615) was sponsored by Rep. Brian Patrick Kennedy in the House, where it did pass, although it failed in the Senate. An important plus for affordable housing was provided in the fiscal year 2004 state budget when $5 million for the Neighborhood Opportunities Program (NOP) was approved by the General Assembly.

Several bills relating to historic preservation were proposed by one or both houses of the General Assembly, but none of them became law. Many involved efforts to provide new incentives to promote growth in designated urban mill restoration areas. The failure to pass the efforts to strengthen the Mill Building and

Restoration Act was clearly a negative in furthering the cause of smart growth in Rhode Island, but Grow Smart believes the state's 30 percent historic preservation tax credit is a better stimulus for mill revitalization in the long run.

Three transportation bills were proposed, all originating in the House. While all would have been a positive in meeting Rhode Island's transportation challenges, none cleared the General Assembly. H 5754 would have provided for employer-sponsored parking subsidy programs that give the employee the option of receiving subsidized parking or a monthly transit pass. Cities and towns could then "grant appropriate reductions in parking requirements otherwise applicable to new and existing commercial developments." H 6330 would have required that funds be appropriated to the Rhode Island Public Transit Authority to maintain service, and H 6160 would have created a 17-member special legislative commission to make recommendations regarding the mission of the Public Transit Authority and the challenges facing public transportation in the state.

Action by the 2003 General Assembly on economic development involved H 6577, which created a House Commission of 16 members charged with studying the status of the state's policy formulation and planning for the environmental management and sustainable economic development of Rhode Island's bays and watersheds. This Special House Commission would then report back to the House by March 9, 2004, and would expire on May 9, 2004, or upon passage of a joint House–Senate resolution with the same charge. The work of such a commission, especially if it evolves into a joint legislative body, clearly has a smart growth potential.

Grow Smart's strong push for a coordinated effort in this area has continued. By fall 2003, the Making Good Land Use Decisions program had been conducted in 25 communities. Training in this area is led by Derwent J. Riding of Rhode Island Statewide Planning, Sheila Brush of Grow Smart, and several others from the private sector. Beginning in fall 2003, three more training programs were slated to be added: Affordable Housing; Conservation Development; and Site Plan Review. Response to the training programs has been positive (Grow Smart 2003e, 1).

The historic tax credit program, which became effective in January 2002, was pushed hard by Grow Smart and many of its partners, and has shown a strong return on investment. The Rhode Island Historic Preservation and Heritage Commission, which administers the state and federal historic tax credit programs, noted that 56 proposed projects won approval up to mid-2003 involving a proposed investment of $189 million and the creation of 8,500 new jobs. In contrast to the 24-month period before the Historic Tax Credit Program was enacted, the number of projects employing historic tax credits has tripled and investment in commercial preservation has increased tenfold. The program has also had a strong positive effect on Rhode Island's housing shortage. The number of low- and moderate-income housing units rehabbed by using historic tax credits had doubled to 193, and market rate units increased even more (from 8 to 750) (Grow Smart 2003e, 1).

Rhode Island Economic Policy Council: Embracing Smart Growth Principles

Rhode Island Economic Policy Council (RIEPC), the state-funded nonprofit, is cochaired by Governor Carcieri who took a strong leadership position in his economic plan of September 12, 2003. The plan "focuses on expanding large and small businesses, increasing the number of businesses in the state without creating urban sprawl, and building the state's reputation as a friendly place for businesses to present new ideas." The governor held that "This body is a policy body sitting on top of our whole economic plan" (Stape 2003, 2).

Grow Smart's executive director Scott Wolf, while fully supportive of Carcieri's economic strategy, held that "the key is to translate these smart growth principles into action steps." As he put it:

> we look forward to working with the administration on several specific policy initiatives in support of this strategy, including targeting state investments in mixed-use "growth centers," full adherence by the State Properties Committee to requirements for prioritizing the siting of state facilities in distressed or downtown areas, new incentives for brownfield development, expanding appropriately sited affordable housing opportunities, developing new long term funding strategies for both land conservation and affordable housing, and reducing the state reliance on the sprawl inducing property tax. (Grow Smart 2003a, 1–2)

There is both good and bad news in Wolf's strategy to implement Carcieri's economic strategy. The good news is that Grow Smart and its coalition are clearly able to work in harmony with the governor and his administration to further the cause of smart growth in Rhode Island. The bad news, or at least the challenging news, is that there is a substantial unfinished agenda that will not be easy to put in place.

Grow Smart has continued to work with its partners, the governor and state agencies in the area of state government's facility siting policies and procedures. One of the key challenges remaining was raised by Wolf in asking if the State Properties Committee was adhering to a segment of Rhode Island General Law, Chapter 37-6-2, "that requires the Committee to use siting criteria that give a preference to sites in enterprise zones census tracts or in 'blighted and/or substandard areas' or in 'downtown commercial areas where such facilities would make a significant impact on the economic vitality of the community's central business district.'" In fall 2003 Grow Smart was in the process of analyzing actions by the State Properties Committee in that regard (Wolf 2003, 1).

Conclusion

A substantial number of smart growth initiatives are under way in Rhode Island, with Grow Smart the clear leader in these efforts. For example, in legislation effective on January 1, 2002, Rhode Island created economic incentives to promote redevelopment and reuse of an estimated 900 historic commercial properties in cities, towns and villages throughout the state. A study commissioned by Grow Smart based on 111 projects enrolled through September 23, 2004, showed that this Historic Preservation Investment Tax Credit program was returning historic properties to municipal tax rolls, generating employment and housing where they are most needed, and leveraging substantial private investment that otherwise would not occur (Grow Smart 2005). Property owners can earn state income tax credits equal to 30 percent of qualified rehabilitation expenditures. This multiyear investment is estimated at $145 million, and it is expected to generate $795 million in economic activity.

Scott Wolf notes, "At a time when Rhode Island's open space and farmland are still under tremendous development pressure and our cities and towns are struggling to expand their tax base...[this program] is helping to address both of these challenges. Rehabilitation and reuse of historic buildings is smart economic development that plays to our strength" (Grow Smart 2005). This powerful revitalization tool is also providing significant assistance to meet overall housing needs, particularly affordable housing. Wolf's continued leadership of these and other smart growth initiatives in Rhode Island was recognized in May 2005 when he was elected chairman of the Growth Management Leadership Alliance (GMLA), a national network based in Washington, DC, that seeks to shape and implement smart growth policies and actions.

Within the state political structure, there is strong evidence that Governor Carcieri, as a moderate Republican, is able to work well with the heavily Democratic General Assembly and with the broad-based coalition represented by Grow Smart and its allies. Even with these positive signs, major challenges remain in making the administrative and statutory changes that will be needed, and in finding the added revenues to implement them. The combination of private- and public-sector forces now supporting smart growth holds hope for a strong economy and a healthy environment in Rhode Island's future.

Rhode Island References

Arsenault, Mark. 2002. Grow Smart R.I. lobbies to keep state's charm. *Providence Journal.* July 19, A1, A6.

Design/Build. 1999. New subcode saves old buildings in New Jersey. October.

Dodge, James H. 2001. Letter to Governor Lincoln Almond. November 19.

Grow Smart Rhode Island (Grow Smart). 2000. *Status report on Rhode Island Training Coalition convened under the auspices of Grow Smart Rhode Island.* Presented to the Growth Planning Council's Growth Planning Institute Subcommittee. June 20.

———. 2001a. *Grow smart!* December.

———. 2001b. Major Grow Smart year 2001 activities and accomplishments.

————. 2002a. A strategy for saving Rhode Island from sprawl and urban decay: Grow Smart Rhode Island's candidates' briefing book. July.

————. 2002b. *Grow smart!* April.

————. 2003a. Embrace of smart growth principles in Carcieri economic strategy praised. September 18. News release.

————. 2003b. House Corporations Committee testimony by Scott Wolf, executive director, Grow Smart Rhode Island, in support of H 6492, An Amendment to the Rhode Island Low and Moderate Income Housing Act. June 11.

————. 2003c. Minutes of board of directors meeting. June 25.

————. 2003d. Smart growth e-briefs. July.

————. 2003e. Smart growth e-briefs. August.

————. 2003f. Smart growth e-briefs. November.

————. 2005. Study quantifies substantial return on historic tax credit. E-alert. April 7. http://www.growsmartmartri.com/tax.html

————. Undated a. Strengthening our economy, expanding opportunity, protecting our special places. Providence, RI.

————. Undated b. The case for Rhode Island's adoption of a rehabilitation code for existing buildings (modeled on New Jersey's recent success). Providence, RI.

H. C. Planning Consultants, Inc. and Planimetrics, LLP. 1999. The costs of suburban sprawl and urban decay in Rhode Island. Prepared for Grow Smart Rhode Island. December.

Hiss, Tony. 1989. Reflections encountering the countryside. *New Yorker*. August 21.

Holtzman, Robert. 1988. The land-use commission delivers a landmark bill. *Ocean State Business*. April 11–24, 14–18.

Providence Business News. 2003. RI gets brownfields grant. June 30–July 6.

Providence Journal. 2000. Almond names council to study land development. February 23.

Rhode Island. 1995. The Local Planning Assistance Program, Office of Municipal Affairs. *Comprehensive plan status reports*. Prepared for the State Planning Council. October.

————. 2000. An Act Relating to the State Building and Fire Code, 00-S 2885. Lc03010/2, in General Assembly, January session.

————. 2001. H 5547, An Act Relating to Historic Structures—Tax Credits.

————. 2002a. H 7489 Sub-A, An Act Relating to Remediation of Brownfields.

————. 2002b. S 2283, An Act Relating to Cities and Towns—Zoning.

Rhode Island Department of Administration (RIDA). 1998a. *Statewide Planning Program, Report no. 96*. November.

————. 1998b. *Transportation 2020: Ground transportation plan*. November.

————. 2000. *Information Services, Work Program, FY 2001, Statewide Planning Program*. June.

Rhode Island Department of Administration, Division of Planning (RIDA/DP). 1988. *Grant application and management handbook, no. 17*. December.

————. 1989a. *Data catalogue for the local comprehensive plan, no. 18*. October.

————. 1989b. *Handbook on the local comprehensive plan, no. 16*. June.

————. 1989c. *Land use 2010: State land use policies and plan. State Guide Plan Element 121, no. 64*. June.

————. 1990. *State agency goals and policies, no. 19*. April.

————. 1994. *1991 Zoning Enabling Act. Monthly progress report, no. 364*. December 1–3.

Rhode Island Department of Administration, Statewide Planning Program (RIDA/SPP). 2001. *Governor's growth planning council 2001: State programs and sustainable development inventory, analysis and recommendations report*. March.

Rhode Island Economic Development Corporation (R.I. EDC), Statewide Planning Program (SPP) and Rhode Island Department of Environmental Management (R.I. DEM). 2001. *Governor's growth planning council annual report 2001*. June.

Rhode Island Office of the Governor. 2000. Executive Order 00-2, Creation of growth planning council. February 17.

Rhode Island Rivers Council and State Planning Council, State of Rhode Island and Providence Plantations. 1998. *Rivers policy and classification plan, State Guide Plan element 162, report no. 92*. January.

Sabar, Ariel. 2000a. N.J. touts its success with building codes. *Providence Journal*. March 22, B1.

————. 2000b. Proposed bill would clear way for faster rehab of old buildings. *Providence Journal*. April 5.

Stape, Andrea L. 2003. Rating R.I.: State's visionaries map goals. *Providence Journal*. September 17. http://www.projo.com/cgi-bin/bi-gold_print.cgi.

U.S. Census Bureau. 2002a. Projections of the total population of states: 1995 to 2025. http://www.census.gov/population/projections/state/stpjpop.txt.

————. 2002b. State and county QuickFacts: Rhode Island. http://quickfacts.census.gov/qfd/states/44000.html.

Varin, Dan. 1995. *The consistency doctrine in Rhode Island*. Monthly progress report, no. 366. Rhode Island Department of Administration, Division of Planning. February, 1–3.

Wolf, Scott. 2001. Remarks in support of releasing appropriated funds for the neighborhood opportunities program. Grow Smart Rhode Island. November 20.

————. 2003. Memorandum to Grow Smart Rhode Island board of directors re recent developments in state government's facility siting. October 24.

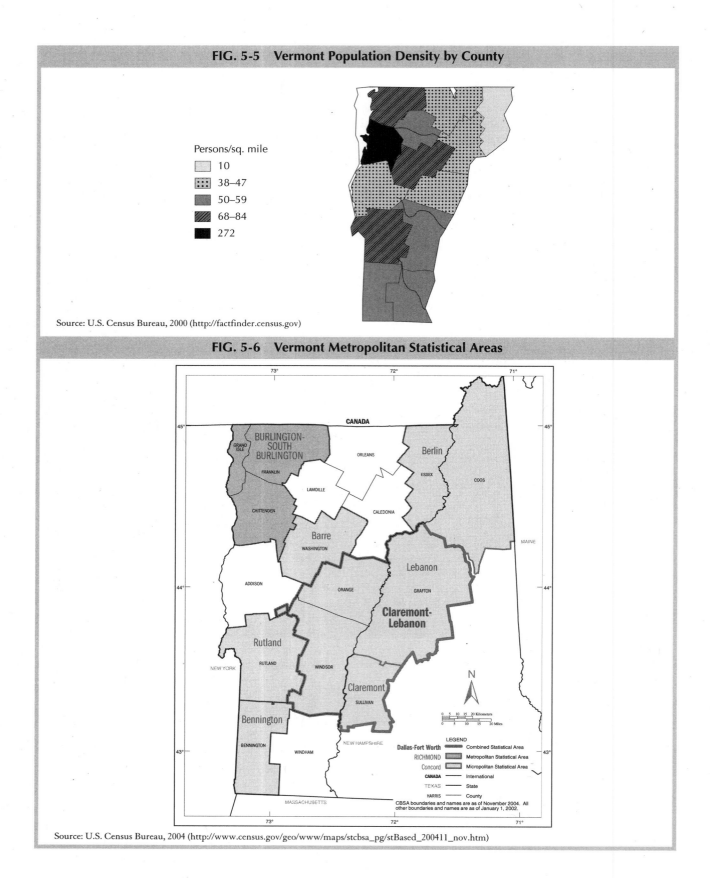

FIG. 5-5   Vermont Population Density by County

Persons/sq. mile
- 10
- 38–47
- 50–59
- 68–84
- 272

Source: U.S. Census Bureau, 2000 (http://factfinder.census.gov)

FIG. 5-6   Vermont Metropolitan Statistical Areas

Source: U.S. Census Bureau, 2004 (http://www.census.gov/geo/www/maps/stcbsa_pg/stBased_200411_nov.htm)

Vermont

The Struggle to Manage Growth in the Green Mountain State

The Issue Context

It has become increasingly clear that Vermont, for all its efforts to manage its growth (under Act 250, the State Land Use and Development Act, adopted in 1970; and Act 200, the Growth Management Act of 1988), has not escaped the downsides of sprawl development so foreign to the "vision" many associate with Vermont: small towns and a relatively undisturbed rural countryside. Vermont's population in 2000 was 608,827, an increase of 8.2 percent from 1990, and it is projected to grow to 662,000 by 2015 and 678,000 by 2025 (U.S. Census Bureau). Sprawl comes in many forms in Vermont, as it does elsewhere: in the strip developments seen on Route 7 around Burlington and Rutland, and in the big-box retail development around Colchester and Williston.

Vermont's economy traditionally was based on low-productivity and low-income hill farms, which later were supplemented by better-paying manufacturing jobs, especially textiles that used hydroelectric power from the state's numerous rivers. In the nineteenth century, water and later rail transportation allowed manufacturing and agricultural products to be moved cheaply to markets throughout the nation and abroad. But those advantages declined in the first half of the twentieth century, leaving Vermont one of the poorer states in the nation by 1950. By the end of that decade, agriculture, lumbering and mining employed almost a quarter of the state's workforce. The state's 10,000 small farms were mostly family-owned. At the time, interstate highways had not reached the state's borders; although skiing development had begun, tourism was centered on the summer season (Governor's Commission 1988).

Vermont in the late 1950s was not especially healthy, either environmentally or economically. Dairy farms and textile mills polluted the rivers and streams, and young people typically left the state for better job opportunities elsewhere. All that started to

change in the 1960s, when the state's population began to increase, and tourism, manufacturing and second-home development boomed. Two factors supported these new developments: the linking of Vermont to New York and Boston through the completion of the interstate highway system; and the rise of environmental values that made Vermont's natural beauty a major attraction for both tourism and permanent relocation of urban dwellers from nearby metropolitan centers.

Growth Pressures Leading to Act 250 in 1970

The surge of growth during the 1960s resulted in higher land values and the appearance of large mobile home parks, as well as strip development along highways. These developments strained municipal services and increased property tax rates (Governor's Commission 1988). Vermont residents were worried about increasing numbers of year-round vacation homes and other development. The state responded to these concerns by establishing the Scenery Preservation Council, the Vermont Planning Council, and laws banning billboards and regulating municipal landfills. The rising tide of citizen protest continued into the administration of Governor Deane C. Davis, who convened a Governor's Conference on Natural Resources. In 1969 he established the Governor's Commission on Environmental Control, an 18-member group chaired by Representative Arthur Gibb (Vermont DHCA 1999, 6).

The Gibb Commission proposed the State Land Use and Development Act, Act 250, which passed the legislature in 1970 with the strong support of the governor and little debate or change. Act 250 was conceived as a three-part program: stage one, the development and adoption of an interim plan to guide initial regulatory activity; stage two, a land capability and development plan; and stage three, a state land planning law.

The state adopted the interim plan with little opposition in 1972, and adopted stage two in 1973. Proponents of the controversial 1973 plan had to overcome opposition from a new landowners' steering committee that opposed a strong state role in growth management. The adoption of stage two strengthened Act 250's environmental criteria, clarified the relationship between the act and local governments, and added a key provision that allowed the regional Environmental District Commissions to reject a project because of the burden placed on local governments in providing public facilities.

Ultimately, the economic recession of the mid-1970s and a widespread perception that the plan would amount to state zoning defeated those advocates who sought to complete the third stage and adopt a state land use plan. Even without the final planning component, the Act 250 process worked well in many ways, but it was understaffed and underfunded, and it addressed only about one-third of the total development taking place in Vermont. A three-member lay board for each Environmental District Commission used the policies of the land capability and development plan as criteria by which to assess and approve, approve with conditions, or deny projects of a certain scale. The small staff involved at both the regional and state levels sharply limited monitoring and enforcement of conditional approvals (DeGrove 1984).

Renewed Concern in the 1980s

As the economic boom and population growth pressures increased again during the 1980s, the state's per capita personal income reached an all-time high of 93 percent of the U.S. average in 1988, compared to 86 percent in 1980. It was increasingly obvious that while Act 250 was a good approach for specific developments, it could not deal with cumulative impacts because it lacked a planning context. With explosive growth occurring in certain parts of the state, Act 250 was under siege and its shortcomings were becoming widely recognized and, more important, widely discussed. Had growth pressures not revived, perhaps the deficiencies of Act 250 as a permitting process would not have been sufficient to generate a change in the system. As it was, Act 250 permits were growing steadily, from 532 in 1981 to 848 in 1986.

The increasing growth and a renewed concern for protecting Vermont's unique quality of life resulted in the passage of several laws between 1985 and 1987,

including statutes addressing groundwater classification, toxic materials and pesticides, water quality and wetlands, and solid waste. But by 1988 it seemed that even the addition of these resource protection statutes to the Act 250 process was not enough. Continuing frustration with the act and Vermonters' fear of renewed influx of "outsiders" led Governor Madelaine Kunin to undertake what would be Vermont's second attempt at a state role in managing growth and change (VNRC 1988).

On September 22, 1987, Governor Kunin created by executive order the Commission on Vermont's Future, which concentrated on the state's incomparable heritage of natural resources, scenic landscapes and livable communities. The executive order advocated a new stimulus for desirable and orderly growth at each level of government, focusing especially on planning at the regional level, where local and state interests are reconciled most effectively (State of Vermont 1987).

The governor charged the 12-member commission with providing

■ an overview of growth patterns in Vermont and an assessment of the effectiveness of existing laws and practices in managing that growth;

■ a statement of goals and principles for the preservation of Vermont's character, with special attention to preserving agricultural land, and providing affordable housing and jobs for all of Vermont's citizens; and

■ recommendations on how to use the goals and principles to guide state, regional and local decisions.

Between October and December 1987 the commission held a series of public hearings around the state, recording what Vermonters were worried about and what they wanted to preserve. In short, the commission was seeking some kind of general consensus. Visits to various communities were carefully planned, beginning with a focus group to listen to a particular group's concerns and ideas, followed by a meeting of the commission to discuss what was significant and noteworthy, and concluding with a public hearing focused on the issues in that particular region. The process, which included 11 public hearings and nine focus group meetings, was highly successful, with strong support from citizens and the media. Overall, the commission met with more than 2,000 Vermonters and received hundreds of letters and several hundred pages of testimony, revealing a core of values shared by Vermont's citizens, including thoughts about the state's community life, agricultural heritage, environmental quality and economic opportunity (Governor's Commission 1988). At the end of the hearing process, commissioners agreed to draw on the best statements, representing consensus on an issue. They were willing to set aside their individual roles for the common good.

Recommendations of the Governor's Commission

The *Report of the Governor's Commission on Vermont's Future: Guidelines for Growth* (Governor's Commission 1988) documented the threats to the shared values of Vermont's citizens.

- A sharp decline in farms and farming
- Lack of an effective growth management system to protect natural resources in the face of strong growth pressures
- Skyrocketing housing prices with inadequate affordable housing programs
- Economic growth dominated by the service and trade industries where jobs typically pay low wages

The commission organized its recommendations around five major areas: the planning process, economic development, natural resources, agriculture and affordable housing. Throughout the report, it emphasized planning, noting that the "adoption of the recommended planning process would provide the single greatest improvement to the practice of regulation" (Governor's Commission 1988, 20).

The first two steps in the process would provide the foundations for planning at all levels: (1) the adoption of state guidelines to serve as a policy framework for planning; and (2) the collection and dissemination of land use data and inventories of regional needs. Based on this information, towns, regional planning agencies and state agencies could prepare plans concurrently. To ensure consistency with the guidelines and with regional needs, newly restructured Regional Planning Commissions (RPCs) would carry out the review of local plans.

In line with the governor's emphasis on the regional level and with the commission's findings of inadequate regional or statewide authority to resolve intertown planning disputes, the commission recommended substantial changes in the practice of regional planning in Vermont, including mandatory membership of all towns in RPCs, whose boards would be composed of elected local officials (Governor's Commission 1988, 18). Under the commission's recommendations, RPCs would have important new responsibilities in regional planning, local plan review and technical assistance, and would be responsible for identifying regional resources and needs in the areas of "critical environmental sites," water and earth resources, agricultural and forestry resources, affordable housing and solid waste disposal.

In addition, a regional land use plan, developed as town plans were being made, would be used to "integrate and unify the town plans while reflecting the state guidelines." RPCs would "review and acknowledge" town plans, working with towns to resolve differences. The commission also assigned to RPCs the unenviable task of recommending locally unpopular land use (LULU) sites. The report suggested additional funding to enable RPCs to carry out their new duties, which also included the major responsibility of providing direct technical assistance to towns (Governor's Commission 1988, 18–20, 22).

The key integrating governance mechanism of the planning process would be a Council of Regional Commissions (CRC), composed of a representative from each of RPCs and five governor-appointed members from state agencies. This council would review regional and state agency plans to ensure consistency with the state guidelines. The Department of Housing and Community Affairs (DHCA) would staff the council and provide expanded technical help to communities (Governor's Commission 1988, 19). This was indeed powerful medicine, with a strong role for the state and especially the regional levels (too strong, as it turned out, for the legislature to digest).

Finally, the commission's recommendations would require Vermont's 246 towns and 57 incorporated villages to develop comprehensive plans and implementing strategies consistent with state guidelines and regional needs. The commission noted that while 75 percent of the towns and 9 percent of the villages had plans, they were typically brief and incomplete. State financial and technical assistance from RPCs (including help in obtaining adequate data for planning and regulation) was an important complement to the mandate for local plans.

The commission also recommended expanded town regulatory power, which included new authority for site-plan review and, in accordance with a comprehensive capital plan and budget, assessment of impact fees. The commission maintained that local planning and regulatory processes must be strengthened in order to make other regulatory changes possible. These included a streamlined Act 250 process, increased regional involvement in that process, and improvements to ease the burden on overloaded District Environmental Commissions (Governor's Commission 1988, 18–22).

In the area of economic development, the commission encouraged growth centers through targeting state funds for infrastructure and expediting permitting processes at all levels of the system. A number of factors specified in regional plans—infrastructure capacity, population density and existing patterns of growth—would provide a basis for locating these growth centers. The result, it was hoped, would be compact urban development patterns and the protection of natural resource values in the rural countryside. In order to "shore up the foundation of our economy, and ensure high-paying employment opportunities in the future," the commission also recommended a series of steps to bolster economic development, including linking state infrastructure allocation to economic development incentives (Governor's Commission 1988, 21–25).

Addressing natural resources, the commission recommended the standard litany of things to protect (e.g., land, air and water), but there was a notable emphasis on implementation and on unusual strategies for resource protection, such as the Vermont Housing and Conservation Trust Fund (begun in 1987). The commission pointed with approval to the trust fund board's innovative use of its initial $3 million appropriation, which helped protect farmland

with minimal investment, and called on the legislature to provide substantial additional monies to the fund, including an annual appropriation (Governor's Commission 1988, 25–26).

In a separate section on agriculture, the commission report laid the groundwork for addressing what many observers felt was the issue that carried Act 200 through the legislature. Noting that support for agriculture was a "dominant theme" in its public hearings, the commission stated that the economic, scenic and recreational value of farming to the state was sufficient reason for aggressive implementation of existing and development of new agricultural protection programs.

Affordable housing received equal treatment, through the commission's endorsement of DHCA's Housing Policy and Plan for Action in June 1987. The commission called for regional and town plans to address affordable housing and stressed the need to support nonprofit housing programs, especially in growth centers (Governor's Commission 1988, 27–28).

The commission report concluded with a call to action for funding the growth management system. A recommended increase in the property transfer tax was intended to support, in part, additional funding for the Housing and Conservation Trust Fund—a $20 million bond issue and a $5 million annual appropriation. The commission proposed an additional increase in this tax, plus an increase in permit fees, to support an annual funding level of $3–$5 million for the planning process. The money would strengthen local and regional planning capacity, support data collection and development of a geographic information system (GIS), and strengthen the legal and planning capacity of state government. Finally, the commission recommended an expanded Agricultural Loan Fund, possibly funded by a one-year increase in the sales tax, as an immediate measure to slow the loss of farms due to economic distress (Governor's Commission 1988, 28–29).

Drafting and Adopting Act 200

Governor Kunin unveiled the commission's report in her 1988 State of the State address and made the passage of a law embodying the report's recommendations her first priority. The report went immediately to the Office of Policy Research and Coordination, where it was eventually converted into the Growth Management Act of 1988 (Act 200). The key recommendations of the commission were included in the three subsections of the proposal: the planning process, proposals for tax sharing and subsidies for agriculture. The House considered the bill first, as is usual with major legislation in Vermont. But, instead of sending the bill to a standing committee, the governor and the House leadership agreed on the formation of an informal growth committee with representatives from all the relevant standing committees. At the growth committee hearings held around the state, the public response was somewhat more mixed than the overwhelmingly positive response to the 1987 Governor's commission.

Paul Pourier, the House Growth Committee chair, decided that the planning, tax sharing and farm subsidy proposals should be considered together in one bill, with the hope that agricultural support would help carry the package. Subcommittees were established in each of the major areas. The planning subcommittee struggled with the issue of whether to make town planning mandatory, as recommended by the commission report. In addition, there was a question of how to bring state agencies into the system while avoiding a potential constitutional issue involving the separation of powers between the executive and legislative branches. The solution was to require carefully defined compatibility (not strict consistency) between state agency plans and state goals.

There was considerable legislative debate over the state goals themselves. The Senate incorporated several of Act 250's policies into the new legislation as goals, increasing the number from the 12 approved by the House to a total of 32, and creating potential confusion between planning and regulation. There was much debate over agricultural supports. Ultimately, both the House and the Senate versions of the bill approved a temporary dairy subsidy and longer-term tax abatement program.

In the Senate, the related issues of private property rights and local control versus regional authority were hotly debated. The House and Senate generally differed over the scope of authority granted to RPCs.

The Senate supported a narrow regional role limited strictly to issues of regional concern, while the House supported a broader regional authority in review of local plans. The general political environment in which Act 200 passed included bipartisan support, but with a strong Democratic tilt. The deliberations of the conference committee went down to the wire, but when the law passed, Vermont at last put stage three of Act 250 into law in the form of Act 200, albeit with not nearly as strong a state and regional framework as recommended by the Governor's commission.

The major differences in the final bill compared to the commission report reflected the Senate's concern over local control and home rule. The final bill dropped the mandatory local planning provision and abandoned the regional and statewide tax sharing proposals. Opposition to tax sharing came even from towns that would have benefited from such a provision but felt it was an erosion of home rule. The key interests that had supported the commission report generally continued to support the legislation as it developed, and the dairy farm subsidy and tax abatement program held the backing of the agricultural community. Most development interests continued to be supportive, although the law did not address full integration of permitting (as in Act 250) and planning, which they hoped would add more certainty to the development process.

Environmental groups, especially the Vermont Natural Resources Council (VNRC), remained powerful and active proponents of the House versions of the bill and the law as it was passed. The Vermont Land Trust (VLT) did not take an advocacy role, but the success of the Housing and Conservation Trust Fund was a positive force in encouraging the passage of Act 200.

The role of the Vermont League of Cities and Towns was mixed. The league's representative on the Governor's commission supported its report, with its emphasis on bottom-up planning and new growth management tools for local governments, but other league representatives saw a potential for ultimate devolution of Act 250's regulatory authority to local governments. The league's opposition to the final bill centered on the uncertainty as to how truly bottom-up the planning process would be and the failure to integrate the Act 250 process with the planning process in a way that would lead to ultimate local control.

Close observers agreed that Act 200 would never have gotten off the ground without the governor's support. Many in the legislature wanted planning legislation, since Act 250 was never designed to be a planning program but rather a permitting program built around a planning process. It seemed that every issue that came up at the legislature's Natural Resources Committee became a state issue because of the lack of local and regional planning.

Act 200: A Summary of Key Provisions

Governor Kunin signed Act 200 into law on May 19, 1988. According to a citizens' guide, published shortly thereafter, the new system significantly strengthened the process of integrating plans on local, regional and state agency levels (Vermont DHCA 1988). It also increased the resources available to towns and regions for planning and provided substantial and sustained funding for the Housing and Conservation Trust Fund. The act authorized communities to assess impact fees and set up two programs to assist Vermont's working farmers (Vermont DHCA 1988).

As in the systems of Maine and Rhode Island, a series of state goals and policies, addressing both procedural and substantive concerns, framed the Vermont growth management system. Passed in 1988, Act 200 ended up with 32 goals addressing such policy areas as the planning process, quality and use of resources, public and private investment, planning for growth, economic development, agriculture and forestry, planning for housing, transportation systems and public utilities.

Consistency and Concurrency Policies

Act 200 did not require municipalities to prepare local plans, nor did it require higher agencies to review the plans for consistency with state goals. The law did stipulate, however, that local plans, in order to be approved or confirmed, had to be consistent with state goals. The law defined the term *consistent with* in this context as "substantial progress toward attainment

of the goals." In addition, the law generally required local plans to be compatible with the plans of their regions and of neighboring towns. The definition of *compatible with* was that the town's plan "would not significantly reduce the desired effect of the implementation of the other plan." If a town plan were not compatible with a neighbor town's plan, it could still be confirmed upon being found to meet certain criteria. Finally, an approved plan would have to conform to all the other procedural and substantive requirements of Act 200.

The more substantive provisions of Act 200 detailed plan requirements, including "a statement of objectives, policies and programs of the municipality to guide the future growth and development of land, public services and facilities, and to protect the environment." The content requirements called for a plan that mapped out current and future land uses, detailing the nature of any development and its provision for services (a "concurrency" provision). The act set forth similar substantive requirements for elements on transportation, utilities and facilities, natural and historic resources, education facilities, energy and a housing element linked to regional needs as identified by RPC.

Vermont's Act 200 offered substantial incentives to encourage municipalities to participate in the planning and review process, including grants and increased planning and regulatory authority. One such incentive was the authority to levy impact fees, granted only to those municipalities with an approved and adopted plan. Once approved or confirmed, a town's plan would gain official status in Act 250 review procedures and the proposal would be reviewed for consistency with the local plan.

The Role of Regional Planning Commissions

Whether or not a municipality chose to participate in the Act 200 process, all municipalities within a designated region were considered members of an RPC. The Act 200 planning process gave RPCs several new responsibilities in three major areas: identification of regional resources and needs for use in local planning efforts; local plan coordination, mediation, and review and approval; and preparation and adoption of a regional plan. In the first area, RPC duties included a mandatory regional housing needs assessment; identification of areas of regional significance (i.e., historic sites, earth resources, rare and irreplaceable natural areas); use of a land evaluation and site assessment system to identify viable agricultural lands; and development of a regional database linked to the state GIS.

The duties of RPCs in coordinating and mediating local planning efforts included leading plan coordination among towns; reviewing at least every five years the compatibility of municipal plans with each other; and heading up voluntary and mandatory mediation to end conflicts between regional and municipal plans. RPCs' new plan review responsibilities included checking member local governments' plans for consistency with state goals and compatibility with the regional and other municipalities' plans. In order to assist local governments in meeting the standards of review in a timely fashion, the act required RPCs to prepare guidelines for consistency review and affordable housing, and data sharing on affordable housing with cities, towns and the state.

Finally, the act charged RPCs with preparing and adopting a regional plan consistent with Act 200 goals and compatible with approved municipal and adjoining regional plans. In prescribing the elements of the regional plan required for consistency with state planning goals, Act 200 put a strong emphasis on policies that protect important agricultural lands. The regional plan was to indicate areas with the potential to sustain farming and make recommendations for maintaining them.

To adopt the regional plan, there was a major effort to secure citizen and organizations' input by distributing the draft plan to municipalities, and business, conservation, low-income advocacy and other groups. A vote of 60 percent of the regional commissioners representing municipalities was required for adoption, and the first regional plans under Act 200 were to be submitted to the Council of Regional Commissions (CRC) for review by the end of 1992. According to Act 200, a majority vote of the municipalities in the region could reject a plan, but, in any case, the plan was to be transmitted to the council. At least every five years, RPCs were required to submit their plans to the council for review.

Act 200 represented a giant leap forward in the roles and responsibilities of RPCs in Vermont. Membership by municipalities became mandatory, though the membership criteria remained the same. Regional plans and local plan review responsibilities were heavy, and, as outlined below, the act provided funding to support these new responsibilities. In the implementation process, the question has been: "How well can these traditionally voluntary regional agencies adapt to a substantial expansion of their responsibilities?" To a considerable extent, the success of Act 200 depended on regional commissions becoming effective partners in the new intergovernmental system.

State Agency Roles and Responsibilities

Act 200 charged all state agencies that have programs or take actions affecting land use with developing plans and implementing strategies to ensure consistency with the Act 200 goals. Vermont thus clearly required that state agencies become part of the growth management system. Plans mandated by state agencies must be consistent with state planning goals and compatible with regional and approved municipal plans. A detailed process for achieving these objectives was spelled out in Act 200, including required hearings, public, regional and local government participation and adoption procedures.

Bringing state agencies into an integrated growth strategy is one of the most difficult challenges in implementing growth management systems, and in Vermont the key to achieving this goal is CRC. The council membership includes a municipal representative from each RPC, three state agency heads and two public members, all appointed by the governor. The council has a major role in determining the degree of success in implementing Vermont's growth strategy. It is a deliberate attempt to make the system acceptable to local governments by putting much of the consistency and compatibility review process in the hands of an agency dominated by municipal government members. The duties of CRC include

- acting as impartial mediator in disputes between or among municipalities, RPCs or state agencies;

- reviewing regional plans and amendments according to consistency and compatibility criteria, including review on request of a municipality;

■ reviewing state agency plans and amendments according to a set of criteria detailed in the law;

■ establishing by rule three-person panels of council members, with membership restrictions to avoid conflicts of interest; and

■ developing a procedure for formal review of RPC determination of approval or disapproval of local plans, with broad standing for citizens and involved agencies.

Act 200 gave CRC administrative support from the state DHCA, which received additional staff and money to support its new responsibilities. A new position of special counsel was created to work on land use matters to support the council as it reviewed and rendered opinions on the legality of existing or proposed municipal plans and ordinances.

In addition to these provisions for integrating state agencies into the growth management system, Act 200 provided for special state agency roles in agricultural and natural resource protection. In keeping with Act 200's emphasis on saving Vermont's working farms, the commissioner of agriculture was directed to establish guidelines for municipal and regional planning commissions in identifying agricultural lands.

The Agricultural Land Development Rights Acquisition Program directed the commissioner to develop, with the advice and consent of the Housing and Conservation Board, a two-part program for selecting and recommending agricultural land development rights suitable for acquisition by the state, and for developing criteria for the board to review those recommendations. The thrust of the program was to ensure that

■ in municipalities with an approved plan under the new law, the board acquire rights only to land designated for agricultural use under a land evaluation and site assessment (LESA) system;

■ the board only acquire land designated in a local government's approved plan for that purpose; and

■ after development rights are acquired, the land shall be taxed upon the fair market value of the remaining rights or interests to which title is retained.

Act 200 gave state and local governments maximum flexibility to acquire or otherwise protect agricultural and natural resource lands. It spelled out the authority of other state agencies, including Natural Resources, Transportation and Agriculture, to purchase land for these purposes. It also addressed the agencies' right to acquire fee title or lessor rights, rules for exemption from taxation of such lands, and definitions of rights and interests in property.

Three specific programs aimed directly at alleviating immediate and long-term pressures on Vermont's agricultural economy crowned Act 200's agricultural preservation efforts: Working Farm Tax Abatement Program; Farm Tax Reimbursement Program; and Dairy Industry Income Stabilization Program. The tax abatement program extended the existing use-value taxation system to include farm buildings and improvements as well as land. The property taxes lost by a municipality because of the new system were to be reimbursed in full. Participation by farmers was voluntary, and there was a $13,000 annual limit on property tax abated. Certain restrictions applied, such as a requirement for a forest management plan for enrolled forest land of more than 25 acres, and a stipulation that enrolled property meet all municipal or regional planning criteria. Act 200 spelled out in some detail procedures for enrolling land in the system, the assessment of the property at fair market value to determine tax rebates due municipalities, and procedures for removing land and improvements from the program.

Act 200 gave the Housing and Conservation Board the right of first refusal to purchase farm or forest land being removed from the tax abatement program at the same price as a bona fide arms-length offer to the owner or according to a prescribed appraisal process. If land were converted without the required notification to the board, it would still have a right to purchase the land, or the seller would be subject to a penalty. If an owner removed land from the program and the state did not buy it, substantial payment would be required.

The tax reimbursement program refunded property taxes paid by farmers in 1988, except for farmers receiving benefits from the Dairy Industry Income

Stabilization Program. A "farmer" was defined as a person receiving at least one-half of an annual income from farming and whose net farm income did not exceed $32,000. Reimbursements could not exceed $5,000. The dairy income stabilization program was a one-year effort to give special help to dairy farmers and to enroll them in the permanent tax abatement program. The definition of dairy farmers was the same as in the tax abatement program, and the program tied the amount of payments to the federal market price of milk.

The Rocky Road to Implementation, 1988–1991

Act 200 gained major support during Governor Kunin's commission hearings and for the most part sustained that support through the legislative debate and into the early months of the implementation process. The combination of the governor's commitment; strong backing in the legislature; and generous funding for planning, Housing and Conservation Board activities, and agricultural industry activities all seemed to point to a reasonably smooth implementation effort. The first year followed that script well. Immediately after Act 200 passed, a study committee was organized to report to the governor and legislature on a number of issues in November 1988. In August DHCA began publishing a newsletter that documented implementation activities on a continuing basis up to and including a backlash against Act 200 in fall 1989 (Vermont DHCA 1989b, 1–8).

Policy and working committees were ready to plan the development of a GIS, supported by a $1 million allocation. In an effort to integrate state agencies into the program, Kunin issued an executive order in November 1988 outlining how they should make their plans and programs compatible with regional and local plans and consistent with Act 200's planning goals. The commissioner of agriculture contracted with the Vermont Land Trust to develop the criteria for the Department of Agriculture and the Housing and Conservation Board to select agricultural lands for priority purchase of development rights.

DHCA was developing a Housing Data Bank to assist RPCs in creating a housing element in regional plans that would identify the need for housing at all economic levels in the region and communities (Vermont DHCA 1989a).

Act 200 provisions for municipal planning did not go into effect until July 1, 1989. In the meantime, DHCA was concerned with bringing municipalities into the planning process. The first few months of activity in implementation focused on getting planning dollars into the hands of towns and RPCs. The first-year local planning money included $1 million in regular planning grants to be distributed on a straight per-capita basis. In addition, municipalities with special planning needs could compete for other grants; subsequent funding for local governments was to be distributed based on a formula developed by DHCA.

For the second year, DHCA devised an allocation formula of some complexity and adopted it as a rule. Two-thirds of the $1.57 million in local planning funds was to be distributed on a per capita basis, and the remaining funds were distributed according to local growth in relation to the state average, the level of development activity in adjacent municipalities, and community need. Local governments could use the funds for a variety of planning and plan implementation activities, however, they could not use the money to pay RPC dues or to substitute for local dollars previously committed to planning.

Of the $1.59 million in regional planning funds for 1989, each of the 12 RPCs received a base funding of $80,000. Sixty percent of the remaining funds was allocated on the basis of population and 40 percent on the basis of the number of municipalities served. Act 200 provided that if the earmarked funding source for planning funds (the property transfer tax) produced expected increases in revenues in the future, the base allocation would increase to $100,000 for RPCs. DHCA authorized RPCs to spend the funds in accordance with a work plan and annual contract with DHCA, focusing on tasks consistent with the new requirements of Act 200 and RPCs' carryover duties. RPCs were also in charge of the confirming process, in which each municipality's planning activities would be reviewed to establish that it was consistent with the goals of Act 200 (Vermont DHCA 1989a).

Act 200 substantially increased Vermont's funding of local and regional planning through the provision of an earmarked funding source: 40 percent of the 1988 increase in the state's property transfer tax was to go into a Municipal and Regional Planning Trust Fund. This had the effect of raising available funding from $860,000 annually in 1988 to $2.99 million in 1989 and $3.5 million in 1990 (Vermont DHCA 1989b, 1–8). The first year of implementing Act 200 was full of positive activity and high hopes, and progress was made on a number of fronts. By July 1989 almost all of Vermont's cities and towns (an estimated 238 out of 246) had been confirmed by RPCs as engaged in a planning process that would lead to adoption of an Act 200 consistent local plan. The second round of special planning grants by DHCA saw $350,000 available in 1990 to add to the $400,000 distributed the first year. Furthermore, state agencies, with a strong push from the governor, were moving toward full review of their plans by the CRC. In spite of this progress, there was a bitter struggle by Act 200 opponents to repeal or drastically weaken the new system.

The Backlash Against Act 200

In September 1989 a group organized as the Citizens for Property Rights (CPR) sponsored a meeting in Morrisville, Vermont, which some saw as the kickoff of a campaign against Act 200. The major theme was signaled by the name of the group: the charge that private property rights would be taken away if Act 200 were implemented. A second charge was that the Act 200 process really constituted top-down planning, which would ultimately shift most control of growth to the state or regional level.

A major organizer of CPR was Senator John McLaughery, who had led a similar (and successful) attack against the adoption of the third stage of Act 250 (the state land use plan). McLaughery was from Vermont's sparsely populated Northeast Kingdom, which had always viewed planning and zoning as, at best, an improper attempt to take away private property rights and local control. The CPR group was well-funded and well-organized, and it produced some effective pamphlets attacking Act 200 as an unconsti-

tutional assault on private property and a thinly disguised effort to take away the right of Vermont's cities and towns to manage their own affairs.

Town meetings in Vermont are traditionally held in March, and CPR orchestrated its assault on Act 200 at that time using carefully drafted resolutions to say that a given town did not wish to participate in the Act 200 planning process. The effort was amazingly successful, and around 100 of Vermont's 250-plus towns and villages approved such resolutions in either their regular town meetings or special meetings. The naysayers were largely but not exclusively rural and located in the Northeast Kingdom; they represented perhaps 25 percent of the state's population. The state's attorney general ruled that the resolutions of nonparticipation were advisory only, but the backlash was still a shocking negative reaction to a law that had had strong support when it passed the 1988 legislature, and whose first year of implementation went forward with little controversy. Part of the success of CPR and other opposition groups may have been related to the way the resolutions were worded. Questions such as "Shall the town prepare a State Land Use Plan?" or "Shall the town prepare a land use plan in compliance with the Growth Control Bill?" were a distortion of both the letter and spirit of Act 200, but the tactic was successful.

Some felt that the governor's office was responsible in part for the backlash by not supporting citizens' groups that could have defended the Act 200 program. Instead, the state itself tried to lead the defense. Because the opposition to some extent focused on the governor, this approach was not always effective.

The revolt was generally seen as antigovernment, antiregulation and especially antizoning. Opposition to regional review of local plans was really aimed at killing effective land use controls. A League of Cities and Towns leader made it clear that while the league supported CPR on some of its agenda, such as weakening or eliminating the regional review role, it could not support CPR's opposition to all planning and zoning. In this tense political environment, the 1990 session loomed at a time of great danger for Act 200, made worse by Vermont's declining economy.

As expected, McLaughery led the assault in the Senate with a motion simply to repeal Act 200. The

Senate defeated the motion, but the battle continued, now focused on limiting regional review of local plans and on reducing the number of goals. It was clear that the votes were there for some sort of "easing up" on regional review, and the act's supporters were concerned that the law would be drastically weakened by eliminating regional review entirely. The Senate narrowly defeated the proposal, and the compromise was an amendment in which RPCs could not reject a plan but only approve or approve with conditions. Thus, local governments submitting plans found inconsistent with state planning goals would benefit from most of the incentives under Act 200. They would continue to be eligible for state planning funds, including the right to apply for special grants, and have the authority to levy impact fees, subject to other requirements for a capital improvements program. Finally, plans approved with conditions would have standing in the Act 250 review process.

After much discussion, the 1990 legislature reduced the original 32 goals approved in 1988 to 12 "soft goals," and weakened their authority. The essential elements of the growth management system were retained. But in other changes, the revised law added the option of electing, as well as appointing, municipal planning board members. Towns were authorized to request RPCs to coordinate how a town plan addressed regional issues, and they were required to show they had solicited comments from abutting towns and RPCs. Per the revised law, RPCs had to define those issues believed to be of substantial regional impact and to consider those impacts in state regulatory proceedings. To ensure timeliness in state-agency plan compatibility with local plans, the law required CRC to review state agency plans every two years.

The compromises worked out in the Senate were approved by the governor. As a result of the amendments, senators and representatives could go home and say that they "had done something about Act 200," but still had not gutted the law. Some supporters of the act felt that although the changes weakened the law somewhat, the alternative was to risk repeal. The key was to keep the planning process moving and hope that RPCs would grow stronger over time.

Act 200 and the Politics of Survival

Republican Richard A. Snelling, an original supporter of Act 250, was elected governor in 1990. He seemed generally supportive of Act 200, although he expressed some reservations about the regional review process prior to the 1990 amendments. His term in office was cut short by his untimely death in August 1991. Democratic Lt. Governor Howard Dean became governor and was reelected governor every two years until he chose not to run in 2002. There was no question that without Dean's readiness to veto efforts to weaken or destroy the 1988 growth management system, it might have suffered even more serious damage over time. His leadership with regard to the Housing and Conservation Trust Fund and the Industrial Development Fund were particularly important in sustaining funding for those key components of the system.

The supporters of Act 200 who fashioned the legislative compromises in 1990 felt they were necessary to avoid outright repeal or drastic weakening of the system. But what about the 100 or more towns that resolved not to participate in the Act 200 planning process? They were still involved, since more than 70 applied for planning funds subsequent to passing those resolutions and were continuing to plan under the Act 200 process. The 1990 amendments, as was intended, made it easier for them to do so. As of April 1992, approximately 100 of the 271 municipalities had completed plans; only 15, however, had submitted their plans to RPCs, and 14 were approved.

The decline in planning funds because of the transfer tax shortfalls was a problem, but some dollars continued to flow to towns, cities and RPCs to move forward in the process. The Housing and Conservation Board also continued to receive funds to implement the several agricultural programs passed in 1988. In 1992 Governor Dean requested a $14 million bonding appropriation for the Housing and Conservation Trust Fund that would triple the fund's budget; he received $11.6 million from the legislature. A state agency planning implementation committee, composed of members of the governor's office and other administration officials, was formed to oversee the process.

Many supporters of Act 200 felt the backlash against the program would run out of steam and that supporters of the law could rally to ensure its future. Indeed, a bill for repeal of Act 200, filed in the 1991 session, received no substantial support.

A Defensive Battle to Save the Growth Management System, 1991–1995

While some positive planning and implementation actions did take place in the first half of the 1990s, the dominant developments involved efforts by Governor Dean and others to defeat attempts by a legislature urged on by property rights groups to repeal or drastically weaken the growth management system.

Cutbacks in state funding caused by the recession of the early 1990s were the main reason the goals of Act 200 were not fully accomplished. Here we find a parallel with Maine and Rhode Island, which also cut the generous allocation of earmarked funding sources for their growth management systems. In Vermont, funding for Act 200 came from the property transfer tax, which was increased initially by three-fourths of a percent, with the proceeds to be split between the Housing and Conservation Trust Fund and the Municipal and Regional Planning Fund. DHCA received significant resources to increase its planning division to seven staff. Before the recession and the subsequent cutbacks, the earmarked funding source allowed some $3.3 million to be spent on local and regional planning. When the fiscal crunch hit, the legislature took all the proceeds of the property transfer tax and put the dollars into the general fund. Even if those revenues had been preserved for municipal and regional planning, the recession had reduced the value of the proceeds from a range of $11–$14 million in the late 1980s to about $6 million by late 1995.

The staff and dollar cutbacks at DHCA's planning division made it impossible to provide the two remaining staff with support needed for components of the system such as the CRC, which was charged with resolving disputes between towns and regions and towns and state agencies. In another example of Act 200 suffering from the financial crisis, publica-

tions, including a quarterly newsletter with a technical assistance insert, were cancelled or not updated, thus hampering DHCA's ability to promote Act 200 in a proactive way, something that was badly needed by the towns that lacked planning expertise.

Support groups and, above all, Governor Dean blocked repeated efforts by the legislature to weaken or repeal the law. The most serious threat to Act 200, other than outright repeal efforts, involved proposed legislation limiting the authority of RPCs over town plans. The most extreme version, which proposed that regional approval of municipal plans be eliminated, passed the Senate in 1994 (VPA 1995). A more moderate House bill would have removed the regional review provision, but not until after 1996. The governor vetoed the 1994 effort, but the politics of the situation had shifted somewhat as a result of the 1992 elections, when Dean easily won his first full two-year term. The Democrats strengthened their majority in the House, but Republicans won a surprising 16 to 14 majority in the Senate. Supporters of Act 200 saw little hope of preventing an override of the governor's veto in the Senate, so they focused on advocating a strong regional role in the House and were successful in finding support of the veto. By focusing on the regional review fight, attention was diverted from repealing Act 200 outright (Dodd 1992, 2; VNRC 1994b, 8; 1995a, 27; 1995a).

On the positive side, the fight in 1994 over Dean's reappointment of three members to the Act 250 Environmental Board, which hears appeals of Act 250 decisions, resulted in both a political victory over Lt. Governor Barbara Snelling (widow of the former governor) and a reconstitution of the Environmental Board in a way that better linked Act 250 with Act 200. Snelling's role in stopping Dean's appointments, all well-respected board members, including one well-known Republican, did not serve her well when she ran against Dean in the November 1994 election; she was soundly defeated.

A figure from the past, 85-year old Arthur Gibb, who in 1969 headed the commission that led to the adoption of Act 250, was called back to serve as interim director of the Environmental Board in 1994. Governor Dean then confounded the anti–growth management forces by appointing as board chair

John Ewing, a retired bank president and former district commissioner with a favorable reputation in both the business and environmental communities. There was general agreement among all but the most extreme conservatives and private property rights advocates that the Act 250 process needed to be streamlined to simplify and expedite the process of getting a permit.

DHCA at this time was to direct growth into designated growth centers and wanted to strengthen that process by forging a formal link with Act 250; if a town's growth center plan met Act 200 standards, the Act 250 permit approval process would be made much simpler. Governor Dean supported the downtown centers–Main Street program pushed by DHCA. For his part, Ewing was open to amending the Environmental Board rules so as to delegate to towns some of the Act 250 permit approval power that had resided with the board. Not only did Act 250 seem safe from further efforts to weaken it, but its positive links to Act 200 seemed to almost ensure its implementation (VNRC 1994a, 7; 1995c, 1–2).

Another positive step took place in the mid-1990s, when, as part of an economic progress law, a Growth Centers Pilot Project was financed to examine how development could be encouraged in downtown areas and other growth centers (DHCA 1999, 14). A number of proposals included in DHCA's *Growth Center Pilot Project Summary* report were adopted by the legislature.

Key Developments, 1995–2000

By the mid-1990s concerns about sprawl and its impact on Vermont's economy and quality of life were becoming a constant theme. The Vermont Forum on Sprawl, funded by the Orton Family Foundation in 1998, had a goal to curb sprawl and promote "a working rural landscape in Vermont through research and education." The work of the Housing and Conservation Trust Fund and the Vermont Land Trust has conserved thousands of acres of conservation and farmland, and provided thousands of affordable housing units. In the legislature, an onsite sewage committee developed a proposed bill that would have cured the infamous 10-acre exemption for septic tanks, which tended to promote sprawl because the exemption gave developers an incentive to divide land into lots just over 10 acres. The bill passed in at least one legislative chamber in two successive sessions, but was always defeated in the other (DHCA 1999, 15).

A DHCA recommendation involving property tax reform would have led to better land use planning, but it was not approved by the legislature until 1997, when a Vermont Supreme Court ruling found the state's system of funding education unconstitutional. Act 60 set up a statewide revenue sharing system as a way of equalizing educational funding across towns with different levels of local revenue. While not aimed directly at land use, Act 60 was seen by DHCA as a potential plus for sound planning under Act 200 because it would eliminate the need for towns to compete with each other for commercial development. Such a revenue sharing process, if fully implemented, could make it easier for towns to coordinate their planning and land use decisions.

Support for the Environment and Downtowns

Governor Dean's 1998 State of the State and budget address illustrated both his rising concern with the impact of sprawl and his support of the Vermont Housing and Conservation Trust Fund and other efforts to acquire or protect environmentally sensitive land and water resources. On the subject of poorly managed development leading to sprawl, Dean stated, "I believe that unplanned growth in a booming economy will change the state forever in ways the vast majority of Vermonters will not support" (Dean 1998, 7–8). He went on to praise the Trust Fund for preserving land and providing affordable housing for Vermonters. Dean also acknowledged the Agency of Natural Resources (ANR) for negotiating the conservation of more than 260 acres of land protected with the help of the private sector and nonprofits, including the Vermont Land Trust.

Founded in 1977, the Vermont Land Trust (VLT) is a nonprofit land conservation organization considered one of the most effective land trusts in the country. By 1999 it had helped conserve 602 projects for a total of 184,186 acres, approximately 3.6 percent of Vermont's privately owned open space. Its primary tool for conserving land is conservation easements; typically, VLT does not own land but provides legal, technical, mapping, stewardship and financial support to land trusts and state agencies to help them achieve their conservation priorities (VLT 1999c, 1). Working with VLT, the Housing and Conservation Trust Fund has acquired thousands of acres in the state, with the goal of returning the land to private ownership with VLT retaining permanent conservation easements and public recreation access rights before it is resold to private developers. The organization seeks to protect critical habitat, sensitive areas and open forest land for recreational uses.[1]

Dean's strong support for preventing sprawl by protecting lands along roadways and interstates led to his reinstatement of the Scenery Preservation Council and the adoption of an Interstate Highway Interchange Development Policy, both in 1999 (DHCA 1999, 16). Another act proposed by the governor and passed by the 1998 legislature, called the Downtown Bill, provides additional incentives for downtown development and revitalization, making such areas eligible for special tax credits and rebates, planning grants and transportation funding. The downtowns also would get training and technical assistance from DHCA (DHCA 1999, 15).

Beginning in 1997, an effort to increase municipal and regional planning funds was led by advocacy groups such as the Vermont Planners Association, RPCs and other supporters of planning within the framework of Act 200's goals and objectives. Sharp cuts took place from 1990 to 1994, when all municipal planning dollars were eliminated, and the zero funding level held until the 1997 legislative session. The pro-Act 200 planning groups, working with key members and committees in the legislature, pushed for renewed funding and steady increases through 2001, though the level of municipal funding remained at about one-half its 1989 level.

---

1. See the Vermont Land Trust website (http://www.vlt.org/) for information on how VLT's conservation easement program works. The critical monitoring and enforcement process is explained in some detail and is worth a careful reading by other states who plan to use this tool as a way to protect farm and forest lands and other important natural areas.

By the end of 2000 Vermont was moving in a direction that could knit that state's growth management effort back together by reviving the planning component of the system (Act 200) and integrating it with a streamlined Act 250. However, a number of items on the unfinished agenda still needed to be addressed to achieve a fully integrated system that could sustain the values of Vermont's rural countryside while channeling population pressures into designated growth centers. That, in turn, would ensure healthy urban systems and arrest the sprawl widely recognized as a major threat to the state's sustainable future.

CRC, the major vehicle for ensuring a state and regional framework for the decisions made by Vermont towns, had not been refunded or staffed and was no longer a key player in the system. Further, Vermont had no state planning office, and the Planning Division of DHCA had not increased its staff since the reductions in the early 1990s. Given the lack of planning capacity in most of Vermont's towns, technical assistance is a must if local and regional plans that meet the goals of Act 200 are to be realized (DHCA 1999, 16–17; Schonberger 2000, 82–83).

A key part of the smart growth agenda continues to be the Downtown Program administered through DHCA's Division of Historic Preservation. Based on the National Main Street model, this program promotes downtown revitalization tax credits, sales tax rebates and transportation-related infrastructure. The 2000 legislature approved a $4 million appropriation proposed by Dean to capitalize grants and loans for downtown infrastructure, streetscape and facade improvements, and building rehab to address code and access issues. A second key piece adopted by Dean in 1999 addressed land use at or around limited access highway ramps. While not opposing all development around the ramps, the policy seeks to block development that would either have a negative impact on the health of nearby downtowns or on the aesthetic quality of the landscape.

A third major development was a 2000 executive order creating a Governor's Development Cabinet chaired by the governor or a designee to ensure collaboration and consultation among state agencies and departments, "by supporting and encouraging

Vermont's economic development and conserving and promoting Vermont's traditional settlement patterns, its working and rural landscape, its strong communities and its healthy environment" (State of Vermont 2000, 2).

The November 2000 Elections

In mid-2000 a political wildcard entered the picture that some felt challenged the assumption that Dean would easily win the November reelection. That wildcard was a civil unions law adopted by the legislature in 2000. The law grew out of a state Supreme Court ruling in 1999 that couples of the same sex could not be denied the same benefits and protections afforded to married opposite-sex couples (Vermont Supreme Court 1999). After months of debate, the legislature with strong support from Dean adopted the civil unions law, and although the issue deeply divided the state, no repeal effort got moving.

The law's impact on Vermont's smart growth agenda had to do with the possibility that Dean could be defeated in his bid for another term, or that one or both houses would be taken over by Republicans. According to supporters of Act 200, either outcome would end any further movement to implement Act 200. Dean's Republican opponent, Ruth Dwyer, was a strong conservative. If the civil unions political turmoil had resulted in her winning, or if Republicans had gained full control of the legislature, some feared a return of previous efforts to repeal both Act 250 and Act 200. The worst fears of smart growth supporters were not realized, however. Dean defeated Dwyer by a margin of just over 51 percent of the vote, although the legislature was split, with 16 Democrats and 14 Republicans in the Senate, and 82 Republicans, 63 Democrats, four Progressives and one Independent in the House.

Building on Smart Growth Initiatives, 2001–2003

The combination of VLT, the Housing and Conservation Board and supportive environmental and government agencies resulted in remarkable progress over the 2001–2003 period, in spite of budget shortfalls and the general uncertainty brought on by the attacks of September 11, 2001. VLT president Darby Bradley noted the statistics: "1,212 properties protected; at least one completed project in 225 of Vermont's 251 towns; 396,937 acres conserved for 6.7 percent of all the land in the state. The more interesting question to ask is: What difference has this work made for the people and communities involved?" (VLT 2002a, 6–7; 2002b, 5). Bradley stressed VLT's strong commitment to partnering with the owners of conserved lands. This approach is important because landowners either sell their development rights or donate conservation easements that are in fact monitored and enforced by VLT on a long-term basis. To assure that it has the resources to aggressively purchase land and conservation easements, VLT launched a capital campaign—Vermont at the Crossroads—with a goal of raising $25 million (VLT 2002a, 6–7; 2002b, 5).

The Housing and Conservation Board remains the only group in the nation that combines funding for affordable housing and land conservation projects, both fundamental pieces of building livable communities. According to Bradley, "Affordable housing groups have become neighborhood and community revitalization organizers, incorporating business incubator space and neighborhood parks into their housing programs" (VLT 2002c, 3–4).

Sewage reform finally passed in 2002, closing the 10-acre exemption and allowing alternative strategies to help establish wastewater treatment in many unserviced village centers. Due to concern that the alternative systems could expose more land to development and foster sprawl, the alternatives are allowed only in municipalities that have an RPC-approved plan and zoning regulations.

Governor's Executive Order on Smart Growth

Governor's Executive Order 01-07 (September 2001), combined with an EPA Sustainable Development Challenge Grant supporting the implementation of the executive order, was an ambitious smart growth initiative to manage land use policies and regulations at interchanges along Vermont's interstate highway system. This sweeping effort sought to bring all relevant state and regional agencies, local governments, the private sector and nonprofits such as VLT into the planning and implementation equation. According to the executive order, which was scheduled to sunset on October 1, 2010, unmanaged development at interchanges "may diminish the scenic character of the landscape, impair critical natural and agricultural resources...pull commerce away from traditional villages and growth centers; and undermine the economic vitality of Vermont's downtowns" (State of Vermont 2001, 1).

The EPA challenge grant focused on four targeted interchanges ("sprawl hot spots": exits 4, 7, 11 and 17 off I-89). DHCA was to put together a coordinating team to find ways local governments at all levels could work together to manage land use and transportation at interstate interchanges. They were also to collaborate with the four towns on subgrants, with local government and regional officials handling the changes and working with contractors where appropriate (DHCA 2002, 2–3). A number of project tasks were identified.

- The ANR will contract with consultants to assess and map the critical natural resources at each of the four targeted exits.

- DHCA will contract with a consultant to develop model design guidelines for land use, development and conservation at the interchanges.

- DHCA will work to summarize activities and results of this project into one document designed to pull the four separate projects into a common format.

- Following public review, DHCA will develop a final report...for distribution to the many other communities facing similar challenges. (DHCA 2002, 3)

Assuming that the Project Work Plan can be fully implemented, its significance for Vermont's smart growth agenda is clear. The challenge grant from the

---

Mandates of Executive Order 01-07, 2001

- All agencies and departments shall coordinate their participation in Act 250 cases with the Agency of Natural Resources (ANR) in order to achieve Vermont's land use goals in interstate interchanges.

- ANR shall review any proposal for sewer or water infrastructure funding in and around interchanges utilizing the criteria established in the wastewater priority points system, and shall deny those projects that would result in development that is incompatible with Vermont's land use goals and growth center planning.

- The Agency of Transportation, prior to allocating federal or state transportation funds, including but not limited to TEA-21 funds, and prior to approving additional means of vehicular access (curb-cuts, drives, highways, rights-of-way) near interstate interchanges or other limited access highways, shall investigate whether land near said exchanges should be protected from development and protected for conservation, scenic and recreational uses.

- DHCA shall support, through department grant funds, community planning and zoning projects that seek to preserve the unique values of lands around interstate interchanges.

- The Governor's Development Cabinet, acting through the DHCA, in collaboration with property owners, state agencies, and municipal and regional planning and development entities, shall inventory interstate interchange lands and monitor development proposals at interstate interchanges.

- The Governor's Development Cabinet, acting through DHCA, shall evaluate prime interstate interchange lands for conservation efforts.

- After completion of an inventory of interstate interchange lands, DHCA shall work collaboratively with ANR, the Department of Agriculture, Food and Markets, the Department of Buildings and General Services, RPCs, the Association of Vermont Conservation Commissions, and interested nonprofit conservation organizations to determine which lands present important conservation, agricultural, scenic and recreational values.

- If parcels near interstate interchanges contain multiple conservation values, the Governor's Development Cabinet, acting through DHCA, shall work with the Housing and Conservation Board and the Board's public and nonprofit conservation partners to assemble the resources necessary to conserve priority parcels.

- All agencies, departments and instrumentalities of the State of Vermont with missions or responsibilities that affect development of lands near interstate interchanges, including, but not limited to the Agency of Transportation, ANR, DHCA and the Department of Buildings and General Services, shall provide information and resources for conservation efforts of priority parcels at interstate interchanges.

Source: State of Vermont, 2001, 2–3

EPA amounted to a substantial enough sum to ensure meaningful results.

Downtown Programs

As discussed above, the Vermont Downtown Program provides technical assistance to local entities for revitalization efforts; maintains a Downtown Resource Library; holds an annual conference and quarterly meetings to allow for updates and networking; and coordinates a local Comprehensive Training Program. The 1998 Downtown Development Act supported revitalization through tax credits and loans and grants from various state agencies (Vermont Division for Historic Preservation 2002, 1–2). The 2002 Second Downtown Development Act, adopted as H 208 and signed into law in May 2002, included the following major provisions:

■ Expand the existing 5 percent income tax credit to a 10 percent tax credit, which is added to an existing 20 percent federal tax credit for substantial rehabilitation of qualified historic buildings.

■ Create a 50 percent income tax credit for construction of elevators, lifts and sprinkler systems.

■ Ease the threshold triggering Act 250 jurisdiction for housing projects that provide for mixed income or mixed uses.

■ Allow special assessment taxes to be used for operating funds as well as capital projects.

■ Create a priority for state buildings to locate facilities in Village Centers. (State of Vermont 2002; Vermont ACCD 2002, 1)

H 208 also created new processes for designating development areas to be known as New Village Centers and New Town Centers. In the case of New Village Centers, a number of added benefits were to be made available:

■ Create a 5 percent income tax credit, to be added to an existing 20 percent federal tax credit for the substantial rehabilitation of qualified historic buildings.

■ Create a 50 percent income tax credit for code improvements made to commercial buildings.

■ Create a priority for village centers within the Municipal Planning Grant program and the state's Consolidated Plan for HUD funding (including the Community Development Block Grant [CDBG] program).

■ Allow special assessment taxes to be used for operating funds, as well as capital projects.

■ Create a priority for State Buildings to locate facilities in Village Centers. (Vermont ACCD 2002, 1)

In New Town Centers, special assessment taxes could be used for operating funds and capital projects, and a priority was created for locating state buildings in New Town Centers (Vermont ACCD 2002, 1). H 208 also amended several processes and procedures of the Department of Labor and Industry and called for the establishment of an advisory committee to lend assistance to the department.

Smart Growth Moves by the Agency of Natural Resources

As noted earlier, ANR plays an important role in the implementation of Act 250. While the state land use plan scheduled to be a part of Act 250 never passed, the ANR has been the key state agency working with the District Environmental Commissions to approve, approve with conditions, or deny projects of a certain scale. Two smart growth initiatives of note are an agency executive order issued in 2002 by Scott Johnstone, secretary of ANR, and the adoption of new environmental protection rules involving municipal pollution control (Vermont ANR 2002b; 2002a).

The purposes of Chapter 2: Municipal Pollution Control Priority System as part of the ANR Department of Environmental Conservation's Environmental Protection Rules are to

■ obtain and maintain state water quality standards;

■ make efficient use of scarce public funds by providing financial assistance only to Publicly Owned Treatment Works (POTW) and Municipally Sponsored Privately Owned Wastewater System (MSPOWS) projects that: abate existing public health and/or environmental problems, and serve locally designated growth centers, unless there are

Smart Growth Principles Introduced by the Agency of Natural Resources

1. ANR shall work to identify, inventory, conserve, protect, manage and restore in a sustainable manner the state's natural resources in order to undertake and assist in land use planning efforts at all levels, and address issues related to scattered development. The state's natural resources include, but are not limited to: (1) air quality; (2) water quality; (3) biological diversity; (4) plants; (5) fish and wildlife; (6) ecosystems; (7) natural communities; and (8) geological formations.

2. ANR shall inform, educate, coordinate and cooperate with municipal governments, regional planning commissions and nongovernmental organizations, as well as other state agencies, regarding the identification, conservation and protection of natural resources within communities and working rural landscapes. This will include identifying and efficiently resolving resource protection conflicts.

3. ANR shall only support and provide public investments and incentives for public infrastructure that provides public health and environmental protection, does not contribute to scattered development and is consistent with the Agency's Growth Center and Growth Management Guidance Document.

4. ANR shall incorporate, as appropriate, smart growth concepts and principles into all relevant statutes, policies, procedures, guidance and practices related to regulatory review, land acquisition and other activities.

5. ANR shall support economic development that protects and conserves the state's natural resources, rural character, traditional working landscapes and traditional settlement patterns. This includes, but is not limited to, a sustainable and diversified agricultural and forest products economy that protects and enhances the state's natural resources.

6. ANR shall support dispersed outdoor recreation, and the cultural traditions associated with the public's use and enjoyment of fish and wildlife resources by discouraging scattered development and thus the loss of access and opportunities in the rural landscape for hunting, trapping and fishing and recreational activities.

7. ANR shall incorporate these smart growth principles in a manner that enhances the efficient and effective operations of the Agency.

Source: Vermont ANR, 2002b, 1

health and/or environmental problems outside of growth centers; and

- ensure appropriate controls on the use of ANR funded treatment for utilities in order to minimize polluted runoff from unplanned land development, the state's fastest growing source of water contaminants; and to prevent scattered development and its negative impacts on surface and ground waters, wetlands, air quality, wildlife habitats, natural areas, threatened and endangered species, and land use patterns within the host and adjacent communities. (Vermont ANR 2002a, 1–2)

The rule established a priority system for use by ANR's Department of Environmental Conservation in providing federal and state monies for POTW and MSPOWS projects. A grant or loan for an existing wastewater treatment facility and/or a sewer line extension can only go to a "project designed to serve only a locally designated growth center, unless there are significant health and environmental problems located outside of a growth center" (Vermont ANR 2002a, 2).

While the Municipal Pollution Control Rule involved a complex set of mandates for municipalities, there were also strong incentives aimed at drawing municipalities into the game. To be eligible for federal and/or state funds, municipalities were required to take measures to strengthen their local plans and development regulations in a smart growth direction. In 2002 ANR issued a document to help public and private entities understand the new rule and to persuade Vermont's municipalities that they could in fact benefit from smart growth (ANR 2002c, 1).

The smart growth moves ANR introduced in 2002 through Secretary Johnstone's executive order are impressive. The key will be how effective ANR and its allies are in implementing them over time. In the next several years, a key question will be whether sufficient funds can be found to help bring the main actors, especially municipal governments, into the game.

The 2002 Elections

When Dean chose not to run for reelection in 2002, a tight race for governor ensued. Democratic candidate Lt. Governor Doug Racine was seen by supporters of smart growth as an excellent choice, given his long record as a strong advocate of strengthening the planning function in Vermont. Republican Jim Douglas, Vermont's State Treasurer, was viewed as a moderate. After a very tight race, Racine conceded to Douglas. In the legislature, Democrats maintained a strong majority in the Senate (19–11) and Republicans managed to keep a thin majority in the House (74 Republicans, 69 Democrats, four Progressives and three Independents).

Advocacy Groups Report on Pros and Cons, 2003–2004

Vermont Natural Resources Council

The Vermont Natural Resources Council (VNRC) cites continuing failure by the governor, legislature and other actors to address key issues needed to strengthen Vermont's smart growth action tools. As VNRC and its allies saw it, "The real problems—insufficient planning, lack of coordination and implementation, and negligible foresight into the long-term environmental impacts of development—are never really addressed" (VNRC 2004, 1). Bringing this gloomy picture into the 2003 legislative session, VNRC referred to a permit reform proposed by the Douglas administration to limit citizen participation in Act 250 proceedings. VNRC held that proponents of the change could not give one good reason by example or otherwise "why citizens should be cut out of the Act 250 dialogue" (VNRC 2004, 2).

VNRC took the position that a series of major changes were needed to address the larger problem of the development review process, which is "the lack of planning by state agencies and poor coordination among local, regional and state agencies" (VNRC 2004, 3). VNRC cited four principles that must be followed in changing Vermont's development review process.

1. Protection of Vermont's natural resources, working landscape and communities

2. Predictable and consistent timeframes and outcomes

3. Fairness and equality to all applicants and interested participants

4. Effectiveness in preserving Vermont's character and quality of life (VNRC 2004, 3)

To adhere to the above principles, VNRC then called for specific actions:

- expedite the permit process for development defined and designated in Growth Opportunity (GO) Centers while protecting valuable resource lands

- improve predictability of the permit process through better planning by
  - reestablishing Vermont OSP
  - strengthening regional and state agency planning
  - investing state dollars in GO centers
  - reviewing cumulative impacts
  - strengthening state planning
  - createing town master plan permit
  - requiring project master plans in Act 250

The above recommendations amount to a far-reaching call for strong action to strengthen Vermont's planning and growth management process, all focused in one way or another on smart growth strategies. The fact that such drastic steps are needed to get Vermont firmly on a smart growth path illustrates how difficult the unfinished agenda really is.

Smart Growth Progress Report

The Vermont Smart Growth Collaborative (VSGC) was formed in 2001 to strengthen state policy, public education and community strategies for encouraging smart growth in Vermont. Its 10 members include a broad cross-section of public, private and nonprofit groups: Association of Vermont Conservation Commissions, Conservation Law Foundation, Friends of the Earth, Housing Vermont, Preservation Trust of Vermont, Vermont Bicycle Pedestrian Coalition, Vermont Businesses for Social Responsibility, Vermont Forum on Sprawl, Vermont Natural Resources Council, and Vermont Public Interest Research Group (VSGC 2003). In preparing its *Smart Growth Progress Report* in 2003, VSGC "selected a sample of state programs that have major land use implications," and through an extensive research process assessed how Vermont was doing in furthering smart growth policies. Some agencies were singled out as doing well, others poorly.

The report cited a "lack of overall planning and coordination of state expenditures and policies to ensure that they are directed toward smart growth" (VSGC 2003, 2). Act 200 requiring that state agency plans "be developed and updated every two years is not being implemented by state agencies or enforced. The enforcement entity for Act 200 compliance, the Council of Regional Commissions, has not met in years and does not have an appropriation to provide staff support" (VSGC 2003, 2). Where state agency plans do exist, their spending, contrary to Vermont law, is not always aligned with those plans. As an example, "VTrans' expenditures are more heavily weighted toward roadway construction than is recommended in the Long Range Transportation Plan" (VSGC 2003, 2).

The VSGC holds that Vermont "does have a good planning enabling statute [Title 24, Chapter 117, Act 200] supportive of smart growth local and regional planning" (VSGC 2003, 3). Other positive smart

growth programs in Vermont include the Downtown Program, Housing and Conservation Board, Transportation Enhancements and the Bicycle/Pedestrian Program. On the negative side, the progress report holds that Vermont does not participate in several smart growth programs being tried in other parts of the country, such as Live Near Your Work, Safe Routes to School Programs, state investments targeted to growth centers or a "workable" brownfields development program (VSGC 2003, 3).

The progress report also includes a series of state agency profiles, including their missions, smart growth connection, conclusions on their understanding of and adherence to smart growth principles, and how they could strengthen their record of adherence. The Vermont Economic Progress Council got low ratings, with only about one-fourth of its investments supporting smart growth. From 1998 to 2000 VEPC

Selected Smart Growth Progress Report Recommendations

Compliance with Existing State Laws, Executive Orders and Rules

- The Governor's Office should convene the Development Cabinet regularly and staff the Cabinet to ensure state agencies meet their responsibilities under Title 3, Section 2293.

- Through the Development Cabinet and the state agency plan requirements of Act 200 the state agency plan requirements should be reinvigorated and state investments should be made to comply with these plans.

- VSGC should periodically update this report and measure the progress of the state of Vermont in implementing smart growth practices.

Coordination Among State Agencies

- Through the Development Cabinet all economic development investments should be coordinated with affordable housing investments, water and sewer, and transportation investments to insure that all are well-connected and consistent with smart growth principles.

- Through the Development Cabinet, interagency smart growth initiatives, such as the Safe Routes to School program between the Department of Education, Department of Health, and VTrans, should be coordinated.

State Agency Planning

- A consistent definition of growth centers as found in the ANR sewer fund rule guide and in the State Consolidated Plan should be used by all state agencies. Through the Development Cabinet, the state should develop procedures to insure that growth centers are supported in investment decisions.

- Citizen priorities, as established in valid statewide surveys, public discussions and stakeholder groups, and coordination with regional and local plans should be part of every state agency plan.

- VTrans should recognize the important role of coordinated land use and transportation planning for achieving smart growth. For example, compact growth centers facilitate public transit use and pedestrian accessibility.

Education and Training

- Training of local and regional planners and district environmental coordinators on the concept of growth centers and how to implement them should be supported by ACCD, regional planning commissions, Vermont Planners Association and VSGC.

New Initiatives

- The Vermont Legislature should adopt the proposed amendments to Chapter 117 that the Vermont Senate passed in 2003 in order to support smart growth planning and regulation at the local and regional levels.

- The Vermont Legislature with the help of ANR should adopt legislation for a more effective brownfields redevelopment program that includes provisions to insure that brownfields developments are integrated into plans for the surrounding areas of the community.

- ACCD should explore a public-private partnership that would develop incentives for a Live Near Your Work program.

Source: VSGC, 2003, 3–4

provided $18.1 million in income tax credits for smart growth projects, but $46.2 million for sprawl projects over the same time period (VSGC 2003, 11, 15).

In contrast, the Agency of Transportation Enhancement Grants program got a high rating, with the state exceeding the requirements of the Federal Highway Administration (FHWA). FHWA set a goal of obligating 75 percent of available funds. With a national average of 69.8 percent at the end of fiscal year 2001, Vermont had obligated 89.3 percent (VSGC 2003, 21). The projects in Vermont "typically reflect smart growth principles," often involving "pedestrian improvements in downtown and village centers, scenic easements, historic preservation and other smart growth actions" (VSGC 2003, 20, 21, 23).

Not surprisingly, Vermont's Housing and Conservation Board ranked high in both its affordable housing and farmland conservation dimensions as significant smart growth programs. From 1998 to 2002, $30.8 million was invested by VHCB in affordable housing projects, of which $23.2 million went to "downtown or existing growth centers on rehabilitation or new construction." Only $3 million was spent on projects in sprawl locations (VSGC 2003, 30). During the same period, VHCB spent $19.6 million for farmland preservation, $11.9 million for open space/natural areas/recreation projects, and $500,000 for historic preservation. Over the five-year period, VHCB spent more than $62 million, with less than 5 percent going to projects in sprawl locations, a definite plus for smart growth in Vermont (VSGC 2003, 30).

The progress report also includes profiles of the two federal agencies whose programs could have an impact on smart growth strategies in Vermont: the U.S. Small Business Administration (SBA) Loan Guarantee Program and the U.S. Army Corps of Engineers Section 404 Permits regarding state water quality certification. According to the report, the SBA, which is required by the National Environmental Policy Act (NEPA) to consider and mitigate environmental impacts, "had failed [in its loan activity] to satisfy any of the NEPA obligations, either site-specific or programmatic." The collaborative concluded that since SBA failed to meet NEPA obligations, it was unable to determine whether its loans undermined

or supported smart growth. In August 2000, Friends of the Earth filed a lawsuit against SBA seeking to require compliance with NEPA, and in July 2002 SBA agreed to comply (VSGC 2003, 34-35).

The U.S. EPA administers the Clean Water Act and authorizes the Army Corps of Engineers to regulate discharges into U.S. waters, including wetlands (VSGC 2003, 35). Vermont's ANR reports to the U.S. EPA about all waters that are too polluted to attain designated water-quality standards. The VSGC assessed all 542 development projects from 1998 to 2002 requiring a 404 Permit, of which 167 involved rivers and streams designated as impaired. The VSGC found that the analysis of cumulative impacts was not available for public review, even though it is required by law. In November 2002, the Corps issued a new Section 404 General Permit for the State of Vermont. The VSGC felt the Corps analysis of the permit (showing the direct, indirect and cumulative impacts) was inadequate. The Corps simply concluded that "without reviewing the required impacts...the General Permit was not a major federal action significantly affecting the quality of the human environment." The new Section 404 Permit, given the above, allows projects that release dredge and fill material into wetlands even though they are listed on the Vermont 303(d) list of polluted waterways that fail to meet U.S. EPA water-quality standards (VSGC 2003, 36).

With regard to the Corps' activities in this area:

> The Collaborative recommends that the Corps satisfy its legal obligations and review the direct, indirect, and cumulative impacts of its general permit. In addition, the Corps should not approve projects that impact wetlands located in watersheds designated as having impaired water quality under the General Permit without first confirming that the project will not contribute to the further degradation of water quality in the watershed. (VSGC 2003, 36)

VSGC, with its broad base of membership, is clearly a powerful force for effecting the changes it advocates.

Vermont Land Trust

The Vermont Land Trust (VLT) has been a champion of smart growth in the state for more than two decades. Since its founding in 1977, VLT has helped conserve more than 418,000 acres of productive farm and forest land. As of December 31, 2003, VLT had closed 1,129 projects, adding up to 418,507 acres (VLT 2004, 1). Led by its president Darby Bradley, VLT has expanded its mission: "Clearly, we need all types of land, from urban areas to wilderness, and we need them in the right places. And we must see them as linked." Bradley is certain that this broader mission will make VLT's work more complex and difficult, but feels that anything less would be falling short of their ethical responsibilities (VLT 2004, 3–4). This broader view is evidenced through VLT's capital campaign, Vermont at the Crossroads. With a goal of $25 million, as of February 2005, $23.5 million had been raised. Each of four funds has a special purpose: conservation, stewardship, land acquisition and land protection (VLT 2005, 9).

In light of the concerns raised in 2005 by the U.S. Senate Finance Committee's hearings on land trust practices, Bradley wrote that "the biggest challenge for the land trust community long-term will be the stewardship of its land holdings and easements" (VLT 2005, 3). He noted that Vermont is fortunate in that regard because the Vermont Housing and Conservation Board (VHCB) preceded the formation of most local land trusts and modeled its conservation easement after VLT's standard document, thus providing the kind of uniformity, accountability and stewardship often lacking in other states.

Conclusion

In assessing the future of smart growth strategies in Vermont, there are encouraging factors. Leading the list are the Vermont Natural Resources Council, the Vermont Smart Growth Collaborative and the Vermont Land Trust, which is now focusing on conservation of farms and forestland in a way that better supports smart growth. The membership of these organizations stretches across and embraces all key stakeholders in Vermont (public, private and non-profit), certainly a positive factor in bringing smart growth to Vermont for the long-term future.

Turning briefly to the governor and legislature, we find a mixed picture. Will Governor Douglas follow through to ensure a smart growth future for Vermont? One major smart growth advocate is doubtful that the governor will attempt to build on smart growth policies and programs already in place, and his administration has advocated some changes strongly opposed by the VNRC and other smart growth advocates.

However, the 2004 election returned strong Democratic Party majorities to the Vermont House and Senate, which helped ensure action on strengthening the state's planning capability. To bolster this result, in August 2004 the Vermont Council on Rural Development formed a Vermont Planning Council to reexamine the horizontal and vertical structure of land use planning and make recommendations for improvements in 2005.

It may be too soon to predict whether Vermont will succeed in fighting off the downsides of sprawl. The legislature still needs strong leadership from the governor to support smart growth policies and programs. There is reason for optimism that the breadth and depth of groups supporting smart growth will win the day as the economy recovers and more funds can be channeled into incentives and disincentives to bring local governments, state agencies and the private sector fully into the game.

Vermont References

Dean, Howard. 1998. State of the state and budget address. January 6.

DeGrove, John M. 1984. *Land, growth and politics*. Chicago, IL: American Planning Association.

Dodd, Philip K. 1992. Publisher's corner. Vermont Property Owners Report 7 (December–January 1993):2.

Governor's Commission on Vermont's Future. 1988. Report of the governor's commission on Vermont's future: Guidelines for growth. Montpelier, VT: Agency of Development and Community Affairs.

Schonberger, Benjamin. 2000. *Locally grown: Statewide land use planning in northern New England*. Thesis for master's degree in city planning. Cambridge, MA: Massachusetts Institute of Technology.

State of Vermont. 1987. Office of the Governor. Executive order no. 50. September 22.

————. 2000. Office of the Governor. Executive order 01-00. February 9.

————. 2001. Office of the Governor. Executive order 01-07. September 13.

————. 2002. H 208, An act relating to the Vermont downtown development board.

U.S. Census Bureau. State and county QuickFacts: Vermont. http://quickfacts.census.gov/qfd/states/50000.html.

————. Projections of the total population of states: 1995 to 2025. http://www.census.gov/population/projections/state/stpjpop.txt.

Vermont Agency of Commerce and Community Development (ACCD). 2002. H 208 summary. May 15.

Vermont Agency of Natural Resources (ANR). 2002a. Environmental protection rules: Chapter 2: Municipal pollution control priority system (adopted August 30).

————. 2002b. Vermont Agency of Natural Resources: Agency of Natural Resources Smart Growth Principles. December.

————. 2002c. Vermont Agency of Natural Resources: Growth center and growth management guidance document. September.

Vermont Department of Housing and Community Affairs (DHCA). 1988. A citizens guide: Vermont's new Act 200 for growth management.

————. 1989a. Allocation of municipal planning funds. Vermont Municipal and Regional Planning Assistance Program. Rule adopted July 1, 1989.

————. 1989b. Vermont's future: An update on Act 200 and planning.

————. 1999. *History of planning in Vermont*. December.

————. 2002. EPA Sustainable Development Challenge Grant project workplan.

Vermont Division for Historic Preservation. 2002. *Downtown program*.

Vermont Land Trust (VLT). 1999a. Conservation easement donations.

————. 1999b. Conservation groups announce Champion lands purchase and president's report: A "champion" resource for Vermont's future.

————. 1999c. News (http://www.vlt.org/news.html) and Facts (http://www.vlt.org/fact.html).

————. 2002a. 2001–2002 annual report.

————. 2002b. Autumn report 2002.

————. 2002c. Winter report 2002.

————. 2003. 2002–2003 annual report.

————. 2004. Winter report.

————. 2005. Winter report.

Vermont Natural Resources Council (VNRC). 1988. The laws that roared: A status report on the implementation of Vermont's new conservation laws (1985–1988). Montpelier, VT: VNRC.

————. 1994a. Environmental board debacle. Vermont Environmental Report (Spring/Summer).

————. 1994b. VNRC opposes changes to Act 200. Working together for Vermont: Vermont Natural Resources Council 1994 annual report. Montpelier, VT: VNRC.

————. 1995a. Act 200: Governor and house hang tough. *Vermont Environmental Report* (Spring/Summer): 27.

————. 1995b. Act 250: Weakening efforts still alive. *Vermont Environmental Report* (Spring/Summer): 27.

————. 1995c. Legislative platform '95. *VNRC Bulletin* (Winter).

————. 2004. VNRC bulletin and legislative platform. January.

Vermont Planners Association (VPA). 1995. *1995 legislative summary*.

Vermont Smart Growth Collaborative (VSGC). 2003. State of Vermont smart growth progress report. October.

Vermont Supreme Court. 1999. *Stan Baker et al. v State of Vermont*, 98-032. December 20.

Appendix

Maine

Governors

Joseph E. Brennan (Democrat)	1979–1987
John R. McKernan Jr. (Republican)	1987–1995
Angus S. King Jr. (Independent)	1995–2002
John E. Baldacci (Democrat)	2002–present

Acronyms

CPAC	Community Preservation Advisory Committee
DECD	Department of Economic and Community Development
DEP	Department of Environmental Protection
GIS	geographic information system
LURRC	Land Use Regulatory Reform Committee
MDOT	Maine Department of Transportation
MEREDA	Maine Real Estate and Development Association
MMA	Maine Municipal Association
NRCM	Natural Resources Council of Maine
OCP	Office of Comprehensive Planning
SPO	State Planning Office

Contacts

Friends of Midcoast Maine
88 Elm Street
Camden, ME 04843
207-236-1077
http://www.friendsmidcoast.org/

GrowSmart Maine
81 Bridge Street
Yarmouth, ME 04096
207-847-9275
http://www.growsmartmaine.org

Maine Municipal Association (MMA)
60 Community Drive
Augusta, ME 04330
207-623-8428
http://www.memun.org/

Maine Real Estate and Development Association (MEREDA)
2 Market Street, 5th Floor
Portland, ME 04101
207-874-0801
http://www.mereda.org/

Maine State Planning Office
38 State House Station
184 State Street
Augusta, ME 04333
207-287-3261
http://www.state.me.us/spo/

Natural Resources Council of Maine (NRCM)
3 Wade Street
Augusta, ME 04330
207-622-3101 or 800-287-2345
http://www.maineenvironment.org/

State of Maine
http://www.state.me.us

Rhode Island

Governors

Edward D. DiPrete (Republican) (three two-year terms)	1985–1991
Bruce G. Sundlun (Democrat) (two two-year terms)	1991–1995
Lincoln C. Almond (Republican) (two four-year terms)	1995–2003
Donald L. Carcieri (Republican)	2002–present

Acronyms

LUC	land use commission
NOP	Neighborhood Opportunities Program
RIDA	Rhode Island Department of Administration
SPP	Statewide Planning Program
TDR	transferable development rights

Contacts

Grow Smart Rhode Island
235 Promenade Street, Suite 550
Providence, RI 02908
401-273-5711
http://www.growsmartri.com

Rhode Island Department of Administration
Statewide Planning Program
One Capitol Hill
Providence, RI 02908-5870
401-222-1220
http://www.planning.state.ri.us

Save the Bay
100 Save the Bay Drive
Providence, RI 02905
401-272-3540
http://www.savebay.org

State of Rhode Island
http://www.info.state.ri.us

Vermont

Governors

Deane C. Davis (Republican)	1969–1973
Madelaine Kunin (Democrat)	1986–1990
Richard A. Snelling (Republican, deceased)	1990–1991
Howard Dean (Democrat)	1991–2002
Jim Douglas (Republican)	2002–present

Acronyms

ACCD	Agency of Commerce and Community Development
ANR	Agency of Natural Resources
CPR	Citizens for Property Rights
CRC	Council of Regional Commissions
DHCA	Department of Housing and Community Affairs
GIS	geographic information systems
OPRC	Office of Policy Research and Coordination
RPC	Regional Planning Commissions
VHCB	Vermont Housing and Conservation Board
VLT	Vermont Land Trust
VNRC	Vermont Natural Resources Council
VSGC	Vermont Smart Growth Collaborative

Contacts

State of Vermont
http://www.vermont.gov

Vermont Agency of Natural Resources (ANR)
Secretary's Office, Center Building
103 South Main Street
Waterbury, VT 05671-0301
802-241-3600
http://www.anr.state.vt.us/

Vermont Department of Housing and Community Affairs (DHCA)
Planning Division, National Life Building, 6th floor
Drawer 20
Montpelier, VT 05620
802-828-3211 or 800-622-4553
http://www.dhca.state.vt.us/Planning/index.htm

Vermont Forum on Sprawl
110 Main Street
Burlington, VT 05401
802-864-6310
http://www.vtsprawl.org

Vermont Land Trust (VLT)
8 Bailey Avenue
Montpelier, VT 05602
802-223-5234
http://www.vlt.org

Vermont Natural Resources Council (VNRC)
9 Bailey Avenue
Montpelier, VT 05602
802-223-2328
http://www.vnrc.org

Vermont Smart Growth Collaborative (VSGC)
c/o Vermont Forum on Sprawl
110 Main Street
Burlington, VT 05401
http://www.vtsprawl.org

6

Georgia

Contents

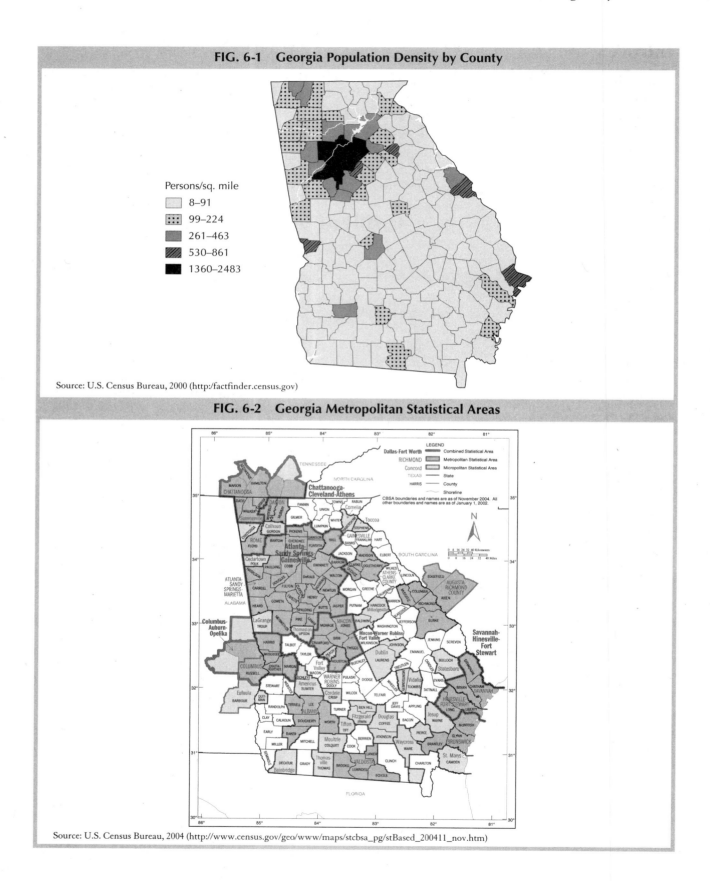

FIG. 6-1   Georgia Population Density by County

Persons/sq. mile

8–91
99–224
261–463
530–861
1360–2483

Source: U.S. Census Bureau, 2000 (http:/factfinder.census.gov)

FIG. 6-2   Georgia Metropolitan Statistical Areas

Source: U.S. Census Bureau, 2004 (http://www.census.gov/geo/www/maps/stcbsa_pg/stBased_200411_nov.htm)

Introduction

Georgia has been viewed by many as an unlikely state to mobilize the forces needed for developing and passing a major planning and growth management law. Yet, a close look at the state reveals a record of progressive leadership and a joining of public and private resources to address these challenges successfully. What is particularly remarkable about Georgia is that, unlike states such as Florida, Maryland and Oregon, it attempted to achieve its goals, not through a "top down" or "command and control" process, but through a series of incentives and disincentives created or supported by leadership from the state's highest office.

When Governor Joe Frank Harris proposed and the General Assembly adopted Georgia's growth management statute—the Georgia Planning Act of 1989—the state undertook a unique experiment that continues today. The key features of this nationally significant effort to achieve a comprehensive, coordinated growth management system included

■ a unique consensus building process that resulted in broad-based support among a wide range of stakeholders;

■ a bold effort to achieve, in some 700 local governments, comprehensive plans and land development regulations consistent with each other and with regional and state plans, without directly mandating them. The intent was to guarantee a comprehensive system with incentives and disincentives that depended heavily on the support of the governor to ensure full state agency participation in the process; and

■ the attempt to use both voluntary and mandatory mediation to fully implement the integrated system and to identify and protect regionally important resources (RIRs) and developments of regional impact (DRIs).

The ultimate goal was a state comprehensive plan that would be consistent with regional and state agency plans. The success or failure of the effort to implement this system would test whether an incentive-based approach could achieve an integrated, comprehensive system of growth management.

By the late 1990s major weaknesses emerged at the local, regional and state levels to threaten the viability of the system. Failure to replace low-density sprawl with compact, mixed-use development supported by public transportation systems led to the needless destruction of natural systems and the undermining of existing urban centers as sprawl eroded their vitality. This has been especially true in the fast-growing Atlanta region. Key participants in and observers of the efforts to implement Georgia's planning act concluded that the system could not work comprehensively unless it was substantially strengthened.

This view came to be shared by a wide range of public and private sector stakeholders, and a series of specific actions was proposed to strengthen the system for Georgia and the Atlanta region. Georgia elected Democrat Roy Barnes as governor in November 1998, and a number of key groups presented the new governor and General Assembly with significant recommendations for changing the system. Barnes took a strong leadership role in a number of actions during his four years in office. Winning the election by a wide margin, Barnes was in a position to push for several smart growth initiatives to strengthen Georgia's growth management system.

In gaining approval for major new smart growth actions, Barnes earned the support of public and private sector interests, and of long-time advocates of smart growth such as Joel Cowan, chair of the original Growth Strategies Commission (GSC) in the late 1980s; John Sibley, executive director of that commission and head of the Georgia Conservancy; and Jerry Griffin, executive director of the Association of County Commissions of Georgia (ACCG). The result was a remarkable number of new initiatives to strengthen Georgia's growth management system, led by the Georgia Regional Transportation Authority (GRTA).

All of this new momentum was called into question in 2002 by Republican Sonny Perdue's surprising defeat of Barnes in his bid for reelection. During Perdue's first year in office, many of Barnes's smart growth actions came under fire or were repealed, but near the end of 2003, Perdue took a number of actions supportive of smart growth principles.

The Growth Management Context

Georgia is the largest state east of the Mississippi River, with a land area of nearly 60,000 square miles. Its four distinct geographic areas are the Blue Ridge Mountains of north Georgia; the gently rolling hills of the Piedmont; the fertile coastal plains; and a coastal area terminating in a wide expanse of marshes and sea islands along the Atlantic coast. These four areas encompass a wealth of land and water resources: 25 million acres of heavily forested timberlands, 8 million acres of farmland (mostly in the coastal plains), and 4 million acres of forested wetlands, including one of the largest swamps in North America, the 660-square-mile Okefenokee Swamp.

The state has experienced tremendous population growth in the last several decades, ranking fourth or fifth in percent of increase in the nation between 1970 and 2000. About half of this growth was due to in-migration and half from births over deaths. A substantial part of Georgia's growth occurred in the Atlanta region, which became home to nearly one-third of the state's residents by 1980, with projections approaching 45 percent in the early decades of the twenty-first century.

Georgia's economy expanded with its population, again concentrated in the Atlanta region and along the coast, but more than 30 rural counties have lost jobs in recent decades as forestry, fisheries and agricultural services declined. A combination of factors has made Atlanta the major trade, business and financial center in the southeastern United States, including the development of the Hartsfield International Airport, one of the busiest in the nation. Between 1970 and 1980 employment grew by almost one-third, to a total of 2.38 million; by 1990, to 3.12 million; and by 2002, to 4.07 million (Georgia DOL Undated).

The Atlanta region has emerged as a strong political force as well, leading to friction between Atlanta and the cities and towns outside the region. Any major new public policy initiative is seen by some as reinforcing Atlanta's dominance and placing the rest of the state at a disadvantage. Tension also is evident in the development of growth management, since the 10 counties of the Atlanta Regional Commission (ARC) make up well over 80 percent of the 20-county Atlanta Metropolitan Statistical Area (MSA). ARC's supporters have crafted key features of the system to overcome ARC's tendency to dominate regional agencies (ARC 1994). However, the conflict is not only between the Atlanta region and the rest of the state: land use issues, environmental concerns and interjurisdictional conflicts within and among the counties in this region are chronic.

By the late 1980s, unmanaged and often substantial growth in the outer counties of the region had produced predictable infrastructure shortfalls, most often taking the form of traffic congestion and inadequate water and sewer capacity (Georgia Governor's GSC Undated, 93). In 1987–1988 there were more than 30 sewer moratoria around the state, threatening the ability of the development industry to thrive.

Traffic on the interstates in the greater Atlanta region showed good capacity downtown, even at rush hour, but real problems on the perimeter. Discussion of an outer perimeter beltway to relieve congestion was alarming to proponents of the growth management system; they believed it would exacerbate an already serious urban sprawl problem (DeGrove 1992, 100). As the outer perimeter solution moved to the planning stage, it emerged as a key issue in how best to address the problem of moving people around and through the Atlanta region. By the mid-1990s, battle lines were drawn on whether to build all or part of the outer perimeter system.

Water was another compelling issue in Georgia in the mid-1980s. The drought of 1984 was not a crisis, but underscored the fundamental mismatch between water supply and growth in the state: relatively abundant ground water and surface water supplies in the coastal plains of south Georgia, but the highest growth areas in north-central Georgia around the Atlanta region (Georgia Governor's GSC Undated, 27–30).

Interjurisdictional issues heightened environmental and infrastructure problems and made their solution extremely difficult. For example, uncoordinated transportation planning in the counties of the Atlanta region resulted in major highways changing from two lanes to four, or vice versa, as they crossed jurisdictional boundaries. A highly public fight between Atlanta's fastest growing county (Gwinnett) and its downstream neighbor (Rockdale County, also growing) over pollution of their common water source illustrated the problems of interjurisdictional conflict and the need for better intergovernmental coordination. New federal mandates (clean air and water, wetlands protection), coinciding with declining federal dollars, demanded better coordination of planning and implementation at all levels of Georgia's intergovernmental system (DeGrove 1992, 100–101).

Governance capacity (and sometimes the lack thereof) also supported action to change the system. In 1956 Georgia amended its constitution to authorize the delegation of zoning powers to local governments, rather than to the General Assembly, as had been the case. The Planning and Zoning Enabling Act of 1957 established procedures and standards for local governments to exercise that power. For the next 20 years, the state took this "constitutional approach" to planning and zoning, but in 1976 it approved another amendment that placed zoning *exclusively* in the hands of local government. The second amendment specifically provided that the General Assembly could not regulate, restrict or limit the planning and zoning powers of any county or municipality. A later opinion by the state attorney general held that this provision invalidated at least some portions of the earlier planning and zoning enabling acts. Thus, in 20 years the state had gone from one extreme to the other, from total state power to no state role in zoning. As a result of this vacuum, after 1976 the courts were increasingly called on to decide local zoning issues (Godschalk, Knopf and Weissman 1978, 87–102).

Georgia made an effort to balance the situation in 1981, when a complete revision of the constitution included an amendment that again allowed the state to adopt procedures governing the exercise of planning and zoning powers by local government. The state designed its new system to focus on process and procedures rather than on substance, however. There is difficulty separating procedure and substance, but the constitutional mandate for the state's protection and preservation of "vital areas" (wetlands, watersheds and mountain slopes) demanded substantive standards.

Georgia has almost 700 active local governments, including 159 counties and 533 cities. All have the authority to provide basic urban services, such as water and sewer systems, and to regulate land use

through planning and zoning powers. However, as of 1986, less than one-fifth of these jurisdictions had adopted comprehensive plans; only one-third had adopted land use plans; and about half of the cities and nearly two-thirds of the counties had not even adopted zoning ordinances. During the 1980s decreases in federal funding for planning activities further weakened the state's system, particularly the regional Area Planning and Development Commissions (APDCs). Weak regional agencies, hundreds of local governments acting in isolation from one another, and lack of coordination among state agencies created a fragmented system incapable of addressing the growth issues facing the state. In a broad sense, sustaining economic development in the greater Atlanta area and other, especially rural, areas of the state was always part of a statewide planning and growth management program (DeGrove 1992, 101).

It is fair to say that the problems faced by Georgia in the 1980s were no greater than those of other states that took no action toward establishing a comprehensive growth management system. Why and how Georgia chose to adopt such a system, with every major public and private stakeholder in the state supporting it, is truly a remarkable story.

The Roots of Georgia's Growth Management Legislation

The effort to put in place a comprehensive and integrated planning system for Georgia has a surprisingly long history, dating back at least to Governor Jimmy Carter, who named a Planned Growth Commission in 1973. Although no policy changes resulted from that effort, two members of the commission continued to play major roles in the development and adoption of the new system: Joe Frank Harris, a legislative representative on the commission who became governor in 1983; and commission chair Joel Cowan, who chaired the Governor's Growth Strategies Commission in 1987.

In 1982, near the end of Governor George Busbee's last term in office, the General Assembly passed a law creating a commission to study growth issues. This was left to Governor Harris to implement. However, the new governor's main priority was to improve the quality of basic education in the state, and growth issues were set aside for the time being. Another relevant event was the development of a strategic plan by the Georgia Municipal Association (GMA), which, surprisingly, called for a statewide development policy to be put in place by the General Assembly. Finally, in 1986 ARC made an effort to get a bill through the General Assembly giving the agency a strong "review and comment" authority over large-scale projects in the Atlanta metropolitan area. ARC already had mandatory review and comment authority over such projects, but the proposed legislation asked only that local governments be required to consider, accept or reject ARC comments, and then report back to ARC on their action. Modest as it was, the proposal evoked a storm of protest, interpreted by many as foreshadowing little chance for any statewide growth strategy.

At the end of Governor Harris's first term (late 1986), a small group representing both public and private interests met to discuss improving Georgia's ability to manage its growth. The group was remarkable for its composition alone: cities, counties, the corporate sector, developers and environmentalists. They were convened informally by Leonard Ledbetter, commissioner of the state Department of Natural Resources (DNR), who was motivated by extreme frustration with what he considered to be local land use issues coming to his office as state environmental issues, because there was no other way to deal with them. Maintaining good quality of life and continuing economic growth demanded a better system for coordinated planning at the state, regional and local levels. The governor accepted this idea and announced his intention (if he were reelected) to appoint a group to study growth strategies for the state.

Consensus Building in the Growth Strategies Commission

Harris was reelected, and in his State of the State address in January 1987, he formally introduced his growth strategies initiative, which became the major public policy focus of his second term. By June 1987 he had appointed a 35-member Growth Strategies Commission (GSC). It was chaired by Joel Cowan, head of an Atlanta-based investment and develop-

ment organization, who had a broad vision and was committed to growth where appropriate as well as to environmental protection. GSC included 16 members in the business and development sector; eight state legislators; seven local elected officials; two academics, including one in the public school system; a citizen activist; and a former county commissioner (Georgia Governor's GSC 1988c, 2).

Members were sworn in on June 16, 1987, and given 18 months to design and present a blueprint for Georgia's future state growth strategy. The GSC's work was divided into three stages: studying the issues, developing strategies, and taking short- and long-term actions. Four task forces were then formed to address economic development, capital investments, land use and natural resources (Georgia Governor's GSC 1988d, 1).

Even before the commission was named, the governor had recruited John Sibley, an attorney with experience in private practice and state government. Sibley turned to Dr. Joseph Whorton, director of the Institute of Community and Area Development at the University of Georgia, who specialized in facilitating community development and other consensus-building efforts. The process started with a retreat in September 1987 for an advisory panel of staff and political leaders. Participants included Jim Burgess, director of GMA, and Jerry Griffin, director of ACCG. Other noncommission members joined equal numbers of commission members on each of the four task forces. The general consensus later was that the commission's approach to coalition building was favorably accepted by a broad spectrum of stakeholders, from the development community to environmental organizations.

Recommendations of the Growth Strategies Commission

By the end of its work period in late 1989, GSC had produced three documents whose points were incorporated into the Georgia Planning Act of 1989, offering recommendations in the areas of governance, economic development, resource management and coordinated planning (Georgia Governor's GSC 1988a; 1988b; 1988c). The final report identified two

Implementation of the Nine-Point Strategy
Addressing Human Needs
1. Develop an education culture
2. Strengthen and coordinate programs for human resources
Building Capacity for Growth
3. Integrate the state's transportation network
4. Create a regional reservoir program
Safeguarding the Environment
5. Enhance protection of natural and historic resources
Strengthening Local Communities
6. Increase support for local infrastructure needs
7. Improve business access to capital
8. Accelerate community development efforts and support for "home grown" jobs
Coordinating Efforts
9. Establish a three-tiered partnership for planning
Source: Georgia Governor's GSC, 1988c, 6

major goals: to "accommodate the inevitable growth of the future without allowing a deterioration in the quality of life" and to "upgrade the quality of life in low-growth areas through realistic and innovative economic development programs" (Georgia Governor's GSC 1988c, 4). It also addressed five major areas, with implementing steps and funding estimates attached to each of nine strategies.

The report, although brief, managed some rather specific recommendations. For example, to ensure a long-term water supply to support development, the commission proposed establishing a system of regional reservoirs to be acquired, constructed, financed and managed by DNR, with costs to be recovered by fees from those contracting to use the water. A three-tiered planning process would be an integral part of that effort. To ensure protection for watersheds, water quality (especially for aquifers) and wetlands, state minimum standards and regional review of local compliance with those standards were recommended. Similar recommendations were made for aquifer recharge areas, sensitive and vital areas, and air quality.

To strengthen local communities, the commission recommended

- an increase in the loan program of the Georgia Environmental Facilities Authority (GEFA) (for water, sewer, community reservoirs and solid waste facilities);

- the authorization of impact fees;

- programs to develop a comprehensive approach for generating more capital;

- development of a Georgia employment incentive program by 1990 for recommendation to the general assembly; and

- funding for a Community Improvement Program to bolster development in low-growth areas. (Georgia Governor's GSC 1988c, 11–12)

In the commission's words, "The keystone for the Quality Growth Partnership is comprehensive, integrated, and coordinated planning at local, regional, and state levels" (Georgia Governor's GSC 1988c, 13). The state would begin a coordinated planning process by establishing a planning framework that would include

- goals for the state (the vision);

- minimum standards and procedures for planning as well as minimum criteria for critical areas;

- identification of areas requiring regional coordination; and

- a coordinated database that included information provided by local, regional and state entities and the private sector. (Georgia Governor's GSC 1988c, 13)

The governor would act as the state's chief planner, and a comprehensive statewide policy plan, updated annually and tied to the state budget, would emerge from local, regional and state agency plans. The governor also would head a new development council, with assistance from a new board for the Department of Community Affairs (DCA), the lead state agency for the new coordinated planning system.

Local governments were to prepare and implement comprehensive local plans; if a city did not plan, the county plan would apply. Local governments also were required to actively participate in and pay dues to the regional body, adopt regulations consistent with the minimum state standards and procedures, and construct capital improvements consistent with the local plan. Local governments, however, would maintain their jurisdiction over land use decisions having a local impact. Zoning would remain a local function (Georgia Governor's GSC 1988c, 14).

Newly established regional development centers (RDCs), actually reconstituted APDCs, would carry out the regional role. Their assigned duties were substantial: reviewing and commenting on local plans to ensure coordination and consistency; preparing regional plans, including mediating conflicts between local plans; providing technical assistance to local governments; and preparing local plans if contracted to do so.

The commission recommended that the state provide funding for basic planning at the state and regional levels, with local governments contributing the funding for basic local planning and part of the funding to operate RDCs. The system would have no "hammer" to force compliance, but the commission did propose that local governments whose plans were not consistent with state and regional plans would be ineligible for state funds for infrastructure.

Provisions of the Georgia Planning Act of 1989

House Bill 215, the legislation to implement the GSC's recommendations, was presented to the General Assembly in January 1989 and passed easily (155–13 in the House and 55–9 in the Senate). The General Assembly mandated that its 1990 session would have to approve the standards and criteria to guide the local plan-making process. The planning act is organized into five main parts:

1. Purpose of the legislation and creation of a new Governor's Development Council

2. State role, especially the new responsibilities of the DCA

3. Role of RDCs

4. Local role

5. Mandate to DNR to develop minimum standards for certain natural resource areas, subject to legislative review and approval

Governor's Development Council

The Governor's Development Council (GDC) was created to promote coordinated and comprehensive planning by all levels of government. The governor served as chair of the 17-member council and also could authorize up to three additional members. The council was to meet at least once a month to oversee state agency planning and to require cooperation among state agencies in any way necessary to ensure coordinated planning, including the siting and building of public facilities based on considerations at the state, regional and local levels.

State Role

The legislation describes the state's role in general, with a particular focus on establishing a new DCA board and substantially expanding the responsibilities of that lead agency for the coordinated planning system. Where a local government failed to gain certification as a qualified local government (QLG) or take part in the mediation process, DCA could condition its grants to that local government.

DCA was to incorporate its minimum standards and procedures for local governments with those of

---

DCA Planning Responsibilities, HB 215

- "Developing, promoting, and establishing standards and procedures for coordinated and comprehensive planning," and assisting counties, municipalities and RDCs with implementation

- Acting as "the state's principal department for developing, promoting, maintaining, and encouraging coordinated and comprehensive planning"

- Determining the boundaries of the RDCs (subject to approval by the General Assembly)

- Certifying local governments (including RDCs) as "qualified" under the system

- Taking the lead role in working with other state agencies, RDCs and local governments to compile and make available a Georgia database and information network

- Reviewing and reporting to the governor the plans of state agencies, RDCs and local governments developed under the new system

- Establishing procedures and guidelines for mediation or other methods of conflict resolution

Source: Georgia 1989, 50-8-1 through 50-8-12

DNR regarding natural resources, the environment and vital areas, with the authority to differentiate among local governments and regions on the basis of demographic, geographic and fiscal factors. While the planning system attempted to focus on process and procedure, the difficulty of avoiding substance is well illustrated by this point. For example, local governments had to include DNR standards on buffer areas, groundwater, watersheds, wetlands and aquifer recharge areas in developing, preparing and implementing their comprehensive plans. So, a plan must be reviewed under established procedures and meet specific substantive standards for protection of these vital areas. Finally, DCA was charged with identifying and establishing, with DNR, review and mediation procedures for regionally important resources (RIRs) and developments of regional impact (DRIs).

Regional Role

The regional role to be carried out by the newly established RDCs included reviewing local plans and local government behavior for conformity with minimum standards and procedures, for the presence of regulations "and for participation in mediation or other means of resolving conflicts," all of which determine whether a local government receives qualified status; preparing a regional plan; managing the mediation of conflicts between local plans; and providing technical assistance to local governments in preparing their plans, and preparing local plans if contracted to do so (Georgia 1989, 50-8-30 through 50-8-46).

The regional role also changed the regional board structure in important ways: membership in RDCs was mandatory, and minimum dues were required.

Local Role

The basic local planning framework must include an inventory and assessment of existing conditions, a statement of needs and goals, and an implementation strategy. The rule required six local planning elements: population; economic development; natural and historic resources; community facilities; housing; and land use. Considerable detail was provided on what would be required for each element. For example, the natural and historic resources element must meet DNR's minimum standards by addressing coastal resources, steep slopes and prime agricultural and forest lands. The community facilities element must identify existing levels of service for 11 facilities; reflect a decision as to what future level of service a community wants for each facility; and provide sources of funding to remedy any shortfalls. The land use element must include existing and future land use maps, with appropriate details for each. Requirements for an implementation strategy, to ensure plans will be used to guide decision making, included five-year, short-term work programs and community and economic programs (Georgia DCA 1992).

Municipalities and counties would pay dues to the RDC within whose boundaries they lie, and participate in compiling a statewide database and network. Local governments were not required to prepare a comprehensive plan, but any plan had to be reviewed by the RDC for consistency with the planning system (including DCA, DNR and RDC minimum criteria). If a local government failed to become a QLG through participation in the planning and plan review process, grants from DCA and certain other grant and loan programs could be withheld, a disincentive strong enough to draw almost all local governments into the system.

The Implementation Record, 1989–1995

Planning for the implementation effort began well before HB 215 passed. In October 1988 Governor Harris asked DCA for help in drafting the legislation and an implementation strategy. DCA continued the same open, inclusive process GSC had used and set up teams for planning standards and procedures and for a data network. A third group explored ways to distribute grant money to help ensure full implementation of the system.

By May 1989, shortly after the governor signed the Georgia Planning Act into law, DCA adopted and the General Assembly ratified the rules on planning standards and procedures. In the meantime, the Office of Coordinated Planning (OCP) was created within DCA and headed by Lynn Thornton, who had worked with GSC and helped draft the legislation. The OCP's responsibilities were broad and its staffing modest—24 positions, of which 13 were transferred from other divisions. All of DCA's responsibilities under the law were assigned to OCP's planning and data sections, including preparation of minimum standards and procedures (which included purpose, definitions, duties and responsibilities, local planning standards, and additional planning and procedural elements); establishing and monitoring the mediation process; defining and later designating DRIs and RIRs; establishing the state data network; implementing the state's new building codes; and developing a draft state plan for review and adoption by the governor and his development council (Georgia DCA 1992).

Participants in the early implementation of the growth strategy saw the establishment of the GDC as the key to the system's success in securing local government compliance to the planning act. The council was established to coordinate compatibility among state, regional and local plans and to integrate agencies at all levels into the growth management system. Implementing this aspect of growth management has been problematic, however, because of a somewhat fragmented executive structure, in contrast to a state like New Jersey, where the governor appoints all state agency heads. For example, a board selected by the Georgia General Assembly from congressional districts names the head of the Department of Transportation (DOT), resulting in the agency being widely recognized as part of the problem in implementing Georgia's growth management system, especially in the Atlanta region. Governor-appointed boards select many other state agency heads, including that of DCA, the lead agency for the growth management system.

The 1990–1991 transition to the new governor, Zell Miller, was expected to be smooth, since he had been lieutenant governor with Harris, served on the Growth Strategies Commission, and had a longstanding interest in protecting the mountain areas of north Georgia (his home district) from inappropriate land uses. Miller reorganized GDC, which seemed to serve two purposes: strengthening the potential effectiveness of the council through changes in membership

from 17 to 12; and giving him direct "ownership" of the growth strategies system. However, the recession of the early 1990s and a budget crisis kept Miller from devoting full attention to the growth management system, despite his clear support for it, and the GDC gradually faded from the picture until its revival by the Barnes administration in 1999.

Until the 1995 legislative session, DCA and OCP received their fair share of the budget in bad years and good. A September 1995 DCA overview of the state's growth management system provided an excellent record of the implementation of the planning act up to that point (Georgia DCA 1995b).

Local Comprehensive Planning

The compliance record of Georgia's nearly 700 local governments is remarkable, considering the fact that local governments are not required to prepare plans at all. Even if plans are prepared, they are not required to be "qualified" or consistent with the legislatively sanctioned minimum planning standards and procedures prepared by DCA's and DNR's environmental planning criteria. Nevertheless, by the end of 1995 almost all local governments had submitted plans to DCA and the RDCs.

Because local government compliance with the new planning system was tied to eligibility for a substantial list of state grants, DCA awarded all local governments in Georgia qualified status at the beginning of the process. Then, in the course of the plan submission and review process, a local government could lose its status in one or more of five ways:

1. Failure to submit a plan by the assigned date. In effect, local governments were given something of substantial value either to keep or lose.

2. Submitting a plan that failed to meet the standards required by the law. The local government could then regain qualified status when it brought the plan up to minimum standards.

3. Failure of the local government to mediate in good faith.

4. Failure to adopt and implement development regulations consistent with its own local plan.

5. Failure to submit a DRI for review.

For communities with local plans already in place, preexisting plan consideration and determination had to occur within the first year of the new law's implementation. The communities were given six months to submit the plan and another six months for DCA to either certify the plan or find it not in compliance. If the plan did not meet the compliance test, the local government reverted to its regularly assigned date within the five-year period.

Local governments without preexisting plans (about half of the total) had a maximum of five years (by the end of 1995) to present a plan meeting the requirements of HB 215 to remain a QLG. After the fourth round of plan submission and review, 579 of the total local governments had plans reviewed by DCA. All but 56 of those plans met the requirements and were recertified as qualified. By September 1995 those 56 plans were still in the review process, and another 96 plans were due for submission. Twenty-one local governments were still unaccounted for, most of which had not submitted plans. Assuming that the 10 percent figure for plans unsuccessful in recertification is correct, only 67 local governments had not yet been recertified as QLGs.

Three factors account for this strong level of participation. First, unlike any other state considering a comprehensive planning and growth management system, Georgia's local governments, through their state associations, strongly supported the adoption of such a system. Two key local government organizations, GMA and ACCG, were positive influences on the process. Both are well organized, active in the public policy and political areas, with well-respected executive directors who supported the Georgia Planning Act—Jerry Griffin with the ACCG and Jim Burgess (and later, Jim Calvin) with the GMA.

The second and perhaps strongest incentive for local governments to comply was the requirement of QLG certification to be eligible for a variety of local government grants and loan-funding programs. DCA and other state agencies were sending the message that noncompliance could be costly, and they used the law to deny grants to local governments unless they achieved QLG status. An agency cooperating in the grant and loan eligibility system determines whether

---

Examples of Grants and Loan Funding Programs Available Only to Qualified Local Governments

- Appalachian Regional Commission Infrastructure Funds
- Capital Felony Grant Program
- Community Development Block Grants
- Business Development Revolving Loan Fund
- Employment Incentive Program
- Immediate Threat and Danger Grants
- Local Development Fund
- Water and Sewer Loan Program
- State Revolving Loan Program
- Recreation Grants
- Historic Preservation Grants

Source: Georgia DCA, 1993, 2

---

a local government applying for a grant is a QLG. If not, the application is still considered on its merits, but the local government is warned that the grant cannot be awarded unless and until it is reinstated as a QLG. However, some critical funding sources, such as the Georgia DOT, did not make its funds subject to the QLG process.

A third major factor in bringing local governments into compliance was the extensive technical assistance effort of OCP and the agency's flexibility in interpreting and applying the rules. Many local governments were too understaffed to prepare plans that met the requirements of HB 215, but OCP sought to provide technical assistance to local governments, and prepared comprehensive data books and maps for each city and county that included information needed to prepare each element (Georgia DCA 1990a). DCA, during the first four years of local plan preparation, also published a series of guidebooks and produced more than 45 articles about the act for publication in the newsletters and magazines of many organizations.

Developments of Regional Impact

In late 1990 DCA adopted *Submittal and Review Procedures: Developments of Regional Impact*, which outlined local government and RDC responsibilities when applying for approval of a project triggering the DCA regional impact thresholds (Georgia

DCA 1990b). The document proposed differential thresholds based on characteristics for three regions: Atlanta, other metropolitan areas and nonmetropolitan areas. For example, the threshold for housing was 500 new lots or units in the Atlanta region; 400 in the other metropolitan areas; and 250 units in nonmetropolitan areas. The land use categories to which the developments of regional impact (DRI) requirement applied included office, commercial, wholesale and distribution, hospitals, housing, industrial, hotels, mixed-use developments, airports, attractions and recreational sites, and postsecondary schools. RDCs could adopt more restrictive criteria with the approval of the DCA board.

In determining whether a project was a DRI, RDC would look at whether it met or exceeded established thresholds and whether it would have interjurisdictional impacts, including the extent of its infrastructure impacts on other jurisdictions. With data provided by the applicant and the local government, RDC could consider six regional impact categories: environmental and natural resources; the economy; water and sewer; solid waste or other public facilities; public transportation; and housing. If the review showed that all negative impacts had been accounted for, RDC would make a finding to that effect. If there were impacts not accounted for, RDC could bring all parties to the table for informal conflict resolution before the formal public hearing on the project. After the conflict resolution effort, RDC was required to make one of two possible findings: the proposed action either will or will not be "in the best interests of the state" (Georgia DCA 1990b, 3). A local government that cooperates in the review and mediation process may opt to not mitigate the negative impacts and lose its qualified status.

During this second phase of implementation of the Georgia Planning Act, most DRIs were in the metropolitan Atlanta area; others were in smaller metropolitan areas and a few rural areas. By fall 1995 a total of 101 projects had been reviewed, including all solid waste disposal facilities, which are automatically DRIs. In those cases, the legislation limits the local government's ability to control the siting process of a landfill. The law provides for a Facilities Issues Negotiating Process, under which local government

and citizens negotiate on where the landfill should be located. In the end, the state's Environmental Protection Division determines the solid waste facility site.

Regionally Important Resources

The DCA board adopted the *Procedures for the Designation and Review of Regionally Important Resources* on January 1, 1991. A regionally important resoursce (RIR) is defined as "a natural or historic resource which has natural boundaries extending beyond a single local government's jurisdiction or has value to a broad constituency and which is vulnerable to the actions and activities of man" (Georgia DCA 1991, 1). Natural resources include geographic areas from the mountains (mountain ridges and steep slopes) to the sea (marshlands, estuaries and beaches) and areas in between (e.g., rivers, streams, lakes, prime forest and agricultural lands, rare and irreplaceable natural communities, unique scenic areas). Historic resources include "unique historic properties, districts, and sites as well as archeological and cultural resources" (Georgia DCA 1991, 1–2).

Local governments, citizens and the members of GDC were asked to make RIR nominations, including an analysis of value and vulnerability as defined in the procedures, by June 1992. After the first round, no additional nominations could occur before July 1997. RDCs were required to prioritize potential RIRs and submit their top candidates to DCA for potential designation. The DCA board was responsible for selecting RIR candidates and approving a resource management strategy, defined as "a set of policies and practices specifically designed to manage and conserve or protect a particular RIR and may include such measures as buffers and setbacks, cluster development with open space, or other best management practices" (Georgia DCA 1991, 3). Upon completion of a draft strategy, DCA was charged with distributing the draft and a location map to all affected parties for review and comment. After a public hearing for additional input, the DCA board could make a decision to designate or not to designate (Georgia DCA 1991, 3).

In Georgia, as in Florida, any citizen, group or government agency may make a nomination for designation. Unlike Florida, the ability of DCA to enforce the management strategy is not clear, even though the link with DNR may make certain parts of the management plan enforceable. Furthermore, there still was a question of the circumstances under which a local government's failure to be consistent in its plan and regulations with the resource management strategy for RIRs would cause it to lose its qualified status.

Between 1991 and 1993 there were about 160 nominations during the window of opportunity, of which only four were given full consideration by the DCA board. Eventually, only one was designated as an RIR: the Augusta Canal, which runs through Columbia County, the city of Augusta and Richmond County. Efforts failed to carry these designations forward through the resource management plan and full implementation stage. In short, in late 1998 the RIR process was virtually nonoperative and was to be examined by the Growth Strategies Reassessment Task Force. RIRs and DRIs shared with other elements of the Georgia Planning Act a question of how effective a system based on incentives and disincentives could be.

Regional Planning Process

The transformation of RDCs from the earlier regional system of APDCs in many ways strengthened the regional level, making RDCs key actors in defining and implementing the state's planning and growth management system. Local government payment of dues and membership became mandatory, and their involvement in both developing and reviewing local plans was significant. The name change signaled the RDCs' assumed importance in the area of economic development, as did RDCs' participation in RIRs and DRIs. They also were assigned the role of developing regional plans as a follow-up to the preparation and adoption of local plans. In turn, these regional plans clearly were meant, under the law, to be the building blocks for the state plan, completing the three key elements of plan making under the Georgia Planning Act.

Despite the important role assigned to RDCs, there was substantial skepticism from the beginning about the boundaries and number of RDCs (18), which were essentially carried over from the former APDCs. An analysis of the boundaries concluded that some RDCs had neither the geographic area nor the fiscal economic base to carry out the responsibilities assigned to them. A recommendation was made to reduce their number to 12 by redrawing the boundaries with an eye to more logical and effective regional units. The politics of this seemingly rational proposal resulted in no action to change RDC structure, although concern about the viability of some RDCs proved well founded.

As the initial round of local plan development neared an end in late 1995, and the time approached for the development of regional plans, the sense of urgency rose in finding a solution to the RDC problem. Governor Miller's unhappy experience with a coastal RDC apparently convinced him that RDCs were more trouble than they were worth. Economic development was without question a primary goal of the state planning act, and the RDCs were presumably a major vehicle for achieving that goal. However, in early 1996 Miller established 11 economic development districts (EDDs) with roughly the same boundaries as the proposed 11 or 12 RDCs, aimed at promoting economic development although their relationship to the planning act was not clear. To further complicate the matter, in the early 1990s, two RDCs had succumbed to fiscal insolvency.

The solution to the regional dilemma seemed obvious to many supporters of the Georgia planning system: return to the concepts of the 1989 study of regional boundaries and reduce the number of RDCs. EDDs would be merged with the newly drawn RDC boundaries to reflect geographically logical and economically and fiscally viable RDCs that could play the expected regional role in carrying out their responsibilities under the Georgia Planning Act. DCA could then determine and establish, from time to time, the territorial boundaries of RDCs (Georgia DCA 1995a). These boundary changes, however, required approval by a joint resolution of the General Assembly.

Most supporters of the act felt that the RDC problem would ultimately be sorted out, with the number reduced to 11 or 12, and hoped the governor would then support the merging of EDDs with the reduced number of RDCs, with perhaps some further integration of other regional functions into those same boundaries. However, the planning law (HB 215) had no language about EDDs reporting directly to the GDC. Furthermore, EDD regions had no staff or source of funds, and those that were effective were already associated with the RDCs in their region. EDD regions were never set up as nonprofits; they were not public agencies and had no legal standing even to receive dollars from the state.

State Initiatives and Implementation through 1998

Local Government Plans

The local planning phase of Georgia's three-tiered growth management system was completed in September 1995, with 683 local governments (99 percent) preparing plans that met the requirements of the planning act. As of June 1998, some 232 local governments had completed the first required updates of their plans by finishing short-term work programs and reporting on plan implementation during the first five years since adoption.

The most significant way the state helped local governments under the Georgia Planning Act was by providing funding to RDCs to carry out their duties. By 1993 about $9.6 million had been provided, and by 1998 more than $22 million, including special grants for RDC regional planning from 1996 through 1999. The total provided by DCA to the RDCs in the 1990–1999 period was $20.7 million (for the growth strategies support and special projects category), while the grants for the preparation of regional plans totaled just under $1.9 million. Other funding provided computer software and hardware so RDCs could be an active part of the Georgia data network. DCA monitored RDC performance under their contracts, including development of a detailed RDC Performance Evaluation Network (Georgia DCA 1993, 5–6; 1998a).

The key DCA staff in OCP thought its data books and map packets and other technical assistance efforts established a good relationship with local governments, especially since DCA was not passing dollars directly to local governments for planning. Plan making had gone well, but implementation had

not, and momentum began to build to find ways to strengthen it. Regulations to protect mountains and river corridors had been especially weak. The state, through DCA and DNR, required implementation of protection measures by a certain deadline, but whether that effort would result in meaningful action was in doubt (Georgia DCA 1998b, 1).

Mediation

A mixed picture was also evident regarding DRIs, RIRs and the mediation process. DRIs have had the most success, with some 641 large-scale developments being subject to DRI review between 1992 and November 2003 (Smith 2003). Certainly, such reviews have resulted in increased communication among local governments on issues involving more than one jurisdiction. In the final analysis, the current system cannot force a local government in a DRI to mitigate greater-than-local impacts; thus, the efforts to protect significant natural or historic resources have failed.

A large number of RIRs were presented to the DCA board for designation. However, RIRs have been the most difficult component to implement. A task force appointed to assess the RIR program found a number of basic problems:

- Given Georgia's constitutional home rule provisions, local governments are the primary entities to control development activities that may be detrimental to a particular RIR located wholly or partially within their respective jurisdictions.

- These local governments cannot effectively implement a coordinated enforcement of land use controls, such as zoning.

- Local governments have no incentives to do any of this.

The task force concluded that without critical state incentives, the RIR program was basically unworkable, and since the state has not produced money or incentives, there has been little interest in RIRs since the mid-1990s. A DCA effort to simplify and streamline the process to get more local government support for RIR designations had not produced results as of late 2000 (Georgia DCA 1998b, 1–2). By the end of 2003 further efforts to revive the process had not resulted in additional nominations, and the

Augusta Canal remained the only designated RIR (Miness 2003).

The process for mediating local government planning disputes (often involving land use issues) has been equally disappointing, as local governments have resisted using the process. By late 1998 only a few local governments had initiated mediation, with three completing it, but even then the results were not clear. DCA adopted new rules for mediation in 1997, but as of late 2003 these had not stimulated more support from local governments (Georgia DCA 1998b, 1–2). In 2001 Cobb County and Paulding County completed the first successful mediation. The dispute revolved around the two counties' different land use concepts for a proposed mixed-use DRI that straddled their borders. The counties agreed to provide early notification to each other, relative to their future local development permitting of this large project (Georgia DCA 2003b, 4).

Use of development impact fees also has been rare in local comprehensive plan implementation. To levy such fees, the planning act required local governments to have a comprehensive plan with fees to be linked to improvements listed in the capital improvements element (CIE) in that plan. As of late 2003, impact fees were being collected by 26 local governments, 11 of which had amended their comprehensive plans to include the capital improvement element. DCA was in the process of reviewing CIE amendments for two additional local governments and had reason to believe more submittals would be received in the near future (Basso 2003). Proposed changes in impact fee implementation to make them more attractive to local governments were not approved by the General Assembly (Georgia DCA 1998b, 1–2).

Regional Planning Update

Phase two of the three-tiered planning system, set out in the 1989 planning act, began shortly after the September 1995 deadline for local plans to be completed. The logic of a further realignment of RDC boundaries was still compelling, if RDCs were to play their assigned role in the system. Recognizing this, the 1998 General Assembly put $750,000 in DCA's budget as an incentive fund to get certain counties to move from one RDC to another and facilitate the

merger of some RDCs to create the fiscal strength and geographic cohesion needed for an effective regional system. Following DCA's planning standards, as of June 1998 five RDCs had completed their plans, eight more would finish by December 1998, and the remaining three in 1999. DCA's contracts with the regions to prepare the plans included required matching grants to RDCs that varied by region (Georgia DCA 1998a; 1998b, 2).

From the perspective of the DCA staff working directly with RDCs, the results were very disappointing. Each region got $145,000 initially. An RDC committee was supposed to examine the way the process was working, in light of DCA's standards, especially in terms of dealing effectively with intergovernmental challenges that could lead to real solutions to the tough regional issues. For the most part, the RDC staff did not point out the weaknesses or propose solutions, so regional plans typically went to the RDC boards without challenging them to develop a strong regional perspective. Any progress on this front has been a function of new initiatives under the Barnes administration post-1998.

The Service Delivery Strategy Act

In 1995 the Georgia General Assembly created the 30-member Georgia Future Communities Commission (GFCC) to offer new ideas on how communities could create an environment conducive to an improved quality of life and economic prosperity. By summer 1996 the commission had agreed that "the lack of a clear legal distinction between cities and counties since 1972 has fostered inefficient service delivery systems and unhealthy conflict in too many of our communities" (ACCG et al. 1997, foreword). In October 1996 and September 1997, the commission made wide-ranging sets of recommendations that led to passage of the Local Government Service Delivery Strategy Act and establishment of the Growth Strategies Reassessment Task Force (GFCC 1996; 1997).

By late January 1997 the commission reached a consensus embraced by the boards of the city and county associations, and the 1997 General Assembly passed HB 489, the Service Delivery Strategy Act. The act called for 159 service delivery strategies, one for each county, with the counties charged with initiating the process by January 1, 1998. There are repeated references throughout the requirements of HB 489 regarding the importance of reconciling and eliminating land use conflicts between counties and their cities (GMA et al. 1997). Every strategy was to include

- identification of all services presently provided in the county by cities, counties and authorities;

- assignment of which local government will be responsible for providing which service in what area of the county;

- description of how all services will be funded; and

- identification of intergovernmental contracts, ordinances, resolutions, etc., to be used in implementing the strategy, including existing contracts. (ACCG et al. 1997, 1)

HB 489 aimed at no less than a potentially far-reaching realignment of service delivery within a given county, to "develop a more rational approach to allocating delivery and funding of these services among the various local governments and authorities in each county" (ACCG et al. 1997, 1). The required criteria include

- elimination of unnecessary duplication; of arbitrary water and sewer rate differentials; and of double taxation of municipal property owners for services provided by the county primarily for the benefit of the unincorporated area;

- compatible land use plans;

- water and sewer extension consistency with land use plans (in which any provision for extraterritorial water and sewer extensions by a jurisdiction must be consistent with "all applicable land use plans and ordinances"); and

- resolution of annexation disputes over land use. (ACCG et al. 1997, 13)

Another requirement mandated that a process be established by July 1, 1998, for resolving land use classification disputes between counties and cities over property to be annexed. Local governments within a county were to amend their land use plans to assure compatibility or put in place one land use plan for the entire county. This issue was deemed important because incompatible land use plans do not protect citizens who reside in one local government from incompatible uses by a neighbor government (ACCG et al. 1997, 12). HB 489 is one of a number of efforts to bring about land use compatibility between and among local governments, without directly requiring it through a regulatory process, presumably barred by Georgia's Constitution.

Another significant requirement involved the resolution of land use classification disputes when the county objected to a proposed annexation of county land into a city. The 1998 General Assembly amended the annexation statute, narrowing the grounds on which counties can stop such annexation (GMA et al. 1998). By July 1, 1998, cities and counties were to adopt the conflict resolution process consistent with a change in that process in HB 1603 (an amendment to the annexation statute), outlining the grounds on which a county could object to a land use classification involved in an annexation.

Local governments had until July 1, 1999, to adopt a service delivery strategy, and the final deadline for a verified strategy, including extensions, was October 29, 1999. Local governments that did not comply would lose their eligibility for state funding and permits (GMA 1998, 1, 12). The large majority of Georgia's 159 counties met the deadline and finally had a plan verified by DCA, and thus, at a minimum, service delivery efficiency within those counties was significantly strengthened. However, there still remains the challenge of achieving *regional* smart growth strategies across county lines, especially in the difficult area of land use.

The regional challenge was addressed again through 1998 budget recommendations and action by the General Assembly establishing another set of regional jurisdictions in Georgia. HB 1650 determined the boundaries of 11 state development regions and appropriated some $2 million to set them up. The boundaries of the 11 regions outside Atlanta were similar to those DCA Commissioner Jim Higdon and others had tried to establish previously. Beginning July 1, 1998, DCA and the Department of Industry, Trade, and Tourism opened 11 new regional offices with staff from the two agencies. The need to overcome the "two Georgias" division of the mid-1980s continued; many in rural Georgia felt that too much state effort was focused on growth in the Atlanta region and too little on the rest of the state. The new regional offices would reinforce economic development opportunities in rural Georgia with new technologies (Higdon 1998, 33).

Two things in particular stand out about the state development regions. First, this is yet another effort by the state, and especially Higdon, to gain fuller implementation of the Georgia Planning Act, by stressing the need for stronger incentives and disincentives in the face of the constitutional prohibition against the state directly mandating growth management measures (land use controls) on local governments, except in the "vital areas" category. Second is the continuing emphasis on stronger incentives and disincentives to persuade and assist local governments to join together to find regional solutions to regional problems.

The Growth Strategies Reassessment Task Force

There was a growing conviction that unsuccessful efforts to implement plans to achieve the goals of the Georgia Planning Act were a major weakness of the system. At the request of the GFCC, DCA's Division of Planning and Environmental Management drafted a proposal for a task force to explore the implementation problems (Georgia DCA Undated). While 99 percent of Georgia's local governments had comprehensive plans in place, many simply were not implementing them. A 1995 survey conducted by DCA revealed that only about half the counties and one-third of the municipalities responding had a zoning ordinance, a typical means to implement a land use plan. The intergovernmental coordination measures aimed at yielding compatible land use decisions by neighboring jurisdictions were seen as disappointing. No state or regional muscle existed to bring a reluctant local government into the game (Georgia DCA Undated, 1–2).

In October 1997 GFCC called for a statewide planning and growth management policy group to suggest changes in the planning act "as well as other legislative initiatives to support a more cohesive and results-oriented planning and growth management framework for the state" (Georgia DCA Undated, 2). With the strong support of DCA, this challenge was taken up by the appointment of a 30-member Growth Strategies Reassessment Task Force (GSRTF) that began meeting in late summer 1998. The task force included elected and appointed officials from cities and counties, home builders, state agencies (including DOT), the heads of GMA (cities) and ACCG (counties), business groups, state elected officials, the Georgia Conservancy and others. It was chaired by Joseph Whorton, who had long held that the 1989 planning act was a critical first step, but that additional measures would have to be taken to make the system adequate to cope with the heavy growth pressures in Georgia, especially the Atlanta region. Staff for the task force came largely from DCA's Division of Planning and Environmental Management (GFCC 1997, 7–11).

The task force submitted its final report in December 1998, just as newly elected Governor Roy Barnes was taking office, and many of the recommendations were crafted for his attention. The predominant theme was that the governor must be the source of leadership that takes the state from growth strategies to growth management. The report's message was clear and consistent with longstanding criticisms: the requirements and incentives were sufficient to get local governments to make and adopt plans, but they were not sufficient to overcome the forces pushing local governments to plan and act in isolation from one another. Furthermore, local entities such as school boards and special authorities in areas such as housing, water, sewer and other infrastructure were not drawn into the process.

The task force recommendations were organized into eight categories: state vision; financial support; regionalism; limiting sprawl; local planning requirements; local plan implementation; participation in local planning; and environmental protection (Georgia GSRTF 1998, 3–4; Goldberg 1998a, E1). The report states that GDC should be reestablished as the governor's primary resource in marshaling state resources and guiding state agencies and other organizations in implementing the state vision. At state, regional and local levels, agencies would have to report regularly to the council on their actions to carry out the state vision. Other organizations receiving state assistance (e.g., school systems, and public development and housing authorities) would be subject to the same requirement. Any government failing to comply would be subject to major financial sanctions (Georgia GSRTF 1998, 7–9).

The financial support section was clear: incentives and disincentives were not strong enough. The key was to provide a base level of funding for standard good compliance, but making significant special incentives, fiscal and otherwise, available for those who moved beyond the minimum. Regions and regionalism also were high on the list for significant strengthening, with the state (as usual) leading the way to implement a number of initiatives to strengthen regional coordination by all relevant local actors. Stronger RDCs would oversee the regional plan and institute a meaningful review of local government plans regarding consistency with the regional plan (Georgia GSRTF 1998, 10–12).

Incentives to contain sprawl were cited as inadequate, and the report urged the state to take the lead in making them stronger. Instituting minimum density zoning, establishing urban services areas, providing incentives for infill development, and implementing traffic-calming measures were among the tools proposed to limit sprawl (Georgia GSRTF 1998, 13–14).

The three sections on local planning (requirements, implementation and participation) represented quite a divergence from the existing bottom-up, largely voluntary system. Coordination among key local and regional agencies in making and implementing fully coordinated local and regional plans would be required, and all state permits or funding would be withheld from local governments failing to comply. State agency funding and permits would also be withheld from any local or regional projects not consistent with local comprehensive plans (Georgia GSRTF 1998, 15–18).

Finally, the section on environmental protection called for the expansion and strengthening of the "vital areas" provision of the state constitution. The DNR did develop standards, but shared the fate of other parts of the planning act: inadequate imple-

mentation. The report also suggested the state should develop an enhanced program for environmental protection to ensure implementation of existing "vital areas" provisions for river corridors, watersheds and mountains, and newly added components such as historic and coastal resources (Georgia GSRTF 1998, 20–21). The report was completed in December 1998; however, since newly elected Governor Barnes was focusing his attention on his Georgia Regional Transportation Authority (GRTA) initiative, he did not receive the task force's recommendations until later in spring 1999.

The Atlanta Regional Commission

The Atlanta region is the dominant demographic, economic and political force in Georgia, and thus provides a kind of secondary case study to understand the strengths, obstacles and issues inherent in the state's growth management system. Technically, the Atlanta Regional Commission (ARC) was one of the 18 RDCs established by the Georgia Planning Act of 1989. The other 17 were former Area Planning and Development Commissions (APDCs), but the Atlanta commission traditionally had been a "first among equals" in Georgia's regional agency system.

ARC was authorized in 1971 as the state's only Metropolitan Area Planning and Development Commission for a region containing a population of more than one million. ARC's original jurisdiction matched the seven-county boundary of the Standard Metropolitan Statistical Area (SMSA) for the Atlanta region, but the SMSA has since expanded to 20 counties, while ARC still consists of only 10 counties. The region's population has increased from 2.88 million in 1995 to 3.4 million in 2000, with a projected increase to more than 3.7 million by 2010 and 4.4 million by 2025. By that time it will comprise over 44 percent of the total state population (ARC 1996a, 17; 1996b, 9, 33, 36–39; Soto 1998).

A Brief History and Early Accomplishments

The first ancestor of ARC was the Metropolitan Planning Commission (MPC), which was founded in 1947 and included the city of Atlanta and DeKalb and

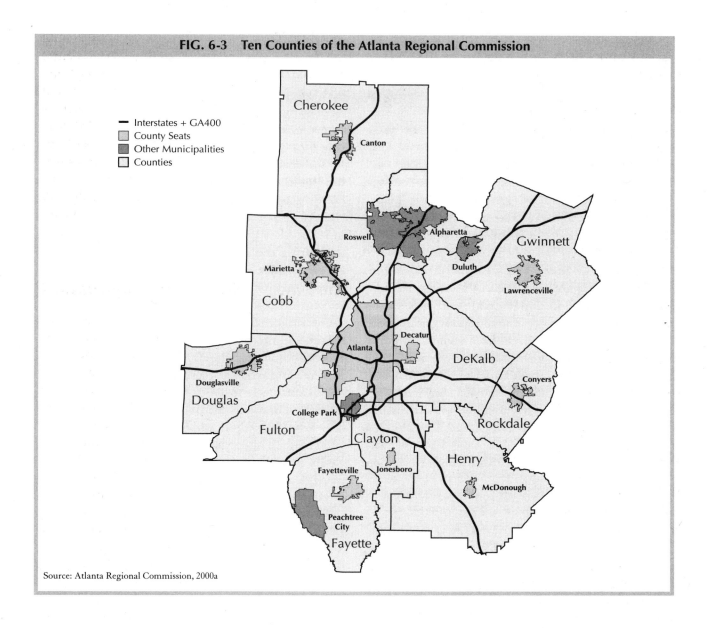

FIG. 6-3   Ten Counties of the Atlanta Regional Commission

Source: Atlanta Regional Commission, 2000a

Fulton counties. MPC was the first publicly supported multicounty planning agency in the U.S., and was the only regional planning agency in the state for more than a decade. In 1960 the boundary was expanded to include Clayton, Cobb and Gwinnett counties, and the MPC was reconstituted as the Atlanta Region Metropolitan Planning Commission (West 1992, 16). During the 1960s three additional areawide planning organizations were created, each with a separate board and work program, and the resulting fragmentation made interagency and local government coordination difficult.

To correct the problem, the General Assembly passed special legislation (Act 5) in 1971 to consolidate the work of those agencies under a new regionwide Metropolitan Area Planning and Development Commission. As a result, Douglas and Rockdale counties were added to the Atlanta APDC, making it a seven-county region (ARC 1989). The ARC governing board was composed of 39 public and private members, and the state DCA board had a nonvoting representative (ARC 1989). Funding for ARC's activities came from local, state and federal sources, including mandatory dues from member governments.

Act 5 designated ARC as the region's comprehensive planning agency for transportation, land use, and environmental, aging and human services in the region. It also authorized the preparation of comprehensive "development guides," or regional plans, consisting of policy statements, goals, standards, programs and maps. Those plans were to take into account future developments including land use, water and sewerage systems, storm drainage systems, parks and open spaces, and the land needs and location of airports, highways, transit facilities, hospitals and public buildings, in addition to other facilities and services.

Within those functional areas of responsibility, ARC's planning authority was to be advisory only, limited to review and comment on area plans, which were defined as proposals for action by government and public agencies that could have regional impacts. There were no enforcement provisions, but the commission had broad authority to determine if an action constituted an area plan. The agency used its discretion in this area to have the maximum impact possible on local land use decision making (West 1992, 18–19). However, the determination of many local governments to act in isolation from each other or the region remained a challenge.

Development Reviews

Environmental degradation of the Chattahoochee River corridor, due to increasing development there, was a pressing regional issue when ARC began operations in late 1971. A citizens group, Friends of the River, had unsuccessfully sought legislation to protect the river in 1970 and 1971. The river supplied hydroelectric power and a broad range of recreational uses, and was a major source of drinking water for the region. In a 1972 resolution, ARC declared any plan or proposal involving government action or expenditure of public funds that could affect the Chattahoochee River corridor to be an area plan under the provisions of Act 5. The corridor was defined to include all land within 2,000 feet of the riverbanks for a length of about 48 miles (ARC 1978).

Pursuant to Act 5, ARC prepared the Chattahoochee Corridor Study in July 1972. Shortly after adoption of the ARC plan, then-Governor Jimmy

Carter signed the Metropolitan River Protection Act into law, enabling ARC to prepare a comprehensive land and water use plan to protect the river corridor. Local government actions affecting the corridor were required to be consistent with the ARC plan, as determined by ARC through a review and comment procedure. The act helped ensure compliance with ARC recommendations by requiring approval by the Environmental Protection Division of the state DNR for any action ARC deemed inconsistent. ARC readopted its 1972 corridor study as the official plan in 1973 (ARC 1978).

During the 1970s ARC used its general review authority most effectively for the protection of proposed transportation corridors for both highway and transit systems. In the 1980s ARC identified a proliferation of large-scale developments as having significant intergovernmental and regional impacts, and established thresholds for residential, office, commercial, industrial, mixed-use, hotel and hospital uses. From 1984 to 1990, ARC reviewed 174 large-scale developments, 62 hotels and a combined total of nearly 359 million square feet of office, industrial and commercial space (ARC 1991).

By 1986 the limitations of ARC's review authority over large-scale development under Act 5 became increasingly evident and unsatisfactory. Implementation of proposed projects depended on voluntary cooperation by the submitting agency. There was no requirement for compliance with, or even serious consideration of, ARC's recommendations. Furthermore, there was no required feedback to ARC even if the comments were considered and acted upon.

Proposed legislation in 1986 would have strengthened ARC's review authority by requiring a local governing body to consider ARC's comments, accept or reject them by a majority vote and notify ARC of its action. This bill, however, met with strong opposition from other regions and their local governments, and failed to pass. In the same year, Governor Harris initiated a process that would grant ARC even more authority than that proposed in the failed legislation. In a campaign speech in 1986, Harris pledged that if he were reelected to a second term, he would appoint a blue-ribbon commission to study growth management and regional planning issues statewide, an action that led to the adoption of the Georgia Planning Act (HB 215) in 1989.

Impacts of the Georgia Planning Act on ARC

Many of ARC's activities continued after the Georgia Planning Act was passed, including conducting special studies and offering high-quality technical assistance to member governments. ARC began reviewing existing local plans in 1991 and found that many were basically land use plans rather than comprehensive plans, and did not meet the new standards. Only three local governments were able to take advantage of the law's provisions for adoption of preexisting plans, and even those required work before being approved (West 1992, 25).

In 1991 ARC extended the scope of its work from assisting local communities to exerting its influence regionally. Under the planning act, the DRI process expanded ARC's review role to more projects, and mandated a designation by ARC as to whether a project was in the best interest of the region. In the early 1990s, Harry West, ARC executive director, saw this as a powerful new tool for injecting a regional perspective into the local planning and land use decision-making process, something the region had struggled long and hard to achieve. In spite of positive new developments, that objective was not fully accomplished (ARC 1992b, 30; West 1992, 22). The nomination of RIRs provided another opportunity for promoting a regional perspective. ARC sought to continue its ongoing efforts to protect the region's resources as it proceeded to identify RIRs for nomination (ARC 1992c, 30; West 1992, 26).

Under the planning act, ARC's regional plan was, for the first time, subject to state review. The act required the regional plan to consider local plans and be consistent with DCA's minimum regional planning standards, although meeting those standards did not pose any great difficulty. For ARC the challenges of the new system resided in the meaningful integration of the regional and local plans and moving from plan making to implementation when local governments were reluctant to do so. By taking a creative approach to the change in the direction of regional planning, the ARC staff hoped to avoid ending up with a regional plan that was merely a composite of local plans.

Vision 2020: A New Participatory Process

In early 1992 ARC launched Vision 2020, to ensure the growth management system's bottom-up emphasis would enhance the regional perspective that had always driven its planning process. Vision 2020 was a long-term participatory process to develop a vision for the region's future and guarantee implementation of the vision's key components by 1994.

The Vision 2020 process was intended to involve a cross-section of the region's citizens in developing the vision, to build strong links between local and regional plans, and to set the direction for the region's development during a time of renewed growth challenges. The region had begun to recover from the 1990–1991 recession, and growth had resumed by 1993. Some employment losses were reversed or offset by other gains. For example, Lockheed employment increased in the 1990s, and Holiday Inn decided in 1991 to relocate its North American headquarters to Atlanta, to join its international headquarters.

In the early 1990s, ARC began to develop a plan for a comprehensive transportation system to meet the needs generated by the 1996 Olympics, although the pending games were only part of a larger regional traffic and transportation problem (ARC 1992b, 28, 32). ARC undertook a number of studies to investigate transportation alternatives and the feasibility of extending rail transit to various sections of the region. Plans were produced for reducing traffic tie-ups and

---

Vision 2020 Recommendations

- Work with ARC to modify the transportation planning process
- Implement transit–land use changes to support transit-pedestrian development
- Create incentives and regional policies to promote livable communities
- Develop a regional transportation–land use institute
- Improve connections between truck, rail and air freight facilities
- Develop intermodal passenger connections and equalize accessibility

Source: ARC 1995, 60–65

establishing a computerized traffic management system that would use synchronized traffic signals, closed-circuit TV cameras and electronic signs on freeways.

The federal Intermodal Surface Transportation Efficiency Act (ISTEA) of 1991 expanded ARC's role as a regional forum for decision making, and placed new emphasis on alternative transportation modes (ARC 1992b, 32–33). A new multimodal transportation center was planned for downtown Atlanta to serve as a central terminal for intercity and commuter rail and other transit modes. In the transportation context, the Vision 2020 process included background research, a public awareness campaign, public opinion surveys and a planning process, culminating in policies to guide development in the region (ARC 1992d).

The initial research phase began with a survey conducted by Ketchum Public Relations of New York. The results, presented at a public meeting in May 1992, identified potential obstacles to addressing regional growth issues effectively. A persistent concern was disharmony among the many municipal and county governments. Some panelists suggested that government services be consolidated to prevent duplication, cope more effectively with future growth and distribute tax burdens more equitably. Others urged local governments and the private sector to cooperate in developing a comprehensive regional plan dealing with growth management, public education and environmental protection. One proposal encouraged public transit and less dependence on private automobiles, and the implementation of stricter emissions controls. Another suggested a regional growth strategy to promote compact urban development and discourage sprawl (ARC 1992b, 6, 9–10, 16).

The Vision 2020 steering committee began a visioning process of its own, asking participants to identify their choices for the most critical issues facing the region. The comprehensive public opinion surveys of that phase, which targeted audiences representing civic, business and community interests, led to the last phase of developing a final vision for the region (ARC 1992d). Community forums were held in each of the region's counties to move toward a preferred vision to be released at ARC's May 1993 Outlook conference (ARC 1992a, 1–4). The survey results

were organized and presented under three major headings: creating livable communities, establishing a strong economic foundation, and attaining a better quality of life (ARC 1993, 1–3). In late January 1994, the implementation phase of Vision 2020 was formally launched (West 1992, 26).

The Vision 2020 final report recommended a remarkably wide range of actions aimed at improving the quality of life of all sectors of the Atlanta region (ARC 1995). It called for initiatives in such areas as community leadership and citizen involvement; cultural arts; health systems; housing and community development; human services; media forum; natural resources; public safety; a regional center for educational excellence and workforce development; and transportation–land use. The most direct call for ending sprawl development patterns and substituting more compact livable communities included linking transportation and land use to change the shape and character of growth in the Atlanta region.

Despite Vision 2020's early success, it was not clear whether its goals could be implemented. For example, opponents of an outer perimeter beltway, a $5 billion interstate proposed by Georgia DOT, were concerned that it would only exacerbate the region's serious sprawl problem. A joint study by the Georgia Conservancy and the Greater Atlanta Chamber of Commerce showed that stakeholders were uncertain as to whether the outer loop should be built in whole in or part (Georgia Conservancy 1994, 6).

State Representative Ron Slatin, of the Atlanta region, introduced Senate Bill 2 to the 1996 legislative session. The bill would change the Governor's Road Improvement Program (GRIP) and make other transportation improvements to existing routes. Another Slatin bill focused on transportation planning and construction to stress transit systems and other alternatives to the automobile. Neither was acted on by the General Assembly. The battle over the outer perimeter (or outer loop road) was far from over, with many observers convinced that the road would not be built. The battle was directly related to the implementation of Vision 2020 and at least indirectly to the implementation of the Georgia Planning Act (Allison 1995).

The vision for the Atlanta region to radically alter growth patterns by linking transportation, land use and air quality was just that at the close of the Vision 2020 process in 1995—a vision with all the right components but without clear evidence that implementation would be possible. At the same time, two closely related developments were taking place, one focused on the Atlanta region and the other on the state as a whole. For the Atlanta region, it was the designation of the 10-county ARC region and the three adjacent counties as nonattainment areas for air quality under the federal Clean Air Act, with a resulting withholding of federal transportation dollars until a Regional Transportation Plan (RTP) and a Transportation Improvement Program (TIP) could be put in place to correct the problem.

On the state level, assessments of the state's growth management system throughout the late 1990s led to a conclusion that major executive and legislative changes were needed to move Georgia in a smart growth direction that would give it sustainable natural and urban systems into the new century. It had become clear that changes necessary for the Atlanta region and for Georgia as a whole were closely related.

Legislative and Political Actions during the Barnes Administration, 1999–2003

The results of the November 1998 gubernatorial election were a pleasant surprise to the Democrats, as Roy Barnes won unexpectedly by a wide margin. Democrats gained one seat in the House and stayed even in the Senate, holding majorities in each chamber. Barnes asked Joel Cowan, chair of the original Growth Strategies Commission (GSC) in the late 1980s, and John Sibley, executive director of that commission, for post-election input on how to strengthen the system. In an *Atlanta Journal-Constitution* interview, Barnes restated his intention to work toward the creation of a state transportation authority to deal with mass transit and air quality problems in Georgia. He also reaffirmed his support for having the governor appoint the members of the DOT board, instead

of their selection by the General Assembly (Walston 1998, H-8).

Barnes made it clear early on that any local governments that did not achieve and maintain a QLG status would not receive funds from any state agency over which the governor had control. His leadership triggered a series of initiatives to strengthen Georgia's system for managing growth and change both in the Atlanta region and statewide. Implementing those initiatives, however, would challenge the autonomy of the DOT and its influence on intergovernmental coordination, the ability of local governments to decide where development could go, and the autonomy of developers who often had acted alone on development decisions.

Stakeholder Support for Smart Growth

Public, private and nonprofit sector leadership in the Atlanta region, and to a lesser degree throughout the state, supported Barnes's new initiatives for smart growth. The Republican minority leader in the state Senate and many other legislators declared their support of efforts to begin to deal with urban sprawl, although with considerable caution. Some feared that home rule and private property rights would be undermined, while others feared that Barnes would not move far or fast enough to get on top of the problem. Key support also came from Jerry Griffin, executive director of the ACCG, who noted, "the problem has to be solved on a regional basis. It can't ever be done county by county" (Goldberg 1999a, D5).

Some advocates of change felt that early movement on all the components of Barnes's initiatives would be best. However, full implementation of the transportation initiative, in particular, would radically change growth management in the 10-county Atlanta region and three adjoining counties under the federal Clean Air Act mandate to improve their air quality or lose federal transportation funding. Barnes himself saw creating a new transportation agency as "only a start at coming to grips with the quality-of-life, environmental, and economic consequences of poorly managed growth" (Goldberg 1999a, D5).

The Metro Atlanta Transportation Initiative (MATI), formed in June 1998 by the Metro Atlanta Chamber of Commerce, was one of the leadership groups that supported new initiatives for smart growth (Goldberg 1998b, D5). MATI was viewed by John Sibley of the Georgia Conservancy (the only nonbusiness entity asked to participate) as containing the key "heavy hitters" in business and industry in the Atlanta region. Another group with significant potential was a legislative committee named by the powerful House Speaker Tom Murphy to review ARC's overall structure and responsibilities (Goldberg 1998b, D5). This committee seemed destined to be a major player, since Murphy strongly supported Barnes.

The Georgia Conservancy emerged by the mid-1990s to reexamine and support major changes in Georgia's growth management system, and has remained a key player in moving Georgia and the Atlanta region in a smart growth direction. Some of its programs, such as its Watershed Initiative, looked at water quality and quantity statewide, and encouraged citizen groups to build and sustain support for watershed plans and implementing regulations (Boring 1997, 1–4). The conservancy's Blueprints for Successful Communities program clearly took smart growth beyond an environmental agenda (Georgia Conservancy 1997a, 6–7). The program grew out of the organization's 1995 effort to collaborate with private sector groups in examining the pros and cons of the outer beltway, strongly supported by the Georgia DOT, and linked air quality, water quantity and quality, traffic and other problems directly to sprawl. The program selected a number of communities where workshops were held to address specific development issues. Key players representing diverse interests assisted a community to develop a vision for the future (Georgia Conservancy 1997b). The entire community would then be invited to address the options for growth and development and reach consensus with regard to goals (Georgia Conservancy Undated, 1–2).

The Blueprints program also cosponsored a smart growth conference on September 11–12, 1998, in Atlanta, attended by more than 350 people. One of the key features was a call by Jim Chaffin Jr., president of the Urban Land Institute and leader of ULI's Smart Growth Initiative, for a new approach to enable all stakeholders to agree on smart growth planning and practices. The key questions explored at the conference were, "What sustainable practices can Georgia's communities adopt?" and "How can those practices move from vision to reality?" At the end of the conference, participants agreed on a list of recommendations to be forwarded to DCA, the Growth Strategies Reassessment Task Force, MATI and Governor-elect Barnes.

■ Establish a state vision and corresponding guidelines that reflect sustainable land use practices and environmental integrity.

■ Ensure local comprehensive plans reflect the vision.

■ Coordinate actions of all state agencies so they reflect the state vision.

■ Pass a state constitutional amendment to allow use of gas tax revenues for projects other than roads and bridges. (Georgia Conservancy 1998, 1, 6–7)

The Georgia Regional Transportation Authority

During fall 1998 Barnes was involved in drafting a proposal for a Georgia Regional Transportation Authority (GRTA). Introduced in the Senate on January 25, 1999, the proposal called for a 15-member board, appointed by the governor without Senate approval, to oversee the new agency. Initially, GRTA's authority would extend to ARC's 10 counties and three adjacent counties only, subject to the air quality standards that, if not met, would block federal transportation dollars. The authority would, however, extend its control to other urban areas such as Macon, Columbus and Augusta, if they failed to meet the stricter new federal air quality standards. DOT would become mainly the department of rural roads. The authority as proposed did not have direct taxing power but could issue up to $2 billion in bonds to be repaid by revenue generated by the authority. Supporters, cautious and otherwise, included ARC's Harry West and business leaders who served on the board of MATI (Goldberg 1999b, 5D).

The critical first question about GRTA was whether it could win a majority vote in both houses of the General Assembly without being rendered "toothless." The answer, a resounding *yes*, illustrated that most legislators recognized the need for tough measures to reverse the traffic congestion–air quality–sprawl crisis that threatened the state's economic and environmental future. To the surprise of many, GRTA (introduced as SB 57) passed both houses by a large margin (41–12 in the Senate; 158–14 in the House), with no crippling amendments (Georgia 1999). GRTA clearly could be one of the most powerful land use–transportation–air quality agencies in the nation. To counter some business concerns, however, Barnes assured the state that GRTA would not shut down development, but would promote growth "that is served by infrastructure" (Firestone 1999).

As the process moved forward, the governor named a number of outstanding civic, business and corporate leaders to the GRTA board. Joel Cowan was named chair, and John Sibley, now president of the Georgia Conservancy, was named one of the 15 members. GRTA seemed to have the key ingredients of a regional agency with teeth: support of the governor; the power to reject local governments in nonattainment areas; large amounts of money to initiate actions to further its regional goals; and the support of private, public and nonprofit sector interests. Still uncertain was whether that support could be maintained when GRTA said *no* to local governments on land use and transportation issues they had been deciding for themselves for more than 30 years. Nevertheless, the determination to change land use and transportation decisions in the direction of smart growth did advance on several fronts.

GRTA has been described by Alan Ehrenhalt as follows:

> The law places Barnes at the head of a sprawl-fighting super-agency that can practically dictate land-use decisions all over the Metropolitan area. It can tell the state Department of Transportation not to build a highway. It can tell a county not to allow a new shopping mall within its borders. If it wants to, it can build and operate a mass transit system in any of the jurisdictions surrounding Atlanta. It can then force those jurisdictions to pay for it by threatening to take away their state financing. (Ehrenhalt 1999, A29)

Ehrenhalt predicted that "something like the GRTA debate will soon surface elsewhere. Public officials, citizen activities and chambers of commerce throughout the nation have begun to talk about sprawl in terms they used to reserve for pornography or communism." He continued by noting that the broad-based support for the assault on sprawl had produced a counterattack by freemarket think tanks, "in which they argue that sprawl is actually a good thing." But, he said, "They're too late. The American people are coming to the conclusion that sprawl is to blame for a good deal of the discontent...and this change of mind will shake up politics in many ways in the first decade of the 21st century" (Ehrenhalt 1999, A29). Ehrenhalt's prediction is in effect a central theme of this book—that movement in the direction of smart growth has deep roots and broad support, and will be reflected in the development and implementation of smart growth initiatives across the nation.

Another analysis of the remarkable scope of GRTA saw the legislation as having "the power to veto almost any new transportation project and control regionally significant development in the Metro Atlanta area, as well as the power to shape growth throughout the remainder of the state" (Cohen and Kirk 1999, 1). That analysis highlighted a number of other GRTA powers that have been or seem likely to be important to Georgia's continuing smart growth efforts:

- In a provision that could greatly expand GRTA's already major revenue bonding authority, GRTA may direct GEFA "to issue revenue bonds, bonds, notes, credit agreements or other obligations to finance any GRTA project within the GRTA jurisdiction."

- Barnes' designation of the GRTA board as the Governor's Development Council gives it wide-ranging powers to "coordinate, supervise and review planning by state agencies, including the coordination of long-range planning and the location and construction of public facilities pursuant to the statewide plan that GRTA will develop with assistance from the Department of Community Affairs."

- The act authorizes GRTA to "make grants or loans to a local government to pay all or part of the cost of any 'project,'" with "project" broadly defined to include meeting "land use and public transportation needs and environmental standards to aid in the accomplishment of the purposes of [GRTA]."

■ The act provides that any local government under GRTA's jurisdiction that "fails or refuses to plan, coordinate, or implement services as provided in the Act...is deemed ineligible to receive any state grant of any kind," with certain exceptions regarding the well-being of the residents. Georgia DOT funds or federal transportation funds may not be expended if the "local government is non-cooperative with the mission of GRTA," again with narrowly drawn exceptions. (Cohen and Kirk 1999, 9, 10)

GRTA and Smart Growth in the Atlanta Region

GRTA's first major action was in connection with its approval of ARC's three-year Transportation Improvement Program and its commitment to ensure that the region's local governments implemented the transportation–land use actions. The federal DOT and EPA had asked the region's ten counties and three adjacent counties to commit to pay their share of the transportation projects included in the plan, and to adopt land use policies to support the projects. The response was minimal, and GRTA told local governments to adopt land use policies consistent with the transportation strategies in the Regional Transportation Plan and its three-year implementation compo-

nent, or suffer the consequences. GRTA's Cowan made it clear that GRTA could and would withhold federal and state dollars for local road projects (Simmons 2000, H3; Seabrook 2000a, E5).

ARC finally produced an RTP and TIP that found favor with both GRTA and the federal DOT and EPA. In addition, ARC designed a series of related policy initiatives to draw local governments fully into the implementation process. The details of ARC's proposed 25-year, $37 billion RTP hold the key to why it ultimately, with the help of GRTA, won approval at the federal level as a plan that could move the region from a nonattainment status for air quality and, in the process, move it in the direction of smart growth.

Developed in 1998 and presented in 14 public forums for citizen comment, the RTP and the TIP were adopted on March 22, 2000. The $37 billion

---

Relationship Among Various ARC Initiatives

Vision 2020
↓
The Regional Development Plan (RDP)
↓
The Regional Transportation Plan (RTP)
↓
The Transportation Improvement Program (TIP)
↓
Land Use Strategy
↓
Livable Centers Initiative
↓
Critical Choices Project
↓
Community Choices in 2000

Revised Policies of the RDP

1. Encourage new development to be more clustered in portions of the region where such opportunities exist.
2. Strengthen and enhance the residential and mixed-use character of the central business district and city and town centers.
3. Strengthen and enhance the residential and mixed-use character of existing and emerging activity centers.
4. Encourage mixed-use redevelopment of corridors where public services are currently available.
5. Encourage transit-oriented development.
6. Support the preservation of stable, single-family neighborhoods.
7. Encourage focused infill and redevelopment where acceptable to communities.
8. Encourage mixed-use development.
9. Encourage traditional neighborhood developments.
10. Protect environmentally sensitive areas.
11. Align local policy and regulation to support these policies.
12. Support growth management through local and state institutional arrangements.
13. Encourage the utilization of best development practices.
14. Create an ongoing regional land use coordinating committee.

Source: ARC, 1999b, 3–7

RTP and $1.9 billion TIP represented a sharp shift in transportation investments from roads to public transportation (rail and bus systems) and extensive new sidewalks and bicycle lanes. Of the $37 billion RTP, $20 billion was earmarked for transit facilities and $500 million for new bicycle and pedestrian facilities, plus a "massive investment" in land use strategies that will support the pioneering transportation initiatives found throughout the TIP. The $1.9 billion TIP, over three years for the initial priority projects for the RTP, allocated some 40 percent of that amount for transit facilities, including $20 million for regional bus purchases and $178 million for commuter rail. ARC projected that its 10-county region would gain one million new residents by 2025, for a total of 4.4 million, so key elements of the plan included vehicle emission control strategies, investments in alternatives to the automobile and new, smarter growth land use policies. The TIP also included $23 million for "smart growth studies" and initial implementation of plans through the Livable Centers Initiative (ARC 1999c, 3–4; 2000f, 4; 2000b, 1–2).

The ARC board, headed first by Harry West and later Charles "Chick" Krautler, moved aggressively to draft and implement strategies that would move the Atlanta region in a smart growth direction. At its May 24, 2000, meeting the board adopted a land use strategy that included an implementation timetable aimed at helping local governments make their comprehensive plans consistent with ARC's RTP and TIP (ARC 2000a, 2; West 2000, 3–4). The June 2000 board meeting of GRTA signed off on ARC's TIP. In a closely related action, ARC's Livable Centers Initiative supported the updated RDP, which had been approved by the board in May 1999. That was a revision of the plan first developed in 1997 as a way to implement Vision 2020.

As we assess the ARC initiatives, it is important to keep two things in mind. These initiatives are connected to each other to assure the full implementation of the RDP, the 25-year RTP and the three-year TIP. All are aimed at promoting a smart growth agenda for the Atlanta region and all of Georgia. Add to this scenario GRTA, which had the power and, while Barnes was governor, the will to see that local governments would actually do their part in implementing the smart growth strategies emerging out of the goals of the RDP, the RTP and the TIP. Krautler and other key actors in this drama stressed at every turn the critical importance of linking land use and transportation planning and implementation in very specific ways (Krautler 2000, A11).

ARC's development of the 1999 RDP was a parallel and closely tied to development of the RTP and TIP. The 14 revised policies of the RDP were to guide the region's growth in the future. The last four policies ensured that the first 10 are implemented, including support for the recommendations of the state's Growth Strategies Reassessment Task Force (Policy 12). Taken together, these policies articulate all the key elements of smart growth for the Atlanta

---

Livable Centers Initiative Goals

1. Provide funding for development of activity/town centers that showcase the integration of land use policy and regulation for transportation investments and urban design tools.

2. Encourage a diversity of medium-to-high-density neighborhoods, employment, shopping and recreation choices at activity/town centers.

3. Provide access to a range of travel modes, including transit, roadways, walking and biking to enable access to all uses within the study area.

4. Encourage integration of uses with transportation investments to maximize use of alternate modes.

5. Through transportation investments, increase the desirability of redevelopment of land served by existing infrastructure at activity/town centers.

6. Preserve the historical characteristics of activity/town centers; create a community identity.

7. Develop a community-based TIP at the activity/town center level that will identify capital projects, which can be funded in the annual TIP.

8. Provide transportation infrastructure incentives for jurisdictions to take local actions to implement the resulting activity/town center study goals.

9. Provide for development and implementation of Smart Growth initiatives and Best Development Practices at the study area, local government and regional levels.

10. Develop a local planning outreach process that promotes the involvement of all stakeholders, particularly low-to-moderate income and minority citizens.

Source: ARC, 2000e 2

region, and are supported by the other initiatives as well (ARC 1999b, 3–7).

The Livable Centers Initiative made substantial planning and implementation dollars available to the region's local governments on a competitive basis—$5 million over a five-year period starting in 1999. The planning phase, titled Activity Center/Town Center Investment Policy Studies (ACTIPS), preceded allocation of $350 million in implementation funds from TIP resources. A local match of 20 percent was required to be provided by the sponsoring local government or nonprofit sponsor. This initiative was under way by 1999–2000, with the first 12 communities and nonprofits awarded a total of $800,000, from a total of 51 applications. A lively discussion ensued over how some of the $350 million could go to local governments or nonprofits with developed plans that would meet the criteria for the implementation grants (Saporta 2000, C3). The key point is that significant dollars were being put on the table for planning and implementing projects that met a smart growth model throughout the region.

The Community Choices initiative aimed at taking the Quality Growth Principles from the RDP to the citizens of the region, focusing on "diverse citizen involvement to include more of the region's residents, particularly low-income and minority populations who are typically underrepresented at the planning table" (ARC 1999a 3; 2000d). Tools included GIS software, such as video display methods and graphic 3D visualization tools, to help citizens participate in the planning process. Another program initiated in 1999 was ARC's Developments of Excellence Awards, designed to honor developments that reflected initiatives such as mixed uses, traditional neighborhood developments and other principles of smart growth.

ARC's Job Access Transportation Coalition was supported by a $400,000 grant in federal funds "to plan and develop an integrated multi-year Regional Job Access Plan to improve access to employment opportunities for individuals transitioning from welfare to work, as well as other low-income populations in the Atlanta Region." The 65-member task force was to develop a comprehensive plan addressing job access and reverse commute (ARC 2000c, 4).

A report by the Brookings Institution Center on Urban and Metropolitan Policy (2000) deserves a brief assessment because it listed three actions needed by the Atlanta region in order to address the issue of sprawl.

1. A transportation agenda that embraces an alternative vision of land use and invests in public transit as a competitive necessity.

2. An ambitious housing agenda that stimulates the development of affordable housing for low-, moderate- and middle-income households.

3. An economic development agenda that leverages public and private sector investments in the slow-growing portions of the city and nearby counties.

The report also stressed the need "to recognize the pervasive role of race in shaping metropolitan growth patterns and undertake sustained efforts to give African-Americans and other minorities greater access to educational and economic opportunities" (Brookings Institution 2000, 4–16).

Other Legislative Actions, 1999–2002

The approval by the 1999 General Assembly of Barnes's proposal for GRTA was seen as the major output of that session, and was a clear demonstration of support for the governor in the General Assembly, including from some moderate Republicans. Leading up to the 2000 General Assembly, however, the governor was engaged in his first priority for the session: a major revamping of the state's education system.

On the environmental front, in August 1999 Barnes announced his intention to propose a Greenspace Initiative and named a broad-based Greenspace Committee to produce a specific proposal for the 2000 legislative session. As recommended by the committee and later approved by the General Assembly as SB 399, "Georgia's 40 fastest-growing and most populated counties are eligible to share in state grants to purchase and permanently protect 20 percent of their undeveloped land" (Georgia 2000; Seabrook 2000b, C2). Participating counties must amend their comprehensive plans to be consistent with the goals of the program and to realize the 20 percent goal through their land acquisition and zoning regulations. The program is voluntary, and a city within the county may also participate.

The act and rules adopted by the Georgia Board of Natural Resources make some types of land not eligible for development (ballfields, large lakes) and stressed that "undeveloped property that harbors scenic beauty or provides 'informal recreation'" was desirable (Seabrook 2000b, C2). The $30 million appropriated by the 2000 General Assembly for fiscal year 2001 would support the first round of grants, and the governor indicated that he would ask for an annual $30 million for future years. In July 2000 Barnes named a five-member Community Greenspace Commission, which was responsible for making the decisions on fund distribution to the counties (ACCG 2000, 14).

Another significant initiative sponsored by Barnes and approved by the 2000 General Assembly was the OneGeorgia Authority (SB 398), which created a new state agency headed by the governor as chairman and an executive director appointed by Barnes. The authority was to earmark about one-third of the state's $4.8 billion settlement from Georgia's lawsuits against tobacco companies to assist with economic development activities for the poorest counties in the state. With other Barnes initiatives such as GRTA focused at least initially on the greater Atlanta region, this program addressed the "two-Georgias" dilemma and broadened Barnes's base of support outside the Atlanta region (Pruitt 2000, D5).

All of these Barnes initiatives passed the 2000 legislative session with ease. So what happened to the hard-core conservative Republicans in the Georgia General Assembly? As might be expected, they were biding their time in the hope that Barnes and the Democrats would somehow self-destruct so they could further their agenda of tax cuts and other limitations on government. While the Republican minority leadership did not expect to gain control of either house in the 2000 General Assembly, they seemed convinced that redistricting would put them in a position to win at least one legislative chamber in the 2002 elections.

Governor Barnes continued to make education his top priority in the 2001 legislative session, including expansion of the Promise Scholarship Program,

providing forgivable loans to those who commit to becoming teachers. Barnes also proposed legislation to speed up GRIP to improve roads in rural Georgia, started by Governor Harris more than a decade earlier. Barnes's goal was to finish GRIP within seven years instead of previous projections of 17–22 years. On the urban transportation side, the governor asked the legislature to support a reduction to 10 years for Atlanta metro area's highest priority transportation needs, with a special focus on high occupancy vehicle (HOV) lanes, buses and rail, to assure that the region would meet the air quality standards set at the federal level. Barnes also pledged continued support for the OneGeorgia Authority to bring better times to Georgia's poorest counties. Finally, Barnes offered a legislative package aimed at correcting the state's water quality and quantity problems, including a study committee to recommend statewide policies for water management (GMA 2001, 3).

Lt. Governor Mark Taylor asked the General Assembly to strengthen the work of the Georgia Rural Development Council (GRDC), which he chaired, by providing $500,000 to DCA's budget for a statewide Leadership Collaborative and a Leadership Initiative carried out through the state university system to help rural areas improve their economies and quality of life (GMA 2001, 3). Taken together, Barnes's and Taylor's legislative agendas for the 2001 session continued their strategy of combining good policy with good politics by building support in both rural and urban areas (especially the Atlanta region).

Key Developments in the 2002 Legislative Session

What follows is a very selective account of actions by the 2002 Georgia Senate and House focused on matters relating to smart growth prospects for Georgia. Public Transit Actions, HB 1245, involved the Metropolitan Atlanta Regional Transit Authority (MARTA) and brought about a key change in the funding ratio in the use of the 1 percent sales tax dollars collected for MARTA, the largest transit system in Georgia serving the Atlanta region's central counties. The original ratio, in place for three decades, worked well for a long time, but by 2002 the original 50 percent for capital improvements and 50 percent for operating costs "threatened MARTA's service and affordability and thus its ridership. To prevent immediate loss of service routes and immediate fare increases, a bill was introduced to allow operating costs to rise to 55 percent of total revenues" (Georgia Conservation Voters 2002). The bill passed the House by a 98–64 vote margin and the Senate by 43–5. While not solving all funding problems for the system, HB 1245 was a critical short-term action to promote smart growth development in the Atlanta region.

Another bill that passed the legislature, HB 587, would have had the effect of making "certain kinds of pollution legal, even if the pollution is known to be unhealthy to certain populations." The Georgia Environmental Protection Division (GEPD) was to conduct a cost-benefit analysis that could have blocked "new, beneficial regulations that account for the current scientific understanding of the effects of toxic pollution by miring the state government in 'paralysis by analysis.'" Governor Barnes vetoed the bill, however, and the veto was not overridden (Georgia Conservation Voters 2002).

SB 59 addressed the subject of billboards and would have eased "the restrictions on billboard advertisements by reducing the distance between billboards…and decreasing the time between rotations of multiple messages from ten seconds to six seconds." Considered a very bad bill by smart growth advocates, who felt that Georgia had a bad reputation across the country for the number and size of its billboards, SB 59 passed the Senate by a 30–20 vote and easily passed the House 98–66. Again Barnes vetoed it, on May 17, 2002, and his veto was not overridden.

From the perspective of the Georgia Municipal Association, SB 438, *Greenspace Trust Fund: Allocation to Cities,* was a strong positive. The bill

> allows cities located in counties that receive an annual amount over $500,000 from the Georgia Community Greenspace Trust Fund to apply for direct matching grants for city greenspace projects. The matching grants funds will come from 10 percent of the host county's share of appropriated greenspace funds. This legislation would affect grants beginning in fiscal year 2003. (GMA 2002, 1)

SB 438 is singled out as an important tool to support urban greenspace, an important smart growth component. Another action favored by GMA was the passage of HB 1002, which provided for Georgia's fiscal year 2003 budget to include "$1.5 million in funding to the Georgia Cities Foundation…[and] provides Local Development Funds for the Department of Community Affairs" (GMA 2002, 3).

As the election for governor and the legislature approached in 2002, the prospects for sustaining Georgia's move to smart growth seemed as good or better than those of any other state we have examined in this book. The state appeared to have in place all the key ingredients for crafting, sustaining and ultimately implementing a smart growth system: a governor strongly committed to moving the state to smart growth; a General Assembly demonstrably supportive of the governor's initiatives; and critical support from the private sector. Finally, broad-based coalitions brought all key stakeholders to support smart growth initiatives. The popular support for Barnes's reelection in 2002 seemed strong, and while there were naysayers in the General Assembly and elsewhere, it seemed unlikely that they could stop Georgia's move to smart growth.

Political Upheaval in the 2002 Elections

A poll conducted by the *Atlanta Journal-Constitution* in late September and early October 2002 showed Governor Barnes leading his Republican opponent George Ervin "Sonny" Perdue III by a 49–42 margin. Support for Barnes was strongest among African-American voters, but the poll did not show an easy win. Those who said they were certain to vote were more likely to be white and Republican, a group giving Perdue a 47–44 percent lead, which made the race too close to call (Salzer 2002). Barnes's most far-reaching and well-known initiative was legislative approval for GRTA to develop and implement regional traffic plans that helped the Atlanta region gain billions of dollars in federal transportation money. However, Perdue argued in his campaign that he had not seen any results from GRTA.

The Republicans shocked most outside observers and themselves by winning the governor's race, capturing that office for the first time in 130 years; gaining eight of thirteen congressional seats; and winning a U.S. Senate seat against Democrat Max Cleland, considered an almost sure winner. Republican Perdue defeated incumbent Barnes by a margin of 52–46 percent (Snow 2002). Lt. Governor Taylor, reelected in 2002, still presides over the Senate, and no coalition of Republicans and Democrats has come together in an attempt to use Senate rules to replace him as presiding officer. Democrats kept a solid majority in the House (106 to 73 Republicans and one Independent), but one of the greatest shockers occurred when House Speaker Murphy lost his first election in 42 years. Independently elected state officials such as the Secretary of State, Lt. Governor, Labor Commissioner and Insurance Commissioner were all reelected.

Some saw the key factor in the outcome as "the national Republican tide" of 2002, but voter turnout also played a significant role. In Barnes's five highest vote-producing counties, all with heavy African-American populations, the average turnout was 52 percent. In Perdue's five top counties, mostly white suburbs of Atlanta, the average turnout was 59 percent. Across the state, Barnes won in a majority of Georgia counties in 1998, but he lost or tied in a majority in 2002 (Tammam and Galloway 2002).

Ongoing Policy Challenges and Smart Growth Actions

For the Atlanta region and Georgia as a whole, any chance for a sustainable future seems tied to a major new revenue source to link land use and transportation in a way to assure Georgia a smart growth future (Hairston 2003). Governor Barnes set aside $90 million over three years to buy greenspace in Georgia's fastest growing counties, a program that Perdue supports, as he does Barnes's water supply and conservation initiatives. However, *Georgia Trend* magazine saw governor-elect Perdue confronted with "a unique set of problems. To keep his campaign pledges…he must tear down and put aside many of the accomplishments of exiting Gov. Roy Barnes" (Shipp 2002, 122).

In spite of the unexpected change in gubernatorial leadership, some smart growth measures and organizations continue to have a strong presence in Georgia. One positive effort to promote smart growth

strategies is the Georgia Quality Growth Partnership (GQGP), "a collaboration among diverse public and private entities that provides local governments and citizens with the tools and knowledge to transform the way we define, create and sustain high quality Georgia communities" (GQGP Undated). The 33 founding members included home builders, universities, the Metro Atlanta Chamber of Commerce, the Trust for Public Land, DCA, GMA, GRTA, the Georgia Conservancy and many others.

Formed in March 2000, GQGP has expanded its services and membership with expertise in a wide range of topics (GQGP Undated). Realizing that what works for one community might not work for another, GQGP offers solutions in the form of options, not one-size-fits-all tools. Tool-kit subjects are constantly evolving and building a comprehensive set of growth management solutions. In addition to sharing cutting-edge information through its Web site, the GQGP has teams of volunteer experts who

---

Guiding Principles of GQGP's Quality Growth Tool Kit

1. Ensure equitable access for all citizens to a range of options for education, transportation, housing, employment, human services, culture and recreation.

2. Create opportunities for citizens to learn more about community planning and actively encourage their involvement in public decision-making.

3. Respect and protect our natural resources—wildlife, land, water, air and trees.

4. Shape appealing physical environments that enhance walkability and positive social interaction.

5. Recognize that community decisions have an impact on neighboring jurisdictions and, therefore, must be made from a responsible regional and statewide perspective.

6. Incorporate practices learned from our local experience as well as from other communities and cultures.

7. Preserve and enhance our cultural and historic places for future generations.

8. Provide for the efficient and economical use of public infrastructure.

9. Employ the principles of sustainability and balance to ensure the economic viability of all communities and to enhance the state's economic competitiveness.

Source: GQGP, Undated

visit communities on request to help with growth and development issues.

Another positive sign of a continued smart growth presence is that Georgia's DCA has not been dismantled or somehow merged into oblivion, as has happened to planning agencies in some other states. While some key staff have left state service, others are actively promoting smart growth initiatives under Rick Brooks, director of DCA's Planning and Environmental Management Division.

Under the Georgia Planning Act of 1989, DCA is charged with adopting minimum standards for local governments to adhere to in their comprehensive planning efforts. DCA's Minimum Planning Standards Task Force recommended proposed changes, adopted in November 2002, to substantially strengthen Georgia's ability to plan and manage its growth. Local plan updates will have to be consistent with the new standards after they go into effect on January 1, 2004.

The new minimum standards rule includes two key changes that strengthen the requirements for local comprehensive planning and provide greater flexibility in terms of planning level thresholds. One change allows regional development centers (RDCs) to add another planning element to currently mandated comprehensive planning elements. Any new requirements for local planning adopted by RDCs will apply to their member governments only, including mandated consistency with the regional plan. The second, more far-reaching change, established three-tiered standards to address the fact that the size and rate of growth of communities result in their having different needs: *basic*, very similar to the current standards; and *intermediate* and *advanced* that have additional requirements, including a much needed transportation element that links transportation and land use. Taking the planning standards revisions as a whole (and given that they will be implemented between 2004 and 2008 as all local governments prepare major required updates to their plans), they constitute a very significant strengthening of smart growth strategies for Georgia (Georgia DCA 2003a, 1–6).

Looking again at the Atlanta region, forecasters are predicting that "the 10-county Atlanta area will be home to more than 6 million people by the year 2030,

2003 ARC Smart Growth Strategy

1. Provide development strategies and infrastructure investments to accommodate forecasted population and development growth more efficiently.
2. Guide an increased share of new development to the central business district, transportation corridors and activity/town centers.
3. Increase opportunities for mixed-use development, infill and redevelopment.
4. Increase transportation choices and transit-oriented development (TOD).
5. Provide a variety of housing choices throughout the region to ensure housing for individuals and families of diverse incomes and age groups.
6. Preserve and enhance existing residential neighborhoods.
7. Advance sustainable development.
8. Protect environmentally sensitive areas.
9. Create a regional network of greenspace that connects across jurisdictional boundaries.
10. Preserve existing rural character.
11. Preserve historic resources.
12. Inform and involve the public in planning at regional, local and neighborhood levels.
13. Coordinate local policies and regulations to support the Regional Development Plan.
14. Support growth management at the state level.

Source: ARC, 2003, 3

an increase of nearly 2.3 million new residents" (ARC 2003, 1). The challenge is clear: how to absorb that much growth and enhance the quality of life for the region's urban, rural or suburban residents. In March 2003 ARC's board incorporated 14 new policies into its RDP. Those same policies could well comprise the key components of a smart growth strategy for a complex and rapidly growing region anywhere in the nation.

Mobility 2030 is the new name for ARC's 25-year plan addressing transportation goals. ARC noted that "the region is currently slated to invest nearly $40 billion through 2025 to provide a host of new transportation options.... Even at this level of new investments, our traffic congestion challenges are not solved over the next 25 years" (ARC 2003, 6). Scheduled to be adopted by the ARC board in late 2003, it is obvious that new sources of revenue will be needed to ensure

Mobility 2030's implementation. After developing a draft plan during 2003, ARC conducted extensive public outreach in each county in the region to refine the program and build stakeholder support for the solution.

This outreach effort, known as the Platforms for Progress program, involved a public opinion poll, conducted in concert with the Carl Vinson Institute of Government, to identify the residents' priorities in the region. Those surveyed were asked to rank 22 goals in the areas of "civic engagement, regional prosperity, education, air quality, transportation and environment. On a scale of 1 to 10 (with 1 being unimportant and 10 extremely important), the 22 goals averaged 8.1, with none scoring less than 7.0" (ARC 2003, 2). Improving the quality of education got the highest score: 9.3 on the 10-point scale. ARC's Platforms for Progress team began traveling around the region to present survey findings to key members of the public, private and community sectors.

A second initiative involved new efforts to meet the region's housing needs, and in March 2003 ARC cosponsored the Regional Housing Forum, a series of workshops intended to share information about housing research and tools. The problem, certainly not unique to the Atlanta region, grows out of "a combination of rising housing costs, flat wages, and government spending cuts," causing families to "spend more of [their] income on housing while lower-income workers and even police officers, fire fighters, and teachers are...priced out of the areas they serve, unable to afford the housing costs where they work" (ARC 2003, 2). John McIlwain, a senior housing fellow at the Urban Land Institute and keynote speaker at the first Regional Housing Forum, suggested several ways to provide more affordable housing, all of which have been effective in areas around the nation. Among his recommendations were inclusionary zoning and green-taping, where a developer willing to build affordable housing "moves to the front of the line" in getting permitted (ARC 2003, 2).

The Atlanta region's long history of transportation problems and its testing of key provisions in federal clean air and transportation laws reached a legal conclusion in 2003 after more than four years of litigation. In early 1999 the Southern Environmental

Law Center (in concert with the Georgia Conservancy, Georgians for Transportation Alternatives, and Georgia's chapter of the Sierra Club) filed a lawsuit in federal court "aimed at holding the local, state and federal transportation officials accountable for air pollution resulting from future highway construction." The suit was prompted by what the plaintiffs viewed as illegal actions by Georgia DOT, ARC and the USDOT in 1997 in using loopholes in the Clean Air Act to approve over 60 transportation projects, many of which were deemed to actually exacerbate problems with air quality and traffic congestion.

On June 16, 2003, the 11th U.S. Circuit Court of Appeals in Atlanta ruled that "the EPA should not have granted the metro area more time to clean up its polluted air." As a result, the ten-county Atlanta region and three adjacent counties were redesignated a "severe" ozone nonattainment region effective January 1, 2004. The court "rejected EPA's argument that it could administratively extend the 1999 statutory deadline for 'serious' nonattainment areas to meet the one-hour ozone standard" (Farren 2003). EPA's Deputy Regional Administrator Stan Meiburg stated that he was pleased with the court decision "because it clarifies the agency's role in approving state air quality plans" (Shelton 2003). This will bring greater pressure to bear on the Atlanta region to strengthen its capacity to keep the air clean or lose its eligibility for federal transportation dollars as a key source of funds to support major investments in public transit. The demand for a well-funded regional approach is made more urgent by the latest U.S. Census Bureau figures that show the Atlanta MSA expanding to 28 counties (Georgia State University 2003), making it very likely that more than the present 13 counties will be subject to the stricter air quality standards.

Another old transportation issue, addressing interstate highway links around the region, also seems to have been resolved. The Northern Arc connecting I-85 and I-75 was the only part of the former outer perimeter project not removed from state and regional plans back in the mid-1990s. On August 18, 2003, the *Atlanta Journal-Constitution* noted, "Gov. Sonny Perdue has declared the Northern Arc dead, but the final bullet won't be fired until late next year. Perdue has thrown out the road's funding plan and ordered the state Department of Transportation to stop work on the project." Perdue and longtime anti–Arc activists want the 59-mile toll road removed from Metro Atlanta's long-term transportation plan, but that will take time. ARC will not vote on the plan until fall 2004, and Jane Hayse, ARC chief transportation planner, stated that it's "highly unlikely" the road will be in the revised plan. According to Hayse, one stretch of the Northern Arc in Gwinnet County will be recommended. At a transportation town hall meeting in Forsyth County, Perdue repeated his promise that the highway is dead, "I'm a Baptist, and I don't believe in reincarnation." As for the future use of the Northern Arc, Jeff Anderson, president of the Northern Arc Task Force, a citizen group that has been given major credit for killing the road, favors converting the property "into a greenway with trails" (Stanford 2003).

In late 2003 and early 2004, Governor Perdue took a number of other actions that are directly relevant to a smart growth future for Georgia and have brought strong praise from environmental groups in Georgia and beyond. The Georgia Environmental Action Network (GEAN), an online collaborative effort among environmental and conservation organizations throughout the state, singled out three actions by Perdue as being positive for Georgia's environmental future.

1. The appointment of Dr. Carol Couch, a biologist and ecologist, to direct the Georgia Environmental Protection Division, the first time a woman or a scientist has held that position.

2. Naming the Georgia Land Conservation Partnership to promote land conservation statewide, and an advisory panel that will work to identify priorities statewide for land preservation, develop a statewide land conservation plan, and recommend changes in the law to further enhance land preservation efforts.

3. A pledge to support passage of a bill by the 2004 legislature to create a statewide water plan. The governor had created the Georgia Water Resources Council to ensure coordination, cooperation and communication among state agencies

and their water-related programs and activities. (GEAN Undated)

These actions, each a critical component of any state's smart growth strategy, were especially significant coming from a governor from whom most Georgia smart growth advocates had expected negative, not positive, actions.

On December 23, 2003, Perdue announced that GEFA would be restructured to allow communities across the state greater access to infrastructure loans based on a sliding population scale. The City of Atlanta, for example, will have access to up to $500 million over 10 years, or $50 million a year, for sewer infrastructure improvements. Perdue stressed that, "This is not just about Atlanta. It is part of my vision for clean and adequate water resources through an environmentally sound statewide water plan" (Office of the Governor 2003). Lee Thomas, president of Georgia Pacific and former head of the U.S. EPA, was named chair of a task force to monitor the Atlanta sewer project. This initiative is of critical significance to Atlanta Mayor Shirley Franklin's effort to correct the long-neglected Atlanta sewer system that has been an environmental disaster in the making.

Conclusion: A Smart Growth Path for Georgia?

In January 2004 Neely Young, editor and publisher of *Georgia Trend,* put forward a strongly negative view of the political framework for supporting smart growth strategies in Georgia, specifically focused on the governor's capacity for exercising the leadership that will be needed to follow through on smart growth moves. As Young saw it, "Gov. Sonny Perdue is occupying the weakest position the governor's office has had in the history of modern state politics." He went on to list a number of "sea changes" that have weakened the governor's position.

■ Loss of Perdue's lawsuit against Attorney General Thurbert Baker over congressional reapportionment, when the Georgia Supreme Court ruled that "the governor could not tell the attorney general what to do on any subject." Therefore, Young argued, Perdue "lost any direct influence over other constitutional offices [that] make up a huge part of state government involving millions of dollars."

■ Rejection of Perdue's "call for a tax increase, along with most of his other proposals" by Senate Republican majority leader Eric Johnson.

■ Lack of support for the governor's plans in the House, controlled by Democrats and Speaker Terry Coleman.

■ Diminished influence because the governor "does not have the Big Stick—money. There is no money to pass around for favors to influence senators or representatives for pet projects back home." (Young 2004, 122)

Young concluded that these factors were the reason nothing was really accomplished during the 2003 session of the legislature, and that, unless the governor's "momentum changes, we will get more of the same this year [2004]" (Young 2004, 122). Young did not once refer to those positive actions taken by Perdue and his administration that produced added dollars for smart growth initiatives.

We can say with some certainty that a smart growth future for Georgia was made much more uncertain by the results of the 2002 elections. Even in the best political environment, funding a sustained series of smart growth initiatives would be difficult, given the budget shortfalls faced by the state. Sonny Perdue's election as governor and a Republican majority in the Senate, achieved in part because four Democratic Senators switched to the Republican ranks, made selective tax increases seem highly unlikely. However, all is not gloom and doom in early 2004. At the end of his first year in office Governor Perdue took some actions, including recent key appointments, that have pleasantly surprised many supporters of smart growth in Georgia.

An editorial in the *Atlanta Journal-Constitution* made it clear that more than transportation dollars will be required to assure a smart growth future for the greater Atlanta 13-county region. Spending $50 billion and even more without major changes in the region's "helter-skelter land-use patterns" won't do the job (*Atlanta Journal-Constitution* 2004, E8). The key missing ingredient is in integrating "well intentioned transportation improvements . . . with carefully considered commercial, residential and recreational land-use planning." To achieve that goal, an historically unprecedented level of regional cooperation will be necessary.

And so we conclude with the question, "Is there a smart growth future for Georgia?" No absolute answer to that question is possible. There are some positive indications, including the support of the corporate and business community, and the Georgia Quality Growth Partnership. There are also some negative factors, notably the continued failure to act on the critical need for major new investments in the land use–transportation area.

References

Allison, David. 1995. Bills affecting highways to be discussed. *Atlanta Business Chronicle*. November 6, 17B.

Association of County Commissioners of Georgia (ACCG). 2000. The 2000 Georgia legislature: Hot-button issues for counties. *Georgia County Government*. February.

Association of County Commissioners of Georgia (ACCG), Georgia Municipal Association (GMA), Georgia Department of Community Affairs (DCA), and Carl Vinson Institute of Government, The University of Georgia. 1997. Charting a course for cooperation and collaboration: An introduction to the Service Delivery Strategy Act for local governments. June.

Atlanta Journal-Constitution. 2004. When money flows, traffic still doesn't. August 22: E8.

Atlanta Regional Commission (ARC). 1978. Chattahoochee corridor plan refinement: Evolving issues. Staff working paper. December.

———. 1989. Guide to Atlanta Regional Commission.

———. 1991. *Action* 20.2. February.

———. 1992a. *Action* 22.11. November.

———. 1992b. Atlanta region outlook.

———. 1992c. Atlanta's regional economy.

———. 1992d. Fact sheet for Vision 2020 participants.

———. 1993. *Action* 23.5. May.

———. 1994. *Action* 24.6. August/September.

———. 1995. A community's vision takes flight: Vision 2020, key initiatives for the future.

———. 1996a. 1996 annual report.

———. 1996b. Atlanta region outlook. October.

———. 1999a. *Action* Special edition, 1999 annual report.

———. 1999b. A framework for the future: ARC's Regional Development Plan. October.

———. 1999c. New options on the horizon for Atlanta region travel. *Action* 29.6. November/December.

———. 2000a. ARC adopts innovative land use strategy. *Action* 30.4. July/August.

———. 2000b. ARC board approves long and short-term transportation plans. *Action* 30.3. May/June.

———. 2000c. Coalition formed to develop job access and reverse commute plan for the region. *Action* 30.5. September/October.

———. 2000d. Community choices: The state of smart growth in the Atlanta region, innovative development regulations of local governments. March.

———. 2000e. Livable Centers initiative, project vision and outcomes. March.

———. 2000f. The public has spoken on ARC's transportation plan and program. *Action* 30.2. March/April.

———. 2003. *Action* 33.3. May/June.

Basso, Daniel. 2003. Georgia Department of Community Affairs. Development impact fees? E-mail to Ann Carlson, November 14.

Boring, Lindsay. 1997. Downstream effects of sprawl motivate Georgia communities. *Panorama* 27.4. July/August.

Brookings Institution. 2000. *Moving beyond sprawl: The challenge for metropolitan Atlanta.* Washington, DC: Center on Urban and Metropolitan Policy.

Cohen, Mark H. and David C. Kirk. 1999. *The Georgia Regional Transportation Authority: Implications for planning and development.* Atlanta: Troutman Sanders LLP.

DeGrove, John M. 1992. *The new frontier for land policy: Planning and growth management in the states.* Cambridge, MA: Lincoln Institute of Land Policy.

Ehrenhalt, Alan. 1999. New recruits in the war on sprawl. *New York Times.* April 13, A29.

Farren, J. David. 2003. Atlanta air quality. E-mail to Ann Carlson, November 24.

Firestone, David. 1999. Georgia setting up tough anti-sprawl agency. *New York Times.* March 25.

Georgia. 1989. HB 215, The Georgia Planning Act of 1989. Official Code of Georgia, ch. 70, art. 1, S. 36-70-1.

———. 1999. Georgia Regional Transportation Authority Act, signed into law as SB 57, sec. 7, and codified as O.C.G.A. 50-32-1-70.

———. 2000. SB 399, to amend Title 36 of the Official Code of Georgia Annotated, relating to local government, so as to provide for state and local government activities with respect to preservation of Greenspace.

Georgia Conservancy. 1994. Issue monitor. *Panorama* 24.1. January/February.

———. 1997a. *Blueprints for successful communities: A guide for shaping livable places.*

———. 1997b. Workshop Covington: Results of a community design workshop for Covington, Georgia. November.

———. 1998. "Smart Growth in Georgia!" Two-day conference addresses growth challenges here and abroad. *Panorama* 28.6. November/December.

———. Undated. About the Georgia Conservancy's "Blueprints for Successful Communities." http://www.gaconservancy.org/SmartGrowth/SG_issue01.asp.

Georgia Conservation Voters. 2002 Legislative scorecard. http://www.protectgeorgia.org/2002%20Vote%20Descriptions%20Senate.htm.

Georgia Department of Community Affairs (DCA). 1990a. Data for city planning. Prepared for Peachtree City. October.

———. 1990b. Submittal and review procedures: Developments of regional impact (DRIs) (as adopted by the Board of Community Affairs, January 9).

———. 1991. Procedures for the designation and review of regionally important resources.

———. 1992. Minimum standards and procedures for local comprehensive planning to implement Georgia laws 1989, 1317–1391, Act 634. As amended by the Board of Community Affairs. April.

———. 1993. Growth strategies implementation: Accomplishments of the Office of Coordinated Planning in meeting the requirements of Georgia Planning Act of 1989. May.

———. 1995a. DCA Board resolution. December 13.

———. 1995b. Status of comprehensive planning. September.

———. 1998a. DCA funding: Regional development centers: 1990–1999.

———. 1998b. Status of comprehensive planning. June 1.

———. 2003a. Comparative summary of planning standards revisions, 2003 Edition–2004 Edition.

———. 2003b. Georgia Department of Community Affairs: Status of comprehensive planning. June.

———. Undated. Proposal for planning and growth management task force. Division of Planning and Environmental Management.

Georgia Department of Labor (DOL). Undated. Labor force, employment and unemployment data in Georgia. Georgia QuickStats. http://quickstats.dol.state.ga.us.

Georgia Environmental Action Network (GEAN). Undated. Environmental community thanks Gov. Perdue. http://actionnetwork.org/gean/alert-description.tcl?alert_id=2072797.

Georgia Future Communities Commission (GFCC). 1996. Promoting prosperity in Georgia's communities: A new charter for the 21st Century, preliminary recommendations. October.

———. 1997. 1997 preliminary recommendations: Cooperation, innovation, and shared problem solving. September.

Georgia Governor's Growth Strategies Commission (GSC). 1988a. Interim report—Policy recommendations. June.

———. 1988b. Preliminary report on implementation of coordinated planning. August.

———. 1988c. Quality growth partnership: The bridge to Georgia's future. Final report. November.

———. 1988d. Report of the Task Forces on Economic Development, Capital Investments, Land Use and Natural Resources. Executive summary. March.

———. Undated. A report addressing Georgia's population trends, land and water resources, government structure, economic development, and infrastructure.

Georgia Growth Strategies Reassessment Task Force (GSRTF) 1998. Georgia's future: Beyond growth strategies: Recommendations. December.

Georgia Municipal Association (GMA). 1998. First service delivery strategy deadline fast approaching. *Georgia's Cities* 9.5: May 11.

———. 2001. *Georgia's Cities* 12.2. February 14.

———. 2002. 2002 Legislative session: Summary of key municipal issues.

Georgia Municipal Association (GMA), Association of County Commissioners of Georgia (ACCG), Georgia Department of Community Affairs (DCA), and Carl Vinson Institute of Government, University of Georgia. 1997. HB 489 Information Bulletin #1: Drafting a service delivery strategy: Getting started—Some ideas and suggestions. December.

———. 1998. HB 489 Information Bulletin #2: Establishing an Annexation Dispute Resolution Process. April.

Georgia Quality Growth Partnership (GQGP). Undated. Georgia Quality Growth Partnership website: http://www.georgia qualitygrowth.com/aboutgqgp.html.

Georgia State University. 2003. Race and ethnicity map of Atlanta-Sandy Springs-Marietta MSA. AtlantaCensus2000.

———. Undated. Guiding principles. http://www.georgia qualitygrowth.com/aboutgqgp.html.

Godschalk, David R., Bruce J. M. Knopf and Seth G. Weissman. 1978. *Guiding growth in the South*. Research Triangle Park, NC: Southern Growth Policies Board.

Goldberg, David. 1998a. State urged to prescribe healthier growth: Final report. *Atlanta Journal-Constitution*. December 12, E1.

———. 1998b. Trying to get a grip on the sprawl. *Atlanta Journal-Constitution*. July 12, D5.

———. 1999a. 1999 Georgia legislature: Can Barnes loosen the traffic choke hold? *Atlanta Journal-Constitution*. January 11.

———. 1999b. Detailed road plan en route to state Senate. *Atlanta Journal-Constitution*. January 24.

Hairston, Julie B. 2003. Metro Atlanta encroaches on larger chunk of state. *Atlanta Journal-Constitution*. July 11, A1–A7.

Higdon, Jim. 1998. Fuel for rural development. *Georgia County Government*. May/June.

Kraulter, Charles C. 2000. ARC transit plan a direct route to relief. *Atlanta Journal-Constitution*. August 14, A1.

Miness, Deborah. 2003. E-mail re RIRs (Georgia DCA) to Ann Carlson, November 12.

Office of the Governor. 2003. Governor Perdue provides greater access to community infrastructure loans. Press release. December 23.

Pruitt, Kathey. 2000. Another clean sweep. *Atlanta Journal-Constitution*. March 26, D5.

Salzer, James. 2002. *Atlanta Journal-Constitution*/WSB-TV Poll: Cleland, Barnes lead in new poll, governor's approval rating rises. *Atlanta Journal-Constitution*.

Saporta, Maria. 2000. ARC planning grants stir debate. *Atlanta Journal-Constitution*. August 7, C3.

Seabrook, Charles. 2000a. Air cleanup isn't just for Atlanta. *Atlanta Journal-Constitution*. July 1, E5.

———. 2000b. Rules ok'd to get greenspace grants. *Atlanta Journal-Constitution*. July 27, C2.

Shelton, Stacy. 2003. Court: Fix air or else. *Atlanta Journal-Constitution*. June 18, A1, A6.

Shipp, Bill. 2002. Mandate to deactivate. *Georgia Trend* December: 122.

Simmons, Kelly. 2000. GRTA oks three-year traffic plan. *Atlanta Journal-Constitution*. June 16, H3.

Smith, Elizabeth. 2003. Additional DRIs? (Georgia DCA). E-mail to Ann Carlson. November 12.

Snow, Wayne. 2002. GOP becomes grand new party. *Atlanta Journal-Constitution*. November 10.

Soto, Lucy. 1998. Metro area keeps growing and growing. *Atlanta Journal-Constitution*. August 14.

Stanford, Duane D. 2003. Last rites awaited for ARC. *Atlanta Journal-Constitution*. August 18. http://www.ajc.com/ monday/content/epaper/editions/monday/business_ f3049511036a22c20080.html.

Tammam, Maurice and Jim Galloway. 2002. Election 2002: Rural areas revolted, experts say; State wakes up to "historic realignment." *Atlanta Journal-Constitution*. November 7.

U.S. Census Bureau. Undated. State and county QuickFacts: Georgia. http://quickfacts.census.gov/qfd/states/13000.html.

Walston, Charles. 1998. A talk with Georgia's new governor. *Atlanta Journal-Constitution*. November 8, H8.

West, Harry. 1992. The evolution of growth management in Georgia, *Environmental and Urban Issues* 24:3. Fort Lauderdale, FL: FAU/FIU Joint Center for Environmental and Urban Problems.

———. 2000. West offers parting advice. *Georgia Cities* (GMA) 11.3 March 16: 3–4.

Young, Neely. 2004. Centers of power. *Georgia Trend* 19.5. January.

Appendix

Governors

James Earl (Jimmy) Carter (Democrat)	1971–1975
George D. Busbee (Democrat)	1975–1983
Joe Frank Harris (Democrat)	1983–1991
Zell Bryan Miller (Democrat)	1991–1999
Roy E. Barnes (Democrat)	1999–2002
George Ervin "Sonny" Perdue, III (Republican)	2003–present

Acronyms

ACCG	Association of County Commissioners of Georgia
ACTIPS	Activity Center/Town Center Investment Policy Studies
APDCs	Area Planning and Development Commissions
ARC	Atlanta Regional Commission
CIE	capital improvements element
DCA	Department of Community Affairs
DNR	Department of Natural Resources
DOT	Department of Transportation
DRI	development of regional impact
EDD	economic development district
GDC	Governor's Development Council
GEAN	Georgia Environmental Action Network
GEFA	Georgia Environmental Facilities Authority
GEPD	Georgia Environmental Protection Division
GFCC	Georgia Future Communities Commission
GMA	Georgia Municipal Association
GQGP	Georgia Quality Growth Partnership
GRDC	Georgia Rural Development Council
GRIP	Governor's Road Improvement Program
GRTA	Georgia Regional Transportation Authority
GSC	Growth Strategies Commission
MARTA	Metropolitan Atlanta Regional Transit Authority
MATI	Metro Atlanta Transportation Initiative
MPC	Metropolitan Planning Commission
MSA	Metropolitan Statistical Area
OCP	Office of Coordinated Planning
QLG	qualified local government
RDC	regional development centers
RDP	Regional Development Plan
RIR	regionally important resource
RTP	Regional Transportation Plan
TIP	Transportation Improvement Program

Contacts

Alliance for Quality Growth
University of Georgia
Athens, GA 30602
http://aqg.ecology.uga.edu

Atlanta Regional Commission
40 Courtland Street, NE
Atlanta, GA 30303
404-463-3100
http://www.atlantaregional.com

Georgia Conservancy
817 West Peachtree Street, Suite 200
Atlanta, GA 30308
404-876-2900
http://www.gaconservancy.org/Home/Home.asp

Georgia Cool Communities
204 Broad Street, Suite A
Rome, GA 30161
706-295-7540
http://www.coolcommunities.org

Georgia Department of Community Affairs (DCA)
60 Executive Park South, NE
Atlanta, GA 30329
404-679-4940
http://www.dca.state.ga.us

Georgia Department of Natural Resources (DNR)
2 Martin Luther King Jr. Drive S.E.
Suite 1252 East Tower
Atlanta, GA 30334
404-656-3500
http://www.gadnr.org

Georgia Environmental Action Network
% Georgia Conservancy
http://www.gaconservancy.org/Home/Home_GEAN.asp

Georgia Municipal Association
201 Pryor Street, SW
Atlanta, GA 30303
404-688-0472
http://www.gmanet.com

Georgia Quality Growth Partnership
http://www.georgiaqualitygrowth.com

Georgia Regional Transportation Authority (GRTA)
245 Peachtree Center Avenue N.E., Suite 900
Atlanta, GA 30303
404-463-3000
http://www.grta.org

Institute of Community and Area Development
University of Georgia
1234 S. Lumpkin Street
Athens, GA 30602-3350
706-542-3350

Metropolitan Atlanta Transportation Initiative (MATI)
℅ Metro Atlanta Chamber of Commerce
235 Andrew Young International Boulevard N.W.
Atlanta, GA 30303
404-880-9000
http://www.metroatlantachamber.com

The Nature Conservancy, Georgia Field Office
1330 West Peachtree Street, Suite 410
Atlanta, GA 30309-2904
404-873-6946
http://nature.org/wherewework/northamerica/states/
   georgia/

The Regional Business Coalition
235 Andrew Young International Boulevard
Atlanta, GA 30303
404-586-1920
http://www.rbcatlanta.org

State of Georgia
http://www.state.ga.usv

University of Georgia
Carl Vinson Institute of Government
201 North Milledge Avenue
Athens, GA 30602
706-542-2736
http://www.cviog.uga.edu

7

Maryland

Contents

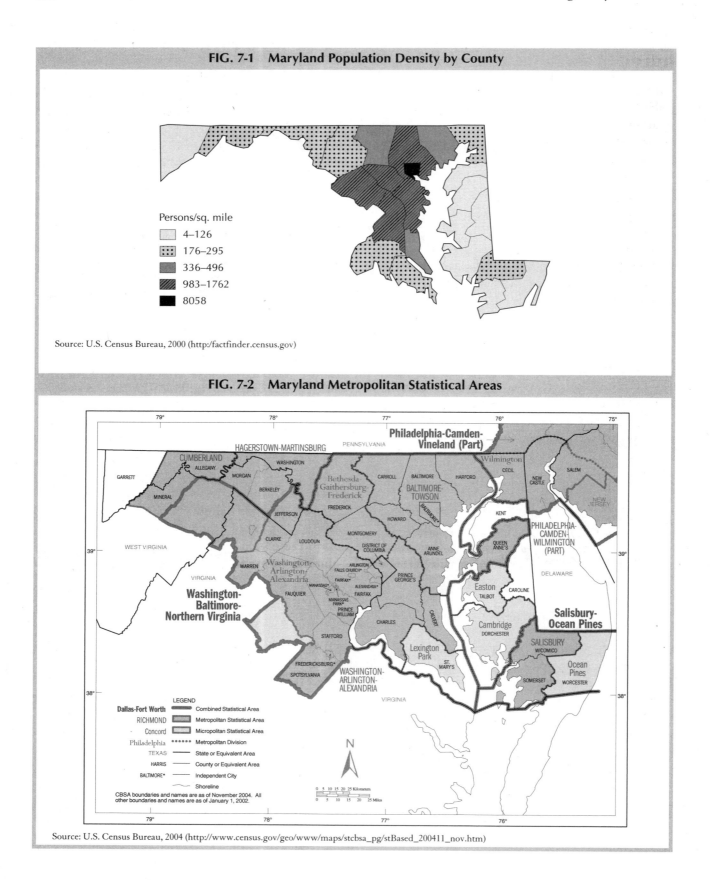

FIG. 7-1   Maryland Population Density by County

Persons/sq. mile

- 4–126
- 176–295
- 336–496
- 983–1762
- 8058

Source: U.S. Census Bureau, 2000 (http:/factfinder.census.gov)

FIG. 7-2   Maryland Metropolitan Statistical Areas

Source: U.S. Census Bureau, 2004 (http://www.census.gov/geo/www/maps/stcbsa_pg/stBased_200411_nov.htm)

Introduction

Former Maryland governor Parris Glendening (1995–2003) has been widely recognized as a leader of the smart growth movement across the nation. In his State of the State address to the Maryland General Assembly in January 1997, Glendening challenged himself, the citizens of Maryland, local governments and private and public interest groups to "work together to meet one of the most pressing challenges of our time: suburban sprawl." Glendening was seeking support for his newly articulated Smart Growth and Neighborhood Conservation Initiative "to protect our cities and our rural areas for tomorrow . . . stop urban sprawl that sacrifices our environment . . . keep farming a vital enterprise . . . and pay the tab for infrastructure improvements needed to support suburban sprawl" (Glendening 1997).

The governor detailed the disastrous impacts of past government policies that had encouraged sprawl, taking "thousands of acres of fields where corn and soybeans and other crops once grew . . . [and turning] them into housing developments . . . consuming thousands of acres of woodlands and wetlands." In the process of this headlong sprawl into the countryside, the governor warned, "we are leaving and losing our downtowns" (Glendening 1997). His urgency in halting such alarming trends was not new. In a June 1996 speech to the Maryland Municipal League, he called for major new efforts to support the full implementation of the Maryland Economic Growth, Resource Protection, and Planning Act of 1992 (also known as the Growth Act or the Planning Act) as a series of smart growth initiatives. The main components of these initiatives were passed by the 1997 General Assembly, though not without some tough battles and some important modifications to the original proposals by the governor himself.

The key to Maryland's successful efforts to manage growth seems clear: a strong, sustained commitment by the governor, his state agencies and the Maryland Department of Planning (MDP) to contain sprawl, protect natural resources, insure livable urban areas, and sustain and expand a healthy economy. Glendening's reelection in November 1998 allowed him to begin implementing his smart growth initiatives by strengthening his own team and by taking action to stop highway bypasses and encourage the siting of government facilities in existing urban or priority funding areas (PFAs).

Glendening's administration focused on demonstrating the effectiveness of the state's smart growth strategy, and on crafting and gaining legislative approval of a budget that focused spending by all key state agencies to support Maryland's smart growth principles. The administration and the Maryland Economic Growth, Resource Protection, and Planning Commission prepared an ambitious agenda for the 2000 legislative session. Five major pieces of legislation were proposed, and all were approved by the legislature essentially intact. The 2001 legislature was also a spectacular success from the perspective of the Glendening administration and smart growth advocates. The General Assembly supported additional smart growth initiatives essentially as the administration proposed them, and on the budget side provided the funding to assure implementation.

During the campaign and after his election in 2002, Governor Robert L. Ehrlich Jr. stressed his intent to go "places Republican candidates have never gone before," referring to his plan to continue Governor Glendening's smart growth policies. In October 2003 Ehrlich issued an Executive Order to put his own stamp on Maryland's smart growth initiatives, while keeping Glendening's core principles intact. As noted later in this chapter, this Executive Order established the Maryland Priority Places strategy, with all six components aimed at strengthening Maryland's smart growth system. The new governor also made a number of changes, such as moving the Office of Smart Growth from the governor's office in Annapolis back to the Maryland Department of Planning office in Baltimore. That move was strongly objected to initially by smart growth advocates in and out of Maryland, and especially by Senate President Thomas V. Milba, but new MDP Secretary Audrey Scott noted that her staff did all the implementing of the smart growth planning initiatives, and that it made more sense to locate the two staffs closer together.

The Roots of Growth Management, 1970–1985

Like many states, Maryland has a long history of involvement in planning and land use. The Maryland State Planning Commission, established in 1933, is the oldest state planning commission in the country. The original commission's staff was formalized as the State Planning Department in 1959, and became a cabinet-level Department of State Planning in 1969. The Maryland Office of Planning (MOP) was created in another reorganization in 1988. In 2000 the office was restored to department-level status as the MDP.

Early planning efforts in Maryland did not lead to a comprehensive state growth management strategy capable of assuring livable urban places and protecting important natural systems, especially the unique and greatly prized (and abused) Chesapeake Bay. However, over the years these entities have addressed a wide range of important public policy issues, including critical wetland issues (tidal and nontidal) (Noonan and Moran 1996, 2–8).

Environmental Concerns in the Chesapeake Bay

The Chesapeake Bay is described as the "largest and most productive estuary[1] in the United States...involving some 7,000 miles of shoreline, a surface area of 2,200 square miles" (doubled if tributaries are included) and providing habitat to "more than 200 fish species and 2,700 plant and animal species" (Baer and Bishop 1996, 1). The bay varies in width from 4 to 30 miles, with an average depth of only 21 feet. Maryland passed a wetlands act in 1970 to protect tidal wetlands, but by the early 1970s the vast, unique and ecologically diverse bay area was experiencing a deterioration in water quality and habitat destruction.

FIG. 7-3   Chesapeake Bay Watershed Area

Source: Based on map prepared by Chesapeake Bay Foundation

---

1. Estuaries are "semi-enclosed coastal bodies of water having a free connection to the open sea and within which seawater is measurably diluted with fresh water derived from land drainage" (Baer and Bishop 1996, 1).

In 1975 concerns about the future of the bay caused the U.S. Environmental Protection Agency (EPA) to launch a five-year $25 million study of this critical estuary. By 1983 the EPA had analyzed data from some 40 scientific studies that documented a variety of problems with the bay, including reductions in submerged aquatic vegetation, striped bass and shad fisheries, and shellfish. These problems were associated with excessive nutrient levels (i.e., phosphorous and nitrogen), excessive sediment loads and high levels of toxic metals and compounds (USEPA 1983).

The Chesapeake Bay Commission was founded in 1980, under a bistate agreement between Maryland and Virginia, following recommendations of the Chesapeake Bay Legislative Advisory Commission on the need for improved interstate coordination of baywide management. Pennsylvania joined the commission in 1985. The commission continues to help the legislatures of the three states evaluate and respond to problems relating to the Chesapeake Bay; encourages coordinated resource planning and action among the executive agencies of the three member states; and serves as liaison to the U.S. Congress.

The commission has 21 members (seven from each signatory state). Five from each state are state legislators whose terms coincide with those of their office. Of the Maryland legislative members, two are senators named by the Senate president and three are delegates chosen by the Speaker of the House of Delegates. The governor or a designee also serves as a member. The seventh member, neither a legislator nor a member of the executive branch, is selected jointly by the Senate president and the Speaker of the House. Nonlegislative members serve no longer than four years unless reappointed. The commission chair and vice chair are selected by the members and alternate annually among the delegations from the three states. Each state contributes equally to the annual budget.

The alarming results of the 1983 EPA report motivated the first in a number of actions to mobilize relevant stakeholders in a regional effort to save the bay. In 1983 the historic Chesapeake Bay Agreement was signed by the EPA, Virginia, Maryland, Pennsylvania and the District of Columbia, to serve as the basis for a regional approach to reversing the decline of the bay's biological systems. These jurisdictions stated their commitment to preparing specific plans to reverse the decline of the bay's water quality and the living resources dependent upon clean water. Over time, the Chesapeake Bay Agreement led to a number of initiatives, some successful, some less so, all instigated by a concern for the bay's healthy future. This goal has been a unifying and driving force in Maryland's efforts to craft and implement a comprehensive growth strategy.

The 1983 agreement led to the 1985 Chesapeake Bay Restoration and Protection Plan, which committed the participating states, as well as seven federal agencies, to a set of goals aimed at "reducing nutrients, reducing toxins, protecting living resources,

focusing environmental programs on Bay impacts, and establishing cooperation among institutions. The plan specified that these goals would be linked to state environmental programs" (Chesapeake Executive Council 1985).

The Critical Area Act of 1984

The critical role of current land use patterns in the Chesapeake Bay region emerged as a central issue in Maryland. Two state laws—the Maryland Critical Area Act of 1984 and the 1992 Growth Act—were especially important in the evolution of a comprehensive growth strategy for Maryland that linked land, water, air and transportation in an interconnected system. The state's current smart growth program is rooted in these laws, which focused on containing sprawl development patterns by a system of incentives and disincentives aimed at encouraging growth in designated areas, especially in and around existing urban communities.

While the main focus of this chapter is on the 1992 Growth Act and on more recent efforts to strengthen the implementation of its goals, the Critical Area Act of 1984 deserves some attention because it "was Maryland's first attempt to provide inter-jurisdictional management of land use patterns through common land use criteria" (Baer and Bishop 1996, 6). Overall, the act provided for land use policies that regulate the location, density and type of development within 1,000 feet of the tidal water's edge or from the landward edge of adjacent tidal wetlands and the lands under them. This translated into some 640,000 acres, or about 10 percent of Maryland's total land area. The focus on tidal areas reflected the strong growth pressures in many of those areas. During the early 1980s, "nearly 20 percent of all development was within a thousand feet of the edge of the Bay and its tidal rivers" (Baer and Bishop 1996, 7).

The statute had a number of goals, but one was particularly important in terms of the evolution of growth management in Maryland: to "establish land use policies for development in the Critical Area that accommodate growth, while acknowledging that, even if pollution is controlled, the number, movement, and activities of persons in an area can create adverse environmental impacts" (Baer and Bishop 1996, 7).

The law was supported by a commission charged with significant mandates and responsibilities, and drew from the 60 local governments around the bay that fell within the 1,000-foot zone.

The act was and continues to be administered by the Chesapeake Bay Critical Area Commission, whose responsibilities include

- developing critical area criteria guidelines for local governments to follow as they create and submit their own critical area program to the commission, which included zoning regulations and ways to minimize the negative impacts of growth;

- reviewing local governments' critical area programs. Using maps and data showing agricultural lands, wildlife habitats, soil types, endangered species habitats, streams and fish spawning areas, the local governments were required to establish three land classification types: intensely developed areas (IDAs), limited development areas (LDAs) and resource conservation areas (RCAs); and

- reviewing development projects in the critical area after local protection programs had been approved. The commission was authorized to intervene in court if a local government failed to carry out its programs.

The criteria for development in each land classification category were surprisingly specific. For example, densities in IDAs had to be four or more units per acre. New development in LDAs was limited to one unit per acre with strong requirements for vegetative buffers. Future intense development was strongly encouraged outside the coastal area, and a long list of criteria aimed at "environmentally friendly" development was included in the commission's recommendations. Development criteria also required farmers within a critical area to use defined "best management practices" to limit bay pollution.

Although these rules and regulations held promise for protecting the bay, the gains were limited by a number of statutory loopholes: one exempted between 8,000 and 10,000 lots from the Critical Area Act; another allowed local governments to develop 5 percent of RCAs to IDAs or LDAs, which enabled inappropriate development of "islands" in those areas. Despite these loopholes, there is general agreement

that the law greatly reduced the negative impacts of development on the bay during that time (Horton and Eichbaum 1991; Chesapeake Bay Critical Area Commission Undated; Maryland Department of the Environment 1995).

Recognizing Problems and Acting to Change Future Growth Patterns, 1987–1992

Year 2020 Panel and Barnes Commission Reports

Despite the positive impacts of the actions to protect the Chesapeake Bay in the 1970s and early 1980s, the 1983 Chesapeake Bay Agreement was expanded in 1987 to include additional and more specific goals for the region. For example, it featured a goal to reduce the 1985 nitrogen and phosphorous levels by 40 percent by the year 2000, and a set of strategies to address the pollution problems in the bay's tributaries. Most notable in terms of Maryland's overall growth management history is that the 1987 agreement sought to look at the issue of growth statewide, and commissioned a one-year study "to evaluate anticipated growth issues through the year 2020," to be carried out by the Year 2020 Panel: "a distinguished panel . . . assigned the task of developing strategies to alter traditional growth patterns" (Tierney 1994, 465).

In December 1988 the Year 2020 Panel presented its report to the Chesapeake Executive Council, which had been established by the Chesapeake Bay Agreements of 1983 and 1987 to coordinate the work of restoring and protecting the bay (Year 2020 Panel 1988). This report has proven to be a key document in the still-unfolding history of growth management in Maryland. The panel concluded that current development patterns—characterized by unmanaged growth and state and local government agencies that acted in isolation across the 64,000-square-mile watershed—would not lead to the restoration of the bay's water quality. Indeed, such development could only cause further decline in water quality.

The panel framed its recommendations within six visions for the future of the bay and charged Mary-

Visions of Year 2020 Panel					
Vision I	**Vision II**	**Vision III**	**Vision IV**	**Vision V**	**Vision VI**
Development is concentrated in suitable areas	Sensitive areas are protected	Growth is directed to population centers in rural areas and resource areas are protected	Stewardship of the Bay and the land is a universal ethic	Conservation of resources, including a reduction in resource consumption, is practiced throughout the region	Funding mechanisms are in place to achieve all other visions

Source: Year 2020 Panel, 1988, 4–8

land, Virginia and Pennsylvania with crafting and implementing growth strategies to implement these visions. The reactions of the three states were decidedly mixed: Pennsylvania rejected the recommendations outright; Virginia established a commission, chaired by Virginia legislator Tayloe Murphy, which worked for several years, but ultimately was unable to gain the support of the General Assembly and governor; Maryland's reaction was swift and positive.

Maryland Governor William Donald Schaefer responded in October 1989 by appointing the Governor's Commission on Growth in the Chesapeake Bay Region, representing all key public and private stakeholders. Also known as the Barnes Commission, it was led by former Maryland congressman Michael D. Barnes. The commission agreed that the six visions of the 2020 Panel would guide the future growth of Maryland in terms of protecting its environmental values, especially the bay, and generating viable (sustainable) urban communities and a healthy economy. With strong support from the governor and MOP, the commission developed a set of recommendations to carry out the charge of the Year 2020 Panel, although the evolution of consensus on key elements of proposed legislation took longer than many of the players had hoped. The report was published in January 1991, and the proposed legislation was introduced to the General Assembly by the governor as the 1991 session convened (Governor's Commission 1991). The legislation, incorporating SB 227 and HB 214, was known collectively as the 2020 bill because it embraced the essence of the Year 2020 Panel's visions. Tierney (1994, 466) observed:

> The Barnes Commission spent sixteen months conducting evaluations of development strategies and holding public hearings throughout Maryland. Its report, published in January 1991, concluded

that Maryland's population will increase by one million by the year 2020, that sprawl development is a major contributing factor in the loss of farms and forests and pollution of the Bay, and that the threat of unmanaged growth to the Bay watershed is so substantial that a statewide land use regulatory system is needed to successfully implement the visions of 2020.

The initial consensus of the Barnes Commission and the unquestioned support of Governor Schaefer were diluted by the governor's strained relationship with the 1991 General Assembly, and several factors united to block passage of the 2020 bill that year. First, the lateness of the final recommendations did not allow some stakeholders on the commission time to gather their constituents in support of the proposed legislation. Second, the specifics of the proposed legislation surprised many stakeholders, especially local governments that were required to implement the standards in their planning and regulatory processes. For example, designated growth areas had to have an average net density of 3.5 dwelling units per acre, and residential development outside of growth areas had to be at a maximum density of one unit per 20 acres. Criteria for the protection of specified sensitive areas were also included. Third, the governor strongly advocated other controversial laws in that session, and his outspoken reaction to opposition aggravated his relationship with many legislators.

Opposition to the 2020 bill formed quickly in a number of sectors, including local governments, development interests and the agricultural community. The environmental community was generally supportive, but many felt the bill's provisions should have been even stronger. When it became clear that the legislation could not prevail despite the governor's backing, the legislative leadership agreed to establish two standing committees to consider what might be done to reach consensus on growth management for the 1992 legislative session. While relegation to an interim study status often means the end of a legislative initiative, in this case new life was breathed into the effort.

With the governor's continued support, the MOP worked with the key groups that had balked at the relatively strong bill in 1991, including local governments, the General Assembly and (less successfully) some environmental groups. The office sought to find common ground for a "passable" bill, although heated political interactions led to the passage of legislation that became quite complex.[2] Local governments preferred an entirely permissive law that set forth the visions with an admonition that they should be implemented through state, local and private-sector efforts, and most agricultural and development interests shared that view. Many environmental groups took the position that unless a "strong" bill could be passed, it would be better to do nothing, since a "weak" bill would end any hope of passing a stronger bill in the near future.

Supporters of the 1992 legislation argued that a modest start in the right direction (that is, adopting a growth policy for the state) was better than nothing and could still help contain sprawl, thus benefiting both the environment and the development of livable urban places. In the end, advocates of "half a loaf is better than none" carried the day, and the 1992 Growth Act passed easily in both houses. In accordance with the act's requirements, Governor Schaefer, on December 11, 1992, signed an executive order that established procedures for the review of state projects for consistency with the planning policy and with local comprehensive plans.

The Economic Growth, Resource Protection, and Planning Act of 1992

The six visions for Maryland's future, as articulated by the Year 2020 Panel, generated strong support from a broad spectrum of interest groups and citizens, and they remained the key elements set forth in the 1992

legislation. A seventh vision was added to ensure achievement of the visions, encourage economic growth and streamline regulatory mechanisms. These seven visions were incorporated to guide the behavior of local governments through an amendment to Article 66B of the Annotated Code of Maryland, the basic planning and zoning enabling legislation for local governments. The law mandated, among other things, the incorporation of the visions into local comprehensive plans, a mandatory "sensitive areas" element in local plans, and provision for the "streamlining of development regulations in areas suitable for growth" (Noonan and Moran 1996, 4). A deadline of July 1, 1997, was set for each local government's comprehensive plan, as well as for amendments to land development regulations consistent with the plan.

Given Governor Schaefer's strong support of a state growth policy, the executive order provided for the widest scope possible under the statute in its application to relevant state agencies. It set procedures for consistency with the planning policy and put in place "three key provisions to guide state-level implementation of the act" (Noonan and Moran 1996, 6). First, the policy was to guide all state agency decisions not prohibited by statute or the Maryland Constitution. After opting for the broadest possible coverage, the order established an agency project review process in which each agency was to make consistency findings and report them to an interagency committee; any unresolved policy issues were to be raised within certain time limits.

Second, each agency was to establish regulations to implement the policy, such as "streamlining permit review procedures within designated growth areas, creating flexible development regulations, and directing economic growth through the use of innovative strategies" (Noonan and Moran 1996, 6). The MOP, working with other state agencies, produced an elaboration of the policy (MOP 1993).

Third, the act created an Economic Growth, Resource Protection, and Planning Commission, whose mandate was to track the progress toward implementing the visions and goals of the act, identify weaknesses and recommend new legislative or other actions. Its findings would be reported to the governor and General Assembly annually.

---

2. This account of the 1991 and 1992 legislation is based in part on the author's role as an adviser to Governor Schaefer and the Office of Planning, and on his interviews with key public officials.

Evaluation of the 1992 Growth Act: Strengths, Weaknesses and Recommendations

Economic growth and resource protection often have been put forward as competing goals, but the full title of the Maryland law rejects that idea and embraces the premise that managing growth wisely leads to a healthy environment *and* a strong economy. In citing the strengths of the law, Tierney (1994, 469–470) pointed out that it included "a new comprehensive growth policy, mandatory application of the policy on local governments, a state oversight mechanism to monitor compliance, a consistency requirement, and a new authorization for use of flexible techniques." If fully implemented, the visions in the state growth policy constituted a powerful attack on sprawl development patterns. The visions required local governments to concentrate development in "suitable areas" where public facilities and services already existed, to protect "sensitive areas" (with a specific requirement for a sensitive areas element in local comprehensive plans), and to direct growth to population centers, so that resource areas could be protected.

The Economic Growth, Resource Protection, and Planning Commission

A key provision of the 1992 Growth Act that proved in the long run to be a major factor in its success was the establishment of a new state agency, the Maryland Economic Growth, Resource Protection, and Planning Commission (known as the Growth Commission). Appointed in March 1993, the commission had 17 members representing geographic regions and public and private stakeholders across the state. The House of Delegates and Senate appointed one member each, and the other 15 were appointed by the governor from categories named in the statute: two from the Maryland Association of Counties (MACO), one from the Maryland Municipal League (MML), one member-at-large, and eleven members from seven regions. The statute suggested that the governor include representatives with diverse backgrounds, including business, finance, agriculture, forestry, environmental, civic, planning and real estate interests.

The Growth Act required the commission to have four subcommittees whose duties and membership were outlined in the law: the Subcommittees on Inter-jurisdictional Coordination; on Planning; on Planning Techniques; and on the Environment and Economic Development. The Subcommittee on the Review of Planning and Zoning Legislation was established later, to examine the effectiveness of local government enabling ordinances. Over time, the commission and its subcommittees have emerged as critical sources for developing recommendations and mobilizing support for strengthening the Growth Act (Tierney 1994, 471–472).

After his election in November 1994, Governor Glendening was steadfast in his support of the 1992 Growth Act and acted promptly to enable the newly formed commission to carry out its mandate. In November 1995 he made a request that was significant for two reasons: it signaled his concern about whether the act was working as it should and gave the commission an opportunity to review the law and recommend changes for overcoming weaknesses that had been identified by the commission and its subcommittees. The commission established "growth indicators intended to measure the effectiveness of state and local policies and actions affecting land use and development streamlining" (Growth Commission 1996, 3).

Under the law, a full review of the 1992 Growth Act was not technically required until 2002, but from the beginning the commission enjoyed vigorous leadership under its chair, Florence Beck (Becki) Kurdle, who had been active at the local planning level and later became an executive in the private sector. As a result, the commission may fairly be described as one of the strongest forces of objective assessment of the progress, or lack therof, in achieving the visions and goals of the act, as well as an increasingly powerful source of recommendations for strengthening the process.

1996 Annual Report of the Commission

The Growth Commission's 1996 annual report serves as an excellent vehicle for understanding the strengths and weaknesses of Maryland's growth management system at the close of 1996. The report is organized under four headings: historical perspective; summary of the act; strengths and weaknesses; and recommendations. It highlights, among other things, the work of the following subcommittees:

- *Subcommittee on Interjurisdictional Coordination*: Studied how to strengthen urban growth boundaries to support growth management and to develop a conflict resolution process.

- *Subcommittee on Planning*: Highlighted two key 1995 accomplishments: an awards program and an "effects of sprawl" slide show. Recommendations included focusing on a planning commissioner training program and creating the nonprofit 1000 Friends of Maryland.

- *Subcommittee on Planning Techniques*: Provided a "Critique of Planning Tools: Strengths and Weaknesses" in June 1996, recommending development of a State Development Policy Plan.

- *Subcommittee on the Environment and Economic Development*: Reviewed sensitive areas protection and regulatory streamlining. Goals for 1996 included focusing on incentives for development in designated growth areas; strengthening efforts to identify the true cost of sprawl and to impose that cost on sprawl development.

- *Subcommittee on the Review of Planning and Zoning Legislation*: Charged with examining existing enabling acts and recommending needed changes. This subcommittee was temporary and ceased to exist in July 1998.

- *Subcommittee on Transferable Development Rights*: Sought to contain sprawl by recommending a market-driven program for late 1996. It was appointed in September 1996 to examine options for establishing a statewide or regional transferable development rights (TDRs) program and provide recommendations to the commission. (Growth Commission 1996)

The fundamental principles that guided the development of the 1992 Growth Act reveal the weaknesses the governor and others tried to overcome without alienating key constituencies, especially local governments. The commission analysis asserted that these principles were, in fact, strengths that should be preserved. In illustrating the principle of preserv-

ing local land use authority, however, it noted that local land use controls were the best way to conduct basic land use planning, provided "that local plans minimize parochial perspectives, account for plans of neighboring jurisdictions, and are consistent with regional objectives and state policies" (Growth Commission 1996, 4). This is a very significant proviso, and the commission's analyses question whether it could overcome the firm determination of most local governments to plan in isolation from each other.

The report also stressed the importance of consistency: the principle that local implementation tools (regulations) be consistent with the local plans and that "plan consistency [was] required for capital funding" (Growth Commission 1996, 5). The commission thought this was a "very strong provision of the act

---

Fundamental Principles of the 1992 Growth Act

- Local governments retain responsibility to make land use decisions.
- Substate regions vary, so one size does not fit all.
- The state considers the growth implications of its actions, including the use of infrastructure funds.
- The planning process should include annual reports to the governor and General Assembly and after a period of implementation, should be studied to determine its successes and weaknesses.
- The state should act to coordinate land use efforts affecting economic development, interjurisdictional conflicts, regional arrangements and environmental issues.

State and Local Government Requirements of the 1992 Growth Act

- By July 1, 1997, local governments must adopt comprehensive plans and implementation "tools."
- The local plans must "implement the seven visions, encourage regulatory streamlining, flexibility, and innovation."
- The local plans must contain a "sensitive areas" element.
- By executive order, state agencies must "pursue the seven visions through their various programs and agencies."
- State and local governments "may not spend state or federal pass-through dollars for capital projects unless the project is consistent with local comprehensive plans and the visions." An exception can be made for "extraordinary circumstances with no feasible alternative."

Source: Growth Commission, 1996, 4

and could be used by the state and local governments to influence local land use planning and decisions."

The 1996 annual report also detailed the emerging weaknesses of the planning system as it neared July 1, 1997, when all local plans and regulations were scheduled to be in place and consistent with the visions, including implementing regulations. The commission cited the lack of definitions for terms used in the visions, such as *rural* or *growth areas,* as a significant barrier to translating the visions into major changes in development patterns. For example, the requirement to set growth boundaries did not include a consistent definition of what densities were appropriate where. In Baltimore County, rural meant one dwelling unit per 50-acre minimum density; Charles County had a three-acre minimum; and Washington County used one dwelling unit to the acre (Tierney 1994, 473).

Thus, a basic goal of the Growth Act (to limit sprawl development) had not been carried out, except where local governments had already done so before 1992. Even with the sensitive area requirement, local governments could and did use widely varying definitions in developing that element for their comprehensive plans. All of this complicated the commission's ability to monitor how local governments and state agencies were attempting to implement the planning policies laid out in the law.

Even the visions were found to be unclear. Vision I stated that development be "concentrated in suitable areas," but does not define "concentrated" or "suitable." Descriptive terms, such as *existing communities, growth centers, stabilized areas, revitalization areas* and *infill development* would have been specific, and Vision I's goals (directing growth to older areas, away from greenfields) would have been realized. Vision III (protecting rural and resource areas) did not clearly define its terms, either. It could have been strengthened by adding terms such as *critical masses of farm and forest land, mineral resource lands* and *nongrowth areas* (Growth Commission 1996, 6).

Another hindrance in turning the 1996 report's concerns about the visions into reality involved the lack of a formal statewide coordinating body. In spite of what the commission described as "various informal attempts to bring agencies together," and the broad authority given the state by the Growth Act "to

influence growth management...it appears that the state is not using the authority in relation to the visions in a coordinated, consistent, and concerted manner" (Growth Commission 1996, 7). The commission's accurate critique then offered the principal tool by which development patterns at all levels could be altered in the direction of more compact patterns in both rural and urban areas: infill and redevelopment potential maximized by concerted state actions.

By the end of 1996, Maryland's 23 counties and Baltimore City had adopted procedures to review local construction projects that included state funds for consistency with local comprehensive plans. They had also submitted time schedules for compliance with the plan and its implementation requirements. Eight counties had plans in place and six were in the review process; the other counties and Baltimore City had plan updates in process. At the municipal level, 145 jurisdictions had review procedures in place, and 104 of the 107 municipalities that had planning and zoning authority had submitted schedules: 25 had adopted updated plans, 17 were in the formal review process and 62 municipalities were in some stage of plan preparation (Growth Commission 1996, 29). While many jurisdictions did not meet the deadline, all eventually did amend their plans in accordance with the act.

In offering specific recommendations based on its analysis of the 1992 Growth Act's strengths and weaknesses, the commission responded directly to perceived weaknesses. First, the commission repeated its

---

MdProperty View

An electronic mapping tool, known as MdProperty View, was developed by the Maryland Department of Planning (MDP) in 1996 and continues to be upgraded each year. It simplifies the way property information for Maryland's 23 counties and Baltimore City is gathered and utilized. This visually accessible database allows users to view information using geographic information systems (GIS) software.

Some of the maps and data included in the program are current property tax maps and assessment data; monthly reports of property sales and transfers; extracted information on commercial/industrial, tax-exempt, agricultural and unimproved residential parcels; statewide road maps; land use and land coverage data; and boundaries for census tracts, ZIP code areas, and legislative and congressional districts. See http://www.mdp.state.md.us/data/index.htm.

call for more detailed definitions of the visions and for development of a statewide policy plan to serve as the basis for fully mobilizing state resources to implement the Growth Act. While reasserting its commitment to the guiding principles framing the act, the commission also stressed the coordination of local plans on a regional level (Growth Commission 1996, 8).

The commission's recommendations to curtail sprawl proposed an interjurisdictional TDR program. The goal was to "maximize and facilitate a developer's ability to construct in areas designated for growth by the local comprehensive plan, in exchange for a developer's participation in protecting Maryland's important rural resources such as farmland, forest land, rural landscapes and environmentally sensitive areas" (Growth Commission 1996, 9).

This set of recommendations included the establishment of purchase of development rights (PDR) programs by local governments to complement and supplement the state PDR program administered by the Maryland Agricultural Land Preservation Foundation (MALPF), which had been created in 1977 to counter the potential threat to Maryland's agricultural economy. It worked (and continues to work) with local subdivisions in an effort to slow land encroachment by establishing agricultural preservation districts. Once in a district, a landowner could apply to the foundation to sell an agricultural land preservation easement to the state in order to preserve the land in perpetuity for agricultural use. In an important part of its TDR recommendation designed to complement MALPF and local TDR and PDR programs, the commission cautioned that "the program must be structured so that local governments do not undermine its success by liberal use of zoning variances and other procedures" (Growth Commission 1996, 10).

Finally, the commission's report made a "first effort" to develop a series of "growth indicators" to identify and track "changes in the location, impact and magnitude of development" (Growth Commission 1996, 12). The indicators were described as a form of benchmark, intended to provide baseline data from which to track the impact of the planning system on development patterns in Maryland. The indicators were grouped into five broad categories associated with one or more of the visions: development patterns, land preservation, development potential, targeting infrastructure resources and economic growth. The commission applied these indicators to six geographic regions of the state, ranging from the Baltimore metropolitan region to the Eastern Shore, southern Maryland and the Washington suburban region.

The report stated clearly that its data indicated a continuing trend toward sprawl patterns of development. While low-density residential land accounted for 31 percent of all development in 1973, that figure had increased to 40.7 percent by 1990 (Growth Commission 1996, 19). Another dismal statistic involved substantial overzoning for the population increase projected to 2020: 1.4 million households versus 634,000 needed to accommodate the projected population growth.

Even the most generous analysis of Maryland's planning system could not claim that it had successfully put in place, at local and state levels, the needed implementation actions to achieve the goals (visions) incorporated into Maryland law by the Growth Act. Nevertheless, the state's effort to channel infrastructure dollars into growth areas demonstrated some positive effects, as illustrated by the state's school construction program. In 1991, 62.5 percent of construction money was spent on new schools, but by 1997 the distribution "was altered drastically, with 85 percent of all construction money going to renovation of existing schools" (Growth Commission 1996, 20).

Emboldened by Governor Glendening's request for an early assessment of the Growth Act (that is, in 1996 instead of 2002) and his intention to develop a set of smart growth initiatives for submission to the 1997 General Assembly, the commission developed a very strong case for strengthening the implementation of the act to ensure the visions would be translated from high hopes to firm reality.

Governor Glendening's Smart Growth Initiative

Glendening began his leadership role in 1994 with a "triple E" agenda: education, economy and the environment. He also developed a six-point directed growth initiative to focus on reining in sprawl, consistent with discussions on "land use, growth management, and stewardship of our landscapes" (Matuszeski 1996, 16). After an October 1995 meeting of the key leaders of the Chesapeake Bay Agreement, Glendening "went public" with his proposals in a speech to the Maryland Municipal League in June 1996. He stressed economic development and committed his administration to using state agency infrastructure dollars in existing urban areas. He also called for a stepped-up fight on crime and the strengthening of the education system to promote growth in urban and urbanizing areas. In commenting on the need for Maryland to continue to grow, he added:

> How we grow is critical. The answer largely depends on how well local governments manage growth, how well we use existing infrastructure, how well we conserve and reinvigorate our existing neighborhoods, and how often we stretch our imaginations and use our creativity to modernize and use what already exists instead of building something new. (Glendening 1996)

Signaling his intention to develop a major legislative package for the 1997 General Assembly, Glendening promised a proposal on Neighborhood Conservation and Smart Growth initiatives to be drafted by fall 1996 (Matuszeski 1996, 16–17). Ronald L. Young and Ronald Kreitner of the MOP headed the effort to develop and seek support for the initiatives. Kreitner had experienced the relatively strong state growth management effort of 1991, and both men helped broker the scaled-down effort that produced the 1992 Growth Act. They understood the deep-seated opposition from private- and public-sector interests, and thus the need to mobilize all possible support in the effort to strengthen the 1992 law.

The outreach effort to build strong grassroots support for the governor's initiatives was aimed at bringing key interests and the General Assembly into line through "extensive outreach to community, business, environmental, farm, local government and other groups and organizations." All were asked to make specific recommendations that would help prevent sprawl and make neighborhoods more livable. The responses comprised a "book" of approaches, which was distributed to all relevant parties for their reactions.

Six Elements of the Smart Growth Initiative

When the dust settled on the outreach effort, the key components of the Smart Growth and Neighborhood Conservation Initiative fell into place and were outlined in Glendening's State of the State address in January 1997. "For at least half a century, government policies have supported sprawl.... It has turned thousands of acres of fields...into housing developments, [losing] not only the productivity of the farms but their rolling beauty as well." He highlighted the loss of woodlands and wetlands, "our natural buffers against man's many assaults on the air we breathe and the water we drink." If the current trend of sprawl continued, he said, "over the next 25 years we will lose over 500,000 acres of forests and farmlands" (Glendening 1997).

The governor noted that in addition to the destruction of natural systems, urban areas and the economy are suffering: "As residents and employers flee to the suburbs, they leave behind boarded-up storefronts, the jobless poor, higher welfare caseloads, and increased crime." He cited the excessive cost ("hundreds of millions of dollars") to taxpayers for infrastructure to support sprawl, then presented his vision for the future:

> As our constituents move further and further from the city centers, we are forced to use our money... to build more roads, new water and sewer systems, to clean up failed septic systems, to construct new fire and police stations and to provide other infrastructure demanded by development. We do this even as we abandon the roads, the sewer systems, and our schools in established neighborhoods.
>
> We are changing. For example, we changed the way we spend our money for school construction. Today we focus our funding on existing schools, renovating and expanding their capacity, or building at new sites only in areas designated by local governments for growth and development.... We've made a start, but it has taken us half a century to get to this point and we are not going to turn it around overnight, or even in a year or two. (Glendening 1997)

The governor then characterized the overall tone of his Smart Growth and Neighborhood Conservation Initiative, combining a bow toward home rule that at the same time revealed the teeth in the initiatives: "Our proposal is not a 'no growth' or even a

Six Elements of the Smart Growth and Neighborhood Conservation Initiative

1. Priority funding areas (PFAs, or smart growth areas) are locations where state and local governments would encourage and support economic development and new growth. PFAs would be the beneficiaries of state funds for both capital and operating programs: roads and highways, business development financing, most housing programs, schools and other infrastructure needs.

2. The Rural Legacy Program was designed to enhance existing agricultural and open space land acquisition programs, such as local Program Open Space allocations and the Maryland Agricultural Land Preservation Foundation's easement purchase program.

3. The Brownfields Program was similar to other developments across the country where infill and redevelopment combat urban sprawl and encourage sustainable compact urban systems. Its mandate was to track proposals in other states, as well as new initiatives by the EPA, to encourage responsible cleanup and redevelopment of contaminated sites and create new job opportunities. These areas often make up a substantial part of available property in areas earmarked for redevelopment and infill, and can be very significant in relieving the pressure to sprawl.

4. The Job Creation Tax Credit, administered by the Department of Business and Economic Development, promotes job creation and revitalization, especially for small business owners. It grants an income tax credit to companies in certain industry sectors that create at least 25 new jobs within a PFA that also meet other guidelines.

5. The state's existing Right to Farm Law was proposed to be strengthened, so the types of activities currently protected from nuisance suits would be expanded to include activities relating to the preparation, processing, and transportation of farm products for sale. It did not, however, override any local laws relating to processing activities on farms.

6. The Live Near Your Work (LNYW) Program was implemented by the Department of Housing and Community Development to encourage people to live in older neighborhoods near their jobs. Participating employers (businesses, nonprofits, colleges or universities, government agencies) must set eligibility requirements, promote the program to their employees and provide matching resources.

Source: MOP, 1997a

'slow growth' proposal. It is a smart growth proposal. It builds on the growth act passed by this assembly in 1992." The governor noted that local governments would still have the authority for planning and zoning, but the state would "only fund projects in smart growth areas." The original legislative package contained elements that would constrain local power, especially the state's role in designating the smart growth areas.

The Smart Growth and Neighborhood Conservation Initiative can be described as a potentially bold and far-reaching effort to combine a rich mix of incentives and disincentives to arrest sprawl development patterns by channeling population growth and targeting state infrastructure dollars into designated growth areas while protecting the rural landscape (MOP 1997a, 7–14).

Smart Growth Meets the 1997 General Assembly

Introduced and read for the first time on January 27, 1997, the bill was entitled "An Act Concerning 'Smart Growth' and Neighborhood Conservation—Rural Legacy Program," with proposed administrative amendments incorporated on February 26, 1997. The bill was referred to the Economic and Environmental Affairs and Budget and Taxation Committees.

Both positive and negative factors came into play as Glendening's smart growth package made its way through the 1997 General Assembly. First, the most massive outreach effort ever mounted by Maryland, one that equaled or exceeded anything attempted in other states, won friends and support from more than 600 organizations around the state. Surprisingly, some of these supporters had been opposed to every previous effort by Maryland to establish a strong growth management framework.

This intense lobbying succeeded in weakening some coalitions opposed to any kind of growth management. For example, the outreach effort was responsible for splitting the bankers off from the home builders and realtors (who never came around), and for splitting county commissioners of the MACO state board in a 10–10 tie vote on the governor's program. The result was that while MACO leaders closed ranks and opposed the legislation as introduced, they also tried to find ways to make the proposals more acceptable to their constituents. MACO's executive director praised Glendening's administration for its "good faith efforts to accommodate our concerns."

Further, the outreach effort did not simply soften up diehard opponents of a strengthened state role in growth management: it created a strong core of active supporters who appeared at committee hearings and flooded legislators with messages of support at critical times in the legislative process.

Another factor that boded well for the passage of the governor's smart growth initiatives was a Senate generally amenable to the package, especially the Senate Economic and Environmental Affairs Committee, which was assigned to review the PFAs and brownfields proposals. In contrast was the much more resistant House, where neither the Speaker nor key committees were receptive to the governor's efforts. According to one report, "The House produced what 'smart growth' advocates considered a watered-down version of the legislation that was more favorable to rural interests. Even in the Senate, the bill underwent substantial changes...when the Budget and Taxation Committee offered certain amendments to scale back the initial plan" (Inside Washington 1997, 16).

Final Passage of the Smart Growth Initiative

In the end, all but one of the six elements of the governor's smart growth initiative were passed by the 1997 General Assembly, although the final products differed, sometimes markedly, from the initial language proposed by the administration. An overall assessment by the Office of Planning of what finally passed was that "we came out in pretty decent shape." The defeat of the expanded Right to Farm proposal was particularly surprising because originally it was considered to be a "sure pass." Its demise can be attributed to the concerns of environmental groups that it would open the door to environmental abuse.

From the beginning the designation of PFAs was the most controversial element of the proposed legislative package. In the view of the MOP, the "politics of reality" in Maryland would not support a straightforward state requirement for urban growth boundaries as the key requirement for containing sprawl. The incentive-based approach of targeting state funding to designated areas, combined with the Rural Legacy Program and other components of the package, were seen as the best hope for containing most growth within designated areas while protecting the rural countryside from inappropriate development. Key stakeholders (e.g., MACO and the Farm Bureau) were determined to change a number of issues pertaining to the criteria for PFAs, and MACO took the lead in pushing for changes to make this part of the package more acceptable to its members. Negotiations involved five primary issues.

1. State versus county role in designating PFAs

Under the administration's proposal, counties would submit PFAs that presumably met the criteria; the state would review the submissions and certify them as PFAs if they met the criteria. MACO considered the state's role as undue state control over the process, and it was ultimately agreed that counties could submit any area they wanted as a PFA. It is debatable whether this made the process essentially meaningless in controlling sprawl and promoting economic development and growth in the "right" places. The answer is probably *no, it did not*, especially in light of how the politics of implementation have played out.

Knowing that the governor was committed to channeling state dollars to PFAs, MACO fought for as little state oversight as possible. However, if counties submitted PFAs that did not meet the criteria, the state was not required to channel dollars to them. Since there will be more PFAs nominated than state dollars available to support their development, the state could simply *not* fund those that fail the certification test. The key was how and to what extent the governor kept pressure on state agencies to integrate their state dollars for maximum support to "certifiable" PFAs, while giving little or no support to the others.

Related to the priority funding issues, the administration was able to retain a "legislative blessing" for the governor's existing policy of shifting education funds to renovate and expand existing schools rather than directing education construction dollars to new schools at the edge. From 1995 to 1996, 83 percent of education construction dollars went toward investment in existing schools. The continuation of that policy, strongly objected to by some county and development interests, was and is critical to both stopping the "push" of sprawl and making the Smart Growth and Neighborhood Conservation Initiative work.

2. *Allowable densities in the PFAs*

This issue involved an effort by the Glendening administration to assure that development in PFAs would be reasonably compact (dense) and not simply involve more sprawl (low densities) inside the PFAs. Ongoing efforts to strengthen incentives and disincentives to assure moderate densities to support compact development patterns have been more successful in recent years. Only if appropriate densities are assured will population growth be largely accommodated in PFAs and existing urban areas, rather than continue the sprawl into the rural countryside.

3. *Water and sewer in new PFAs*

The issue of mandating both water and sewer facilities in newly designated PFAs led to a compromise requiring central sewers and water for growth areas. For existing communities, there was some compromise that allowed sewer *or* water as a qualifier. However, in areas permitting water only, state projects could be funded only if they maintained the character of the existing community and did not support growth. MACO and others fought for having all existing industrial areas designated as PFAs, whether or not they had water and sewer facilities. The compromise was that any newly designated industrial areas would be required to have both services.

4. *Rural villages as PFAs*

Rural counties viewed the governor's smart growth initiatives as a threat to their ability to grow at all, and many small town officials felt they were not being involved in the process. To accommodate that concern, a rural villages designation was added to the PFAs list, making it clear that some development would be allowed in rural areas and would be eligible for state support. The MOP did not see this addition as a major concession, since there was an assumption all along that some development would occur in rural areas.

5. *Infrastructure requirements for PFAs*

An interesting and potentially significant element of the governor's initiative involved the requirement of a needs assessment for infrastructure in designated PFAs, including an estimate of the costs of the needed

facilities. The governor's original proposal called for counties to develop a capital plan that identified the source of the county's share of infrastructure funds. MACO objected, and the state countered by requiring that before state infrastructure dollars were committed to a PFA, local governments would either have their share of needed infrastructure in place or provide it concurrent with the development. The state welcomed MACO's compromise—a proposal that included the local government's ability to pay for the needed infrastructure—as stronger than its own. The issue of assessing the "when" and "how" of infrastructure needs in PFAs was and is an important move in the direction of a concurrency provision in Maryland.

The other elements of the governor's initiative drew more broad-based support from most of the key stakeholders. The Rural Legacy Program was introduced as SB 388 on January 27, 1997, and referred to the Committee on Budget and Taxation. Supported by agricultural interests and environmental groups, the proposed amendments survived the legislative process essentially intact, with some reduction in available funding for implementation. The state's Program Open Space would continue to use its funds for the purchase of parks, wildlife management areas, scenic rivers, greenways, Chesapeake Bay access and other such areas. This new initiative would

> redirect *existing* state funds into a focused and dedicated land preservation program specifically designed to limit the adverse impacts of sprawl on our agricultural lands and natural resources. The Program will reallocate state funds to purchase conservation easements for large contiguous tracts of agricultural, forest, and natural areas subject to development pressure. (MOP 1997b, 4)

Proposed funding for fiscal years 1998 through 2002 was substantial: general obligation bonds ($90 million); a 10 percent increase in the real estate transfer tax already funding Program Open Space ($35.4 million); and the statewide land acquisition budget for Program Open Space ($38 million), for a total of $163.4 million. The most significant feature of the Rural Legacy Program is the way it builds on and augments existing programs aimed at containing sprawl by making rural lands off-limits to inappropriate development (MOP 1997b, 4).

The Brownfields Voluntary Cleanup and Revitalization Program received support from all quarters, with one member of the MOP calling the reaction to the proposal a "love fest." This program was introduced as SB 340 (on July 2, 1997) and assigned to the Committee on Economic and Environmental Affairs. The bill passed essentially as proposed by the administration.

The proposed major amendments to existing legislation included "clear liability protection for purchasers and lenders who acquire and clean up brownfield sites; clean-up standards that ensure public heath and safety are protected; and authority for the state to continue to hold certain parties responsible where new or previously undiscovered contamination is discovered after a liability release is granted" (MOP 1997b, 4). The Brownfields Program was seen by the governor as a major step toward revitalizing existing neighborhoods and industrial areas, preventing unnecessary sprawl and providing new economic development opportunities, including job creation" (MOP 1997b, 13).

The Job Creation Tax Credit legislation was introduced on January 17, 1997, as SB 229A, and referred to the Committee on Budget and Taxation. As with the Rural Legacy Program, the committee amended existing legislation. The governor's objective was to target a part of the existing Job Creation Tax Credit that

> grants an income tax credit to companies in certain industry sectors that create 60 or more new full-time jobs, unless the jobs are high paying jobs averaging $29,000 a year in which case the threshold is 30 jobs. The one-time tax credit equals 2.5 percent of the wages of qualifying employees (capping at $1000 times the number of qualified employees) in non-revitalization areas, and 5% of the wages of qualifying employees (capped at $1500 times the number of qualified employees) in the revitalization areas designated by the Department of Housing and Community Development. (MOP 1997b, 2)

The smart growth initiatives would lower the job creation threshold to 25 jobs when businesses locate in a smart growth area, in the hope of encouraging mid-size and smaller firms to locate in areas "with existing infrastructure that needs reinvestment." As passed in final form, the administration's proposal remained essentially intact.

The final successful bill in the administration's package was the Live Near Your Work (LNYW) Program. It was approved by the General Assembly as part of its budget bill to provide funds for cash grants of $3,000 to homebuyers moving into targeted communities near their work places; those eligible for the grants must live in the LNYW area for at least three years (MOP 1997a, 14). Local governments designate such areas with the concurrence of the Department of Housing and Community Development.

Implementing the Smart Growth Initiative, 1997–2001

Despite the legislative success of the smart growth initiative, the on-the-ground experience implementing its mandates was more problematic. Volume I of the Economic Growth, Resource Protection, and Planning Commission's 1997 annual report summarized the status of counties and cities in adopting comprehensive plans: 16 of the state's 23 counties reported adopting revised comprehensive plans and of the 105 municipalities with planning and zoning powers, 62 had adopted revised plans as of December 1, 1997. The report made it clear that the commission had not thoroughly reviewed the quality of the revised plans in terms of incorporating the key elements of the 1992 Growth Act. It promised in the coming months, presumably to be ready for inclusion in the 1998 annual report, "to thoroughly analyze the comprehensive plans...to better assess compliance with the growth act" (Growth Commission 1997, 14).

The commission committed itself to "review implementing ordinances adopted to achieve consistency with the new plans" (Growth Commission 1997, 14). Changes made to comprehensive plans were seen as ranging from "significant strides" to "minimal" or "cosmetic" (Growth Commission 1997, 16). The thorough review was not ready for the 1998 report either, and in addition, the 1997 report revealed that the necessary changes had not been made to assure that comprehensive zoning and subdivisions ordinances would be consistent with the new comprehensive plans.

The commission also proposed a thorough revision of Article 66B, the source of planning and zoning enabling authority for noncharter counties and most municipalities, with some provisions applying to all local governments. Article 66B had not had a thorough review since 1970, and many of its provisions were based on model legislation proposed by the U.S. Department of Commerce in the 1920s. The law often did not permit local governments to use "new zoning and planning tools to create diverse and attractive communities and to achieve economic development in an environmentally responsible manner" (Growth Commission 1997, 42).

Revisions to Article 66B were the product of a commission subcommittee that had begun its work in 1994. The subcommittee included a broad range of stakeholders: local elected officials and planners; MACO; and MML. Input was received from the Maryland Home Builders Association, the APA's Growing Smart project and the Chesapeake Bay Foundation. The proposed redraft aimed at "establishing greater uniformity in the ground rules of land use regulation, providing local governments with opportunities to be flexible in land development regulation...and for streamlining permitting processes while maintaining review standards" (Growth Commission 1997, 42). This kind of flexibility was and still is critical to achieving the goals of the 1992 Growth Act and the 1997 Smart Growth Initiative, and contributed to the laws adopted in the 2000 legislative session.

Addressing one of the governor's success stories, the 1997 annual report noted that the school construction program had begun to shift from supporting new schools in ever-expanding sprawl suburbs to supporting the growth management principles in the 1992 Growth Act and the 1997 Smart Growth Initiative revisions. In fiscal year 1999, 75 percent of school construction dollars was allocated to renovations and additions to existing schools; in 2001, 78 percent was spent on aging schools; and for fiscal year 2002, 71 percent was dedicated to existing schools.

The 1997 report had set forth some ambitious goals, but many of them had not been realized by the time the 1998 report was issued. For example, the 1998 report noted that cities and counties still had a long way to go in such areas as making major changes to zoning and subdivision ordinances; strengthening local plan policies to contain sprawl in agriculture and resource areas; and strengthening weak regulations to contain sprawl.

The commission also continued to push the development and legislative adoption of a state development policy plan. The goal of an indepth review of the process and substance of local comprehensive plans remained unfinished and the commission's 1999 agenda included reaching agreement on the goal statement and benchmarks, with input from various state agencies and committees on "the identification and analysis of state policies and procedures" (Growth Commission 1998, 13).

The summary assessment in the 1998 annual report, however, included several positive examples of emerging smart growth policies in a number of cities and towns, including the adoption of a sensitive areas element to apply to development projects initiated in local governments after June 30, 1998. It also cites the importance of several publications and planning tools in reaching the goals of the smart growth initiative. For example, the Office of Planning focused on approaches to setting meaningful urban boundaries and keeping them current over the long-term implementation process (MOP 1998). Another potential implementation tool is the use of TDRs in conjunction with the Rural Legacy Program. The commission's Task Force on Transferable Development Rights organized a workshop in March 1998 to examine a variety of ways to make more effective use of TDRs. Progress in this area was taken up by the 2000 legislature.

Glendening's Crucial Role and His 1998 Reelection

Backing his rhetoric and enthusiasm for smart growth planning, Glendening signed an executive order issued on January 23, 1998, to mobilize state agencies to fully realize the goals of the 1992 Growth Act through the smart growth legislation approved by the 1997 General Assembly. Replacing and building on Governor Schaefer's executive order following the passage of the 1992 Growth Act, Governor Glendening's 1998 executive order included

- a series of mandates aimed at achieving the goals of the smart growth initiatives through a wide range of proactive moves by state agencies;

- the formation of a Smart Growth and Neighborhood Conservation Subcabinet with membership by nine state agencies, the director of the MOP and two representatives from the Governor's Office. The MOP director chaired the meetings, which must be attended by the agency heads or deputy heads fully authorized to act for the head;

- a specific list of procedures for review and coordination of projects and activities in PFAs; and

- a provision that agencies report to the governor annually on the implementation of the 1997 smart growth legislation with a list of specific items the reports must contain.

In the months and weeks prior to the 1998 primary, the governor's race between Democrat Glendening and Republican candidate Ellen Sauerbrey was assessed as a dead heat, with the edge going to Sauerbrey. Yet, Glendening's job approval rating rose from 42 to 56 percent and later to 61 percent over this time, and when the votes were counted after the November 3 general election, Glendening won over Sauerbrey: 56 to 44 percent (Smith 1998).

During his first administration, Glendening was untiring in his efforts to encourage smart growth in Maryland, and he intended to carry those efforts into a new term. Starting with his 1999 State of the State address, the governor sent a series of clear signals about his position on the future prospects of his smart growth initiative (Glendening 1999). A *Baltimore Sun* editorial reported, "Smart Growth, the governor's pride and joy, dominates his environmental package." The editorial listed $46.5 million to preserve greenspace and farmland, $1.5 million to help reclaim contaminated industrial sites, $18 million for neighborhood redevelopment, $8 million to "rejuvenate downtown Silver Spring, and $6 million to recycle Memorial Stadium." In addition, the budget included $12 million to help clean up the Chesapeake Bay and its tributaries (*Baltimore Sun* 1999).

The governor's 1998 executive order was a strong start to making sure state dollars were targeted as directly and fully as possible to PFAs. But it was in the fiscal 2000 budget that his intention to put teeth into his smart growth initiative became clearer. The budget cut highway and other projects across the state, such as in western Maryland, the Baltimore suburbs and the Eastern Shore. Five long-planned highway projects, a major police training center and other projects were included in the cuts (Dresser 1999). By omitting these projects from his budget, the governor demonstrated that smart growth would involve action, not just talk. As Glendening's spokesman asserted, "the governor's policy is to strictly enforce the law's prohibition on state construction spending outside priority funding areas" (Dresser 1999).

Furthermore, all state agencies had been directed to review projects for consistency with the law. This was particularly evident in the actions of the Maryland DOT, whose director of planning promised, "these are not the last of the projects to be eliminated." These projects tended to be bypasses, which the administration viewed as contributing to sprawl. The executive director of 1000 Friends of Maryland also noted, "bypasses are the old solution that killed downtowns" (Dresser 1999). Despite Glendening's strong stance, communities whose projects were eliminated typically reacted with disappointment and even outrage. For example, the elimination of a $13 million bypass for the small town of Brookeville in Montgomery County even stirred the opposition of former Governor Schaefer, then the state comptroller (Thomson 1999). Clearly, observers noted, political heat would be generated as the list of projects canceled or substantially redesigned grew longer (Dresser 1999).

Glendening demonstrated his continuing support of the smart growth system by appointing three new department heads (Housing, Economic Development and Transportation) committed to getting their departments in line with smart growth priorities. By early 1999, key departments were looking at their spending patterns much more closely, to assure that their dollars were spent in support of smart growth priorities. The new campus for the University of Maryland at Hagerstown was a defining smart growth project because it addressed the issue of locating major public facilities downtown as a way to revitalize existing urban areas, rather than on the outskirts as had been the traditional pattern for such large projects.

Other examples included the addition of $3 million for transit station area developments, stronger efforts to keep schools in existing urban areas or PFAs, and more state dollars from the DOT for sidewalks connecting transit areas with adjacent neighborhoods.

The governor asked for no new smart growth legislation in 1999, but established a study group to develop legislation for the 2000 session. He aimed to show the effectiveness of the smart growth strategy. He crafted his entire 1999 budget to reflect spending by all key departments that would support smart growth principles, and that approach was endorsed by the General Assembly in acting on the budget. The Glendening administration did not push for a separate Smart Growth Infrastructure Trust Fund, as many other states have done, because the administration saw it as a tempting target for raiding by the General Assembly. However, the strategy was generally considered to be working well, although many local governments, which are pushing or being pushed for growth in existing urban areas or PFAs, believe that an important need is not being met: funding for sewer treatment plant expansion and the upgrading of old or construction of new sewer lines. With the governor using his power to bargain with key legislative leaders and committees to achieve his objectives, support from the General Assembly was mostly positive.

The Continuing Role of the Growth Commission

The 17-member Economic Growth, Resource Protection, and Planning Commission has been a major force in moving Maryland's smart growth initiative toward full implementation. In 1999 Michael Barnes, who had chaired Governor Schaefer's 1989 Commission on Growth in the Chesapeake Bay Region, took over as chair from Becki Kurdle. His return to the scene gave additional support to the smart growth program. The clear message of the commission's 1999 annual report (seventh in the series) is signaled in the executive summary: "There are many accomplishments to recognize, to applaud. But, much more should be addressed, for we have only begun to tackle

the problems which have developed over decades" (Growth Commission 1999, 5).

Frustration with and determination to do something about the failure to bring many local governments fully into the growth management system were also reflected in the annual report. In July 1999 commission members agreed that they "should be more central and relevant to the development of future efforts and recommendations in the field of Smart Growth and of growth management in general" (Growth Commission 1999, 29). Acting on that commitment, the commission used considerable effort in the late summer and autumn to move smart growth initiatives to the next level. The commission examined activities for the coming year, including the broader issues of growth areas; urban revitalization; lack of adequate funding to support growth; conflicts among federal, state or local programs that affect growth and the environment; the need to focus on economic growth and removing obstacles to growth; and changes to codes and regulations that prevent appropriate densities in PFAs.

The commission's Subcommittee on the Environment and Economic Development addressed the shortage of funds to meet the infrastructure needs of Maryland's smart growth system since the adoption of the initial growth management legislation in 1992. A MOP infrastructure needs survey in 1998 documented the need for at least $41 billion to cover the cost of infrastructure over the next 20 years, with sprawl development patterns a major cause of the substantial gap between needs and available funds.

The commission also endorsed the subcommittee's proposal for a smart growth infrastructure fund to "provide money to local governments to address infrastructure deficits and provide for infrastructure needs within [PFAs]" (Growth Commission 1999, 10). The fund's design involved a major step toward drawing local governments fully into the smart growth system. State dollars allocated from the fund would be limited to needed infrastructure in PFAs. To be eligible for such funding, local governments would be required to develop a Capital Improvements Program (CIP) that identified eligible projects. Higher ranking was given to projects promoting the revitalization of distressed areas and existing PFA infrastructure deficiencies.

Special status would be given to projects that removed Adequate Public Facilities Ordinance (APFOs) restrictions "that stop or retard development in PFAs; or involve the renovation or rehabilitation of existing infrastructure" (Growth Commission 1999, 11).

The commission saw the establishment and implementation of the infrastructure fund as achieving several goals considered essential to the full development of smart growth for Maryland: "It would first establish a source of funding to provide needed infrastructure in the targeted development areas. It would leverage local investments by requiring a match by county and municipal government" (Growth Commission 1999, 12). Continuing with its justification for such a program, the commission stressed several concerns.

■ While Adequate Public Facilities Ordinances (APFOs) are a necessary tool for assuring public facilities in growth areas, unless new financing structures were established, APFOs have been used to block development in the very areas where growth needs to go, such as existing urban areas and PFAs.

■ The long success of Maryland's smart growth system depends on channeling new development and redevelopment into designated growth areas, which in turn requires ordinances, codes, and other regulations (such as the Smart Codes legislation passed by the 2000 General Assembly).

■ Proposed changes would require a regular inventory of infrastructure shortfalls in their PFAs, targeting funds from state and local sources to those areas. (Growth Commission 1999, 13)

One reason for the considerable attention given to these recommendations is that without strengthening Maryland's smart growth system, especially in the funding area, the full implementation of its goals will not be achieved. This attention also illustrates the ongoing determination of the growth commission to work with the governor and other supporters of the system to bring about the needed changes, legislative and otherwise. The 2000 General Assembly approved important steps in that direction, but with some items still on the unfinished agenda.

On another front, Michael Barnes resigned in early 2000 as chair of the Growth Commission to be replaced by Paul Zanecki, a long-time associate of the governor with a background in public and private practice concentrated on land use, zoning, real estate and environmental law. He was expected to push at least as hard as Barnes did for a strong role for the growth commission.

Executive and Legislative Actions in 2000

The Glendening administration proposed five key pieces of legislation to the 2000 session of the Maryland General Assembly, and all five were approved essentially as proposed. Each was a major step forward in implementing Maryland's smart growth initiative. Just as important, they illustrated the governor's ability to mobilize support for sustaining and strengthening the implementation process.

1. Smart Codes—Maryland Building Rehabilitation Code

This bill addressed a problem common to almost all attempts to implement smart growth approaches: lack of uniformity, unpredictability and inflexibility of rehabilitation codes that often make it difficult to implement initiatives such as upgrading existing structures and recycling abandoned buildings. The Maryland Building Rehabilitation Code is based on a model code developed by the U.S. Department of Housing and Urban Development and the National Association of Home Builders. While the rehabilitation code would operate statewide, local jurisdictions could amend its provisions—a potential major weakness in the code. To overcome that problem without a rigid top-down requirement, the state would "provide financial incentives for localities that choose not to amend the...Code, including $17 million annually in the Maryland Department of Transportation's Neighborhood Conservation Program; $10 million in the State's Rural Legacy Program; and new low interest mortgage loans through the Maryland Department of Housing and Community Development" (Strocko and Hopkins 2000, 1, 6). Another part of the legislation established a Rehabilitation Code Advisory Council, charged with drafting and updating the code; issuing advisory opinions to resolve issues that arise in the implementation process; and "oversee[ing] training for code officials, design professionals, and others in the construction industry" (Strocko and Hopkins 2000, 1, 6–7).

2. Smart Codes—Models and Guidelines—Infill Development and Smart Neighborhoods

The second smart codes bill was intended to promote infill development in existing communities and new development in PFAs. The Planning Office was charged with promoting infill development and mixed use through additions to its ongoing Models and Guidelines series. The infill model includes "community compatibility standards that deal with land use transition, building orientation, privacy, and building materials." The aim of the smart neighborhoods model is to accommodate "population growth by encouraging communities to develop with a mix of housing, employment, and community services that encourage pedestrian traffic...[and] encourage attractive, livable communities." Another goal was to increase flexibility in development standards by "establishing floating zones, overlay zones, or new zoning categories" addressing such issues as building height and setbacks, lot size, density, bulk and scale, street widths and parking requirements and open space/landscaping (Strocko and Hopkins 2000, 7).

3. Natural Resources—Transferable Development Rights—Rural Legacy Program

This bill is a major move toward implementing Maryland's smart growth goals, because it provides significant fiscal incentives for both local governments and the development community to utilize TDRs as a tool in promoting smart growth. For the first time, there will be a powerful incentive for developers to purchase and counties to sell TDRs.

To illustrate how this legislation will work, county "X" has been allocated $10 million under the Rural Legacy Program. The county sells development rights to a developer for $10 million, half of which goes to infrastructure improvements, typically to help support the increased density for the development in a PFA. The other $5 million goes back into the Rural Legacy pot in that county. With that $5 million, the county can repeat the process, selling development rights,

with half ($2.5 million) earmarked for needed infrastructure and the other $2.5 million going back into the Rural Legacy fund. The county can ultimately leverage the $10 million up to $30 million ($20 million from developer purchase of TDRs and the original $10 million Rural Legacy allocation to the county).

4. Home Ownership Opportunities for Teachers

An important part of Maryland's smart growth agenda has been reallocating state education funding from the outer suburbs, and developing new and rehabilitating existing schools in urban areas and in PFAs. SB 206 adds a unique increment to ensure schools are not only located in the right place, but are also staffed by the right teachers.

In this bill, the General Assembly declared its intent that the Department of Housing and Community Development "develop a program to promote home ownership opportunities for teachers in consultation with the state Board of Education and local boards of education." The legislation passed the Senate (30–12) and the House (136–0) in early April 2000. The findings section of the legislation found that to attract and retain teachers, the state needed to increase home ownership opportunities by developing a program that authorized the department to dedicate up to $25 million over five years to provide mortgage loans to teachers at interest rates below the prevailing rate of interest for similar programs. Some of the conditions for a teacher to participate would be to agree to teach in Maryland for a minimum of three years, be a first-time home buyer, and purchase a property located in a PFA.

5. State Government—Department of Planning

The fifth Glendening proposal approved by the 2000 legislative session was SB 204, which converted the Office of Planning to the Department of Planning, "making it a principal department of state government." With the passage of SB 204 (its counterpart in the House was HB 286), the state government unit that had taken the lead in developing and implementing Maryland's smart growth system achieved full cabinet status.

As of July 2000, Ron Kreitner left state employment; Ron Young became the deputy director of the new department; and Harriet Tregoning, formerly at the U.S. EPA, became secretary of planning for Maryland. At EPA, Tregoning helped found and coordinate the National Smart Growth Network, a national partnership program designed to inform and accelerate innovative smart growth policies and practices.

The New Chesapeake Bay Agreement

The continued work of the Chesapeake Bay Program both directly and indirectly supports Maryland's efforts to manage its growth better. As noted earlier in the chapter, the program is a partnership that includes the states of Pennsylvania, Maryland and Virginia; Washington, DC; the Chesapeake Bay Commission; and the EPA representing the federal government. Since 1983 it has increased its attention on nonpoint source pollution as the bay's greatest enemy—one that could be corrected only by a radical change in land development patterns to reverse sprawl, thereby protecting farms, forests and wetlands, and reducing the pollutants flowing into the bay. Unfortunately for that agenda, only Maryland has risen to the challenge of the program, although Pennsylvania began moving in that direction under Governor Tom Ridge's leadership.

The signatories to the Chesapeake Bay Program were faced with EPA's putting the bay on its "dirty waters" list, an action that requires a cleanup plan called Total Maximum Daily Load. In early 1999 those actors agreed to draft a new Chesapeake Bay 2000 Agreement to be debated by all key stakeholders, including a request for the Alliance for the Chesapeake Bay to provide input on the draft. The alliance includes environmentalists, business representatives, government officials and others committed to the protection of the Chesapeake Bay. Its monthly publication, the *Bay Journal*, carried a detailed account of the efforts to produce a draft Chesapeake 2000 Agreement and put it out for review, leading to its formal adoption in June 2000.

The agreement "lays out a vision for protecting the Bay and its watershed for the next decade" and must be adopted by the Bay Program's executive council (Blankenship 2000b). While all sides favored specific goals and implementing measures—and in

most areas the final version to be adopted by the council met that goal—the sticking point, as usual, involved land use issues. The draft agreement called for reducing the rate at which farms and forests are converted to development by 30 percent annually by

---

Smart Growth Actions of the 2001 Legislative Session

- *GreenPrint*. Five-year program funded at $145 million to protect ecologically sensitive lands. Composed of a "statewide network of large ecologically significant 'hubs' bound together by greenway corridors." Hubs will support and provide protection and safe passage for a wide variety of native wildlife. Another goal is to maintain quality of streams and wetlands by protecting nearby vegetation. Initial funding for FY 2002 was $35 million. (MDP 2001, 9)

- *Community Legacy Program*. Added component of existing revitalization efforts that targeted severely distressed areas. Funded at $10 million for capital projects; $1 million for planning. The goal is to help communities avoid falling into further decline and enable them to make the most of their positive assets. (MDP 2001, 12–13)

- *Neighborhood Parks and Playgrounds*. New competitive program funded at $11 million for FY 2002. Allows the establishment or renovation of parks and playgrounds by communities located in PFAs. (Maryland Office of the Governor 2001b, 3)

- *Transit Initiative Program*. Aimed at making the governor's goal of "doubling the number of daily transit users by 2020" a reality. Proposals called for investing more than $500 million over six years to upgrade mass transit service and infrastructure. Increases approved for transit funding nearly equaled funds proposed for roads, a first for Maryland, with demand rapidly outstripping supply. Funding for the new transit investments will come from general fund transfers and some toll increases. (MDP 2001, 16–17; Maryland Office of the Governor 2001b, 4)

- *Investing in Education*. More than any state in the union, Glendening's administration focused on upgrading and building new schools in urban and PFAs, rather than at the edge where schools encourage sprawl. New funding for FY 2002 totaled $250 million for classroom modernization and construction (Maryland Office of the Governor 2001b, 2–3). Many state school systems, in the face of losing state dollars for "nonsmart growth" spending, have adjusted their projects to reflect the state's new approach. Quality schools in the "right" places are recognized as critical to channeling growth into designated growth areas, but no state has gone as far as Maryland in putting the dollars on the line to implement this.

Source: MDP, 2001, 24–25

2010. Council members were split on such a specific land use goal, with Glendening stating, "anything that is not specific on the goal for reduction of sprawl and the loss of agricultural and forest land will be too soft" (Blankenship 2000b, 1).

Virginia Governor Jim Gilmore understood the importance of the land conversion issue, but felt that he did not have the authority to impose this kind of land use policy decision on the localities of his state. Supporters of the goal saw land use as the Achilles heel of the Bay restoration effort. As EPA's Bill Matuszeski put it, "The last thing left to hang our hat on was the conversion goal. Everything else had been sort of swept off the table" (Blankenship 2000b, 1–2). "Everything else" in this case included such things as limits on vehicle miles traveled, targets for farmland or forest preservation, or caps on impervious surfaces such as pavement and rooftops, all of which had been taken off the table. However, Matuszeski and others were not too discouraged by having to fall back on the 30 percent land conversion goal, seeing it as a "surrogate for other land use issues: it's hard to reduce the rate at which farms and forests are developed unless efforts are made to consolidate development, address where roads are built and a range of other growth issues" (Blankenship 2000b, 2).

The final version of the new Chesapeake Bay 2000 Agreement did keep the land conversion goal, pledging to "slow the rate that 'harmful sprawl' development consumes farms and forests by 30 percent by 2012" (Blankenship 2000a, 1). In a related land use issue, the agreement's goal specified protecting 20 percent of the watershed as open space by 2010. Part of the agreement's success related to the public comments that "overwhelmingly supported efforts to curtail sprawl" (Blankenship 2000a, 1–2; 2001).

Taken as a whole, the new Chesapeake Bay 2000 Agreement is a major plus for the smart growth approach in one of the nation's most significant watersheds. The process leading to its adoption has placed greater pressure on states in the watershed to work together for a more regional approach. Much discussion about having other relevant states such as New York, Delaware and West Virginia formally join the program may cause this to happen in the near future—an action supported by the Alliance for the Chesapeake Bay. As chair of the Chesapeake Bay Executive Council, Governor Glendening took a leadership role in seeing that Chesapeake 2000 "focused on the root causes of the Bay's decline: poor land use and sprawl development, excess nutrients and habitat destruction" (MDP 2001, 20–21).

Actions in the 2001 General Assembly

Developments during and following the 2001 legislative session strengthened the implementation of Maryland's already cutting-edge smart growth strategies. The General Assembly approved the governor's programs essentially as proposed, including the establishment of the Governor's Office of Smart Growth (OSG) and a smart growth subcabinet.

In July 2001 the governor warned, however, that "Smart growth will help restore our downtown economies, our sense of community, and our environment. This is neither an easy nor a quick task. It will take a fundamental change in thinking" (MDP 2001, 1). Clearly, the governor recognized that the full implementation and sustaining of Maryland's smart growth initiatives would take longer than his term-limited tenure in November 2002. His strategy was to assemble a team of nationally recognized smart growth leaders, including Harriet Tregoning, his special secretary heading OSG; Roy Kienitz, secretary of the Maryland Department of Planning (MDP); and Ron Young, deputy secretary of MDP. For his part, the governor saw that this new team and new approach would correct the fact that, despite Maryland's leadership in the area, "Smart growth projects are still too often the exception rather than the rule...our new approach will change this" (Maryland Office of the Governor, 2001a).

In another action, Glendening announced in May 2001 that the state would use its longstanding legal authority to participate in local government land use proceedings that have significant smart growth implications. The state's planning agencies have had that authority since 1974, and at the governor's direction will now intervene to oppose local government actions that are clearly inconsistent with smart growth and will support local governments whose attempts to implement smart growth policies have been challenged (Maryland Office of the Governor

2001a, 2–3). The first three interventions taken by the MDP were

■ filing a motion in support of the Kent County Planning Commission's decision to turn down a proposal for a WalMart, based on the view that WalMart would have a negative impact on the business district in the city of Chesterton;

■ supporting a transit-oriented development project known as Parklands with transit dollars, and assisting in the development of a pedestrian-scale environment, provision of mixed uses and design that takes advantage of nearby transit; and

■ "supporting the conceptual framework of Acton's Landing, an infill redevelopment project…in downtown Annapolis that exemplifies the appropriate use of Smart Growth and Smart Code policies." (MDP 2001)

Given the generous funding the state had at its disposal at that time, the use of its intervention authority via MDP in coordination with the OSG had the potential to substantially strengthen the implementation of the state's smart growth strategies. The changes to Maryland's smart growth system, and especially the actions of the 2001 legislature in supporting Glendening's rich menu of initiatives, went far toward reinforcing Maryland's status as one of the leading states in the nation in crafting, implementing and sustaining a comprehensive smart growth system. The question then arose as to whether the broad-based implementation of those strategies could be sustained in the face of the economic downturn, aggravated by the events of September 11, 2001, and the unexpected and far-reaching changes in Maryland's political framework.

Transition to a New Administration, 2002–2003

The 2002 General Assembly took no action that directly impacted Maryland's smart growth strategies, but it did pass SB 247/HB 301, which extended development protections under the Chesapeake Bay Critical Areas Act to other coastal bays in the state.

Lt. Governor Kathleen Kennedy-Townsend had no opposition in the Democratic primary, but her Republican opponent, Robert L. Ehrlich Jr., had a long record of public service in Maryland as a state legislator and member of Congress. Early in the campaign, Ehrlich stated, "I'm going places Republican candidates have never gone," referring in part to "his praise for and pledge to continue…Glendening's comprehensive Smart Growth policy, including urban redevelopment, farmland conservation and open space protection." Ehrlich did criticize Glendening for his administration's use of a policy of withholding funds from local governments, or threats to do so, to block local zoning decisions by local governments that do not support smart growth (*Baltimore Sun* 2002a).

Both gubernatorial candidates were taking care "to confirm a widely held view that whoever wins will have to follow…Glendening's environmental and Smart Growth policies, but their apparent accord on some principles ends at practicalities." Ehrlich even declared, "We have a common goal. There's just differences on how to get there." But, Kennedy-Townsend stated, "It makes a difference who the governor is. You can have laws on the books, and you can decide whether to enforce or not to enforce" (*Baltimore Sun* 2002b).

While the smart growth strategies developed by the Glendening administration seemed to have broad support in Maryland, the election results, to the surprise of many, resulted in a win for Ehrlich (51 percent) over Kennedy-Townsend (48 percent). Both Houses of the Maryland General Assembly remained in the Democrats' camp, with substantial majorities (97–44 in the House and 33–14 in the Senate).

The Ehrlich administration's decision to move the OSG from the Office of the Governor back to the Department of Planning was defended as a way to avoid duplication and increase efficiency, although smart growth advocates in and out of Maryland strongly objected. Senate Democratic President Thomas V. Miller saw the OSG as Glendening's "greatest legacy" and attacked the move as undercutting its "land and resource protection strategy," and as "an example of politics over reason, partisanship over common sense, small-mindedness over what's best for the citizens of Maryland" (*Baltimore Sun* 2003).

The strongest defense for why moving the office did not represent a step backward for smart growth came from Erlich's new MDP secretary, Audrey Scott, a former Prince Georges County council member, mayor of the City of Bowie and affordable housing administrator at the U.S. Department of Housing and Urban Development. Scott noted that the OSG under Harriet Tregoning had only six people who had been transferred from the MDP. While the OSG was in Annapolis reporting directly to the governor, its key mission was to promote smart growth. However, Scott felt there was some hostility toward the office, since the MDP staff in Baltimore did all the implementation of the smart growth planning initiatives. Seeing it that way, Scott and the governor's office decided to move OSG back under the MDP.

Scott, on one hand, saw the focus of the Glendening administration to be preserving open space, the part of his initiative that received most of the funding. The Ehrlich administration, on the other hand, inherited a major deficit and decided to prioritize its focus by shifting attention to established urban communities by expanding such programs as brownfields and wastewater treatment facilities. To Scott, that amounted to expanding Maryland's smart growth program.

In the 2003 session of the General Assembly, the MDP cited some positive bills that passed, such as HB 0131, "authorizing the governing bodies of two or more counties to designate a priority funding area under State smart growth laws; requiring that the area designated be located in contiguous parts of each of the designated counties." The department also endorsed other legislation that favored smart growth, supporting Scott's assertion that the Ehrlich administration was not against smart growth (MDP 2003, 1).

In October 2003 Governor Ehrlich issued an executive order to put his stamp on Maryland's smart growth initiatives, but at the same time keeping Governor Glendening's core principles intact (Ehrlich 2003). The executive order established the Maryland Priority Places Strategy for MDP to implement by developing strategies to

- ensure that state programs, regulations and procedures, and funds are used strategically to achieve the goals of local comprehensive plans and state planning policy, and provide for the infrastructure necessary to support planned growth;

- better enforce existing laws, regulations and procedures designed to ensure mutually supportive public investments and actions;

- streamline state regulations and procedures to make quality, well-designed growth easier to build inside PFAs;

- identify key plans and functions of state government that affect growth and development and make appropriate changes to those plans and functions to better support the goals of the Maryland Priority Places Strategy;

- encourage resource protection and production outside PFAs of environmental protection, recreation, tourism, forestry, and agricultural purposes; and

- enhance existing brownfield cleanup and redevelopment, transit-oriented development, and community revitalization efforts. (Ehrlich 2003, 2)

The order also established a Development Capacity Task Force charged with producing a Development Capacity Study that complements Priority Places; the task force's final report was delivered to the governor on July 1, 2004. In announcing this strategy, Ehrlich called it "a little more than a tweak but certainly not a sea change." Ehrlich also reemphasized his support for the core principles of Glendening's smart growth program that focused on urban areas: community revitalization, redevelopment of brownfields, transit-oriented development, and streamlining regulations to make it easier to develop planned growth areas (Dresser 2003a). Reaction to Ehrlich's executive order was mixed, with most outside observers willing to wait and see what happened once they had more details. Responding to some concerns that the order would undermine PFAs, Scott commented that "There is no backing off the commitments to PFAs. It certainly won't be on my watch" (Dresser 2003a; 2003b, 1B, 5B).

Conclusion

As one long-time participant-observer put it, Governor Ehrlich's administration had a rough start. Upon taking office, he was faced with a major budget crisis that called for drastic cuts in agency budgets unless some taxes were raised. The General Assembly crafted a budget that included some tax increases to avoid budget cuts for key programs, but Ehrlich vetoed it. After a big battle, a compromise of sorts was reached. Several other participants in Maryland's smart growth efforts agreed that the MDP seemed to have support from the Ehrlich administration, that a number of top professionals in the MDP had been retained, and there seemed to be no effort to dismantle the smart growth program. However, major smart growth initiatives requiring large investments can not go forward until the budget crisis is eased.

So, what can we say about the future of Maryland's landmark smart growth system? It is too soon to know just what will happen. Assuming the budget deficit resolves itself through increased revenues, growth in the economy or increased taxes, will the Ehrlich administration walk the walk and not just talk the talk in implementing Maryland's smart growth system?

Parris Glendening is continuing his efforts to promote smart growth nationwide as president of the Smart Growth Leadership Institute housed at the nonprofit Smart Growth America in Washington, DC. In a speech in February 2003, Glendening stressed that "States are spending millions of dollars to subsidize sprawl.... If we're going to deal successfully with poverty and crime and the segregation of education, then you have to deal with the fundamental issue of sprawl" (Frankston 2003, 2).

References

Baer, David and Joe Bishop. 1996. *Cleaning up the Chesapeake Bay through Maryland's Critical Area Act of 1984*. May 2. Unpublished paper.

Baltimore Sun. 1999. Glendening's vision for the 21st century: Ambitious agenda: Education, environment, equality top the list, but can we afford it all? January 23.

———. 2002a. Maryland gubernatorial candidates agree to follow smart growth policies, but paths may vary. October 21.

———. 2002b. Smart growth program will continue, pledges Maryland Republican gubernatorial nominee. May 1.

———. 2003. Gov. Ehrlich defends dismissal of state smart growth officers. June 23.

Blankenship, Karl. 2000a. Bay leaders agree to curb sprawl, protect open space. *Bay Journal* 10.4 (June). Alliance for the Chesapeake Bay.

———. 2000b. Bay partners split on policy for land conversion. *Bay Journal* 10.1 (March). Alliance for the Chesapeake Bay.

———. 2001. Bay states must protect 1.1 million more acres to meet goal. *Bay Journal* 11.1 (March). Alliance for the Chesapeake Bay.

Chesapeake Bay Critical Area Commission. Undated. Critical areas and you: The Chesapeake's first line of defense. Annapolis, MD.

Chesapeake Executive Council. 1985. Chesapeake Bay Restoration and Protection Plan. Annapolis, MD.

Dresser, Michael. 1999. Smart growth plan's 1st bite. *Baltimore Sun*. January 24.

———. 2003a. Ehrlich sets priorities for smart growth. *Baltimore Sun*. October 10.

———. 2003b. Ehrlich's smart growth plan praised by national advocate. *Baltimore Sun*. October 11.

Ehrlich, Robert L. 2003. Executive Order 1010.2003.33, Maryland's Priority Place Strategy. October 8.

Frankston, Janet. 2003. Governors enter sprawl fray; "Smartgrowth" debate: More states taking steps to control development. *Atlanta Journal-Constitution*. February 17.

Glendening, Governor Parris. 1996. Remarks to the Maryland Municipal League. In *Smart growth and neighborhood conservation in Maryland*, 6–7. Maryland Office of Planning.

———. 1997. State of the State Address. Smart growth and neighborhood conservation in Maryland. Baltimore, MD: Maryland Office of Planning.

———. 1998. Executive Order 01.01.1998.04: Smart Growth and Neighborhood Conservation Policy. January 23. Annapolis, MD.

———. 1999. State of the State Address: Preparing Maryland for the next century: An education blueprint for our future.

Governor's Commission on Growth in the Chesapeake Bay Region. 1991. *Protecting the future: A vision for Maryland*. Baltimore, MD.

Horton, Tom and William Eichbaum. 1991. *Turning the tide: Saving the Chesapeake Bay*. Washington, DC: Island Press.

Inside Washington Publishers. 1997. *State Environmental Monitor* 2(5) May:16.

Maryland Department of the Environment. 1995. *The state of the Chesapeake Bay, 1995*. Washington, DC: U.S. Government Printing Office.

Maryland Department of Planning (MDP). 2001. Maryland Department of Planning takes action in support of smart growth; First use of long-standing intervention authority. August 23.

———. 2003. Legislative status report, 2003 session. June 26.

Maryland Economic Growth, Resource Protection, and Planning Commission (Growth Commission). 1996. Annual report, vol. I: Recommendations and report. Baltimore, MD.

———. 1997. Annual report: vol. I: Recommendations and report. December. Baltimore, MD.

———. 1998. Annual report, vol. I: Recommendations and report. December. Baltimore, MD.

———. 1999. Annual report, vol. I: Recommendations and report. December. Baltimore, MD.

Maryland Office of the Governor. 2001a. Governor Glendening appoints new secretaries for Office of Smart Growth and Department of Planning.

———. 2001b. 2001 Legislative session: A solid record of success; a solid foundation for Maryland's future.

Maryland Office of Planning (MOP). 1993. Managing Maryland's growth: Procedures for state project review under the Planning Act of 1992. January. Baltimore, MD.

———. 1997a. Managing Maryland's growth—What you need to know about smart growth and neighborhood conservation. May. Baltimore, MD.

———. 1997b. *Smart growth and neighborhood conservation in Maryland.* Baltimore, MD.

———. 1998. Managing Maryland's growth—Models and guidelines, sizing and shaping growth areas. December. Baltimore, MD: Subcommittee on Planning Techniques.

Matuszeski, Bill. 1996. Mature approach to land use could ease growing pains. *Bay Journal* 6.5 (July–August):16–17. Alliance for the Chesapeake Bay.

Noonan, James T. and Gail Moran. 1996. Implementation of Maryland's Economic Growth, Resource Protection, and Planning Act. *Environmental and Urban Issues* 23 (4):2–8. Fort Lauderdale, FL: FAU/FIU Joint Center for Environmental and Urban Problems.

Smith, C. Fraser. 1998. Governor wins with new tactics, old allies. Early Sauerbrey edge melted under scrutiny of her voting record. *Baltimore Sun*. November 4.

Strocko, Ed and Johns Hopkins. 2000. General Assembly passes smart codes legislation. *Planning Times*. Maryland Office of Planning. Spring.

Thomson, Candus. 1999. Montgomery town battles for bypass. *Baltimore Sun*. February 8.

Tierney, Philip J. 1994. Bold promises but baby steps: Maryland's growth policy to the year 2020. *University of Baltimore Law Review* 23.2 (Spring): 461–520.

U.S. Environmental Protection Agency (USEPA). 1983. *Chesapeake Bay: A profile for environmental change.* Annapolis, MD.

Year 2020 Panel. 1988. Population growth and development in the Chesapeake Bay watershed to the year 2020. *The report of the Year 2020 Panel to the Chesapeake Executive Council.* December. Annapolis, MD.

Appendix

Governors

William Donald Schaefer (Democrat)   1987–1995
Parris Glendening (Democrat)   1995–2003
Robert L. Ehrlich Jr. (Republican)   2003–present

Acronyms

APFO   Adequate Public Facilities Ordinance
APA   American Planning Association
CIP   Capital Improvements Program
DOT   Department of Transportation
IDA   intensely developed area
LDA   limited development area
LNYW   Live Near Your Work
MACO   Maryland Association of Counties
MALPF   Maryland Agricultural Land Preservation Foundation
MDP   Maryland Department of Planning
MML   Maryland Municipal League
MOP   Maryland Office of Planning
OSG   Office of Smart Growth
PDR   purchase of development rights
PFA   priority funding area
RCA   resource conservation area
TDR   transferable development rights

Contacts

1000 Friends of Maryland
1209 N. Calvert Street
Baltimore, MD 21202
410-385-2910
friends@friendsofmd.org
http://www.friendsofmd.org

Alliance for the Chesapeake Bay
6600 York Road, Suite 100
Baltimore, MD 21212
410-377-6270
http://www.acb-online.org

Chesapeake Bay Foundation
Philip Merrill Environmental Center
6 Herndon Avenue
Annapolis, MD 21403
410-268-8816
http://www.cbf.org

Chesapeake Bay Program
410 Severn Avenue, Suite 109
Annapolis, MD 21403
800-YOUR-BAY
http://www.chesapeakebay.net

Maryland Department of Natural Resources
Watershed Service
(formerly Education, Bay Policy and Growth Management Unit)
Tawes State Office Building, E-2
580 Taylor Avenue
Annapolis, MD 21401
410-260-8710
http://www.dnr.state.md.us

Maryland Department of Planning
301 West Preston Street, Suite 1101
Baltimore, MD 21201-2305
410-767-4500
http://www.mdp.state.md.us/contacts.htm

Maryland Governor's Office of Smart Growth
301 West Preston Street, Suite 1101
Baltimore, MD 21201-2305
410-767-4500
http://www.smartgrowth.state.md.us

Maryland Municipal League
1212 West Street
Annapolis, MD 21401
410-268-5514
800-492-7121
http://www.mdmunicipal.org/mmlhome/index.cfm

MdProperty View
http://www.mdp.state.md.us/data/index.htm

National Center for Smart Growth Research and Education
University of Maryland
Preinkert Fieldhouse
College Park, MD 20742
301-405-6788
http://www.smartgrowth.umd.edu/

State of Maryland
http://www.mec.state.md.us
http://www.maryland.gov

8

Washington

Contents

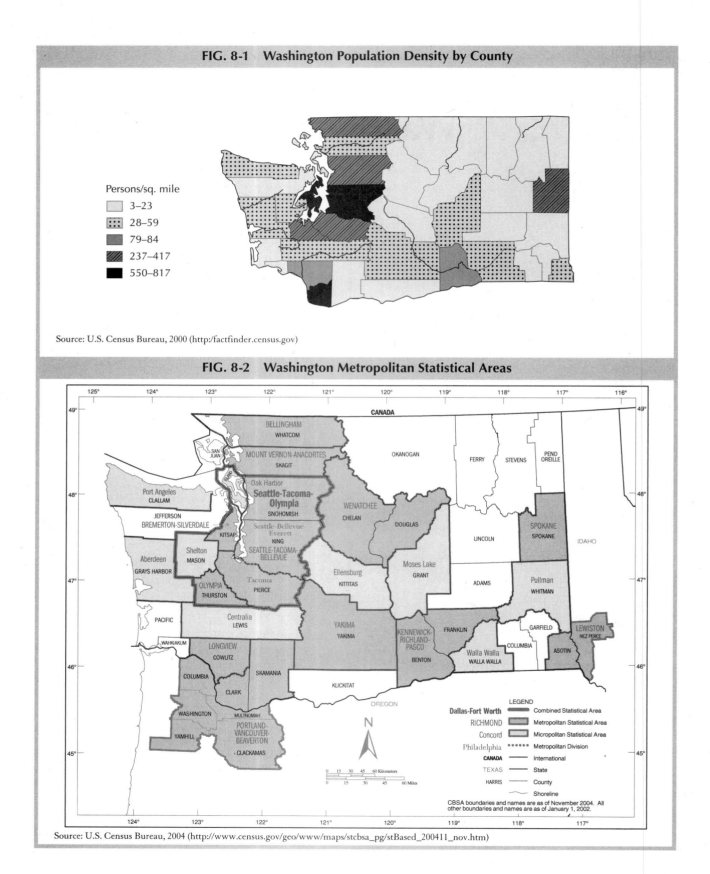

FIG. 8-1   Washington Population Density by County

Persons/sq. mile
- 3–23
- 28–59
- 79–84
- 237–417
- 550–817

FIG. 8-2   Washington Metropolitan Statistical Areas

Introduction

Analyzing growth management systems in the late 1990s and early twenty-first century challenges the reader to understand the impact of major upheavals in the nation's politics and governance. These forces have threatened to weaken, and in some cases destroy, state and regional growth management systems that appeared reasonably secure at the beginning of the 1990s. The antigovernment, antiregulation mood of many Americans fed the extreme property rights movements that in the mid-1990s had a chilling impact on efforts to implement comprehensive growth management systems.

Washington is an especially interesting case because the 1995 legislature passed a highly restrictive property rights compensation statute that questioned whether the state's recently established growth management system could be implemented effectively. The broad-based advocacy group 1000 Friends of Washington and an environmental coalition led by the Washington Environmental Council (WEC) headed the effort to nullify the law. However, the property rights statute was drawn up to prevent a veto by the governor, thus making the initiative process the only strategy available to void it. Sufficient signatures were collected to place the initiative on the ballot, and in 1995 voters repealed the law by a wide margin. Many believed the vote was a defining moment in the state, suggesting that the legislature was out of step with the citizens on growth management issues.

Washington was the first state in the early 1990s to adopt a comprehensive growth management system, after a struggle that extended over two legislative sessions (1990 and 1991). The efforts to pass the Growth Management Act (GMA) succeeded at the last minute in each of the sessions, only by adopting ambiguous and contradictory language that could be interpreted in a variety of ways by the key interests opposing and supporting the system. Nevertheless, the system provides for oversight and enforcement, seeks to manage growth pressures better in some sections of the state, includes a special effort to foster growth and economic development in others and mandates protection of environmentally sensitive areas statewide. The result was a blend of goals and policies designed to address complex growth challenges in a state with two distinct regions: booming western Washington dominated by Seattle and the four-county Puget Sound region, and slow- or no-growth eastern Washington, eager to share in its western cousin's prosperity (DeGrove 1992, 117–135).

There have been times when Republicans and Democrats joined to advance the system, but that has been the exception rather than the rule. Republicans have generally opposed Washington State's growth management system while Democrats have supported it. Initiatives have played a key and largely negative role in the decade-long struggle to implement the system. Many supporters believe that initiatives can be used to overcome some of the most severe threats to the GMA's full implementation, especially to stop some of the negative past initiatives.

The ability of Washington's growth management program to proceed at all after its hard-fought adoption is largely due to the determined support of former governors Booth Gardner, Mike Lowry and Gary Locke. They have done more to sustain the program than any other single factor, despite efforts in several legislative sessions to dismantle it. The road to full implementation of the state's system has been a rough one, however, with a continuing need to integrate all relevant state programs and strengthen the ties for full participation of local governments in the system.

In November 2000 Governor Locke handily won his bid for a second term, ensuring continued strong support for the system. But on the negative side, it has not been possible to bring together all key stakeholders, public and private, to champion the full and fair implementation of that system.

State Profile

Washington has grown substantially since World War II. The 1950 population of some 2.4 million was a dramatic increase (about 37 percent) over the 1940 figure of slightly higher than 642,000, and the decades of the 1950s and 1960s both increased by about 20 percent. Since 1970 growth has continued at more than 500,000 each decade. The state's 2000 population was 5,894,121, and projections for the future show population growth reaching 6.26 million by 2005; 7.1 million by 2015; and 7.8 million by 2025 (U.S. Census Bureau Undated d).

Much of the growth in Washington has taken place in the greater Seattle region: King, Pierce, Snohomish and Kitsap counties. In 1990 this region included 63 municipalities; 11 other incorporations were added from 1990 to 1996. When combined with annexations that have added to existing cities (especially in the suburbs), the result has been to lower the percentage of the population in unincorporated areas. The 1997 population of the region reached 3.1 million—a 12.8 percent increase from 1990 and a 38.4 percent increase from 1980. By 2000 the region's population was 3.28 million, approximately 55.8 percent of Washington's population (PSRC 2001a; U.S. Census Bureau Undated a). The region is projected to grow to 3.8 million by 2010 and 4.26 million by 2020. Growth in eastern Washington has been slow, with Spokane, the only densely populated county, having 361,364 in 1990 and 417,939 in 2000 (U.S. Census Bureau Undated b).

Washington's population growth in the 1980s, before the passage of the 1990–1991 GMA, mostly represented a sprawl pattern of development common to all growth states in the nation, whereas Seattle, the state's preeminent city, managed to grow only from 516,259 in 1990 to 563,374 in 2000 (U.S. Census Bureau Undated c). This sprawl has been described as resulting in a "continuous, connected urban area" in the central Puget Sound region. One focus of this chapter is whether the GMA and the growing strength of the Puget Sound Regional Council (PSRC) have been effective in altering these sprawl patterns of development (King County 1989; PSRC 1997a, 4).

The Economy

From 1974 to 2000 the number of private-sector jobs in Washington increased by 187 percent, and one industry, aerospace, dominated the state's economy. Boeing is the state's largest private-sector employer, and "its fortunes are correlated with those of this city and the entire state economy" (Northwest Policy Center 1990, 18). Washington's overall employment growth rate in 2000 was 2.6 percent, a slight increase from

1999 but a considerable decrease from the 1996–1998 period, which had an unprecedented total employment growth rate, due primarily to expansion in the aerospace industry (Washington State Office of the Forecast Council 2001, 4). Washington is also home to Microsoft and a host of other technology-based industries, which provided close to 286,000 jobs in 2000. Such jobs accounted for approximately 10.8 percent of total state employment between 1974 and 2000 (Technology Alliance 2001).

Starting in the early 1980s, Washington saw a continual economic expansion and fared much better than most other states during the recession of the early 1990s. The advent of high-tech companies in the area, coupled with high paying jobs in manufacturing, helped boost Washington's economy and cause a boom in population. However, at the start of the twenty-first century, Washington's economy is in decline and is predicted to gain strength more slowly than the rest of the country. The state's promising international trade prospects have been severely hampered by the decline in Asian markets. With the technology sector already in a slump, the events of September 11, 2001 hit the state's aerospace industry hard. By March 2002 Washington's unemployment rate rose above 7 percent and the state was facing a 20 percent budget deficit.

In January 2003 Governor Locke noted that Washington had the third highest unemployment rate in the country and was facing the state's biggest deficit ever: $2.4 billion (Locke 2003, 1). A September 2003 report by the state's Office of the Forecast Council pointed out that Washington's boom in the information technology sector prior to the 2001 recession only meant that the state's economy had farther to fall. While most economic indicators for the state were seen as having worsened since September 2002, the report noted that between 1998 and 2002, Washington's average employment growth rate was 1.1 percent, just about on par with the national average of 1.2 percent. Most of the indicators for quality of life, education and skills of the workforce, infrastructure and cost of doing business showed improvement over the past year, perhaps a sign that Washington may be on the road to recovery (Washington State Office of the Forecast Council 2003, 1, 6).

The Puget Sound Region

The Puget Sound region, with more than half the state's population, has developed a unique partnership among federal actors such as the U.S. Department of Transportation (DOT) and the Environmental Protection Agency (EPA) and the state, notably the Washington State Department of Transportation (WSDOT). All have played key roles in helping the Puget Sound Regional Council craft and implement a smart growth system for the region. After more than a decade of implementing efforts, the system has survived but not thrived, and major challenges remain, especially efforts to fund continued smart growth.

The Puget Sound economy is still subject to the vagaries of Boeing. In July 2003 "Boeing announced another round of layoffs, raising the total aerospace job cuts in the region to 28,000 since September 11 and 53,000 since 1998." It is clear that Boeing "will continue to have a big say in economic matters for some time to come" (Conway and Pederson 2003, 1).

Whatever Boeing decides to do, another major corporate enterprise, Microsoft, found the region, and Seattle specifically, an ideal location. In a February 23, 2003, interview in the *Seattle Times*, Microsoft Chair Bill Gates noted, "We are very happy that we chose to be in Seattle…a lot of companies in the Northwest are among our best customers" (Conway and Pederson 2003, 6). Another economic plus for the region was biotechnology leader Amgen's decision to locate its cancer research center in Seattle. Thus, the Puget Sound region continues to be a good place to do business, with the most important sectors being transportation equipment (principally aerospace) and information (software and telecommunications).

The Puget Sound regional economy has experienced many cyclical ups and downs over the past several decades, as heavy dependence on natural resources and transportation has been replaced by a more diverse economy. Further, "VISION 2020, adopted under the state's Growth Management Act (GMA), is the region's growth management, economic, and transportation strategy that responds to these issues…. VISION 2020's primary stated economic goal is to have a strong, vital, growing regional economy…. The plan's economic policies are based on the fundamental growth management strategy of containing this growth, and reinforcing and diversifying the region's existing urban areas and urban centers." The strategy supports "economic activity throughout the region with a wide variety of improved transportation infrastructure" (PSRC 2003a, 2).

The Growth Management Context

The negative impacts of unplanned growth in Washington during the 1970s and 1980s are not unique. Prior to 1990 Washington's unmanaged growth led to congested roads, especially in the Puget Sound area; sprawl development patterns that threatened open space, farmlands and natural systems; and increased air and water pollution. Underlying it all, however, was the misuse of land resulting from lack of a land use planning system capable of containing sprawl and providing infrastructure. Above all, there was no way to coordinate the management of growth among the 39 counties, almost 300 cities and more than 1,000 special districts across the state. In the state's periodic growth surges from the 1960s onward, the response of local governments was no planning at all, or planning in isolation from each other. Regional issues, even if recognized, could not be addressed, except in the area of environmental regulation, where Washington emerged as an early leader with the adoption of its Shoreline Management Act (SMA) in 1970.

An excessive commitment to home rule produced a cumulative failure to deal with greater-than-local problems. For example, most of the 31 cities in King County (which includes Seattle and 150 special districts) were planning individually, but were unable to address some of the bigger (countywide or regional) questions. Furthermore, since the 1970s, the failure to invest in adequate infrastructure, especially transportation, contributed to citizen dissatisfaction with the status quo. The loss of available open space emerged as a quality of life issue, as city and suburban dwellers, accustomed to "escaping" easily to a beautiful, rural countryside, found themselves fighting traffic to get there and then finding just another suburb. An environmental leader observed that different segments of the population were upset about different issues, ranging from crowded highways and schools to loss of forest land (10,000 acres per year to suburban development) to wetland losses that also eliminated open space.

Such negative impacts became more obvious in the mid-1980s and produced a mix of political forces that pushed Washington in a direction it had long resisted: toward the adoption of a comprehensive growth management system. Mandates were to be established for local and regional levels and carried out within the framework of state goals and state oversight. The key supporters of the system—political officials, environmental leaders and others—repeatedly cited the cumulative negative impacts of unmanaged growth as the fuel that drove the engine of change in the painful struggle to establish the new system from 1988 to 1991.

Growth Management Act, Part I: The 1990 Legislation

In the early 1970s Washington's Republican Governor Daniel J. Evans led the adoption of a number of significant environmental laws. The SMA made Washington the first state to win approval by the federal Office of Coastal Zone Management for its coastal regulation program. The second major act, the State Environmental Policy Act (SEPA), called for the environmental review of state and local actions that might adversely affect the environment. These acts made Washington a leader in the nationwide environmental movement, but they were not framed by a growth management system that linked them to land use.

Evans strongly supported statewide land use planning, building on efforts dating back to the early 1960s. A state land planning act based on the Model Land Development Code of the American Law Institute passed the House in 1973 and 1974, but could not clear the more conservative Senate (Scates 1990; Settle and Gavigan 1993, 875–876). After the high point of the early 1970s, however, land use reform was moved off the agenda for a decade by the election of Democratic Governor Dixy Lee Ray. Growth management did not return as a significant public policy issue until the late 1980s brought a booming

economy and renewed fears of a population invasion from California and elsewhere.

Getting Growth Management on the Public Policy Agenda

By 1989 the negative impacts of substantial unmanaged growth in western Washington had attracted considerable support in both the public and private sectors for a growth management system. Settle and Gavigan (1993, 879–880) summarized the weaknesses of the existing system:

> [U]nder pre-GMA law, local governments were largely autonomous in the realms of general land use and public facility planning and development regulation. At the same time, planning and regulatory actions were subject to SEPA's extensive environmental review process requirements, and quasijudicial regulatory actions were subject to rigorous judicially imposed procedural requirements. As a result, Washington land use law has been long on procedure and short on substance.

The private sector's newfound concerns about the negative impacts of unmanaged growth surfaced at the 1989 Leadership Conference of the Greater Seattle Chamber of Commerce. At the conference, Governor Booth Gardner, not previously known for his advocacy of land use reform, warned that not acting to manage growth better risked "strangulation or stagnation," and issued a challenge to find a way to "take advantage of growth without hurting our quality of life" (DeGrove 1992, 120).

With the citizens of the Puget Sound area becoming increasingly alarmed at the rapid and visible deterioration of their quality of life, the political system, by 1989, was poised to respond. The leadership for promoting a growth management system came from House Speaker Joe King, who was especially interested in transportation and land use linkages. In 1988 and 1989 King was pressed hard by building and development lobbyists to increase the gas tax to build more roads; he decided to use the increase as a starting point for reforming land use planning. The increases proposed in the 1989 legislative session ranged from three cents (the governor's proposal) to nine cents (recommended by a citizens' committee) per gallon.

Through King's leadership, the House passed HB 2140, which set up a Growth Strategies Commission

(GSC) charged with recommending a strategy for Washington that would focus on better coordination between land use and transportation. Half the proceeds of any gas tax increase would go to creating and funding the commission. The Republican-controlled Senate opposed any gas tax increase, however, and HB 2140 died.

King's proposal for a GSC was kept in the 1989–1991 biennium budget bill, which created a 17-member GSC, to be appointed by the Speaker of the House and president of the Senate.[1] It was "directed to develop strategies for (1) accommodating and guiding the state's growth, focusing on the Puget Sound region and fast-growing counties elsewhere; (2) linking transportation and land use planning; (3) enhancing regional planning; and (4) coordinating state and local governments" (Settle and Gavigan 1993, 883). The GSC would be staffed by the Department of Community Development (DCD), with $350,000 appropriated for that purpose.

Governor Gardner vetoed the 1989 legislative action directing him to establish a GSC, on the grounds that it was an improper legislative invasion of executive authority. At the same time, he stated his support for such a commission and his intent to establish it along the lines of the legislative directive. After some delay, the governor, by executive order, created the Washington GSC to recommend ways to preserve the environment and high quality of life that Washingtonians value, while maintaining steady economic growth throughout the state. The commission, including 13 citizens and 4 legislators, was directed to provide both interim and final reports during 1990 (Washington State Office of the Governor 1989; DeGrove 1992, 119–120).

The Growth Strategies Commission (GSC)

The GSC convened in October 1989 under its chair, Dick Ford, a respected civic leader. The 17-member commission functioned as a group of distinguished leaders who would reach out to relevant stakeholders in the course of its work. During 1989 the GSC hired staff and heard briefings on growth management issues in Seattle and Spokane. Five subcommittees— governance, infrastructure, shared economic growth, land use and housing—completed their reports early in 1990 (Washington State GSC 1990c, 1).

The GSC did not become involved in the 1990 legislative debate over a growth management bill, on the grounds that such involvement would divert the commission from its central charge. Ford was willing to expand the commission's outreach and was instrumental in holding the GSC together in support of what many viewed as a surprisingly strong final report.

The GSC issued its interim report in July 1990, in time to acknowledge its additional charge contained in the 1990 legislature's growth management law (Washington State GSC 1990a). The report envisioned a statewide growth strategy and outlined recommendations for fast-growing cities and counties subject to the full-scale planning mandates in the report. The strategy would involve all state agencies, create mechanisms to address regional issues, and offer timeframe and funding recommendations. Local plans would include such elements as character and design, environmental management, open space and parks, land use–infrastructure linkage and housing.

The governor played a crucial role in ensuring the proposed growth management system's success, and would be responsible for making certain state agency planning and implementation activities complied with the overall strategies. The interim report outlined a process by which the state would review, monitor and participate in the development of plans, resolve disputes and enforce compliance; it also emphasized the need to fund the mandated planning system (Washington State GSC 1990a; DeGrove 1992, 121).

The 1990 Growth Management Act (GMA I)

Before GSC had completed its work, the 1990 legislature adopted HB 2929, which became known as GMA I. Speaker King led the charge, determined to achieve what he had failed to get in the 1989 legislature. He saw an opportunity in the rising tide of resentment at the failure to manage growth in the Puget Sound region, which had led to the defeat of

---

1. Washington State enacts budgets for a two-year cycle, beginning on July 1 of each odd-numbered year and ending June 30 two years later. The governor is required by law to submit his biennial budget in December, one month prior to the convening of the legislature. During any legislative session, the legislature can modify the adopted biennial budget by changing the original appropriations.

several veteran local government officials and altered the political environment in favor of a growth management law. These events sent shockwaves through the Republican Party, which had a one-vote majority in the state Senate. With senatorial elections coming up in the fall of 1990, several Republican incumbents from the Puget Sound area faced reelection, and the loss of the party's Senate majority appeared to be a real threat.

King and his growth management supporters saw a chance to speed up the process and narrow the range of issues facing the GSC. The tough implementation and governance issues had been forwarded to the commission for inclusion in its final report and for action by the 1991 legislature. A retreat the previous year, involving 60 representatives from statewide city and county planning directors groups, resulted in a persuasive report calling for a growth strategy to end weak state and local planning and replace it with a vision for the state's future. The report included a mandated planning process consistent at all levels with goals and policies, an effective regional governance system, concurrency and an appeals process to resolve intergovernmental conflicts (Washington City Planning Directors 1989, 1).

As King saw it, the key purposes of a progrowth management bill would be to get transportation concurrency and adopt policies to curb urban sprawl and protect wetlands, leaving the tough governance and implementation issues for the GSC to resolve. King and his staff met with environmentalists (who had a strong bill of their own and were threatening a growth management ballot initiative if it did not pass), home builders (who wanted a gas tax increase with as little else as possible) and other groups. When King's bill was introduced early in the session, most Republicans were convinced it could not pass in 1990 but were nervous about the possible consequences if it did not. Opponents recognized that they could not kill the effort in the House and instead focused on the Senate (DeGrove 1992, 122–123).

An informal legislative committee was established, made up of the chairs of six House committees: Trade and Economic Development; Local Government; Transportation; Natural Resources and Parks; Environmental Affairs; and Housing (Settle and

Gavigan 1993, 884). Representative Marie Cantwell coordinated the effort, and each chair presided over drafting an aspect of the system, introduced as HB 2929 on January 26, 1990, as four separate bills. Four relevant committees held hearings and sent the results to the Appropriations Committee, which conducted no substantive review of the bills and then consolidated them back into one bill, which passed 72–3, on February 15, 1990 (Settle and Gavigan 1993, 884–885).

In the Senate, most Republicans opposed any growth management bill, and they passed a weak bill destined to die in conference. When HB 2929 went to the Senate it was referred to the Government Operations Committee, the traditional "killer committee" for bills unloved by leadership. After only one hearing on the bill, the committee struck everything after the enacting clause, substituting a new bill bearing little resemblance to HB 2929. The Senate passed the watered-down version the next day on a 35–12 vote.

In short, King got what he wanted from the House, but the Senate substitute for HB 2929 was generally more permissive toward development. While it required planning in all 39 counties, the bill included a largely procedural checklist of what had to be in the plans with little or no state oversight (DeGrove 1992, 123). The House and Senate conferees started with the House version in a special session called by the governor immediately following the end of the regular session on March 8, 1990. On the final day of the special session, the conferees reached agreement on ESHB 2929, and it passed the Senate 32–16 and the House 72–21.

In the end, the Washington State Growth Management Act of 1990, the first part of the state's comprehensive system, passed both houses of the legislature on April 1, 1990, and was signed into law on April 24. It was far stronger than the Senate bill, yet not as strong as King or the Washington Environmental Council/Citizens for Balanced Growth coalition would have liked. The law included important new funding for both planning and infrastructure, but left the task of strengthening the law's implementation requirements to the 1991 session (DeGrove 1992, 123).

Given broad skepticism that the Senate would accept any legislation of substance, the GMA (HB 2929) was a surprisingly strong document with substantive requirements of major importance. It included a concurrency requirement that apparently applied only to transportation; mandated "regionally coordinated levels of service"; and attempted to harmonize land uses and transportation systems. Municipalities or counties were required to identify funding capacity, transportation backlogs and future needs within a 10-year timeframe. The law authorized Regional Transportation Planning Organizations (RTPOs) charged with coordinating the plans of all cities and counties in a region and a transportation policy board to support that effort.

HB 2929 clearly mandated the establishment of urban growth areas (UGAs). The bill's criteria were similar to Oregon's for urban growth boundaries, with the UGAs including cities and urbanized or urbanizing unincorporated areas, and densities high enough to meet 20-year population projections. Each county was required to work with its cities in establishing UGAs, but if agreement could not be reached, the county would designate the UGA boundaries. Cities were authorized to appeal to DCD for mediation, with amendments allowed once a year consistent with the law. Development regulations were required to be in place one year after the adoption of a local plan and had to be consistent with and implement the plan. At least every 10 years, counties were required to review the UGAs and, if necessary, increase densities to accommodate the projected population growth.

HB 2929 provided for funding and technical assistance to local governments, with DCD as the administering state agency. The legislature appropriated more than $7 million to assist local governments in preparing mandated plans, and DCD received an additional $1 million to bolster its planning-related technical assistance efforts. Furthermore, cities and counties collecting .25 percent of excise taxes on each sale of real property were required to use those dollars for capital facilities or housing relocation allowances. The law also authorized a city or county to levy an additional .25 percent excise tax on each sale of real property, solely to fund infrastructure costs needed to implement local plans.

Sewerage and water districts were required to prepare plans consistent with local government plans mandated under the law, which stated that such districts could not provide for the extension or location of facilities that were inconsistent with urban service areas. A similar provision applied to annexations, which were forbidden beyond a UGA. HB 2929 included the rules of the game for levying impact fees, incorporating most of the standard requirements dictated by the courts to meet the rational nexus test. The governor vetoed some items in this section that developers badly wanted, since these would have limited total liability for developments in meeting the costs of infrastructure occasioned by new development.

The law mandated that the state's most populous, fastest growing counties, and the cities within them, adopt comprehensive land use plans and development regulations. Those not meeting the growth-rate criteria could opt to be included but were not allowed to withdraw—this became an issue in the mid-1990s when some counties regretted opting in and wished to pull out. Plans were to be adopted on or before July 1, 1993, or three years after a given county and its cities either chose to come under the system or grew into mandatory participation. All counties were required to inventory agricultural and forest lands and other critical areas, then make zoning consistent with comprehensive plans. Critical area designations and land development regulations to conserve such lands were to be in place one year after the adoption of the plans, and the law prohibited land uses and developments inconsistent with those goals.

In the first phase of the law's implementation, the goal of horizontal consistency among plans was an important requirement for city and county comprehensive plans, although a process to ensure consistency with the state goals (vertical consistency) was not provided for. The law contained substantial language about the character and content of local plans, however, including maps and descriptive texts that would set forth objectives, principles and standards used to develop the plan. All planning was required to be consistent with the future land use map, and would include land use, housing, capital facilities, utilities, rural, and transportation elements, with the ability to provide optional and subarea elements as well. Major sections of the law addressed hard-to-site facilities, the establishment of open space corridors, and natural resource and critical area designations.

HB 2929 was a bold leap forward for a state that had long resisted a comprehensive, integrated system of planning, but it did not address the linked issues of governance, implementation and state oversight. In 1991 GSC was to explore and recommend additional legislative action steps needed to

- ensure that cities, counties, special districts and state agencies develop plans and programs consistent with the goals and provisions of HB 2929;

- define the state's role in growth management;

- address the issues of land and resources of state-wide significance;

- identify state funds to be withheld to ensure local government compliance with HB 2929;

- address the vested rights and affordable housing issues and promote linkages between land use and transportation; and

- recommend dispute resolution procedures for the setting of UGAs.[2]

The Growth Strategies Commission's Final Report

The legislature's passage of a growth management law while the GSC was still at work might easily have become a divisive issue, but in fact the GSC had already begun to struggle with the very governance and implementation issues given to it by HB 2929. The GSC's final report (Washington State GSC 1990b) reflected an acceptance of the legislature's challenge and proposed a state oversight system emphasizing the governor's role and leaving no doubt about the need to ensure the full and fair implementation of such far-reaching policies as concurrency and urban service areas.

The final report is a remarkable document and a tribute to the hard work of the commission's members

and staff and, above all, its chair, Dick Ford. The report recommended the formation of a governor-appointed Growth Strategies Advisory Council that would include state agency, local government and private-sector representatives to assist in the development of guidelines enabling every governmental level to "achieve legislative goals." While the legislature's 1990 session did not follow the commission's exact recommendations on state oversight, it did place the ultimate responsibility with the governor.

The commission recommended strengthening some of HB 2929's goals and adding new ones. In support of the overall goal of consistency, the report recommended that "plans, regulations, and actions of state governments, counties, cities, and special districts should conform to and support" the specific goals of the law. New growth targets within UGAs to ensure a jobs-housing balance and a positive urban environment augmented the existing goals for those areas. Furthermore, the report recommended the stipulated densities needed for affordable housing and transit. Goals for open space and protection for significant lands and resources were new, as was a fair-share goal that involved not just traditional NIMBYs but "low income and special needs housing" (Washington State GSC 1990b, 20).

Growth Management Act, Part II: The 1991 Legislation

Initiative 547: The Political Context

While the GSC completed its work in mid-1991, events in Washington on the growth management scene were unfolding rapidly, sometimes with contradictory results. When the legislature adopted HB 2929, environmental groups, led by the Washington Environmental Council (WEC) and the Citizens for Balanced Growth, faced a tough decision, because GMA I contained many but not all of the goals supported by these groups. The WEC had filed its own bill in 1989, calling for a "comprehensive statewide land use planning [system]—one with teeth" (WEC 1989). But when the Senate passed a "nothing" bill, with strong requirements for local planning but no

---

2. The above analysis of HB 2929 is taken from DeGrove (1992, 123–125). Settle and Gavigan's (1993, 885–889) analysis of GMA I listed 13 key provisions of HB 2929 as originally introduced and traced the legislative process that produced the final version of HB 2929, including a list of 12 "important questions unanswered" by HB 2929.

state oversight or enforcement authority, environmental groups were not pleased.

David Bricklin, WEC's leader, was familiar with events in Florida, Georgia and Oregon that

---

Key Goals for Washington's Statewide Growth Strategy

- Protect the environment
- Connect greenways and separating cities
- Conserve agricultural and forest lands
- Preserve land and resources of statewide significance
- Share economic growth
- Make cities more livable
- Designate UGAs and provide services
- Provide affordable housing
- Link land use and public facilities
- Resolve NIMBY (not in my back yard) problems

Source: Washington State GSC, 1990c, 20

Recommendations of the Growth Strategies Commission

- Listed implementation measures to translate goals into reality
- Called for strengthening planning and for stronger coordinating links at all levels
- Estimated funding needed to support new institutions or mandated new duties
- Expanded planning and regulatory requirements for all counties and cities
- Called for stronger actions to combat sprawl through compact urban development patterns inside UGAs
- Expanded HB 2929's consistency provision in transportation to include other public facilities (parks, schools, sewage, water supply) with increased funding at all levels
- Called for a dispute resolution system backed by a governor-appointed independent panel for binding arbitration, with sanctions imposed by the governor if an arbitration order was not followed
- Recommended the boldest effort by any state to locate hard-to-site facilities, i.e., airports, prisons, landfills and other locally unwanted land uses
- Struggled with regional issues by recognizing the need for better regional planning; broadened its scope from transportation to open space, UGAs and siting; brought special districts into the consistency requirement; and gave the regional coordination task to the state

Source: Washington State GSC, 1990c; DeGrove, 1992, 127

---

had greatly strengthened state and regional roles in growth management (WEC 1989, 1). But, deciding whether to mount an initiative that would repeal HB 2929 and substitute a much tougher growth management law was a close call. The group's board met twice, first rejecting the idea of an initiative and then voting to proceed, acting out of both fear and concern that the conservative Senate would block any effective implementation bill, just as it had recently failed to pass a wetlands protection measure. Many believed the initiative would not get on the ballot, but if it did, they believed it would pass easily in the fall 1990 elections. They were wrong on both counts. The signatures were collected in an amazingly short time, and the fight was on. The initiative's goals were more specific than HB 2929, which many supporters considered an advantage. All cities and counties would have been mandated to plan, with state agencies as well as local governments complying with the goals.

When the smoke cleared, however, Initiative 547 had been overwhelmingly defeated. The fatal blow was the opposition of two champions of growth management: Speaker King and Governor Gardner. Both called for waiting to give the 1991 legislature a chance to pass a bill dealing with the key issues, and the governor promised to fight for passage of a new initiative if the legislature failed to act. Some people voted against the initiative, fearing that if HB 2929 (and the funding it provided for infrastructure and open space) were repealed, the legislature would not reenact it. Another factor in the initiative's defeat was the issuance of the powerful final report by the Growth Strategies Commission in September 1990, midway in the campaign. Because King and Senate Majority Leader Jeannette Hayner had pledged to address the GSC's call to strengthen HB 2929, the commission report caused many supporters of a stronger growth management act to vote against the initiative (Citizens for Balanced Growth 1990, 1–3; DeGrove 1992, 129).

Adoption and Key Provisions of HB 1025

The GSC's blueprint, later proposed as HB 1025 in the 1991 legislature, was acceptable to most growth management advocates. As in 1990, the question centered on whether a bill with any muscle could clear the Senate, which kept its one-vote Republican margin after the fall elections. King and Hayner had publicly committed themselves to addressing the commission's recommendations to strengthen the 1990 law if Initiative 547 were rejected.

The governor's staff drafted the proposed growth management bill for the 1991 session, including most of the GSC's major recommendations. The governor's bill was introduced into the House in mid-January, and the informal committee on growth management was reconstituted. Each of the six policy committees worked on the bill and sent their results to the House Appropriations Committee, where the separate bills were consolidated and passed out of Appropriations to the floor in early March 1991. Majority and minority leaders reached an agreement on the bill; it was approved by the House on March 20 and sent to the Senate. As in 1990, the bill went to the Government Operations Committee, not friendly territory, where an attempt was made to weaken the House bill. In the end, the Senate took no action on HB 1025 during the regular session.

Gardner continued his leadership role by organizing legislative leaders and his staff to agree on a bill that could clear the legislature. The so-called Five Corners Committee was composed of the governor's staff and representatives from each of the four legislative caucuses. Negotiations ended after almost a month of trying to agree on a bill. Legislators then asked developers, business interests and local government leaders for their input, which led to reconvening the Five Corners Committee. The committee subsequently agreed on a proposed bill, but it was different in important ways from the business and local government proposal. When it looked as though the negotiated agreement would come apart, Senator Hayner helped fend off the attacks on the Five Corners agreement (Settle and Gavigan 1993, 892–895).

When HB 1025 passed 70 to 22 in the House and 29 to 15 in the Senate, some environmentalists, still recovering from Initiative 547's defeat, were surprised to get anything meaningful out of the session. However, the Washington legislature had indeed enacted part II of its Growth Management Act, and the governor signed the bill into law on July 16, 1991 (DeGrove 1992, 130; Settle and Gavigan 1993, 895–896). The second effort was much like the first: strong support from King and House Democrats and limited support or opposition from Senate Republicans. The *Seattle Post-Intelligencer* (1991) summed it up nicely, "King, the liberal Democrat, and Hayner, the conservative Republican, in this case at least, showed that partisanship can and should be set aside when the interests of the state are paramount. That they have done so over the issue of growth management merits them high praise."

The main thrust of HB 1025 was to provide state oversight and enforcement provisions that had been missing from HB 2929, even with minor modifications by the 1991 legislation. The GSC recommended giving enforcement responsibility to the governor, and HB 1025 generally followed that approach. If fully implemented, the sanctions could have been the most powerful of any state growth management system, since they included state agency actions.

The new law's centerpiece provided for a Growth Management Hearings Board for each of three major regions: eastern Washington, central Puget Sound and western Washington. Appointed by the governor, the boards were to hear challenges to any state agency, county or city plans alleged not to be in compliance with the act. The act specified processes and timeframes; defined challenges to plans or development regulations; listed evidence to be considered; and

---

Central Purposes of the Growth Management Act (HB 2929 and HB 1025)

- Avoiding sprawling settlement patterns by concentrating new development in UGAs

- Ensuring adequate public facilities to serve new development through infrastructure planning and concurrency requirements

- Protecting critical areas from environmentally harmful activities and natural resource lands from incompatible development by directing it elsewhere

- Achieving regional responsibility among governmental units by coordinating local plans and regulations to ensure fair and efficient allocation of locally undesirable but regionally essential resources, while compelling state agencies to comply with local plans and regulations

Source: Settle and Gavigan, 1993, 904–905

empowered the hearings boards to rule on compliance. In the event of noncompliance, the governor could apply a wide range of sanctions that essentially involve the withholding of state funds.

Under HB 1025 all counties and cities in Washington were required to adopt regulations to protect agricultural, forest and mineral lands as defined in HB 2929. A county could not designate lands inside a UGA for long-term commercial or forestry use unless that county had adopted a transferable development rights (TDR) system to protect landowners' rights. The law continued the resource protection theme by mandating a temporary Committee on Natural Resources of Statewide Significance, made up of state agency heads, local government officials and citizen members. Charged with preparing a report by the end of 1991, the committee would develop criteria to be used in identifying significant natural resources, minimum standards to protect them, and justification of the need to acquire such resources to protect them. The law defined as significant those resources possessing "outstanding natural, ecological, or scenic values, and . . . of the highest quality and most significant of their type" (DeGrove 1992, 131).

HB 1025 thus continued Washington's struggle to address problems on a regional basis. Unless applied to just one county, the concept of regional governance appears even more controversial in Washington than in most states, and HB 1025 addressed it in a less-than-bold fashion. The bill called for countywide planning policies, with counties recognized as "regional governments" within their boundaries. The law established a process in which a county convenes its cities in a "collaborative process" to hammer out the policy framework within which the county and all cities in it would develop their plans.

A countywide planning policy, once adopted, may be appealed to the appropriate Growth Management Hearings Board by the state, cities or eligible private-sector groups. The governor may also impose sanctions if a county misses the deadline for initiating the plan development process. This critical component of the system lays out a mandatory process that leads to horizontal consistency across a single county, with enough state oversight to ensure implementa-tion (DeGrove 1992, 131). Regional coordination is addressed in HB 1025 by mandating development of multicounty planning policies by counties with populations of at least 450,000. This provision applies to the Puget Sound region counties of Snohomish, King and Pierce. Presumably a multicounty planning policy would contain the same elements as the single-county "regional" policy. In some ways, this approach is similar to Oregon's, which mandates regional coordination only in the three-county area constituting the boundaries of Portland Metro.

HB 1025 assigned a wide range of responsibilities to DCD, making it the lead state agency for implementing the GMA. Even after a 1995 merger of state agencies under Governor Mike Lowry that created the Department of Community, Trade and Economic Development (DCTED), the GMA unit remained intact in the new department. Its responsibilities included administering financial and technical assistance; the adoption of procedures and assisting local governments in formulating plans in compliance with the law; and providing mediation services to local governments. The act also required state agencies to comply with local plans and regulations where such plans comply with state GMA goals and policies (DeGrove 1992, 131–132).

A challenge for any state growth management system that mandates confining urban development to specified boundaries is what to allow outside those boundaries in the way of urban development, without undermining the central concept of separating rural and urban uses. Oregon's SB 100 allows almost nothing, but there have been substantial difficulties in sustaining that policy, and the Florida growth management system is fuzzy on the issue. In HB 1025 Washington developed policies to allow "fully contained communities" and "master planned resorts" outside UGAs, under certain conditions. To mitigate damage to farm and forest lands, and to maintain rural densities, HB 1025 listed conditions on compact development, transit orientation, buffers and land use regulations, and also mandated that such developments be within 25-year population projections. Giant economic players in Washington, such as Weyerhauser and Boeing, which own large amounts of land in rural areas, may have had a special interest in these developments outside of UGAs (DeGrove 1992, 132).

Reaching consensus on the issue of economic development and how it will fit into a growth strategy for Washington continues to be difficult. Everyone agrees that any growth management system should include the promotion of economic development in areas that need it, in this case, primarily in eastern Washington. In a state dominated by one metropolitan region, the issue takes on added significance. HB 2929, the GSC and HB 1025 have supported "spreading the wealth" as the state grows. The central approach of HB 1025 combined a wide range of economic assistance to local governments—the "managing to grow" aspect of growth management—within the implementation of the system itself. Funding comes from the Public Works Assistance Account; grants and loans for facilities to control water pollution; and other state agency loans or grants, with eligibility limited to local governments in compliance with the act's requirements (DeGrove 1992, 132).

No other state's growth strategy has addressed the NIMBY issue so directly. HB 1025 requires each county and city subject to the full requirements of the act to develop a comprehensive plan to include the siting of essential public facilities. While there is a provision that forbids counties and cities from excluding such facilities in their plans, the law does not go as far as the GSC's recommendation to provide a "siter of last resort" at the state level, if local governments are unable or unwilling to designate sites.

Although HB 1025 did not fully implement the GSC's recommendations, Washington's quest for a comprehensive growth management system was changed in substantial ways—above all in the areas of state oversight and sanctions to assure compliance with the law. The 1991 "window of opportunity" that many feared would be lost if the bill had failed was salvaged. Thanks to gubernatorial and legislative leadership, the system was essentially complete, though some gaps and ambiguities remained. The challenge, as Washington moved to the first stage of responsible growth management, was to keep up the momentum, just as a national recession was beginning to affect the state (DeGrove 1992, 132).

Implementation: 1991–1995

Enough time has passed to analyze the early implementation of GMA's mandates and to evaluate its strengths and weaknesses, but it remains difficult to assess the system's effectiveness in reflecting the broad objectives and policies that fall under the GMA's goals. While HB 1025 moved in the direction of meaningful state oversight of the system, implementation of the GMA was made more difficult by the lack of detail and the great responsibility placed on local governments. The Growth Management Hearings Boards, and ultimately the courts, emerged as important groups to provide statutory definition and clarification.

Given the negative public attitude toward government in general and government regulations in particular during most of the 1990s, any major statutory strengthening of the law appeared unlikely. Indeed, the whole implementation effort could have been thrown into chaos if the public had endorsed Initiative 164, related to regulation of private property, in the November 1995 elections. Voters rejected this initiative, however, and while the struggle with a hostile legislature continued into the late 1990s, strong support from two governors prevented any major weakening of the system as the implementation process continued.

State and Local Government Requirements

By the end of 1991 Washington's growth management system included 26 counties and the cities within them, identified because of their size and population growth rate (13 counties); a population increase of 20 percent or more in the past 10 years (three counties); or because of a county's governing body vote to abide by the growth management requirements (10 counties). The state's counties made up 85 percent of the population, and since 1991 three more counties have come under the law's requirements.

The act required the original 26 counties and their cities to complete comprehensive plans by July 1993, containing at least six elements: land use, housing, utilities, transportation, capital facilities and rural development (for counties only). Counties whose population placed them in the mandated planning category in the future had three years to complete the planning process. Cities and counties were required to bring their development regulations into consistency with their comprehensive plans one year after the plans were in place. Once a county opted to plan under the law, all cities within it were mandated to plan according to the act.

The state's remaining 10 counties, largely rural and in eastern Washington, also were required to carry out three major responsibilities under the act: to classify and designate natural resource and critical area lands by September 1991, with DCD authorized to extend that deadline by six months; to adopt regulations to protect critical areas by March 1992, with a similar 180-day extension authorized; and to make their zoning and other development regulations consistent with their comprehensive plans by July 1992.

During the last half of 1990, the lead state agency for growth management, DCD (later, DCTED), worked to meet a number of deadlines established in the law. The most pressing was to assist in the legislative mandate to move first under the act to protect natural resource and critical area lands. The legislature directed the establishment of a Temporary Committee on Natural Resources of Statewide Significance, with DCD's Growth Management Division serving as staff. By late 1990 DCD had prepared guidelines for local governments, which were ultimately responsible for their own designation decisions (Washington State DCD 1990; 1991c). The initial designation of areas and the adoption of regulations were temporary and subject to change upon incorporation into the development regulations that would implement the comprehensive plans. The committee issued its final report at the end of January 1992 (Washington State DCD 1992b).

Dr. Gary Pivo, director of the University of Washington Growth Management Planning and Research Clearing House, reported on some of the strengths and weaknesses of the first stage of the GMA implementation, focusing on "the adoption of development regulations to protect critical areas and conserve resource lands" (Pivo 1993). Local governments received grants from DCD to help them meet the terms of the act. The 1990 legislature appropriated $7.4 million for such grants, and the 1992 legislature

added $6.8 million. The first round of grants to 24 counties amounted to $75,000 each and increased to $100,000 each in 1991. Grants were shared with the cities within each county. Pivo noted that a stronger role was needed "to balance state and local interests at the local level" by having a systematic process for checking consistency (Pivo 1993, 1143, 1146, 1177–1179).

The March 1992 deadline was met by about three-fourths of the local governments; by 1994 there were still a few holdouts; and by 1995 a few still were not in compliance, some because their approvals were held up by appeals to one of the three hearings boards. Implementation of the second and third stages (countywide and multicounty planning policies, and county designation of UGAs, respectively) produced a large number of appeals initiated by cities objecting to their county's actions. Appeals in the fourth and last stages (the development and adoption of comprehensive plans) came largely from citizen and public interest groups.

Strategies, Progress and Problems

Many supporters of Washington's Growth Management Act believed, or at least hoped, that the 1992 legislative session would be a positive one, but, in fact, it turned out to be a time of renewed crisis. The session focused mainly on funding issues, with the governor and legislature facing the need to make significant budget cuts. Washington's economy had held up well compared to the national scene, but revenues were down. The governor reduced his budget request for GMA planning funds for local governments to $6.8 million, but the legislature reduced that even further to $5.7 million.

A public outcry against legislative cuts for local government planning grants no doubt contributed to the governor's exercising his veto to raise the DCD's planning dollars back to $6.8 million. The governor also used his veto power to restore the full $1.9 million to get the Growth Management Hearings Boards under way by May 1992, instead of postponing their establishment until September. That action was of special importance, for the hearings boards have emerged as the key source of clarifying and detailing the requirements of the act, as they hear appeals by citizen groups, local governments and the state, regarding the adequacy of local government efforts to comply with the law. Funds to support SEPA's pilot projects to test ways to integrate SEPA's environmental permitting approach with the GMA were cut completely, and the legislature did not fund this effort until 1994 (DeGrove 1992, 134).

The strategy of the Growth Management Division of DCD was to work with any local government making a good faith effort to comply with the GMA, without regard to strict deadlines. Some felt the division was too permissive, but there was considerable agreement that the implementation effort was going well, given the short timeframe and limited resources. The first major tasks included preparing guidelines for resource and critical area designations and a series of guidebooks to help local governments comply with the law (see Washington State DCD 1991a; 1991b; 1991c; 1992a; 1992c; 1992d). Other guidebooks were prepared by Forward Washington (1992) and Young (1990). A joint effort by DCD and DCTED, in July 1993, was meant to help communities achieve viable, sustainable economic development through the growth planning process, and to encourage collaboration among community leaders representing diverse interests.

By July 1995, 140 draft plans had been received, 128 reviews were completed, 81 comprehensive plans adopted and 77 adopted plans received, with most reviewed by Growth Management Services of DCTED. Contrary to popular belief, DCTED does review and comment on draft and final comprehensive plans and development regulations completed in whole or part by local governments. Local governments were notified that an appeal to a hearings board was possible when plans were seriously deficient. The line was clear between "review and comment," and certification for consistency. Given the possibility of an appeal and ultimate sanctions for noncompliance, most local governments typically responded by making the changes to achieve compliance.

Growth Management Hearings Boards

The component of Washington's GMA process that elicited the most optimism about the full implementation of the act was the establishment of Growth Management Hearings Boards. Leaders of the GSC, 1000 Friends, WEC and other groups agreed that the initial rulings of the boards gave promise of filling in the gaps and clearing up the ambiguities of the system to establish standards and criteria. By doing so, the boards championed success in achieving an integrated, consistent system of managing growth and change in Washington. Noting that the boards' appeals decisions were just beginning, former GSC chair Dick Ford observed that hearings boards had forced some counties to face the cost realities of opening huge areas to development, and thus limited their irresponsible behavior.

Other observers noted that the boards consistently took a broad view of their tasks, writing expansive and long decisions to fill in many details not strictly necessary for the particular case. For example, in designating UGAs, the boards read into the law the requirement for a land capacity analysis as part of the justification for the UGA boundary. Board appointments, in the eyes of the law's supporters, were strong under governors Gardner, Lowry and Locke.

Fears that the three boards—central Puget Sound, western and eastern Washington—would fragment and weaken the law have not been manifested. The law requires the three boards to meet annually, but apparently they meet more often. As a result of their communication and a strong sense of taking a common approach to interpreting the law, the three boards' decisions to date have been consistent.

If a hearings board finds a plan lacking, it is sent back to the city or county, which has up to 180 days to bring it into compliance. The board then holds a compliance hearing. If compliance has not been achieved, sanctions come into play by cutting off funds from various agencies. Some sanctions apply automatically if a plan is not in compliance, with no further action needed (including state grants for public works and clean water funds). Another strategy places noncomplying areas at the bottom of the eligibility list for some 76 state discretionary funds. Finally, the governor can act directly if the growth management agency asks him or her to apply sanctions; local governments stand to lose five state-levied taxes to which they would otherwise be entitled. Recent governors have been reluctant to apply sanctions—their main role to date has been to "persuade" local governments to comply with the act. In this way, the threat of sanctions has been significant.

The Evolving Growth Management System, 1995–1998

This section reviews legislative actions, budget challenges and other matters related to implementing Washington's growth management system during a period of political and economic turmoil.

The 1995 Legislative Session: Property Rights and Regulatory Reform

Just after the November 1994 elections, many growth management supporters feared the result of a legislature whose leadership did not support the GMA. The state legislature appeared to reflect the national mood, with Republicans holding a majority in the House and the Democrats a one-vote majority in the Senate. More than 50 bills were introduced in the 1995 session that could harm the GMA in major or minor ways, and several would have done major damage to the system. In the end, however, only one law passed that had the potential to affect the GMA seriously: Initiative 164, the Private Property Rights Regulatory Fairness Act.

To prevent the governor's veto, the legislature handled the proposed law as an initiative. Overwhelming support came from business interests, including builders, realtors and timber companies, which contributed 87 percent of the almost $300,000 raised for the effort. By any standard, Initiative 164 was an extreme private property rights measure that would require "taxpayers...to compensate landowners whenever public policies prevent land from attaining its greatest possible market value. If zoning or other regulations reduce the greatest possible value by even one cent, the public would have to pay" (1000 Friends 1994).

The legislators implemented Initiative 164, effective July 23, 1995, but opponents had 90 days after the session to obtain the necessary signatures to force a referendum. Opponents, including 1000 Friends, the statewide organizations of cities and counties, and many other groups, moved immediately with a petition drive. More than 230,000 names were collected in a short period of time, well above the required 95,000. Thus, Referendum 48, by forcing a vote on the initiative in the November 1995 election, stayed the enforcement of the initiative.

Opponents of the private property rights proposal campaigned vigorously against the initiative, stressing the cost to the average taxpayer of implementing its provisions. All major and most minor newspapers opposed it, and even the Environmental Land Use Committee of the state bar opposed the initiative. The result was a stunning 60–40 percent defeat. Initiative 164 would have had a far-reaching negative impact on the GMA and on any effort to plan and manage land use. Negative reaction to the law and the successful effort to repeal it negated what was the worst output of the 1995 legislative session for Washington's growth management system (1000 Friends 1995, 1). Most other growth management-related bills passed by the legislature in 1995 were either technical, neutral in their impacts or favorable to the law (Washington State DCTED 1995, 8–9).

In 1994 the legislature had provided $1.35 million to DCTED to provide financial and technical assistance to local governments to explore innovative ways to integrate SEPA and GMA. Six grants were made to counties and cities, with the results used to guide the implementation of the new law (Washington State DCTED 1995, 7). The 1995 legislature moved the process along with the passage of ESHB 1724, to integrate growth management planning and environmental review. In 1993 the governor had set up a Regulatory Reform Task Force to produce recommendations for integrating environmental permitting under SEPA and comprehensive planning and regulation under the GMA. His strategy was to force a consensus between private property rights and extreme regulatory reform advocates on one hand and environmentalists who feared giving up any permitting under SEPA on the other. Most environmental leaders and other advocates of the GMA supported regulatory reform in principle, but many were concerned that it would weaken environmental protections. As signed into law, ESHB 1724 required that cities and counties include their shoreline master program in their comprehensive plans; adopt proceedings combining environmental review with project review by March 31, 1996; and establish an integrated and consolidated development permit process for all projects involving two or more permits by March 31, 1996.

Local governments are to "provide for enhanced review of their comprehensive plans or subarea plans and/or development regulations to reduce or eliminate much of the environmental analysis or permit applications or project environmental impact analysis." An environmental review loan fund was established with a $3 million appropriation to help with these tasks and locally imposed environmental analysis fees were authorized (Washington State DCTED 1995, 8). Other requirements called for the Department of Ecology to establish a state permit assistance office to aid in the consolidation and simplification process, and the creation of a 14-member Land Use Study Commission.

The November 1995 vote on Initiative 164 was a watershed in the evolution of the implementation phase of Washington's GMA. The increasing strength and stature of 1000 Friends, Washington Environmental Political Action Committee (now called Washington Conservation Voters), and the WEC indicated broad-based citizen support for the GMA, yet the legislature continued to be hostile. "What would be the outcome of this seeming disconnect?" was the critical question for Washington's GMA, as preparation began for the 1996 legislature.

The 1996 Legislative Session: Hearings Boards

A summary of actions by the 1996 legislature noted that it "defeated the usual number of bills that sought either to repeal the GMA entirely or to abolish the GMA [Hearings] Boards" (Washburn 1996, 1). One defeated bill, which would have mandated greater integration of water resource and supply planning with GMA planning, could have evolved into a more comprehensive growth management system for the state. This issue continued to be discussed and debated after the 1996 legislature and was considered again in the 1997 session.

Another bill, SB 6637, would have significantly weakened the hearings boards, viewed by many as critical to giving direction to local governments as they prepared plans and development regulations under the GMA. It passed the 1996 legislature, but Governor Lowry vetoed the section of the law that would have diluted the impact of hearings board decisions on local plans and regulations, so that the final bill contained relatively minor housekeeping measures.

The degree to which hearings boards have engaged the wrath of GMA opponents can be understood by looking at key decisions where actions of counties or cities have been challenged for not meeting the requirements of the law. The boards have required detailed justification of any UGA reaching beyond municipal boundaries. The boards have applied a "bright-line rule" that allows the inclusion of 25 percent more land than required to accommodate the 20-year population projection. Anything more than that is subject to increased scrutiny. County actions outside UGAs that promote urban rather than rural growth have been rejected. While the term *rural uses* in the GMA is not clearly defined, the GMA boards have specified what is rural as opposed to urban: generally, one dwelling unit per 10 acres or greater is rural, one dwelling unit per acre is not.

For urban areas, the hearings boards have focused on promoting compact urban development. Efforts to include low density inside UGAs, generally defined as one dwelling unit per acre or less, have been rejected, while four units per acre are seen as clearly urban. One decision held that cities could not use local neighborhood policies to reduce densities otherwise required under GMA. Furthermore, the boards have been consistent in requiring cities "to fully analyze and include in their plans the detailed transportation and other capital facilities issues set forth in the GMA statutes" (Washburn 1996, 1–2).

In *Taxpayers for Responsible Government v Oak Harbor*, for example, the Western Washington Hearings Board "imposed a stiff requirement for cities and counties to clearly specify in the comprehensive plans how capital facilities will be funded. A general list of revenue sources fails to comply with GMA"

(Washburn 1996, 1–2). Going even further, the board brought the GMA concurrency requirement closer to Florida's by ruling that the concurrency provision need not apply to transportation only, "but to all public facilities (water, sewer, etc.) necessary to support development, leaving it to the discretion of the local government to determine which specific public facilities are necessary to support development" (Washburn 1996, 2). Given the kinds of decisions being rendered by GMA boards, it is not surprising that they have become the focus for substantially weakening the GMA implementation process. In the 1997 legislature, opponents of the GMA again zeroed in on hearings boards, in their ongoing efforts to weaken the system.

1997 Legislative Modifications to GMA (ESB 6094)

The 1997 legislative session focused on the work of the Land Use Study Commission, created by the 1995 legislature to succeed Governor Lowry's 1993 Regulatory Reform Task Force. Newly elected Governor Gary Locke made it clear coming into the 1997 session that the commission's work, largely reflected in ESB 6094 (Growth Management Modifications), would be his benchmark in responding to legislative action on the state's growth management system. Locke held that if the legislature strayed too far from the commission's recommendations, he would use his veto pen freely.

ESB 6094's major provisions focused on what would be appropriate for rural areas, including Growth Management Hearings Boards, and a number of provisions on the status of local government plans and regulations where local governments were under question because of a hearings board action. The bill also included annexation changes strongly supported by cities; strengthened public participation provisions; and provided funding for a buildable lands project to determine whether countywide planning policies left enough land to accommodate growth projections.

The rural lands element of the GMA, which was largely the result of negotiations between the WEC and the Association of Washington Business, has remained one of the most hotly debated components of

the law, and a large percentage of appeals to hearings boards on local comprehensive plans have involved this element. The Land Use Study Commission concluded that "a key element of improving the GMA was providing greater guidance to the counties and the boards about what development was appropriate in rural areas." In some ways the law gives counties added flexibility about how to define rural, taking account of local conditions. With this added authority, however, came added responsibility, including taking actions to protect rural character, such as "controlling development, assuring visual compatibility, reducing sprawl, protecting critical areas, and protecting against resource conflicts" (Washington State DCTED 1997a, 1). Not only did ESB 6094 contain definitions of terms such as *rural character*, *rural development* and *rural government services*, it also amended the definition of *urban growth* to clarify the relationship between rural and urban.

ESB 6094 spelled out the following circumstances under which exceptions would be made to the rule that development in rural areas could not be urban in nature: (1) infill in areas already developed, such as crossroads or hamlets; (2) new or redeveloped small-scale recreational or tourist use, with no residential development allowed; and (3) further development of existing nonresidential uses in isolated locations, such as cottage industries or small-scale businesses, provided counties imposed controls to guard against the spread of such uses into adjoining rural areas. If fully implemented, those changes would help ensure the maintenance of rural lands and resources, without fostering a one-size-fits-all straightjacket on local governments. Hearings boards would be relieved of much of the need for interpreting a vague substantive requirement.

Even the governor took the position that some added flexibility should be allowed so local governments could prepare plans and regulations to meet the requirements of the system. The Land Use Study Commission recognized the need for limited but not substantial changes to hearings boards, and recommended several key changes that were included in ESB 6094. First, the standard of review was changed from the "preponderance of evidence" to "clearly erroneous in view of the entire record...and in light of the goals and requirements" of the GMA. Whether this change would weaken the hearings boards' ability to rule on recalcitrant local governments remained to be seen, depending on how the boards used and the courts interpreted the new standard.

A second change pushed by opponents of hearings boards was to remove them from enforcing the law by allowing unrestricted direct appeals to the courts. While they were not fully successful in that effort, ESB 6094 allows a case involving a challenged local plan to be heard in the Superior Court rather than before a hearings board if both parties to the appeal agree. However, the strengthening of the public participation element affirmed a finding of the courts on Chelan County, where the county, after being sanctioned for noncompliance, made major changes to its plans and regulations with no public participation. Other provisions of the law strengthened the requirement that boards follow the Administrative Procedures Act; gave boards more flexibility to extend time limits on decisions and compliance hearings; and clarified the ability of cities or counties under an invalidity order to adopt interim controls, upon approval by the hearings board.

ESB 6094 also required all counties with more than 150,000 residents in 1995 to implement a system by September 1, 2002, and every five years thereafter, to track the intensity of development to determine "whether a county and its cities are achieving urban densities sufficient to meet the state growth projections" (Washington State DCTED 1997a, 3, 8). This section of the law was similar to another requirement in ESB 6094, the Buildable Lands Project, which required six western Washington counties—the four in the Puget Sound region, and Thurston and Clark counties—to determine whether they were meeting planned residential densities and uses. The push for a buildable lands project stemmed from the conviction of the business and development community that densities and intensities within UGAs were not sufficient to handle the 20-year population projections. The Growth Management Services staff welcomed the provision, since their incomplete, anecdotal data suggested the opposite might be true: that UGAs could actually shrink when all data were in place and

a monitoring system was functioning. Establishing and maintaining such a system would be an expensive proposition involving standardizing data collection in a GIS format.

The six-county project was funded by a $2 million appropriation by the 1997 legislature; the governor's budget request for the 1998 budget had additional funding for the buildable lands project. The complexity, cost and need for such a monitoring system was compelling; no real assessment of the size of UGA boundaries could be made without it. Yet local governments were concerned they would get the mandate without the funding to carry it out. With the combined support of the governor, the business and development communities and the legislature, funding for the project seemed likely to continue (Washington State DCTED 1997a, 3, 6, 9).

Other provisions in ESB 6094 included

- encouraging innovative techniques to protect important agricultural lands;

- a mandate on property tax collections preventing a county assessor from using sales of lands converted to nonforest, open space or agricultural uses within five years after the sale in valuing designated natural resource lands;

- a series of "technical corrections" to ESB 1724, to further promote the integration of SEPA with the GMA; and

- a provision for tax incentives for multifamily housing to the largest city or county planning under the GMA, even if there is no town or city with a population of more than 100,000. (Washington State DCTED 1997a, 5–6)

The 1997 legislature passed a substantial number of other laws that affected Washington's growth management system. For the most part, they were aimed at providing greater flexibility to state agencies and local governments in administering the system. The legislature also had many bills that would have severely weakened the GMA, but in an understanding of the "rules of the game" with the governor, those bills stood alone as separate sections of ESB 6094 or as separate bills, and were subsequently vetoed (Washington State DCTED 1997c).

This political situation again raises the question of the apparent disconnect between the attitudes of the citizens and the majority in the 1997 legislature. A statewide poll conducted in the summer of 1996 surveyed some 900 residents to gauge support for growth management and environmental issues. Eighty-two percent believed that managed growth was necessary "to control property taxes, traffic congestion, and maintain quality of life in their communities." Furthermore, growth and development were rated "the most significant environmental problem facing the state" (1000 Friends 1996, 6).

Budget Complexities

The budget picture for GMA was mixed, partly because of the legislature's determination to cut the funds available for further implementation of the growth management law. In addition, DCTED and growth management supporters had difficulty convincing the governor that an adjustment was needed to the provision wherein state grants to local governments to carry out the GMA's mandate would be available only within a four-year window from the time they were subject to the act's requirements. Many supporters of the GMA thought there was a compelling case for increasing the funds available to local governments to develop plans meeting these requirements and to establish the regulations necessary to ensure the implementation of the plans. Adhering strictly to the four-year timeframe was seen as keeping local governments, which had come late to the process for political reasons, from receiving the state incentive dollars to get their plans and regulations in place.

From its inception in 1990 the GMA included funds for local governments to support part of their costs to prepare plans to meet the act's requirements. For most jurisdictions the four-year window ended in 1994, but not all the 179 cities and 29 counties required to develop plans under the act met that deadline. By the end of 1996, 132 municipal plans had been adopted, with 14 county plans in place. Another 47 plans were being reviewed by the state prior to local adoption, leaving 15 city or county plans as holdouts. From 1990 to 1996, DCTED and its predecessor DCD made grants to cities and counties totaling $43.2 mil-

lion, covering an estimated one-third of the cost of compliance with the act.

DCTED's Growth Management Division pushed for continued support for regulation as well as plan preparation outside the four-year timeframe, as long as a given local government was moving toward compliance. While this approach was criticized by some as too passive, it was clearly consistent with the approach favored by governors Lowry and Locke.

DCTED is the only Washington state agency funded for GMA responsibilities, yet some 20 state agencies participate in the Interagency Work Group on Growth Management. Six state agencies review and comment on local plans and provide technical assistance on plan development and implementation: Ecology; Transportation; Health; Fish and Wildlife; Natural Resources; and the Department of Social and Health Services. Failure to provide at least some funding to these agencies is a clear deficiency in a system where they must ensure that local plans meet the act's requirements. This is an area where failure to follow the recommendation of the GSC has weakened the implementation process.

DCTED funds for the Growth Management Division were not reduced by the 1997 legislature; however, it appeared that the division did not have the resources necessary to make the system work effectively, and it was inadequately staffed to meet its responsibilities (Washington State DCTED 1997b, 15). DCTED asked the governor for $7 million, the governor requested $3.5 million, and when negotiations were over, the total received for grants was about $3 million. DCTED did receive planning grant support dollars for three counties and newly incorporated cities at the same rate as the 1995–1997 support. In effect, this maintained the support for these local governments within the four-year framework for planning stipulated in the original 1990 law. In addition, more than $900,000 was carried forward into the new fiscal year to be used as incentive grants by DCTED to support planning in cities and counties after the four-year framework. This budget amounted to a substantial reduction over the 1995–1997 biennium, primarily due to the transfer of $3 million from the growth management planning grant to a new watershed planning program. In addition, the Buildable

Lands budget was allocated $2 million, and $120,000 was approved for Puget Sound water quality technical assistance.

DCTED was charged with continuing its efforts to further integrate GMA, SEPA and the Shoreline Management Act, and was funded for a series of pilot projects in the 1995–1997 biennium with $3 million, through the Planning and Environmental Review Fund. Some 40 local governments were given grants to conduct pilot projects. While the mandate for furthering integration was still there, the governor's request for $2 million to enhance the effort was not supported by the legislature (Washington State DCTED 1997d, 2).

1998 Legislative Challenges, Administrative Reorganization and Elections

Republicans remained in control of the 1998 legislature, with a strong majority in the House and a smaller margin in the Senate, as supporters of Washington's land planning efforts faced another session in which the legislature passed bills to weaken the system. The good news was that Governor Locke was able to veto some bills that threatened vital parts of the system, such as SB 5185, another attempt to weaken the power of the Growth Management Hearings Boards, and HB 2542, which would have allowed counties under 50,000 to opt out of planning under the GMA. This bill was aimed at smaller counties that originally had opted into the system, with some of those now wanting to opt out. 1000 Friends pointed out that all but two of the eleven counties affected by the proposed legislation had, in the last decade, grown at a rate that would require them to plan under the act anyway.

The Republican majority passed HB 2894, a five-year transportation-funding package with 20 years of bonds to be repaid from the general fund, instead of a gas tax increase supported by the governor and proponents of the GMA seeking to raise funds for transportation, especially public transportation. HB 2894 laid out a system of deriving added revenue for transportation that was strongly objected to for two reasons. First, the implementation of HB 2894 was subject to a November vote, Referendum 49, to prevent a governor's veto. Second, the way of deriving the dollars was seen as reducing the state's general

fund by almost a half-billion dollars in the 1999–2001 biennium. It would also deplete the state's reserve funds and undermine funding for a number of essential state services, by having the state issue $1.9 billion in general obligation bonds to finance highway construction. This was seen as risking dollars needed "for essential programs funded out of the general fund: K–12, higher education, salmon recovery, social services, corrections, and aging services" (Pope and Gould 1999, 1–2).

Critics saw Referendum 49 as harmful to the environment, not solving traffic problems, and hurting labor, higher education and the capital budget (Pope and Gould 1999, 2–4). However, it passed in November 1998, and the governor was forced to commit almost all the funds generated in the 1999–2001 transportation budget to highway construction (77 percent), while 9 percent went to improve the ferry system, 7 percent for local highways and 7 percent for rail capital (Washington Research Council 1999). The funding sources forced on the governor by the referendum sharply contrasted the governor's original proposal to increase the gas tax to provide only minimal increases for new, sprawl-inducing highways and maximum dollars for public transportation improvements.

On another regionally important topic, a number of laws were passed on the listing of salmon under the Endangered Species Act (ESA) and the recovery plan being developed under that act. Just how the federal mandate under the ESA would mesh with the GMA was not clear in late 1998, but a number of analyses concluded that the full implementation of the GMA was crucial to restoring the salmon, especially in the Puget Sound region.[3]

In July 1998 an administrative reorganization was put in place that eliminated DCTED's Growth Management Division. It became Growth Management Services, one of four units under the larger Local Government Division, which addressed not only the preparation of local plans but also their implementation. The other units focused on infrastructure

---

3. For more about the 1998 legislative session, see 1000 Friends (1998, 6) and Washington State DCTED (1998b, 6). For an understanding of the link between salmon protection and the GMA, see Washington State DCTED (1998a, 8).

finance through a billion dollar Public Works Trust Fund that is competitive for local governments and special districts; funding through the Federal Safe Drinking Water Act for local government units and private water districts; and Community Development Block Grants earmarked for low- and moderate-income housing. Bringing all these units into the same division resulted in better coordination and a sharing of resources that have largely corrected the shortage of staff and represent a maturing of the growth management program with a stronger focus on implementation.

The 1998 election featured a heavy turnout and important gains for Democrats in the state legislature, U.S. Congress and local elections, surprising both parties. The shift in the state legislature gave Democrats a 26–23 margin in the Senate, and the House ended in a 49–49 tie. The Democrats gained two seats in the U.S. House, giving them a 5–4 edge in the delegation. The final election results showed that 62 percent of the state's 3.1 million registered voters had cast their votes, the highest turnout in a midterm election since 1982, a result attributed by some to the state's mail ballot system. At the local level seven counties had replaced anti-GMA county commissions with a pro-GMA majority. Supporters of the full implementation of the GMA would not have to fight bills aimed at weakening the system, or work with Governor Locke to veto the worst of them. After the November 1998 elections, the more positive political environment for the growth management system led many supporters to conclude that there would be time to focus on a positive agenda for strengthening it.

Struggling to Move Smart Growth Forward, 1999–2003

The struggle to move Washington's smart growth strategies forward over the 1999–2003 period was characterized by a mix of positive and negative developments. The reelection of Governor Locke in November 2000 was positive because he continued his strong support for the implementation of the state's smart growth agenda, which called for substantial funding for public transportation and drew

local governments fully into meeting the mandates of the Growth Management Act. However, the closely divided legislature could not be persuaded to support that new funding. Smart growth supporters such as 1000 Friends and the WEC never tired of fighting for ways to strengthen their smart growth agenda. They were stymied, however, by the strong anti–smart growth forces in the legislature and in some parts of the business and corporate community.

Legislative Developments in 1999–2000

Referendum 49 was approved in 1998 to authorize the use of the motor vehicle excise tax to pay off highway construction bonds (*Olympian* 2002). With its repeal by the passage of Initiative 695 in 1999, much of Washington's transit funding was lost. As 1000 Friends noted, "The passage of I-695 is taking a terrible toll on efforts to create a more balanced transportation system.... Transit agencies around the state face 30 to 60 percent cuts," which was a severe blow to growth management. Added to these negative impacts of I-695, fiscal challenges for stronger public transportation in the state as a whole and the Puget Sound region in particular constituted a major roadblock to bringing smart growth to Washington (1000 Friends 1999, 5).

While no "bad" bills passed the closely divided legislature during 1999–2000, neither was there much legislation to strengthen the system. The most significant item was the Rural Economic Development Act (ESSB 5594). Supported by 1000 Friends, the law included a number of important elements that strengthened the system either directly or indirectly.

- It named a working group, including representatives from DCTED, Department of Revenue, Department of Agriculture and the Economic Development Council, whose goal was "to promote economic development and business diversification throughout the state with special attention given to the economic difficulties of rural counties."

- State agencies "considering a request for a grant or loan for public facilities from a county or city planning under the GMA" must give preference to those local governments "that have adopted comprehensive plans and development regulations" that have been approved by DCTED. Full implementation of this provision could provide powerful incentives for local governments to comply with the GMA. Similar actions in other states, for example, Maryland, have been important. The law also applied these requirements to special purpose districts in GMA jurisdictions.

■ The law also had provisions to promote more affordable housing, especially in rural areas, by increasing the debt limit of the State Housing Trust Fund and by establishing a "one-stop clearinghouse within DCTED...to coordinate state assistance to growers and nonprofit organizations to develop housing for agricultural employees." (Washington State DCTED 1999, 6)

Several bills involving Washington's continuing efforts to respond to the challenges of salmon species being listed under the Endangered Species Act were enacted, including 2E2SSB 5595, which established a 10-member Salmon Recovery Board "to make grants and loans for salmon habitat projects and...recovery activities." The law required that a statewide strategy be developed for submission to federal regulatory agencies by September 1, 1999. The potential significance of salmon protection efforts to the GMA is in linking land use and other provisions of the GMA to salmon restoration efforts (Washington State DCTED 1999, 6).

Two other laws with potential relevance for the GMA were ESHB 2091, Forest Practices and Aquatic Resources, which would coordinate forest practices with the Salmon Recovery Act by authorizing the Forest Practices Board to adopt rules for protecting aquatic resources; and SHB 1204, Environmental Restoration, to make such actions compatible with salmon protection. An advisory committee to WSDOT was created to synchronize the acquisition of state land with environmental projects, including identifying funding sources for such projects (Washington State DCTED 1999, 6).

Legislation that did not pass in 1999 illustrated the impact of a closely divided legislature that blocked important efforts to strengthen the GMA. SB 5101 would have strengthened the state's capacity to protect farmland from sprawl, but it died in the Senate.

ESSB 5914 would have expanded the provision and funding for affordable housing in King County and around the state, but it failed in a House committee. SSB 5677 would have drawn special districts into the GMA by requiring that they collaborate with cities and counties to "cause their decisions to further the requirements of the GMA," but it failed in the Senate. Another negative note for moving toward smart growth was the legislative budget, in which some 85 percent of transportation funds went toward road maintenance and expansion (1000 Friends 1999, 3; Washington State DCTED 1999, 6).

1000 Friends proposed a number of funding sources for public transit and other bills for consideration by the 2000 legislature, but none were adopted (1000 Friends 2000, 1, 6). The only statute affecting the growth management system that did pass was the National Historic Towns Designation, which allowed the redevelopment of historic towns on the national register and in rural areas. The bill initially applied only to one partially abandoned town, allowing it to be redeveloped as "a limited rural area of more intense development." For future implementation, the legislation laid out requirements meant to prevent such designations from leading to rural sprawl. While rural legislators (largely in eastern Washington) attempted to weaken the GMA, no such bills passed.

On May 15, 2000, Governor Locke directed that DCTED be split into two offices with two separate functions. The change, which went into effect in 2001, but lasted for only a brief time, resulted in the Washington State Office of Community Development (OCD), with primary responsibility for coordinating growth management and a focus on the basic needs of a "viable community" (food, housing and the environment); and the Washington State Office of Trade and Economic Development (OTED), which is charged with creating new job opportunities, expanding Washington's economic base and promoting the sale of the state's products abroad (Washington State Office of the Governor 2000).

On the political front, Locke's easy reelection in November meant that a governor supportive of smart growth would be in office for another four years. His Republican opponent, John Carlson, had strongly favored substantial weakening of the GMA by allowing counties to opt out of the act (Thomas and Postman 2000). In his inaugural address in early January 2001, Locke called for bold action to move Washington toward smart growth. Speaking on transportation, education, energy and water, Locke set out an aggressive agenda that called for substantial new revenues (Wall 2001).

Locke noted that "the state should not have a transportation system that's out of gas" (Wall 2001). He also has noted that without substantial transportation improvements, the state was on a collision course with reality, since city traffic congestion was resulting in a loss in productivity of $2 billion per year. The transportation improvements Locke called for focused on essential transit services, adding high-occupancy vehicle lanes, as well as making major improvements to the ferry system. Pledging that Washington would not have "paved troughs that pass for rivers in Los Angeles," Locke called on the 2001 legislature to join him in far-reaching reform of the state's water laws (Wall 2001).

Key Developments in 2001–2003

As viewed by 1000 Friends, the 2001 legislative session also accomplished little to further the cause of smart growth in the state and in fact failed to pass a long-term strategy for funding transportation. Perhaps more important, growth management advocates defeated several bills that would have drastically weakened the GMA by

- allowing all but urban counties to opt out of the GMA and choose a convoluted, weaker law;

- repealing the updated Shorelines Guidelines;

- rescinding the Hearings Boards' review authority;

- compensating landowners for all regulations that reduce property values (another try at an extreme private property "wrongs" law); and

- allowing development of farmlands, despite agricultural significance. (1000 Friends 2001a, 1)

GMA supporters and 1000 Friends did succeed in passing three bills in the area of smart growth, although their significance will be determined in part by future levels of state funding available for the projects (1000 Friends 2001b). ESSB 5748 inte-

grated land use planning criteria to the process for selecting transportation projects for funding. Among its provisions, the Highway Improvement Program and Transportation Improvement Board must consider how potential projects support existing communities, help implement locally adopted population density requirements and promote transportation choices. The Multimodal Transportation Plan must also emphasize preserving existing investments and downtowns, the ability to attract economic enhancement and accommodate planned population.

The second bill, SHB 2648, requires the Office of Financial Management (OFM) to consider environmental protection, community revitalization and growth management information, when deciding which capital projects to fund. It discourages state funding of construction projects that contribute to sprawl. In its capital budget instructions, OFM must ask for the following information, among other questions, from applicants regarding proposed major capital projects:

- Is there regional cooperation?

- Are local or additional funds leveraged?

- Is the reduction of negative environmental impacts considered?

- Is the project identified in the comprehensive plan, development regulations or capital facilities plan (if GMA jurisdiction)?

- Is the project located within the UGA? (1000 Friends 2001b)

The third bill, SHB 2758, creates a program within the Washington Conservation Commission to gather, hold and distribute monies for the sole purpose of buying agricultural development rights that run in perpetuity with the land. It also requires the commission to actively pursue funds and regularly report to the legislature (1000 Friends 2001b).

A number of other developments in 2001 were significant for Washington's struggle to implement a smart growth agenda. According to the 2001 annual report of Growth Management Services (GMS, formerly located in OCD and now housed in the Local Government Division of DCTED), grant funds totaling more than $1.1 million were given to local governments during fiscal year 2001 in seven grant categories: GMA compliance, critical areas, rural communities, urban livability, economic opportunities, conservation and special needs. A total of 54 grants ranging from $2,500 to $50,000 were awarded out of 152 applications for grants totaling $6 million (Washington State DCTED 2002b, 13). In addition, the report announced that the legislature had approved a one-year $5 million grant program to preserve and restore riparian, estuarine and marine areas serving as critical habitat for fish and wildlife in four different locations (Washington State DCTED 2002b, 21).

Washington's Buildable Lands Program is required for the urban counties of Clark, King, Kitsap, Pierce, Snohomish and Thurston, and their cities. The program was moved forward with FY 2001 awards totaling $1,220,499 (Washington State DCTED 2002b, 9). The report also noted the publication of *Achieving Growth Management Goals: Local Success Stories* (Washington State DCTED 2000), in observance of the GMA's tenth anniversary. In April 2001 several programs for local government officials addressed the difficult issues around the concurrency requirements of the GMA. Another workshop examined the theoretical and practical methods, techniques and benefits of integrating the State Environmental Policy Act (SEPA) and GMA (Washington State DCTED 2002b, 12).

In its summary of statewide GMA actions, the report noted that as of June 30, 2001, all of the state's 39 counties and 258 of the 277 cities reported they had set in place the designation and protection of critical areas, a requirement for all local jurisdictions, and that 35 of the 39 counties had also designated resource lands. Twenty-five of the counties had adopted comprehensive plans and 21 of those had established development regulations that were consistent with the plans. Of the cities, 210 had put comprehensive plans in place and 186 had adopted development regulations that were consistent with those plans. Ten counties and 191 cities met all GMA compliance requirements (Washington State DCTED 2002b, 6).

Governor Locke convened the Governor's Competitiveness Council in July 2001 to examine and recommend ways to improve the business climate while considering the importance of other quality of life issues. The council's Regulation and Permitting Subgroup made a powerful recommendation: establish independent state leadership for comprehensive regulatory and agency reform. A secretary of regulatory reform was recommended, independent from the environmental agencies, with authority to "force" changes within those agencies. The secretary would be responsible for coordinating and consolidating the environmental permitting process to lead to a single consolidated environmental permit. Environmentalists might see such a powerful agency as a danger to environmental protection, but with Locke's strong support for the GMA, including environmental protection, this should not be a problem. Anyone familiar with how difficult it is to get state agencies to work in harmony toward a common goal recognizes this set of recommendations as a radical move in achieving a critical objective (Foster, Pepper & Shefelman 2002, 1, 3–4).

Changes in the governance status of DCTED were considered by the 2002 legislature, but when those bills failed to pass the governor opted to keep the department under a single director. GMS remained within DCTED, with its mission to help communities reach their growth management goals. Most supporters of effective growth management in Washington see this as making it easier to coordinate all of the functions involved, and thus favor the governor's move (Washington State DCTED 2002a, 5).

The 2002 legislature passed SSB 5841 to extend the September 1, 2002 deadline for local governments to meet requirements for comprehensive plans and development regulations under the GMA. In addition, review deadlines were extended for those jurisdictions that had to plan for critical areas and resource lands only. In order to be eligible for grants and loans from the state's Public Works Trust Fund and Centennial Clean Water Fund, and receive preferred status for other grant or loan monies to finance public facilities, jurisdictions must fulfill the requirements according to the revised schedule. The deadlines range from 2003 to 2007, with all counties in the Puget Sound region and several others coming first. Supporters of the full implementation of the GMA see SSB 5841 as a major new tool to bring all local governments fully into the game with plans and development regulations that meet the full requirements of the GMA (Washington State DCTED 2002a, 4, 13–14).

SSHB 2697 added economic development and parks and recreation as two new required elements for comprehensive plans under the GMA. While those elements have not gone into effect due to lack of funding, communities are being encouraged to incorporate them when updating their plans. Generally, reductions in the state's budget are creating hardships for local governments as they go about complying with the GMA. For example, Buildable Lands program funds were not available in 2002, but monies from other grants administered by GMS were not impacted.

On another front was a Washington Supreme Court decision involving the petition method of annexation for municipalities to bring unincorporated territory *within* UGAs, so they become part of the municipality and receive urban services. The court found the petition method unconstitutional, and the state asked for reconsideration. The court's decision was seen as negative by GMS, and local governments inside the UGAs were urged to team up and plan for transition in urban levels of service in the future (Washington State DCTED 2002a, 5–7).

In March 2002 the Washington state legislature submitted to the voters a 10-year, $7.8 billion transportation funding proposal that included a nine-cent increase in the gasoline tax. (Some say the legislature took that action out of fear of angering voters by passing a tax increase.) That proposal took the form of Referendum 51, whose proponents included labor, business, many political interests, Governor Locke and former U.S. Senator Slade Gorton. Opponents included 1000 Friends and WashPIRG, who eventually joined forces with others to come up with an alternative, the Washington Mobility Strategy. They cited as reasons for their opposition the fact that Referendum 51 was "a road building measure, pure and simple...study after study has shown that just building more roads to address traffic congestion without making adequate investments in transit will not reduce traffic" (1000 Friends 2002).

In spite of the $4.4 million spent by backers to get it passed, Referendum 51 was resoundingly defeated on November 5, 2002, by a margin of 62 percent to 38 percent. Those on both sides of the issue were stunned by the results, which were attributed to the failure of backers to gain voter confidence and the declining economy (Shannon 2002). The defeat of Referendum 51 boded ill for the future of WSDOT, which has relied on paying for road improvements through bonds since the passage of Initiative 695 in 1999; projections showed up to 600 WSDOT employees losing their jobs by the end of 2005 (Cook 2002). It is fair to say that, while the 2002 legislative session took potentially positive actions in a number of areas, it did not comprehensively address the lack of funding to implement Washington's smart growth strategies.

According to 1000 Friends, "The 2003 legislative session involved an unprecedented attack on growth management." Fortunately for proponents of smart growth, 25 antigrowth management bills were stopped or "neutralized." Among the most offensive were SB 5022, which would have allowed amendments to comprehensive plans as often as once every six months; SB 5152, which would have required the Columbia River Gorge Commission to compensate landowners when certain zoning changes were made; and SB 5160, which would have allowed counties in certain areas of the state to withdraw from planning under the GMA. SB 5507, which did pass, clarified who had standing at hearings of the Growth Management Hearings Boards. The environmental community and other smart growth supporters were pleased with the passage of SB 6012 that codified rules for shorelines (1000 Friends 2003a).

On April 26, 2003, the Washington legislature passed a transportation funding package that raised the gas tax by five cents, increased truck weight fees by 15 percent and added a 0.3 percent sales tax on car sales. The appropriation included $3.7 billion (89 percent) for highways and auto ferries and $475 million for passenger and freight rail and public transportation. Also included were $25 million for clean air programs and $20 million for trains and nonroad recreation (1000 Friends 2003c).

Washington's legislature went into special session on May 12, 2003, primarily to address the state's $2.6 billion budget shortfall. Among the positives for growth management were

- $4.6 million in local planning grants to low-population counties, administered by DCTED to local governments for the required review and possible update of comprehensive plans;

- $3 million to fund the Growth Management Hearings Boards, the only enforcement mechanism of the Growth Management Act; and

- $2 million in shoreline grants to assist identified cities in writing and updating their shoreline master plans in accordance with the new guidelines enacted by SB 6012. (1000 Friends 2003b)

The Puget Sound Regional Council

As in several other states, Washington's progress in developing and implementing its growth management system has been concentrated largely in a strong geographic region with an established regional organization. In this case, the Puget Sound Regional Council (PSRC) was formed in October 1991 by four counties and 55 local governments as a forum for making key decisions on regional growth and transportation issues. King, Kitsap, Pierce and Snohomish counties cover an area of 6,288 square miles and are home to more than 56 percent of the state population. Among other functions, PSRC has been designated by the federal government and the state as the Regional Transportation and Metropolitan Planning Organization, which is responsible for maintaining the growth and transportation strategies for the region (PSRC 1992, 1).

Embracing a Vision

The Puget Sound Council of Governments, the predecessor of the PSRC, spent three years developing Vision 2020, the framework for the future growth and change of the region, and adopted it in 1990. PSRC embraced the vision and has been modifying, updating and implementing it ever since. PSRC also had to adjust the implementation of Vision 2020 by integrating the requirements of both the federal Intermodal Surface Transportation Efficiency Act (ISTEA) and the state GMA, in the process gaining considerable strength as a regional agency, drawing real power from those two laws. In March 1993 PSRC's Gen-

eral Assembly began meeting the requirements of the GMA by adopting phase one of its multicounty planning policy, "the first step in integrating Vision 2020 ... with the countywide planning policies for King, Kitsap, Pierce and Snohomish counties" (PSRC 1993a, 2).

PSRC took advantage of ISTEA, and later, the Transportation Equity Act for the 21st Century (TEA-21) funds, by competing for a share of federal transportation improvement funds (TIFs), updating Vision 2020 to merge transportation and land use in the region, and adjusting the council's structure to advance that effort. Regional Transportation Planning Organizations (RTPOs) must develop Regional Transportation Plans (RTPs), and the transportation element of local plans must be reviewed for consistency with RTPs. Local comprehensive plans must also be reviewed for compatibility with the region's growth management provisions, as expressed in Vision 2020. Developing the process for consistency review was under way by late 1993 (PSRC 1993b, 2).

In examining the PSRC process for reviewing local plans for consistency with regional plans and policies, the potential "muscle" available to the council becomes evident. Certification of transportation in local comprehensive plans is a two-step process in which the PSRC reviews the draft local plan for both consistency with the adopted RTP and the requirements of the GMA. After the local government adopts its final plan, PSRC reviews the local transportation element again, and if it is not certified as acceptable, the local government is not eligible for dollars from "all projects funded with federal transportation dollars" (PSRC 1994a, 2). Furthermore, under HB 1928, a law adopted by the 1994 legislature, PSRC is authorized to "develop a process for certifying that countywide planning policies and the adopted RTP are consistent" (PSRC 1994a).

In July 1994 PSRC conducted four growth management and transportation planning open houses, one in each member county, to discuss the Vision 2020 and Metropolitan Transportation Plan (MTP) update "within the context of related planning being done at the state, regional and local levels" (PSRC 1994b, 3). The draft plan identified issues of growth management in four types of locations: outside of centers; on vacant land within UGAs; in conjunction with high capacity transit station areas; and in rural areas.

The Vision 2020 draft addressed policies and objectives under each major growth management area. One striking issue was how to cope with a forecast population increase of 1.4 million and employment growth of 700,000 jobs over the next 25 years. The Vision 2020 plan and the integration of the MTP upon final adoption in 1995 aimed at providing a clear and compelling framework for integrating land use and transportation planning by the region, its four counties and more than 50 cities. The General Assembly of PSRC approved the *Vision 2020/1995 Update* and the 1995 MTP at its May 25, 1995 meeting. Updating Vision 2020 was necessary in order to make it consistent with city and county planning under the state GMA; add the MTP, so jurisdictions in the region can remain eligible for federal transportation funds; fill in gaps or flesh out areas lightly treated in the original Vision 2020; and add a performance monitoring system to see if Vision 2020 is having desired effects (PSRC 1995b, 1).

This PSRC action was the high point in integrating land use and transportation in the Puget Sound region. The requirement that PSRC must certify local plan transportation elements, and that failure to gain certification will cause local governments to lose eligibility for all federal funds, is a powerful incentive for local governments in the PSRC territory to develop their plans according to Vision 2020. The core goals and policies of Vision 2020, as expressed in the *1995 Update*, illustrate the breadth, scope and above all the interrelated nature of a comprehensive regional growth management strategy:

> The vision is for diverse, economically and environmentally healthy communities framed by open space and connected by a high-quality multimedia transportation system that provides effective mobility for people and goods. Vision 2020 calls for locating development in growth areas so services can be provided efficiently, and farmlands, forests, and other natural resources are conserved. Within urban areas, it supports creation of compact communities with employment and housing growth focused in centers. The strategy is designed to ensure that development in our communities makes it easier to walk, bicycle,

and use transit. Vision 2020 also aims to preserve rural areas by supporting rural lands for farming and forestry, low-density housing and other uses consistent with rural character.

> In adopting Vision 2020, the elected officials that make up the Regional Council recognize the jurisdictions in the region are increasingly interdependent. The decisions we make regarding how we accommodate growth, the kind of transportation system we provide, and our economy are inextricably linked. Vision 2020 is an integrated regional growth management, economic and transportation strategy, which addresses issues that cannot be comprehensively addressed within a single jurisdiction. (PSRC 1995c, 1)

The Implementation Challenges

PSRC's capacity to implement the core goals of Vision 2020 hinged on the development of local plans consistent with the GMA's goals, along with mandates from PSRC's review of local government plans and regulations, countywide planning policies and the requirements of the MTP. The substantive requirements, as listed in PSRC (1997c), include the following points that constitute the key ingredients of any smart growth system:

- *Urban growth.* Concentrate new development inside UGAs, preferably within urban centers or compact communities.

- *Public facilities and services.* Ensure public facilities and services are coordinated with planned patterns of growth.

- *Housing.* Provide choice in housing types, including an adequate supply of low and moderate income, and special housing needs, throughout the region.

- *Rural.* Preserve rural character, protect critical areas, conserve natural resources and preserve lands and resources of regional significance.

- *Economy.* Promote economic opportunity, stability, sustainability and vitality.

- *Transportation.* Develop a transportation system that emphasizes accessibility, choice and efficiency.

By June 1997, 77 of the 84 jurisdictions within PSRC's boundary had completed and adopted comprehensive plans, and 52 transportation elements in local plans had been certified as consistent with the MTP. Development regulations consistent with the plans were in place and had a favorable compliance review in King (January 1995), Pierce (July 1995) and Snohomish (July 1995) counties. Kitsap County's initial plan (submitted December 1994) was found not in compliance; the new plan was adopted in December 1996 and under compliance review by mid-1997. Certification of the transportation element was significant for local governments, since consistency with the MTP by July 24, 1997, was a prerequisite for local governments to participate in the 1998–2000 Transportation Improvement Plan (TIP) funds (PSRC 1997b, 2). The 1998–2000 TIP was adopted by PSRC's executive board on September 25, 1997, and contained more than $260 million in new spending on transportation projects in the four Puget Sound counties (PSRC 1997d, 3).

To proceed, transportation projects receiving federal funds for any regionally significant project must be adopted in the regional TIP. The 1998–2000 TIP, for example, included $140 million in new federal funds allocated by PSRC and another $100 million in federal and state funds allocated or sponsored by WSDOT. The TIP then went to Governor Locke and then to the U.S. DOT for final approval. Given the close coordination among the key players in preparing the TIP, those approvals posed no problem. To have all those funds available for spending, Congress needed to reauthorize ISTEA, but failed to do so by mid-November 1997. Temporary spending authority was authorized as a stopgap measure until Congress could reconvene and adopt the ISTEA reauthorization (PSRC 1997d, 3).

The U.S. Congress approved TEA-21, the nation's largest highway and mass transit bill, on May 22, 1998. The six-year package amounted to $203 billion, and the bill substantially increased both highway (40 percent over the six years) and mass transit funding (an increase to $36 billion over the six years). Clearly, the new federal transportation legislation created an even more compelling incentive for local governments to meet the certification requirement. It should be remembered that the transportation element of the local plans must also be consistent with the requirements of the GMA, creating a powerful

transportation–land use link for the Puget Sound region (PSRC 1997a, 1; 1997d, 3).

Local governments establish their UGAs as part of developing their comprehensive plans. By 1995 local government UGAs in the region totaled 16 percent of the total land area and 86 percent of the population. Kitsap County had the largest percentage of its land area designated as UGAs (30 percent), and Snohomish, the smallest (8 percent). King County, with about 22 percent of its land area in UGAs, had more than 90 percent of its population in UGAs, reflecting its pre-GMA commitment to managing its growth. Encouraging growth within urban centers is a major goal of Vision 2020, and the four counties and their cities have designated 21 such centers, comprising 2 percent of the UGA, with 4.7 percent of the population and 29.7 percent of the region's jobs. The goal is to accommodate 8 percent of the population and 31.8 percent of the jobs, thus moving in the direction of a jobs–housing balance (PSRC 1997c, 29–30).

The PSRC devised a six-year strategy, focused on "nontraditional" transportation planning and ways to finance such strategies, for consideration by the 1997 legislature as well as future legislatures, since the capacity to implement nontraditional transportation options depended on finding new revenue sources (PSRC 1996b, 9–15). The baseline data for this effort were included in the costs of transportation study, which for the first time compiled for the region how much government, businesses and citizens spend on transportation. During 1996 the council supported 16 transportation enhancement projects requested by local governments, 10 of which were funded by the state, with lower matching requirements negotiated by the council for bicycle, pedestrian and other enhancement projects. In a major move on a contentious issue, in July 1996, the General Assembly approved a third runway at the region's major airport, Sea-Tac, "upon satisfaction of environmental review and permit processes and authorization by the Port of Seattle Commission . . . with additional noise reduction measures" (PSRC 1996a, 5).

The council certified transportation elements in 20 municipal comprehensive plans, gave conditional certification to four cities, and fully certified Pierce County's countywide policies, putting these jurisdictions in a position to compete for federal and state transportation funds. The importance of the federal ISTEA was highlighted in the report, noting that it had allowed PSRC to manage more than $600 million in federal transportation funds over the past five years (PSRC 1996b, 6–14).

Creating new and revitalizing old urban centers are key components of Vision 2020. To support the implementation of the regional greenways network, PSRC was developing a regional greenspace database to document the efforts of all actors (cities, counties, state agencies, nonprofits and land trusts). The goal was to produce a regional map of all existing greenspaces, highlighting opportunities for linkages (PSRC 1996b, 14–17). Putting a UGA in place is a key action. Monitoring will be done through the PSRC's policy and plan review process, its review of regionally significant public and private development projects, and the review of transportation projects for inclusion in the TIP. Performance monitoring aims at documenting whether implemention actions are producing the intended results; for example, whether the establishment of a UGA has led to a pattern of compact urban development and the protection of rural areas (PSRC 1996b, 17).

A final cautionary word about the prospects for the future in achieving sustainable urban and natural systems has to do with funding to implement the preferred goals and policies of the MTP. Without major changes in the availability and allocation of dollars for transportation improvements, traffic congestion in all parts of the region will go from bad to worse by 2020 (PSRC 1995a, 30–32). Full implementation of the MTP is projected to produce modest improvement in a number of factors by 2020, but congestion will still be worse than current conditions. The MTP calls for an optimum performance strategy to be studied over the next several years that if funded would shift transportation choice away from single occupancy vehicles and toward carpools and transit (PSRC 1995a, 81).

The key question looming over whether the 1995 MTP could be implemented was the availability of dollars to do the job. By 2020, with an additional 1.4 million people living in the region, funds needed to

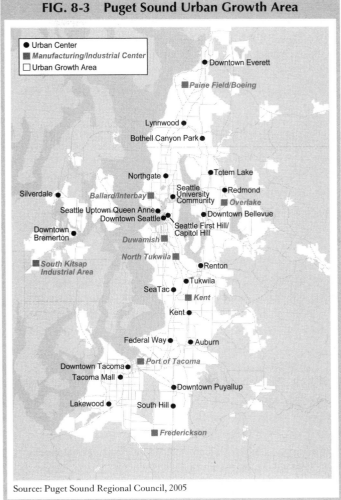

FIG. 8-3   Puget Sound Urban Growth Area

- ● Urban Center
- ■ *Manufacturing/Industrial Center*
- ☐ Urban Growth Area

Downtown Everett ●
■ *Paine Field/Boeing*
Lynnwood ●
Bothell Canyon Park ●
Northgate ● ● Totem Lake
Silverdale ● *Ballard/Interbay* ■ Seattle University Community ● Redmond
Seattle Uptown Queen Anne ● *Overlake*
Downtown Seattle ● ● Downtown Bellevue
Downtown Bremerton ● Seattle First Hill/ Capitol Hill
Duwamish ■
■ *South Kitsap Industrial Area* *North Tukwila* ■
● Renton
● Tukwila
SeaTac ● ■ *Kent*
Kent ●
Federal Way ● ● Auburn
■ *Port of Tacoma*
Downtown Tacoma ●
Tacoma Mall ● ● Downtown Puyallup
Lakewood ● South Hill ●
■ *Frederickson*

Source: Puget Sound Regional Council, 2005

maintain the current system, when added to revenues needed to implement the MTP, would amount to $58.3 billion, a shortfall of $21 billion compared to expected revenues. The 1995 MTP identified four options to try to close the gap: reduce costs through better system management and maintenance programs; postpone improvements; identify new revenue sources; or a combination of the three.

Options for new revenues included using local option taxes (authorized but not yet used); adjusting the state transportation tax distribution formula to benefit the region; indexing the state motor fuels tax; and/or adopting transportation pricing measures such as regional congestion road pricing. WSDOT and the State Transportation Commission supported indexing the motor fuels tax by nine cents per gallon, with five cents for state purposes and four cents for local purposes. As of early 2002, the legislature was not willing to support such measures, although Governors Lowry and Locke had supported various revenue proposals to enhance transportation revenues.

When asked in 1997 to reflect on how local governments in the region were responding to the tightening requirements of Vision 2020 in their plan and regulation development, Mary McCumber, executive director of PSRC, was cautiously optimistic. Ironically, Kitsap County, which had been most resistant to the GMA goals and thus to Vision 2020, volunteered to join PSRC, a decision some county officials later appeared to regret. While stresses in devising local plans and regulations can be found in almost all the region's local governments, it was McCumber's view that most were making significant progress in conforming to the federal, state and regional requirements.

From 1998 to 2000 PSRC continued its aggressive efforts to implement Vision 2020. In early 1999 the council's executive board announced a new six-year action strategy with three major goals: strategic corridor investments, reversing congestion trends and keeping pace with growth. Key to the action plan was identifying gaps between what is planned and what is possible with existing resources. A financial summary of the dollar requirements to meet the needs of the action program showed $9.49 billion available, leaving a $6.42 billion shortfall. Some 456 projects were included in the action plan, all described as "consistent with local comprehensive plans and, supported by the region's long-term plan" (PSRC 1999, 1–2). The six-year action strategy and the shortfall of dollars in implementing it continued to be the central challenge into the new century: well-conceived plans with implementation strategies that did not have the funding to carry them out.

In October 2002 PSRC's executive board asked staff to prepare regional criteria and designation processes for new regional growth centers and manufacturing-industrial centers to ensure consistency across the region. The Policy Board recommended that the processes establish more formal roles for the policy and executive boards in the review and final approval of proposed regional growth and manufacturing cen-

ters. The board believed that a lack of clarity in the existing processes and criteria had resulted in designations that were not consistent with each other or with the objectives of Vision 2020. In January 2003 the draft criteria were distributed for a 45-day public review period, and after taking public comments into consideration, the board approved the new process and criteria on June 26. They became effective the same day. Unless the board takes other actions in the future, the new criteria will not affect the existing 21 regional growth centers or eight manufacturing/industrial centers (PSRC 2003c).

Destination 2030

The determined optimism of PSRC is illustrated by the development of Destination 2030, adopted on May 24, 2001, by its General Assembly as "a transportation action plan for the next 30 years of growth." The region's elected officials and business and community leaders worked together to draft the plan, using Vision 2020 as a foundation. It would be hard to overestimate the importance of the development and unanimous adoption of Destination 2030, or of the challenge of finding the resources to implement that program to move the Puget Sound region and all of Washington strongly in the direction of smart growth.

The strategy behind Destination 2030 was to (1) sustain existing plans that called for investing billions of dollars of public monies in the transportation system; and (2) make certain that future decisions for the region ensure balanced choices for all modes of transit. The plan focused on system improvements in the Metropolitan Transportation System (MTS) in the following areas: freeways and regional arterials; transportation system management; state ferries; regional transit; nonmotorized transportation; freight and goods; aviation and intercity rail. Additional recommendations included investigating tools for greater regional coordination; pursuing sustainable transportation finance; conducting a value pricing demonstration project in the region; refining regional growth strategies; and supporting subregional plan refinements (PSRC 2001b, vii–xii).

Destination 2030 also detailed current traffic trends and estimated how the performance of the

Destination 2030 Executive Summary

Over the next decades, the region will grow by an additional 1.5 million people, add over 800,000 new jobs, and need to accommodate over 60 percent more travel, putting even more strain on our transportation system. To ease current congestion and prepare for future growth, the region must expand its transportation system and complete key missing links. With smarter, more strategic transportation investments, traffic movement can be improved by the year 2030, even with additional people and increased use of our roads, buses, trains and ferries. With an expanded set of transportation choices offered by a more fully developed system, the region can prepare for continued economic growth, while protecting and enhancing its celebrated quality of life.

Source: PSRC, 2001b, v

transportation system would be affected by implementing the plan. With the region's air quality a top priority, the plan was designed to conform to federal and state clean air standards (increasing the likelihood of additional transportation funding). Finally, the plan set forth procedures for establishing benchmarks and performance standards for the MTS and Destination 2030 to ensure the plan's implementation went forward in accordance with expectations (and changed early in the process if problems were encountered) (PSRC 2001b, xiv–xv).

More than 2,200 projects are set out in Destination 2030, including more than 2,000 miles of new and improved state and regional roads; improved public transit; new incentives for car- and vanpools; and more than 2,000 miles of new walking and biking paths. The cost of providing the recommended roads, bridges, buses, rails and ferries and other transportation–land use improvements would involve $105 billion over the next 30 years, requiring "almost double the annual rate of transportation tax dollars spent in 2001." The plan outlines ways to reduce spending and use technology to improve management, and calls for new taxes and fees in the area of transportation, so that those who use the transportation system the most pay the most. Over the 30-year period, $49.5 billion is needed for system expansion; $53.9 billion is required for basic needs. Projected current law revenues over the 2001–2030 period are $57.2 billion, leaving a shortfall of $40.0 to $45.0 billion (PSRC 2001b, xii, xiii).

The 2001 PSRC annual report noted that the council's highest priority was to see that Destination 2030 was financed, since implementation of the plan would result in strengthening the region's economy and keeping it competitive (PSRC 2002a, 1). The report sets out the following plans with regard to Destination 2030:

- *Transit.* Local bus service would increase 40 percent by 2010; 80 percent by 2030. Initial phase of light rail between downtown Seattle and Sea-Tac Airport will be running by 2010, along with more frequent commuter rail service between Tacoma and Everett, and express bus service throughout the region. More than 25,000 park-and-ride spaces and 800 more vanpools will be added.

- *Ferries.* Six new passenger ferries and four new auto ferries will be added to the fleet to provide faster and more frequent trips across Puget Sound from better terminals.

- *Freight.* Projects to fix rail and road conflicts, ease freight truck movement and improve access to the region's ports, to help maintain our competitive position in national and international trade.

- *Travel options.* Improved access to public transit for people without cars. Drivers will have more reason to leave their cars at home. More than 2,000 miles of new walkways and bikeways planned to connect communities with transit. (PSRC 2002a, 3)

Initial funding pluses included a federal transportation bill signed by President George W. Bush in December 2001 that would mean an additional $190 million targeted at transportation projects in Washington State in 2002. Six projects totaling $83 million in the central Puget Sound region were funded from this source. Looking to the future, Governor Locke convened a group to help rewrite TEA-21, which expires in 2004, to strengthen the state's ability to compete for federal monies through 2010 (PSRC 2002a, 4).

PSRC received a $2.98 million grant from the Federal Transit Administration, for transit services and programs providing better access to employment and "reverse commute" services enabling people to get to job centers in the suburbs. Of the total grant, PSRC received $50,000 for administration; the remaining $2.93 million was divided among Community Transit, King County Metro and Kitsap, Pierce and Sound Transits (PSRC 2002a, 6).

PSRC is the MPO for the central Puget Sound region and as such prepares the Transportation Improvement Program (TIP). In September 2001 the council, in a major amendment to the TIP, approved 41 new projects related to transportation. The Transit Station Communities Project was funded by a Federal Highway Administration (FHA) grant and aimed at promoting "transit-oriented development near major regional bus and rail stations and ferry terminals" (PSRC 2002a, 6, 7). In 2001 the council also moved to strengthen the region's growth management planning by linking it to Destination 2030.

In reviewing the policies and plans of local governments and agencies in the region to ensure consistency with state and regional planning goals, a requirement of the GMA, the council revised its Plan Review Questionnaire used in the certification review of local plans to incorporate the provisions of Destination 2030. During 2001, 14 jurisdictions submitted amendments for certification, with the transportation plans for four towns certified for the first time. Kitsap County, a long-time holdout, is conforming with the requirements of the transportation plan and GMA, and adopted amendments in 2001 that led to its countywide planning policies being certified for the first time. Snohomish County's updated transportation element was also certified (PSRC 2002a, 9).

Washington's long struggle to gain a consensus on how to find the funds needed to implement smart growth initiatives in transportation linked to land use was the focus of the "Conference on Value Pricing in Transportation," cohosted by PSRC in May 2002. The conference was part of a series coordinated by FHA and the Hubert H. Humphrey Institute at the University of Minnesota. Value pricing was defined as a technique to "help cut congestion during rush times by charging fees or tolls on congested routes." Such charges during the morning and afternoon rush hours were seen as encouraging drivers to shift trips to a less congested time or to use transit or carpool during peak hours (PSRC 2002c, 2). The council received a

$1.88 million grant from the FHA's Value Pricing Pilot Program to conduct a value pricing demonstration project starting in fall 2002, and to be completed in 2005 (PSRC 2002d, 1).

The 2002 state legislature passed several bills that strengthened the financial incentives advocated in PSRC's Destination 2030. SHB 2466 was designed to encourage new multifamily housing in cities, by forgiving the property tax payments for 10 years and lowering the population threshold for its use from 50,000 to 30,000, thus allowing numerous midsize cities to be eligible for the tax break. Tax increment financing was not authorized at all in Washington State until 2001 with the passage of ESHB 1418, which promoted community revitalization, and revisions to that act in the form of SHB 2592 in 2002 made it clear that local governments could issue long-term revenue bonds not considered as general obligation indebtedness. By creating a separate structure for generating and paying back the revenue bonds, SHB 2952 helped protect local governments (PSRC 2002c, 3).

Also on a regional level, E2SSB 6140 authorized the formation of a Regional Transportation Investment District (RTID) in June 2002 by King, Pierce and Snohomish counties, to pay for regional transportation projects directly with local taxes and fees. The bill provides a tool for the region to choose transportation investments utilizing elected county representatives and existing local, county and state transportation agencies. A planning committee (composed of all 25 council members from the counties, with the secretary of transportation, a nonvoting member, serving as chair) is charged with putting the transportation investment plan before the voters. An executive board made up of three council members from King County, two from Pierce and two from Snohomish is to formulate the plan. According to RTID's timeframe, the draft plan would be ready by October 2003; public outreach regarding the draft plan would be held through January 2004; and adoption of the final plan by the board would be in April 2004. County adoption was scheduled for May and June 2004, with the plan being on the ballot for voter approval in fall 2005 or later (RTID 2003).

PSRC's TIP draft for 2003–2005 focuses on ensuring designs for urban centers and that manufacturing centers take into account the transportation corridors that will link them. The council issued its called for projects in March 2002 and received funding requests for 28 projects totaling almost $156 million (PSRC 2002c, 1). The council's executive board then approved six of the projects for a total of $37 million (PSRC 2002d, 2). Federal funds will come from TEA-21.

The TIP undergoes routine amendments by PSRC at its monthly meetings to consider new projects or projects currently in place that do not need air quality analysis. It usually takes eight to twelve weeks for such amendments to be approved and incorporated into the state TIP. The Annual Air Quality Amendment, on the other hand, includes the addition of a new project that is of "regional significance" or changes to an existing project (in a current or previous regional and state TIP) that requires a finding of regional air quality conformity. Applications for the annual amendments are usually due in June of each year, after which the council makes recommendations that are subject to public comment for 30 days. The Transportation Policy Board then reviews public comments and makes recommendations to the PSRC's executive board that subsequently adopts the amended TIP. Final state and federal approval are generally granted the following December or later.

The 2003 Air Quality TIP amendments, due to be adopted by the board in September, included 19 projects calling for $1.9 billion in federal, state and local funds. The proposed projects included Seattle's monorail project; improvements to interchanges, roadways, traffic signals and I-90 in the Seattle/Mercer Island areas; and the South Lake Union streetcar (PSRC 2003f; PSRC 2003d). In June 2003 the PSRC board also appropriated $12.2 million in FTA monies for projects in King, Kitsap, Pierce and Snohomish counties. The 16 projects awarded funding included bus replacements, ferry boat purchases, monorail car restoration and a pedestrian bridge (PSRC 2003b; 2003e).

The challenge still remains to find more funding sources to bring the many aspects of the Destination 2030 vision to reality. The excellent leadership of PSRC's Mary McCumber, with support from the governor and other key state and regional leaders, have been the pluses, but to date a mixed response in the legislature and ill-conceived initiatives leave a substantial unfinished agenda in place. Destination 2030 is a bold, far-reaching plan that is clearly the right smart growth strategy for the Puget Sound region, but a substantial increase in funds is required to support its implementation.

Conclusion

With growth pressures still strong, what can we expect in the future for a sustainable smart growth system for Washington? Key components for the full implementation of such a system will be continued strong gubernatorial leadership and a successful regional and statewide coalition of key stakeholders including state agencies, nonprofit groups such as 1000 Friends of Washington (renamed Futurewise in 2005), citizens and a legislature supportive of smart growth initiatives. Even with the current budget shortfall caused by major weaknesses in the economy, the basic components of a strong economy in Washington still exist, and as the economy recovers, the ability to support the smart growth system will grow with it. There is good reason to be optimistic, with much depending on success in providing the most critical element for ensuring a smart growth future for Washington—new and sustained funding to support the implementation of the key components of the state's smart growth system.

The major roadblock standing in the way of creative solutions is the fact that the legislature has a substantial number of members who are strongly opposed to any smart growth system for Washington. While their efforts to completely dismantle the system have not succeeded, they have blocked attempts to put in place major new funding. This is especially significant in the area of transportation–land use, where dollars could be taken away from sprawl-inducing highway expansion and put into public transportation initiatives as part of Washington's overall smart growth strategy.

Finally, there still seems to be a disconnect between broad-based support for Washington's Growth Management Act and the regional smart growth strategies developed by the Puget Sound Regional Council versus the continued strength of those dedicated to dismantling the system. Eventually, however, the actions needed to implement the state's growth management system are capable of moving Washington into the front ranks of the smart growth states in the nation. Whether or not this will happen cannot be predicted at this time.

References

1000 Friends of Washington. 1994. *Outlook*. Spring.

———. 1995. State legislature ends session. *Outlook*. June 22.

———. 1996. *Outlook*. Winter.

———. 1998. 1998 legislative session yields mixed results. *Outlook*. Spring.

———. 1999. 1000 Friends of Washington annual report: Promoted smart transit options. *Outlook*. July.

———. 2000. *Outlook*. February.

———. 2001a. 2001 Legislative overview.

———. 2001b. Legislative details.

———. 2002. Alternative fixes fatal flaws in Referendum 51: Washington Mobility Strategy makes most of rare opportunity. Press release. September 24.

———. 2003a. Attack on growth management halted.

———. 2003b. Special session.

———. 2003c. State transportation package.

Citizens for Balanced Growth. 1990. Initiative 547: Keep Washington livable! Press release. September 25. Seattle, WA.

Conway, Dick and Doug Pederson. 2003. *Economic Forecaster* 11.3: September. Seattle, WA: Conway Pederson Economics, Inc.

Cook, Rebecca. 2002. DOT boss has bleak forecast. *Olympian*. November 15.

DeGrove, John M. 1992. *The new frontier for land policy: Planning and growth management in the states*. Cambridge, MA: Lincoln Institute of Land Policy.

Forward Washington. The voice for statewide economic vitality. 1992. Preparing for economic vitality: A guidance document for including economic considerations in local comprehensive plans. February 19. Tacoma, WA.

Foster, Pepper & Shefelman. 2002. Governor's competitiveness council makes environmental regulation and permitting recommendations. *Land Use & Environmental News*. Seattle, WA.

King County. 1989. King County 2000: The need for improved regional governance: Final report and recommendations. August 3.

Locke, Gary. 2003. State of the State Address. January 14. Olympia, WA: Washington State Office of the Governor.

Northwest Policy Center and U.S. Bancorp. 1990. *Northwest portrait: 1990 annual economic review and outlook*. Seattle, WA: University of Washington Graduate School of Public Affairs.

The Olympian. 2002. Ref. 51 failure leaves transportation future in limbo. November 10.

Pivo, Gary. 1993. Is the growth management act working? A survey of resource lands and critical areas development regulations. *University of Puget Sound Law Review* 16.3: Spring, 1141–1179.

Pope, Jernae and Jon Gould. 1999. *Why oppose Referendum 49: The transportation financing plan (EHB 2894)*. October 13. Fax from authors.

Puget Sound Regional Council (PSRC). 1992. *Regional View*. December.

———. 1993a. *Regional View*. April.

———. 1993b. *Regional View*. November.

———. 1994a. Consistency review...working cooperatively so it all works together. *Regional View*. June.

———. 1994b. Initial draft of Vision 2020 Update and Metropolitan Transportation Plan released. *Regional View*. October.

———. 1995a. *1995 Metropolitan Transportation Plan*. May.

———. 1995b. *Regional View*. June.

———. 1995c. *Vision 2020/1995 update*.

———. 1996a. 1996 Amendment to the Metropolitan Transportation Plan for the Central Puget Sound Region. Adopted July 11, 1996.

———. 1996b. *Your Regional Council 1996*.

———. 1997a. Puget Sound trends: Population of cities, towns, and unincorporated areas 1990–1997. *Regional View*. September.

———. 1997b. *Regional View*. February.

———. 1997c. *Regional View: Monitoring change in the Central Puget Sound Region*. September.

———. 1997d. *Regional View*. November.

———. 1999. *Regional View*. February.

———. 2001a. Decennial change in population and land area of cities, towns, and counties in the Central Puget Sound: 1990–2000. http://www.psrc.org/datapubs/census2000/pl94-171/popchange.pdf.

———. 2001b. Destination 2030: Metropolitan Transportation Plan for the Central Puget Sound Region. May 24.

———. 2002a. 2001 Puget Sound Regional Council annual report. March.

———. 2002b. Region in motion. *Regional View*. May.

———. 2002c. Lawmakers act on some financial incentives to support centers. *Regional View*. July.

———. 2002d. Regional council wins $1.8 million transportation technology grant. *Regional View*. August.

———. 2003a. Central Puget Sound Regional Economic Profile 2003. March.

———. 2003b. Designation criteria for regional growth and manufacturing industrial centers. Adopted by the PSRC executive board, June 26, 2003.

———. 2003c. Executive board approves new regional centers designation criteria. June.

———. 2003d. PSRC seeking public comment on transportation projects. August 14.

———. 2003e. Regional council approves $12.2 million for transit projects. Press release. June 26.

———. 2003f. TIPINFO-4, Making changes to the regional and state TIP. June.

Regional Transportation Investment District (RTID). 2003. RTID: A Puget Sound investment in Transportation. Seattle, WA.

Scates, Shelby. 1990. Growth in Washington: 1962 report was very prophetic. *Seattle Post-Intelligencer*. January 18.

Seattle Post-Intelligencer. 1991. June 30.

Settle, Richard L. and Charles G. Gavigan. 1993. The growth management revolution in Washington: Past, present, and future. *University of Puget Sound Law Review* 16.3(Spring): 867–948.

Shannon, Brad. 2002. Ref. 51 backers say they failed to ensure voter confidence. *Olympian*. November 6.

Technology Alliance. 2001. The economic impact of technology-based industries in Washington State in 2000. Seattle, WA.

Thomas, Ralph and David Postman. 2000. Locke, Carlson exchange jabs in gubernatorial debate. *The Seattle Times*. October 12.

U.S. Census Bureau. Undated a. Census 2000 PHC-T-3. Ranking tables for metropolitan areas: 1990 and 2000. http://www.census.gov/population/cen2000/phc-t3/tab01.pdf.

U.S. Census Bureau. Undated b. Census 2000 PHC-T 5. Ranking tables for incorporated places of 100,000 or more: 1990 and 2000. http://www.census.gov/population/cen2000/phc-t5/tab01.pdf.

U.S. Census Bureau. Undated c. Census projections of the total population of states: 1995 to 2025. http://www.census.gov/population/projections/state/stpjpop.text.

U.S. Census Bureau. Undated d. Table 1: Metropolitan areas and their geographic components in alphabetic sort, 1990 and 2000 population, and numeric and percent population change: 1990 to 2000. http://www.census.gov/population/cen2000/phc-t3/tab01.pdf.

Wall, Nicole. 2001. Memorandum to OCD—Office of Community Development re Gov. Locke's inaugural address. January 11. Olympia, WA: Washington State Office of the Governor.

Washburn, Tayloe. 1996. Growth Management Act 1996 update: Feet to the fire—no legislative relief in sight. *Land Use & Municipal News*. August. Seattle: Foster Pepper & Shefelman.

Washington City Planning Directors Association and Washington State Association of County and Regional Planning Directors. 1989. Toward a growth strategy for Washington. Kirkland, WA.

Washington Environmental Council (WEC). 1989. *Alert*. October/November.

Washington Research Council. 1999. Policy brief: 1999–2001 transportation budget—Referendum 49 impacts. January 29. Seattle.

Washington State Department of Community Development (DCD). 1990. Minimum guidelines to classify agriculture, forest, mineral lands and critical areas. Seattle, WA.

———. 1991a. *Implementation Briefs* 3. August.

———. 1991b. Planning data source book for resource lands and critical areas.

———. 1991c. Toward managing growth in Washington: A guide to community visioning. October.

———. 1992a. Issues in designating urban growth areas: Part I, Providing adequate urban area land supply. March.

———. 1992b. Natural resources of statewide significance: Final report of the temporary committee on natural resources of statewide significance. January 31.

———. 1992c. Paying for growth impacts: A guide to impact fees. January.

———. 1992d. The art and science of designating urban growth areas: Part II, some suggestions for criteria and densities. March.

Washington State Department of Community, Trade and Economic Development (DCTED). 1995. Legislature passes growth management related laws. *About Growth*. Summer. Olympia, WA.

———. 1997a. *About Growth*. Summer.

———. 1997b. Briefing for DCTED director Tim Douglas. June 24.

———. 1997c. Land use study commission, comparison of land use study commission recommendation with ESB 6094 (as passed legislature). June 9.

———. 1997d. Transition issue brief: Growth management.

———. 1998a. Let's build on growth management to save salmon. *About Growth*. Summer.

———. 1998b. New laws offer options for watershed planning, fund watershed projects. *About Growth*. Summer.

———. 1999. 1999 growth management-related legislation. *About Growth*. Summer.

———. 2000. Achieving growth management goals: Local success stories. December.

———. 2002a. Growth management services annual report, July 1, 2000–June 30, 2001. June.

————. 2002b. Legislative update. *About Growth*. Summer. Draft.

Washington State Growth Strategies Commission (GSC). 1990a. A growth strategy for Washington State: Preliminary discussion draft. July.

————. 1990b. A growth strategy for Washington State: Final report. September.

————. 1990c. *Commission Update*. April.

Washington State Office of the Forecast Council. 2001. Washington State economic climate study, vol. VI. September.

————. 2003. Washington State economic climate study, vol. VIII. September.

Washington State Office of the Governor. 1989. Executive Order EO 89-08: Establishing the Washington State Growth Strategies Commission.

————. 2000. Governor's Directive No. 00-03. May 15.

Young, Randall L. 1990. Special study and background materials: Capital planning workshop. Prepared for Washington Department of Community Development (DCD). Palm Harbor, FL. October.

Appendix

Governors

Daniel J. Evans (Republican)	1965–1977
Dixy Lee Ray (Democrat)	1977–1981
John D. Spellman (Republican)	1981–1985
Booth Gardner (Democrat)	1985–1993
Mike Lowry (Democrat)	1993–1997
Gary Locke (Democrat)	1997–2005
Christine Gregoire (Democrat)	2005–present

Acronyms

DCD	Department of Community Development
DCTED	Department of Community, Trade and Economic Development
DOT	Department of Transportation
FHA	Federal Highway Administration
GMA	Growth Management Act
GMS	Growth Management Services
GSC	Growth Strategies Commission
ISTEA	Intermodal Surface Transportation Efficiency Act
MTP	Metropolitan Transportation Plan
MTS	Metropolitan Transportation System
NIMBY	Not in my backyard
OCD	Office of Community Development
OFM	Office of Financial Management
OTED	Office of Trade and Economic Development
PSRC	Puget Sound Regional Council
RTID	Regional Transportation Investment District
RTP	Regional Transportation Plan
RTPO	Regional Transportation Planning Organization
SEPA	State Environmental Policy Act
SMA	Shoreline Management Act
TDR	transferable development right
TEA-21	Transportation Equity Act for the Twenty-First Century
TIFs	transportation improvement funds
TIP	Transportation Improvement Plan
UGA	urban growth area
WEC	Washington Environmental Council
WSDOT	Washington State Department of Transportation (formerly WASHDOT)

Contacts

1000 Friends of Washington
(renamed Futurewise in 2005)
1617 Boylston Avenue, Suite 200
Seattle, WA 98122
206-343-0681
http://www.futurewise.org

Association of Washington Business
1414 Cherry Street S.E.
Olympia, WA 98507
360-943-1600
http://www.awb.org

Puget Sound Regional Council (PSRC)
1011 Western Avenue, Suite 500
Seattle, WA 98104-1035
206-464-7090
infoctr@psrc.org
http://www.psrc.org/contact.htm

Regional Transportation Investment District (RTID)
1941 26th Avenue
Seattle, WA 98112
206-709-9040
http://www.rtid.dst.wa.us

Washington Environmental Council (WEC)
615 Second Avenue, Suite 380
Seattle, WA 98104
206-622-8103
info@wecprotects.org
http://www.wecprotects.org

Washington Research Council
108 S. Washington Street, Suite 406
Seattle, WA 98104-3408
206-467-7088
http://www.researchcouncil.org

Washington State Web Site
http://access.wa.gov

Washington State Department of Community, Trade and Economic Development Web Site
(formerly Office of Community Development)
http://www.cted.wa.gov

9

Conclusion

Support for Smart Growth Matched by Challenges

From the Introduction to this concluding chapter, I have traced the evolution of legislation and related public and private planning efforts to manage growth and change in nine states. The overarching goal has been to contain sprawl patterns of development so that sustainable natural and urban systems can be established and maintained over time. None of these state endeavors has been fully successful, but in every case a careful assessment shows that growth management systems leading toward stronger urban areas and better protection of natural resources, as imperfect as they may have been, are better than what would have occurred without such frameworks.

The momentum to establish what we now commonly call smart growth systems has occurred within different governance structures and changing political cultures, but since the early 1970s states have adopted remarkably consistent principles and goals. The first wave of state growth management systems concentrated on protecting the environment, and later efforts focused more on what came to be called quality-of-life issues, such as traffic congestion and the loss of walkable, livable communities, fed by the failure to keep up with the costs of growth. The need to put infrastructure in place to meet the impacts of growth concurrent with the occurrence of those impacts has been a special challenge. Roads, potable water, sanitary sewers, storm water management, solid waste disposal, park and recreation facilities, and other community facilities have been at the core of those concerns.

Through the 1980s and 1990s, there was a growing recognition that sprawl development patterns to accommodate population increases (or simply population shifts without overall increases) were draining the life out of city centers and other existing urban areas, as well as destroying natural systems, including valuable wetlands, uplands, farms and forests. The remarkable strengthening of concerns about sprawling development in the last half of the 1990s and early 2000s forms the substance for the central findings of this book: smart growth approaches have penetrated every corner of the nation, sometimes in quite unexpected places, and the wide range of public, private and nonprofit stakeholders supporting these approaches are committed to pursuing them into the foreseeable future.

Past Efforts to Manage Growth and Change

The first wave of states attempting a more or less comprehensive approach to managing growth and change with a substantial focus on implementation included Oregon, Florida and Vermont. Concern for the environment was the key factor in mobilizing the political muscle to pass legislation that was a radical departure from the hands-off approach that states had previously taken to land use issues at the local level. If local planning and implementation actions occurred at all, they were not within a statewide framework, however limited.

Because home builders, developers, local governments and other private sector groups are often opposed to any action at the state or regional level, leadership by governors and key legislators has been critical in almost every successful effort since the 1970s. Governors have been significant leaders in both establishing new systems and defending established systems against efforts to destroy or weaken them by hostile legislatures and the aforementioned groups.

Further analysis of the first-wave states shows that, however mixed the implementation record, both state and local governments gained authority from their growth management systems. Although some regional and local governments were reluctant to exercise their roles fully, these states clearly assumed new and important precedents in planning and land use. There were weaknesses, such as failing to make permitting systems consistent with the comprehensive planning and land management systems. Furthermore, monitoring and enforcement often fell short of what was called for in the statutes and implementing regulations. Nevertheless, these systems evolved in the face of new demands, and other states joined the movement.

There is a connection between efforts to better manage growth and change in the first-wave states and those in the second wave (New Jersey, Georgia, Maine, Maryland, Rhode Island and Washington State) that either returned to the drawing board to strengthen their systems or acted for the first time during the 1980s and early 1990s. That connection held true for innovative smart growth approaches that emerged in the last half of the 1990s and dominated the national scene in the early twenty-first century. The second wave of state efforts focused in part on the redefinition of growth management as a broader concept that included "managing to grow" as well as improved management of existing growth pressures. The statewide initiatives from the 1970s to the early 1990s resulted in at least three important outcomes: (1) redefining the practice of planning; (2) redefining state/regional/local relations, including reallocating authority and responsibility for important public policy issues; and (3) moving funding issues associated with growth management into the public policy agenda.

As the process of adopting new or revising old comprehensive planning and growth management systems advanced, the early definition of growth management evolved from a narrow growth control–no growth-slow growth matter, a label associated with early one-at-a-time local government efforts in

California and elsewhere. The new definition can be described as "a commitment to plan carefully for the growth that comes to an area so as to achieve a responsible balance between the protection of natural systems—land, air and water—and the development required to support growth in the residential, commercial, and retail areas" (DeGrove 1992, 1).

My earlier prediction—that the smart growth approaches then underway would survive and be implemented, and that others would come on line within a state and regional framework—was based on a number of key factors.

- The bipartisan nature of the support for smart growth approaches, especially from governors in both major parties taking the lead in establishing and implementing these systems;

- The remarkably broad base of support for smart growth approaches across the public, private and nonprofit sectors, including the expanding strength of advocacy groups such as New Jersey Future and 1000 Friends organizations;

- The sometimes overlooked but key role of the federal government in furthering smart growth approaches, especially during the Clinton-Gore administration from 1992 to 2000; and

- The leadership of many governors, often combined with key legislative leaders, to shape a friendly climate for smart growth approaches, even in the face of hostility from legislatures and extreme private property rights and antigovernment advocates.

The argument was never that it would be easy to implement smart growth strategies to contain sprawl, revitalize existing urban areas, apply smart growth principles in new urban centers, and restore and protect significant natural systems and rural areas. The argument was that new, broad-based coalitions were being formed across the nation that promise powerful and sustained support for smart growth approaches—the newest and most promising evolution of the decades-long effort to better manage growth and change.

Assuming that this prediction about the staying power of smart growth approaches is accurate, there remains the task of fully implementing their goals, policies and regulations. Given that most of these approaches depend heavily on incentives and disincentives, the implementation challenge involves committing the substantial funding needed to ensure their effectiveness. Developments at the national, state and local levels, as well as worldwide events following the September 11, 2001 attacks, call for a reassessment of previous, more optimistic assessments for a smart growth future for our nation and the world. In spite of earlier advances, the George W. Bush administration, since 2000, has taken actions that weakened the federal role in smart growth planning and development across the nation. Many states also have responded to changing social and economic priorities that have resulted in diverting resources away from comprehensive land use planning systems.

Other State Initiatives

In addition to the nine states in this volume, many other states and regions have developed smart growth systems that illustrate the best principles of smart growth and are supported by broad-based coalitions. A few of them are described briefly to illustrate the diversity of approaches and degrees of success in implementing their goals and objectives.

Minnesota

The Metropolitan Council of the Twin Cities of Minneapolis and St. Paul was established in 1967 and long viewed as one of the most important and successful regional governance systems in North America (along with Metropolitan Toronto). Over time, however, the Met Council has faced increased difficulty in achieving its goal of limiting urban development patterns to a defined seven-county region, and protecting the area's natural resources. The system called for a definite breakpoint between urban and rural areas to achieve its intended purpose. The difficulty with these bold goals was that the Met Council lacked both the political support and adequate funding to make the vision a reality. Some important steps were taken in the 1970s, such as the Metropolitan Land Planning

Act and the Metropolitan Revenue Distribution Act, but the Met Council struggled to implement key elements of its smart growth strategies.

Several aggressive land use planning efforts in the 1990s seemed to founder for the lack of a meaningful statewide growth management system. When 1000 Friends of Minnesota and its allies finally gained passage of the Community Based Planning Act in 1997, it was the first significant move in Minnesota toward a state land use planning framework. Leadership was provided by Curtis Johnson, first as chief of staff for Governor Arne Carlson in the early 1990s and then as Met Council chair from 1996 through 1998. In spite of lukewarm support from Carlson, Johnson put together a bipartisan coalition in the 1998 legislature for a bill to strengthen the Met Council through an earmarked incentive fund for affordable housing, more dollars for brownfield redevelopment and support for public transportation initiatives.

Other successes were the formation of the Minnesota Smart Growth Network, led by 1000 Friends of Minnesota, which included a variety of key stakeholders; publication of reports establishing smart growth principles; and surprising support for a series of implementing actions by Governor Jesse Ventura's administration from 1998 to 2002. Leadership by the governor clearly was the key. As 1000 Friends (1998, 2) put it, "The energy and excitement to make ideas a reality are coming straight from the governor."

Utah

Utah offers an instructive example of a smart growth initiative that is the product of strong leadership by former Republican Governor Mike Leavitt (appointed Administrator of the U.S. Environmental Protection Agency in late 2003 and Secretary of the U.S. Department of Health and Human Services in January 2005). The broad-based Coalition for Utah's Future, sponsor of the organization Envision Utah, is composed of state and local officials, business leaders, developers, conservationists, landowners, academics, church groups and citizens. This public-private partnership was established in 1997 with Governor Leavitt as honorary cochair. A key to its early success was the involvement of the governor and his Office of Planning and Budget.

Over the past eight years, Envision Utah has developed a Quality Growth Strategy to preserve critical lands, promote water conservation and clean air, improve regionwide transportation systems, and provide housing options for all residents. That strategy focuses on the Greater Wasatch area, stretching for 100 miles north and south of Salt Lake City on both sides of the Wasatch Mountains. The corridor contains 80 percent of the state's population and is projected to grow by about one million residents over the next 15 years to reach 2.7 million by 2020 and 5.0 million by 2050.

In the late 1990s, initiatives by the Office of Planning and Budget and Envision Utah led to the Quality Growth Act of 1999 (HB 199) and impressive action in the legislature to increase funding for components of a broad-based smart growth initiative. However, the political environment for smart growth in Utah has been complex, as Republican majorities in both houses are reluctant to implement the smart growth agenda of the former governor and Envision Utah.

Pennsylvania

Pennsylvania began moving toward smart growth in the mid-1990s, in large part due to the strong leadership of former Republican Governor Tom Ridge (until he was appointed Secretary of the Department of Homeland Security in January 2003). Ridge, the Pennsylvania legislature and an impressive array of nongovernmental groups faced one of the most complex governance arrangements in the nation, featuring 2,568 municipalities—townships, boroughs and cities—and 67 counties. All municipalities have land use planning and zoning authority, although 31 percent have a population of less than 1,000 and 80 percent have less than 5,000. The ability of these municipalities to collaborate on issues at a greater-than-local scale is made almost impossible by complex problems with the Municipal Planning Code, which require legislative action to correct them. Over the past several decades, efforts to change the governance system have faced strong resistance by local governments, private property groups, realtors, home builders and others.

During his first term (1994–1998), Ridge moved aggressively to attract new jobs to the state, increase spending on areas such as education, and give tax breaks to low-income working families. Before his reelection, Ridge developed Growing Greener and Growing Smarter initiatives that included successful efforts to designate significant funds to implement these smart growth goals. Ridge and his administration also joined forces with nonprofit and private sector groups to push a smart growth agenda for Pennsylvania.

Ridge shared his 21st Century Environment Commission's view that land use changes needed to be addressed first. Recognizing the political delicacy of making real changes in land use to limit sprawl and all that goes with it, he tried to build bipartisan cooperation in the legislature for the funding and changes needed to implement his Growing Smarter initiative. While the initiative enjoyed broad-based support, many municipalities fearful of losing home rule powers, extreme private property rights advocates, and some, though not all, developer and home builder groups remained opposed.

Following debate and negotiation, the General Assembly in April 2005 sent legislation to Governor Edward G. Rendell for a ballot measure, known as Growing Greener II, to authorize bonds up to $625 million to support environmental cleanups and the preservation of farms and open spaces. This initiative would broaden the original Growing Greener program, and Rendell saw it as a victory for the state's continuing stewardship of the environment. In the May 2005 election, 61 percent of Pennsylvania voters supported the measure. While this is a major step for smart growth in the state, many details must be worked out to determine how the funds will be used (*Bay Journal* 2005, 11).

Tennessee

Leadership for the effort to move toward smart growth in Tennessee came not from Republican Governor Tom Sundquist (1996–2003) but from a legislature controlled by Democrats, the Tennessee chapter of the American Planning Association (APA), through the national APA Growing Smart Project, and other groups such as the Tennessee Advisory Commission on Intergovernmental Relations (TACIR). The central issue that mobilized this coalition was similar to that of other states: a rising concern with the negative impacts of decades of sprawl development patterns. This trend of development moving into rural areas made Tennessee one of the top 10 states in the loss of valuable farmland.

Tennessee's permissive annexation policies over previous decades "evolved from annexation by private act to annexation by general law, and finally, through Public Chapter 1101, to annexation by general law within the framework of a comprehensive growth policy" (Tennessee Advisory Commission 1999, 5–12). In the postwar period of the 1950s and 1960s, friction between core cities and their suburbs increased in conjunction with the extent of urbanization. Core cities were losing much of their economic vitality to the suburbs and subsequently moved to annex them. The state's 1998 Growth Policy Act (Public Chapter 1101) moved the state strongly toward smart growth by requiring it to establish urban growth boundaries, planned growth areas and rural areas drawn within the framework of a comprehensive growth policy for each county and the cities within it.

Tennessee defies the more typical combination of leadership by the governor and strong fiscal incentives from the state that are the keys to many other smart growth initiatives. The effort in Tennessee is bipartisan, with the Democratic House and Senate firmly committed to giving the Growth Policy Act a chance to test its effectiveness before major changes are made to its requirements.

Governor Sundquist's need to confront a serious deficit by proposing a drastic change in Tennessee's tax structure complicated the picture in the early 2000s, but this has not affected the state's role as a significant player. State agencies and the University of Tennessee system provided valuable technical assistance and published reports to help local governments comply with the process. In any event, Tennessee tells us that the path to smart growth can take a variety of turns, but the constant in all such initiatives is the focus on ensuring sustainable natural and urban systems by containing sprawl and revitalizing urban areas through creative infill and redevelopment initiatives.

The Central Role of Governors

As indicated by the key role of governors in three of the four states described above (Minnesota, Utah and Pennsylvania), elected state executive leaders have generally supported growth management systems against efforts to destroy or weaken them by hostile forces including their own legislatures, local governments or private sector groups.

Florida is a good example of a long-established system regularly threatened with major weakening by a hostile legislature and others. The governor's role has been the critical factor in the system's survival. From the early 1970s through the late 1990s, Florida's growth management system was strongly supported by governors who were Democrats. Republican Governor Bob Martinez (1987–1991) had a mixed record. Since the 1998 elections, when Republicans took control of both houses of the legislature, Governor Jeb Bush's actions have sent confusing messages with regard to his support (or lack of support) for sustaining and even improving Florida's system for managing growth and change.

Given the ultraconservative leadership in the Florida House of Representatives, where a clear majority of Republicans seem intent on dismantling or at least drastically weakening the system, the role of the governor remains crucial. While Governor Bush made some pro–smart growth appointments and has voiced support for some smart growth actions, such as restoring and sustaining the Everglades ecosystem, he will not support the increased revenues essential for implementation.

For example, in the 2005 session of the Florida legislature, Governor Bush supported strengthening the state's growth management system, including additional funds to cover the costs of Florida's continuing development. However, the governor and many legislators do not seem ready to support a critical funding ingredient that would increase the sales tax on services. Senate President Tom Lee (R-Brandon), one of a number of Senate Republicans who have prevented the dismantling of the state's growth management system, has made it clear that the Senate will not support the governor's proposed changes in the growth management system, unless substantial new funding to pay for the costs of growth is included.

A breakthrough of sorts took place on April 21, 2005, in a meeting of the Budget Conference committee during which all sides compromised, although none was completely pleased and many details remain to be worked out. House Republicans do not like hoped-for tax cuts being reduced in favor of a commitment to fund growth management measures to address the backlog of road, school and water projects (Dunkelberger and Follick 2005).

However, Lee's objection to tax cuts without new funding sources (i.e., tax increases) is apt to remain his core principle in funding the costs for the state's projected growth. The U.S. Census Bureau's latest projections lend strength to Lee's position, showing Florida replacing New York as the nation's third largest state. Florida's population is projected to reach 20 million by 2010 and to top 21 million by 2015. By 2030 those 65 and older will make up 27.1 percent of the state's population, up from 17.6 percent in 2000. Florida will be one of 10 states where retirees will outnumber school children (*Gainesville Sun* 2005, 6-B).

The central challenges that must be resolved if Florida's system for managing growth and change is to be realized remain a steady source of funding and positive leadership from the governor's office to set funding priorities for effective smart growth implementation.

Even the highly praised Oregon growth management system has been challenged by recurring attempts to weaken or even destroy its comprehensive efforts to manage growth and change within a state and regional framework. From the late 1990s into 2005, key Democratic governors have struggled with a hostile Republican legislature and ill-conceived initiatives in attempts to ward off the drastic weakening or even destruction of the Oregon system.

In the election of 1994, Democratic Governor John Kitzhaber, a strong supporter of the system, battled the Republican House and Senate, whose leadership was actively opposed to the program. In 1995, 1997 and 1999, Republican-controlled legislatures mounted major assaults on the system, and in each case Kitzhaber, reelected in 1998, vetoed the worst of the bills. Most supporters would agree that Kitzhaber's vetoes,

and other actions to support the system, kept it from being destroyed.

Hostile forces in the legislature and such groups as Oregonians in Action are still active, and Governor Ted Kulongoski, elected in 2002, faced the most serious threat to Oregon's smart growth future in 2004. Measure 37, a ballot initiative that would drastically alter the state's well-established land use planning practices and regulations, passed by a 60–40 margin, and won a majority in 35 of 36 counties. Bob Stacey, executive director of 1000 Friends of Oregon, made it clear that supporters of the system would continue to fight to keep it intact. Kulongoski has asked cities and counties to minimize or deny any waivers requested under the new measure until the his office and legislature can develop a strategy to protect key features of the existing system and address the need for substantial new financial resources to meet the expected legal challenges from property owners. What the future holds for the Oregon system remains to be seen.

Washington State also exemplifies states whose governors, typically but not always Democrats, must push hard for the implementation of a potentially effective smart growth system without support from the legislature. Former Governor Gary Locke, a Democrat strongly supportive of the state's smart growth strategies, persisted over three terms (1993–2005). His leadership attempted to protect the Washington system from being destroyed or weakened by a hostile Republican legislative majority in one or both houses, as bad bills were proposed in large numbers. The further challenge of winning support for funding needed to provide incentives and disincentives to support the system still has not been met, complicated by a severe recession in the early 2000s. While we cannot declare victory for Washington's smart growth system, without Locke's leadership the system might not have survived at all.

Former Maryland Governor Parris N. Glendening is recognized as one of the most successful governors in terms of developing and implementing smart growth initiatives. When he left the governor's office after two terms, he vowed to continue to support smart growth nationwide. He now heads the Smart Growth Leadership Institute housed at the nonprofit Smart Growth America in Washington, D.C., with a goal of providing resources to elected officials struggling with growth problems. Following the surprise defeat of Glendening's Lt. Governor Kathleen Kennedy Townsend by her Republican opponent in November 2002, the new governor, Robert L. Ehrlich Jr., pledged to continue Glendening's comprehensive smart growth policies. He has kept that pledge, even in the face of a severe budget crunch that forced some adjustments yet sustained the core principles of the program.

Political Action, Collaboration and Economic Incentives

Factors other than gubernatorial leadership have been important to the progress of smart growth strategies over the past several years. The attacks of September 11, 2001, unfinished business in Afghanistan and the invasion of Iraq have diverted the Bush administration's attention from many domestic issues, including support for smart growth initiatives. In spite of the gloomy prospects for the implementation of comprehensive smart growth strategies at the federal level and in individual states in 2005, analysis from other states shows that innovative programs do have broad support from a cross-section of public and private interests.

Notwithstanding some disastrous results in the 2004 elections, there was generally "a coast to coast groundswell of support for smart growth, transit funding, and land protection" (Greenbelt Alliance 2005b, 2). Voters approved 162 state and local land conservation measures (75 percent of those proposed), allocating $4.1 billion for open space protection, including protecting agricultural and ranch land, improving water quality, and providing additional parks and recreational resources. These measures passed in large numbers in Arizona, California, Florida, Massachusetts, Michigan, New Jersey, New York and Texas, indicating broad local support for land conservation, regardless of the red state–blue state political dichotomy of 2004 (The Trust for Public Land 2005).

In California's Solano County, for example, a combination of actions, led by the San Francisco Bay Area's Greenbelt Alliance, resulted in assisting the City of Vacaville to create an urban growth boundary that will protect 30,000 acres of surrounding open space. The Alliance also defeated that county's Measure A, a "highway-heavy transportation sales tax measure" that "would have funded highway expansion with no growth controls and no funding for transit...a recipe for sprawling growth" (Greenbelt Alliance 2005a).

While it is clear that there was still much to be done to protect the Greater San Francisco Bay region, the Alliance cited a list of other successes.

- Designation of transportation sales tax measures in San Mateo and Marin counties for transit and safer roads for cyclists and pedestrians;

- Withdrawal of a proposal to build a casino on threatened wetlands on San Pablo Bay in Sonoma County, and permanent protection of bayfront lands by the Sonoma Land Trust;

- Adoption of inclusionary housing ordinances in Sonoma and Contra Costa counties, increasing the supply of affordable homes for those making less than the local median income; and

- Expansion of the Mid-Peninsula Open Space District's jurisdiction, enabling protection of forests and farmlands across the peninsula to the coast. (Greenbelt Alliance 2005a)

Collaboration is another overriding theme showing promise in many states. It is highly questionable whether any small town or county governments can survive without dramatic increases in joint service districts and shared tax bases, and those actions will require state intervention (Peirce 2004). Maine's immediate past governor, Angus King, and his planning director, Evan Richert, pinpointed the downsides of the lack of coordinated planning among many small towns, including unplanned sprawl and rising costs due to duplication of many public services. For example, King's economic development director drew a 20-mile circle around the capital of Augusta and found 91 fire trucks serving 95,000 people, with none of them—priced from $100,000 to $500,000—jointly owned (Peirce 2004).

Charles Colgan, an economist at the University of Southern Maine, projects that "it's going to be collaborate or collápse." Maine's current governor, John Baldacci, is putting in place a regionalization program involving "cash incentives for localities that agree to curb local tax rates through sharing services between towns or school districts" (Peirce 2004). The twin cities of Lewiston and Auburn have agreed to collaborate to rebuild their economies devastated by the loss of textile and shoe factories along the Androscoggin River. The leaders of these two historically rival cities have negotiated 23 intercity agreements, including jointly developing the local airport, an economic growth council and recycling programs, and they are looking at other similar mergers (Peirce 2004). In conclusion, Peirce poses the question, "From historically icy independence to a new fraternalism? If it can start in turf protective New England towns, then why not everywhere?"

Stimulating economic development through tax incentives that also enhance historic preservation is another strategy used in many states. Grow Smart Rhode Island, for example, commissioned a study of the Rhode Island Historic Preservation Investment Tax Credit Program, which is "returning historic properties to municipal tax rolls, generating employment and housing where they are most needed, and leveraging substantial private investment that otherwise would not occur" (Grow Smart 2005b). Through legislation made effective on January 1, 2002, the state created economic incentives to stimulate the redevelopment and reuse of some 900 historic commercial properties in city, town and village centers across the state. Owners of these properties can earn income tax credits equal to 30 percent of qualified rehabilitation expenditures.

The study was based on 111 projects in the program, through September 23, 2004, showing a proposed investment of over $484 million. It concluded that the state's multiyear investment in the tax credit (some $145.47 million) generated a total of $795.25 million in economic activity. That is, each $1 of state tax credit investment is leveraging $5.47 in total economic output. In addition, the program is estimated to add $245 million to the tax base of local communities and generate a present value base of $179.4 million in additional property tax revenue and $42.14 million in sales and income tax revenue (Grow Smart 2005a).

Scott Wolf, executive director of Grow Smart, noted, "At a time when Rhode Island's open space and farmland are still under tremendous development pressure and our cities and towns are struggling to expand their tax base, the Historic Preservation Investment Tax Credit is helping to address both of these challenges.... Rehabilitation and reuse of historic buildings is smart economic development that plays to our strengths" (Grow Smart 2005b). The study report notes that 70 percent of the projects and 83 percent of the investments are in census tracts where family income levels are below the statewide median of $52,781. Data in the report confirm that the tax credit is "helping to ease the state's housing affordability crisis." Wolf concludes, "This is the single best economic development and neighborhood revitalization tool the state has seen in decades. This is about new jobs, new residents and new vitality" (Grow Smart 2005b).

Concluding Remarks

This volume illustrates examples of what is needed at a statewide level to sustain, strengthen and revitalize smart growth strategies that will ensure a sustainable future in terms of a strong economy, a healthy environment and a good quality of life for all citizens. Envision Utah, Grow Smart Rhode Island and the many 1000 Friends groups are examples of broad-based coalitions that include the public sector, nonprofits and the corporate sector. The key in all such efforts is to encourage relevant actors to find a way to agree on the fundamental components of a smart growth strategy, put it in place and implement it through a full and fair process. This assumes that the most common missing ingredient—adequate long-term funding to support the incentives and disincentives needed to attract the stakeholders—is available to ensure a sustainable future at the community, regional, state and federal levels. A strong economy and a healthy environment are not at odds with each other but in fact are dependent on each other. In the end, we just can't have one without the other.

Political leadership by governors, state legislatures, the president and the U.S. Congress needs to support implementation of smart growth strategies. When that support is missing at any level, as it is currently under the George W. Bush administration, the challenge is to find a way to bring about a change in the political environment. I would never give up on our collective efforts to establish and implement smart growth strategies that lead to a sustainable future. There are no losers in such a scenario. The challenge is to bring the doubters to the table and convince them that this is the case.

The evidence presented in these chapters is strong that the smart growth movement and its core principles for managing growth and change enjoy broad-based support across the nation, especially from coalitions of public, private and nonprofit interests that have not previously been assembled in such large numbers. There are many positive indicators that this movement will sustain itself through the first decade of the millennium and beyond. In short, I choose to believe that right reason will prevail, and as a nation we will recognize that smart growth has the right stuff and is here to stay. This has to assume that the political environment will support the kinds of changes needed to make this optimistic view a reality.

References

1000 Friends of Minnesota. 1998. Ventura administration begins to flesh-out smart growth initiatives. *Land Patterns* 4.3:2.

Bay Journal. 2005. Pennsylvania voters saw green on environmental bond issue. Seven Valleys, PA: Alliance for the Chesapeake Bay. June.

DeGrove, John M. 1992. *The new frontier for land policy: Planning and growth management in the states.* Cambridge, MA: Lincoln Institute of Land Policy.

Dunkelberger, Lloyd and Joe Follick. 2005. Budget talks can progress: Deal made on funds for growth, tax cuts. *Gainesville Sun.* April 22: 1-A, 4-A.

Envision Utah. Introduction to Envision Utah. http://www.envisionutah.org/

Gainesville Sun. 2005. Florida may be no. 3 in population by 2030, April 22, 6-B.

Greenbelt Alliance. 2005a. 2004 Annual Report. http://www.greenbelt.org/.

———. 2005b. *Greenbelt Action.* Winter.

Grow Smart Rhode Island. 2005a. Rhode Island Historic Preservation Investment Tax Credit: Economic and financial analysis. Prepared by Lipman, Frizzell & Mitchell LLC, Columbia, MD. http://www.growsmartri.com/tax.html.

———. 2005b. Study quantifies substantial return on historic tax credit. E-alert. April 7. http://www.growsmartri.com/tax.html.

Peirce, Neal. 2004. Collaborate or collapse—Tough New England message. http://www.postwritersgroup.com/archives/peir0417.htm.

Tennessee Advisory Commission on Intergovernmental Relations (TACIR). 1999. *Implementation of Tennessee's Growth Policy Act: The history of Public Chapter 1101 and the early stages of its implementation.* Staff policy report. March: 5–12.

The Trust for Public Land. 2005. *LandVote 2004.* Boston: The Trust for Public Land Conservation Finance Project and Land Trust Alliance.

Acknowledgments

Many individuals in many places helped make this book a reality, and I would like to express my deepest appreciation to them for their willingness to share their experiences and expertise, and for their unfailing patience and graciousness. My special thanks are extended to:

Ann Carlson, program coordinator, The John Scott Dailey Florida Institute of Government at Florida Atlantic University (FAU), without whom I would not have been able to bring the book to closure. She has been a key to keeping us on track from start to finish.

Also at FAU I thank Angela Grooms, coordinator of research information at FAU's Center for Urban and Environmental Solutions (CUES), for her invaluable assistance in gathering background information; the late Annie Reagan, research assistant at CUES, who undertook the initial task of transcribing interview tapes; and Linda Adams, administrative assistant at CUES, for her help with logistics and record-keeping.

Deborah Miness, assistant director of the Office of Planning and Quality Growth at the Georgia Department of Community Affairs, helped me in arranging and conducting interviews and collecting data. She has always been willing to go far beyond what could be considered major help in updating what was happening in states across the nation, with a special focus on Georgia.

The dedicated staff at the Lincoln Institute of Land Policy, in particular Armando J. Carbonell, senior fellow and cochairman of the Department of Planning and Development and Ann LeRoyer, senior editor and manager of publications, have shared invaluable financial, editorial and moral support during the long process of putting this book together. Others affiliated with the Lincoln Institute who contributed to the editing and production of these chapters are Kathy Foulger, Julia Gaviria, Maureen Lempke, Donna McDaniel, Emily McKeigue, Joseph Ryan, Anna Snow and Michael Snow.

There is no way I can thank my wife, Gail, enough for her patience and assistance in a variety of ways as we have moved to bring the research to a close.

Thank you as well to the countless men and women who made themselves available for sometimes lengthy interviews. I want to acknowledge those whom I have interviewed, sometimes many times over the past 15 years. They are listed by state, usually with their affiliations at the time of our conversations. Naturally, many of them have moved on to other positions or agencies, and I offer my apologies to those whom I have referenced inaccurately or omitted unwittingly.

Florida

James Murley, director, Center for Urban and Environmental Solutions, Florida Atlantic University; former executive director, 1000 Friends of Florida; former secretary, Florida Department of Community Affairs

Tom Lee, Florida State Senate

John MacKay, former president, Florida State Senate

Charles Pattison, executive director, 1000 Friends of Florida

Thomas Pelham, former secretary, Florida Department of Community Affairs

Nathaniel Reed, former chair, Commission on the Future of Florida's Environment

William Sadowski, former secretary, Florida Department of Community Affairs

Linda Loomis Shelley, former secretary, Florida Department of Community Affairs

Charles J. Zwick, chair, State Comprehensive Plan Committee

Georgia

Rick Brooks, division director, Administrative Division, Georgia Department of Community Affairs

Jim Burgess, former executive director, Georgia Municipal Association

T. J. Connolly, Georgia Development Alliance

Joel Cowan, chair, Growth Strategies Commission; chair, Georgia Regional Transportation Authority

Michael Gleaton, division director, Planning and Environmental Management Division, Georgia Department of Community Affairs

Jerry Griffin, executive director, Association of County Commissioners of Georgia

Bob Kerr, executive director, Georgia Conservancy

John Sibley, president, The Georgia Conservancy; former executive director, Growth Strategies Commission

James Skinner, Atlanta Regional Commission

Elizabeth Smith, senior planner, Planner Section, Georgia Department of Community Affairs

Lynn Thornton, former director, Office of Coordinated Planning, Georgia Department of Community Affairs

Harry West, executive director, Atlanta Regional Commission

Joseph Whorton, chair, Growth Strategies Reassessment Task Force

Howard Zeller, former executive assistant to the commissioner, Georgia Department of Natural Resources.

Maine

Jerry Bley, former resource specialist, Natural Resources Council of Maine

Everett "Brownie" Carson, executive director, Natural Resources Council of Maine

John DelVecchio, legislative liaison, Maine State Planning Office

Dr. John Kortecamp, executive director, Maine Real Estate Development Association

Theodore S. (Ted) Koffman, Maine state representative; Eco-Eco Maine, College of the Atlantic

Chris Lockwood, executive director, Maine Municipal Association

Michael Michaud, U.S. representative; former Maine state senator and chair, Commission on Land Conservation and Economic Development

Delia May Perras, former staff, Natural Resources Council of Maine

Kay Rand, former policy director, Office of the Governor; former director, Office of Comprehensive Planning, Department of Economic and Community Development; former staff, Natural Resources Council of Maine

Evan Richert, former director, Maine State Planning Office; associate research professor, Muskie School of Public Service, University of Southern Maine

Maryland

Thomas L. Bass, Communications and Legislative Affairs, Maryland Office of Planning

Bob Beckett, Maryland Department of Natural Resources

Ron Kreitner, former director, Maryland Office of Planning

Florence Beck Kurdle, former chair, Economic Growth, Resource Protection and Planning Commission

Jack Miller, Maryland Farm Bureau

Audrey E. Scott, secretary, Maryland Department of Planning

Harriet Tregoning, former secretary, Maryland Office of Smart Growth; executive director, Smart Growth Leadership Institute

Ronald N. Young, former director, Maryland Office of Planning; former deputy director, Maryland Office of Planning; former deputy secretary, Maryland Department of Natural Resources; former deputy director, Maryland Office of Planning

New Jersey

Candy Ashman, State Planning Commission

Martin Bierbaum, executive director, Municipal Land Use Center, The College of New Jersey; former administrator, New Jersey Department of Environmental Protection and Energy

Peter Buchsbaum, attorney, Greenbaum, Rowe, Smith, Ravin & David

Sue Burrows, assistant executive director, New Jersey Future

William Dressel, executive director, New Jersey League of Municipalities

Cary Edwards, former chief counsel to Governor Kean

John Epling, executive director, New Jersey State Planning Office

James G. Gilbert, former chair, New Jersey State Planning Commission

Barbara Lawrence, former director, New Jersey Future; executive director, Henry and Marilyn Taub Foundation

Chet Mattson, executive director, Bergen County Department of Planning and Economic Development

Thomas O'Neil, Partnership for New Jersey

Ingrid Reed, Woodrow Wilson School, Princeton University

Judy Shaw, former chief of staff, Office of the Governor

Herbert Simmons, director, New Jersey Office of State Planning

Gerald Stockman, state senator

Jack Trafford, director, New Jersey League of Municipalities

Tim Touhey, chair, New Jersey State Planning Commission

Oregon

Carl Abbot, Portland State University

Blair Batson, staff attorney, 1000 Friends of Oregon

Mark Bello, senior planner, City of Portland

Richard Benner, executive director, Land Conservation and Development Commission

Earl Blumenauer, U.S. Representative

Mike Burton, elected executive, Portland Metro

Arnold Cogan, managing partner, Cogan Owens Cogan LLC; former director, Department of Land Conservation and Development

Andy Cotugno, planning director, Portland Metro

John Fregonese, Fregonese Calthorpe Associates and former director, Growth Management Services Division, Portland Metro

Charles Hales, Portland City Council member; former vice president, Portland Home Builders Association

Mike Hoagland, regional planning director, Portland Metro Planning Department

John Kelley, director, Transportation and Growth Management Program

Robert Liberty, former executive director, 1000 Friends of Oregon

Henry Richmond, director, Growth Management Institute; former executive director, 1000 Friends of Oregon

Mitch Rohse, communications manager, Department of Land Conservation and Development

Ethan Seltzer, director, Institute of Portland Metropolitan Studies, Portland State University

Robert Stacey Jr., executive director, 1000 Friends of Oregon

Mark Turpel, senior planner, Portland Metro

Rhode Island

Robert Bendick Jr., former director, Division of Environmental Management

Robert A Cioe, president C. O. Construction Company, Inc.; Rhode Island Land Use Commission

Thomas Evans, Rhode Island State Library

John O'Brien, chief, Rhode Island Statewide Planning Program

Derwent "Derry" Riding, principal planner, Rhode Island Statewide Planning Program

Daniel Varin, former director, Division of Planning; ex-officio member, Rhode Island Land Use Commission

Robert Weygand, former state representative and chair, Rhode Island Land Use Commission

Scott Wolf, executive director, Grow Smart Rhode Island

Vermont

Darby Bradley, president, Vermont Land Trust

Greg Brown, former planning director, Vermont Department of Housing and Community Affairs; former commissioner, Department of Housing and Community Affairs

Tim Burke, former Vermont State Representative and Member, House Special Growth Committee and Conference Committee on Act 200

Douglas Costle, former chair, Governor's Commission on Vermont's Future: Guidelines for Growth; former dean, Vermont Law School

Peg Elmer, director, Planning Division, Department of Housing and Community Affairs

Ned Farquhar, former executive director, Vermont Natural Resources Council

Stephen J. Holmes, director, Sustainable Communities Program; Vermont Natural Resources Council; former commissioner of Housing and Community Affairs

Steven Jeffrey, executive director, Vermont League of Cities and Towns

Doug Racine, former chair, Senate Natural Resources Committee

Washington State

David Bricklin, president, Washington Environmental Council

Steve Clagett, former executive director, 1000 Friends of Washington; Department of Community, Trade, and Economic Development, Growth Management Division

Richard Ford, former chair, Governor's Growth Strategies Commission

Kjristine Lund, executive director, Regional Transportation Investment District

Michael McCormick, former assistant director, Washington Department of Community Affairs

Mary McCumber, former executive director, Puget Sound Regional Council; former executive director, Governor's Growth Strategies Commission

Betty Jane Narver, director, Institute for Public Policy and Management, University of Washington

Gary Pivo, assistant professor, Department of Urban Design and Planning, University of Washington

Norman Schwab, former assistant director, Governor's Growth Strategies Commission

Steve Wells, assistant director, Washington State Local Government Division; Department of Community, Trade, and Economic Development, Growth Management Division; former director, Growth Management Services.

Others

Jonathan Barnett, Department of City and Regional Planning, University of Pennsylvania

David Goldberg, Smart Growth America

Bruce Katz, Center on Urban and Metropolitan Policy, Brookings Institution

Arthur (Chris) Nelson, Metropolitan Institute, Virginia Tech

Douglas R. Porter, Growth Management Institute

Robert D. Yaro, Regional Plan Association

Index

About the Author

John M. DeGrove

John M. DeGrove, AICP, is the first holder of the John M. DeGrove Eminent Scholar Chair in Growth Management and Development at Florida Atlantic University's College of Architecture, Urban, and Public Affairs. The primary purpose of the named chair is to promote the development and implementation of smart growth initiatives that will contain sprawl, revitalize central city and other urban areas, and protect natural systems. Dr. DeGrove assumed this position on January 5, 1999, and retired in January 2000.

Dr. DeGrove began his academic career at Florida Atlantic University (FAU) in 1964, and he served as director of the Florida Atlantic University/Florida International University Joint Center for Environmental and Urban Problems from 1971 until his retirement. He was also a professor in FAU's departments of Political Science, Public Administration, and Urban and Regional Planning, and served as Dean of the College of Social Science. Prior to joining FAU, Dr. DeGrove taught at the University of Florida and the University of North Carolina. He received his Ph.D. in Public Administration from the University of North Carolina, his M.A. in Political Science from Emory University, and his B.A. in History from Rollins College. He also served in the U.S. Army Infantry from 1942 to 1946, starting as a private and ending as a lieutenant via a battlefield commission.

Dr. DeGrove has been a leading figure in Florida growth management since the early 1970s, and is a nationally recognized authority in the fields of planning and public administration. He served as Secretary of Florida's Department of Community Affairs (1983–1985) and was instrumental in the conception and passage of the 1985 Growth Management Act, the State Comprehensive Plan, and other components of Florida's system. He was a member of the Governor's Commission for a Sustainable South Florida from 1994 to 1999. Dr. DeGrove was a founding member of 1000 Friends of Florida, the state's nonprofit growth management watchdog group; starting in 1986, he served as vice president, became president in 1993, and was named president emeritus in 2000.

His involvement with the Lincoln Institute began in the early 1980s and he served on the Board of Directors between 1990 and 1996. In addition to his contributions to Lincoln Institute publications, his research has been published by the American Planning Association, the Urban Land Institute and many journals and law reviews.

About the Lincoln Institute of Land Policy

The Lincoln Institute of Land Policy is a nonprofit and tax-exempt educational institution founded in 1974 to improve the quality of public debate and decisions in the areas of land policy and land-related taxation. The Institute's goals are to integrate theory and practice to better shape land policy and to provide a nonpartisan forum for discussion of the multidisciplinary forces that influence public policy. Inspired by the work of Henry George as expressed in the book *Progress and Poverty* (1879), the Lincoln Institute introduces his thinking and ideas into the contemporary land and tax policy debate to advance a more equitable and productive society.

The work of the Institute is organized in three departments: Valuation and Taxation, Planning and Development; and International Studies. We seek to inform decision making through education, research, dissemination of information, and demonstration projects in the United States and internationally. Our programs bring together scholars, practitioners, public officials, policy advisers, and involved citizens in a collegial learning community. The Institute does not take a particular point of view, but rather serves as a catalyst to facilitate analysis and discussion of land use and taxation issues—to make a difference today and to help policy makers plan for tomorrow.

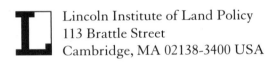

Lincoln Institute of Land Policy
113 Brattle Street
Cambridge, MA 02138-3400 USA

Phone: 1-617-661-3016 x127 or 1-800-LAND-USE (800-526-3873)
Fax: 1-617-661-7235 or 1-800-LAND-944 (800-526-3944)
E-mail: help@lincolninst.edu
Web: www.lincolninst.edu